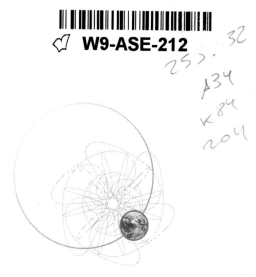

REAL WORLD ADOBE INDESIGN CS5

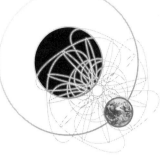

Real World
Adobe InDesign CS5

by
Olav Martin Kvern
&
David Blatner
&
Bob Bringhurst

Adobe

Peachpit
Press

∞

for Amy and Max
&
Gabriel and Daniel
&
Wendy

REAL WORLD ADOBE INDESIGN CS5
Olav Martin Kvern, David Blatner, and Bob Bringhurst

PEACHPIT PRESS
1249 Eighth Street
Berkeley, California 94710
(510) 524-2178
(510) 524-2221 (fax)

Find us on the web at: *www.peachpit.com*
Peachpit Press is a division of Pearson Education
Real World Adobe InDesign CS5 is published in association with Adobe Press

Production editor: Lisa Brazieal
Indexer: Jan C. Wright
Cover design: Charlene Charles-Will
Cover illustration: John Weber
Interior design, illustration, and production: Olav Martin Kvern, David Blatner, and Bob Bringhurst

CREDITS
Thanks to the Seattle Gilbert and Sullivan Society and their photographer, Ray O. Welch, for giving us permission to use some of their archival photographs as example images. Thanks to Minette Layne for the sea critter pictures. And special thanks to the late Ed Poole for the free use and abuse of his moustache.

ISBN 13: 978-0-321-71305-6
ISBN 10:   0-321-71305-2

9 8 7 6 5 4 3 2 1

Printed and bound in the United States of America

CONTENTS

INTRODUCTION

We're desktop publishers—just like you. We've been through the long shifts (some of them longer than 70 hours), entering and editing text, setting type, drawing paths, importing images, and trying to get files to print. On most of those late nights and early mornings, we could have been home in bed if we had known just one key piece of information. But we weren't. There was no one there to tell us.

We're here to tell you.

If some piece of information in this book saves you one late night, one early morning, or gets your document to print on the first pass through the imagesetter instead of the second or third, we will have succeeded in our purpose.

How This Book Was Produced

To answer the question we've been asked so many times: Yes, we produced this book in Adobe InDesign. We wrote some sections in Microsoft Word, saved them as RTF files, and imported them into InDesign. We wrote other sections using InDesign's Story Editor. We captured screens using Snapz Pro and SnagIt. To produce other graphics, we used InDesign's tools, Photoshop, and Illustrator.

David and Bob used 15-inch MacBook Pro laptops running Mac OS 10.6 (and Windows 7 under VMWare Fusion). Ole laid out chapters on a homebrew system (he's a gamer—what do you expect?) running Windows XP and on a Thinkpad T61p running Windows 7.

We used Adobe's Minion Pro family for our body text—a workhorse typeface that manages to look both modern and classical at the same time. It takes years to really get to know a typeface, and we've reached a point of happy familiarity with this one. For code, we used TheSansMonoCondensed, by Lucas de Groot (from lucasfonts.com). We think it is the best monospaced font available for setting code (much, much better than the Courier everyone else uses.

Real World Concerns

Since this is a "Real World" book, we're going to talk a bit about some or our real world challenges. It's not just the kids, our spouses/partners, and various life events that seem to make producing a book difficult. It's the macroeconomic climate and how it affects the microeconomy of writing and producing a computer book.

First, you may have noticed some large-scale economic changes in the last few years. Due to the World Economy falling off a cliff, everyone's either broke or scared, and, either way, they're not spending any money on software upgrades or third-party how-to books. Next, printed books just aren't doing that well as a market or medium. Finally, the cost of paper, relative to the total cost of printing, has gone through the roof.

If we wanted to publish this book, we were told, we'd have to cut pages. About a hundred pages. While adding all of the new features in InDesign CS5.

This meant not only cutting jokes and charming anecdotes, but making really tough decisions about what sections to pull out of the book; what sections to reduce to their bare essentials, and what sections to put online (see "Bonus Materials," below).

We considered publishing this as an entirely online book. We considered breaking it into separate chapters and selling them *a la carte*. We thought about keeping the CS4 version in print and creating a shorter "What's New?" title that covered only the differences since the earlier version. We couldn't think of a way that made any kind of economic sense, given the time frame that we had.

We're still thinking about it. We think we came up with the right blend of cuts, additions, and online bonus materials, but we're open to new ideas. If you have an opinion on what future form this information should take, please let us know.

Bonus Materials

We cut a lot of information out of this book to keep the size down. Bonus materials include XML workflow information (an entire chapter), scripting resources, and more. To access this material on the web, you will need to register your book. Go to this link:

www.peachpit.com/realworldindesigncs5

After you've registered, click "Access to protected content" next to the book title in your registered products list.

Welcome, Bob!

Ole and David's circumstances have changed since the last edition—changed in ways that make it difficult for them to crank out another book as they have in the past. Ole's job at Adobe has become much more demanding—he doesn't have any "slow times" anymore (as he usually did after a Creative Suite release in his previous position). David…well, it's hard to describe just how chaotic and demanding David's life and work are right now. We were thinking that we wouldn't be able to write and update an edition for InDesign CS5, and had pretty much decided not to do it.

With that, David and Ole would like to introduce Bob Bringhurst, our new co-author. Bob is a definite partner, and brings a fresh voice to the book. He's a fantastic guy, and great to work with. We're delighted to have him with us.

As an Adobe employee for the last 12 years, Bob has written documentation for every InDesign version since InDesign 1.0. He has been the *only* InDesign writer since InDesign CS2. Bob had also written third party software books and magazine articles (on WordPerfect and Word) before working at Adobe.

The figures lying in the snow in some of the new images in this edition are Bob's children, not members of the Franklin Expedition or Scott's doomed attempt to reach the South Pole.

Acknowledgments

Thanks to Adobe's InDesign team and all the other folks at (or *formerly at* Adobe—another sign of the economic hard times we referred to) Adobe who helped support this book—including Michael Ninness, Lynly Schambers-Lenox, Whitney McCleary, Chad Siegel, Bur Davis, Angie Hammond, Matt Phillips, Tommy Donovan, Douglas Waterfall, Eric Menninga, David Stephens, Jonathan Brown, Alan Stearns, Dov Isaacs, Zak Williamson, Paul Sorrick, Mark Niemann-Ross, Christine Yarrow, John Hake, Adrian O'Lenskie, and the other members of the Adobe Developer Technologies group (especially Lee Huang, Ole's long-suffering neighbor).

We appreciate the growing web of InDesign users and trainers with whom we love to trade cool tips and tricks, including Bob Levine, Anne-Marie Concepción, Sandee Cohen, Claudia McCue, Steve Werner, Pariah S. Burke, Scott Citron, Rufus Deuchler, Diane Burns, Avery Raskin, Dave Saunders, Branislav Milic, Mordy Golding, Mike Rankin, Michael Murphy, Pam Pfiffner, and Ted LoCascio.

Thanks to Jan C. Wright, Queen of Indexing, for our index. She won the 2009 ASI/H.W. Wilson Award for Excellence in Indexing, sometimes referred to as the "Pulitzer Prize of Indexing" for a previous edition—the first time a technical book has ever won the award.

Thanks to our friends at Peachpit Press for their patience, support, professionalism, patience, and understanding (and did we mention patience?), including Nancy Ruenzel, Nancy Davis, our editor Susan Rimerman, Lisa "see myk" Brazieal, and Charlene Will.

DAVID: "My deepest appreciation to my wife and partner, Debbie Carlson, as well as to our sons Gabriel and Daniel, who ensured that sanity wouldn't gain the upper hand. My thanks, too, go to Anne-Marie, Niyaz, Ted Falcon, and many other friends and helpers."

OLE: "Thanks to my incredible friends, to my partner, Amy Lanset, and to my son, Max Olav Kvern, for their love and support."

BOB: "All my thanks go to my wife Wendy, as well as to my twin sons Luke and Max, who agreed to be ignored for a few months while I worked on this book."

Olav Martin Kvern
okvern@ix.netcom.com

David Blatner
david@indesignsecrets.com

Bob Bringhurst
bobbringhurst@gmail.com

CHAPTER 1

Workspace

Come on in! Let us show you around. We'll be your tour guides to the world of InDesign. We're here to tell you what's what, what's where, and how it fits together. This chapter is all about InDesign's user interface—the myriad windows, panels, menus, and other gadgets InDesign displays on your screen. It tells you what they all are, and what we call them. This is important, because not everything in InDesign is clearly labeled—as you read through the techniques in this book, you need to know that we mean this button *over here*, and not that button *over there*.

This chapter also contains lots of tips and tricks for working with InDesign's user interface. These are the "little things" that make all the difference between enjoying and hating the time you spend working with InDesign (or any other program, for that matter). The point is to get you up to speed with all of these new tools so that you can get on with your work.

If you have used earlier versions of InDesign, you're no doubt wondering: *does Adobe have to change the user interface with each new version*? We don't know. Probably.

Ready? Let's start the tour.

A Note About Keyboard Shortcuts: Throughout this book, we will refer to keyboard shortcuts using the format: Mac OS/Windows, as in "Command-Z/Ctrl-Z" (this is not necessarily in our order of platform preference, but it is in alphabetical order).

Another Note About Keyboard Shortcuts: Since you can redefine most of the keyboard shortcuts in InDesign, we can't guarantee that your keyboard shortcuts will match ours. And we can't follow every keyboard shortcut in the text with the disclaimer, "…or the shortcut you've defined for this action." As you read this, bear in mind that we're using the shortcuts from the default keyboard shortcut set.

Yet Another Note About Keyboard Shortcuts: A few of InDesign's default keyboard shortcuts—especially those for selecting tools—do not use a modifier key (by "modifier key," we mean Command, Control, Option, Ctrl, Alt, Shift, and so on). If you're editing text, you can't use these keyboard shortcuts without deselecting the text, or you'll end up entering characters in the text.

The keyboard shortcut to switch to the Pen tool, for example, is "P." If you press the shortcut while the cursor is in text, you'll enter the character "P." If you use InDesign to set type (as most of us do), you'll almost certainly want to add a modifier key to the unmodified keyboard shortcuts you use most often.

Layout and Story Windows

When you open or create an InDesign document, you view and work on the publication using one or more windows (see Figure 1-1). InDesign windows come in two flavors: *layout windows* give you a view of a page or spread; *story windows* show a section of text in a document. You can have multiple windows of either type open at once. We'll cover story windows in more detail in "The Story Editor," in Chapter 3, "Text."

The view of the document you see in a layout window can be magnified or reduced, and each layout window can be set to a different magnification. Since magnification is primarily a way of moving around in your publication, we'll cover it later in this chapter, in "Publication Navigation."

Application Frame   On the Mac OS, you can choose to have InDesign keep its windows inside a single frame or to treat each window as a separate item. Turn on the Application Frame option from the Window menu to do the former; turn it off if you prefer to accidentally switch out of InDesign by clicking on the desktop or a window belonging to some other application. If you turn this option off, the close/minimize/maximize buttons will disappear from the Application Bar and appear on each window.

FIGURE 1-1
InDesign Windows

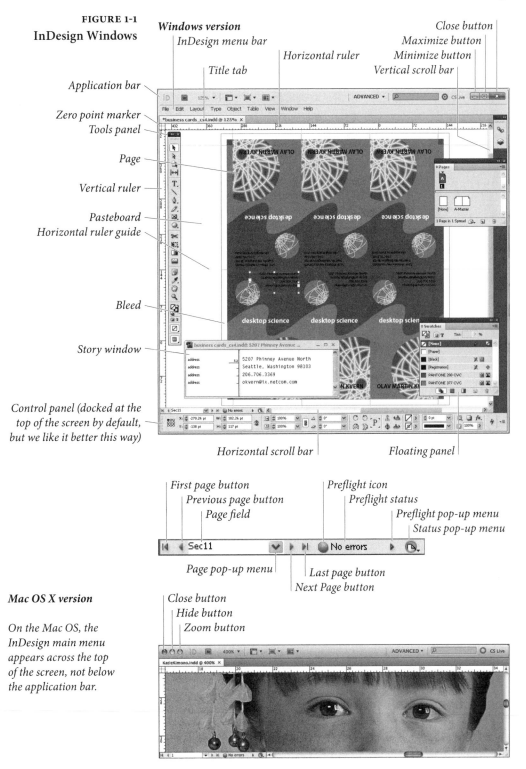

Windows version

InDesign menu bar

Title tab

Horizontal ruler

Close button
Maximize button
Minimize button
Vertical scroll bar

Application bar

Zero point marker
Tools panel

Page

Vertical ruler

Pasteboard
Horizontal ruler guide

Bleed

Story window

Control panel (docked at the top of the screen by default, but we like it better this way)

Horizontal scroll bar

Floating panel

First page button
Previous page button
Page field

Preflight icon
Preflight status

Preflight pop-up menu
Status pop-up menu

Page pop-up menu

Last page button
Next Page button

Mac OS X version

Close button
Hide button
Zoom button

On the Mac OS, the InDesign main menu appears across the top of the screen, not below the application bar.

Application Bar   At the top of the screen, you'll usually see the Application Bar (see Figure 1-2), which contains controls for changing the workspace and window arrangement, changing window magnification, launching Adobe Bridge, and searching Adobe's online InDesign help.

The appearance of the Application Bar differs slightly between the Windows and Mac OS versions of InDesign. In Windows, you'll see the control menu, close/minimize/maximize buttons, and you might see the main menu (if the window is maximized). The main menu on the Mac OS appears at the top of the screen, and is not associated with the window.

On the Mac OS, you can turn the Application Bar on or off—it's an option on the Window menu (when Application Frame is off).

FIGURE 1-2
Application Bar

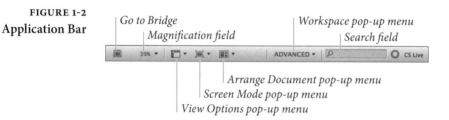

Title Bar   At the top of a document window you'll see the title bar or title tab, which contains the name of the document. If the document has not been saved, an asterisk (*) appears next to the name.

To close a window, press Command-W/Ctrl-W (or Ctrl-F4 in Windows). To close all windows, press Command-Option-Shift-W/Ctrl-Alt-Shift-W. If you have unsaved changes in any of the documents you're closing, InDesign will ask if you want to save them.

Pasteboard   Like most other page layout programs, InDesign is built around the metaphor of the traditional layout table. In the days before this desktop publishing fad came along, we would lay out our pages on a table, drafting board, or desk. As we did our layout, we'd place our waxed galleys of type and artwork on the pasteboard, an area off the page. We would then move the items onto our layout as they were needed. The pasteboard is the same in InDesign—an area off the page on which you can place elements for future use (see Figure 1-3).

The pasteboard is not a fixed size, as it was in PageMaker, and it's not shared between spreads—each spread has its own pasteboard (as in QuarkXPress). You can use areas of the pasteboard for temporary storage of the elements you're working with—just drag the elements off the page, and they'll stay on the pasteboard until you need them (again, this is just like an old-fashioned layout board).

FIGURE 1-3
Pasteboard

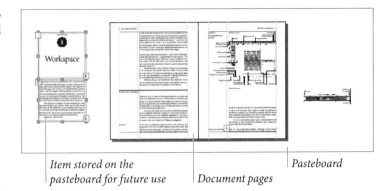

Item stored on the
pasteboard for future use   Document pages   Pasteboard

By the way, you can also make the height of the pasteboard larger (providing more space above and below the page); we cover that in "Guides and Pasteboard Preferences," later in this chapter.

Scroll Bars   The most obvious, least convenient, and slowest way to change your view of your publication is to use a scroll bar (that is, to click in a scroll bar, drag a scroll handle, or click the scroll arrows). For more on better ways to get around, see "Publication Navigation," later in this chapter.

Page Field and   The Page field/pop-up menu and its attached navigation buttons give
Page Buttons   you a way to get from one page to another. Click the Previous Page button to move to the previous page in your publication, or click the Next Page button to move to the next page. Alternatively, you can click the First Page button to go to the first page in the publication, or the Last Page button to go to the last one.

   If you know exactly which page you want to go to, choose the page number from the Page pop-up menu or enter the page number in the Page field. You can jump directly to the Go To Page dialog box by pressing Command-J/Ctrl-J.

Zoom Level   Enter a magnification percentage in this field in the Application Bar, or choose one from the attached pop-up menu, and InDesign magnifies or reduces the view of the document you see in the window. There are better ways to do this, as we show in "Publication Navigation," later in this chapter.

Preflight   The Preflight area (the icon and related pop-up menu) in the lower-left of window shows you the preflight status of the document. For more on the Preflight feature, refer to Chapter 11, "Printing."

Status Pop-Up Menu The Status pop-up menu lets you display the document in its folder, in Bridge, or in Mini Bridge. Choose Reveal in Finder (Mac OS) or Reveal in Explorer (Windows) to open the folder containing the document. Choose Reveal in Bridge to display the folder in Bridge. Choose Reveal in Mini Bridge to display the folder in Mini Bridge.

Rulers Pressing Command-R/Ctrl-R displays or hides InDesign's rulers—handy measuring tools that appear along the top and left sides of a publication window (see Figure 1-4). The rulers are marked off in the units of measurement specified in the Units & Increments Preferences dialog box. The increments shown on the rulers vary with the current magnification; in general, you'll see finer increments and more ruler tick marks at 800% size than you'll see at 12% size.

As you move the cursor, lines in the rulers (we call them "shadow cursors") display the cursor's position on the rulers (see Figure 1-5).

To change the units of measurement used by a ruler, Control-click/Right-click the ruler to display the Context menu. Choose a new measurement system from the menu, or choose Custom to enter a custom measurement increment (if you do this, InDesign displays the Custom Measurement Unit dialog box, where you can enter the measurement unit you want to use).

Zero Point The intersection of the zero measurement on both rulers is called the zero point. To change the location of the zero point, drag the zero point marker (see Figure 1-6).

As you drag, intersecting dotted lines show you the position of the zero point. Stop dragging, and the rulers will mark off their

FIGURE 1-4
Rulers

The Context menu on the rulers is the quickest way to change measurement units.

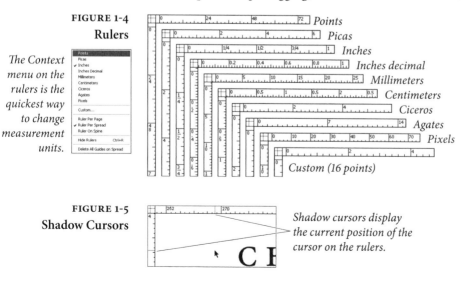

Points
Picas
Inches
Inches Decimal
Millimeters
Centimeters
Ciceros
Agates
Pixels
Custom...
Ruler Per Page
Ruler Per Spread
Ruler On Spine
Hide Rulers Ctrl+R
Delete All Guides on Spread

Points
Picas
Inches
Inches decimal
Millimeters
Centimeters
Ciceros
Agates
Pixels
Custom (16 points)

FIGURE 1-5
Shadow Cursors

252
270

Shadow cursors display the current position of the cursor on the rulers.

FIGURE 1-6

Moving the Zero Point

Position the cursor over the zero point marker.

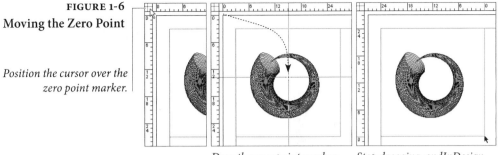

Drag the zero point marker.

Stop dragging, andInDesign moves the zero point.

increments based on the new position of the zero point marker. To reset the zero point to the default location, double-click the zero point marker.

To lock the position of the zero point, use the Context menu. Point at the zero point, then hold down Control and click (Macintosh) or click the right mouse button (Windows). Choose Lock Zero Point from the Context menu (see Figure 1-7). To unlock the zero point, display the Context menu and turn off Lock Zero Point.

FIGURE 1-7

Locking the Zero Point

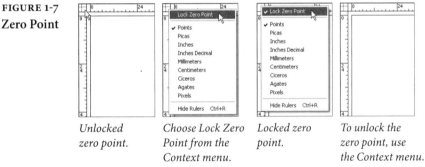

Unlocked zero point.

Choose Lock Zero Point from the Context menu.

Locked zero point.

To unlock the zero point, use the Context menu.

Managing Multiple Windows

To open more than one window on a document, choose "New Window" from the Arrange submenu of the Window menu. Now that you have two windows open, you can arrange them by choosing either Tile Windows Horizontally or Tile Windows Vertically from the Arrange submenu of the Window menu (see Figure 1-8). Choose Cascade from the Arrange submenu of the Window menu to stack the open document windows on top of each other. You can other arrangement options from the Arrange Documents pop-up menu on the Application bar.

FIGURE 1-8
Window Views

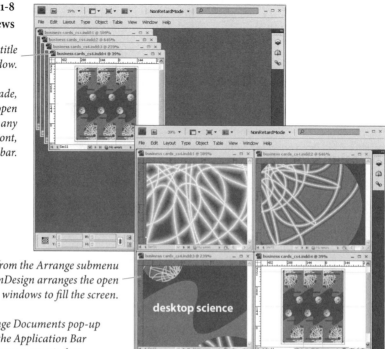

InDesign highlights the title bar of the active window.

When you choose Cascade, InDesign stacks the open windows. To bring any window to the front, click its title bar.

In either view, you can rearrange and resize windows to create custom views.

When you choose Tile from the Arrange submenu of the Window menu, InDesign arranges the open windows to fill the screen.

The Arrange Documents pop-up menu on the Application Bar provides even more window arrangements.

To switch from an active document window to an inactive document window, click any part of the inactive window or choose a window name from the listing of open windows at the bottom of the Window menu. Or, better yet, press Command-`/Ctrl-` (accent grave) to switch from one open window to the next.

Sometimes it's easier to display pages in multiple windows than it is to scroll or zoom from page to page. Think about using multiple windows on a single document in the following situations:

▶ When you find yourself jumping back and forth between two or more locations in a publication.

▶ When you need to copy an object or objects from one page to another page that's several pages away. Dragging the objects from one publication window to another is faster than scrolling and dragging or cutting and pasting.

▶ When you're trying to fit copy into a story that spans several pages. Make one window focus on the end of the story, and you can view the end of the story as you edit text.

There's no trick to removing a view—simply close the window, and it disappears from your Windows menu.

You can also have as many different documents (files) open as you like. You switch from one publication to another by choosing a window name from Window menu, or by clicking on their windows.

To close all open windows, hold down Option as you click the Close box (Macintosh) or hold down Alt as you click the Close button (Windows). Or press Command-Option-Shift-W/Ctrl-Alt-Shift-W.

InDesign's Panels

Can you see your page? If not, it's probably due to InDesign's omni-present panels—there are plenty of them. Don't rush out to buy a larger screen—you don't have to have all of the panels open all of the time. The best way to work with InDesign's panels is to have the minimum number of them open at once, to combine panels into functional groups and workspaces, and to learn and master the keyboard shortcuts for working with and navigating through panels. That's what this part of the book is about.

InDesign's panels work two ways—they display information about the document or the selected object, and they provide controls for changing the publication and the objects in it.

Note: You've probably noticed that most of the panels in our illustrations use proper capitalization, rather than the ALL CAPS default. To make your panels look like this, add an empty folder named "NoAllCaps" to your InDesign application folder.

All About Focus   When a particular window, field, or control is active, we say it has "focus"—it's receiving any keystrokes you might press. If you're pressing keys, and yet no text is appearing in the selected text frame, it's because something else—another window or field—has focus.

Understanding and manipulating panel focus is very important—especially when you're working with text.

When you choose a menu option or click a button in a panel, InDesign applies the change and returns focus to your page layout. When you press Tab to move ahead one field (or Shift-Tab to move back one field), InDesign applies any change you made and shifts focus to the next (or previous) panel field.

InDesign offers a number of keyboard shortcuts for controlling keyboard focus:

▶ Press Enter/Return to apply a value you've entered in a panel field and return focus to your page.

> ▶ Press Shift-Return/Shift-Enter to apply the value you've entered in a panel field and keep that panel field in focus.

> ▶ You can return to the last-used panel field by pressing Command-Option-~/Ctrl-Alt-~ (tilde; that's the key in the upper-left corner of the keyboard). The panel must be visible for this to work. If you want to change this, look for the "Activate last used field in panel" feature in the Views and Navigation product area of the Keyboard Shortcuts dialog box (see "Keyboard Shortcuts," later in this chapter).

> ▶ In any of the "list" panels (the Swatches panel or Character Styles panel, for example), press Command-Option/Ctrl-Alt and click in the list. This transfers focus to the list—you'll see a heavy outline appear around the list. Press the up and down arrows, or type the name of an item to select that item from the list.

> ▶ When you double-click the name of an item in many of the panels (the Layers, Paragraph Styles, and Tags panels, for example), you can edit the name of the item.

Displaying and Hiding Panels

You can use keyboard shortcuts to show and hide panels and save yourself lots of mouse movement (see Table 1-1). If a panel is open, but is hiding behind other panels in a group, pressing the keyboard shortcut brings the panel to the front of the group. To close a panel, press the shortcut again, or click the Close button on the panel's title bar (the "X").

Zipping and Unzipping Panels. It's easy to run out of room on your screen to see anything *but* the panels. You can shrink a panel down to just its tab and title bar by clicking the area at the top of the panel, away from the title tab (see Figure 1-9). When you want to display the entire panel, click the area at the top of the panel again.

Hiding All Panels. Press Tab, and all of the panels currently shown disappear; press it again, and they reappear. This shortcut won't work

FIGURE 1-9
Zipping and Unzipping Panels

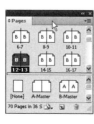

Click the area at the top of the panel...

...and InDesign "zips" the panel. Click again to restore the panel to its original size.
You can also do this by clicking the little minimize/ maximize button (the "-" near the top right corner of the panel). It's a lot harder to hit.

TABLE 1-1
Panel Keyboard
Shortcuts

To display this panel:	Press:
Align	Shift-F7
Attributes	None/Alt-W, B
Character	Command-T/Ctrl-T
Character Styles	Command-Shift-F11/Shift-F11
Check Spelling	Command-I/Ctrl-I
Color	F6
Control	Command-Option-6/Ctrl-Alt-6
Find/Change	Command-F/Ctrl-F
Effects	Command-Shift-F10/Ctrl-Shift-F10
Glyphs	Shift-Option-F11/Shift-Alt-F11
Gradient	None/Alt-W, D
Index	Shift-F8
Info	F8
Layers	F7
Links	Command-Shift-D/Ctrl-Shift-D
Object Styles	Command-F7/Ctrl-F7
Pages	Command-F12/F12
Paragraph	Command-Option-T/Ctrl-Alt-T
Paragraph Styles	Command-F11/F11
Pathfinder	None/Alt-W, J, P
Preflight	Command-Shift-Option-F/ Ctrl-Shift-Alt-F
Preview	Command-Shift-Return/ Ctrl-Shift-Enter
Scripts	Command-Option-F11/Ctrl-Alt-F11
Story	None/Alt-T, R
Stroke	Command-F10/F10
Swatches	F5
Table	Shift-F9
Tabs	Command-Shift-T/Ctrl-Shift-T
Text Wrap	Command-Option-W/Ctrl-Alt-W
Tools	None/Alt-W, T

when you have text selected or have an active text cursor in a text frame (it'll enter a tab character, instead). Press Shift+Tab to hide panels without hiding the Tools panel.

Reducing a panel to an icon. Zipping a panel makes it smaller, but to make it smaller still, you can reduce the panel to an icon. To do this, double-click the bar at the very top of the panel or click the very tiny Collapse to Icons button (see Figure 1-10).

FIGURE 1-10
**Reducing a
Panel to an Icon**

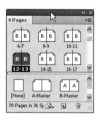

Click the bar at the top of the panel…

Collapse to Icons button

…and InDesign collapses the panel to an icon.

Click again to expand the panel.

Displaying options. Many of InDesign's panels can be set to display all of the available options for a particular feature, or a subset of those options. To expand the panel to show all its features, select Show Options from the panel menu, or click the little arrow icon to the left of the panel name (see Figure 1-11).

FIGURE 1-11
**Showing/Hiding
Panel Options**

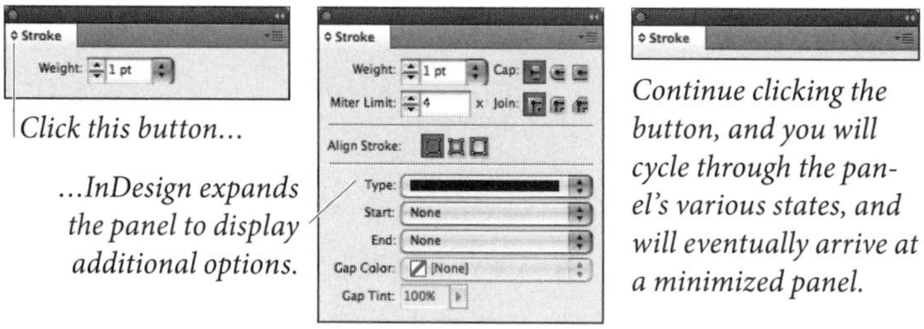

Click this button…

…InDesign expands the panel to display additional options.

Continue clicking the button, and you will cycle through the panel's various states, and will eventually arrive at a minimized panel.

Resizing panels. To resize a panel, drag the Resize box at the panel's lower-right corner (see Figure 1-12). If a panel doesn't have a Resize box, you can't resize it. You can drag the sides of some of the panels.

FIGURE 1-12
Resizing Panels

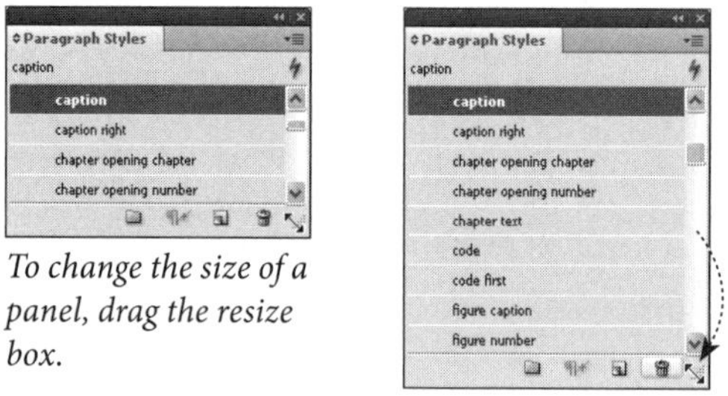

To change the size of a panel, drag the resize box.

Snapping panels into position. When you drag a panel near the edge of another panel, InDesign snaps the edge of the panel you're moving to the closest edge of the other panel. This makes it easy to arrange and resize panels in relation to other panels.

Grouping and separating panels. When you first launch InDesign, you'll notice that some panels are combined. For example, Paragraph Styles and Character styles are grouped together. You can rearrange any of these panels, pull panels groups apart, or combine the panels any way you want (see Figure 1-13). We all have different work habits, and tabbed panels give us a way of customizing InDesign to fit our particular habits and needs.

FIGURE 1-13
Grouping Panels

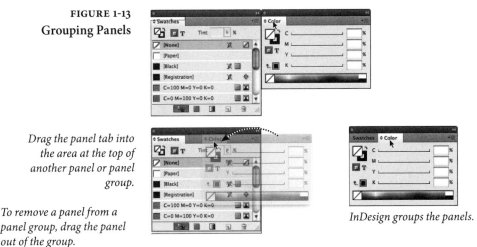

Drag the panel tab into the area at the top of another panel or panel group.

To remove a panel from a panel group, drag the panel out of the group.

InDesign groups the panels.

To combine panels, drag the tab of one panel into the area at the top of another panel (Adobe calls this a "drop zone"). When you combine two or more panels, you are creating a "panel group." A panel group behaves as if it is a single panel—the panels move, resize, and zip/unzip as a unit.

In any panel group, only one panel can be "on top" at a time; only the tabs of the other panels in the group are visible. To display another panel in the group, click the panel's tab or press the keyboard shortcut for the panel.

Stacking panels. Another way to customize the layout of InDesign's panels is to "stack" one panel on another. When you do this, both panels remain visible (in contrast to grouped panels, where only the uppermost panel is visible), and move, hide, display, or resize as a single panel.

To do this, drag the tab of a panel into the area at the bottom of another panel. InDesign highlights the bottom of the target panel. Stop dragging and InDesign stacks the panels (see Figure 1-14).

FIGURE 1-14
Stacking Panels

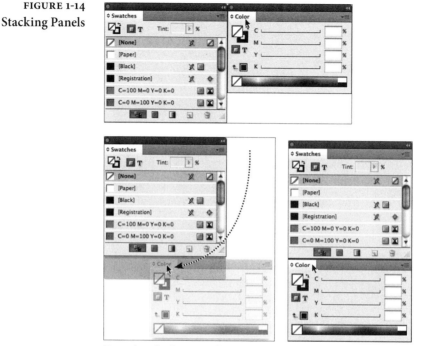

Drag the tab of one panel into the bottom of another panel. InDesign displays a highlight when the panels are ready to stack.

Stop dragging and release the mouse button. InDesign stacks the two panels (they will now move as a single unit).

Docking panels. Another way to show and hide panels is to use InDesign's "dock" feature. When you drag a panel tab within a few pixels of the left or right edge of the screen or the application frame, InDesign adds the panel to a dock, a special area at either side of the screen. Panels in the dock are shown as icons, either with or without the name of the panel, depending on the width of the dock (see Figure 1-15).

To expand a docked panel, click the panel's icon or press the panel's keyboard shortcut. To collapse the panel again, click its tab (or press the keyboard shortcut again).

To dock all of the panels in a panel group, drag the top of the panel group into the dock or hold down Option/Alt as you drag the panel tab into the dock area.

You can't move the Control panel or the Tabs panel into the dock areas at the sides of the workspace. You can, however, dock the

FIGURE 1-15
Docking Panels

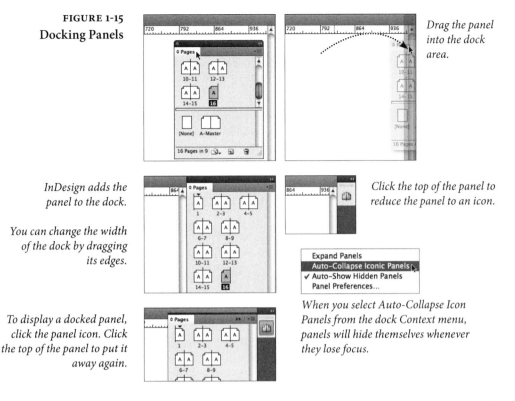

Drag the panel into the dock area.

InDesign adds the panel to the dock.

You can change the width of the dock by dragging its edges.

Click the top of the panel to reduce the panel to an icon.

When you select Auto-Collapse Icon Panels from the dock Context menu, panels will hide themselves whenever they lose focus.

To display a docked panel, click the panel icon. Click the top of the panel to put it away again.

Control panel to the top or bottom. When you do this, the Control panel isn't reduced to an icon.

To turn a docked panel back into a floating panel, drag the panel's icon out of the dock. Hold down Option/Alt and drag a panel group to convert the entire group to a floating panel group.

Small Panel Rows. To reduce the height of each item in any of the "list" panels (such as the Paragraph Styles and Layers panels), choose Small Panel Rows from the panel's pop-up menu (see Figure 1-16).

FIGURE 1-16
Small Panel Rows

Choose Small Panel Rows from the panel menu…

…and InDesign reduces the height of each item.

Overriding Units of Measurement. Being able to switch from one measurement system to another is great, but what do you do when you want to enter a value in a measurement system other than the one currently selected? Do you have to go to the Units & Increments Preferences dialog box and switch to another measurement system? No—all you need to do add a "measurement override" when you enter the value. Want to enter 115.3 points in a field that's currently showing decimal inches? It's easy: enter "115.3 pt," or even "0p115.3" in the field, and InDesign will take care of the conversion for you. You can use these shortcuts in any numeric field in any InDesign panel or dialog box. Table 1-2 shows you how to enter measurement overrides.

You can also cycle through measurement units by pressing Command-Option-Shift-U/Ctrl-Alt-Shift-U when any measurement field has focus (note, though, that this changes the measurement system in all fields and rulers).

Doing Arithmetic in Fields. You can add, subtract, multiply, or divide in any numeric field in any InDesign panel or dialog box. Want an object to be half its current width? Type "/2" after the value in the W (width) field in the Transform panel and press Enter. Want an object to move two picas to the right? Enter "+2p" (yes, all of the measurement unit overrides shown above work with these operations) after the value shown in the X field in the Transform panel. Enter "*" to multiply, or "-" to subtract. You get the idea.

TABLE 1-2
Measurement Overrides

When you want:	Enter:	Example:
points	pt	136 pt
points	0p	0p136
picas	p	1p
picas and points	p	1p6
inches	i*	1.56i
millimeters	mm**	2.45mm
ciceros	c	3c
ciceros and didots	c	3c4
agates	a**	3a
pixels	px	136 px

or "in," or even "inch" if you feel the need to type the extra characters.

*** Oddly enough, you have to type "mm," even though there is no other measurement that starts with "m."*

**** or "ag," if you feel the need to type the extra characters.*

You can also enter percentages as part of any arithmetic operation. For example, if you replace a value with "25%" and press Enter, InDesign enters one quarter of the value for you.

Using the Tools Panel

If the publication window is the layout board where you collect the galleys of type, and illustrations you want to use in your publication, the Tools panel is where you keep your waxer, X-Acto knife, T-square, and bandages. (Note to youngsters: there were tools used in the early days of page layout. You don't have to understand how they work to use the corresponding tools in InDesign. But it helps.)

Some of the following descriptions aren't going to make any sense until you understand how InDesign's points and paths work, and that discussion falls in Chapter 5, "Drawing." You can flip ahead and read that section, or you can plow through this section and figure it out as you go. It's your choice, and either method works.

You can break InDesign's Tools panel (as shown in Figure 1-17) into conceptual sections.

▶ Selection tools (the Selection, Direct Selection, Page and Gap tools) select objects, pages, or space between objects. You can do different things with the objects depending on the selection tool you've used.

▶ Tools for drawing basic shapes (the Rectangle, Polygon, Ellipse, and Line tools) and their equivalent frames (Rectangle Frame, Polygon Frame, and Ellipse Frame tools) draw complete paths containing specific numbers of points in specific positions on the path.

▶ Path-drawing and editing tools (the Pen, Add Point, Delete Point, Convert Point, Pencil, Eraser, Smooth, and Scissors tools) draw paths point by point (or, in the case of the Scissors tool, delete points or split paths).

▶ Transformation tools (the Rotate, Shear, Scale, and Free Transform tools) change the rotation angle, size, and skewing angle of objects on your pages.

▶ Text editing tools (the Type tool and Path Type tool) give you a way to enter and edit text (the latter along a path). The Notes tool adds non-printing notes to text.

FIGURE 1-17
The Tools Panel

Click this button to switch between different Tools panel views (single column, double column, and single row).

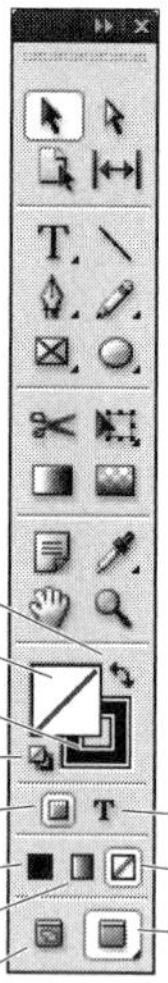

Swap fill/stroke (Shift-X)
Fill (X)
Stroke(X)
Default fill/stroke (D)
Formatting affects container
Apply Color (,)
Apply None (/)
Normal View Mode (W)

Formatting affects text
Apply Gradient (.)
Preview Mode (W)

When you see a tiny arrow in the corner of a tool icon, more tools lurk beneath the surface.

To select a "hidden" tool, position the cursor over a tool, then hold down the mouse button.

InDesign displays a "flyout" menu containing the available tools.

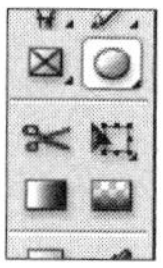

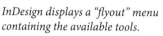

Choose a tool from the menu and release the mouse button.

To switch to any tool temporarily, hold down the shortcut keystroke for that key. When you release the key, the previous tool is selected again.

	Tool name	Shortcut		Tool name	Shortcut
	Selection	V		Rectangle	M
	Direct Selection	A		Rectangle Frame	F
	Page	Shift-P		Polygon	
	Gap	U		Polygon Frame	
	Type	T		Scissors	C
	Path Type	Shift-T		Free Transform	E
	Line	\		Rotate	R
	Pen	P		Scale	S
	Add Point	+		Shear	O
	Delete Point	-		Gradient	G
	Convert Point	Shift-C		Gradient Feather	Shift-G
	Pencil	N		Note	
	Smooth			Eyedropper	I
	Erase			Measure	K
	Ellipse	L		Hand	H
	Ellipse Frame			Zoom	Z

▶ Navigation tools (the Zoom and Hand tools) help you move around in your publication.

▶ Object formatting tools (the Fill and Stroke selectors, the Gradient tool, and the Gradient Feather tool) provide ways to apply formatting to objects.

The tool descriptions below are brief and are only intended to give you a feeling for what the different tools are and what they do. To learn more about entering text with the Type tool, see Chapter 3, "Text." For more on drawing objects with the drawing tools, see Chapter 5, "Drawing." For more on working with the Transformation tools, see Chapter 9, "Transforming."

Tool Hints. The Tool Hints panel not only shows which shortcut activates each tool, but also which modifier keys work with the tool. Choose Utilities from the Window menu, and then choose Tool Hints to open the Tool Hints panel. Then select a tool to see how to use it.

Spring-loaded tools. Here's an Illustrator feature that finally made its way into InDesign. While you're using one tool, you can temporarily switch to another tool. While one tool is selected, press the tool shortcut—and keep holding it down—perform your action, and when you release the shortcut key, the original tool is still active. We love it for quickly using the Direct Selection tool (A) when we're drawing with the Pen tool, or switching temporarily to the Selection tool (V) to nudge an object when we're using the new Gap tool. Try it.

Changing the Tools Panel View. You can display the Tools panel in three different arrangements: single column, double column, and single row (horizontal). You can toggle between these views by clicking the tiny double-arrow icon at the top of the panel.

Tools Panel Keyboard Shortcuts. You can choose most of the tools in the Tools panel using keyboard shortcuts such as "F" for the Frame tool (no Command/Ctrl or other modifier key necessary). This is usually faster than going back across the screen to the panel. Note, however, that you can't press these while you're editing text. That's why we like to add additional keyboard shortcuts (see "Keyboard Shortcuts," later in this chapter) to the tools we use most often; for example, on David's system, Command-Shift-1/Ctrl-Shift-1 switches to the Selection tool when he's editing text.

Selection Tool

The Selection tool is the swiss-army knife of the Tools panel. Use it to select, resize, scale, and rotate objects. You can even manipulate content within frames by dragging that thing that looks like a donut (it's actually called the Content Grabber). Press V to select the Selection tool (when the cursor is not in text). The Selection tool's versatility is why the InDesign team dumped the Position tool and buried the Rotate tool under the Free Transform tool.

When you double-click a text frame with the Selection tool, you'll switch to the Type tool. When you double-click the contents of an object with the Selection tool, you'll switch back and forth between selecting the contents and selecting the frame.

We'll go into more detail on using the Selection tool. See "Selecting and Deselecting," in Chapter 2, "Page Layout," for more about making selections.

Direct Selection Tool

The Direct Selection tool (press A) is for selecting objects that are inside other objects, such as the following.

▶ Individual points on paths. For more on editing the shape of a path, see Chapter 5, "Drawing."

▶ Component paths of compound paths. For more on working with compound paths, see Chapter 5, "Drawing."

▶ Objects inside groups. For more on selecting objects inside groups, see Chapter 2, "Page Layout."

▶ Objects pasted inside other objects. For more on working with path contents, see Chapter 9, "Transforming."

Page Tool

Use the Page tool for creating different page sizes within a document. To create a different page size, press Shift+P to select the Page tool, and click the page in the layout to select it. Then use the options in the Control page to change the page layout.

For more on working with the Page tool, see Chapter 2, "Layout."

Gap Tool

Use the Gap tool to adjust the spacing between objects. If you select the Gap tool and try to use it without knowing what it does, you'll probably get frustrated because it utterly refuses to select objects.

Press U to select the Gap tool, place the pointer between objects, and drag to change the gap between aligned objects. Shift-drag to move the gap between only the two nearest objects; Ctrl-drag/Command-drag to resize the gap instead of moving it; Alt-drag/Option-drag to move the gap and objects in the same direction. Ctrl+Alt-drag/Command+Option-drag to resize the gap and move the objects. Adding the Shift key to any combination affects only the two nearest objects.

For more on working with the Gap tool, see Chapter 9, "Transforming."

Pen Tool

You use the Pen tool to draw paths containing both straight and curved line segments (that is, paths containing both curve and corner points). Illustrator users will recognize the Pen tool immediately, because it's pretty much identical to Illustrator's Pen tool (maybe there's something to all this "cross-product" talk, after all). Click the Pen tool to create a corner point; drag to create a curve point. Press P to select the Pen tool.

Under the Pen tool, you'll find the Add Point tool, the Delete Point tool, and the Convert Point tool.

For more (much more) on working with the Pen tool (and its variants) to draw and edit paths, see Chapter 5, "Drawing."

Type Tool

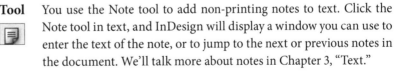

You enter and edit text using the Type tool. To create a text frame, select the Type tool and drag the tool in the publication window; a text frame appears with a flashing text-insertion point (or text cursor) in its first line. To edit text, select the Type tool and click in the text frame. For more on entering, editing, and formatting text, see Chapter 3, "Text." To select the Type tool, press T. Note that when you have the Selection or Direct Select tool chosen in the Tool panel, you can switch to the Type tool automatically by double-clicking any text frame. InDesign places the text cursor as close as possible to where you double-clicked.

Path Type Tool

Use the Path Type tool to enter and edit text on a path (Adobe calls this the "Type on a Path" tool). To add text to a path, select the Path Type tool and click the tool on a path. A flashing text insertion point (or text cursor) appears on the path. At this point, text you enter will flow along the path. See Chapter 6, "Where Text Meets Graphics." To select the Path Type tool, press Shift-T.

Note Tool

You use the Note tool to add non-printing notes to text. Click the Note tool in text, and InDesign will display a window you can use to enter the text of the note, or to jump to the next or previous notes in the document. We'll talk more about notes in Chapter 3, "Text."

Pencil Tool

If you're one of the millions of computer users who find the Pen tool—and the whole process of drawing by manipulating points, line segments, and control handles—confusing, give the Pencil tool a try. With the Pencil tool (press N), you can sketch free form paths. As you drag, InDesign creates a path that follows the cursor, automatically placing points and adjusting control handles as it does so.

If you don't like something about a path you've drawn using the Pencil tool, you can adjust it using any of InDesign's other drawing tools (including that scary Pen tool). You might want to start with the other tools that share the same space in the Tools panel: the Smooth tool and the Eraser tool (see below).

Smooth Tool

Select a path—any path—and drag the Smooth tool over it. It'll get smoother. Not smooth enough yet? Drag again. As you drag the Smooth tool, InDesign adjusts the points and control handles that define the path to create a smoother transition from one line segment to another. InDesign often removes points during this process. If you continue to repeat the smoothing process, we think you'll eventually end up with a simple curve between two points.

Eraser Tool

The Eraser tool erases line segments and points. To use the Eraser tool, select a path, then drag the eraser tool over part of the path. InDesign splits the path and removes the line segments and points where you dragged the Eraser tool.

Line Tool

Use the Line tool to draw straight lines—paths containing two corner points. If you hold down Shift as you drag the Line tool, the lines you draw will be constrained to 0-, 45-, and 90-degree angles. Press \ (backslash) to select the Line tool.

Ellipse Tool

Use the Ellipse tool to draw ellipses and circles. Hold down Shift as you drag the Ellipse tool, and InDesign draws circles. Press L to select the Ellipse tool.

Rectangle Tool

Use the Rectangle tool to draw rectangles. If you hold down Shift as you drag, you draw squares. Press M to select the Rectangle tool.

If you need a rectangle with rounded corners, draw the rectangle using the Rectangle tool, then choose Corner Options from the Object menu to display the Corner Options dialog box (you can also get to this dialog box via the context menu). The Corner Options dialog box can provide a variety of other corner shapes, as discussed in Chapter 5, "Drawing."

Polygon Tool

The Polygon tool makes it easy to draw equilateral polygons, such as pentagons, hexagons, and dodecagons. (Polygons are closed geometric objects that have at least three sides; they're equilateral if all sides are the same length.) You can also use the Polygon tool to draw stars.

To change which polygon the Polygon tool draws, double-click the tool in the Tools panel. InDesign displays the Polygon Settings dialog box (see Figure 1-18). Enter the number of sides you want in the Number of Sides field. If you want the polygon to be a star

FIGURE 1-18
Polygon Settings

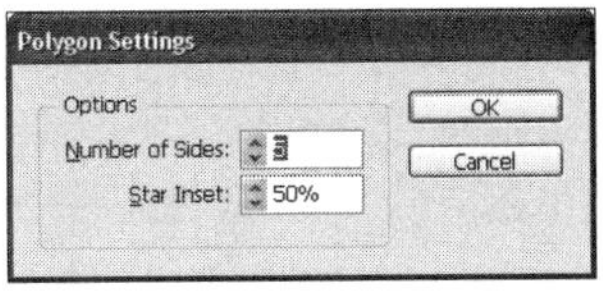

Polygon Settings

Options

Number of Sides: 3

Star Inset: 50%

OK

Cancel

polygon, enter a percentage (from 0 to 99 percent) in the Star Inset field. If you don't want the polygon to be a star polygon, enter 100 percent in the Star Inset field.

Want to impress your friends? Select the Polygon tool and start dragging a shape. Press the left and up arrow keys several times to create a grid of polygons. While still dragging, press the Spacebar, and press the left and up arrow keys again. Because you pressed the Spacebar, the arrow keys adjust the star inset and number of polygon sides. Press the Spacebar again to switch back to grid mode.

Rotate Tool

To rotate the selected object (or objects), select the Rotate tool from the toolbox (press R) and then drag the tool on your page. When you select the Rotate tool, InDesign displays the transformation center point icon on or around the selected object. The center point icon sets the center of rotation (the point you'll be rotating around), and corresponds to the selected point on the Proxy in the Transform and Control panels. Drag the transformation center point icon to a new location (or click one of the points in the Proxy) to change the point.

Hold down Shift as you drag the Rotate tool to constrain rotation to 45-degree increments (as you drag the Rotate tool, InDesign snaps the selection to 0, 45, 90, 135, 180, 225, 270, and 315 degree angles).

Scale Tool

To scale (or resize) an object, select the object, select the Scale tool, and then drag the tool in the publication window. When you select the Scale tool, InDesign displays the transformation center point icon on or around the selected object. The location of the center point icon sets the center of the scaling, and corresponds to the selected point on the Proxy in the Transform and Control panel. Drag the transformation center point icon to a new location (or click one of the points in the Proxy) to change the point you're scaling around.

Hold down Shift as you drag a corner handle to retain the object's proportions as you scale it. When you scale an object that has a stroke and Adjust Stroke Weight When Scaling is turned on in the Transform panel, the stroke may appear disproportional (thicker in some places and thinner in others) and the stroke weight in the Strokes and Control panels appears incorrect. You can fix both of these problems by choosing Redefine Scaling as 100% from either the Transform or Control panel menus.

Shear Tool

Shearing, or skewing, an object alters the angle of the vertical or horizontal axes of the object. This makes it appear that the plane containing the object has been slanted relative to the plane of the publication window. To shear an object, drag the Shear tool (press O) in the publication window. As you drag, InDesign shears the object.

When you shear an object, InDesign distorts the stroke weights of the paths in the selection. The Redefine Scaling as 100% feature mentioned above will fix this distortion, too.

Free Transform Tool

The Free Transform (press E) tool is a combination of the Scale, Rotate, and Selection tools, all bundled into a single tool. What the tool does depends on the position of the cursor. For more on working with the Free Transform tool, see Chapter 9, "Transforming."

▶ When the cursor is above one of an object's selection handles, the Free Transform tool acts as the Scale tool. Drag the Free Transform tool, and you scale the object around its center point.

▶ When the cursor is just outside one of the selection handles, the Free Transform tool behaves as if it were the Rotate tool. Drag the tool to rotate the object.

▶ When the Free Transform tool is inside the bounds of the selection, it acts as a "move" tool—drag the tool to move the object.

Eyedropper Tool

The Eyedropper tool (press I) can pick up formatting attributes (from the fill and stroke of a path to the character and paragraph formatting of text) and apply them to objects, or sample a color in an imported graphic and add it to your Swatches panel.

To "load" the Eyedropper tool, click the tool on an object (the object doesn't have to be selected). If you have an item selected when you click, InDesign applies the attributes of the item under the cursor to the selected item. Then click the "loaded" Eyedropper tool on an object to apply the formatting (see Figure 1-19).

Double-click the Eyedropper tool to display the Eyedropper Options dialog box. Use this dialog box to define the attributes sampled and affected by the Eyedropper tool (see Figure 1-20).

Measure Tool

The Measure tool—which is usually under the Eyedropper tool—gives you a way to measure distances and angles (see Figure 1-21).

To measure the distance between two points, select the Measure tool (press K) and drag it from one point to the other. When you drag the Measure tool, InDesign displays the Info panel. The D field in the Info panel shows the distance between the two points.

FIGURE 1-19
Eyedropper
Tool Options

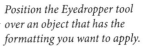

FIGURE 1-20
Eyedropper Tool

Select an object or a series of objects and then choose the Eyedropper tool from the Tools panel.

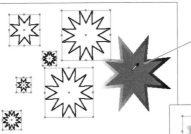

Position the Eyedropper tool over an object that has the formatting you want to apply.

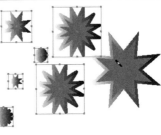

To format text using the Eyedropper tool, select the text using the Type tool.

Click the Eyedropper tool. InDesign applies the formatting of the object beneath the cursor to the selected objects.

Here's another method.

Select the Eyedropper tool from the Tools panel.

Position the cursor over an object and click. InDesign loads the Eyedropper tool with the formatting attributes of the object.

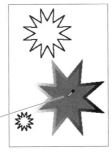

Click another object (it doesn't have to be selected). InDesign applies the formatting attributes to the object.

FIGURE 1-21
Measure Tool

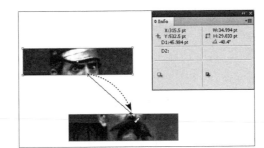

Drag the Measure tool between two points, and the Info panel will show you the distance between the points.

To measure an angle, select the Measure tool and drag it between two points—this creates one side of the angle. Next, hold down Option/Alt and drag from one of the end points of the line created by the Measure tool. This creates the other side of the angle. The Info panel displays the angle in the Angle field (it also displays the length of the two sides of the angle in the D1 and D2 fields).

Gradient Tool and Gradient Feather Tool

Use these tools to apply gradients or gradient feather fills, or to adjust fills you've applied. When you drag the tool, you're setting the location of the beginning and ending points of the gradient. We discuss gradients and blends in Chapter 5, "Drawing."

Scissors Tool

The Scissors tool cuts paths or points. Select a path, choose the Scissors tool (or press C), and then click the path. InDesign splits the path at the point at which you clicked.

Hand Tool

The Hand tool lets you scroll around your page; we explore how best to use it in "Publication Navigation," later in this chapter. Double-click the Hand tool to set the view to Fit Spread in Window.

Zoom Tool

Use the Zoom tool to change the magnification in a publication window. To switch to the Zoom tool, press Z. To switch to the Zoom tool temporarily, hold down Command-Spacebar/Ctrl-Spacebar (when you're done using the tool, InDesign will select the tool you were using before you switched to the Zoom tool).

Once you've switched to the Zoom tool, click the tool on the area you want to magnify, or drag a selection rectangle around it. To zoom out, hold down Option/Alt—you'll see that the plus ("+") inside the Zoom tool changes to minus ("-")—and then click or drag to zoom out.

For more on using the Zoom tool, see "Publication Navigation," later in this chapter. Double-clicking on the Zoom tool jumps to 100-percent View, but pressing Command-1 is easier and faster.

Fill and Stroke

The Fill and Stroke buttons, or "selectors," near the bottom of the Tools panel control what part (the fill or the stroke) of the selected path or text is affected when you apply a color. To make a selector active, click it. Here are two very useful shortcuts:

▶ Swap colors—apply the color assigned to the fill to the stroke, or vice versa—click the swap fill and stroke icon (or press Shift-X).

▶ Press X (when you're not editing text) to switch between the Fill selector and the Stroke selector.

Beneath the Fill and Stroke buttons, you'll see two very small buttons—the Formatting Affects Container button and the Formatting Affects Text button. Click the former button to apply the fill or stroke to the text frame; click the latter to apply it to the text.

As your eye proceeds down the Tools panel, you'll find three more buttons—they're shortcuts for applying colors or gradients, or for removing a fill or stroke from an object. Click the Apply Color button to apply the current color (in the Color panel or Swatches panel) to the fill or stroke of the selected object. The state of the Fill and Stroke selector determines which part of the object is affected. Click the Apply Gradient button to apply the current gradient (in the Swatches panel or the Gradient panel), and click the Apply None button to remove the fill or stroke from the selected object.

As you'd expect, InDesign has shortcuts for these buttons, too.

▶ To apply the most recently used color to the current fill or stroke (which attribute is affected depends on which selector is active), press , (comma—again, this won't work when text is selected).

▶ Press . (period) to apply the current gradient.

▶ Press / (slash) to remove the fill or stroke from the selected object or objects.

For more on applying colors, see Chapter 10, "Color."

Other Panels

Most of InDesign's other panels are discussed in the other chapters of this book. But there were a few (pesky) panels that didn't really fit in the other chapters, so we'll talk about them in this section.

Background Tasks Panel If you're exporting a large file to PDF or IDML format, you can keep working in InDesign during the export. The Background Tasks panel shows the process's status. Choose Utilities from the Window menu, and then choose Background Tasks.

Info Panel The Info panel displays information about the selected object, or, if no objects are selected, about the current location of the cursor (see Figure 1-22).

▶ When you select a character, it shows you the Unicode value of the character. Select text, and, the panel displays a count of characters, words, lines, and paragraphs in the selection.

FIGURE 1-22
Info Panel

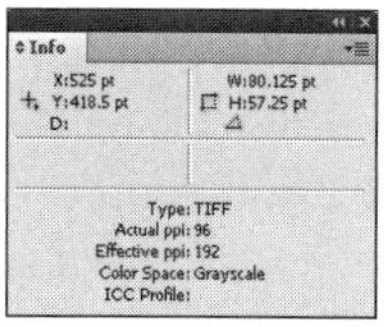

> ▶ When you select a frame or line, the Info panel displays the stroke and fill colors.

> ▶ Select a graphic, and the panel shows the file type (EPS, TIFF, PSD), resolution, and color space (RGB, CMYK, or Grayscale). InDesign can't extract the resolution from EPS and PDF.

Library Panel   Use the Library panel (or panels, as you can have multiple libraries open at once) to store and retrieve commonly used items (see Figure 1-23). Does your company or client have a logo they like to plaster all over every publication you lay out? Put it in a library. Open library files just as you open InDesign documents or book files—using the Open and New options on the File menu.

FIGURE 1-23
Library Panel

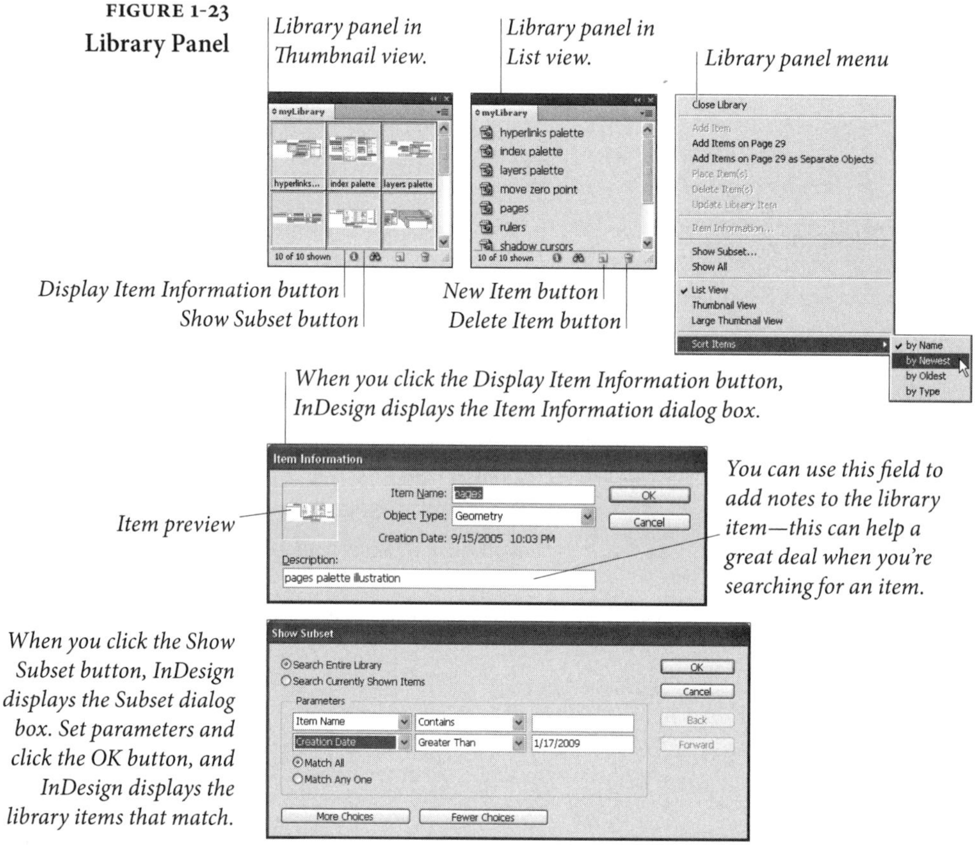

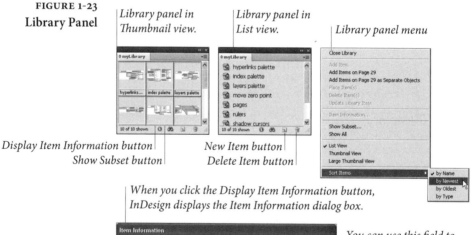

Library panel in Thumbnail view.

Library panel in List view.

Library panel menu

Display Item Information button
Show Subset button

New Item button
Delete Item button

When you click the Display Item Information button, InDesign displays the Item Information dialog box.

Item preview

You can use this field to add notes to the library item—this can help a great deal when you're searching for an item.

When you click the Show Subset button, InDesign displays the Subset dialog box. Set parameters and click the OK button, and InDesign displays the library items that match.

Context Menus

Context menus are menus that pop up at the location of the cursor, and change according to the location of the cursor and the object you have selected (see Figure 1-24). On the Macintosh, you summon a context menu by holding down Control as you click the mouse button. In Windows, click the right mouse button.

Context menus give you a great way to do a lot of things—from changing the formatting of the selected objects to changing your magnification. Let's face it—your attention is where the cursor is, and there's a limited amount of it. Dragging the cursor across the screen to reach a menu or button is distracting and time-consuming.

Many of InDesign's panels (such as the Pages, Paragraph Styles, and Links panels) feature Context menus of their own. These menus, for the most part, replicate the options on the panel menu, but save you a trip across the panel to get at the menu.

Context menus also show the shortcut keys for the commands on the menu—a handy reminder.

FIGURE 1-24
Context Menus

The Context menu looks like this when you have text selected.

Hold down Control and click to display the Context menu on the Macintosh; in Windows, click the right mouse button.

The Context menu looks like this when you have a graphic selected.

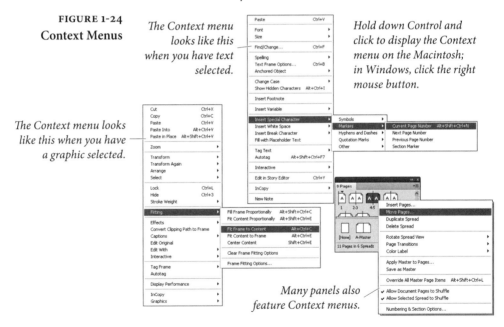

Many panels also feature Context menus.

Keyboard Shortcuts

We hate it when software manufacturers change the keyboard shortcuts we know and love. Especially when they change an easy-to-reach, frequently used shortcut to one that's difficult to use. InDesign gives us something we'd like to see in every application—editable keyboard shortcuts. This means that we can make the program's keyboard shortcuts work the way we think they ought to.

You can redefine those that correspond to menu commands—you can't redefine some of the keyboard shortcuts that modify mouse actions. To define or redefine a keyboard shortcut, follow these steps (and take a look at Figure 1-25).

1. Choose Keyboard Shortcuts from the Edit menu. InDesign displays the Keyboard Shortcuts dialog box.

2. To create a new shortcut set, click the New Set button. To use an existing set, choose the set's name from the Set pop-up menu (if that's all you want to do, you can skip to Step 7). To delete a set, choose the set's name and click the Delete Set button.

3. Choose an option from the Product Area pop-up menu. InDesign fills the Commands list with the available commands for the corresponding area of the program.

4. Select a command from the list. InDesign displays the current shortcut (or shortcuts) assigned to the command.

5. To remove a selected shortcut, click the Remove button. To assign a shortcut to a command, or to replace an existing shortcut, move the cursor to the New Shortcut field and press the keys you want to use for the shortcut.

6. Click the Assign button to assign a shortcut to the command, or (if you had a shortcut selected) click the Replace button to replace the selected shortcut. Note that a single command can have multiple shortcuts assigned to it. If you want, you can save your changes without closing the dialog box by pressing the Save button.

7. Once you've changed all of the shortcuts you want to change, click the OK button to close the dialog box and save the set.

Keyboard shortcut sets are saved in the Presets > InDesign Shortcut Sets folder in your InDesign folder. Want to take your keyboard shortcuts with you to another machine? Take the shortcuts file from your machine and copy it into the InDesign Shortcut Sets folder of the copy of InDesign you'll be using. Open the Keyboard Shortcuts dialog box and choose your shortcut set from the Sets pop-up menu.

To return to InDesign's default keyboard shortcuts, all you need to do is choose the Default set from the Set pop-up menu.

FIGURE 1-25

Editing Keyboard Shortcuts

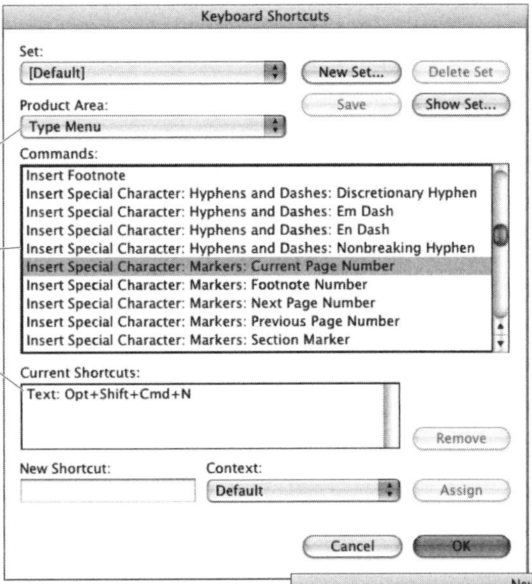

When you select an option from this pop-up menu...

...InDesign displays a list of the available commands.

When you select a command, InDesign displays the shortcut in this field.

Click the New Set button, or choose the QuarkXPress 4.0 shortcut set from the Set pop-up menu.

Keyboard Shortcuts

Set:
[Default]   New Set...   Delete Set

Product Area:
Type Menu   Save   Show Set...

Commands:
Insert Footnote
Insert Special Character: Hyphens and Dashes: Discretionary Hyphen
Insert Special Character: Hyphens and Dashes: Em Dash
Insert Special Character: Hyphens and Dashes: En Dash
Insert Special Character: Hyphens and Dashes: Nonbreaking Hyphen
Insert Special Character: Markers: Current Page Number
Insert Special Character: Markers: Footnote Number
Insert Special Character: Markers: Next Page Number
Insert Special Character: Markers: Previous Page Number
Insert Special Character: Markers: Section Marker

Current Shortcuts:
Text: Opt+Shift+Cmd+N

Remove

New Shortcut: Context:
                       Default   Assign

Cancel   OK

✓ [Default]
  [Shortcuts for PageMaker 7.0]
  [Shortcuts for QuarkXPress 4.0]

  myShortcuts

If you loaded the QuarkXPress 4.0 set, and don't want to edit any shortcuts, click the Save button, then close the dialog box.

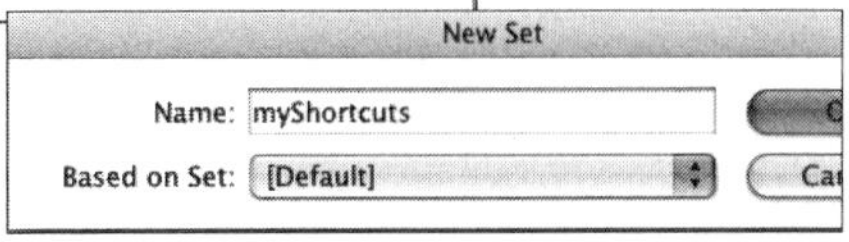

New Set

Name: myShortcuts

Based on Set: [Default]

If you're creating a new set, InDesign displays the New Set dialog box. Enter a name for your set and click the OK button.

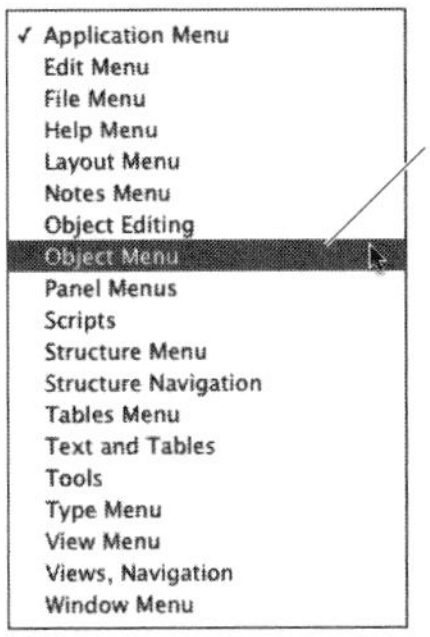

✓ Application Menu
  Edit Menu
  File Menu
  Help Menu
  Layout Menu
  Notes Menu
  Object Editing
  Object Menu
  Panel Menus
  Scripts
  Structure Menu
  Structure Navigation
  Tables Menu
  Text and Tables
  Tools
  Type Menu
  View Menu
  Views, Navigation
  Window Menu

Select an option from the Product Area pop-up menu.

Select a command.

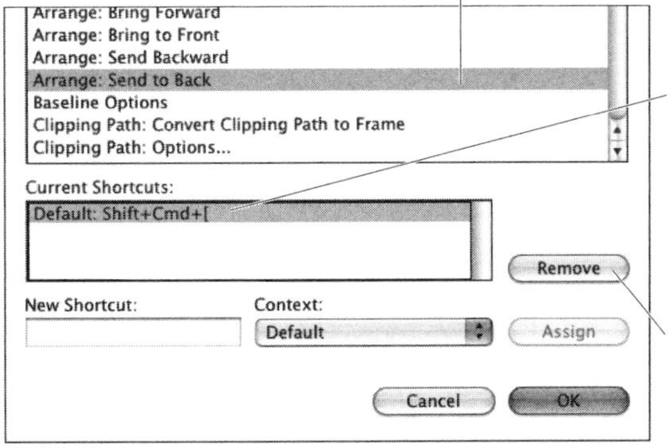

Arrange: Bring Forward
Arrange: Bring to Front
Arrange: Send Backward
Arrange: Send to Back
Baseline Options
Clipping Path: Convert Clipping Path to Frame
Clipping Path: Options...

Current Shortcuts:
Default: Shift+Cmd+[

Remove

New Shortcut: Context:
                       Default   Assign

Cancel   OK

If a keyboard shortcut is already assigned to a command, InDesign displays the name of the command here.

You can remove the existing shortcut by selecting it and clicking the Remove button.

Enter the new shortcut and click the Assign button. If it's already assigned to another command (as it is here), clicking Assign removes the conflicting shortcut.

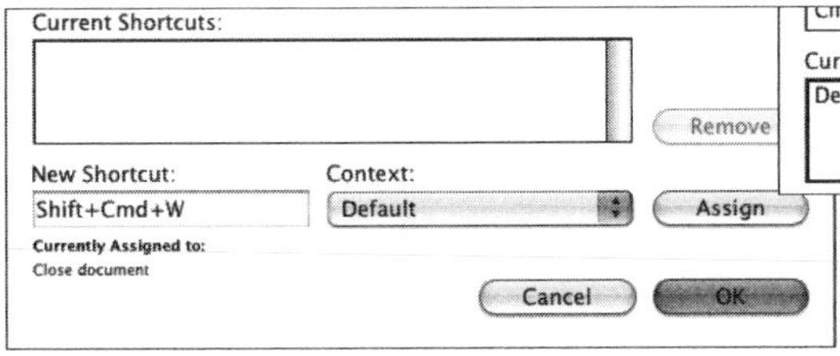

Current Shortcuts:

Remove

New Shortcut: Context:
Shift+Cmd+W   Default   Assign

Currently Assigned to:
Close document

Cancel   OK

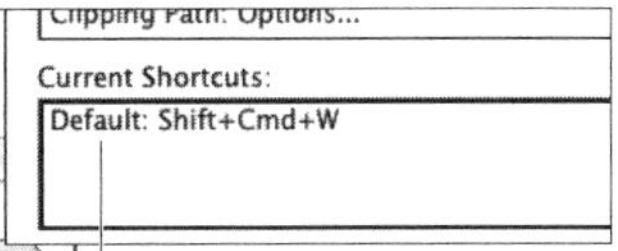

Clipping Path: Options...

Current Shortcuts:
Default: Shift+Cmd+W

InDesign assigns the shortcut to the command.

To view all of the shortcuts in a set, select the set from the Set pop-up menu, then click the Show Set button. InDesign displays a list of the shortcuts in the set using the default text editor on your system (TextEdit on the Macintosh; Notepad in Windows). You can print or save this file for your reference.

Setting the context. You can have a keyboard shortcut do different things. You might want Command-T/Ctrl-T to open the Text Frame Options dialog box when you're editing text and open the Table Options when your cursor is in a table. To do this, select a context from the Context pop-up menu before you click the Assign button.

A few thoughts on making up your own shortcuts. There are two approaches to making up your own keyboard shortcuts. The first is assign shortcuts using a key that has something to do with the name of the command—like "P" for "Print." Usually, these shortcuts are easy to remember. Another, and, in our opinion, better, approach is to analyze the way you work with commands, and then take the commands you use most often and assign them shortcuts that are easy to reach with one hand (usually the left hand, given that the shortcuts for copy, cut, and paste are all on the left side of the keyboard).

What's the most frequently used keyboard shortcut? For us, it's got to be Fit Page In Window, because we navigate by zooming in with the Zoom tool, then zooming out to the Fit Page In Window view, and then zooming in on another part of the spread. The default shortcut for the Fit Page In Window view, Command-0/Ctrl-0 doesn't work for us. It's a long reach for the left hand, and 0 (zero) is a difficult key to hit without looking at the keyboard. Consider using Command-Shift-W/Ctrl-Shift-W—it's an easy, one-handed reach.

Customizing Menus

In addition to being able to customize keyboard shortcuts, you can also change InDesign's menus. That said, you can't change them much. You can hide menu items, and you can change their color, but you can't add them (except via scripting).

To edit InDesign's menus, follow these steps (see Figure 1-26).

1. Choose Menus from the Edit menu. InDesign displays the Menu Customization dialog box.

2. Select a menu set from the Set pop-up menu, if necessary.

FIGURE 1-26
Customizing Menus

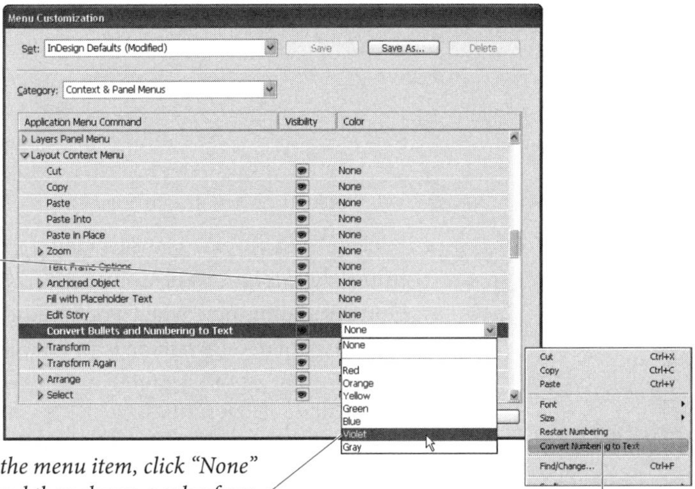

*You can show or hide menu
items by clicking in the
Visibility column (the
"eye" icon indicates that
the menu item is visible).*

*To change the color of the menu item, click "None"
in the Color column and then choose a color from
the pop-up menu that appears.*

*Menu item with a custom
color applied to it.*

3. Select a menu type (Application Menus or Context and Panel Menus) from the Category pop-up menu.

4. Select the menu you want to edit. It can sometimes take guesswork to find the right menu, but keep at it—they're all there.

5. Once you've found the menu item you want, you can hide it by clicking the "eye" icon (or show it by clicking the box in the Visibility column). To change the menu item's color, click the text in the Color column—InDesign displays a pop-up menu you can use to select another color.

6. To save the menu set, click the Save button, or click Save As to save a new menu set.

7. Click the OK button to close the dialog box.

To return to InDesign's menu defaults, choose Reset Menus from the Workspace submenu of the Window menu. Or you can display the Menu Customization dialog box and select the InDesign Defaults menu set from the Set pop-up menu.

To display hidden menu items, hold down Command/Ctrl as you display the menu, or choose Show All Menu Items.

Menu sets are saved as XML and are given the file extension ".inms". If you need to find one, search for the name of the menu set. Only the differences between the default set and the custom set are saved in the file. Ole has (once again) spent way too much time rooting through the menu customization files.

Customizing the Control Panel

The Control panel can take the place of a number of other panels, and thereby save you a great deal of space on your screen. But it's even better than that—you can change the controls that appear in the Control panel. If, for example, you're like Ole and do not care about object effects and text wrap, you can do away with them and save the space for more worthy interface items. Doth the text skewing control offend thee? Pluck it out!

You can turn controls in the Control panel off or on to make it more to your liking. To do this, choose Customize from the Control panel menu. InDesign displays the Customize Control Panel dialog box (see Figure 1-27). You can't change the order in which the controls appear, and you can't add different controls.

FIGURE 1-27
Customizing the Control Panel

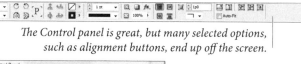

The Control panel is great, but many selected options, such as alignment buttons, end up off the screen.

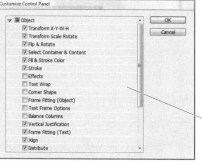

While we're showing a pretty specific customization in this example, the point is that you can reconfigure the Control panel to better suit your needs and workflow.

Also note that we're only showing the right end of the panel; if we reduced it to fit our layout, the controls would be invisible.

To move the alignment buttons farther to the left (and, therefore, make them appear), choose Customize from the Control panel menu.

Use the controls in the Customize Control Panel dialog box to turn off the options you don't use.

Previously hidden buttons now appear.

Saving and Loading Workspaces

Once you've gotten your panels and menus set up just the way you want them, you can save them—their locations and states—to a workspace. You can load that workspace to return to that arrangement.

You can set up special configurations for specific tasks—you might want to have one set of panels for working with paths; another for entering text and typesetting, and still another for creating bookmarks and hyperlinks. With InDesign's workspace management, you can dramatically reduce the number of panels you have on your screen.

To save a workspace, choose Save Workspace from the Workspace submenu of the Window menu. InDesign displays the Save Workspace dialog box. Enter a name for the workspace and press the OK button to save the workspace. InDesign adds the workspace name to the list of available workspaces (see Figure 1-28).

To apply a workspace, choose the workspace name from the Workspace submenu of the Window menu. After a (relatively) brief pause, InDesign resets your panels to the configuration saved in the workspace. You can assign keyboard shortcuts to the workspaces in the Window Menu area of the Edit Keyboard Shortcuts dialog box (see "Keyboard Shortcuts," earlier in this chapter).

Once you have your workspaces set up the way you like them, it's a good idea to back up the file containing them. It's called "Active-Workspace.xml" and you can find it by searching your hard drive.

FIGURE 1-28
Saving a Workspace

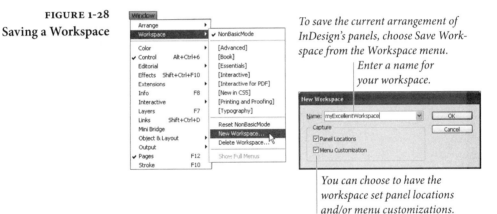

To save the current arrangement of InDesign's panels, choose Save Workspace from the Workspace menu.

Enter a name for your workspace.

You can choose to have the workspace set panel locations and/or menu customizations.

Setting Preferences

Why do applications have Preferences dialog boxes? It's simple: there's often more than one "right" way to do something. Rather than dictatorially decide to limit users, InDesign gives you a choice. Preferences are one way you can control the appearance and behavior of the program. They're a place where you can customize the program to better fit your work habits and personality.

To display InDesign's Preferences dialog box, choose General from the Preferences submenu (under the InDesign menu on the Macintosh, or the File menu in Windows), or press Command-K/Ctrl-K. The Preferences dialog box contains a number of panels—each listed along the left side for you to click on.

Have you ever been frustrated when a preference option doesn't stick? You change a preference, and end up with the old setting when you open a new document. That's because some preference settings affect only the current document, while other settings affect all documents. If you want a preference option to affect all new documents you create, close all documents before changing the settings.

General Preferences   The General pane of the Preferences dialog box (see Figure 1-29) is the "kitchen sink" of the Preferences dialog box universe—it contains the things that didn't fit anywhere else. All options in the General pane are application-specific.

Page Numbering. The options on the View pop-up menu change the way InDesign displays page numbers in the Pages panel. When you choose Absolute Numbering, InDesign numbers the pages sequentially, starting with page one, and pays no attention to the page numbering options of any of the sections in the publication. Choose Section Numbering to have InDesign display page numbers based on the page numbering options you've set up in the Section Options dialog box for each section. For more on setting up sections and numbering pages, see Chapter 2, "Page Layout."

Always Subset Fonts with Glyph Counts Greater than 2000. Whew. This one takes a bit of rapid-fire explaining. When InDesign sends a font to a printer (or into an exported file), you can choose to include all of the characters in the font, or to include only those characters of the font that are used in the document. The latter option is called a font "subset" (see Chapter 7, "Importing and Exporting").

While we generally think that you should include all of the characters in a font (you never know when you might need them, and disk space/network bandwidth are both cheap these days), we have to say that some fonts are *huge*. Some OpenType fonts actually include *tens of thousands* of character glyphs. Turning this option on lets us download complete character sets of standard Western fonts without

フリクリ forcing us to download all of Kozuka Gothic Pro just because Ole felt the need to spell out "furi kuri" in Katakana.

Prevent Selection of Locked Objects. In previous versions of InDesign, you could select locked objects. People complained, so Adobe decided to make a change. In InDesign CS5, you can't select locked objects—unless you uncheck this option.

When Scaling Options. When you scale an object, how should it be reflected in the interface? For example, if you double the scale of a text frame with 12-pt text, what should appear in the Control panel?

FIGURE 1-29
General Preferences

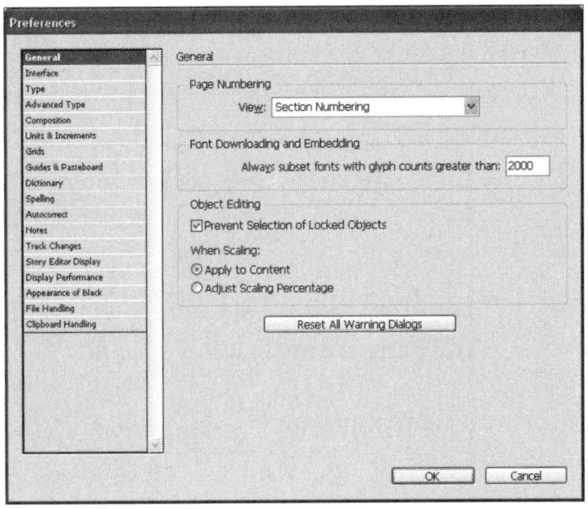

If Apply to Content option is on, "24 pt" appears for Font Size and the Scale values are reset to 100%. If Adjust Scaling Percentage is on, "12 pt(24)" is displayed for Font Size, and the Scale values are 200%. There is one benefit to turning Adjust Scaling Percentage on: You can always reset the text frame to 100 percent size in the Control panel or Transform panel, returning the text to its original, pre-scaled size. When you turn Apply to Content on, it can be hard to get back to the original size. See Chapter 9, "Transforming."

Reset All Warning Dialogs. Many of InDesign's warning dialog boxes include a "never ask me this question again" option. If you have checked this option, and, for whatever reason, want to see the dialog box again, click the Reset All Warning Dialogs button.

Interface Preferences

The Interface pane of the Preferences dialog box (see Figure 1-30) gives you a way to customize a variety of user interface behaviors. these settings affect the application, not individual documents.

Tool Tips. If you're having trouble remembering the names of the tools in InDesign's panels or their associated keyboard shortcuts, choose Fast or Normal from the Tool Tips pop-up menu. When you do, InDesign displays a small window containing a tool's name when your cursor passes over the tool. Tool tips do not work for every tool or control in every panel. Once you're familiar with InDesign, turn this option off—showing tool tips does slow down the application.

Show Thumbnails on Place. When you place a file, you can have the cursor display a tiny preview of the incoming content. To do this, turn the Show Thumbnails on Place option on. To show an icon instead (which is what we strongly prefer), turn this option off.

FIGURE 1-30

Interface Preferences

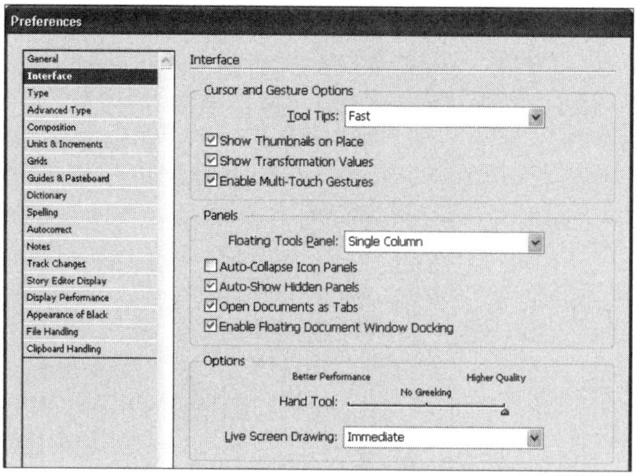

Show Transformation Values. When you're creating or moving an object, notice those numbers in the grey box that show the X, Y coordinates? Those are transformation values (or "smart cursors"), and you can turn them off.

Enable Multi-Touch Gestures. If you're running InDesign in Windows Vista, Windows 7, or on a Mac, you can take advantage of multi-touch gestures when using your mouse. For example, the rotate gesture rotates the spread, and the swipe gesture scrolls up and down.

Floating Tools Panel. You can choose to display the Tools panel in one of three arrangements: Single Row, Double Column, or Single Column. Choose the option you like best.

Auto-Collapse Icon Panels. When you add panels to the dock, you can display the panels as icons. When you turn this option on, InDesign will automatically close docked panels after you use them.

Auto-Show Hidden Panels. When you press Tab or Shift-Tab to hide panels, mousing over the side of the document window shows the panels temporarily.

Open Documents as Tabs. Turn this option off to have documents appear as floating windows; turn it on to have documents appear in tabbed panels.

Enable Floating Document Window Docking. When this option is on, you can dock floating document windows (just as you would dock panels).

Hand Tool. Determine the balance between performance and visual quality when you scroll through a document, which causes text and images to be greeked.

Live Screen Drawing. Do you want the image to redraw when you move an image? If Immediate is in, the image redraws while you drag. If Never is on, dragging an image moves only the frame, and then image is moved when you release the mouse button. If Delayed is on, the image redraws only if you pause before dragging—as in InDesign CS4.

Type Preferences

The Type pane of the Preferences dialog box (see Figure 1-31) contains preferences that affect the way that InDesign formats and displays text in your publications.

Use Typographer's Quotes. Using "typewriter" quotation marks and apostrophes (" and ') instead of their typographic equivalents (", ", ', and ') is one of the hallmarks of amateur desktop publishing design. It's sometimes difficult to remember what keys to press to get the preferred marks. Fortunately, you don't need to remember these obscure shortcuts because when you turn on the Use Typographer's Quotes option, InDesign enters the correct quotation marks for you as you type normal straight quotes. This option is document specific.

Type Tool Converts Frames to Text Frames. When this option is turned on, clicking a frame with the Type tool will convert it to a text frame, even if the content type is set to Unassigned or Graphic. To

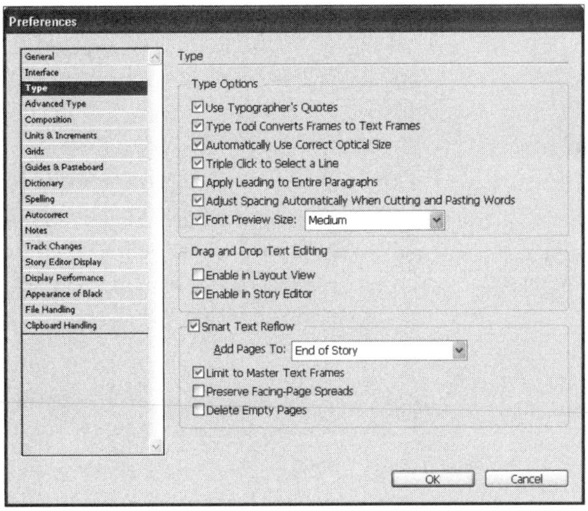

FIGURE 1-31
Type Preferences

prevent the Type tool from converting frames to text frames, turn this option off. This option is application specific.

Automatically Use Correct Optical Size. This setting only comes into play when you're working with multiple master fonts—and then only with those fonts that have a defined optical size axis (not all multiple master fonts do). If your font fits this description, feel pleased that you're among a tiny handful of people on the planet, and that turning on Automatically Use Correct Optical Size forces the font to use an optical size axis that matches the point size of the text, regardless of the optical size axis setting of the instance of the font. When this option is off, InDesign uses the optical size axis setting of the font instance. This option is document specific.

Triple Click to Select a Line. When the Triple Click to Select a Line checkbox is on, triple-clicking the Type tool in text selects the line you're clicking on and quadruple-clicking selects the paragraph; when this option is off, triple-click to select a paragraph and quadruple-click to select the entire story. Since we can't agree on the "correct" setting for this option, we leave it up to you. This option is application specific.

Apply Leading to Entire Paragraphs. While you might, in rare instances, want to vary the leading of lines in a paragraph, you'd probably prefer to use a single leading value for all lines in a paragraph (if you're coming to InDesign from QuarkXPress, Frame-Maker, or Microsoft Word this is the behavior you expect).

By default, InDesign applies leading at the character level, which means that you might accidentally create uneven leading between lines of a paragraph. To force InDesign to use a single leading value for an entire paragraph, turn on the Apply Leading to Entire Paragraphs option. When you do this, the largest leading value in the paragraph sets the leading of the paragraph. Note that this doesn't affect any leading that you set while this preference was turned off—only leading you apply from here on out. That means you can get the best of both worlds: Leave it turned on most of the time and turn it off on the rare occasions that you want to adjust leading on a line-by-line basis. This option is document specific (see Chapter 4, "Type").

Adjust Spacing Automatically when Cutting and Pasting Words. What should InDesign do when you paste a word into text? Should it add space before and after the word, if necessary? If you think it should, turn this option on. Note that InDesign will not insert space before sentence-ending punctuation, regardless of the state of this option. This option also controls whether InDesign removes extra spaces when you press Delete. This option is application specific.

Font Preview Size. This option turns the font preview in the various font menus (in the Control panel, Type menu, and Character menu) on or off, and controls the size of the text used in the menus. We have to mention that turning this option off will dramatically speed up the font menu display, and that you should select typefaces based on printed examples, not from a screen. This option is application specific.

Drag and Drop Text Editing. Turn on the Enable in Layout View option to enable drag and drop text editing in layout view; turn on Enable in Story Editor to make it work in the story editor. These options are application specific. For more on drag and drop text editing, see Chapter 3, "Text."

Smart Text Reflow. The options in this section define the way that InDesign adds pages when you create overset text by editing a story. The Add Pages To pop-up menu defines where you want to add pages: at the end of the story, the end of the section, or at the end of the document.

Turn on Limit to Master Text Frames to force InDesign to add the text to text frames defined on the master pages. Leave this option off to add new text frames based on the area within the margins of the new pages.

The Preserve Facing-Page Spreads option does just what it says it does—if your editing would cause a single page to be added in the middle of the document, InDesign will add a spread to maintain the pagination of the pages following the added page.

Turn this option on to allow InDesign to delete pages when your editing empties the text frames on the page. This option only comes into play when the emptied text frame(s) are the only objects on the page. These options are document specific.

Advanced Type Preferences

The options in the Advanced Type pane provide additional control over text formatting. For more on superscripts, subscripts, and small caps, see Chapter 4, "Type."

Character Settings. When you apply Superscript or Subscript to text, InDesign scales the selected characters and shifts their baseline position. (This doesn't apply to OpenType formatting.) How can you control the amount of scaling and baseline shift? That's where the options in this section come in. The Size fields are percentages of the size of the selected characters (you can enter from 1 to 200 percent); the Position fields are percentages of the leading (you can enter from –500 to 500 percent). When you apply Small Caps formatting to text, InDesign scales the selected characters by the percentage you enter in the Small Cap Size field (from one to 200 percent).

Note that these settings affect all superscript, subscript, and small caps formatting you've applied throughout your current document. (This is the way that QuarkXPress handles these formatting attributes, but it's unlike PageMaker, where superscript, subscript, and small caps formatting options are set at the character level.) These options are document specific. For more on superscript, subscript, and small caps, see Chapter 4, "Type."

Use Inline Input for Non-Latin Text. When you're entering characters that are outside the range of the Western character set (like Japanese, Chinese, or Korean), you can use one of (at least) two methods to get the characters into the text frame. You can use the Input Method Editor (or IME) that comes with your operating system (usually typing characters in a separate floating window), or you can use the inline text entry method (where you type right in the text frame). We think it's much easier to type "inline," along with all the other text. This option is application specific.

Composition Preferences

Composition is the process of making type fit in the columns and pages in your publication. The options in the Composition Preferences pane of the Preferences dialog box relate to various aspects of InDesign's text composition features. Composition preference settings are application specific. To really understand how composition works, see Chapter 4, "Type."

Highlight. The options in the Highlight section help you spot composition problems before they become printed mistakes. All three options work the same way: when they spot a composition problem (a place where InDesign has had to break your rules to lay out a publication, or where InDesign lacks the font to properly compose a piece of text), they "highlight" the text by drawing a colored bar behind it.

▶ **Keep Violations.** In the Keep Options dialog box (choose Keep Options from the Paragraph panel's menu, or press Command-Option-K/Ctrl-Alt-K), you'll see a variety of settings that determine the way a paragraph deals with column and page breaks.

These settings, collectively, are called "keeps." InDesign will sometimes have to disobey your keeps settings. Keeps violations are rare, but you can easily spot them when you turn this option on. When you do, InDesign highlights the problem paragraphs.

- **H&J Violations.** When InDesign composes text, it tries to follow the guidelines you set in the Justification dialog box, but, sometimes, it can't. In those cases, InDesign applies word spacing that's looser or tighter than the minimum or maximum you specified. This is known as an "H&J violation." When you turn this option, InDesign highlights the problem lines by displaying a yellow bar behind the text. The intensity of the tint used to draw the bar gives you a rough indication of the severity of the "violation"—the more saturated the yellow, the greater the variation from your settings. See Figure 1-32.
- **Substituted Fonts.** When you turn on this option, InDesign highlights text that uses fonts that aren't currently have loaded. The highlight color is pink. See Figure 1-33.
- **Substituted Glyphs.** InDesign has various features that replace characters in your text with other characters, such as ligatures, swashes, ordinals, and so on (most of these options are on the Character panel menu). To see the places where InDesign has applied these special characters, turn on the Substituted Glyphs option. The highlight color is purple. See Figure 1-34.

FIGURE 1-32
Highlighting Composition Problems

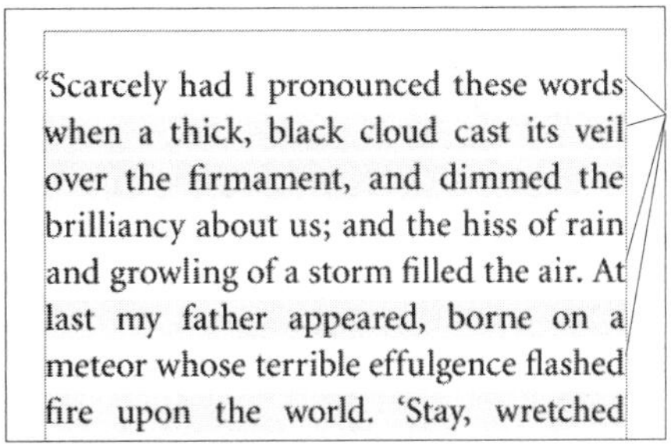
"Scarcely had I pronounced these words
when a thick, black cloud cast its veil
over the firmament, and dimmed the
brilliancy about us; and the hiss of rain
and growling of a storm filled the air. At
last my father appeared, borne on a
meteor whose terrible effulgence flashed
fire upon the world. 'Stay, wretched

When you turn on the H&J Violations option in the Highlight section of the Text Preferences dialog box, InDesign highlights lines of text that break the spacing rules you entered in the Justification dialog box.

FIGURE 1-33
Highlighting Font Substitution

TimeTravelTickets
I Comici Gelosi
1568-1604
TimeTravelTickets
Theatre
I Comici Gelosi
1568-1604

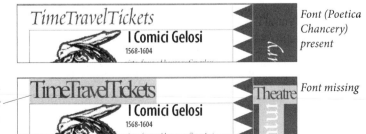

Font (Poetica Chancery) present

Font missing

Highlighted font substitution. The substituted text appears in the default font.

FIGURE 1-34
**Highlighting
Glyph Substitution**

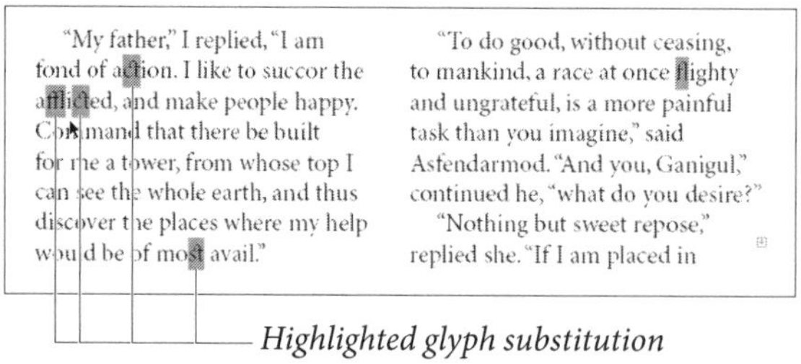

"My father," I replied, "I am fond of action. I like to succor the afflicted, and make people happy. Command that there be built for me a tower, from whose top I can see the whole earth, and thus discover the places where my help would be of most avail."

"To do good, without ceasing, to mankind, a race at once flighty and ungrateful, is a more painful task than you imagine," said Asfendarmod. "And you, Ganigul," continued he, "what do you desire?"

"Nothing but sweet repose," replied she. "If I am placed in

— *Highlighted glyph substitution*

▶ **Custom Tracking/Kerning.** To see the places in your text that have had custom kerning or tracking applied to them, turn on this option. When you do this, InDesign highlights any text containing manual kerning (i.e., kerning that was not applied by one of the automatic kerning methods), or tracking values other than zero with a blue-green tint. See Figure 1-35.

Justify Text Next to an Object. When an object bearing a text wrap appears in the *middle* of a column of text, should InDesign justify the text around the wrapped object? If so, turn on Justify Text Next to an Object. Note that this option has no effect on text wraps that do not split a line into two or more parts. The authors suggest that you never create a design that would cause you to care about this option one way or the other. See Figure 1-36.

Skip by Leading. When a text wrap breaks a text column, and the text in the text column is aligned to a baseline grid, should the text

FIGURE 1-35
**Highlighting
Custom Tracking
and Kerning**

*The paragraph style applied
to this paragraph specifies a
tracking value.*

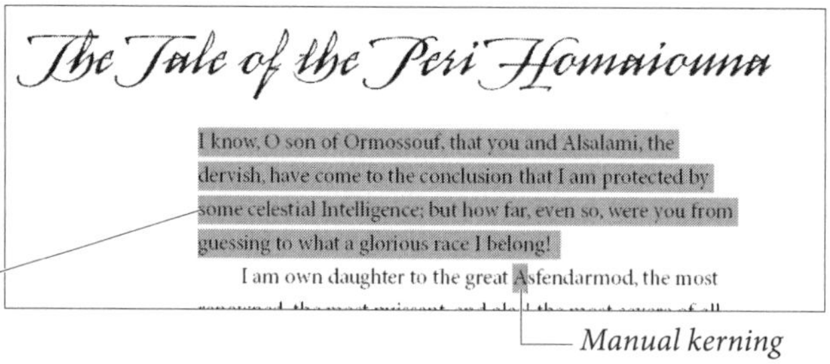

The Tale of the Peri Homaiouna

I know, O son of Ormossouf, that you and Alsalami, the dervish, have come to the conclusion that I am protected by some celestial Intelligence; but how far, even so, were you from guessing to what a glorious race I belong!

I am own daughter to the great Asfendarmod, the most

— *Manual kerning*

FIGURE 1-36
**Justifying Text Next
to an Object**

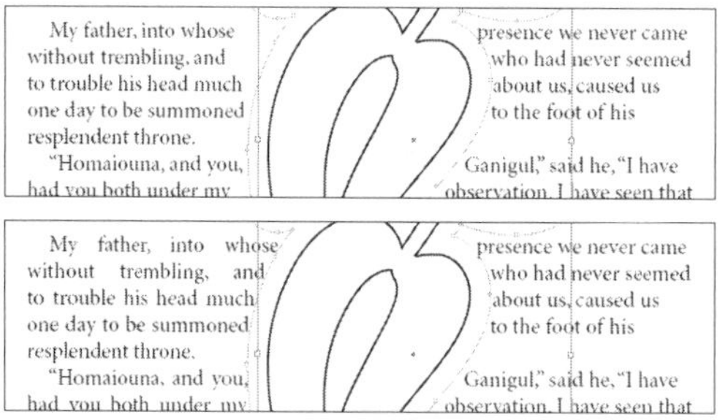

My father, into whose without trembling, and to trouble his head much one day to be summoned resplendent throne.
"Homaiouna, and you, had you both under my

presence we never came who had never seemed about us, caused us to the foot of his
Ganigul," said he, "I have observation. I have seen that

*Justify Text Next to an
Object off*

My father, into whose without trembling, and to trouble his head much one day to be summoned resplendent throne.
"Homaiouna, and you, had you both under my

presence we never came who had never seemed about us, caused us to the foot of his
Ganigul," said he, "I have observation. I have seen that

*Justify Text Next to an
Object on*

continue to align to the baseline grid, or should it get as close to the text wrap boundary as possible? We like to turn Skip by Leading on to make sure the text aligns to the baseline grid. For more on this topic, see Chapter 6, "Where Text Meets Graphics."

Text Wrap Only Affects Text Beneath. Many QuarkXPress users get confused when using text wrap (runaround) in InDesign because text can wrap even when the wrapping-object is underneath the text frame (in the page's stacking order or layer order). If you don't like this behavior, you can turn on the Text Wrap Only Affects Text Beneath checkbox. There are pros and cons to both methods. For more on this topic, see Chapter 6, "Where Text Meets Graphics."

Units & Increments Preferences

We've all got favorite units of measure—Ole is partial to furlongs and stone, while David prefers cubits—so we should be able to choose the measurement system we use to lay out our pages. That's what the Units & Increments pane is for (see Figure 1-37). Units & Increments preferences are document specific.

Ruler Units. The Origin pop-up menu sets the default location of the ruler zero point. Choose Spread to have InDesign position the zero point at the upper-left corner of the spread. Choose Page, and InDesign locates the zero point at the upper-left corner of the page. If you have three or more pages in a spread, you might want to choose Spine to place the ruler zero point at the binding spine.

Use the Horizontal and Vertical pop-up menus to select the measurement units (inches, inches decimal, picas, points, millimeters, agates, ciceros, and pixels) you want to use for the rulers. In addition to the measurement systems, you can use custom increments for either or both rulers. When you choose Custom, you can enter a value in the field (see "Rulers," earlier in this chapter).

As you set up a publication's measurement units, there are two things you should keep in mind:

▶ You can use the Context menu to change ruler units—Control-click (Macintosh) or right-click on the ruler in the document window, and InDesign displays a Context menu containing the same options as you see in the Units & Increments Preferences dialog box.

▶ You can always override units of measurement in any field in any panel or dialog box in InDesign. For more on entering measurement unit overrides, see "Overriding Units of Measurement," earlier in this chapter.

Other Units. The Text Size and Stroke options are new in InDesign CS5 to help create documents for the web. Change the Text Size unit of measurement to display the Font Size and Leading values in points or pixels. Change the Stroke values to Points, Millimeters, or Pixels to affect the Weight value in the Stroke panel and any other place where you can change the stroke width.

Point/Pica Size. This option changes the definition of the size of a point (and, therefore, the size of a pica). The modern (i.e., post-desktop publishing) standard for the size of a point is 72 points per inch.

If using your old Compugraphic E-scale is more important to you than anything else in life, feel free to set this option to something other than PostScript (72 pts/inch). Just don't tell us about it, or insist that we should do the same.

Keyboard Increments. What happens when you push an arrow key? That depends on the settings you've entered in the following fields.

► **Cursor Key.** When you have an object selected using the Selection or Direct Select tool, you can move it by pressing the arrow keys. How far do you want it to move with each key press? Enter that value in this field.

► **Size/Leading.** When you have text selected, you can increase or decrease the size and/or leading of the text by pressing keyboard shortcuts (by default, you press Command-Shift->/Ctrl-Shift-> to increase the size of the text; Command-Shift-</Ctrl-Shift-< to decrease the size; Option-Up arrow/Alt-Up arrow to increase the leading; or Option-Down arrow to decrease the leading). How much larger or smaller should the point size or leading get with each key press? Enter the amount you want in this field.

► **Baseline Shift.** When you have selected text using the Type tool, you can increase baseline shift by pressing (by default) Option-Shift-Up Arrow/Alt-Shift-Up Arrow, or decrease baseline shift by pressing Option-Shift-Down Arrow/Alt-Shift-Down Arrow. How much baseline shift should each key press apply? Enter the amount you want in this field.

► **Kerning.** When the text cursor is between two characters, you can apply kerning by pressing Option-Left Arrow/Alt-Left Arrow or Option-Right Arrow/Alt-Right Arrow. When a range of text is selected with the text tool, pressing this shortcut applies tracking. Enter the kerning amount you want to apply (in thousandths of an em) in this field.

Grids Preferences

InDesign can display two different types of grid: baseline and document. You control various aspects of their appearance using the options in this pane (see Figure 1-38). Both grids are very similar to the guides (ruler guides, margin guides, and column guides), and have a similar effect on items on your pages. Grid preferences are document specific.

Baseline Grid. The baseline grid is an array of horizontal guides that mark off the page in units equal to a specified leading amount (note that the baseline grid isn't really a "grid," as it has no vertical lines).

► **Color.** Choose a color for the baseline grid using the Color pop-up menu.

► **Start.** Enter a value in the Start field to set the distance from the top of the page at which you want the baseline grid to begin.

► **Increment Every.** Enter a distance—in general, the leading value of your publication's body text—in the Increment Every field.

► **View Threshold.** Set the magnification at which the grid becomes visible in the View Threshold field.

Document Grid. The document grid is a network of horizontal and vertical guidelines—something like graph paper.

► **Color.** Choose a color for the grid using the Color pop-up menu.

► **Gridline Every.** Enter the distance you want between grid lines in this field.

FIGURE 1-38
Grids Preferences

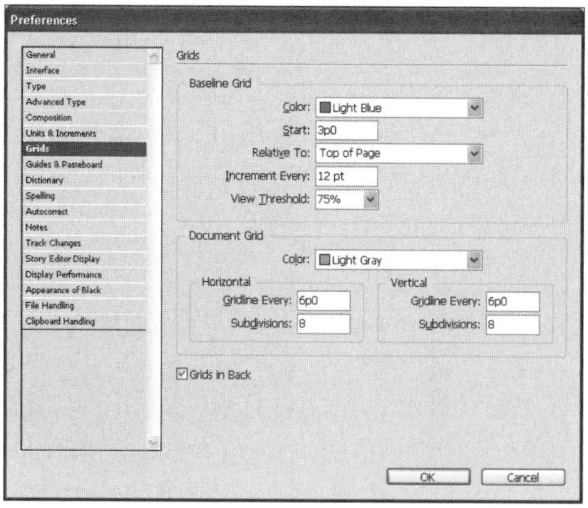

▶ **Subdivisions.** Just as the document grid divides the page, subdivisions divide the grid into smaller sections. The number you enter in this field sets the number of subdivisions between each grid line. If you don't want to subdivide the document grid, enter 1 in this field. InDesign displays the grid subdivision lines using a tint of the color you specified for the document grid.

Grids in Back. Turn on the Grids in Back option to make both grids appear at the bottom of the stacking order rather than on top of your page objects.

Guides and Pasteboard Preferences

Use the Guides and Pasteboard pane of the Preferences dialog box (see Figure 1-39) to set the color for displaying margin, column, bleed, and slug guides, as well as the preview color of the pasteboard. Why isn't there an option for setting the color of ruler guides? Because you don't have to use the same color for all of your ruler guides—you specify the color using the Ruler Guides dialog box. The color preferences are application specific.

(Tip: Changing your pasteboard color to black before showing a client boosts the apparent contrast and looks cool. You could also change the preview color for each stage of a job—first draft could be pink, second draft green, and so on. But remember that any color other than neutral gray may make your page or images look like they have a slight color cast on screen; that's just the way the human eye works.)

Snap to Zone. Use the Snap to Zone option to set the distance, in screen pixels, at which guides begin to exert their mysterious pull on objects you're drawing or dragging. This option is document specific.

FIGURE 1-39
Guides & Pasteboard
Preferences

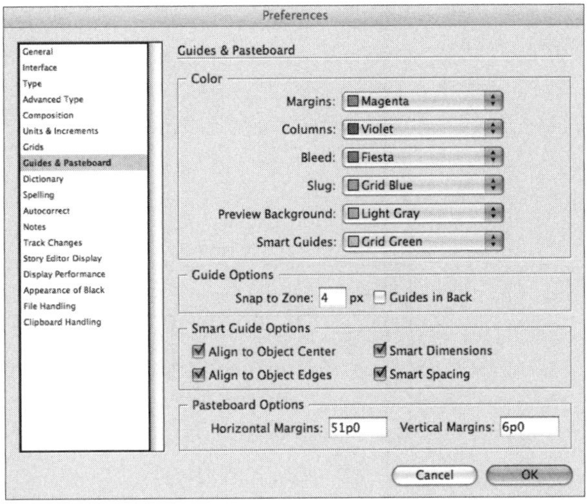

Guides in Back. Turn on Guides in Back to position the guides at the bottom of the stacking order of the layer they're on. We've never figured out a good reason to turn this feature off. This option is document specific.

Smart Guide Options. InDesign's Smart Guides feature displays information about objects as you move, resize, or create them, and gives you a way to snap to other object locations on the page (see Figure 1-40). This is a terrific feature, but bear in mind that it can interfere with snapping to the grid or guides. These options are application specific.

Pasteboard Options. The Vertical Margins field sets the distance from the top or bottom of the page to the outside edge of the pasteboard. To make your pasteboard taller, increase this value; to make it shorter, decrease the value. This option was called Minimum Vertical Offset in InDesign CS4 and is the equivalent of the old Pasteboard XTension for QuarkXPress (but without the associated bugs and troubles). The Horizontal Margins field sets the width of the pasteboard on both sides of the spread. These options are document specific.

Dictionary Preferences

The Dictionary pane of the Preferences dialog box controls the spelling and hyphenation dictionaries used in the document (see Figure 1-41). This looks like it would set the default dictionary for a document, but it does not. It's very rare that you would need to change these, unless you were using a third-party plug-in offering different hyphenation and spelling dictionaries. Choose a dictionary from the

FIGURE 1-40
Smart Guides

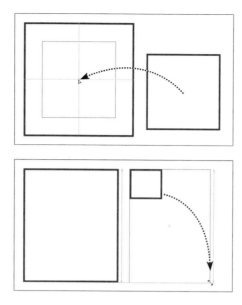

When you turn on Smart Guides, InDesign displays guides as you move objects. In this example, it's showing us that the center of the square we're moving aligns with the center of the larger square.

When your turn on the Smart Dimensions option, InDesign displays guides when nearby objects are the same size. In this example, InDesign shows us that the height of the two rectangles is the same.

Language pop-up menu to choose the vendor of your choice from the Hyphenation and Spelling pop-up menus. You can add additional dictionaries for each language by clicking the New Dictionary or Add Dictionary buttons. The Language setting is application specific; all other Dictionary preferences are document specific

Double Quotes. Enter the pair of characters you want to use for double quotes, or select them from the pop-up menu.

Single Quotes. Enter the pair of characters you want to use for single quotes, or select them from the pop-up menu.

Compose Using. When you add a word to your user dictionary (including changes you make to hyphenation points), InDesign adds the word to the user dictionary's exceptions list. Choose User Dictionary to use the exceptions list in the current user dictionary; choose Document to use the hyphenation exceptions stored in the document; or choose User Dictionary and Document to use both exception lists.

User Dictionary Options. Choose Merge User Dictionary into Document to copy the hyphenation and spelling exceptions list from the user dictionary into each document you open. Clearly, this isn't an option you want to turn on if you frequently open documents created by other people.

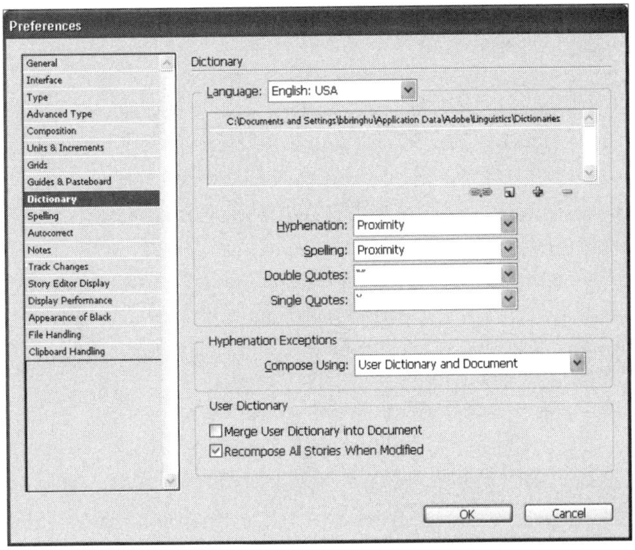

FIGURE 1-41
Dictionary Preferences

Choose Recompose All Stories When Modified to recompose all stories in a document when the user dictionary changes (or when you change the setting of the Compose Using pop-up menu). Recomposing all stories in a document can be a time-consuming process; most of the time, we think you should leave this option turned off.

Spelling Preferences   The options in the Spelling pane of the Preferences dialog box give you control over InDesign's spelling checker and dynamic spelling feature (see Figure 1-42). Spelling preferences are application specific.

Spelling. There's not much to the options in the Spelling section. Turn on Misspelled Words to check for spelling errors. Turn on Repeated Words to check for "the the" and other repetitions. Turn on Uncapitalized Words to check for common capitalization errors, and turn on Uncapitalized Sentences to find sentences that do not start with a capital letter.

Dynamic Spelling. Turn on the Enable Dynamic Spelling option to have InDesign mark possible spelling errors in text (this feature is very similar to the dynamic spelling features in Word or other word processors). You can specify the colors InDesign uses to mark misspelled words, repeated words, uncapitalized words, and uncapitalized sentences using the pop-up menu associated with each type of spelling error. For more on dynamic spelling, see Chapter 3, "Text."

Autocorrect   InDesign's Autocorrect feature can fix misspelled words as you type.
Preferences   To turn the Autocorrect feature on or off, and to add or remove words

FIGURE 1-42
Spelling Preferences

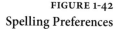

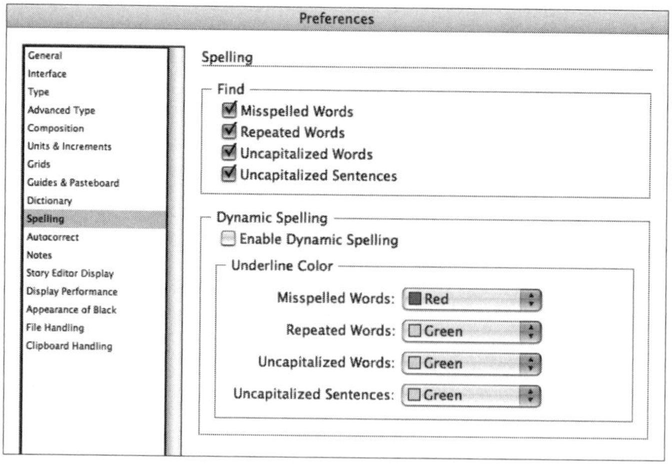

from the list of misspellings and their corresponding corrections (see Figure 1-43). Autocorrect preferences are application specific. For more on using the Autocorrect feature, see Chapter 3, "Text."

Notes Preferences   The option in the Notes pane of the Preferences dialog box control the appearance of notes in your documents. Notes preferences are application specific. For more on using the Autocorrect feature, see Chapter 3, "Text."

Note Color. Choose the color you want to use for notes. You can select either a fixed color or the User Color (which you can define by choosing User from the File menu).

Show Note Tool Tips. When this option is on, you can position the cursor over a note and see a tool tip that includes user information and a short excerpt of the note. With this option turned off, you'll have to open the note in the Notes panel to see this text.

Include Note Content When Checking Spelling. Do you want to check the spelling of the text in notes? If so, turn this option on.

Include Note Content in Find/Change Operations. Do you want to include notes when you find and change text? If you do, turn this option on.

Inline Background Color. Sets the background color for the notes displayed in the Story Editor.

FIGURE 1-43
Autocorrect Preferences

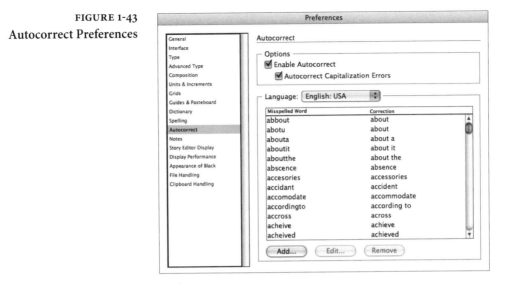

Track Changes Preferences

The options in the Track Changes pane of the Preferences dialog box control the appearance of edited text in the Story Editor (see Figure 1-44). The idea of tracking changes is to see which changes were made by another person so that you can accept or reject them. Or, if you're the other person who jumps into someone else's file, you can turn on Change Tracking to let the author know what you've done to the precious publication. Keep in mind that the change tracking shows up only in the Story Editor, not in the layout. Track Changes preferences are application specific. We'll have more to say about tracking changes in Chapter 3, "Text."

Show. You can change the appearance of Story Editor text that's been added, deleted, or moved when Track Changes is turned on. Turn off Added Text, Deleted Text, or Moved Text if you don't want any of these types of changes to be tracked. For example, if you care only about new text, turn off Deleted Text and Moved Text.

For each option, set the display appearance. By default, all changes have the same Text settings as the Story Editor text—that's what the parentheses in (Text Color) mean. All changes are also highlighted with your user color. (Choose User from the File menu to change the user color.) If Prevent Duplicate User Colors is selected, you may be assigned a color that differs from the one you select in the User dialog box.

By default, Marking is set to None. Unless you have an excellent reason for doing so, don't change the Marking setting for any of the options.

FIGURE 1-44
Track Changes
Preferences

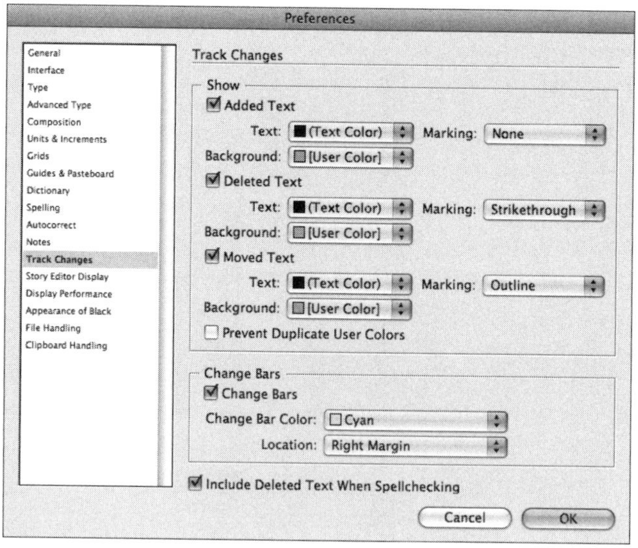

Change Bars. Change bars appear in the margin of the story editor next to any text that is added, deleted, or moved. If the Story Editor looks too busy visually, turn off Change Bars. You can change the color of change bars, and decide whether you want them on the left or right side.

Include Deleted Text When Spellchecking. Depending on your workflow, it can be annoying to include deleted text when you're checking spelling, or it can be annoying not to include deleted text. You decide.

Story Editor Display Preferences

The options in the Story Editor Display pane of the Preferences dialog box control the appearance of Story windows in the document (see Figure 1-45). The idea of the Story Editor is to make text editing easier on your eyes, but it's up to you to decide what that means. They're your eyes, after all. Story Editor preferences are application specific. We have more to say about the Story Editor and story windows, as you'll see in Chapter 3, "Text."

Text Display Options. The options in the Text Display Options section set the font, font size, spacing, and background and foreground colors displayed in story windows. The Theme pop-up menu contains several preset color combinations. The Enable Anti-Aliasing option smooths the edges of text in story windows.

Cursor Options. The options in the Cursor Options section control the appearance of the cursor as it moves through text in a story

FIGURE 1-45
Story Editor Display
Preferences Dialog Box

FIGURE 1-45
Story Editor Display
Preferences Dialog Box

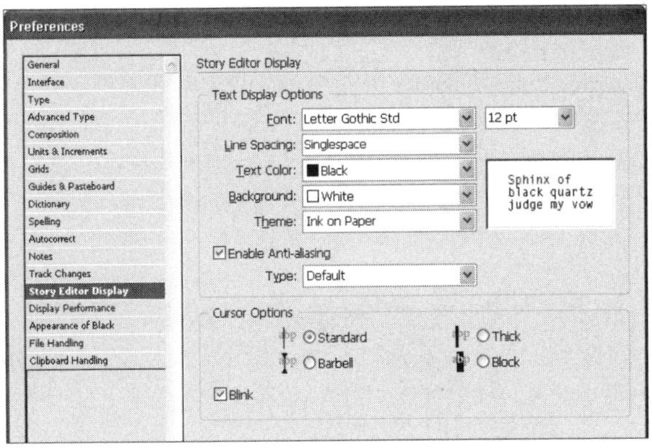

window. Turn the Blink option on to make the cursor blink, or turn it off to prevent the cursor from blinking. We had actually finally expunged the memory of the 1980s Block cursor from our minds when Story Editor brought it all back for us.

Display Performance Preferences

The options in the Display Performance pane of the Preferences dialog box control the way that InDesign draws text and graphics on your screen. The choices you make in this pane can dramatically speed up—or slow down—drawing and redrawing the screen (see Figure 1-46). Display Performance preferences are application specific, and have no effect on printing to PostScript/PDF printers.

Default View Settings. Choose an option on the Default View pop-up menu to set the default view setting for the document. Perhaps we're just middle-of-the-road guys, but we like to choose Typical.

Preserve Object-Level View Settings. The Preserve Object-Level View Settings option tells InDesign to save any display settings you've applied to images when you save the document and then reopen it. When it's turned off, InDesign forgets all the display settings. While it seems like a good idea to turn this on, it can increase the time it takes to open your documents, so we usually leave it off.

Adjust View Settings. You can apply one of three display settings— which are named "Optimized," "Typical," and "High Quality"—to any InDesign window or object, and you can define the parameters of each setting. Note that the names of these settings do not necessarily apply to the quality of the display; "High Quality" can be redefined to produce a lower quality display than "Optimized."

To edit the parameters of a view setting, choose the setting and then adjust the values of the options.

FIGURE 1-46
Display Performance
Preferences

This text changes to Gray Out or High Resolution, depending on the slider setting.

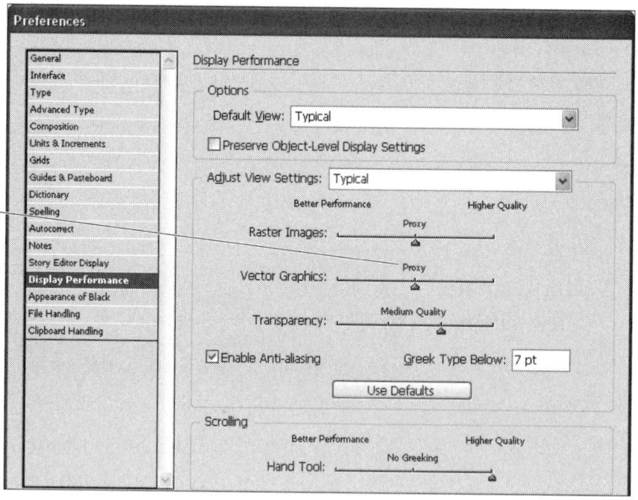

FIGURE 1-46
Display Performance
Preferences

▶ **Raster Images.** This slider defines the method InDesign uses to draw imported bitmap images (TIFF, JPEG, GIF). Note that images saved in the EPS (including DCS) and PDF formats are considered "vector graphics." See Figure 1-47.

Choose Gray Out to draw every image as a gray box. Choose Proxy to have InDesign construct a low-resolution screen version of the imported graphic and use that image for display at all magnification levels. When you choose High Resolution from the Raster Images slider, InDesign gets its information about how to render an image from the original file that's linked to your publication, which means that InDesign renders the best possible display of the image for the current magnification.

This setting has no effect on the way the images print.

▶ **Vector Graphics.** Choose an option from the slider to define the method InDesign uses to display vector graphics (EPS and PDF). See Figure 1-48.

Choose Gray Out to draw every graphic as a gray box. Choose Proxy to have InDesign construct a low-resolution screen version of the imported graphic and use that image for display at all magnification levels. When you choose High Resolution from the Vector Graphics slider, InDesign gets its information about how to render the graphic by reinterpreting PostScript/PDF instructions in the graphic file. InDesign then renders the best possible view of the graphic for the current screen resolution. Note, however that this process can be very time consuming.

FIGURE 1-47
Raster Images
View Settings

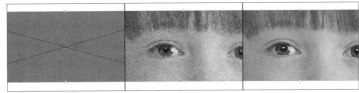

Gray out   *Proxy*   *High resolution*

FIGURE 1-48
Vector Graphics
View Settings

Proxy   *High Resolution*

▶ **Transparency.** The Transparency slider controls the appearance of transparency on your screen—it has nothing to do with the way that transparency prints. Choose Off to omit previews for transparency altogether, or choose Low Quality, Medium Quality, or High Quality to control the accuracy of the preview. See Figure 1-49.

▶ **Enable Anti-Aliasing.** Anti-aliasing smooths the edges of InDesign objects by adding pixels around the edges of the object. See Figure 1-50.

▶ **Greek Type Below.** It takes time to draw text characters, and, frankly, it's not always worth doing. You might have noticed that when you zoom out to the 12.5% page view, InDesign doggedly

FIGURE 1-49
Transparency
View Settings

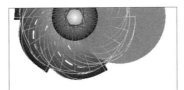   

Off   *Low Quality*

Medium Quality   *High Quality*

FIGURE 1-50
Anti-Aliasing

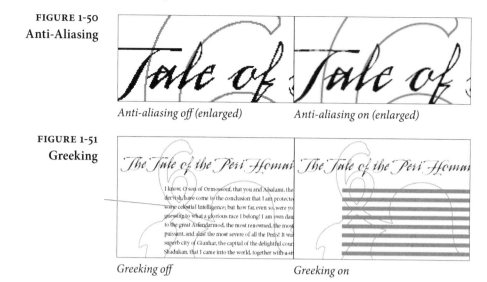

Anti-aliasing off (enlarged)   Anti-aliasing on (enlarged)

FIGURE 1-51
Greeking

Greeking off   Greeking on

attempts to give the best preview it can of the (now very tiny) text on your pages. To tell InDesign not to bother, and to speed up your screen redraw, use greeking.

When you enter a value in the Greek Type Below field that's greater than zero, InDesign displays text characters that are equal to or smaller than that value as a gray bar (see Figure 1-51).

The value shown in the field is in points, but it doesn't refer to the point size of the text. Instead, it refers to the size of the text as it appears on your screen at the current magnification. The advantage of using this option is that the gray bar draws much faster than the actual characters. Greeking has no effect on text composition.

▶ **Use Defaults.** Click this button to return the options for the selected display setting to their default value.

Appearance of Black Preferences

What is the color "black" in your documents? Is it always 100 percent black ink (or "100K black")? Or is it sometimes a "rich black," a color made up of large percentages of other inks? The options in the Appearance of Black pane of the Preferences dialog box control the on-screen, exported, and printed appearance of both 100K black and rich black colors. The best way to understand what the settings in the Appearance of Black panel of the Preferences dialog box (see Figure 1-52) is to look at the example graphics in the dialog box. These preferences are application specific.

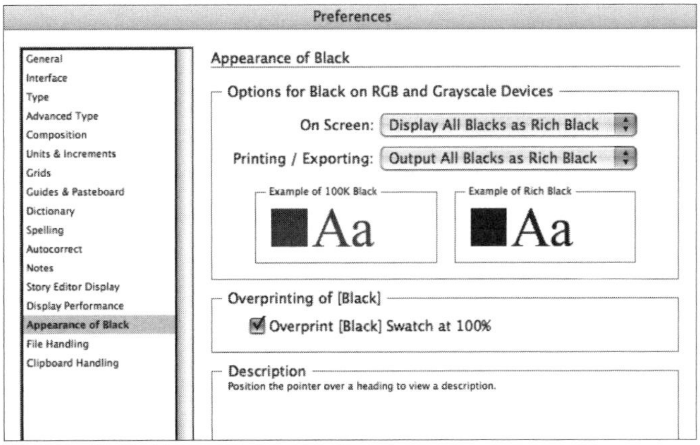

FIGURE 1-52
**Appearance of
Black Preferences**

FIGURE 1-52
**Appearance of
Black Preferences**

On Screen. When you choose Display All Blacks Accurately, InDesign will display 100K black as a dark gray and rich black(s) as RGB black (the darkest color your monitor can represent). When you choose Display All Blacks As Rich Black, both 100K black and rich black(s) will appear as RGB black.

Printing/Exporting. When you choose Output All Blacks Accurately and print to a non-Postscript printer or export to an RGB file format, InDesign will print (or save) 100K black as gray and rich black(s) as RGB black. Choose Output All Blacks As Rich Black, and InDesign will print (or save) both 100K black and rich black(s) as RGB black.

Overprint [Black] Swatch at 100%. If you always want objects colored with the [Black] swatch to overprint, turn this option on. This setting overrides any changes you might make in the Print dialog box. Note that this setting only affects that swatch; it has no effect on any other black swatch (even solid black!), which will print solid black and still knock out whatever is behind it even if this option is on (see Chapter 10, "Color").

File Handling Preferences

The File Handling pane contains options for importing files and setting the location of InDesign's temporary files. All but one File Handling preferences are application specific; the option for creating links applies only to the document.

Document Recovery Data. As you work with InDesign, the program saves information about your preference settings and keeps a record of changes you make to your document. While this makes for a lot of disk-writing activity, it also gives you InDesign's multiple undo and document recovery features.

To change the folder InDesign uses to store its temporary files, click the Choose button. InDesign displays a dialog box. Locate and select the folder you want to use and click the OK button.

Why would you want to change the location? InDesign's temporary files—in particular the file recovery information, can get quite large. You might want to move them to a larger drive to free disk space on your system drive, or to a faster drive to improve performance.

Number of Recent Items to Display. Enter the number of recent files you want to display on the Open Recent submenu of the File menu.

Always Save Preview Images with Documents. Turn this option on to save a preview image of the document with the document file. You can also choose how many pages have preview thumbnails. The preview slightly increases the file size. We leave this turned off.

Snippet Import Options. When you import an InDesign snippet (see Chapter 7, "Importing and Exporting"), you can choose to have the snippet appear at its original location (that is, the position it occupied in its document of origin), or at the current cursor location. To do the former, turn on Position at Original Location; to do the latter, turn on Position at Cursor Location.

Check Links Before Opening Document. Turn this option on to have InDesign check the link status of the imported files in the document as you open the document; turn it off to manage links yourself using the Links panel (see Chapter 7, "Importing and Exporting").

Find Missing Links Before Opening Document. If you have turned on the Check Links Before Opening Document option, you can also choose to have InDesign look for missing links as it opens the document.

Create Links When Placing Text and Spreadsheet Files. When you imported text or Excel files into InDesign 1.x and 2, InDesign always maintained a link to the original file on disk (unless you manually unlinked it in the Links panel). This caused all sorts of confusion, so Adobe made it a preference. Now, by default, imported non-picture files are *not* linked. If you want them to be linked, then turn on the Create Links When Placing Text and Spreadsheet Files option. We discuss this in more depth in Chapter 3, "Text."

Preserves Image Dimensions When Relinking. When you use the Links panel to update or relink a the linked graphic, should the new or updated graphic be scaled to match the dimensions of the existing graphic, or should it take on the same scaling as the existing graphic? To do the former, which can result in the replacement graphic being distorted, turn this option on.

Clipboard Preferences

When you copy data out of an application and switch out of that application, the program writes data to the system Clipboard so that it can be pasted into other applications. Applications often post multiple data formats to the Clipboard in the hope that at least one of them will be readable by the application you want to paste the data into. In InDesign, you use the Clipboard Handling pane of the Preferences dialog box to control the way that InDesign works with the Clipboard. Clipboard preferences are application specific.

Prefer PDF When Pasting. Some applications (notably Illustrator) can put PDF format data on the system Clipboard. InDesign can paste this data as an imported PDF graphic. Whether this is a good thing is debatable—personally, if we want an Illustrator PDF file in InDesign, we'd much rather save it to disk and import it using Place (see Chapter 7, "Importing and Exporting"). However, sometimes we want to paste Illustrator paths into InDesign as editable objects (rather than as a non-editable graphic). If you want to paste paths from Illustrator, turn off the Prefer PDF When Pasting option.

Copy PDF to Clipboard/Preserve PDF Data At Quit. InDesign can put PDF data on the Clipboard, too. This lets you copy something out of InDesign and paste it elsewhere, such as Illustrator (which can convert the PDF into editable objects). If you want InDesign to put PDF data on the Clipboard, turn on the Copy PDF to Clipboard option. Turn on Preserve PDF Data at Quit to prevent InDesign from clearing the Clipboard when you quit.

When Pasting Text and Tables from Other Applications. When you switch from one application to another, copied text typically appears on the Clipboard as both RTF and plain text. RTF carries formatting with it; plain text doesn't. If you want to retain the RTF formatting when you paste text into InDesign from Microsoft Word or some other program, turn on the All Information (Index Markers, Swatches, Styles, etc.) option. To have pasted text take on the attributes of the text you're pasting it into, turn on the Text Only option.

Setting Defaults

"Defaults" are the settings you begin with when you start InDesign. InDesign's defaults control page size, fill type and stroke color, available styles, type specifications, and other details. InDesign has two kinds of defaults—application defaults and document defaults. Application defaults determine the appearance and behavior of all new publications; document defaults control the specifications of objects you create in a particular publication.

Neither document defaults nor application defaults change any existing objects or publications—you can change the defaults at any time without harming publications you've already laid out.

When you create a new InDesign publication, do you immediately add a set of colors to the Colors panel, change the default line weight, display the rulers, and add styles to the Style panel? If you do, you probably get tired of making those changes over and over again. Wouldn't it be great if you could tell InDesign to create new documents using those settings?

You can. To set InDesign's application defaults, close all publications (without closing InDesign), then, with no publication open (what we like to call the "no pub state," or, as our good friend Steve Broback would say, "Utah"), add or remove styles and colors, set type specifications, and otherwise make the changes you've been making in each new publication.

The next time you create a new InDesign publication, it'll appear with the settings you specified.

Some document properties cannot be set as application defaults—you cannot, for example, create a new layer or add master pages.

Reverting to InDesign's Original Defaults

You may occasionally want to delete your preferences and start from scratch. To do this, hold down Command-Option-Shift-Control (on the Mac OS) or Ctrl-Alt-Shift (in Windows) as you start InDesign.

Publication Navigation

InDesign offers three ways to change your view of the publication: zooming, scrolling, and moving from page to page. Zooming changes the magnification of the area inside the window. Scrolling changes the view in the window without changing the magnification.

Zooming

When you zoom in and out on a page, you are using an electronic magnifying glass, first enlarging a particular area of a page and then reducing your screen view so that you are seeing the entire page or pages at once. InDesign lets you magnify or reduce your screen view from 5 percent to 4,000 percent.

Zooming with the View menu. The View menu offers InDesign's "standard" magnifications, or views, and provides keyboard shortcuts for most of them (see Table 1-3). In fact, some of the keyboard shortcuts in the table should probably just be committed to memory, as they don't appear in the View menu—such as Command-2/Ctrl-2 to zoom to 200-percent view, and Command-Option-2/Ctrl-Alt-2 to zoom back to the last magnification you used.

All of these commands except Fit Page in Window and Fit Spread in Window center the selected object in the window. If you don't have an object selected, these shortcuts zoom in or out based on the center of the current view. Fit Page In Window centers the current page in a publication window. This makes Fit Page In Window the perfect "zoom-out" shortcut.

Zooming with the Zoom tool. Another method: choose the Zoom tool, point at an area in your publication, and click. InDesign zooms to the next larger view size (based on your current view—from 100% to 200%, for example), centering the area you clicked on. Hold down Option/Alt and the plus ("+") in the Zoom tool changes to a minus ("-"). Click the Zoom tool to zoom out.

Fit Selection In Window. Another view command we use all of the time is Fit Selection In Window. Don't bother looking for it on the View menu—it's not there. Instead, it appears on the context menu when you have an object selected. It does just what it says—zooms (in or out) on the current selection and centers it in the publication

TABLE 1-3
View Shortcuts

To zoom to this view:	Press:
Actual size (100%)	Command-1/Ctrl-1
200%	Command-2/Ctrl-2
400%	Command-4/Ctrl-4
50%	Command-5/Ctrl-5
Fit Page in Window	Command-0/Ctrl-0
Fit Spread in Window	Command-Option-0/Ctrl-Alt-0
Zoom in	Command-+/Ctrl-+
Zoom out	Command-- (minus)/Ctrl--(minus)
Last zoom	Command-Option-2/Ctrl-Alt-2

window (see Figure 1-53). Press Command-Option-=/Ctrl-Alt-= to zoom to the Fit Selection In Window view. When text is selected, this shortcut fits the text frame containing the text in the window.

Switching to the Zoom Tool. Press Command-Spacebar/Ctrl-Spacebar to temporarily switch from any tool to the Zoom tool to zoom in; or hold down Command-Option-Spacebar/Ctrl-Alt-Spacebar to zoom out.

Zooming with "Power Zoom." We're not kidding—that's what it's called. To use this feature, switch to the Hand tool, then hold down the (left) mouse button. After a second, InDesign displays a red frame in the window. You can move the mouse to change the area selected, and you can make the frame larger or smaller using the mouse scroll wheel. When you release the mouse button, InDesign zooms in or out to fit the area in the window (see Figure 1-54).

The Best Way to Zoom. To zoom in, press Command/Ctrl and hold down Spacebar to turn the current tool (whatever it is) into the Zoom tool, then drag the Zoom tool in the publication window. As you drag, a rectangle (like a selection rectangle) appears. Drag the rectangle around the area you want to zoom in on, and release the mouse button. InDesign zooms in on the area, magnifying it to the magnification that fits in the publication window (see Figure 1-55).

To zoom out, use one of the keyboard shortcuts—Command-0/Ctrl-0 (for Fit Page In Window) is especially handy. It's even better if you redefine the shortcut to make it easier to reach with one hand—why take your hand off of the mouse if you don't need to?

FIGURE 1-53
Fit Selection in Window

It doesn't really matter where the selection is hiding. Press Command-Option-=/Ctrl-Alt-= (or choose Fit Selection in Window from the Context menu)...

...and InDesign will find it and display it front and center.

FIGURE 1-54
Power Zoom

Switch to the Hand tool, then hold down the left mouse button. InDesign displays a red frame in the window (you'll just have to imagine that this is red).

Use the scroll wheel to enlarge or reduce the frame, and move the mouse to change its posion.

Release the mouse button, and InDesign fits the framed area in the window.

FIGURE 1-55
Drag Magnification

Hold down Command-Spacebar/Ctrl-Spacebar to switch to the Zoom tool.

Drag the Zoom tool around the area you want to magnify.

InDesign zooms in on the area you defined by dragging.

Entering a magnification percentage. To zoom to a specific magnification percentage, enter the percentage in the Magnification field and press Return/Enter. InDesign zooms to the percentage you specified (centering the selection, if any, as it does so).

Scrolling

As we mentioned earlier in this chapter, we rarely use the scroll bars to scroll. So how do we change our view of our publications? We use the Hand tool (also known as the "Grabber Hand").

Scrolling with the Hand tool. So how do *you* use the Hand tool? Sure, you can always click on the Hand tool in the Tools panel, or press H to switch to the Hand tool. But it's better to use the keyboard shortcut that always works, no matter what tool you have selected: Option/Alt-spacebar (see Figure 1-56). This shortcut is temporary—release it, and you'll go back to whatever tool you had selected.

The Hand tool even works inside the Pages panel (though you don't need to hold anything down or choose a tool to use it there).

Scrolling as you drag objects. Don't forget that you can change your view by dragging objects off the screen. If you know an object should be moved to some point outside your current view, select the object and do one of the following things:

▶ To scroll down, drag the cursor into the scroll bar at the bottom of the publication window. Don't drag the cursor off the bottom of the screen—InDesign won't scroll if you do this.

▶ To scroll to the right, move the cursor into the vertical scroll bar, or drag the cursor off of the left edge of the screen.

▶ To scroll to a point above your current view, drag the cursor into the horizontal ruler.

▶ To scroll to the left, drag the cursor into the vertical ruler (or off the screen, if the ruler is not visible).

The window scrolls as long as the mouse button is down. Sometimes it's the best way to get something into position.

InDesign won't let you drag objects to an area in the publication window that is behind a panel. If you drag the cursor into any panel other than the Library panel, InDesign displays the "prohibited" symbol. When you drop objects you're dragging into an area covered by a panel, InDesign bounces the objects back to their original locations. You can't hide panels while you're dragging objects, so you might want to hide the panels before you begin dragging.

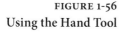
FIGURE 1-56
Using the Hand Tool

Hold down Option-Spacebar/Alt-Spacebar to switch to the Hand tool, then drag the Hand tool to scroll.

When the publication window looks the way you want it to, stop dragging.

Scrolling with a Scroll Wheel. If your mouse has a scroll wheel, InDesign probably supports it (no promises—there are lots of different mice). Move the scroll wheel to scroll the window up and down, or hold down Option/Alt as you move the scroll wheel zoom.

The scroll wheel even works inside panels—this is especially useful in the Pages panel, but it also comes in handy when you need to scroll through long lists of styles in the Paragraph Styles panel.

If you have a fancy mouse and you're running InDesign in Windows Vista, Windows 7, or on a Mac, turn on Enable Multi-Touch Gestures in Interface preferences to do things like rotating the spread using the rotate gesture.

Jump to Page   One of the best navigation shortcuts doesn't appear in the menu: Command-J/Ctrl-J, for Go To Page (it displays the Go to Page dialog box—where you can enter the page you want to jump to).

Two of the most useful page-navigation features in the Layout menu have odd names (Go Back and Go Forward) and are set apart in the menu. How do these work? Let's say you're working on page 9 when you jump to page 25 to make a quick change and then jump to page 81 to see how the change affected the end of the story. Now you can press Command-Up Arrow/Ctrl-Up Arrow (Go Back) to jump back to page 25, and press it again to return to page 9. Want to return to page 25? Press Command-Down Arrow (Go Forward).

Place Icons

When you place (that is, import) a file, InDesign changes the cursor into an icon called a "place icon," or "place gun" (see Figure 1-57). You can click the place icon to specify the position of the upper-left corner of the incoming file, or you can drag the place icon to define the width and height of the file.

We'll talk more about place icons in the next chapter, again in Chapter 3, "Text," and in Chapter 7, "Importing and Exporting."

Managing InDesign's Plug-Ins

Everything you see in InDesign is provided by a plug-in. The "application" itself is little more than a plug-in manager. The functions we traditionally think of as being central to a page layout application—things like text composition, text editing, or basic drawing tools—they're all plug-ins. We're not kidding.

FIGURE 1-57

Place Icons

Text place icon (manual flow)

Text place icon (semi-automatic flow)

Text place icon (autoflow)

Graphic place icon

Image place icon

Text place icon (in frame)

Text place icon (autoflow, in frame)

Image place icon (in frame)

Graphic place icon (in frame)

PDF place icon

Multi-file place icon

This means that you can turn plug-ins on and off to customize InDesign to the way that you work and the publications you work with. Specifically, you can turn off the plug-ins you don't use.

To define the plug-ins InDesign will load the next time you start the program, choose Manage Extensions from the InDesign menu (on the Macintosh), or from the Help menu (in Windows). The Adobe Extension Manager opens. This command used to be called Configure Plug-ins in previous versions. (If you've spent time configuring plug-ins in a previous version, you'll miss the old Configure Plug-ins dialog box. While the Extension Manager works with the other suite programs, it's slower and less versatile than Configure Plug-ins.)

Why would you want to turn plug-ins off? Simple—to reduce the amount of memory taken up by InDesign and to increase the speed of the application (slightly).

Some plug-ins are required by InDesign—they're the ones with the little padlock next to them. But all of the other plug-ins are fair game. Never use the Info panel? Turn it off!

On with the Tour

At this point in the InDesign tour, we've seen most of the sights. Don't worry if you're a little confused—it's hard to take it all in at once. In the following chapters, we'll help you put the tools in context—so far, we've just talked about what the tools *are*. In the rest of the book, we'll talk about what you can *do* with them.

CHAPTER 2

Page Layout

Now that you know what's what, and what's where, in InDesign, it's time to create an InDesign publication and set up some pages. As you work your way through the process of defining the page size, margins, column layout, and master pages for your new publication, think ahead. How will the publication be printed? How will it be bound? Will you need to create a different version of the publication for a different paper size (such as switching from US Letter to A4 for an international edition)? Will you need to create a different version of the publication for online distribution?

We know that having to think about these things and make design decisions early in the process can be boring. And InDesign makes it relatively easy to make changes to your layout late in the production process. Easy, but not without a certain amount of trouble. How high is your threshold of pain? Will it decrease as your deadline approaches? You decide.

Creating a New Publication

When you choose New Document from the New submenu on the File menu, InDesign displays the New Document dialog box (see Figure 2-1). You use the controls in this dialog box to set up the basic layout of the pages in your publication. Don't worry—you're not locked into anything; you can change these settings at any time, or override any of them for any page or page spread in your publication.

▶ **Intent.** Choose Web if you're creating an interactive document and want to use more appropriate settings for the web, such as using a landscape orientation and non-facing pages.

▶ **Number of Pages.** How many pages do you want? We tend to start with one page and add pages as we go along, but you might want to think ahead and add a bunch at once.

FIGURE 2-1
**The New Document
Dialog Box**

*Choose a page size from
this pop-up menu...*

*...or enter a custom page
size using these fields.*

*Enter page margin settings
in the fields in this section.
Note that the margin settings
of individual pages override
these settings.*

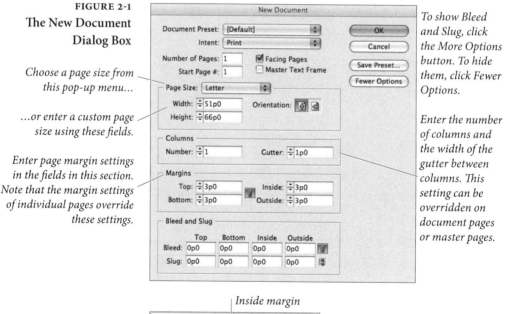

*To show Bleed
and Slug, click
the More Options
button. To hide
them, click Fewer
Options.*

*Enter the number
of columns and
the width of the
gutter between
columns. This
setting can be
overridden on
document pages
or master pages.*

*If you turn off the Facing
Pages option, the "Inside"
and "Outside" fields change
to read "Right" and "Left."*

Inside margin

Outside margin

▶ **Start Page #.** Type the starting number of the page. If you type an even number for Start Page #, the publication begins with a two-page spread—much easier than in previous versions. In InDesign, odd numbers always start on the right-hand page (*recto*) page.

▶ **Facing Pages.** If you're creating a single-sided document—like an advertisement, poster, or handbill—leave Facing Pages turned off. Turn it on for books and magazines, which usually have both left- (*verso*) and right-hand (*recto*) pages.

▶ **Master Text Frame.** Should InDesign create a text frame on the master page? If so, turn the Master Text Frame option on. The width and height of this "automatic" text frame are defined by the area inside the page margins; its column settings correspond to the column settings for the page.

▶ **Page Size.** Pick a page size according to the final size of your document. If this is a print document, that means the size after trimming, not the paper you're printing on. The Page Size pop-up menu lists most of the standard sizes—including common screen resolutions for interactive documents—but you can always enter your own page width and height (when you do this, the Page Size pop-up menu changes to "Custom"). To create a new page size, choose Custom Page Size, specify the settings you want, and click OK. Presto! The page size appears in the list—much easier than editing the New Doc Sizes.txt, which you had to do in previous versions.

▶ **Columns.** When you specify that a document should have more than one column, InDesign adds column guides. Next, enter the amount of space to leave between columns in the Gutter field. Column guides can be overridden on both document pages and master pages.

▶ **Margins.** Use the fields in the Margins section of the dialog box to specify the size of the margins on all four sides of a page. When you turn on the Facing Pages option, "Left" and "Right" change to "Inside" and "Outside." You can always change your margin guides later, on a specific page or for a master page.

Bleed and Slug   If you can't see the Bleed and Slug fields, click the More Options button. These fields let you define guides on the pasteboard and effectively extend the print area of your document.

What's the difference between the bleed and the slug? Usually, people put things in the bleed area that have to do with their design (typically objects that bleed off the edge of the page), and put job tracking and other document information in the slug area. But the real difference, from an InDesign point of view, is that they have independent printing controls. You might choose to include the slug area when printing proofs and then omit the slug when printing your final version. (Here in rainy Seattle, we are very familiar with slugs.)

Document Presets

Do you find that you frequently have to change the settings in the New Document dialog box? If you have particular page sizes and margin settings that you use all of the time, consider making a document preset. The easiest way to make one is to type all the values (page size, margin, bleed and slug settings, and so on) into the New Document dialog box, click the Save Preset button, and give your preset a name.

The next time you want to create a document based on that preset, you can select the name from the Document Preset pop-up menu at the top of the New Document dialog box. You can also make, delete, or edit document presets by choosing Define from the Document Presets submenu (under the File menu). The Define Document Presets dialog box also lets you save presets to disk or load presets from disk—very helpful if you need to send a document preset to someone else in your workgroup.

By the way, for those who care about terminology, the difference between a *preset* and a *style* has to do with how InDesign behaves when you later change the preset or style. Let's say you save a Document Preset, make three new documents based on that preset, and

FIGURE 2-2
The Open a File
Dialog Box

This is the Windows version, of course. The Mac OS version is similar. Sort of.

Choose Normal to open the publication; choose Original to open and edit a file you've saved as an InDesign template file; and choose Copy to open a file as an untitled publication.

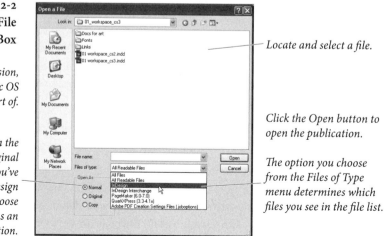

Locate and select a file.

Click the Open button to open the publication.

The option you choose from the Files of Type menu determines which files you see in the file list.

then change the definition of the preset. InDesign doesn't change the documents you already made. Now let's say you define a paragraph style in a document, apply it to three paragraphs, and then go back and change the style definition. InDesign applies the change to all of the paragraphs formatted using that style. (We cover paragraph styles in Chapter 4, "Type.")

Skip the dialog box. If you use a specific document preset all of the time, why in the world should you have to look at the New Document dialog box every time you create a layout? You don't. You can bypass the dialog box by holding down the Shift key while selecting the preset name from the Document Presets submenu (under the File menu). Or, instead of pressing Command-N/Ctrl-N to create a new document, press Command-Option-N/Ctrl-Alt-N. This creates a new document using the settings you used most recently.

Setting New Document Defaults

The Document Preset feature is great, but some people create the same kind of document day in and day out. If you're one of those folks, you should probably change the values in the default New Document dialog box (the way it first opens). You can do this by choosing Define from the Document Presets submenu (under the File menu) and editing the Default preset.

But wait, there's more! If you always want your new documents to have certain paragraph styles, character styles, and colors, create them while no documents are open. Every new document you build from then on will have these settings.

Opening Publications

When you choose Open from the File menu, or press Command-O/Ctrl-O, InDesign displays the Open a File dialog box (see Figure 2-2). Locate and select the InDesign document you want to open, then click the Open button and InDesign opens the selected document in a new window.

There are two "twists" InDesign adds to the standard process. The first has mainly to do with publications you've saved as templates (also known as "stationery" on the Macintosh), or documents you want to treat as templates (later in the chapter, we'll describe templates). To open a copy of the file, turn on the Open Copy option. InDesign opens an untitled copy of the file you selected. To open a template file for editing, turn on the Open Original option.

The second twist has to do with opening files created in previous versions of InDesign. Unlike most programs, InDesign doesn't just open earlier version's files—rather, it actually converts them to InDesign CS5 files. It takes longer than you might expect (though usually not too long), and the file opens with "[Converted]" in the title bar. You can't save converted files; you have to use Save As.

In fact you may find your files open as [Converted] even after installing a minor InDesign update or an update to a plug-in. Again, the theory is that this is all for your safety, so you won't accidentally replace an earlier version, but it can be frustrating at times.

QuarkXPress and PageMaker Files. InDesign can also open some PageMaker or QuarkXPress files. Select the file you want to convert, and then click the Open button. (To do this in Windows, choose the file type you want to open from the Files of Type pop-up menu, or choose All Documents.) InDesign converts the file and opens it as a new, untitled InDesign publication. However, before you convert a file, we strongly encourage you to open it in QuarkXPress or Page-Maker, make sure the images are all linked properly and available on a local hard drive, and perform a Save As to save a clean copy of the file for conversion. And after you open it in InDesign, clean it up by exporting it to IDML format.

How well does this conversion process work? That depends on the publication you're trying to open, but you should never expect the conversion process to be perfect. There are simply too many differences in the capabilities of the different products.

InDesign also does a good job of converting text formatting, though line endings may change. The following sections provide more detail on what you can expect to see when you convert publications from other page layout programs.

QuarkXPress Files   InDesign can open QuarkXPress 3.3-4.11 documents and templates, including multi-language QuarkXPress Passport files. This useful ability is subject to a number of terms and conditions, which we'll outline in this section. First, InDesign cannot open:

▶ QuarkXPress files from version 5, 6, 7, or 8. You can, of course, open a QuarkXPress 4.x document saved from version 5.x.

▶ QuarkXPress documents (any version) created using XTensions that require you have the XTension to open the document (the infamous Pasteboard XT, for example)

▶ QuarkXPress book or library documents

Provided the document you want to convert does not fall into one of the above accursed categories, InDesign will convert the document setup, pages, and page items into their InDesign equivalents as best it can. However, as you might expect, there are still a number of details you need to be aware of.

If you need more details about QuarkXPress conversion issues, please download this file for more information: http://www.indesignsecrets.com/rwid/quark.pdf

PageMaker Files

As you convert, or prepare to convert, publications from PageMaker to InDesign, a few odd things happen for reasons that seem odd but make sense when you consider the differences between the two programs. For example, all pasteboard objects from PageMaker are placed on the pasteboard of the first spread in InDesign, and all master page items are assigned to a layer named "Master."

If you need details about PageMaker conversion issues, please download this file for more information: http://www.indesignsecrets.com/rwid/pagemaker.pdf

Problems with Converted Files?

You may experience odd problems with a document converted from a previous InDesign version or from QuarkXPress or PageMaker. For example, you may not be able to export to PDF or do other tasks that you don't have trouble doing in a different document.

Here's the cure-all—export the file to IDML format, and then open that IDML file and save it. IDML is a purifier of sorts, like the waters of Lake Minnetonka.

Saving Publications

To save a publication, choose Save from the File menu (or press Command-S/Ctrl-S). To save a publication under a different name, choose Save As (or press Command-Shift-S/Ctrl-Shift-S), and InDesign will display the Save File As dialog box. Use this dialog box to set a location for the new file, assign a file name, and decide whether the file should be saved as a publication file or as a template.

If you're trying to save the file in a format other than an InDesign file, use the "Export" command. For more on exporting publications or parts of publications in file formats other than InDesign's native format, see Chapter 7, "Importing and Exporting."

Save with an Extension. Windows users always save files with filename extensions because Windows requires these in order to figure out what files are associated with which applications. InDesign publications, for example, have the four-letter .indd file name extension. InDesign templates (see below) use .indt. We want to encourage Mac OS users to use these suffixes, too. In today's multi-platform world, you just never know when your Mac OS InDesign file will need to be opened on a Windows machine. File-name extensions are ugly, but they're a fact of life.

Saving As a Template

If you need to base a new publication on the design of a publication you've already laid out, and want to make sure you don't save over the original file, create a template.

When you try to open a file that was saved as a template, InDesign automatically opens a copy of the file. If, at that point, you try to save the file, InDesign will display the Save As dialog box. Which means you can proceed with your plan to save the publication under a new name. Remember? Your plan?

To save an InDesign publication as a template, choose Save As from the File menu. In the Save As dialog box, enter a name for the template file and then choose InDesign CS5 Template from the Format pop-up menu (on the Macintosh) or the Save As Type pop-up menu (in Windows). Click the Save button to save the template file.

You can also create a template by locking the file. On the Macintosh, select the file in the Finder, choose Get Info from the File menu (or press Command-I), and then turn on either the Locked or the StationeryPad checkbox in the Get Info dialog box. In Windows, right-click on the file's icon, choose Properties, and turn on the Read-Only feature in the Properties dialog box.

Actually, any InDesign file can act as a template, no matter how you've saved it. When you open any publication via the Open dialog box and turn on the Open Copy option, InDesign opens it in a new, untitled publication, just as though it were a template.

Saving for Earlier Versions of InDesign

InDesign CS5 gives you a way to "save back" to InDesign CS4. To do this, you export a file using the InDesign Markup format, or IDML, and then open that file in InDesign CS4. You should make sure you're using the most recent version of CS4 by choosing Updates from the Help menu or by downloading the file from adobe.com.

Want to save back to an even earlier version? Sorry. You have to play a leapfrog game of opening the file in each lower version and exporting as IDML (or INX, if you need to go farther back).

To export a file as IDML, choose Export from the File menu, select the InDesign Markup format, and then export the file. For more on the IDML file format, see Chapter 7, "Importing and Exporting."

Crash Recovery

It will happen. At some point, your computer will suddenly stop working. Or the software we jokingly refer to as the "operating system" will fail for some unknown reason.

At this point, it's natural to assume you've lost work—and maybe that you've lost the file forever. That is, after all, the way things work in most other programs.

But it's not true for InDesign. InDesign keeps track of the changes you've made to a document—even for an untitled document you haven't yet saved. When you restart InDesign after a system, the program uses the contents of a folder named "InDesign Recovery" to reconstruct the publication or publications that were open when you crashed—even if you hadn't saved them yet. Because of this automatic "backup"system, you'll be right back where you left off.

If you don't want to recover the most recent changes you made to a publication before a crash (which you might want to do if you felt that your changes caused the crash), delete the files in the folder. This folder appears in different places on different operating systems, so the best way to find it is to use your operating system's Search utility to find a folder called "InDesign Recovery."

You should also delete these files if InDesign is crashing on startup as it tries to read the recovery information (this is pretty rare). In this case, a file has been damaged and cannot be opened—you'll have to try opening the original document (or rebuild the document from scratch, if you hadn't saved the file).

Setting Basic Layout Options

You can always change the margins, columns, page size, and page orientation of a publication. You do this using the Margins and Columns dialog box, and you can apply these changes to any page, page spread, or master page in a publication.

Changing Page Size and Orientation

Page size and page orientation affect the entire document (you can't mix page sizes and page orientations in a file), and you use the Document Setup dialog box (press Command-Option-P/Ctrl-Alt-P to display this dialog box, or choose Document Setup from the File menu) to change these settings. To change the page size, choose a new page size for the publication from the Page Size pop-up menu (or enter values in the Width and Height fields); to change the page orientation, click the button corresponding to the orientation you want.

Usually, InDesign centers the page items on the new page size—that is, each page grows equally on all four sides. However, if you have turned on the layout adjustment feature (from the Layout menu), InDesign moves objects and guides on your pages when you change the page size or page orientation, sometimes in unexpected ways. See "Adjusting Layouts," later in this chapter, for more on this topic.

Specifying Margins and Columns

You aren't stuck with the margin and column setup you specified in the New Document dialog box—you can change margin and column settings for any page, at any time. To change margin and column settings, navigate to the page you want to change, then choose Margins and Columns from the Layout menu (see Figure 2-3). Click the OK button to close the dialog box, and InDesign applies the new margin and column settings. While you can make these changes to any page, it's likely that you'll most often be making changes to master pages. Keep in mind that these margin and column settings affect the page, but not text frames. Use the Text Frame Options dialog box to change columns within frames.

You can create columns of unequal width by dragging the column guides (see "Adjusting Column Guides," later in this chapter).

What happens to the objects on a page when you change the margin and column settings for that page? Do they reposition themselves relative to the new margins? Or do they stay put? That depends on the settings in the Layout Adjustment dialog box. See "Adjusting Layouts," later in this chapter, for more on adjusting layouts.

FIGURE 2-3
Margins and Columns Dialog Box

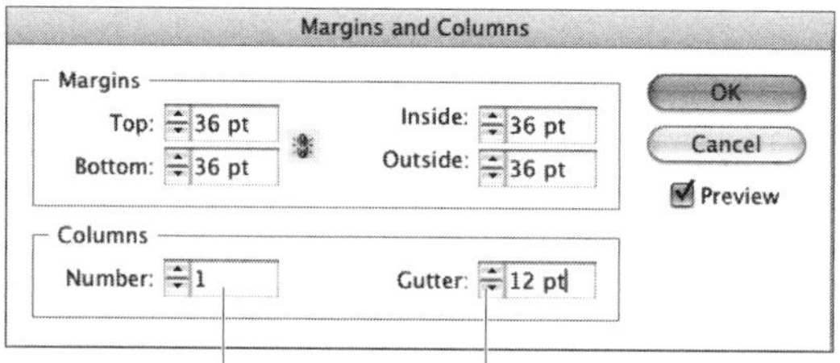

The "Inside" and "Outside" labels have been improperly aligned for several versions now. We don't know why.

The value you enter here sets the number of column guides.

This value sets the distance between column guides.

Pages and Spreads

When you work with a document, you construct the document out of pages and spreads. You won't get far in InDesign without mastering the Pages panel, the primary tool for creating, arranging, deleting pages, and applying master pages. It's also a great way to navigate from one page to another.

Pages Panel Options   The following are brief descriptions of the controls found in the Pages panel (see Figure 2-4).

> ▶ **Spread and page icons.** These icons represent the document pages and master pages in your publication. You can drag these pages around in the Pages panel to change the page order, or apply master pages to document pages (or other master pages), or create new master pages (by dragging document pages into the master page area of the panel).

> ▶ **Edit page size button.** Click this button to apply a different page size to the selected page.

> ▶ **New page button.** Click this button to create a new document page. Hold down Command/Ctrl and click this button to create a new master spread.

> ▶ **Delete page button.** Click this button to delete the selected page or pages.

> ▶ **Master/Document page separator.** This bar separates the master pages in your publication from the "normal" document pages. You can drag the separator up or down.

> ▶ **Resize box.** Drag this icon to resize the Pages panel.

To change the appearance of the panel (and you really should), choose Panel Options from the panel menu (see Figure 2-5). The options in the Panel Options dialog box can be used for good or evil.

> ▶ **Icon Size.** The options on this pop-up menu define the size of the page icons (from Extra Small to Extra Large). in the Pages panel. The Small option remains our perennial favorite.

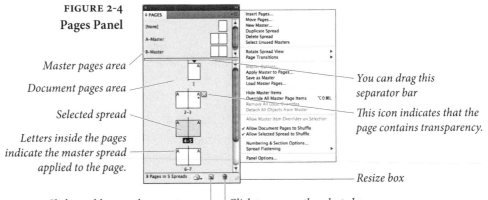

FIGURE 2-4
Pages Panel

Master pages area

Document pages area

Selected spread

Letters inside the pages indicate the master spread applied to the page.

You can drag this separator bar

This icon indicates that the page contains transparency.

Resize box

Click to add a new document page.   *Click to remove the selected page.*

FIGURE 2-5
Pages Panel Options

The Panel Options dialog box (choose Panel Options from the Pages panel menu) gives you a way to control the appearance of the panel.

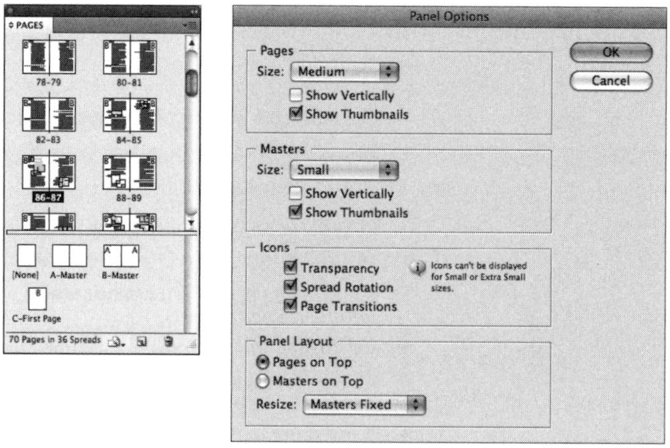

▶ **Show Vertically.** Turn on Show Vertically to arrange the spreads in the Pages panel vertically, centered around the spine. This is similar to the appearance of the corresponding panel in QuarkXPress, but it's also one of the least efficient arrangements available in InDesign. If you want to use the Pages panel for navigation (and you do, believe us), avoid this option.

▶ **Show Thumbnails.** You can show little pictures of the stuff on your pages by turning on the Show Thumbnails option. There is a slight performance penalty to pay for having this turned on, so we usually leave it off.

▶ **Pages/Masters On Top.** This option controls the arrangement of the document/master spreads areas in the panel. If you prefer having the master spreads at the top of the panel (as in QuarkXPress), choose Masters on Top; we prefer Pages on Top since we manage pages far more often than master pages.

▶ **Resize.** Choose Pages Fixed to prevent the document area from resizing, or Masters Fixed (our favorite) to do the same for the masters area of the panel. Choose Proportional to resize both areas by the same amount.

Adding Color Labels   You can apply a little color bar to the page thumbnails in the Pages panel (see Figure 2-6). For example, you can use different color labels for master pages and the layout pages they're applied to.

▶ In the Pages panel, select the pages to which you want to apply color labels. From the Pages panel menu, choose Color Label, and then pick a color.

FIGURE 2-6
Color Labels

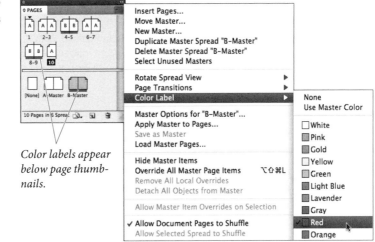

Color labels appear below page thumbnails.

If you apply a color to a master page, all pages to which the master is applied will have the same color by default. If you don't want master color labels to be applied to document pages, choose Color Label from the Pages panel menu, and then uncheck Use Master Color.

Selecting Pages and Spreads

InDesign makes a distinction between *targeting* a page or spread and *selecting* a page or spread (see Figure 2-7):

▶ A page (or spread) is targeted if it is the page onto which the next new objects will be placed.

▶ A page (or spread) is selected if the next page action—such as duplicating the spread or changing its margins—will affect it.

The target page and the selected page can be different pages—you can be viewing one page while your actions affect another. By default, the page you are looking at is the one that is targeted. But if you're zoomed back so that more than one page or spread is visible on screen, you can target *and* select any page or spread by clicking on it.

To select a page, click the page icon in the Pages panel. To select a spread, click the numbers beneath the page icons.

To select more than a single page at a time, select the first spread, then hold down Shift as you select the other pages. Hold down Command/Ctrl as you click pages to select non-contiguous pages.

Double-click a page icon (or the page numbers beneath the spread) to select that page or spread, display it in the publication window, *and* target it. You can hold down Option/Alt as you double-click a page icon, and InDesign changes the page view to the Fit Page in Window view (see Figure 2-8).

**Selecting Pages
and Spreads**

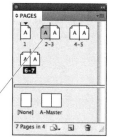

*Double-click the label of a
spread (the name or page
numbers beneath the spread
icon) to select the spread and
make it the active spread.*

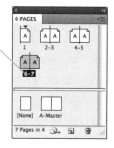

*Click a page icon to select the
page. In this example, page 2
is selected, but pages 6-7 are
the active spread.*

FIGURE 2-8

**Navigating with the
Pages Panel**

*Double-click a page icon
to jump to that page; hold
down Option/Alt as you
double-click to display
the page at Fit Page in
Window view.*

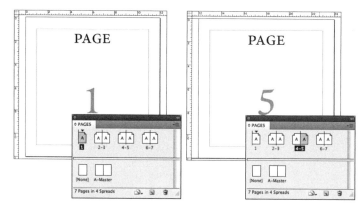

The same goes for master pages. If you're looking at document pages, you can select a master page in the Pages panel (click on it once), open the Margins and Columns dialog box (from the Layout menu) and make changes. The changes are applied to the master page, which then ripple through to the document pages that you see.

Adding Pages

To add a page to your publication, do any of the following.

Click the Add Page button. InDesign adds a page to the publication and displays the new page in the publication window (see Figure 2-9). At the same time, InDesign applies the most recently applied master page to the new page. If you hold down Option/Alt as you click the Add Page button, InDesign displays the Insert Pages dialog box (see below). If you press Command/Ctrl as you click the Add Page button, InDesign adds a new master page.

Choose Insert Pages from the Pages panel menu. InDesign displays the Insert Pages dialog box (see Figure 2-10). Enter the number of pages you want to add in the Pages field. Use the Insert pop-up menu

FIGURE 2-9
The Add Page Button

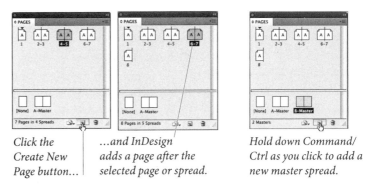

Click the
Create New
Page button...

...and InDesign
adds a page after the
selected page or spread.

Hold down Command/
Ctrl as you click to add a
new master spread.

to select the position at which you want the inserted pages to appear. If you want to apply a master page or spread to the pages, choose that master page from the Master pop-up menu. Click the OK button to add the pages. If you hold down Option/Alt, InDesign turns the Cancel button into the Reset button. Click the Reset button, and the controls will be set back to the state they were in when you opened the dialog box.

Drag a master spread icon into the document pages area of the Pages panel. This creates a new document page or page spread and applies the master page to it. To create a page without applying a master page to it, drag and drop the None master page in the document pages area.

Hold down Option/Alt as you drag a page or page spread icon. Just as you can copy an object on a page by Option/Alt-dragging it on the page, you can duplicate document or master pages by Option/Alt-dragging them in the Pages panel (see Figure 2-11).

Choose Duplicate Spread from the Pages panel's menu. This duplicates the selected spread (including any page objects on the spread's pages) and adds it to the current section.

Arranging Pages

Ordinarily, the pages in your publication are arranged into spreads according to the state of the Facing Pages option in the New Document and Document Setup dialog boxes. If you've turned the Facing Pages option on, InDesign arranges the majority of pages into two-page spreads (the first page is a single page spread). If the Facing Pages option is off, InDesign makes each page in the publication into a single page spread.

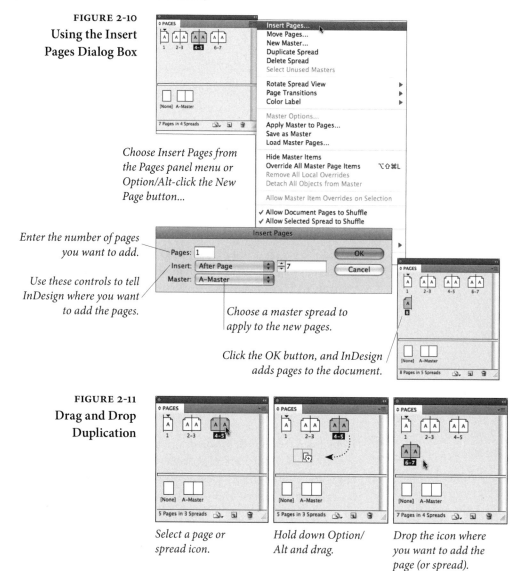

FIGURE 2-10
Using the Insert Pages Dialog Box

Choose Insert Pages from the Pages panel menu or Option/Alt-click the New Page button...

Enter the number of pages you want to add.

Use these controls to tell InDesign where you want to add the pages.

Choose a master spread to apply to the new pages.

Click the OK button, and InDesign adds pages to the document.

FIGURE 2-11
Drag and Drop Duplication

Select a page or spread icon.

Hold down Option/Alt and drag.

Drop the icon where you want to add the page (or spread).

But you're not limited to these arrangements of pages and spreads. At any point, in any section of your publication, you can create a spread—also called an "island spread"—containing anything from one to ten pages.

An island spread pays no attention to the default arrangement of pages, but follows its own whim. It doesn't matter what you do—you can add or remove pages that precede the island spread in a section, and the island spread will remain unchanged.

To create an island spread, select a spread and then turn off Allow Selected Pages to Shuffle from the Pages panel menu. InDesign displays brackets around the name of the spread to indicate that it's an island spread (see Figure 2-12). Selecting more than a single spread before you choose this option converts all of the spreads to separate island spreads; it does not join them into a single island spread.

When you drag a page or spread into an island spread, InDesign adds the pages of the spread to the island spread. When you drag a page out of an island spread, InDesign does not set the page as an island spread (that is, the pages of the island spread do not inherit the spread's "island" quality).

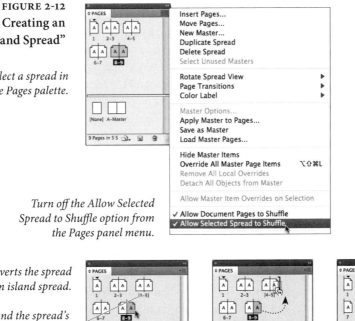

FIGURE 2-12
Creating an "Island Spread"

Select a spread in the Pages palette.

Turn off the Allow Selected Spread to Shuffle option from the Pages panel menu.

InDesign converts the spread to an island spread.

Brackets around the spread's label indicate that the spread is an island spread.

To add a page to an island spread, select a page icon...

...and drag it into or adjacent to the island spread.

InDesign adds the page to the island spread.

Shuffling Pages   Usually, when you drag pages around in the Pages panel, InDesign shuffles all the pages around to accommodate the change. That is, if you add a page in a facing pages document between pages 3 and 4, the left-hand page 4 gets shuffled over to become a right-hand page 5, which pushes page 5 over, and so on. However, you can cause all kinds of curious mayhem if you turn off the Allow Document Pages to Shuffle feature in the Pages panel menu. When this is off, InDesign won't shuffle the pages; rather it just moves and adds pages. For example, in the scenario above, the new page would be added to the spread of either pages 2 and 3, or the spread of 4 and 5 (creating a three-page spread).

Which spread gets the page is subtle: As you drag a page between two spreads in the Pages panel, you'll see a dark vertical line. If you move the cursor a little closer to the spread on the left, the dark line will jog to the left a pixel or two. Move the cursor to the right, and the line jogs to the right. That's the only indication as to which spread (the one to the left or to the right) the page will be added.

Perhaps you want the first page of your facing-pages publication to begin on a left-hand page? Turn off Allow Document Pages to Shuffle, then drag the first page to the left until you see a tiny black arrow pointing to the left. When you let go, the page moves over.

Here's one more time you might want to turn off the Allow Document Pages to Shuffle feature: If you have a facing pages document and you want to bleed an object into the inside of a spread (that is, the object looks like it's bleeding into the binding), you'll need to separate the left- and right-pages in the spread. Turn off Allow Document Pages to Shuffle, then drag one of the pages away from the spread until you see a dark vertical bar. When you let go, the pages will be separated. Of course, if you're going to bleed into the binding, you first need to make sure your printer and their imposition software can handle this correctly.

While dragging pages around in the Pages panel is fun, it's faster and more precise to choose Move Pages from the Pages submenu (under the Layout menu) or from the Pages panel menu. This displays the Move Pages dialog box, which you can use to move pages in the current document, or to other documents (see Figure 2-13).

FIGURE 2-13
Move Pages Dialog Box

Enter the range of pages you want to move...

...and specify the destination for the pages using these controls.

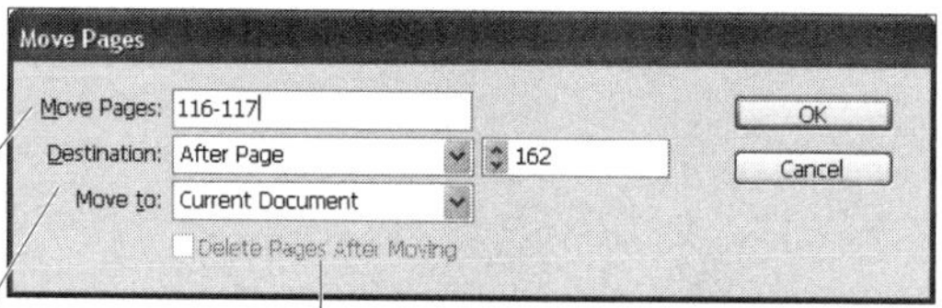

If you're moving the pages to another document, you can choose to delete the pages from the current document as you do so.

Creating pages of different sizes

InDesign now offers a feature that people have been requesting for years—the ability to use multiple page sizes in the same document.

Should you use different page sizes in a document? That all depends on what you're trying to do. To avoid potential printing complexity, you're sometimes better off keeping different page sizes in different documents and using the Books feature to synchronize styles, swatches, and other common design elements. But there are other situations in which having different page sizes in a document saves time and effort. Examples:

Book cover with a spine. You may not know the exact width of the spine until late in the process. Keeping the spine in the same document as the front and back covers allows you to alter the spine width up to the last minute while still sharing the design with the cover pages (see Figure 2-14).

FIGURE 2-14
Multiple Page Sizes
in Same Document

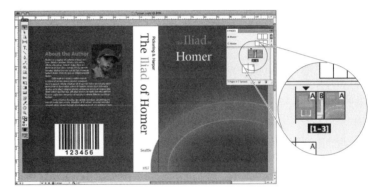

Company stationery. Use the same logo and address block for a letterhead, envelope, and a business card.

Gate fold for a magazine. Does your magazine require a little fold-out flap for the cover? Or a centerfold? Instead of using a separate document for extra wide pages, apply a different page size and use the new widgets in the Print dialog box to print them separately.

Use either of these methods to apply a different page size to pages:

▶ To create a different page size quickly, select the page in the Pages panel. Then choose a preset from the Edit Page Size menu at the bottom of the pages panel.

▶ To take a more advanced approach, use the Page tool to click a page in the layout window (or double-click the selected page in the Pages panel). Then use the options in the Control panel to determine the page dimensions (see Figure 2-15).

FIGURE 2-15
Multiple Page Sizes

Use the Page tool to select one or more pages, and then change the page settings in the Control panel.

As a rule, you should create a master page with a different size, and then apply the master to the document page. That way, you'll avoid a sticky situation in which a master is applied to a document page with different dimensions.

In some cases, you may want one master page to apply to different page sizes. For example, you may want a company logo to appear on a master page, and you want that same logo to appear on an envelope and a business card. In that case, you can use the Master Page Overlay to position the logo properly on the page (see Figure 2-16).

FIGURE 2-16
Master Page Overlay

The header from the master page is cut off on the layout page that has a smaller page size...

...so we turned on Master Page Overlay and dragged the overlay frame to the left .

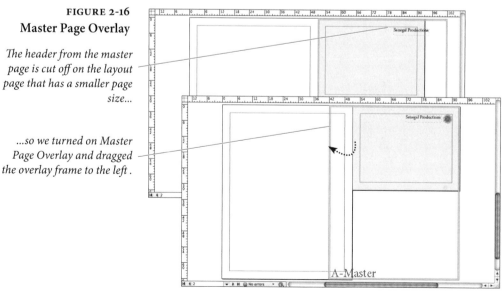

If you try to apply a master to a page that doesn't have its same page dimensions, you have the choice of keeping the custom page size or overriding it with the master's page size.

When you select a page using the Page tool, the Control panel displays options for creating a different page size. Adjust the Y value to determine where the page appears vertically in relation to the rest of the spread.

To create the new page size, specify Height and Width values, or select a preset from the menu. You can also change the orientation by clicking the Portrait or Landscape icon. The Control panel has three check boxes that need their own explanation.

Enable Layout Adjustment. Keeps objects aligned to margins when you change page size. See "Adjusting Layouts" later in this chapter.

Show Master Page Overlay. When the page has a different size than its master page, turning on Master Page Overlay will let you move the master page items.

Objects Move with Page. Select this option if you want the objects to move along with the page when you change the X and Y values or drag the page to move it within the spread. Option/Alt-drag the page using the Page tool to move the page with or without moving objects on the page—the opposite of this option's selection status.

When you send a job to the printer, make sure you let the printer know your document has multiple page sizes. If you need the print the document yourself, the Print dialog box includes a set of icons that lets you select and print all the matching page sizes. We'll talk more about this in Chapter 11, "Printing."

Rotating Spreads

When your design calls for rotated pages or graphics, you can either rotate the page, which we just covered above, or you can use Rotate Spreads feature to rotate only the view of the page. You can rotate any spread (or individual page, in a non-facing pages document) by selecting it in the Pages panel and choosing 90°CW, 90°CCW, or 180° from the Rotate Spread View submenu (in the Pages panel menu, or the Context menu, if you right-click or Control-click on a spread in the panel; see Figure 2-17). In case you're wondering, those "CW" abbreviations stand for "clockwise" and "counter-clockwise."

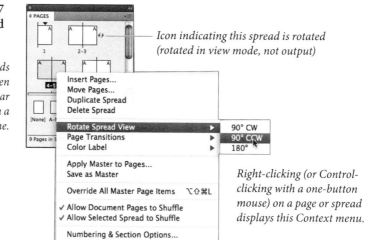

Icon indicating this spread is rotated
(rotated in view mode, not output)

Right-clicking (or Control-
clicking with a one-button
mouse) on a page or spread
displays this Context menu.

Rotating the spread only affects the view; this has no effect on printing or exporting your document. You can save the rotation with your document, but if you plan on handing the document off to someone else, you might consider removing the rotation, just so you don't freak them out—to do that, choose Clear Rotation from the Rotate Spread View submenu. On the other hand, it's a wonderful practical joke to rotate one spread in the middle of a document 180 degrees.

When a spread is rotated, InDesign places a special icon next to it in the Pages panel (unless your icons are set to "Small").

Defining Sections

Sections define ranges of pages in a document, and give you a way to use multiple page numbering styles in a single document. Using sections, you can combine front matter numbered using lowercase roman numerals (*i, ii, iii*) followed by regular pages numbered using Arabic numerals (1, 2, 3).

Sections can also add a page numbering prefix or define section marker text—the sort of thing you'd see in a magazine layout containing a special advertising section.

InDesign's sections features makes setting up these sorts of variations easy. You can have multiple sections in an InDesign document, and each section can have its own starting page number, page numbering system, page numbering prefix, and section marker text. Every InDesign file has one section, beginning on the first page.

To define a new section, follow these steps (see Figure 2-18).

FIGURE 2-18
Defining Section Options

Choose Numbering & Section Options from the Pages panel or Context menu. InDesign displays the New Section dialog box

The options in the Document Chapter Numbering area are related to the Book feature, and are discussed in Chapter 8, "Long Documents."

Turn on the Start Section option.

Select a page numbering style.

Enter the text you want to have appear when you insert a section marker character.

InDesign creates a new section.

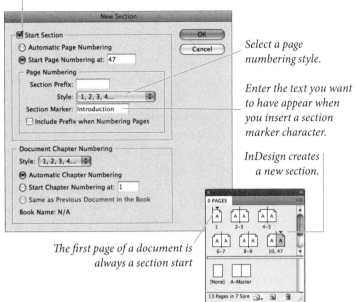

The first page of a document is always a section start

1. Select the page icon in the Pages panel that represents the first spread in the section.

2. Choose Numbering & Section Options from the panel's menu or from the Context menu. InDesign displays the Numbering & Section Options dialog box.

3. Make sure the Section Start option is on, and then use the controls in the New Section dialog box (see descriptions below) to specify the page numbering options of your new section, then click OK. InDesign adds a little black triangle above the page icon in the Pages panel to indicate a section start.

When you want to edit a section, you can repeat the process above or just double-click the black triangle icon in the Pages panel.

Page Numbering. If you want InDesign to continue the page numbering from the previous section, choose the Automatic Page Numbering option. Otherwise, turn on the Start Page Numbering At option and enter a starting page number in the associated field.

Section Prefix. You can enter a label for your section in the Section Prefix field (you can enter up to eight characters). This is primarily helpful when you have multiple sections with the same page numbering. For example, you might have page 1 in Section A and another page 2 in Section B. You could type "A-" and "B-" in the Section Prefix fields. You then have to type the prefix when using the Go To Page feature, or when printing or exporting specific pages.

If you want your prefix to also show up on your documents when you use the automatic page number feature, turn on the Include Prefix when Numbering Pages checkbox.

In some earlier versions of InDesign, the program automatically added the baffling "Sec1:" prefix, which we found incredibly annoying; we're pleased to report that it doesn't do that anymore. Note that this means that you can have both the section prefix text and the section marker text appear on the page (see "Section Marker," below).

Style. Choose the page numbering style you want (roman numerals, Arabic numerals, or upper- or lower-case letters).

Section Marker. If you want InDesign to enter text on some or all of the pages of the section (such as the chapter name) automatically, enter that text in this field. Most of the time, you use this field for the name of the section itself—but you can enter anything (up to around 100 characters). See "Adding Section Marker Text," below.

Numbering Pages

While you can always type the page number of a page into a text frame, there's an easier way to number a page. By entering a page number marker, you can have InDesign automatically number the page for you. If you move the page, or change the page numbering for the section containing the page, InDesign updates the page number.

To enter a page number marker, click the Type tool in a text frame and do one of the following (see Figure 2-19):

▶ Display the Context menu, then choose Auto Page Number from the Insert Special Character submenu.

▶ Choose Auto Page Number from the Insert Special Character submenu of the Type menu.

▶ Press Command-Shift-Option-N/Ctrl-Shift-Alt-N.

If you're on a master page, you'll see the master page prefix (if you're on master page "A," for example, you'll see an "A"); if you're on a document page, you'll see the page number itself.

FIGURE 2-19
Inserting Page Numbers

Click the Type tool in a text frame, and then press Command-Option-Shift-N/ Ctrl-Alt-Shift-N, or choose Current Page Number from the Markers submenu of the Insert Special Character sub-menu of the Context menu.

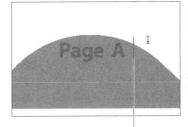

InDesign inserts a page number marker at the location of the cursor.

If the text frame is on a master spread, you'll see a letter corresponding to the prefix of the master spread. On document pages, InDesign displays the actual page number.

Adding Section Marker Text

To have InDesign automatically "type" the section marker text that you specified in the Section Marker field of the Numbering & Section Options dialog box, click the Type tool in a text frame and choose Section Name from the Insert Special Characters submenu (under the Type menu or the context menu; see Figure 2-20). If you're on a master page, however, you'll just see the word "Section." Later, when you change the contents of the Section Marker field, InDesign changes the text on the document pages.

One common use for section markers is running heads at the top or bottom of the page. For example, you could create a single InDesign document with 10 sections—one for each chapter. Instead of creating 10 master pages—each one identical except for the running head that indicates the section name—you could insert a Section marker on a single master page and then simply update the Section field (in the Section & Numbering dialog box) for each section.

To be honest, however, our use of the section marker character has diminished since InDesign added text variables, which can "pull" the text from a heading or a chapter opener and put it in the header even more easily. We cover text variables in Chapter 3, "Text."

Most of the time, you'll probably want to enter automatic page number and section marker characters on your master pages—but you can also enter them directly on document pages.

Working with Master Pages

Master pages (more accurately called master spreads) are the background on which you lay out your publication's pages. When you assign a master spread to a document page, InDesign applies the

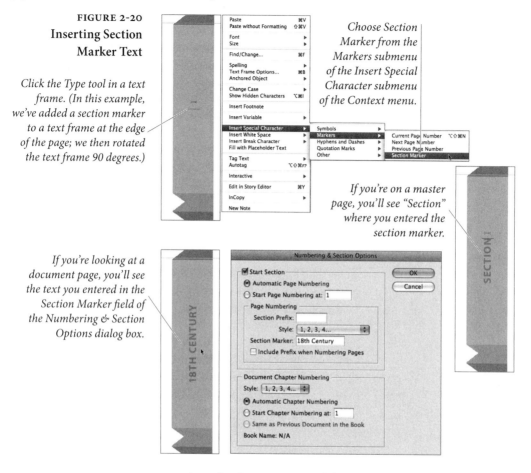

FIGURE 2-20

Inserting Section Marker Text

Click the Type tool in a text frame. (In this example, we've added a section marker to a text frame at the edge of the page; we then rotated the text frame 90 degrees.)

Choose Section Marker from the Markers submenu of the Insert Special Character submenu of the Context menu.

If you're on a master page, you'll see "Section" where you entered the section marker.

If you're looking at a document page, you'll see the text you entered in the Section Marker field of the Numbering & Section Options dialog box.

margin and column settings of the master spread to the page. Any page items on the master spread also appear on the document page, on the layers they occupy on the master spread. Master page items cannot be edited on document pages unless you choose to override the items from the master pages (see "Overriding Master Items").

InDesign Is Not QuarkXPress

If you're a long-time QuarkXPress user, you're probably familiar with the technique of putting items on master pages to use as a "template" for document pages. However, in QuarkXPress, each master page object is immediately accessible ("clickable") on the document page. Therefore, some people used master pages in XPress as a kind of alternative to the Clipboard. That doesn't work very well in InDesign, because InDesign protects master page items so you don't accidentally change them. We cover that in more detail in "Overriding Master Items," later in this chapter.

However, in general, *you should put items on master pages that you do not expect to override on document pages.* In fact, because

InDesign can flow text into the area defined by the margins (a feature QuarkXPress lacks), even master text frames are rarely needed.

Creating Master Spreads

To create a new master spread, use any of the following techniques:

► Hold down Command/Ctrl as you click the Add Page button at the bottom of the Pages panel. InDesign adds a new master spread to the publication. You can display the New Master dialog box by holding down Command-Option/Ctrl-Alt while you click.

► Choose New Master from the Pages panel menu. InDesign displays the New Master dialog box (see Figure 2-21).

► Drag a spread from the document pages section of the Pages panel into the master pages section (see Figure 2-22). If you've already laid out a document page using the layout you'd like to use as a master page, this is the easiest way to transfer that layout to a master page. When you do this, InDesign creates a new master page with the margins, column guides, ruler guides, and content of that document page. The new master spread is based on the master spread applied to the example document pages (see "Basing One Master Spread on Another").

► To duplicate a master page you've already created, hold down Option/Alt as you drag and drop the existing master spread icon in the master pages area of the Pages panel. InDesign creates a copy of the master spread. Alternately, choose Duplicate Master Spread from the Pages panel menu.

Importing Master Spreads

You can also import master spreads from another InDesign document. To do this, choose Load Master Pages from the Pages panel menu. InDesign displays the Open A File dialog box. Locate and select an InDesign document, and click the OK button.

If the document includes master pages with the same name as master pages in the current document, InDesign displays the Load Master Pages Alert dialog box. You can replace the existing master spreads, or rename the incoming master spreads.

If you re-import master spreads from the same document at a later date, InDesign will update the master spreads. This gives you a way to "synchronize" master spreads between documents without having to use the Book feature. (However, if you are using a book panel, using the Synchronize feature may be even easier. We discuss that in Chapter 8, "Long Documents.")

FIGURE 2-21

Choose New Master to Create a Master Spread

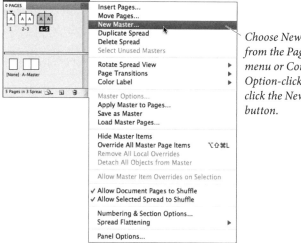

Choose New Master from the Pages panel menu or Command-Option-click/Ctrl-Alt-click the New Page button.

Enter a prefix for the master spread.

Enter a name for the master spread, if you want.

Choose an existing master spread from this pop-up menu to base the new master spread on that spread.

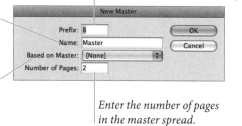

Enter the number of pages in the master spread.

Click the OK button, and InDesign creates a new master spread.

FIGURE 2-22

Basing a Master Spread on a Document Spread

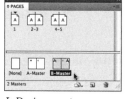

Drag the page spread into the master spreads area of the Pages palette.

InDesign creates a new master spread with the same margins, guides, and page objects.

Copying Master Spreads Between Documents. To copy selected master spreads from one document to another, you can use drag and drop. Select the source document and drag the master page icon from the Pages panel into the other document. Drop the icon, and the master page is copied over.

Alternatively, you can select the master pages and choose Move Pages from the Pages panel menu. This displays the Move Pages dialog box, where you can specify the destination for the pages.

When you copy document pages between documents, InDesign also copies any master pages that were applied to those document pages. If the two documents have master spreads with the same name, the master spread isn't copied.

Basing One Master Spread on Another

Imagine that you produce a catalog, and that, over the course of a year, you produce seasonal issues of the catalog. The basic design elements—the section, margins, columns, and page numbering—remain the same throughout the year, but the colors used, and the page footers change with each issue. Do you have to create a new set of master spreads for each issue? Not when you have InDesign's ability to base a master spread on another master spread, you don't.

When you base a new master spread on an existing master spread, the new master *inherits* the properties of the existing master spread. We refer to the relationship between the original style and the new style as a "parent/child" relationship. Once you've applied a master spread to another master spread, you can add to it or override page elements on the pages of the "child" spread, just as you can from any document page (see "Overriding Master Items," below).

Here's how inheritance works: When you change any of the attributes defined by the "parent" spread, those changes appear in the "child" spread. When the attributes between a "child" spread and its "parent" spread differ, those attributes are controlled by the "child" spread. Take a look at the (somewhat overwrought) example in Figure 2-23 on the next page, and you'll see what we mean.

You can base one master page on another by picking a master page from the Based on Master pop-up menu in the New Master dialog box. Or drag the parent master on top of the child master in the Pages panel.

Applying Master Pages and Master Spreads

To apply a master page or master spread to a document page (or even to another master page), do one of the following.

► Drag and drop the master page spread icon or master page icon on a page icon. Usually, this just affects a single page, but if you move the cursor carefully around the icons until a thick black line appears around the whole spread, the master page is applied to all pages in the spread. This is a slow and tedious process which you'll perform once and then never do again.

FIGURE 2-23

Basing One Master Spread on Another

TimeTravelTickets offers time travel to great performances in history. Their catalog is divided into sections based on the century of the performance, each section is divided into the categories "Theatre," "Music," and "Dance." We've set up master spreads to reflect the organization of the catalog.

Master spread "A" applied to a document page.

Master spread "B" uses a different color scheme and replaces the word "Theatre" with "Music," but is otherwise identical to master spread "A."

Here's an example of master spread "B" in another section (note the differing section text).

Ready to update the catalog? Enter a new season and year in the page footer of the "parent" master spread...

...and that change will be reflected in all of the "child" master spreads.

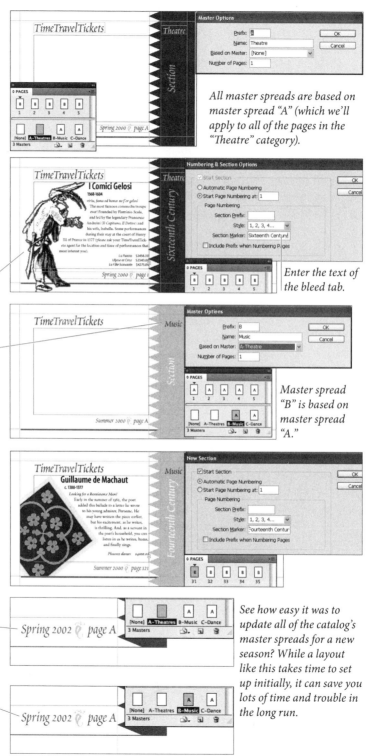

All master spreads are based on master spread "A" (which we'll apply to all of the pages in the "Theatre" category).

Enter the text of the bleed tab.

Master spread "B" is based on master spread "A."

See how easy it was to update all of the catalog's master spreads for a new season? While a layout like this takes time to set up initially, it can save you lots of time and trouble in the long run.

▶ Select a master page in the Pages panel and then choose Apply Master to Pages from the Pages panel menu (see Figure 2-24). Enter the page, or pages, to which you want to apply the master spread. To enter non-contiguous pages, enter commas between the page numbers ("1, 3, 10, 12, 22"), or enter page ranges ("55-73"), or mix ranges and individual pages ("1, 3, 7-13, 44").

▶ Select a page or pages and then Option/Alt-click on the master page. This is the fastest method, period.

FIGURE 2-24
Applying Master Spreads Using the Apply Master to Pages Option

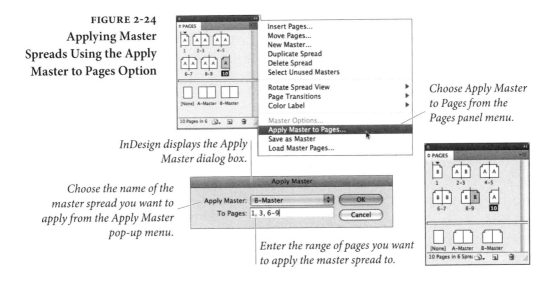

Choose Apply Master to Pages from the Pages panel menu.

InDesign displays the Apply Master dialog box.

Choose the name of the master spread you want to apply from the Apply Master pop-up menu.

Enter the range of pages you want to apply the master spread to.

Editing Master Spreads

To edit the items on a master spread, display the master spread. There are several ways to do this, but the two easiest methods are either to double-click the master spread's label in the Pages panel or press Command/Ctrl-J (to jump to the Page field), type the prefix (such as typing "B" for the "B-Master") and press Enter.

Once you're viewing a master page, you can edit the master spread's margins guides, ruler guides, and page items just as you would any items and attributes of a document spread.

Master Options. You can also select a master page and then choose Master Options from the Pages panel menu to change the master page's prefix, name, or based-on status. Shortcut: click on the master page in the Pages panel, not the icon (to select it) and then Option/Alt-click on the master page's label to open the same dialog box.

Deleting Master Spreads

To remove a master spread from a document, select the master spread in the Pages panel, then choose Delete Master Spread from the Pages panel menu. You can also drag the master page to the Delete button at the bottom of the Pages panel.

Hiding Master Items

Are the items from your master page too distracting? No problem: Select Hide Master Items from the View menu. Later, when you want to see the completed page, select Show Master Items.

Overriding Master Items

Want to modify or delete a master page item from a document page, but leave all of the other master pages items alone? Wait! Don't cover the master page item with a white box! There's a better way. InDesign calls it "overriding" a master page item.

To override a master page item, hold down Command-Shift/Ctrl-Shift and click the master page item (or, if you're using the Type tool, click inside the master page item). InDesign "unlinks" the master page item, so you can select it, format it, or delete it as you would any other page item (see Figure 2-25). You can also override everything on any page(s) selected in the Pages panel by choosing Override All Master Page Items from the panel menu.

FIGURE 2-25
Overriding a
Master Item

In this example, we want to create a new master spread based on the "A-Theatre" master spread. In the new spread, we want to change the word "Theatre" to "Music."

If you click on the frame you want to change, nothing happens. This is probably a good thing, as it prevents you from accidentally changing master items.

So, hold down Command-Shift/Ctrl-Shift…

…and click the object. InDesign copies the object to the current page and marks it as a "local override."

Now you can edit or format the text.

Notice that we put "unlink" in quotation marks above, indicating that the objects aren't really unlinked from their master page. You can return an overridden master page item to its original state by selecting the object and choosing Remove Selected Local Overrides from the Pages panel menu (see Figure 2-26). If you've made some

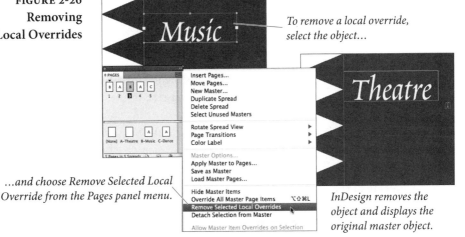

FIGURE 2-26
Removing
Local Overrides

To remove a local override, select the object...

...and choose Remove Selected Local Override from the Pages panel menu.

InDesign removes the object and displays the original master object.

terrible mistake, you can return one or more pages' worth of over-ridden objects by selecting the pages in the Pages panel and choosing Remove All Local Overrides from the panel menu.

Maintaining Some Links. Overridden items are not entirely free of the influence of their master page counterpart. If you override a frame and then move it on the document page, the position of that item is no longer linked to the position of the master page item. However, if you change the fill of the master page item, those changes *do* flow through to the overridden master page.

If you want to totally unlink an object from the master page, so that nothing you do on the master will affect the item on the document page, first override the item, and then—while it's still selected—choose Detach Selection from Master from the Pages panel menu or deselect everything and select Detach All Objects from Master.

Reapplying Master Pages. When you reapply the master page to a document page containing overridden or detached items, the original master page items reappear on the document page, but the over-ridden page items are not deleted. This isn't usually a good thing—it's easy to end up with stacks of duplicated objects.

Adjusting Layouts

What happens when you change the margins of a page, or apply a different master page? Should the items on the affected pages move or resize to match the new page geometry? Or should they stay as they are? You decide. Choose Layout Adjustment from the Layout menu to see the Layout Adjustment dialog box (see Figure 2-27). Here's a quick walk-through of the controls here.

Enable Layout Adjustment. Turn this option on, and InDesign adjusts the position and size of the objects on the affected pages according to the settings in this dialog box. With this option off, InDesign does not change object positions or sizes when you apply master pages, change page size, or otherwise change page geometry.

FIGURE 2-27
Adjusting Layouts

When the Enable Layout Adjustment option is off, InDesign does not change the position or size of page objects when you change the geometry of the page...

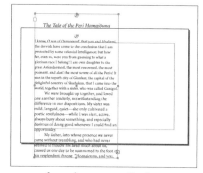

...even for a change as radical as changing page orientation.

Turn on the Enable Layout Adjustment option, and InDesign changes the position and size of page objects in response to changes in page size, orientation, column setup, or margins.

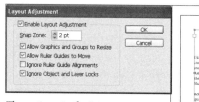

The options in the Layout Adjustment dialog box give you a way to "fine tune" the automated adjustment process.

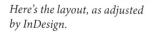

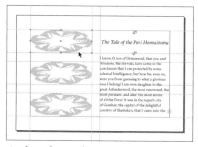

Here's the layout, as adjusted by InDesign.

Ruler guide positions are very important to the layout adjustment feature. In this example, changing the page size changes the shape and position of the graphics—all because of their relationship to the ruler guides that surround them.

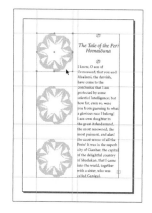

As the ruler guides move, InDesign resizes the graphics you've "stuck" to the ruler guides.

Layout Adjustment can change your file in ways you may not expect. For instance, let's say you have a single-column document with a master text frame. If you change the number of columns to three while Layout Adjustment is enabled, InDesign replaces the single text frame with three threaded frames.

Snap Zone. How close to a guide does an object have to be to be affected by layout adjustment? That's what you're telling InDesign by the value you enter in this field. Objects within the specified distance will move or resize; objects outside that range won't.

Allow Graphics and Groups to Resize. When this option is turned off, InDesign will not resize graphic frames or groups of objects while adjusting layouts. When it's on, InDesign resizes graphic frames and groups when they extend to the edges of the column or margin. Note that InDesign never scales text in a text frame; it may resize the frame itself, but not the text inside it. It will, however, scale graphics. This is quite powerful, but also quite dangerous. If you have a picture that spans from the left margin to the right margin in a single-column document, and you use Margins and Columns to split the page into two or more columns, this option will scale that picture down into the left-most column—probably not what you were hoping for.

Allow Ruler Guides to Move. Should ruler guides move when you change the layout of the page or spread? If you'd like the ruler guides to move, turn this option on; if not, turn it off. How far guides move when you make a layout change depends on a host of issues. (We've tried to figure it out and we're baffled. The best we can say is that InDesign tries to maintain the general look and feel of the page, so if you increase the left margin, the guides all move a bit to the right.)

Ignore Ruler Guide Alignments. When this option is off, InDesign moves and resizes objects to match the positions of ruler guides in the new page layout. When it's on, InDesign does not consider the locations of ruler guides when resizing or moving objects—only the location of margin guides and page edges. The effect of this option also depends on the state of the Allow Ruler Guides to Move option.

Ignore Object and Layer Locks. What should InDesign do while adjusting your layout when it encounters a locked object, or an object on a locked layer? When you turn this option on, InDesign will treat the objects as if they were unlocked. To leave locked objects alone, turn this option off.

It's All in the Guides. The key thing to remember is that InDesign bases all layout adjustment decisions on the positions of margin guides, ruler guides, column guides, and page edges. InDesign cannot know that you want an object to change its size or position unless you somehow associate the object with a guide or a page edge.

Selecting and Deselecting

Before you can act on an object, you have to select it (see Figure 2-28). Sounds simple, but in InDesign you can quickly get in a messy situation if you don't pay attention to what, exactly, is selected on your page and how you selected it. That's why we recommend that even experienced users read through this carefully.

The Selection Tool. The Selection tool is the swiss-army knife of the Tools panel. Use the Selection tool to select, rotate, resize, reposition, crop, and scale frames and frame content. The Content Grabber—the donut that appears when you mouse over a graphic—lets you quickly reposition content within a frame, just by clicking and dragging (see Figure 2-29).

You select objects or groups of objects with the Selection tool by clicking on them, dragging the selection rectangle (marquee) over the objects, or by Shift-selecting (select one object, hold down Shift, and select another object). When you mouse over an object, InDesign highlights the object that will be selected when you click. The selected object's selection handles and the object's bounding box—the smallest rectangular area capable of enclosing the selection. The selection handles on the bounding box also correspond to the points on the proxy in the Transform panel.

You can also select everything on the current spread by choosing Select All from the Edit menu (or pressing Command/Ctrl-A) while using either selection tool.

The Direct Selection Tool. As we noted in "Using the Tools Panel" in Chapter 1, "Workspace," when you click an object using the Direct Selection tool, InDesign displays the points on the object's path—whether it's a line or a frame. You can also use the Direct Selection tool to select objects nested inside other objects (see "Selecting Inside Objects," below). The most common example is selecting a picture inside a graphic frame—the frame and the picture are two separate objects in InDesign, and you can use the Direct Selection tool to select the frame (by clicking on its edge) or the picture (by clicking

FIGURE 2-28
Selecting Objects

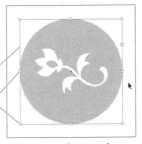 

Bounding box

Selection handles

Proxy

The proxy in the Transform panel and Control panel represents the selection handles of the selected object.

When you select an object using the Selection tool, InDesign displays the objects's selection handles and bounding box.

When you select an object using the Direct Selection tool, InDesign displays the points on the path(s) of the object.

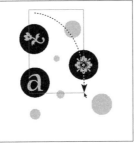 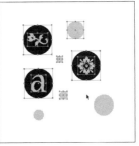

When you drag a selection rectangle around an object or objects...

...InDesign selects all of the objects that the selection rectangle touches.

FIGURE 2-29
Content Grabber

The Content Grabber appears when you mouse over a frame with content using the Selection tool.

Dragging the Content Grabber moves the content within the frame—without switching to the Direct Selection tool.

anywhere inside the frame). You can also select frame contents by clicking the Content Grabber using the Selection tool.

You can drag a selection marquee using the Direct Selection tool, too, just as you can with the Selection tool—InDesign selects the points on the objects within the selection, even if they're in more than one object. To select all the points on a line or frame, hold down Option/Alt while you click the path with the Direct Selection tool.

Deselecting. To deselect all selected objects, click an uninhabited area of the page or pasteboard, or, better yet, press Command-Shift-A/Ctrl-Shift-A. We've developed this keyboard shortcut into something of a nervous tic; there are so many times you need to make sure everything is deselected. For example, when you create a new color, InDesign applies that color to whatever you have selected. If you don't want this, you'd better deselect everything first!

Selecting Through Objects

Sometimes, you have to select an object that's behind another object. You might, for example, need to select and edit a background graphic behind a text frame. Do you need to drag the text frame out of the way? Or hide the layer containing the text frame? There's a better way: Click the Selection tool on the object on top of the stack, then press Command/Ctrl and click again. InDesign selects the next object in the stack. Each successive click selects the next object down in the stack (see Figure 2-30). If you click too far, you can move back up the stack by Command-Option/Ctrl-Alt-clicking.

When overlapping objects are exactly or nearly the same in size, it can be difficult to see which object in a stack is selected. Don't start dragging objects out of the way—look for clues. The color of the selection handles, the state of the Fill and Stroke buttons in the Toolbox, and the Stroke panel all provide information that can help you determine which object is selected.

FIGURE 2-30
Selecting Through Objects

Want to select an object that's behind other objects? You don't need to drag objects out of the way. Instead, hold down Command/Ctrl and click the Selection tool above the object you want to select.

Text frame selected   *Background graphic selected*

The first click selects the object on top of the stack of objects...   *...but each subsequent click selects the next object in the stack.*

Keyboard Selections

InDesign also has menu items and keyboard shortcuts for selecting objects on your page. The menu items live in the Select submenu, under the Object menu, but we only use them if we forget the keyboard shortcuts (below). Note that these features differ from the click-through method; Command/Ctrl-click selects through an object to one directly beneath it. The Select features select from among all the objects on a spread. For example, if you have four small frames, one in each corner of a page (whether they're overlapping or not), you can select among them with these shortcuts.

▶ To select the topmost object beneath the current selection, based on the stacking order on the page (see "Stacking Objects," later in this chapter) press Command-Option-Shift-] / Ctrl-Alt-Shift-] or choose First Object Above from the Select submenu.

▶ To select the object *behind* the currently selected object in a stack of objects, press Command-Option-[/ Ctrl-Alt-[or choose Next Object Below from the Select submenu. Pressing the keyboard shortcut again once you reach the bottom of the stack will select the topmost object.

▶ To select the object above the currently selected object in a stack of objects, press Command-Option-] / Ctrl-Alt-] or choose Next Object Above from the Select submenu.

▶ To select the bottommost object below the selected object, press Command-Option-Shift-[/ Ctrl-Alt-Shift-[or choose Last Object Below from the Select submenu.

Selecting Inside Objects

Sometimes, you need to select an object that you've pasted inside another object, or to select an object inside a group. The Direct Selection tool, as you might expect, is the tool you'll usually use to do this, and the process is called "subselection." (When Ole selects an object that's inside another object, he actually says the object is "subselected." David, who felt subselected through much of his childhood, prefers the term "select-challenged.")

It's important to note that InDesign treats groups and page items that happen to contain other items in the same way. You don't have to ungroup a group, or remove objects from their containing object to select and edit them—you can select them, and then work with them just as you would any other object. To select an object inside another object, you can use any of the following approaches.

▶ Using the Selection tool, click an object to select the group. Double-click an object to select the object (see Figure 2-31). To direct-select the object, press A. Note that in previous versions, double-clicking an object switches to the Direct Selection tool.

▶ Select the Direct Selection tool, and click the element that you want to edit. InDesign temporarily highlights the object as you mouse over it, making it easy to see what will be selected when you click.

FIGURE 2-31
**Subselecting Objects
Inside Groups**

*Press the Escape key to
"back out" of subse-
lected objects, one object
at a time.*

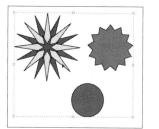

*Click the group with the Selection
tool to select the group.*

*Double-click one of the objects in the
group to select the object.*

▶ Select the group or containing object with the Selection tool,
then choose Content from the Select submenu of the Context
menu. This selects an object. If necessary, choose Next Object or
Previous Object from the Select submenu of the Context menu
until the object you want is selected.

▶ Select the group or containing object with the Selection tool,
then click the Select Content button in the Control panel. If necessary, click the Select Next Object and Select Previous Object
buttons until the object you want is selected (see Figure 2-32).

Guides

InDesign can display four types of guides: margin guides, column
guides, ruler guides, and Smart Guides. Guides are nonprinting
guidelines you can use for positioning objects on the pages and
pasteboard of an InDesign publication. Margin guides appear inside
the page margins for a particular page. Column guides are actually
pairs of guides that move as a unit. The space between the two guides
making up the column guide is the gutter, or column spacing. This
built-in spacing makes these guides good for—you guessed it—setting up columns. A ruler guide is a horizontal or vertical guideline
you can use as an aid to aligning or positioning page items. A Smart
Guide is a guide that temporarily appears on page to help you position an object while you place or move it.

You use guides to mark a position on the page or pasteboard. The
most important thing about guides is not just that they give you a
visual reference for aligning objects to a specific location, but that
they can exert a "pull" on objects you're moving or creating. To turn
on that "pull," choose Snap to Guides from the from the Grids &
Guides submenu of the View menu. When this option is on (it's on by

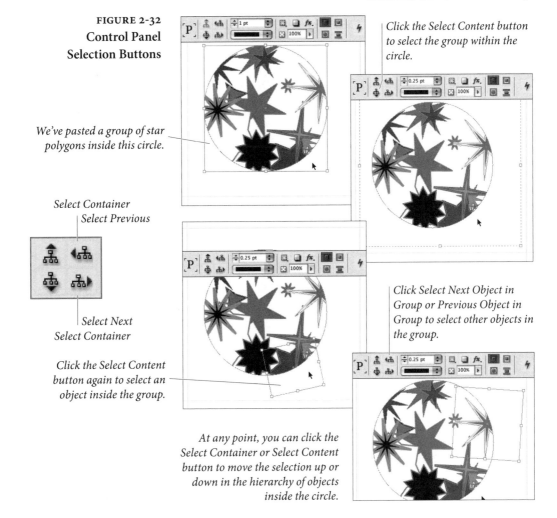

FIGURE 2-32
Control Panel
Selection Buttons

Click the Select Content button to select the group within the circle.

We've pasted a group of star polygons inside this circle.

Select Container
Select Previous

Select Next
Select Container

Click Select Next Object in Group or Previous Object in Group to select other objects in the group.

Click the Select Content button again to select an object inside the group.

At any point, you can click the Select Container or Select Content button to move the selection up or down in the hierarchy of objects inside the circle.

default), and you drag an object within a certain distance of a guide, InDesign snaps the object to the guide.

This is one of our favorite psychocybernetic illusions—as an object snaps to a guide, your nervous system tells you that your hand can feel the "snap" as you drag the mouse. Turning on Snap to Guides can't physically affect the movement of your mouse, of course, but the illusion is very useful.

When you want to drag an object freely, without having it snap to any guides it encounters on its path across the publication window, turn Snap to Guides off. Do not try to align an object to a guide while Snap to Guides is turned off, however—there aren't enough pixels available on your screen to allow you to do a good job of this at any but the highest magnifications (see Figure 2-33).

FIGURE 2-33
Don't Trust Your Screen

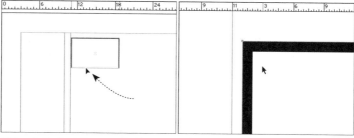

When InDesign's Snap to Guides feature is turned off, it's easy to think that you've gotten an object into perfect alignment with a guide...

...but zooming in will often show you that you've missed the guide. Turning on Snap to Guides can help.

Objects do not snap to guides when guides are hidden. This includes guides that are on a hidden layer. However, they do snap to guides that are invisible due to being in Preview mode.

Also, on the Mac OS, you can disable Snap to Guides temporarily by holding down the Control key while you're dragging—unless Smart Guides is enabled (see "Smart Guides," later in this chapter).

Hiding and Displaying Guides

Tired of looking at all of the guides? To hide all guides, choose Hide Guides from the Grids & Guides submenu of the View menu (press Command-;/Ctrl-;). To display the guides again, choose Show Guides (or press the keyboard shortcut again).

You can also make guides disappear by changing the view threshold (see Figure 2-34). For the document grid, baseline grid, margin guides, and column guides, you set the view threshold using the Grids panel of the Preferences dialog box (see Chapter 1, "Workspace"). For individual ruler guides, use the View Threshold field in the Ruler Guides dialog box (select a guide and choose Ruler Guides from the Layout menu or the Context menu).

FIGURE 2-34
Guide View Threshold

The View Threshold of these ruler guides is set to 100%...

...the View Threshold of these ruler guides is set to the default: 5%.

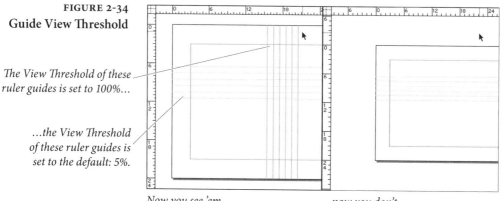

Now you see 'em...

...now you don't.

Adjusting Column Guides

While column guides are very similar to ruler guides, they have an important distinction: they can affect text flow. When you click the text place icon in a column created by column guides, InDesign flows the text into the column. By contrast, ruler guides have no effect on text flow. For more on flowing text, see Chapter 3, "Text."

The method you use to adjust the position of column guides depends on what you're trying to do. If you're trying to divide the area inside the page margins into equal columns, select the page and enter a new value in the Number field in the Columns section of the Margins and Columns dialog box (from the Layout menu).

If, on the other hand, you're trying to get columns of unequal width, you can start by adding evenly-spaced column guides, and then adjust each one by dragging them to the left or right on the page (see Figure 2-35). You might have to unlock the column guides first; see "Locking and Unlocking Column Guides," below.

You can't adjust the distance between the column guides (the "gutter") by dragging—instead, you'll have to go to the Margins and Columns dialog box. To change the gutter width, enter a new value in the Gutter field (see Figure 2-36). When you open the Margins

FIGURE 2-35
Creating Columns of Unequal Width

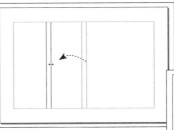

When the column guide reaches the position you want, stop dragging and release the mouse button.

When you create columns of unequal width, InDesign displays "Custom" in the Number field of the Margins and Columns dialog box.

Unlock the column guides (if necessary), then position the Selection tool over a column guide and drag.

FIGURE 2-36
Adjusting Gutter Width

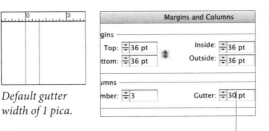

Default gutter width of 1 pica.

Note that the gutter is resized evenly around its center point.

Choose Margins and Columns from the Layout menu, then enter a new value in the Gutter field.

and Columns dialog box after you've set up a custom column guide arrangement, InDesign displays "Custom" in the Number field. Do not enter a number in this field, or InDesign will move your column guides so that they again evenly divide the space between the margins. If you change the gutter width without touching the Number field, InDesign leaves your column guides in their original positions, but changes the space inside each guide.

You should also bear in mind that text frames can, by themselves contain multiple columns of equal width, independent of the Margins and Columns setting. For more on this topic, see Chapter 3, "Text." Sometimes it's easier to work with a single multi-column text frame than with multiple single-column text frames.

Locking and Unlocking Column Guides

You can lock and unlock column guides, just as you can ruler guides. To lock the column guides, choose Lock Column Guides from the Grids & Guides submenu of the View menu; to unlock the guides, choose Unlock Column Guides.

Creating a New Ruler Guide

To create a new ruler guide, position the cursor over one of the rulers (for a horizontal ruler guide, move the cursor to the vertical ruler; for a vertical ruler guide, use the horizontal ruler), then click-and-drag. As you drag, InDesign creates a new ruler guide at the location of the cursor. When you've positioned the ruler guide where you want it, stop dragging (see Figure 2-37). Hold down the Shift key while dragging a guide to make it snap to the nearest increment in the ruler.

Ruler guides can spread across a single page or the entire pasteboard. Release the mouse button while the cursor is over the page, you get a page guide; if the cursor is over the pasteboard, you get a pasteboard guide. You can hold down Command/Ctrl as you drag the guide to force the guide to cross the whole pasteboard. To adjust this type of ruler guide, drag the guide on the pasteboard or with the Command/Ctrl key held down—if you drag it on a page or without the modifier key, InDesign will limit the guide to that page.

You can also double-click a ruler to create a new ruler guide—InDesign creates a guide at the point at which you clicked. While this sounds appealing, we actually find it quite difficult to double-click exactly where we want the guide to be; it's often more precise to drag.

Using Create Guides

Want to add a regular grid of ruler guides to your page? Try the Create Guides option on the Layout menu (see Figure 2-38). The options in the Create Guides dialog box are pretty straightforward—enter the number of rows and columns you want, and enter the distance you want between the rows and columns. You can also choose

FIGURE 2-37
Creating a Ruler Guide

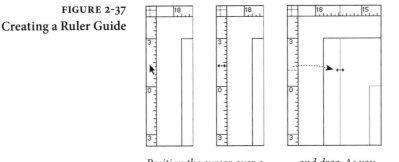

Position the cursor over a ruler, then hold down the mouse button...

...and drag. As you drag, a ruler guide follows the cursor.

When the ruler guide reaches the position you want, stop dragging.

To make a ruler guide snap to the tick marks on the ruler, hold down Shift as you drag the ruler guide.

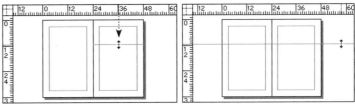

Drag a ruler guide on a page to limit the guide to that page...

...or drag the cursor outside the spread (or hold down Command/ Ctrl) to create a guide that crosses pages in the spread.

FIGURE 2-38
Using Create Guides

Choose Create Guides from the Layout menu. InDesign displays the Create Guides dialog box.

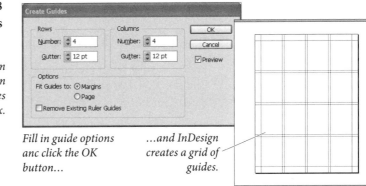

Fill in guide options anc click the OK button...

...and InDesign creates a grid of guides.

to create the guides within the page margins, which is a nice touch. In addition, you can choose to remove all existing ruler guides from the page as you create the new guides.

Snapping Guides to Objects

You can snap a guide to any control handle of an object. To do this, select the object with the Selection or Direct Selection tool, and then drag a guide out and drag the cursor on top of any side or corner handle—the guide will snap to the handle.

Adding Ruler Guides Around an Object

Another way to position ruler guides around a selected object is to use the AddGuides script—one of the sample scripts that come with InDesign. Run the script by double-clicking the script name in the Scripts panel. The script displays a dialog box you can use to set the positions of the ruler guides. Click the OK button, and InDesign adds guides around the selected object or objects. This script is especially useful when you're setting up a publication for use with InDesign's layout adjustment features.

Selecting Ruler Guides

To select a ruler guide, click on the guide using one of the selection tools, or drag a selection rectangle over the guide. This differs from PageMaker and QuarkXPress, where you cannot select a ruler guide as you would any other object. You can select multiple ruler guides at once by dragging a selection rectangle (a *marquee*) over them or Shift-clicking on each guide. If the selection marquee touches an object, InDesign selects the object—you cannot select both ruler guides and objects in the same selection. When a ruler guide is selected, it displays in the layer color of the layer it's on. You can select a locked ruler guide only if the Prevent Selection of Locked Objects is turned off.

You can also select all the guides on a spread with a keyboard shortcut: Command-Option-G/Ctrl-Alt-G.

Editing Ruler Guides

To change the location of a ruler guide, do one of the following.

▶ Drag the guide (using the Selection or Direct Selection tool).

▶ Select the ruler guide and then enter a new position in the X field (for a vertical guide) or in the Y field (for a horizontal guide) of the Transform panel or Control panel.

▶ Select the guide and press an arrow key to "nudge" the guide one direction or another.

You can also select more than one ruler guide at a time, and use the techniques above to move them, as a unit, to a new location (see Figure 2-39).

Moving a Ruler Guide to a Specific Layer

You can assign a ruler guide to a layer as you would any other selected object—drag the Proxy that appears in the Layers panel up or down, then drop it on the layer to which you want to send the guide (see Figure 2-40). The guide will appear on top of other objects. To move the guides behind other objects on the layer, turn on the Guides in Back option in the Guides & Pasteboard panel of the Preferences dialog box.

FIGURE 2-39

Moving Multiple Guides

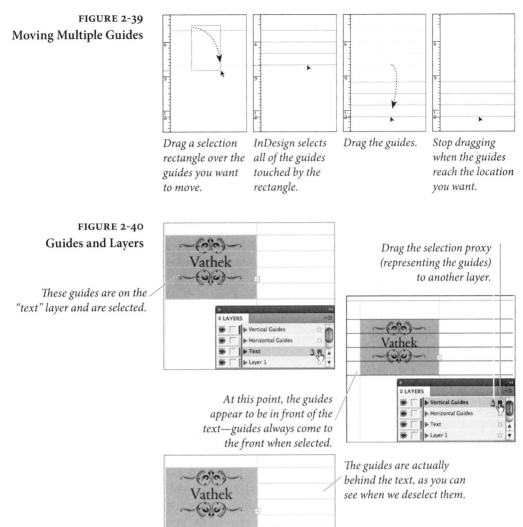

Drag a selection rectangle over the guides you want to move.

InDesign selects all of the guides touched by the rectangle.

Drag the guides.

Stop dragging when the guides reach the location you want.

FIGURE 2-40

Guides and Layers

These guides are on the "text" layer and are selected.

Drag the selection proxy (representing the guides) to another layer.

At this point, the guides appear to be in front of the text—guides always come to the front when selected.

The guides are actually behind the text, as you can see when we deselect them.

Setting Guide Options   When you create a ruler guide, InDesign applies the default guide color (specified in the Guides & Pasteboard panel of the Preferences dialog box) and a default view threshold (usually 5%) to the guide, but you can change these options if you want (see Figure 2-41).

1. Select the ruler guide (or guides).

2. Choose Ruler Guides from the Layout menu or the context menu to display the Ruler Guides dialog box.

3. Choose one of InDesign's preset colors from the Color pop-up menu, or (if you're really finicky) select Custom to create a custom guide color.

FIGURE 2-41

Setting Guide Options

Select a guide, then choose Ruler Guides from the context menu or the Layout menu.

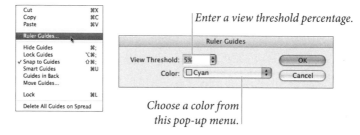

Enter a view threshold percentage.

Choose a color from this pop-up menu.

4. You can also change the view threshold of the selected ruler guide by entering a new value in the View Threshold field. The percentage you enter is the percentage magnification at and above which you want the ruler guide to appear. Enter 5% to make the guide visible at all magnifications. If you change this to 100%, the guide will be visible at 100-percent view or higher (closer), but will be invisible at anything less than 100-percent view.

5. Click the OK button to close the Ruler Guides dialog box. InDesign displays the guide (or guides) in the color you chose.

Why would you want to assign different colors to guides? Guides are such useful tools that we find we use *lots* of them. Color coding guides for different tasks makes it easier for us to see what's going on. One set of guides, for example, might be used for aligning captions in one illustration; another set might be used in a different illustration. Applying colors, changing view thresholds, and assigning guides to layers helps control the way that InDesign draws the guides in the publication window.

Note that guides always take on the layer selection color of their layer when they're selected.

Locking Ruler Guides   To lock the position of a selected ruler guide, choose Lock from the Object menu (or press Command-L/Ctrl-L), or display the Context menu and choose Lock. Once you've locked the position of a ruler guide, you can change the color of the guide, move the guide to another layer, change its view threshold, or copy the guide, but you can't change its position.

To unlock the guide, select the guide and choose Unlock from the Context menu. Of course, you can also lock the position of guides by locking the layer containing the guides.

To lock all guides, press Command-Option-;/Ctrl-Alt-; (or choose Lock Guides from the Grids & Guides submenu of the View menu or the Context menu). When you do this, you're locking more than guide position—you won't be able to select a guide until you choose

Unlock Guides (from the Grids & Guides submenu of the View menu or from the Context menu) or press the keyboard shortcut again.

Deleting Ruler Guides   To delete a ruler guide (or guides), select the guide (or guides) and press the Delete key. Trying to drag the guide onto a ruler or out of the publication window (the technique used in PageMaker and QuarkXPress) simply scrolls your view of the publication window. So don't bother dragging the guide; just press Delete.

If you need to delete all the guides on a spread, choose Delete All Guides on Spread from the Grids & Guides submenu of the View menu.

Copying Ruler Guides   You can also copy selected ruler guides and paste them into other spreads or publications. When you paste, the guides appear in the positions they occupied in the original spread provided the page sizes are the same. If the page sizes are not the same, InDesign gets as close to the original positions as it can.

But wait! It gets better! You can use InDesign's Step and Repeat feature to duplicate ruler guides. For more on Step and Repeat, see Chapter 9, "Transforming." This is a great way to create custom grids, though the Document Grid feature (see below) is even better.

Smart Guides and Cursors   When you're dragging objects around your page, trying to line them up in just the right position, it's sure nice to get a little help. Smart Cursors and Smart Guides to the rescue! The Smart Cursors feature displays measurements alongside your cursor whenever you create a frame (even when placing an image) move an object, or transform it (resize, scale, or skew it; see Figure 2-42).

The Smart Guides feature displays temporary guides as you drag objects around your page (see Figure 2-43). For example, if you drag an object so that its left edge aligns with the left edge of another object on your page, a smart guide suddenly appears, indicating the relationship. Smart guides act as though the Snap to Grid feature is always on, so if you see a smart guide, you can let go of the mouse button confident that the object you were dragging has snapped to the proper alignment.

Note that smart guides only pay attention to objects on the same spread, and only those you can see in the document window. So, if

FIGURE 2-42
Smart Cursors

When resizing

When rotating

For more on scaling, rotating, and so on, see Chapter 9, "Transforming."

FIGURE 2-43
Smart Guides

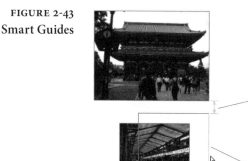

*Smart Spacing guide
with double arrowheads
displays when spacing
between objects is equal.*

*Smart guide indicates that
the right edge of the object
we're dragging is aligned
with the right edge of the
object below it.*

you zoom in so that you can only see objects on the lower half of
your page, the Smart Guides feature ignores objects on the top half.
Similarly, it ignores objects on hidden layers.

Smart Guides also treats the center of each page as an object—as
you drag an object, smart guides will appear when it's horizontally
or vertically centered on the page. These guides are a different color
than normal smart guides; they match your margin guide color.

Smart Spacing. Not only does Smart Guides pay attention to aligning the edges and centers of objects, it also watches the amount of
space between objects. For example, if you have three objects on
a page and start dragging the second one, you'll see smart guides
appear when the space between the first two objects is equivalent
to the space between the second two. These "Smart Spacing" guides
have small arrowheads on them.

Smart Transformations. Smart Guides also watches for similar transformations—what Adobe calls "Smart Dimensions." For
instance, let's say you have an object rotated on your page. Then you
select another object and start rotating it (we discuss the Rotation
tool and other ways to transform objects in Chapter 9, "Transforming"). Smart Dimensions sees the first rotated object and snaps to the
same rotation value. Curiously, this works even if the other object is
on another page (as long as you're zoomed out

Smart Preferences. Like so many other features in InDesign, you can
customize several aspects of Smart Guides so that it better works

for you. First, if you don't like the default lime-green color, you can change that in the Guides & Pasteboard pane of the Preferences dialog box (press Command/Ctrl-K).

In the same place, you'll find four checkboxes: Align to Object Center, Align to Object Edges, Smart Dimensions, Smart Spacing. The first two control what parts of objects InDesign takes into consideration when displaying smart guides. Note that even if you turn off Align to Object Center, objects will still align to the horizontal and vertical centerpoint of each page.

The second two checkboxes enable or disable Smart Dimensions and Smart Space, as described above.

Disabling Smart Guides. As cool as the Smart Guides feature is, it often just drives us batty, kicking in at times we just don't want it to. Fortunately, you can enable or disable it with a quick Command/Ctrl-U. (Or you can do it the slow way and choose Smart Guides from the Grids & Guides submenu, under the View menu.)

When you disable Smart Guides, you may wonder why the X and Y values still appear when you move objects. InDesign doesn't consider that little gray box part of Smart Guides. To get rid of it, turn off the Show Transformation Values in Interface preferences.

Grids

InDesign can display two different grids: the document grid and the baseline grid. Both grids are arrangements of guides spaced a specified distance apart. (The baseline grid is not truly a grid, as it has no vertical guidelines.) You'll find the settings for both grids in the Grids Preferences dialog box, as described in Chapter 1, "Workspace."

To display a grid, choose the corresponding option (Show Document Grid or Show Baseline Grid) from the Grids & Guides submenu of the View menu, or from the Context menu (when nothing is selected, and when a tool other than the Type tool is active). You can also hide or show the document grid by pressing Command-'/Ctrl-'.

If the magnification of the current publication window is below the view threshold of the baseline grid (again, this setting is in the Grids Preferences dialog box), you'll have to zoom in to see the grid (see Figure 2-44).

As we mentioned earlier, the grids aren't very useful without the relevant "snap." The regular Snap to Guides option (from the Grids & Guides submenu of the View menu) affects the baseline grid guides when they're visible, but not the document grid—you'll need to use

FIGURE 2-44
Setting the View
Threshold of the
Baseline Grid

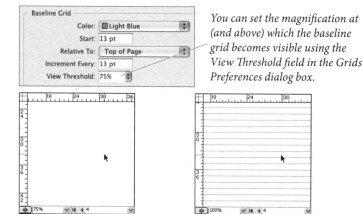

You can set the magnification at (and above) which the baseline grid becomes visible using the View Threshold field in the Grids Preferences dialog box.

If you've chosen Show Baseline Grid, but the baseline grid has not appeared...

...it's because you haven't zoomed in enough to cross the view threshold. Once you do, you'll see the grid.

the Snap to Document Grid feature (on the Grids & Guides submenu of the View menu) for that. In fact, when the Snap to Document Grid option is turned on, objects snap to the document grid even when the grid is not visible. (David likes this because the document grid is useful for aligning objects but distracting to his eye.)

Normally, only frames and lines snap to the baseline grid, but the feature's name implies that you can also snap the baselines of text to these guides—a very useful typesetting feature. We discuss working with text leading grids and the baseline grid in Chapter 4, "Type."

Stacking Objects

Page items on an InDesign page can be arranged in front of or behind each other. You can imagine that every object exists on an invisible plane that it cannot share with other objects, if you like. These planes can be shuffled to place one object above another, or behind another.

Simple stacking isn't the only way to control the front-to-back order of objects on a page—layers are another, and usually better, method (we cover layers in the next section). Arranging objects on a single layer, however, is very similar to tasks we perform every day as we stack and sort physical objects (our lives, for example, seem to revolve around stacks of paper).

Each layer in InDesign has its own stacking order and you can move an object to the front, or send an object to the back of the layer it occupies (see Figure 2-45). To bring an object to the front, Choose Bring to Front from the Arrange submenu (under the Object menu or the context menu). Or you can press Command-Shift-] / Ctrl-Shift-].

FIGURE 2-45
Bring to Front and
Send to Back

To bring an object to the front, select the object…

…and then press Command-Shift-] or Ctrl-Shift-]. InDesign brings the object to the front.

Note that bringing an object to the front or sending it to the back only changes its position in the stacking order of the current layer. Objects on other layers can still appear in front of objects brought to the front; objects on layers behind the current layer will still appear behind objects sent to the back.

To send an object to the back of the current layer, select the object…

…and then press Command-Shift-[or Ctrl-Shift-[.

To send an object to the back, choose Send to Back from the Arrange submenu. Alternately, you can press Command-Shift-[/ Ctrl-Shift-[.

You can also choose to bring objects closer to the front or send them farther to the back in the stacking order of objects on a layer (see Figure 2-46). To bring an object closer to the front (in front of the next higher object in the stacking order), choose Bring Forward from the Arrange submenu (under the Object menu or the context menu) or press Command-] / Ctrl-]. To send an object backward, choose Send Backward or press Command-[/ Ctrl-[.

**Text Wrap and
Stacking Order**

In QuarkXPress, text wrap is affected by the stacking order of objects on the page. If a text box is above a wrapped object, the text avoids the text wrap area; if it's behind/below the wrapped object, the text ignores the text wrap. While there is nothing inherently logical or intuitively obvious about this behavior, many people have gotten used to it.

To make InDesign behave this way, turn on the Text Wrap Only Affects Text Beneath option in the Composition panel of the

FIGURE 2-46
**Bring Forward
and Send Backward**

*Press Command-[or Ctrl-[
to send the object backward.*

*You can also press
Command-] or
Ctrl-] to move the
object forward.*

Select an object.

*Note that the stacking order
includes all of the objects on the
layer containing the object you're
moving. If the next object in the
stacking order does not intersect
the object you're moving, you won't
see any change on your screen.*

*Press the shortcut
again to move the
object farther back
in the layer's
stacking order.*

FIGURE 2-47
**Stacking Order
and Text Wrap**

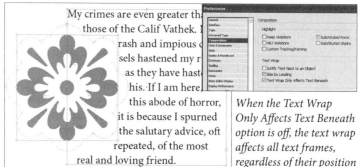

*The text frame is in front of
the wrapped object.*

My crimes are even greater th[an]
those of the Calif Vathek. [...]
rash and impious [coun]
sels hastened my r[uin,]
as they have hast[ened]
his. If I am here, [in]
this abode of horror,
it is because I spurned
the salutary advice, oft
repeated, of the most
real and loving friend.

*When the Text Wrap
Only Affects Text Beneath
option is off, the text wrap
affects all text frames,
regardless of their position
in the stacking order.*

*Note that you can also pre-
vent a text wrap from affecting a text frame by turning
on the Ignore Text Wrap
option in the Text Frame
Options dialog box.*

My crimes are even greater th[an]
those of the Calif Vathek. No [...]
and impious counsels hastene[d]
ruin, as they have hastened his [...]
I am here, in this abode of hor[ror,]
it is because I spurned the salu[tary]
advice, oft repeated, of the most
real and loving friend.

*When the option is off, the
text wrap does not affect
text frames in front of the
wrapped object.*

Preferences dialog box. Once you've done this, the stacking order of
objects on the page will have an effect on text wrap (see Figure 2-47).

For more on working with text wrap, see Chapter 6, "Where Text
Meets Graphics."

Layers

InDesign's layers are transparent planes on which you place page items. You've probably heard that layers are a way to organize your publication (that's what all the marketing materials say, after all). But there's far more to InDesign's layers than just organization—layers give you control over what parts of your publication display and print, and whether they can be edited or not.

Layers Basics
InDesign's layers have a few characteristics you should understand before you start using them. First, layers affect an entire document—not individual pages or page spreads. Next, layers created in one document do not affect layers in another document. As far as we can tell, there's no technical limit to the number of layers you can have in a publication; it's possible to make hundreds or more of them if you have enough memory. But just because you can do that doesn't mean that you should. Too many layers can make a publication difficult to manage.

Layers are especially useful when you're working with pages containing slow-drawing graphics, when your publication features complicated stacks of objects, or when you want to add a nonprinting layer of comments or instructions to a publication. Layers are also helpful when you want to create "conditional" layers containing differing text or graphics (you could create multiple versions of the publication in different languages, for example, and store all of the versions in a single publication).

The Layers Panel
You use the Layers panel to create, edit, rearrange, and delete layers (see Figure 2-49). You can also use the Layers panel to hide, lock, and arrange objects on a layer, and to move objects in and out of groups. To display the Layers panel, choose Layers from the Window menu (or press F7). The Layers panel is chock full o' features; let's look at them one at a time.

New Layer. To create a new layer, click the New Layer button at the bottom of the panel or select New Layer from the Layers panel menu (see Figure 2-48). InDesign normally adds new layers above the layer selected in the Layers panel, but you can tell the program to add the layer immediately beneath the currently selected layer by holding down Command/Ctrl as you click the New Layer button. Hold down Command/Ctrl+Shift as you click the New Layer button to create new layers at the top of the panel.

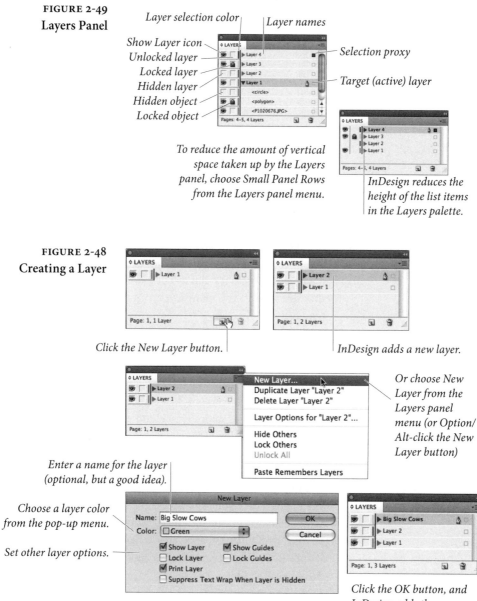

FIGURE 2-49
Layers Panel

Layer selection color

Layer names

Show Layer icon
Unlocked layer
Locked layer
Hidden layer
Hidden object
Locked object

Selection proxy

Target (active) layer

To reduce the amount of vertical space taken up by the Layers panel, choose Small Panel Rows from the Layers panel menu.

InDesign reduces the height of the list items in the Layers palette.

FIGURE 2-48
Creating a Layer

Click the New Layer button.

InDesign adds a new layer.

Or choose New Layer from the Layers panel menu (or Option/ Alt-click the New Layer button)

Enter a name for the layer (optional, but a good idea).

Choose a layer color from the pop-up menu.

Set other layer options.

New Layer
Name: Big Slow Cows
Color: ☐ Green
☑ Show Layer   ☑ Show Guides
☐ Lock Layer   ☐ Lock Guides
☑ Print Layer
☐ Suppress Text Wrap When Layer is Hidden
OK
Cancel

Click the OK button, and InDesign adds the new layer to the Layers palette.

If you want to name the layer (we think you should) or change any other options, hold down the Option/Alt key when you click this button to display the New Layer dialog box. (You can also get to this dialog box by double-clicking the layer after creating it.) We cover the controls in this dialog box in "Layer Options," below.

Delete Layer. Click the Delete Layer button to delete the selected layer or layers (to select more than one layer, hold down Command/Ctrl as you click each layer). If the layer you have selected contains objects, InDesign warns you that deleting the layer will delete the objects.

Collapse/expand arrows. Click the down arrow next to a layer to display the objects that are on that layer and on the current spread. You can hide, lock, and arrange objects on layers (see Figure 2-50).

You can also click the down arrow next to a group of objects to display the objects that make up that group. You can drag other objects into that group to make it part of the group, and you can drag objects out of the group.

FIGURE 2-50
Arranging, Hiding, and Locking Objects within a Layer

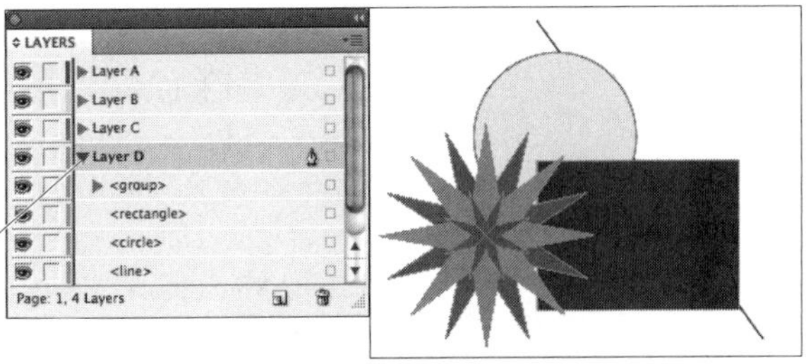

Click the down arrow to display objects on a layer on the current spread.

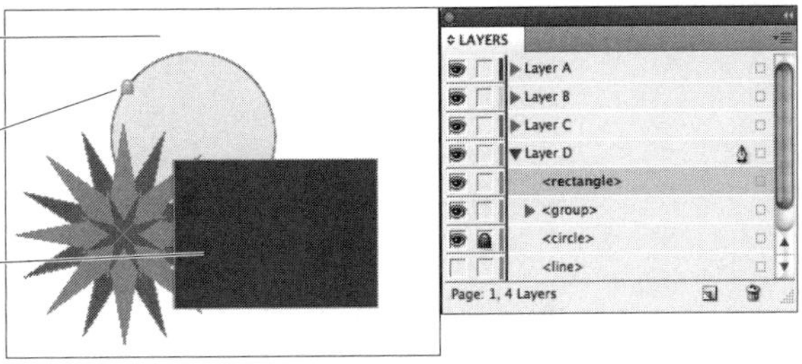

The line is hidden.

The circle is locked, as indicated by the lock icon.

The rectangle moves to the front.

Show/Hide column. When you see an "eye" icon in the left-most column of the Layers panel, that layer or object is visible. When there's no icon next to a layer in this column, all of the objects on the layer are hidden (invisible). If there's no icon next to an object, that object is hidden. Click once in this column to change from one state to another. You can't select or edit objects on hidden layers, and objects on hidden layers don't print.

Often, you want to hide all the layers in a publication except one. It's easy: hold down Option/Alt as you click in that layer's Show/Hide column (or choose Hide Others from the Layers panel menu). Clicking again in the column while holding down Option/Alt will show all layers, which is equivalent to choosing Show All Layers from the Layers panel menu (see Figure 2-51). Use the same Option/Alt trick to show or hide all the objects in a layer except one.

FIGURE 2-51
**Showing and Hiding
Other Layers**

*To hide all but one layer,
follow these steps.*

*Point at the layer's
Visibility icon, hold
down Option/Alt...*

*...and click. InDesign
hides all of the other
layers.*

*Press Option/Alt and
click again to make the
layers visible.*

Lock/Unlock column. Click in the second column to lock a layer or object. InDesign displays the "lock" icon in that column. To unlock the layer or object, click the icon.

You can't select objects on locked layers (so you can't move or format them, either), and you can't assign objects to locked layers. When you want to lock all of the layers in a publication except one, hold down Option/Alt and click in the lock/unlock column (or choose Lock Others from the Layers panel menu). To unlock every layer, hold down Option/Alt and click the lock/unlock column (this is the same as choosing Unlock All Layers from the panel menu).

Target layer icon. The target layer icon (it looks like a little fountain pen nib) shows you which layer is the "target layer"—the layer on which InDesign will place any objects you create, import, or paste. Making a layer the target layer does *not* assign any currently selected objects to that layer.

Selection Proxy. When you select an object on your page, InDesign highlights the name of the layer containing the object and sets that layer as the target layer. In addition, InDesign displays a small square to the right of the layer name. This square is the Selection Proxy, which represents the layer or layers containing the selected objects (just as the proxy in the Transform panel "stands in" for the bounding box of the selection). To move objects from one layer to another, drag the Selection Proxy to another layer (see Figure 2-52).

While this method of moving objects from one layer to another makes it difficult to accidentally move objects, it also makes it difficult to move objects from multiple layers to a single layer. To accomplish this, you'll have to make multiple trips up and down the Layers panel, selecting and moving the proxy for each layer in the selection.

Note that you can also copy an object from one layer to another by holding down Option/Alt and dragging the Selection proxy. Plus, you can even move objects to a locked or hidden layer—to do this, press Command/Ctrl as you drag the selection proxy to the layer. To copy objects as you move them to a hidden or locked layer, hold down Command-Option/Ctrl-Alt as you drag.

FIGURE 2-52
Moving an Object
to a Layer

This object is on the layer
named "D layer."

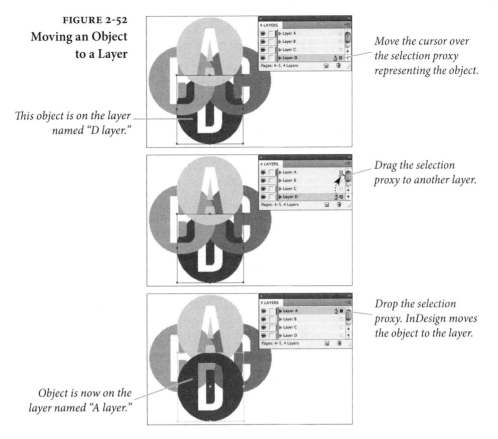

Move the cursor over
the selection proxy
representing the object.

Drag the selection
proxy to another layer.

Drop the selection
proxy. InDesign moves
the object to the layer.

Object is now on the
layer named "A layer."

Layer Options   Here's a quick rundown of each of the controls in the New Layer and
Layer Options dialog boxes.

Layer name. InDesign assigns a default name to each layer you create,
but we think it's better to enter a layer name that means something
in the context of your publication. It's far easier to remember that the
enormous, slow drawing image of grazing Herefords is on the layer
you've named "Big Slow Cows" than it is to remember that you've
placed the image on the layer named "Layer 51."

Layer color. Each layer has its own color that helps you see which
objects are on which layers. When Show Frame Edges (in the View
menu) is turned on, InDesign uses the layer color for the outlines of
frames and other objects. When you select an object, its selection
handles appear in the selection color of that layer. If you don't pick
a color yourself, the program picks one for you automatically. To
change a color later, either double-click a layer in the Layers panel, or
select a layer and choose Layer Options from the Layers panel menu.

We have never felt the need to change a layer's selection color in an actual project, but it's nice to know that you can.

Show Layer. Should the layer be visible, or hidden? This option performs the same task as the show/hide column in the Layers panel.

Lock Layer. Should the layer be locked or unlocked? This option performs the same task as the lock/unlock column.

Show Guides. Remember that you can put ruler guides on layers. But should those guides be visible or hidden? If you want to hide just this layer's guides, turn off the Show Guides option.

Lock Guides. Should the guides on this layer be locked or unlocked? By default they're unlocked; turn this option on to lock 'em.

Suppress Text Wrap When Layer is Hidden. People complained to high heaven because InDesign 2 couldn't turn off the text wrap on objects that were on hidden layers. Fortunately, now you can. This is helpful if you're trying out a number of different designs, each on its own layer. As you hide a layer, you don't want its graphics to affect the other layers!

Paste Remembers Layers. This option doesn't appear in the Layer Options dialog box; rather it's in the Layers panel menu. The Paste Remembers Layers option takes care of a question: "If I copy objects from several layers and then paste, where should the pasted objects end up?" Should they be placed on the target layer (in a stack corresponding to their layer order)? Or should they be placed on the layers they originally came from?

We think you'll turn this option on and leave it on. If you do this, you'll be able to copy layers between publications. To do this, select objects on different layers in one publication, then copy them, and then switch to another publication and paste. When you paste, the layers will appear in the publication's Layers panel.

If layers with the same names already exist in the publication, InDesign moves the incoming objects to the corresponding layers, which is why you might want to turn the Paste Remembers Layers option off. If you don't, and if the layer stacking order is not the same as it was in the publication you copied the objects out of, the appearance of the pasted objects might change.

Deleting Layers To delete a layer, select the layer and choose Delete Layer from the Layers panel menu or click the Delete Layer button. As we noted earlier, if there are any objects on the layer, InDesign warns you first (because deleting a layer also deletes its objects). To delete all of the unused layers (layers that have no objects assigned to them) in a publication, choose Delete Unused Layers from the Layers panel menu.

Changing Layer Stacking Order To change the stacking order of layers, drag the layer up (to bring the layer closer to the front) or down (to send the layer farther to the back) in the Layers panel. As you drag, InDesign displays a horizontal bar showing the position of the layer. When the layer reaches the point in the list at which you want it to appear, stop dragging and InDesign moves the layer (and all the objects on it) to a new location (see Figure 2-53).

FIGURE 2-53
Changing Layer Stacking Order

The selected object is on the layer named "A layer."

Move the cursor over the layer you want to move.

Drag the layer to a new position in the Layers palette.

The layer named "A layer" is now the layer closest to the front.

When the layer reaches the location you want, stop dragging. InDesign changes the layer stacking order.

Merging Layers

To combine a series of layers into a single layer, select the layers and then choose Merge Layers from the Layers panel menu. InDesign merges the layers into a single layer—the first layer you selected (see Figure 2-54). Note that merging layers sometimes changes the stacking order of objects on the merged layers.

FIGURE 2-54
Merging Layers

Select a series of layers and choose Merge Layers from the Layers panel menu.

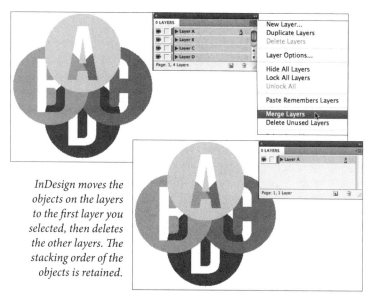

InDesign moves the objects on the layers to the first layer you selected, then deletes the other layers. The stacking order of the objects is retained.

Moving Layers from One Publication to Another

To move a layer from one publication into another publication, make sure you've turned on the Paste Remembers Layers option (on the Layers panel menu), then copy an object from that layer and paste it into the publication that lacks that layer. When you paste, InDesign adds the layer to the list of layers.

Here's a bonus tip: You can select all the objects on a layer by Option/Alt-clicking on the layer in the Layers panel. Now you can copy and paste these objects to copy the contents of the layer to another document.

Layers and Master Pages

In older page layout software (such as QuarkXPress or PageMaker), objects on master pages are always displayed behind document page objects. This means that page numbers often end up being hidden by items on your document pages, and that you may have to copy the master page item to your document page to get it to display or print.

In InDesign, objects on master pages are arranged according to their layer. This means that you can put page numbers on the uppermost layer without worrying about them being obscured by images or other page items on the document pages.

Grouping Objects

What does it mean to "group" objects in a page layout program? When you group objects, you're telling the application to treat the objects as a single object. The objects in the group move and transform (scale, skew, and rotate) as a unit.

To group the objects in a selection, press Command-G/Ctrl-G (or choose Group from either the Object menu or the context menu). Note that you can't have objects in a group when they're each on different layers, so when you group the objects, the group moves to the top-most layer of the selection (see Figure 2-55). To ungroup a selected group, press Command-Shift-G/Ctrl-Shift-G (or choose Ungroup from the Context menu or the Object menu).

To select (or "subselect") an object inside a group, double-click the object using the Selection tool. By the way, don't forget that you can group together groups—each group acting as a single object in the larger group.

An easy way to add objects to an existing group is using the Layers panel. Use the Layers panel to drag items into and out of groups. You can't group objects from different layers.

FIGURE 2-55
Grouping and Ungrouping Objects

Select the objects you want to group.

Groups can come in handy when you've created an assemblage of objects you want to treat as a single object. In addition, grouping objects speeds up screen redraw—InDesign draws selection handles for one object, rather than for all of the objects in the group.

When you select a group with the Selection tool, InDesign displays a dashed line around the group.

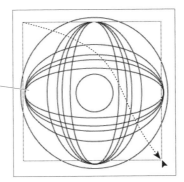

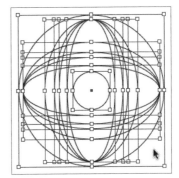

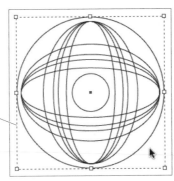

Press Command-G/Ctrl-G. InDesign groups the objects. You can move, scale, shear, or rotate the group as you do any other single object.

To select an object inside the group, double-click the object.

To ungroup, select a group and press Command-Shift-G/Ctrl-Shift-G.

Locking Object Positions

When you want to keep somebody from changing the location of an object, you can lock it by selecting it and then pressing Command-L/Ctrl-L (or choose Lock from the context menu or the Object menu). When an object is locked, the Prevent Selection of Locked Objects option in General preferences determines whether you can select it. If this option is turned on, you can't select locked objects. Just click the lock icon to unlock it, or choose Unlock All on Spread from the Object menu. If the option is turned off, you can select an object, but you can't change its position on the page or pasteboard. You can, however, move the object to another layer (we're not sure why; perhaps it's a bug). When you try to drag a locked object, the cursor turns into a "padlock" icon (see Figure 2-56).

You can also lock the layer that contains the object (see "Layers," earlier in this chapter). Unfortunately, even graphics and text on locked layers can still be changed if you try hard enough: changes made with the Find/Change panel and the Links panel can still affect locked objects and layers (which is usually what you want, anyway).

FIGURE 2-56
Locking and Unlocking Objects

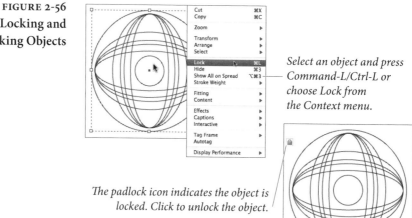

Select an object and press Command-L/Ctrl-L or choose Lock from the Context menu.

The padlock icon indicates the object is locked. Click to unlock the object.

Deleting Objects

Deleting objects on your page is simple: Just select one or more items with the Selection or Direct Selection tools and press the Delete key. If you want a slower method, choose Clear from the Edit menu instead. If you're really trying to kill time, and you're using the Mac OS, you can drag the object from the page into the operating system's Trash icon. Why? Because you can.

Finding and Changing Objects

Have you ever had a client/boss/whatever look at your near-final layout and express a need to make vast, far-reaching changes in the color, stroke weight, or other attributes of the graphic elements on the pages? Have you ever spent the night clawing your way through a document, changing fills and strokes to meet their unreasonable requests?

We have, so we're very happy that InDesign can now find and change objects by their formatting (and other) attributes, just as we can find and change text. (Actually, we now make extensive use of object styles, so our threshold of pain is a little higher than it once was, but the addition of object find/change is still welcome.)

To find and change objects by their attributes, follow these steps (see Figure 2-57).

1. Press Command-F/Ctrl-F to display the Find and Change panel. Click the Object tab if it is not already active.

2. Click the Specify Attributes to Find button to display the Find Object Format Options dialog box. Work your way through the various panels of this dialog box to define the attributes of the object you want to find. Click the OK button to close the dialog box.

3. Click the Specify Attributes to Change button to display the Change Object Format Options dialog box. Work your way through the various panels of this dialog box to set the formatting you want to apply to the objects you find. Click the OK button to close the dialog box.

4. At this point, you can do either of the following:

   ▶ You can choose to have InDesign change the formatting of all of the qualifying objects by clicking the Change All button.

   ▶ You can find each occurrence of the formatting you specified and decide whether to replace it or not. To do this, click the Find button, view the found object, and then click the Find Next, Change, or Change/Find button. The Find Next button moves on to the next instance of the formatting *without* making any changes; the Change button replaces the formatting of the found object and waits to see what you'll do next. The Change/Find button replaces the object, then finds the next instance.

FIGURE 2-57
Finding and Changing Object Formatting

In this example, we want to search for the objects with a gray stroke and change the stroke to black. We also want to reduce the stroke weight.

Please imagine that there are hundreds of these, on dozens of pages.

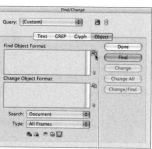

Press Command-F/Ctrl-F to display the Find/Change panel. Click the Object tab, then click the Specify Attribute to Find button.

Use the Find Object Format Options dialog box to set up the attributes you want to find. Click the OK button when you're done, then, back in the Find/Change panel, click the Specify Attributes to Change button.

Use the Change Object Format Options dialog box to set up the replacement attributes, then press OK to return to the Find/Change panel.

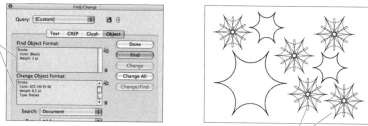

The Find/Change panel displays the formatting attributes you selected. Click the Change All button…

…and InDesign changes the objects whose formatting matches the attributes you selected.

A Good Foundation

Being methodical every now and then can save a lot of trouble later. Setting up master pages, defining layers, creating layout grids and ruler guides are not the most glamorous parts of InDesign, but they're a good place to spend a little organizational energy. Far from cramping your creative style, paying attention to basic layout options—at the very beginning of the production process, if possible—sets the stage on which you produce and direct the play of your publications.

Text

Text is the stream of characters that inhabit your publications. Text is not about what those characters *look like* (that's "type," the topic of the next chapter)—it's about the characters themselves, and the containers that hold them.

All text in an InDesign document exists in one or more stories. A story consists of at least one text container: the container is usually a text frame, but can sometimes be a path text object. A story can be as small as a single, unlinked text frame, or as large as a series of hundreds of linked text frames containing tens of thousands of words and spanning hundreds of pages.

Text frames (see Figure 3-1) are similar to the text "boxes" found in QuarkXPress, and they're also similar to the text "blocks" found in PageMaker. In our opinion, InDesign's text frames present a "best of both worlds" approach—you get the flexibility and fluidity of PageMaker's text blocks combined with the precision of QuarkXPress' text boxes.

Text, in a word, is what publications are really all about. A picture might be worth a thousand words, but they're not very *specific* words. When you create a poster for a concert, for example, the text is what tells the viewer where the concert will be presented, at what time, and on which date. The point of using an image, color, or a stylish layout is to get people to *read the text*.

FIGURE 3-1
Text Frame Anatomy

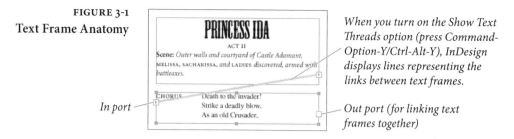

When you turn on the Show Text Threads option (press Command-Option-Y/Ctrl-Alt-Y), InDesign displays lines representing the links between text frames.

In port

Out port (for linking text frames together)

This chapter is all about how to get text into your InDesign documents—how to create and edit text frames, enter text, edit text, and import text files. It's also about creating text variables and conditional text, checking the spelling of the text in your publication, and about finding and changing text.

Creating Text Frames

Before you can add text to your InDesign publication, you've got to have something to put it in: a text frame. To create a text frame, you can use any or all of the following methods.

- ▶ Draw a frame using one of the basic shape tools or the frame drawing tools. To convert the frame to a text frame, select the frame and choose Text from the Content submenu of the Object menu (see Figure 3-2). If you have turned on the Type Tool Converts Frames to Text Frames option in the Type panel of the Preference dialog box, you can also convert the frame by clicking the Type tool inside the frame.

- ▶ Drag the Type tool to create a frame whose height and width are defined by the area you specified by dragging (see Figure 3-3).

- ▶ Drag a text place icon. The text place icon appears whenever you import a text file, or click the in port or out port of a text frame (see Figure 3-4). See "Importing Text" later in this chapter.

- ▶ Deselect all (Command-Shift-A/Ctrl-Shift-A) and then paste text into the publication (or drag it out of another application and drop it into the publication, which accomplishes the same thing). InDesign creates a text frame containing the text.

- ▶ Drag a text file (or series of text files) out of your operating system's file browser (the Finder on the Macintosh, or the Windows Explorer in Windows) and drop it into an InDesign publication.

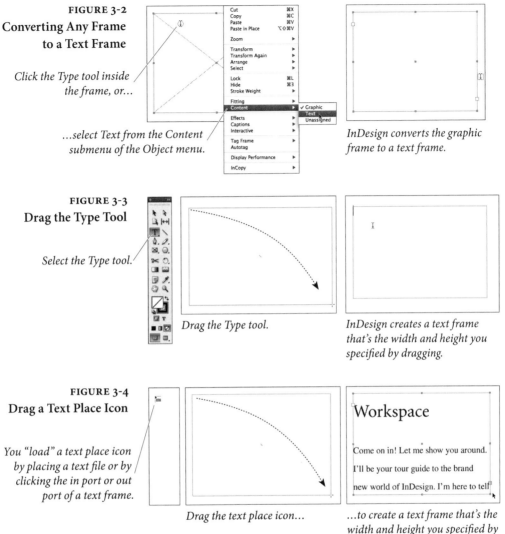

FIGURE 3-2

Converting Any Frame to a Text Frame

Click the Type tool inside the frame, or...

...select Text from the Content submenu of the Object menu.

InDesign converts the graphic frame to a text frame.

FIGURE 3-3

Drag the Type Tool

Select the Type tool.

Drag the Type tool.

InDesign creates a text frame that's the width and height you specified by dragging.

FIGURE 3-4

Drag a Text Place Icon

You "load" a text place icon by placing a text file or by clicking the in port or out port of a text frame.

Drag the text place icon...

Workspace

Come on in! Let me show you around. I'll be your tour guide to the brand new world of InDesign. I'm here to tel

...to create a text frame that's the width and height you specified by dragging.

Note that InDesign does not always require you to create a text frame *before* you add text, as (for example) QuarkXPress does. Most of the text frame creation methods described previously dynamically create a text frame as you enter, import, or paste text.

Once you've created a text frame, you can change its size, shape, and rotation angle just as you would any other object you've created (see Chapter 5, "Drawing" and Chapter 9, "Transforming"). You can also change the shape of the text frame using InDesign's drawing and path editing tools (see Chapter 5, "Drawing").

Text can also appear *on* a path—for more on this topic, see Chapter 6, "Where Text Meets Graphics."

Setting Text Frame Options

Text frames have attributes that are not shared with graphics frames or with frames whose content is set to "Unassigned." To view and edit these attributes, choose Text Frame Options from the Type menu, or press Command-B/Ctrl-B, or hold down Option/Alt as you double-click the frame with either selection tool. InDesign displays the Text Frame Options dialog box (see Figure 3-5).

The controls in this dialog box set the number of columns, inset distances, and first baseline calculation method for the text frame.

Columns and Text Frames

InDesign text frames can contain up to 40 columns—enter the number of columns you want in the Number field. To define the distance between columns, or "gutter," enter a value in the Gutter field.

Column width. InDesign lets you determine the width of a text frame by the width of its columns. When you type the number of columns in the Text Frame Options dialog box and click OK, InDesign divides the current width of the text frame into columns for you. However, if you specify a value in the Width field, then the program changes the width of your text frame so that the columns will fit.

The Fixed Column Width option tells InDesign what to do with your text frame when it gets wider or narrower. When you turn this option on, you'll notice that when you resize the text frame it snaps to widths determined by the fixed widths of the columns (and gutters) it contains (see Figure 3-6). If you leave this option turned off, the column widths change when you resize the frame.

FIGURE 3-5
Text Frame Options

As in many other dialog boxes and panels, the "chain" icon enforces the same spacing in all associated fields.

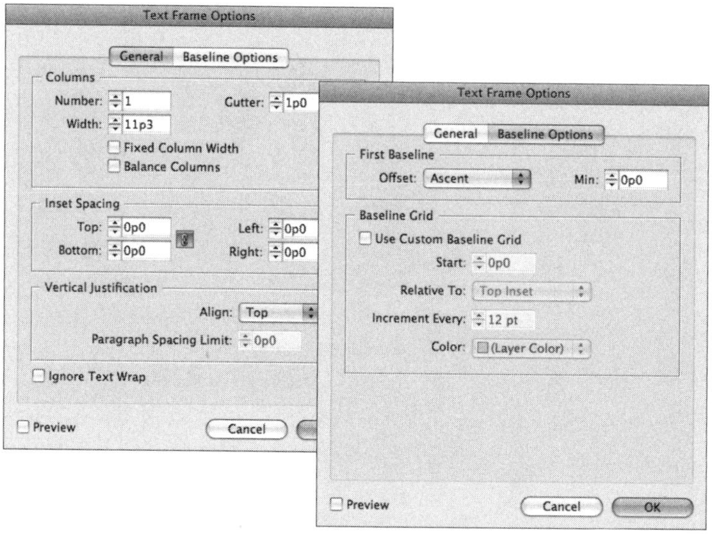

FIGURE 3-6
Fixed Column Width

When you turn on the Fixed Column Width option, InDesign resizes the text frame based on the column width you entered (rather than evenly dividing the width of the text frame into columns of equal width).

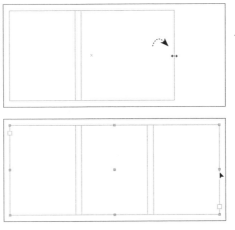

When you resize a text frame that has a fixed column width…

…InDesign will "snap" the frame widths based on that column width. No matter how narrow you make the frame, it will always contain at least one column of that width.

When there isn't enough text to fill a multi-column text frame, the Balance Columns option tells InDesign to keep the height of the columns as close to the same height as possible, leaving empty space at the bottom of all the columns rather than just the last one.

Regardless of the options in this dialog box, we have to point out that a layout created using multicolumn text frames is far less flexible than the same layout using single column text frames. For example, you cannot change the width or height of just one of the columns in a multicolumn text frame.

Setting Text Frame Insets

The values you enter in the Inset Spacing section of the Text Frame Options dialog box control the distances InDesign will push text from the edges of the text frame. You can enter an inset distance from 0 to 8640 points (or about 120 inches). To enter different values for each field, you'll have to turn off the Make All Settings the Same option (the little chain thingy). Unfortunately, you can't enter negative values to make the text hang out of the text frame.

Inset distances work in conjunction with (and in addition to) the margins of the paragraphs in a text frame (see Figure 3-7). In general, we prefer to work with the text inset values set to zero, and use the left and right indent values of individual paragraphs to control the distance from the edges of the text to the edges of the text column. However, these inset features are sometimes helpful when you need to move all the text in a frame up or down slightly without moving the frame itself.

Setting First Baseline Position

The Offset pop-up menu in the First Baseline section of the Text Frame Options dialog box offers five methods for calculating the position of the first baseline of text in a text frame: Ascent, Cap Height, Leading, x Height, and Fixed (see Figure 3-8).

FIGURE 3-7

Text Frame Insets

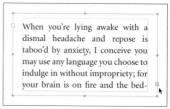

By default, InDesign applies no inset—note that this differs from most versions of QuarkXPress, which apply a one point inset by default.

Enter inset distances in the fields in the Inset Spacing section of the dialog box to push text away from the edges of the text frame.

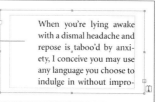

When you select the text frame with the Selection tool, InDesign displays the text inset boundary.

Paragraph indents are applied in addition to the text frame inset distances.

If you use either the Ascent or Cap Height method, the tops of characters in your text frames will touch the top of the text frame (when the top frame inset is zero). Choosing x Height is similar: the tops of the lower-case characters will bump up against the top of the frame. These settings come at a price: it's almost impossible to calculate the distance from the top of the frame to the baseline of the first line of text in the frame (without resorting to scripting).

In addition, using these methods means that InDesign will vary the leading of the first line when you enter characters from different fonts in the line, or change the size of characters, or when you embed inline graphics in the line.

Is that bad? It is, if you care about type.

It's important that you know exactly where the first baseline of text in a text frame will appear, relative to the top of the text frame. Why? Because if you know the position of the first baseline, you can snap the top of the text frame to your leading grid—and rest secure in the knowledge that the first baseline will fall on the next baseline.

FIGURE 3-8
First Baseline Position

Example font is Minion Pro; example leading is 24 points.

All baseline distances calculated using Neo-Atlantean super science, and will vary from font to font.

If you use the Fixed or Leading options, you can know exactly where the first baseline of text will fall in relation to the top of the text frame, regardless of the font or the point size of the text.

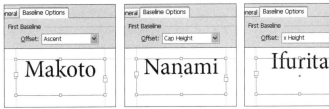

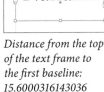

Distance from the top of the text frame to the first baseline: 17.44775390625 points.

Distance from the top of the text frame to the first baseline: 15.6000316143036 points.

Distance from the top of the text frame to the first baseline: 10.4640212059021 points.

Distance from the top of the text frame to the first baseline: 24 points.

Distance from the top of the text frame to the first baseline: 24 points.

To control the location of the first baseline of text in a text frame, choose either Leading or Fixed from the Offset menu in the First Baseline section. When you choose Leading, the first baseline is one leading increment from the top of the text frame—regardless of the size of the characters (or the height of inline graphics) in the line. When you choose Fixed, you can specify exactly how far from the top of the frame the first baseline should fall using the Min field.

The Min field for the Offset settings other than Fixed means, "between the Min value and what the Offset would be ordinarily, use the larger value."

For more on leading, see Chapter 4, "Type."

Ignoring Text Wrap

To keep text in a text frame from obeying a text wrap, select the frame, open the Text Frame Options dialog box, and then turn on the Ignore Text Wrap option (see Figure 3-9).

Note that in this case (where the text was on top of the offending graphic) you could also turn on the Text Wrap Only Affects Text Beneath option in the Composition Preferences dialog box. This preference affects all text wraps in your file (see Chapter 6, "Where Text Meets Graphics").

Vertical Justification

Vertical justification controls the vertical position of the text in a text frame (see Figure 3-10). To set the vertical justification method used

FIGURE 3-9
Ignoring Text Wrap

When you try to place a text frame on top of a graphic that has a text wrap, InDesign pushes the text out of the frame.

Unless, that is, you display the Text Frame Options dialog box (select the text frame and press Command-B/Ctrl-B) and turn on the Ignore Text Wrap option.

Once you do this, text in the text frame ignores the text wrap.

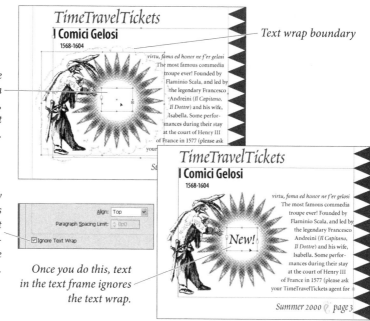

Text wrap boundary

FIGURE 3-10
Vertical Justification

When you choose Center from the Align pop-up menu, you might want to choose the Cap Height or Ascent option from the Offset pop-up menu (in this case, choosing Leading is not a good idea, as it pushes the text away from the visual center of the text frame).

When you choose Justify from the Align pop-up menu, InDesign adds space to force the text to fill the height of the frame. The method InDesign uses is based on the value you enter in the Paragraph Spacing Limit field (you can enter values from 0 to 8640 points).

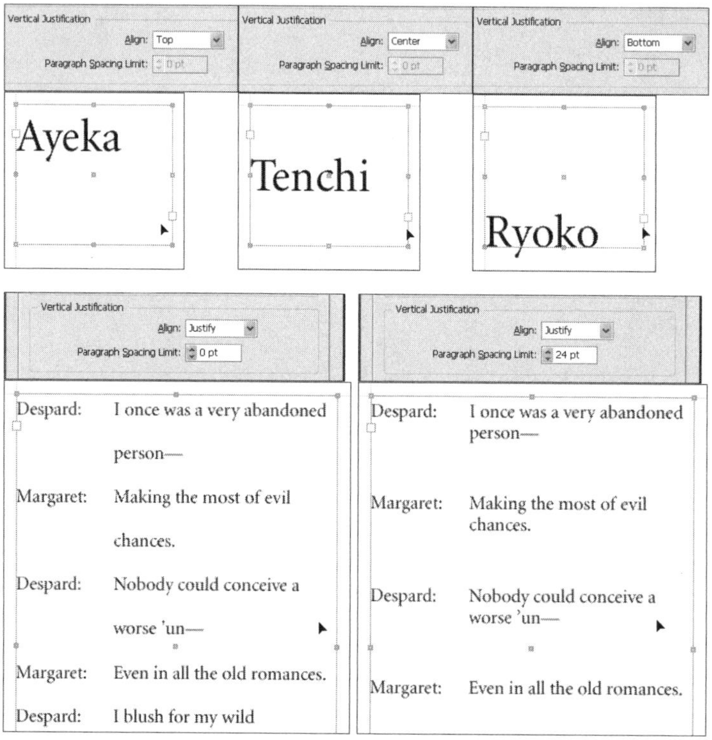

When you enter zero, InDesign applies leading to make the text fill the height of the text frame.

When you enter a value, InDesign applies paragraph spacing up to that amount before changing the leading.

for a text frame, select the text frame, display the Text Frame Options dialog box, and then choose a method from the Align pop-up menu.

▶ **Top.** Aligns the text to the top of the text frame, positioning the first baseline of text in the frame according to the method you've selected from the Offset pop-up menu (see above).

▶ **Center.** InDesign centers the text between the bottom of the text frame and the top of the first line of text (taking the baseline options into account). Note that the text may be mathematically centered, but might not *appear* centered in some cases. In these relatively rare cases, you may have to work with the First Baseline or Baseline Shift settings to center the text.

▶ **Bottom.** Aligns the baseline of the last line of text in the text frame to the bottom of the frame. When you choose this method, the Offset pop-up menu has no effect.

▶ **Justify.** Adds vertical space to the text in the text frame (using paragraph spacing and/or leading to add this space) to fill the text frame with the text. Note that using the Justify method will not pull overset text into the text frame; it only adds space. The first line of the text frame will remain where it was, based on the First Baseline setting.

Paragraph Spacing Limit. When you choose Justify from the Align pop-up menu, InDesign activates the Paragraph Spacing Limit control, which sets the maximum amount of space you'll allow between paragraphs in the text frame. Once the space between paragraphs reaches this value, InDesign adjusts the leading of each line in the text frame, rather than adding space between paragraphs. To keep InDesign from changing leading at all, enter a large value (up to 8640 points) in this field. On the other hand, if you really want InDesign to change the leading instead, enter zero.

Non-Rectangular Frames. The InDesign team fixed a bug in its previous versions that prevented vertical justification from working in non-rectangular frames. If you want to apply vertical justification to elliptical frames or frames with corner effects, go for it.

Spanning and Splitting Columns

In earlier versions of InDesign, if you wanted a heading to span multiple columns, you had to create a separate text frame for the heading.

Now you can span a heading across multiple columns, which is sometimes called a "straddle head" (see Figure 3-11). You can also split a paragraph into multiple columns—especially useful for a list within an article (see Figure 3-12).

▶ To span or split columns quickly, select text, display the paragraph options in the Control panel, and then choose an option from the Span Columns menu.

▶ To span or split columns and bring up a dialog box that lets you adjust the spacing, choose Span Columns from the Paragraph panel menu or the Control panel menu. Or, Option/Alt-click the Span Columns button.

In the Span Columns dialog box, you can specify the number of columns to span or sub-columns to split into, but more important, you can change the spacing before or after the spanning or splitting paragraphs. If you're like us, you probably wonder what the difference is between changing the spacing in the dialog box versus using the Space Before/Space After settings in the Control panel. The answer is a bit odd. If you change the before/after spacing in one

FIGURE 3-11
Spanning Columns

Select the heading you want to straddle...

... and then click the Span Columns button in the Control panel, and choose Span All.

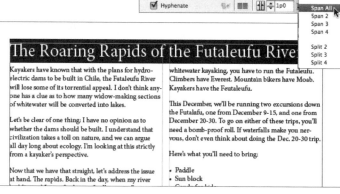

FIGURE 3-12

Splitting Columns

Select the text, and choose Span Columns from the Paragraph panel menu...

...then choose choose Split Column, and fine-tune the spacing settings.

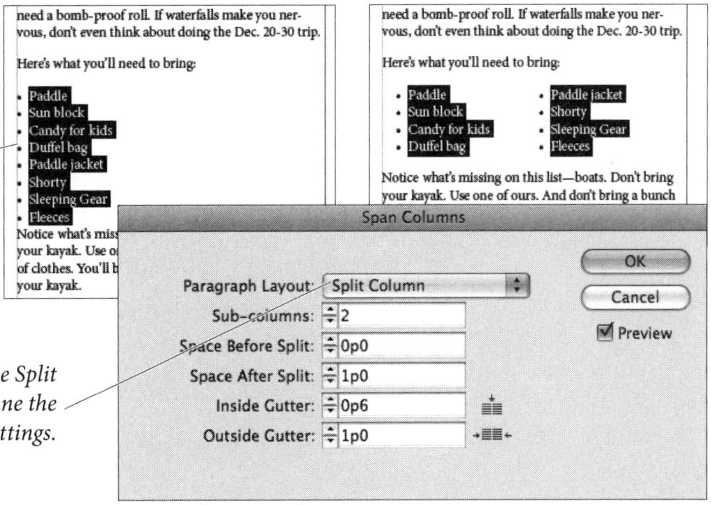

location, the changes in one UI area aren't reflected in the other, and the higher value wins out.

If you're splitting columns, you can also change the inside gutters (the spacing between the sub-columns) and the outside gutters (the spacing between the outside of the sub-columns and the main column's inset).

As a general rule, avoid combining footnotes with paragraphs that split into or span columns. When determining where footnotes should go, InDesign divides a page with spanning or split columns into sections. If you insert a footnote in a split column paragraph, the footnote text appears at the bottom of the split columns, not at the bottom of the text frame. Even worse, if you insert a footnote in text above split paragraphs, the footnote appears above the split paragraphs rather than at the bottom of the text frame. It can get ugly fast.

If you need to add a paragraph to a set of split columns, just choose the same split setting. InDesign combines all paragraphs with the same split setting into the same block.

If you plan on repeating straddle heads or splitting columns in your document, you'll want to create a paragraph style with the settings you need.

Linking and Unlinking Text Frames

You can link one text frame to another to make the text continue—or "flow"—from frame to frame. In InDesign, the controls for linking and unlinking text frames are the "in port" and "out port" icons on the text frames themselves. The process of linking text frames in

InDesign is similar to working with the "windowshade handles" on PageMaker text blocks, and should feel familiar to PageMaker users. There's no need to go to the Toolbox to get a special "linking" tool, as there is in QuarkXPress.

When you link text frames together, you're *threading* stories through the text frames. When you place text to create a series of linked text frames, you're *flowing* text.

The text in a story has a direction—it has a beginning, a middle, and an end. When we speak, in this section, of a particular text frame appearing before or after another, we're talking about its position in the story, not relative to its position on the page.

The way that InDesign displays the in port and out port of a text frame tells you about the text frame and its position in a story (see Figure 3-13).

▶ When the in port or out port is empty, no other text frame is linked to that port. When both ports are empty, the text you see in the text frame is the entire story.

▶ When you see a plus sign (+) in the out port, it means that not all of the text in the story has been placed. The remaining (or "overset") text is stored in the text frame, but is not displayed.

▶ When you see a triangle in the in port or the out port (or both), InDesign is telling you that the text frame is linked to another text frame.

Linking Text Frames   To link one text frame to another, choose the Selection or Direct Selection tool, then click either the in port or the out port of a text frame. InDesign displays the text place icon. Place the cursor over

FIGURE 3-13
In Ports and Out Ports

This text frame contains all of the text in a story. How can you tell?
The in port is empty, and...   *...the out port is also empty.*

This text frame is at the start of a story, because the in port is empty.

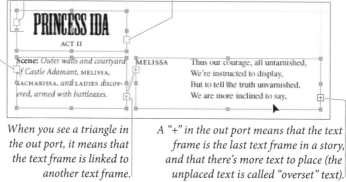

PRINCESS IDA
ACT II

Scene: *Outer walls and courtyard of Castle Adamant,* MELISSA, GACHARISSA, *and* LADIES *discovered, armed with battleaxes.*

MELISSA   Thus our courage, all untarnished,
We're instructed to display,
But to tell the truth unvarnished,
We are more inclined to say,

When you see a triangle in the out port, it means that the text frame is linked to another text frame.

A "+" in the out port means that the text frame is the last text frame in a story, and that there's more text to place (the unplaced text is called "overset" text).

another frame (when you do this, InDesign displays the text link icon, which either looks like a little chain or like some text inside big parentheses, depending on what type of frame you're hovering over) and then click. InDesign links the two frames (see Figure 3-14). That sounds pretty simple, but there are a number of details you should keep in mind:

▶ Unlike QuarkXPress, InDesign can link two text frames when both frames contain text. When you do this, the stories in the text frames are merged into a single story. If the text in the first text frame did not end with a carriage return, InDesign will run the text in the second text frame into the last paragraph of the first text frame (see Figure 3-15).

▶ Unlike PageMaker's text blocks, InDesign frames can be linked when they're empty. This means you can easily set up text layouts without having the copy in hand and without resorting to a "dummy text" placeholder.

FIGURE 3-14
Linking Text Frames

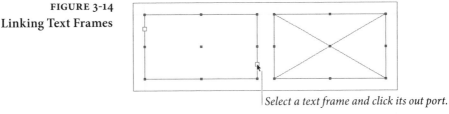

Select a text frame and click its out port.

At this point, you can also create a new text frame by dragging the text place icon. The new frame will be linked to the text frame you clicked.

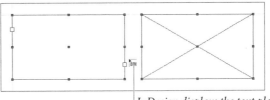

You can also click the in port to load the text place icon.

InDesign displays the text place icon.

Position the text place icon over a frame.

InDesign changes the text place icon to the link icon.

If you've turned on the Show Text Threads option (on the Extras submenu of the View menu), InDesign will display a line linking the out port of one text frame with the in port of another.

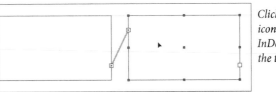

Click the link icon on the frame. InDesign links the two frames.

FIGURE 3-15
Linking Stories

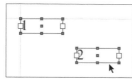

Two unlinked text frames.

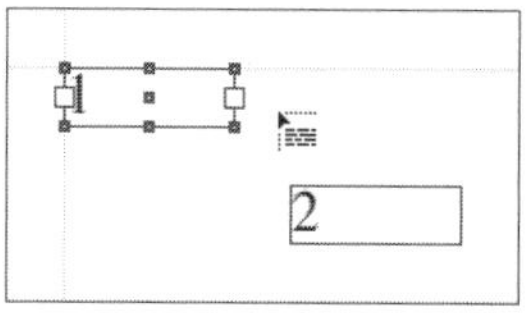

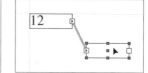

Click the out port of one of the frames to load the text place icon.

If the first frame did not end with a carriage return, InDesign runs the text from the first paragraph of the second frame into the last paragraph of the first frame.

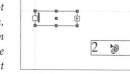

Click the text place icon on the other frame.

InDesign links the two frames.

▶ The port you click (the in port or the out port) sets the position of the link in the sequence of linked text frames making up the story. If you click the out port, the text frame you link to will come after the current text frame. If you click the in port and then another frame, this second frame will come earlier in the story (see Figure 3-16).

▶ When you click the out port of a text frame that contains more text than it can display (that is, an out port that displays the "+" symbol), the additional text will flow into the next text frame in the story (see Figure 3-17).

▶ You don't have to link to another text frame—you can also create a link to a graphic frame or a frame whose content type has been set to "None."

▶ To create a new text frame that's linked to an existing text frame, click the in port or out port of the existing frame and then drag the text place icon.

Link icon   *Unlink icon*

▶ As you link and unlink text, InDesign changes the appearance of the cursor to give you a clue about what you're doing or are about to do.

▶ What if you have a "loaded" text place cursor and then realize that you need to scroll, or turn to another page? No problem—you can scroll, zoom, turn pages, create or modify ruler guides, and create new pages.

▶ To "unload" the text place cursor (disable it, like if you change your mind midstream), click on any tool in the Toolbox (or just press a key to switch tools, like "V" for the Selection tool).

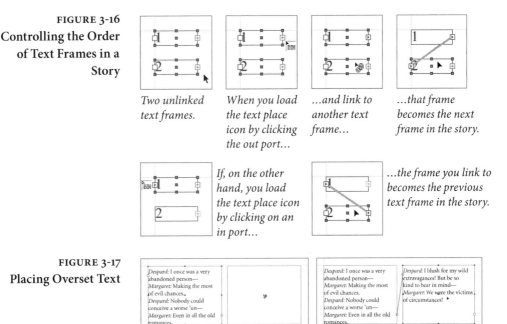

FIGURE 3-16
Controlling the Order of Text Frames in a Story

Two unlinked text frames.

When you load the text place icon by clicking the out port…

…and link to another text frame…

…that frame becomes the next frame in the story.

If, on the other hand, you load the text place icon by clicking on an in port…

…the frame you link to becomes the previous text frame in the story.

FIGURE 3-17
Placing Overset Text

This text frame contains overset text. When you link it to another text frame…

…InDesign places the overset text in the following text frame (in this example, all of the text in the story has been placed).

Unlinking Text Frames

To break a link between text frames, double-click the in port or out port on either side of the link (see Figure 3-18). When you break a link between text frames that have text content, the text usually becomes overset text.

Alternatively, you can click the out port of one frame and then click the next frame in the thread (see Figure 3-19). When you move the text place icon over the next frame, InDesign displays the Unlink Text icon (which is subtly different than the Link Text icon). Click the Unlink Text icon on the frame, and InDesign breaks the link.

When you break a link in the middle of multiple frames, the links before and after the break remain. If boxes A, B, C, and D are linked together, and you break the link between B and C, then C and D will stay linked together (even though there won't be any text in them).

Cutting and Pasting Text Frames

What happens to text frame links when you delete or cut a linked text frame or series of linked text frames? First, InDesign does not delete any text in the story—unless you select all of the frames in the story and delete them. Otherwise, InDesign flows the text contained by the frames you've deleted into the remaining frames in the story. If you want to delete text, you have to select it using the Type tool first. For more on selecting text, see "Editing Text," later in this chapter.

FIGURE 3-18
FIGURE 3-18
Unlinking Text Frames

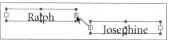

Select a text frame and double-click the out port (or in port).

InDesign breaks the link at the point at which you clicked.

FIGURE 3-19
Another Method

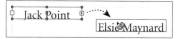

Select a text frame then click the out port (or in port). InDesign displays a text place icon.

Move the text place icon over the next (or previous, if you clicked an in port) text frame. InDesign displays the unlink icon.

InDesign breaks the link between the two text frames.

When you cut or copy linked text frames, then paste, InDesign maintains the links between the duplicated frames—but not between the duplicates and the original frames or any other frames (see Figure 3-20). The copies of the frames contain the same text as the originals.

A side effect of this behavior is that you can copy text frames from a story that are not linked to each other, and, when you paste, the text frames will be linked. This can come in handy when you're trying to split a story that is in multiple frames (see in Figure 3-21).

Adding a New Frame to a Story

It's easy to add a text frame in the middle of a sequence of linked text frames. Just follow these steps (see Figure 3-22).

1. Use the Selection tool to click the out port at the point in the story at which you want to add the new frame.

2. Drag the text place icon to create a new text frame, or click an existing, empty, unlinked frame.

InDesign only lets you link to empty and unlinked frames unless you're adding frames to the beginning or end of your thread.

Flowing Text

When you select Place from the File menu (and then choose a text file), or use the Selection tool to click the in port or out port of a text frame, your cursor changes to the text place icon. You can drag the text place icon to create a text frame, or you can click on an existing frame to flow text into it. Flowing text is all about the care, maintenance, and feeding of the text place icon (see Table 3-1 for more on text place icons).

FIGURE 3-20
Cutting and Pasting Linked Frames

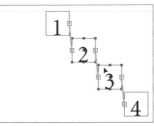

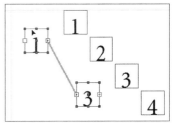

In this example, we've selected the second and third text frames in a story. When we copy and paste...

...InDesign retains the link between the two copied frames.

FIGURE 3-21
More About Copying and Pasting Linked Frames

In this example, we've selected the first and third text frames in a story. When we copy and paste...

...the duplicate frames are linked— even though the frames were not directly connected to each other.

FIGURE 3-22
Adding a New Frame to a Story

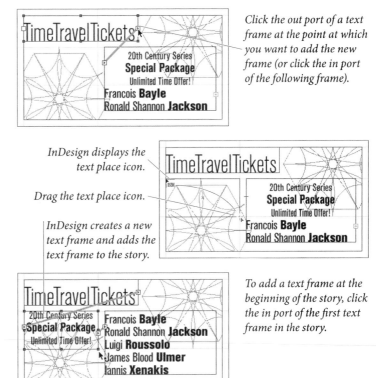

Click the out port of a text frame at the point at which you want to add the new frame (or click the in port of the following frame).

InDesign displays the text place icon.

Drag the text place icon.

InDesign creates a new text frame and adds the text frame to the story.

To add a text frame at the beginning of the story, click the in port of the first text frame in the story.

TABLE 3-1
Text Place Icons

Icon:	What it means:
[icon]	Manual text flow. Click to flow text into a frame; click in a column to create a frame that's the width of the column, or drag to create a frame.
[icon]	Semi-automatic text flow. InDesign "reloads" the text flow icon after each click or drag.
[icon]	Super Autoflow text flow. Click to place all of the text in the story (InDesign adds pages as necessary).
[icon]	Automatic text flow. InDesign flows the story to all empty pages, but does not add pages.
[icons]	The text flow icon is above a guide or grid "snap" point.
[icons]	The text flow icon is above a frame; clicking will place the text in the frame.

The text place icon can also show a preview of the text you're about to place. For more on this, see the description of the Show Thumbnails on Place option in the Interface panel of the Preferences dialog box in Chapter 1, "Workspace."

Once you've "loaded" the text place icon, you can use one of InDesign's four text flow methods: Manual text flow, Semi-automatic text flow, Automatic text flow, or Super Autoflow. These determine what happens when you click or drag the text place icon. Here's the lowdown.

▶ **Manual text flow.** By default, InDesign uses the manual text flow method. When you click the text place icon on your page, or drag the text place icon, InDesign creates a new text frame and flows the text into it (see Figure 3-23). When you click the text place icon in between column guides, the width of the text frame is determined by the width of the column you clicked in; the height of the frame is the distance from the point at which you clicked the text place icon to the bottom of the column (see Figure 3-24). In a one-column document, the text frame reaches from the page's left to right margins. InDesign then flows the text into the new text frame. When you click the text place icon on an existing text frame or series of linked text frames, InDesign flows the text into the frame or frames. In either case, once InDesign is done flowing the text, the text place icon disappears and you're back to whatever tool you had selected before you loaded the text place icon. To continue placing text, click the out port to reload the text place icon.

FIGURE 3-23
Manual Text Flow

Load the text place icon (by placing a text file or clicking the in port or out port of any text frame).

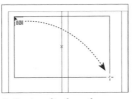

InDesign displays the manual text flow icon. Drag the icon.

InDesign flows text into the area you defined by dragging.

FIGURE 3-24
Manual Text Flow and Column Guides

Load the text place icon. InDesign displays the manual text flow icon.

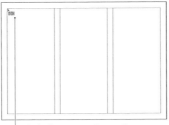

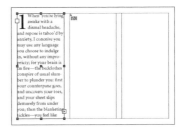

Click the manual text flow icon in a column.

InDesign flows the text into the column. Click the out port to reload and place more text.

▶ **Semi-automatic text flow.** Semi-automatic text flow is almost exactly like manual text flow—the difference is that InDesign reloads the text place icon. The advantage? You don't have to click the out port of a text frame to reload the text place icon. To turn on semi-automatic text flow, hold down Option/Alt when the text place icon is visible. InDesign displays the semi-automatic text place icon (see Figure 3-25).

▶ **Automatic text flow.** Automatic text flow—which you get if you hold down both Option/Alt and Shift—places as much text in the story as can fit on the pages in your document (the cursor looks like a solid down arrow). InDesign adds text frames as necessary on each subsequent column or page (and links them together, of course), but it won't add additional pages to your document.

▶ **Super Autoflow.** Hold down Shift, and the text place icon turns into the autoflow icon. Click the autoflow icon, and InDesign places all of the text, creating new frames and pages as necessary (see Figure 3-26). When you click the autoflow icon in a text frame or series of linked text frames, InDesign duplicates that frame (or frames) on any new pages it creates, automatically links the frames, and places the text in the frames. When you click the autoflow icon in a column, InDesign creates a new text frame in each column (adding pages until it has placed all of the text in the story).

FIGURE 3-25
Semi-Automatic
Text Flow

Load the text place icon.
InDesign displays the
manual text flow icon.

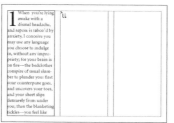

Hold down Option/Alt to switch to
the semi-automatic text flow icon,
then click the icon in a column.

InDesign flows the text into the
column, then automatically reloads
the text place icon.

Click the semi-automatic text flow
icon in the next column. InDesign
creates a new text frame and links it
to the previous text frame.

Repeat this process until you've
placed all of the columns of text you
want to place.

FIGURE 3-26
Super Autoflow

Load the text place icon.
InDesign displays the
manual text flow icon.

Hold down Shift to switch to the
Super Autoflow text flow icon, then
click the icon in a column.

InDesign flows the text into the
available columns or text frames,
and continues adding new text
frames and pages until there's no
more text left to place.

If you want InDesign to add text frames and/or pages as you type, use the options in the Smart Text Reflow section of the Type panel of the Preferences dialog box, as described in Chapter 1, "Workspace."

Shrinking Text Frames

When you want to shrink a text frame so that it's just big enough to fit its content (for a photo caption, for example), you've got a number of different methods you can call on. First, you can press Command-Option-C/Ctrl-Alt-C, to fit the frame to its content. But you can also double-click any of the text frame's edges with the Selection tool to shrink the text frame in a specific dimension (see Figure 3-27).

FIGURE 3-27
Shrinking Text Frames

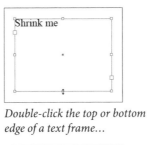

Double-click the top or bottom edge of a text frame...

...and InDesign shrinks the frame vertically.

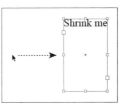

Double-click the left or right edge of a text frame...

...and InDesign shrinks the frame horizontally.

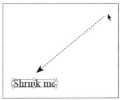

Double-click one of the corners of the text frame...

...and InDesign shrinks the frame horizontally and vertically.

Entering Text

The simplest way to get text into the text frames in your InDesign publications is to type it. To do this, create a text frame by dragging the Type tool, or select the Type tool and click in a frame (again, it doesn't have to be a text frame). You can also double-click with either the Selection tool or the Direct Selection tool to automatically switch to the Type tool. All these methods place a blinking text cursor (or "text insertion point") inside the text frame. Type, and the characters you type will appear in the text frame.

Inserting Special Characters

We don't know about you, but we're not getting any younger, and we have trouble remembering exactly which keys to press to produce certain special characters. If you're like us, you'll appreciate the list of common character shortcuts in Table 3-2. InDesign lists these shortcuts in the Insert Special Character, Insert Break Character, and Insert White Space submenus (under the Type menu, or in the Context menu, see Figure 3-28).

Special character:	What you press:
Bullet (•)	Option-8/Alt-8
Column break	Keypad Enter
Copyright symbol (©)	Option-G/Alt-G
Discretionary hyphen	Command-Shift--/Ctrl-Shift--
Ellipsis (…)	Option-;/Alt-;
Em dash (—)	Option-Shift--/Alt-Shift--
Em space	Command-Shift-M/Ctrl-Shift-M
En dash (–)	Option--/Alt--
En space	Command-Shift-N/Ctrl-Shift-N
Even page break	undefined
Figure space	undefined
Flush space	undefined
Frame break	Shift-Keypad Enter
Hair space	undefined*
Indent to here	Command-\/Ctrl-\
Next page number	Command-Option-Shift-] Ctrl-Alt-Shift-]
Non-breaking hyphen	Command-Option--/Ctrl-Alt--
Non-breaking space	Command-Option-X/Ctrl-Alt-X
Odd page break	undefined*
Page break	Command-Keypad Enter Ctrl-Keypad Enter
Page number	Command-Option-Shift-N Ctrl-Alt-Shift-N
Paragraph symbol (¶)	Option-7/Alt-7
Previous page number	Command-Option-Shift-[Ctrl-Alt-Shift-[
Punctuation space	undefined
Trademark (™)	undefined
Left double quote (")	Option-[/Alt-[
Left single quote (')	Option-]/Alt-]
Right double quote (")	Option-Shift-[/Alt-Shift-[
Right single quote (')	Option-Shift-]/Shift-Alt-]
Straight single quote	Control-'/Alt-'
Straight double quote	Control-Shift-'/Ctrl-Alt-'
Section symbol (§)	Option-6/Alt-6
Thin space	Command-Option-Shift-M Ctrl-Alt-Shift-M
Registered trademark (®)	Option-R/Alt-R

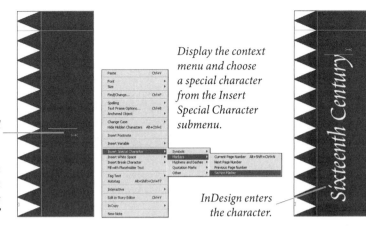

FIGURE 3-28
Entering Special Characters Using the Context Menu

Click the Type tool in a text frame.

In this example, the section marker text (in the Section Options dialog box) is "Sixteenth Century."

Display the context menu and choose a special character from the Insert Special Character submenu.

InDesign enters the character.

All of the keyboard shortcuts for these special characters can be redefined and/or added (for those characters lacking a default keyboard shortcut) by selecting Keyboard Shortcuts from the Edit menu and then navigating to the Type Menu section.

Inserting Glyphs

We're sometimes stumped when it's time to type a dagger (†) or a circumflex (ˆ). And we often spend time hunting through the Character panel (on the Mac OS) or Character Map (in Windows) looking for the right character in a symbol font (such as Zapf Dingbats).

If you also have this problem, you'll love the Glyphs panel. A "glyph" is the term for a specific shape of a character. To open this panel, choose Glyphs from the Type menu (see Figure 3-29).

The Glyphs panel is easy to use: while the text cursor is in a text frame, choose the font, then double-click a character from the list of characters in the Glyphs panel. InDesign inserts the character at the location of the cursor.

Now here's the cool part: If a character can be found inside a font, you can use it—even if the character is outside the range of characters supported by your system. For instance, many fonts have a ½ character, but there's no way to type it on the Mac OS. This seems like a silly feature—after all, why would fonts contain characters that would be inaccessible to any other program? We don't know, mate, but they do. Fonts have all kinds of foreign-language characters, weird punctuation, and even ornaments that simply can't be used in QuarkXPress or other programs. But the Glyphs panel makes it easy to get to them. Characters such as "fi" and "fl" ligatures, which aren't part of the Windows character set, suddenly become available (without switching to an "expert" font). It's well worth your time to trawl through your fonts just to see if there's anything you can use that you haven't been using.

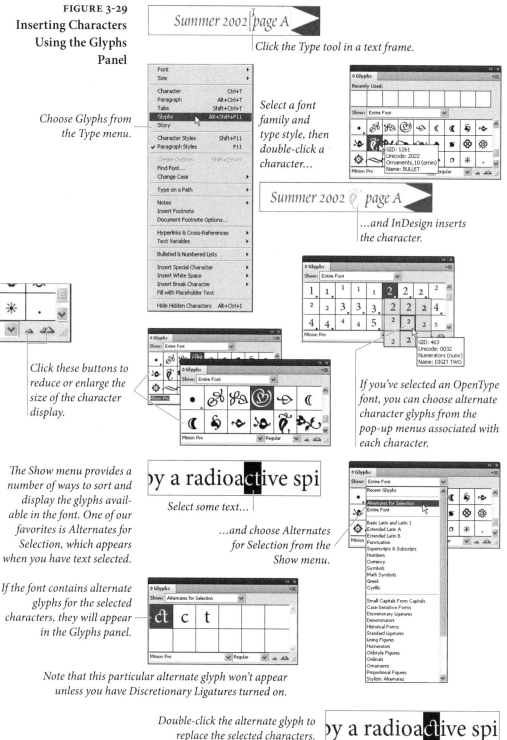

FIGURE 3-29
**Inserting Characters
Using the Glyphs
Panel**

Click the Type tool in a text frame.

*Choose Glyphs from
the Type menu.*

*Select a font
family and
type style, then
double-click a
character...*

*...and InDesign inserts
the character.*

*Click these buttons to
reduce or enlarge the
size of the character
display.*

*If you've selected an OpenType
font, you can choose alternate
character glyphs from the
pop-up menus associated with
each character.*

*The Show menu provides a
number of ways to sort and
display the glyphs avail-
able in the font. One of our
favorites is Alternates for
Selection, which appears
when you have text selected.*

Select some text...

*...and choose Alternates
for Selection from the
Show menu.*

*If the font contains alternate
glyphs for the selected
characters, they will appear
in the Glyphs panel.*

*Note that this particular alternate glyph won't appear
unless you have Discretionary Ligatures turned on.*

*Double-click the alternate glyph to
replace the selected characters.*

Recently used glyphs. The Glyphs panel keeps track of the glyphs you've inserted, and displays them in the Recently Used section of the panel. If you don't see this section, choose Show Options from the Glyphs panel menu. To clear the list, choose Recently Used from the Delete Glyph Set submenu of the Glyphs panel menu.

Missing characters. You've got to keep in mind that just because one font has a particular glyph doesn't mean that another font will. When you use the Glyphs panel, InDesign remembers the Unicode value for that glyph. When you change fonts, the program tries to find the same Unicode value in the new font. If the font designer didn't include that glyph, or assigned a different Unicode value, InDesign displays the dreaded pink highlight instead of the glyph.

Glyph Sets. You've spent hours looking, and you've finally found the perfect ornament characters for your publication. Unfortunately, they're in three different fonts. Wouldn't it be great if you could save those three characters in a special place to access them later? That's where glyph sets come in. To make a new glyph set to store your characters, choose (surprise!) New Glyph Set from the Glyphs panel menu (see Figure 3-30). Then, the next time you find a character you love, click it and choose your set from the Add to Glyph submenu (in the panel menu). You can mix and match fonts in a set, and have as many different sets as you want.

InDesign lists your glyph sets in the View Glyph Set submenu of the Glyphs panel menu; once you select a set, you can insert a glyph into the current text frame by double-clicking it.

By default, glyphs in a set remember what font they came from. So, when you insert a glyph from a set, InDesign assigns the proper font. However, sometimes you want to insert a character in the current font of the selected text. You might want to include the one-half (½) symbol in your set, but want it to appear in the current font. To do this, select the name of the glyph set from the Edit Glyph Set submenu of the panel menu, select the character, and turn off the Remember Font with Glyph checkbox. InDesign indicates that this character can be in any font with a little "u" symbol in the panel.

Dummy Text   The client wants to see the new layout. But the writer won't give you the text. You're stuck—a layout looks, so, well, incomplete without text. And the client, a singularly humorless individual, cannot be appeased by whatever snatches of text from Gilbert & Sullivan, Brecht, or Edgar Rice Burroughs come easily to mind. What you need is something that looks like text, but isn't really text at all.

FIGURE 3-30
Glyph Sets

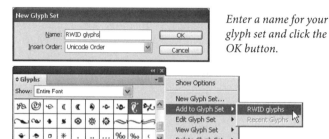

To create a glyph set, choose New Glyph Set from the Glyphs panel menu.

Enter a name for your glyph set and click the OK button.

To add a character to a glyph set, select the character and then choose the glyph set from the Add to Glyph set submenu of the Glyphs panel menu. A glyph set can contain characters from multiple fonts.

To display the glyph set in the Glyphs panel, choose the glyph set's name from the View Glyph Set submenu.

To make changes to the glyph set, select the glyph set name from the Edit Glyph Set submenu of the Glyphs panel menu. InDesign displays the Edit Glyph Set dialog box.

To associate a specific glyph with a specific font, select the glyph and check this option (and choose the appropriate font and font style, if necessary).

Dummy text is a meaningless stream of fake Latin text that *looks* very much like real text. It's just the thing you need to survive your meeting and get that approval your business depends on.

InDesign makes it easy to add dummy text to a text frame—select the text frame using the Selection tool, or click the Type tool in a text frame and choose Fill with Placeholder Text from the context menu (or from the Type menu). InDesign fills the text frame with dummy text (see Figure 3-31). InDesign's dummy text is a random compilation of words taken from the Lorum Ipsum text that many designers have used over the years. If you're using the Mac OS, and turn on Caps Lock as you select Fill with Placeholder Text, InDesign will, instead, fill the box with random words from an oration by Cicero.

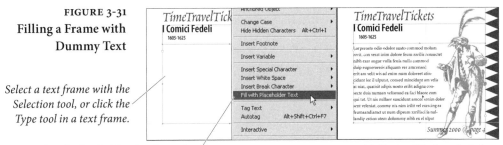

FIGURE 3-31

Filling a Frame with Dummy Text

Select a text frame with the Selection tool, or click the Type tool in a text frame.

Choose Fill with Placeholder Text from the context menu (or from the Type menu)...

...and InDesign fills the selected frame with dummy text.

Even better: If you save a text file in the InDesign folder with the name "Placeholder.txt" the program will use that text instead of the fake Latin. This probably isn't actually useful, but it's fun.

Text Variables

Believe it or not, we've met a number of graphic designers who are scared of the word "variable." It's not that frightening—a variable is simply something that can change. Text variables in InDesign provide a way for you to insert text that can change depending on various factors, such as times, dates, and page references. In a way, the automatic page number special character is a sort of text variable, because it changes depending on the page on which it appears. You're not scared of the automatic page number marker, are you?

It's important to understand the difference between text variables and text variable instances. A text variable is the definition of the variable itself; a text variable instance is the marker in the text that inserts the content of the text variable. It's entirely possible to have a text variable in a document for which no text variable instance exists in the layout (though there's really no reason to).

Text variables come in a variety of flavors, and are subject to a variety of limitations. First, let's take a look at the text variable types InDesign supports.

▶ **Chapter Number.** A text variable that refers to the number of the current chapter (chapter numbering is defined by the book containing the document—for more on books, see Chapter 8, "Long Documents").

▶ **Creation Date.** A text variable that refers to the date and time you created the document (not when you made the variable).

▶ **Custom Text.** A string of any text you can type.

▶ **File Name.** The name of the document.

▶ **Last Page Number.** The number of the last page in the file.

▶ **Metadata Caption.** The metadata of the adjoining (or grouped) image is displayed in the text frame.

▶ **Modification Date.** The date and time of the last modification made to the document.

▶ **Output Date.** The date and time the document was printed.

▶ **Running Header (Character Style).** Refers to the first or last instance of text on the page containing the text variable instance that has been formatted using a specified character style.

▶ **Running Header (Paragraph Style).** Refers to the first or last paragraph on the page containing the text variable instance that has been formatted using a specified paragraph style.

If you work on books, as we do, you're probably curious about using text variables for cross references—this is where the "limitations" come in. You can't refer to an arbitrary string of text using text references, which means that you can't use them for cross references to your figure numbers, or to other sections of a book.

Worse, in some ways, is that text variables are considered as a single character for purposes of text composition. This means that InDesign will not enter a line break inside a text variable instance. This was already true for the composition of section markers and automatic page numbers, but it can be even more of a problem with text variables because they usually more text (see Figure 3-32).

Don't get us wrong—text variables are a great thing. But we point out the problems because we think it's important that you understand how they work. *Before* you're on a deadline.

FIGURE 3-32
Text Variables
and Composition

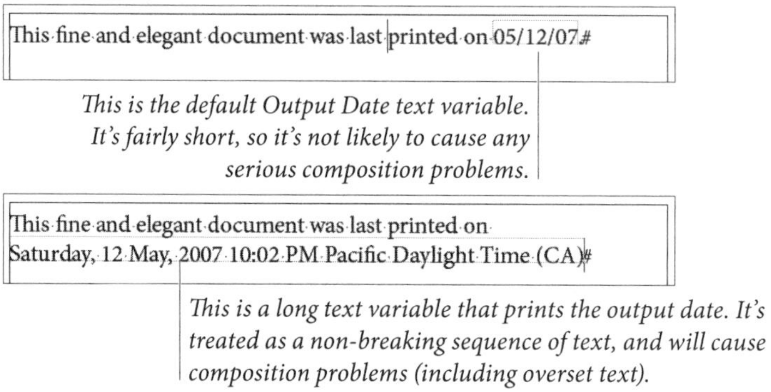

This fine and elegant document was last printed on 05/12/07.#

This is the default Output Date text variable. It's fairly short, so it's not likely to cause any serious composition problems.

This fine and elegant document was last printed on
Saturday, 12 May, 2007 10:02 PM Pacific Daylight Time (CA)#

This is a long text variable that prints the output date. It's treated as a non-breaking sequence of text, and will cause composition problems (including overset text).

Showing Text Variable Instances

When you want to see when text is a text variable instance, choose Show Hidden Characters from the Type menu. InDesign will display a (very pale!) box around each text variable instance in the text.

Text Variable Options

Each type of variable has its own options. Most of the variable types give you the option of adding text before and/or after each variable instance, but almost all of them provide other options, see Table 3-3.

Inserting a Text Variable

Before we get into the details of how to create your own variables, let's look at how you can insert a variable at the current cursor location. Assuming that you have an active text insertion point in a text frame or story, choose the name of the text variable from the Insert Variable submenu of the Context menu (see Figure 3-33) or from the Insert Variable submenu of the Text Variables submenu of the Type menu. InDesign adds the text variable instance.

Creating a Text Variable

The preset text variables are all well and good, but the real fun lies in defining your own. Maybe you just want a more formal time and date format, or maybe you want to enter a custom text variable—either way, it's easy, and the range of possible text variables is vast (even within the limitations we mentioned earlier).

To create a text variable, follow these steps (see Figure 3-34).

1. Choose Define from the Text Variables submenu of the Type menu. InDesign displays the Text Variables dialog box.

2. Click the New button. InDesign displays the New Text Variable dialog box. If you had a variable selected when you clicked the New button, the dialog box will be filled in with the default properties of that variable (as though you duplicated it).

3. Enter a name for the text variable in the Name field.

4. Select a text variable type from the Type pop-up menu. The dialog fills in with the options for that variable type.

5. Changes the options to define your new text variable. When the settings look the way you want them to, click the OK button to close the dialog box and return to the Text Variables dialog box.

6. Click the Done button to close the Text Variables dialog box.

Text variables are stored in the current file. If you want to create a text variable that is available in all new documents, define it when no documents are open. When you do this, the variable will appear in each new document you open.

TABLE 3-3 Text Variables

Variable Type	Option	Definition
All Formats (except Custom Text)	Text Before	Text to enter before the text variable.
	Text After	Text to enter after the text variable.
Chapter Number	Numbering Style	Choose Arabic (1, 2, 3), lowercase Roman (i, ii, iii), uppercase Roman (I, II, III), lowercase letters (a, b, c), or uppercase letters (A, B, C).
Custom Text	Text	Enter the text you want to have appear in the text variable instances.
File Name	Include Entire Folder Path	Set this option to true to include the full path to the document file.
	Include File Extension	Set this option to true to include the file extension of the document file.
Last Page Number	Numbering Style	Choose an option such as Arabic (1, 2, 3) or lowercase Roman (i, ii, iii).
	Scope	Choose Section to specify the last page in the section; choose Document for the number of the last page in the document.
Metadata Caption	Metadata	Choose the metadata to display in the caption. These options are similar to those that appear when you choose File > File Info in Photoshop or Illustrator.
Creation Date, Output Date, Modification Date	Date Format	Enter a date format by selecting items from the pop-up menu. You can enter spaces or punctuation between the time/date placeholders. See Table 3-4 for a list of the placeholders (you can type them or choose them from the menu).
Running Header (Character Style), Running Header (Paragraph Style)	Style	The character or paragraph style to use.
	Use	Choose Last on Page to use the last instance of the style on the page; choose First on Page to use the first instance.
	Delete End Punctuation	Remove the punctuation at the end of the text, if any.
	Change Case	Choose a case option for the text that will appear in the text variable instances.

TABLE 3-4
Date Format Shortcuts

Category	Type	Placeholder	Example
Time	Hour (1-12)	h	1
	Hour (01-12)	hh	01
	Hour (1-23)	H	1
	Hour (01-23)	HH	01
	Minute	m	1
	Minute (00)	mm	01
	Second	s	1
	Second (00)	ss	01
	AM/PM	a*	AM
	Time Zone	zzzz	Pacific Daylight Time**
	Time Zone (Short)	z	PDT
Day	Number	d	1
	Number (01)	dd	01
	Name	EEEE	Tuesday
	Name (Short)	E	Tue
Month	Number	M	4
	Number (01)	MM	04
	Name	MMMM	April
	Name (Short)	MMM	Apr
Year	Number	yyyy	2007
	Number (Short)	y	07
	Era	G***	AD
	Era (Long)	GGGG	Anno Domini

* Simply enters "AM" or "PM," does not provide for other capitalization, punctuation, or formatting options.

** On the Mac OS, "(CA)" is appended to this example. We don't know why, as there are plenty of people who live in this time zone who do not live in California. It's vaguely offensive.

*** Simply enters "AD" or, we assume, "BC." Does not provide for other capitalization, punctuation (e.g., "A.D."), or alternative formats (e.g., "CE" or "BCE"). If your system clock is entering dates from an earlier or later era, there's probably something wrong.

FIGURE 3-33
Inserting a
Text Variable

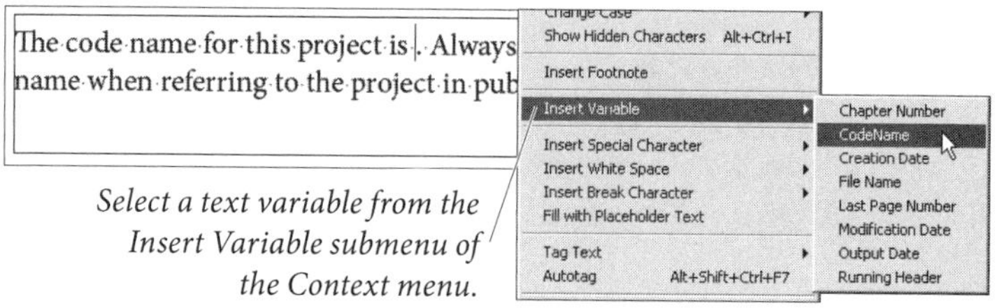

Select a text variable from the
Insert Variable submenu of
the Context menu.

InDesign inserts a text
variable instance in the text.

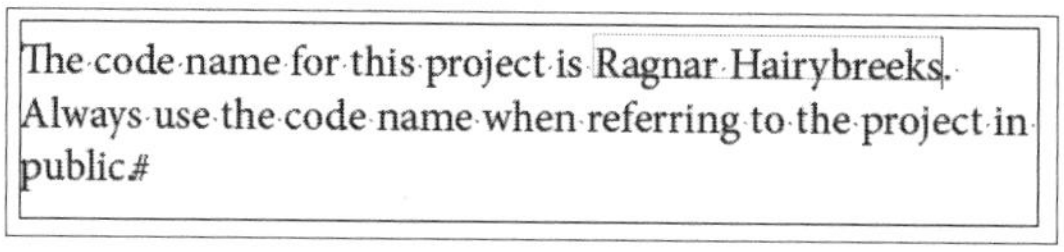

Editing a Text Variable   You can change the definition of a text variable at any time. When
you edit a text variable, all of the text variable instances of that vari-
able will update to reflect the changes you've made. If your variable
instances are inside paragraphs, be prepared for text to reflow and
line endings of composed text to change when you edit a variable.

To change the definition of a text variable, follow these steps.

1. Choose Define from the Text Variables submenu of the Type
   menu. InDesign displays the Text Variables dialog box.

2. Select a text variable and click the Edit button. InDesign opens
   the Edit Text Variable dialog box.

3. Make changes in the Edit Text Variable dialog box. When the
   settings look the way you want them to, click the OK button to
   close the dialog box and return to the Text Variables dialog box.

4. Click the Done button to close the Text Variables dialog box.

At this juncture, we are obligated to point out that you can modify
any of the built-in text variable instances. You could, for example,
change the Chapter Number instance to enter the creation date, as
Ole accidentally did when he first tried to create a new text variable.
We urge you not to do this.

Loading Text Variables   To load text variables from another document, follow these steps (see
Figure 3-35).

1. Choose Define from the Text Variables submenu of the Type
   menu. InDesign displays the Text Variables dialog box.

2. Click the Load button in the Text Variables dialog box. InDesign
   displays the Open A File dialog box.

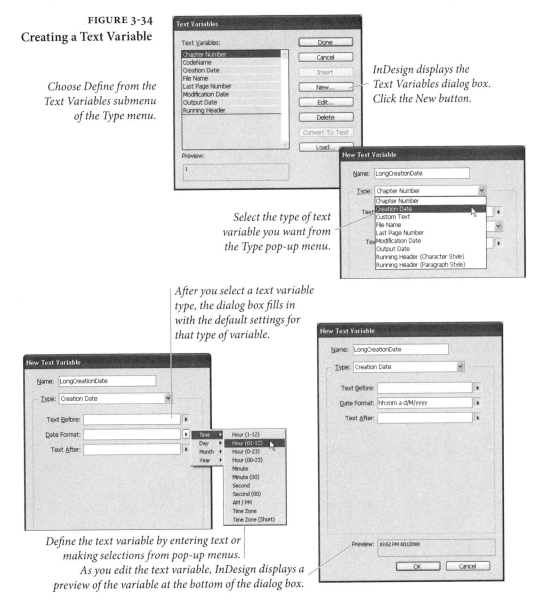

FIGURE 3-34
Creating a Text Variable

Choose Define from the Text Variables submenu of the Type menu.

InDesign displays the Text Variables dialog box. Click the New button.

Select the type of text variable you want from the Type pop-up menu.

After you select a text variable type, the dialog box fills in with the default settings for that type of variable.

Define the text variable by entering text or making selections from pop-up menus. As you edit the text variable, InDesign displays a preview of the variable at the bottom of the dialog box.

3. Locate and select an InDesign document, then click the Open button. InDesign imports the text variables from the selected document into the current document.

4. InDesign will display the Load Text Variables dialog box, which shows a list of the incoming text variables. If the document you've selected contains text variables with the same name as text variables in the current document, you can choose whether to override the definitions of the existing text variables or to

leave them unchanged (by renaming the incoming variable). Click the OK button once you've finished, and InDesign will import the text variables from the selected document.

As usual, if the definition of any text variable used in your text has changed, check for text reflow.

Deleting a Text Variable

To delete a text variable, follow these steps. Note that you can use this process to merge two text variables.

1. Choose Define from the Text Variables submenu of the Type menu. InDesign displays the Text Variables dialog box.

2. Select the text variable you want to delete and click the Delete button. If the variable has been used in the document, InDesign displays the Delete Text Variables dialog box.

3. If you want to replace the text variable with another text variable, select the replacement variable from the Existing Variable pop-up menu. To convert all instances of the text variable to text, select the Text option. To delete all of the text variable instances linked to the selected text variable, select the Nothing option.

FIGURE 3-35
Loading Text Variables

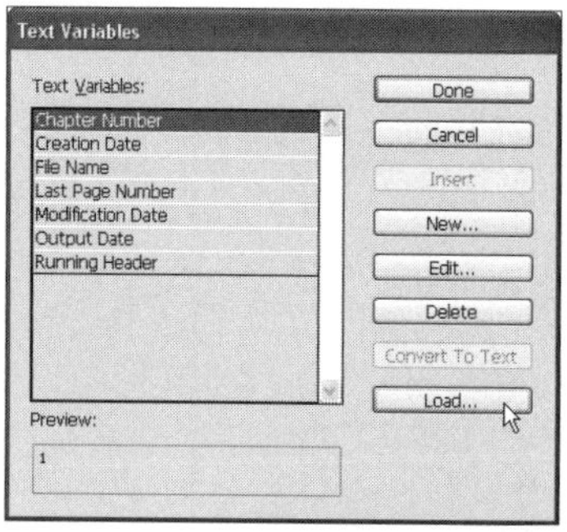

Choose Define from the Text Variables submenu of the Type menu. InDesign displays the Text Variables dialog box.

Click the Load button, then Locate and select the file containing the text variables you want to load.

After you select a file, InDesign displays a list of the text variables in the file. To keep a text variable from being loaded, turn off (uncheck) the option.

If there are text variables in the selected document whose names match the names of text variables in the current document, InDesign shows that there is a conflict.

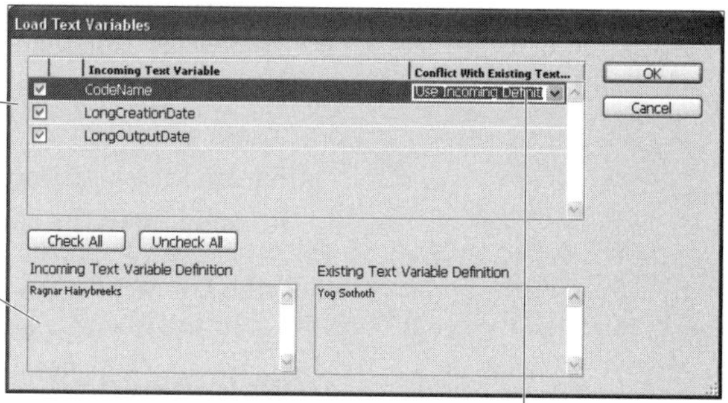

Use the pop-up menu to specify the way you want InDesign to resolve the conflict.

4. Click OK to close the dialog box. InDesign applies the changes you've specified.

You can delete an individual text variable instance as you would delete any other text: Select it and press Delete.

Converting Text Variable Instances to Text

You can, at any time, convert text variable instances to normal text, in effect "freezing" them in their current state. Of course, if the variable instance is inside a paragraph, this will often cause text to reflow, as InDesign is now free to apply its normal text composition rules to the text of the variable. You can choose to convert individual text variable instances to text, or you can convert all of the text variable instances associated with a text variable to text.

To convert an individual text variable instance to text, follow these steps (see Figure 3-36).

1. Select the text variable instance with the Type tool.

2. Choose Convert Variable to Text from the Context menu (or from the Text Variables submenu of the Type menu). InDesign converts the text variable instance to normal text.

To convert all instances of a text variable to text, follow these steps. Note that this does not delete the text variable itself.

1. Choose Define from the Text Variables submenu of the Type menu. InDesign displays the Text Variables dialog box.

2. Select a text variable and click the Convert to Text button. InDesign converts all instances of the text variable to text.

3. Click OK to close the Text Variables dialog box.

FIGURE 3-36
Converting a Text Variable Instance to Text

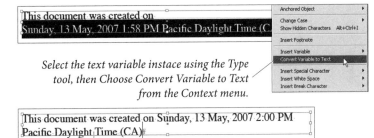

Select the text variable instance using the Type tool, then Choose Convert Variable to Text from the Context menu.

InDesign converts the text variable instance to normal text. This will almost certainly cause text recomposition.

Again, we have to point out that this may cause text recomposition and reflow. Make certain that the line breaks in the document are where they should be after converting the text variable.

You can also use find and change to work with text variable instances—see the section on finding and changing text, later in this chapter, for more information.

Text Variable Examples

In the following sections, we'll present "recipes" that show you how to use text variables for a variety of common page layout tasks.

Creating a Time and Date Stamp. We often like to enter the date and time a file was printed, but we can't always use the built-in time and date stamp from the Print dialog (because the page size is the same as the printer paper size). In the past, Ole has created custom printer's marks files that move the page information up onto the page, but text variables have rendered that bit of esoteric knowledge obsolete. Note, however, that if you plan to omit the time and date stamp from your final printed version, you'll need to make arrangements to suppress the printing of the text variables (such as moving them to a non-printing layer).

To create a text variable that will print the time and date a file was printed, follow these steps.

1. Choose Define from the Text Variables submenu of the Type menu. InDesign displays the Text Variables dialog box.

2. Click the New button.

3. Enter a name for the variable and choose Output Date from the Type pop-up menu.

4. Enter the placeholders and any punctuation or spacing for the date format in the Date Format Field. We use "EEEE, d MMMM, yyyy h:mm a zzzz"—not only does it print the date and time in a civilized format, but it's fun to say aloud.

5. Click OK to close the dialog box, then click Done to close the Text Variables dialog box.

Simple Custom Text. Many people, on first hearing about custom text variables, immediately think that they'd be a good way to enter commonly-used text. Don't do that. There are many other, better ways to accomplish the same end (for example, you can trick autocorrect into entering text for you, as shown in the section on the autocorrect feature, later in this chapter).

Instead, think of custom text variables as a way to enter short pieces of text which might change before your layout is finished. To do this, follow these steps.

1. Choose Define from the Text Variables submenu of the Type menu. InDesign displays the Text Variables dialog box.

2. Click the New button.

3. Enter a name for the variable and choose Custom Text from the Type pop-up menu.

4. Enter the text you want to have appear when you insert the text variable.

5. Click OK to close the dialog box, then click Done to close the Text Variables dialog box.

Page X of Y. Ever wonder why so many financial and legal documents use a page numbering scheme that tells you how many pages there are in the document? For some documents, the simple knowledge that *there is an end* is required to maintain one's sanity.

If, for whatever reason, you need to extend this sort of reassurance to the reader, it's easy to do using text variables. Just enter an automatic page number special character, the text "to," and insert the predefined Last Page Number text variable (see Figure 3-37).

FIGURE 3-37
Creating a Page X of Y Running Header

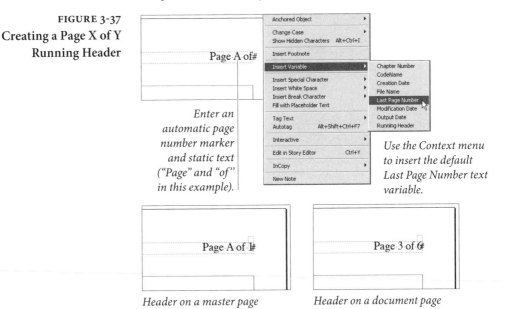

Enter an automatic page number marker and static text ("Page" and "of" in this example).

Use the Context menu to insert the default Last Page Number text variable.

Header on a master page   Header on a document page

Why didn't we enter the "to" as part of the text variable? It's because we're following a general rule of keeping text inserted by text variables to a minimum to avoid potential composition problems. No, you can't specify the last page of a multi-document book.

Running Headers. Many documents feature a layout in which the text of key paragraphs—usually, headings of a given level—appears in the header or footer of each page. Note that this text could also appear in a footer, in a tab on the side of the page, or, really, anywhere on the page. There's nothing special about the text variable type that limits its use to text frames at the top of the page. That said, InDesign refers to this text variable type as a "header," so we will, too.

To do this, you create a text variable, then insert that text variable in text on the page or on a master page. Follow these steps (see Figure 3-38).

1. Choose Define from the Text Variables submenu of the Type menu. InDesign displays the Text Variables dialog box.

2. Click the New button.

3. Enter a name for the variable and choose Running Header (Paragraph Style) or Running Header (Character Style) from the Type pop-up menu.

4. Select the style you want to use from the Style pop-up menu.

5. Choose Last on Page or First on Page from the Use pop-up menu.

6. Set up the controls in the Options section of the dialog box as necessary. For example, you'll almost always want to turn on the Delete End Punctuation option.

7. Click OK to close the dialog box, then click Done.

8. Insert the text variable in text using the Insert Variable submenu of the Context menu.

In some layouts, you might need to create a pair of text variables. In a dictionary-style layout, for example, the left hand page header usually contains the first instance of text in a given style on the page, while the right hand page contains the last instance of the style (see Figure 3-39). If the right hand page is the first page in a section, however, it typically uses the first instance of the specified style (not the last, as would normally be the case for a right hand page). You can change the header of the page manually, or you can create a special master page to accomplish the same task.

FIGURE 3-38
Creating a Running Header Using Text Variables

In this example, we created two text variables using the Running Header (Paragraph Style) variable type. We then inserted text variable instances in text frames on the master spread.

InDesign uses the text from the first or last instance of the specified paragraph style in the header on each document page.

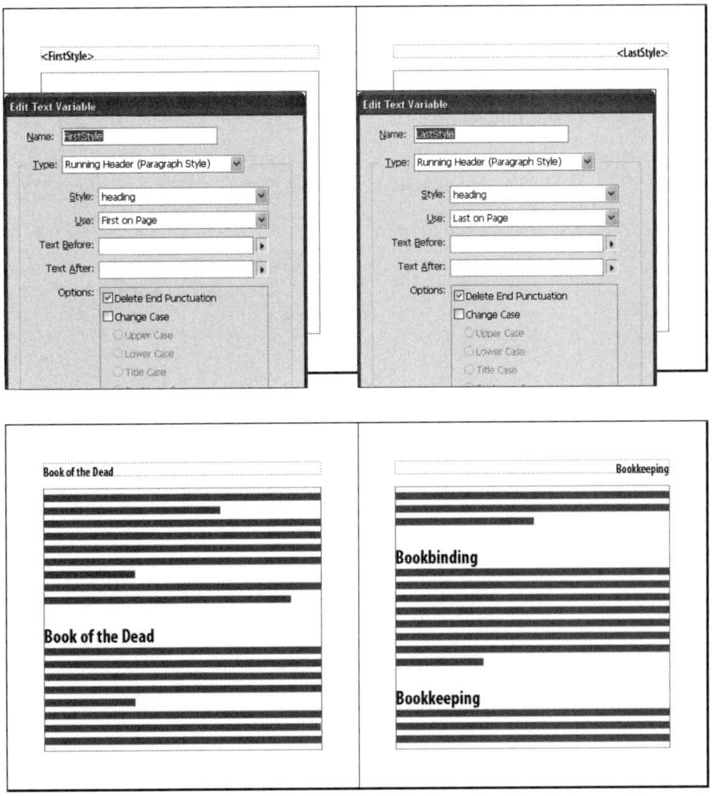

When a page does not contain text formatted with the specified style, the variable in the header repeats the text from the previous instance of the same text variable. However, InDesign will not carry over the last instance of a given style when another instance of the same style appears on the page (see Figure 3-40). If this is the style of running heading your document calls for, you may have to adjust some pages manually.

Phone book Style Running Header. Another use for a running header is to show the range of a certain type of paragraph style on a given page. In a telephone directory or dictionary, for example, the page headers will show you the alphabetical range of names or topics shown on the page. Ole, for example, proudly shares a phone book page containing family names from "Kustyukov" to "Kwok."

To set up this type of running header, you'll need to create two text variables: one for the first instance of a given paragraph or character style on a page, another for the last instance of the same style. Then you create a page header that contains instances of both text variables, as shown in Figure 3-41.

FIGURE 3-39
**Dealing with
Special Cases in
Running Headers**

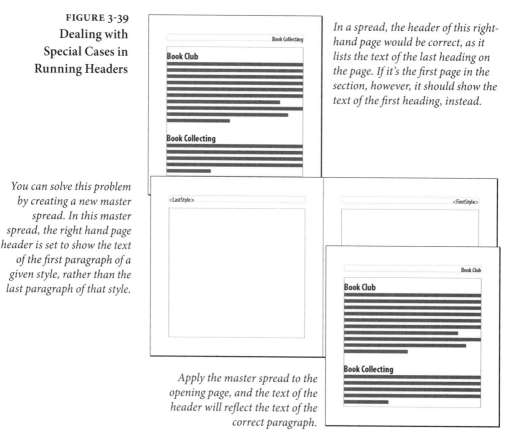

In a spread, the header of this right-hand page would be correct, as it lists the text of the last heading on the page. If it's the first page in the section, however, it should show the text of the first heading, instead.

You can solve this problem by creating a new master spread. In this master spread, the right hand page header is set to show the text of the first paragraph of a given style, rather than the last paragraph of that style.

Apply the master spread to the opening page, and the text of the header will reflect the text of the correct paragraph.

Metadata Caption. A caption variable displays metadata of an image. We talk about metadata elsewhere, but as a quick reminder, you can attach information such as name, creation date, and description for any image or document. This information is called metadata. You can take advantage of image metadata by creating a caption variable that displays whatever metadata you want.

Here's how it works. When the text frame containing the caption variable is placed next to or grouped with an image, the variable displays the metadata of that image. When you create a caption variable, you determine which image metadata is displayed. The most common types of metadata are attributes like Name and Description, but you can dig deeper and display Focal Length or ICC Profile.

For choosing which metadata to display, keep InDesign's limitation in mind when it comes to displaying variables—variables do not break across lines. So if you create a variable that displays the image's Description metadata, make sure the Description text in your images is short enough to fit within a single line of the caption text frame. Otherwise, the description text will be crammed together on a single

FIGURE 3-40
Problems in
Running Headers

*In many designs, the text of
this header should reflect the
text of the previous heading
style, not the text of the first
or last paragraph of that
style on the page. We have
not found a way to do this
using text variables.*

FIGURE 3-41
Phonebook Style
Running Header

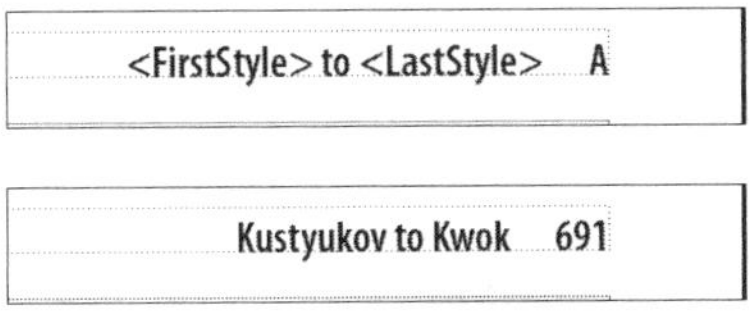

*The header on the master page
contains two text variables and a
page number.*

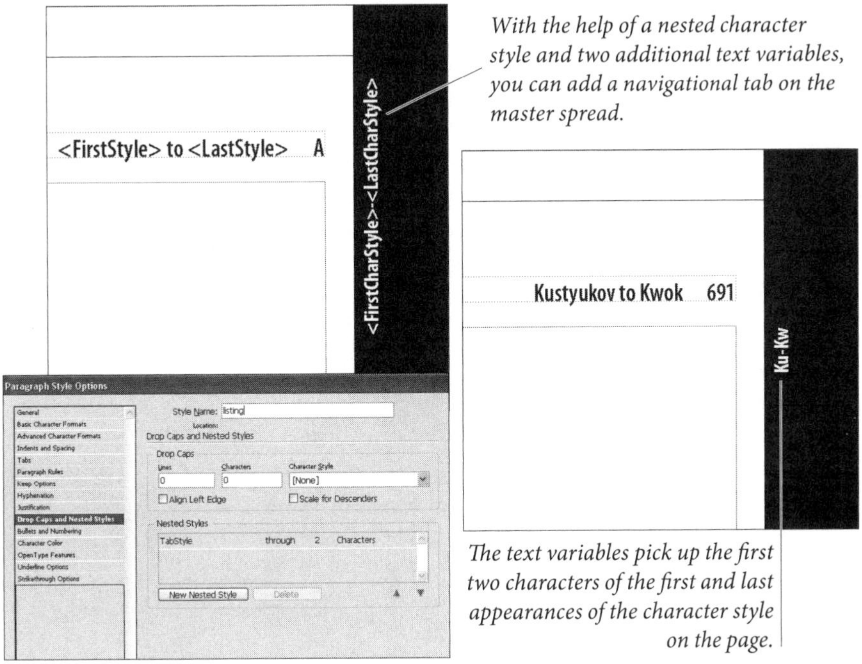

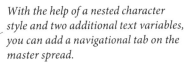

*With the help of a nested character
style and two additional text variables,
you can add a navigational tab on the
master spread.*

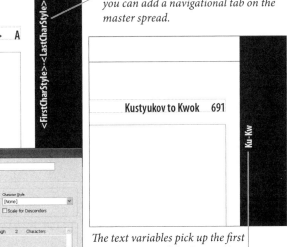

*The text variables pick up the first
two characters of the first and last
appearances of the character style
on the page.*

line. To work around this, you can convert variables into text, but
then you break the connection to the metadata.

1. Choose Define from the Text Variables submenu of the Type
   menu. InDesign displays the Text Variables dialog box (see
   Figure 3-42).

2. Click the New button.

3. Enter a name for the variable and choose Metadata Caption from the Type pop-up menu.

4. Choose the item you want to appear in the variable from the Metadata pop-up menu.

5. Specify the Text Before and the Text After.

   If you want to create a list of running captions in your document, such as Figure 1, Figure 2, and so on, don't do that here. Instead, create a paragraph style that uses a defined list for running captions. See "Applying Numbering" in Chapter 4, "Type."

6. Click OK to create the variable, and then click Done.

7. Insert the caption variable into a text frame, and then move that text frame next to a placed image (or group it with an image).

How do you change the metadata of an image? Open the image in Adobe Bridge, Photoshop, or Illustrator, choose File > File Info, and edit the metadata fields. After you edit the image metadata, remember to update the image using the Links panel.

FIGURE 3-42
Caption Variables

Specify the type of metadata you want to appear in the caption. In this example, we create several variables to use in a caption.

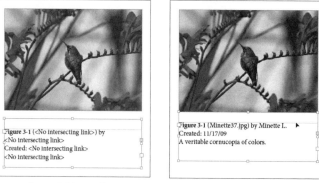

Insert the variables in the caption text frame...

...and then move the text frame next to the image.

For some captions, you want to use several different types of metadata, such as Name, Description, Copyright, and Creation Date: Unfortunately, you can't combine these metadata elements into the same variable. Instead, create a different variable for each.

For more details on working with captions, see "Figure Captions" in Chapter 6, "Text Meets Graphics."

Cross References

Cross references are a type of hyperlink, but we want to make the point that they're incredibly useful for print publishing. We think that they're great for entering text, which is why we'll talk about them in this chapter, rather than in Chapter 13, "Interactive Documents."

Cross references give you a way to insert a marker (which Adobe calls the "source cross reference") in text that refers to another piece of text (which Adobe calls the "destination text"). We'll refer to these two things as the "marker" and "destination," respectively. When the destination changes, the marker can change.

This is a feature that is particularly dear to our tiny hearts, because it means that we can finally number the figures in this book automatically, rather than doing it manually.

A cross reference is really made up of four parts: the marker and destination we've already mentioned, a cross reference format, which defines the appearance of the text in the marker, and the text of the destination itself. The text of the destination determines a great deal about the way you'll construct all of the parts of the cross reference.

Cross reference markers can refer to two types of destinations: the text of a paragraph, or a text anchor. Because text anchors refer to hyperlink text destinations, we'll discuss them later. In this section, we'll talk about using paragraphs as our cross reference destination.

Finally, creating a cross reference pretty much requires that the document use paragraph styles. Again, use paragraph styles.

Creating a Cross Reference

To create a cross reference, follow these steps (see Figure 3-43).

1. Move the text cursor to the location at which you want to insert the cross reference marker (or select text you want to replace with the marker).

2. Choose Insert Cross Reference from the Hyperlinks and Cross References submenu of the Type menu. InDesign displays the New Cross Reference dialog box.

FIGURE 3-43
**Creating a
Cross Reference**

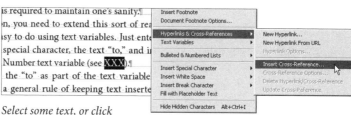

*Select some text, or click
a text cursor in text...*

*...then choose Insert Cross Reference
from the Hyperlinks and Cross References
submenu of the Type menu.*

*Or click the Insert Cross
Reference icon on the
Hyperlinks panel.*

*Select a paragraph
style in this list.*

Choose Paragraph.

Select a document.

*Select a specific
paragraph in this
list (what you see
is the text of the
paragraph).*

*Select a cross
reference format.*

*Click this icon
to create or edit
a cross reference
format.*

*Use the controls in the
Appearance section to
change the format of the
hyperlink, if necessary.*

*InDesign adds the cross
reference marker at the
location of the selection.*

3. Choose Paragraph from the Link To pop-up menu if it's not
   already selected. If the destination paragraph is in another
   document, select the (open) document containing the paragraph
   from the Document pop-up menu.

4. Use the two scrolling lists in the Destination section to set the
   destination paragraph. The list on the left shows the paragraph
   styles in the document; the list on the right displays the text of
   each paragraph in a particular style.

5. Select the cross reference format you want to use from the Format pop-up menu. To create a new format, click the pencil icon to the right of the pop-up menu (see "Creating or Editing a Cross Reference Format," below).

6. The controls in the Appearance section define the format of the hyperlink associated with the cross reference. For most cross references in print publications, we think you'll probably want to select Invisible Rectangle from the Type pop-up menu and leave it at that. For more on hyperlink appearances, see Chapter 13, "Interactive Documents."

7. Click the OK button to insert the cross reference marker.

Creating or Editing a Cross Reference Format

Cross reference formats define the appearance of the marker, including both the text of the marker and the formatting applied to it. Just as applying a character or paragraph style creates a link between the style and the text, applying a cross reference format creates a link between the marker and the cross reference format. If you change the cross reference format, the corresponding markers will change.

Before you create a cross reference format of your own, it's a good idea to look through the existing ones—you might find exactly what you need—and you'll get an idea of how to construct your own.

To create a new cross reference format, follow these steps (see Figure 3-44).

1. Choose Define Cross Reference Formats from the Hyperlinks panel menu (display the panel if it's not already visible). If you're looking at the New Cross Reference dialog box, you can also click the pencil icon to the right of the Format pop-up menu. InDesign displays the Cross Reference Formats dialog box.

2. Click the Create Format (the "+" *below* the list of formats) button to create a new format. The new format will be based on the selected format. InDesign adds a new format to the list. This also displays the definition of the format in the Definition field.

3. Enter a name for the format.

4. Construct the format using the *other* "+" (this one is a pop-up menu, and is known as the "Building Block icon") and the "@" pop-up menu (known as "Special Characters icon"). These two pop-up menus insert text in the Description field. You can also enter the text yourself, once you're familiar with the syntax.

FIGURE 3-44
Creating a Cross
Reference Format

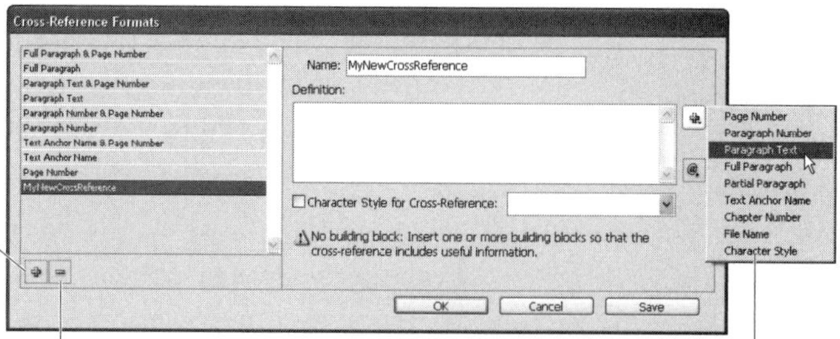

*Click the + button to add a
cross reference format.*

*Click the - button to delete
the selected cross reference
format.*

*Use the + pop-up menu to add cross
reference "building blocks" to the
cross reference format definition.*

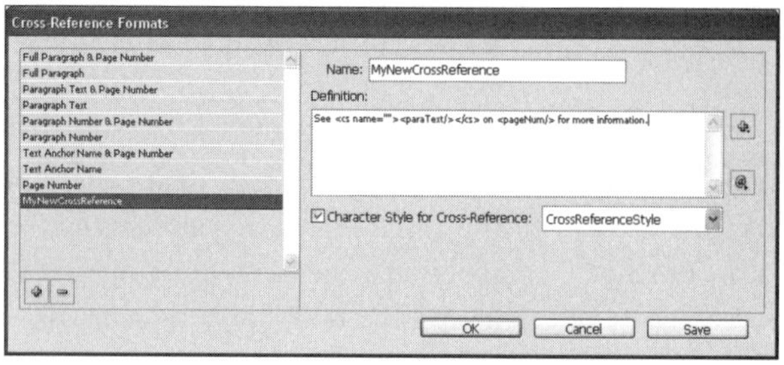

*The cross reference format
definition can look pretty
arcane, but don't let it bother
you: just select building
blocks and then enter the
static text you want.*

5. If you want to apply a character style to the marker, turn on the
    Character Style for Cross Reference option and choose a charac-
    ter style from the associated pop-up menu.

6. Once everything looks the way you want it to, click the Save
    button to save the cross reference format, then click the OK
    button to close the dialog box.

Importing Text

Most of the time, text isn't originally written using a page layout program—it's written using a word processor (such as Microsoft Word)
or text editor (such as BBEdit). To get the text into InDesign, you
must either copy-and-paste or import (or "place") the text files.

Pasting text. A surprising number of people tell us that their primary source of text is their e-mail program or Web browser. The
best way to get text from there into InDesign is to use copy and paste.
InDesign ignores all formatting when you paste from another program. If you want to retain the formatting, turn on the All Information option in the When Pasting Text from Other Applications
section of the Type panel of the Preferences dialog box. This only

affects text pasted from other programs. To paste text that was copied from within InDesign without its formatting, choose Paste Without Formatting from the Edit menu (or press Command/Ctrl-Shift-V).

Placing text. InDesign can import text files in a variety of formats, including Microsoft Word, Microsoft Excel, text-only (ASCII or Unicode), Rich Text Format (RTF), and InDesign tagged text. You can view the complete list of available import filters in the Files of Type pop-up menu in the Place Document dialog box in Windows.

If you don't see your word processor or text editor listed as one of the available import filters, don't despair. InDesign can import text in common "interchange" formats, such as text-only and RTF, and chances are good that your word processor or text editor can save text in one of those formats.

In addition, InDesign's tagged text filter can import formatted text from any application that can write a text-only file. The tagged text format is something like RTF—it's a text-only format that uses special codes to define the typesetting of the text in the file (see "Working with InDesign Tagged Text," later in this chapter).

To place a text file, follow these steps (see Figure 3-45).

1. Choose Place from the File menu (or press Command-D/Ctrl-D). InDesign displays the Place dialog box.

2. Locate and select the text file you want to import.

3. Check Show Import Options to set up the import options you want (if necessary), and/or check Replace Selected Item.

   ► **Show Import Options.** Turn on the Show Import Options checkbox to display another dialog box containing more import options for the specific type of file you're placing. This dialog box appears after you click the Open button to import the text file. We use a shortcut: Hold down the Shift key while clicking the Open button or while double-clicking a text file in the Place dialog box.

   ► **Replace Selected Item.** If you had a frame selected before you displayed the Place dialog box, InDesign makes the Replace Selected Item option available. Turn this option on to replace the contents of the frame (if any) with the text file. If you had text selected, or if you had clicked the Type tool in a text frame, turning the Replace Selected Item option on inserts the text from the file into the text frame.

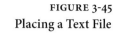

FIGURE 3-45
Placing a Text File

*Select an unlinked frame
(optional), then press
Command-D/Ctrl-D to
display the Place dialog box.*

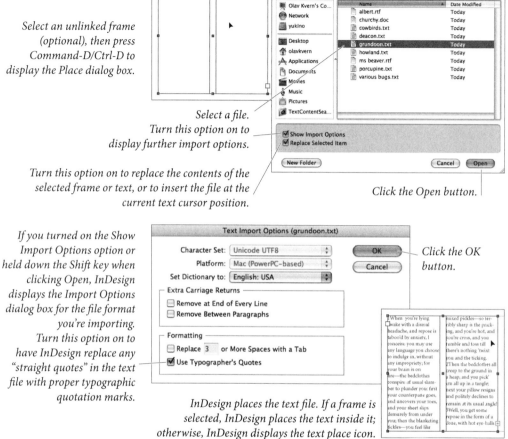

Select a file.
*Turn this option on to
display further import options.*

*Turn this option on to replace the contents of the
selected frame or text, or to insert the file at the
current text cursor position.*

Click the Open button.

*If you turned on the Show
Import Options option or
held down the Shift key when
clicking Open, InDesign
displays the Import Options
dialog box for the file format
you're importing.
Turn this option on to
have InDesign replace any
"straight quotes" in the text
file with proper typographic
quotation marks.*

*Click the OK
button.*

*InDesign places the text file. If a frame is
selected, InDesign places the text inside it;
otherwise, InDesign displays the text place icon.*

4. Click the Open Button. If Show Import Options was on (or you
    held down the Shift key), InDesign displays a dialog box con-
    taining options for the type of file you selected (see below).

5. If no frames were selected, InDesign displays the Text Place
    cursor and waits for you to click on a frame or drag one out (see
    "Flowing Text," earlier in this chapter). If the incoming text file
    contains fonts that aren't currently loaded, InDesign warns you
    of their presence. If you had selected a frame before opening the
    Place dialog box, and you turned on the Replace Selected Item
    checkbox, InDesign fills the frame with the file you selected.

**Word and RTF
Import Options**

InDesign imports the text formatting in Word and RTF text files,
without any page layout ("page geometry") information saved in the
file. This means that InDesign imports paragraph indents, but does

not import page margins. For a more complete list of the formatting imported—or not—by the Word and RTF import filters, see the Filters ReadMe.pdf file at http://bit.ly/d5Knci.

When you turn on the Show Import Options option and place a Word or RTF file, InDesign displays the corresponding Import Options dialog box (see Figure 3-46).

Table of Contents Text. Turn this option on to import the table of contents text (if any) in the Word/RTF file. However, the table of contents entries lose their special qualities. The page numbers appear as they were in the document the last time the file was saved, and do not change as you place the text on the pages of your InDesign publication. The table of contents also loses its navigational (i.e., hyperlink) properties. To InDesign, it's just text. InDesign's Table of Contents feature is not linked with this at all; if you're going to build a table of contents with the InDesign feature, you might as well leave this checkbox turned off.

Index Text. Turn this option on to import an index (or indices) you've inserted in the Word/RTF document. Note that individual index entries that you make in Word are imported whether this option is on or off; this only controls whether any built indexes get imported. We usually leave this turned off.

Footnotes/Endnotes. When you turn on this option, InDesign places any footnotes or endnotes at the end of the story. Leave this option off to omit any footnote or endnote text.

Use Typographer's Quotes. Turn on the Use Typographer's Quotes option to convert any straight quotes (i.e., foot and inch marks) to proper typographic quotation marks and apostrophes.

Remove Styles and Formatting from Text and Tables. When you turn this option on, InDesign strips out any text formatting in your file (paragraph and character styles, font, size, color, and so on) and places the text using the current default formatting.

Preserve Local Overrides. Turn this option on to retain bold, italic, underline, and other local formatting in the incoming text.

Convert Tables To. If you've chosen to remove text and table formatting (see above), you can choose Unformatted Tables or Unformatted Tabbed Text to tell InDesign how to deal with tables.

FIGURE 3-46
RTF Import Options

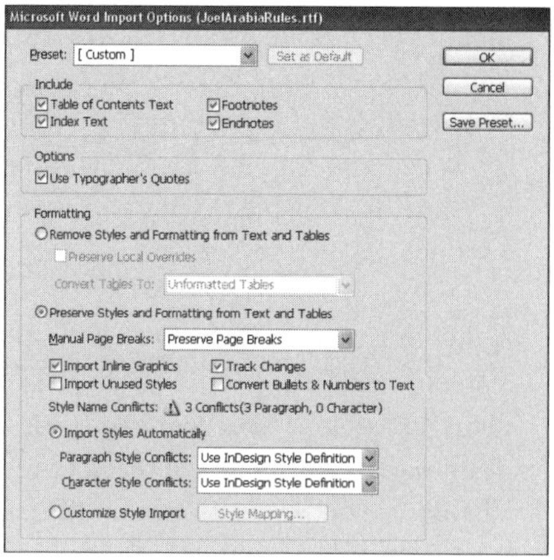

If you find yourself repeatedly making the same choices in this dialog box, click Save Preset—your preset will show up in the Preset pop-up menu. This is especially helpful when using the Customize Style Import mapping feature.

Preserve Styles and Formatting from Text and Tables. When you turn this option on, InDesign will import text formatting used in the Word/RTF document. How, exactly, it does this is determined by the controls that become available when you choose this option.

Manual Page Breaks. What should InDesign do when it finds a page break in the Word/RTF file? We typically want InDesign to ignore these, so we choose No Breaks. However, if those breaks are there for a good reason, you can choose Preserve Page Breaks or Convert to Column Breaks to have InDesign automatically apply the page and column break settings (which is usually done manually using the Start Paragraph pop-up menu in the Keep Options dialog box).

Import Inline Graphics. If you want to include graphics from the Word file, turn this option on. Note, however, that many of the graphics embedded in Word/RTF documents are not suitable for high resolution printing. In general, it's best to save the graphics as separate files (see the file format discussion in Chapter 7, "Importing and Exporting") and then place them in InDesign.

Import Unused Styles. When this option is turned on, InDesign will import character and paragraph styles that are not used in any of the text in the incoming document. When it's off, InDesign does not attempt to import the unused styles.

Track Changes. When this option is turned on, markups added using the Track Changes feature in Word appear in the InDesign Story Editor. InDesign doesn't automatically apply a user color to Word's markup, so the imported Word markups may have a different

FIGURE 3-47
Mapping Styles
on Import

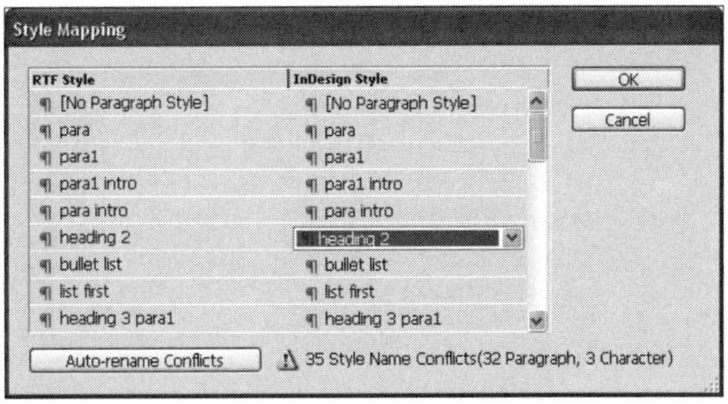

color. To make the markups consistent, select absolute colors (instead of [User]) in Track Changes preferences. We cover tracking text changes later in this chapter.

Import Styles Automatically. The two pop-up menus below this option tell InDesign what to do when character and paragraph styles in the Word document match the names of existing styles in the InDesign document. For both character and paragraph styles, you can choose to use the InDesign style definition, redefine the InDesign style to match the Word style, or to create a new style for each style name conflict. If you choose to take the latter approach, InDesign will automatically generate a new name for each style.

Customize Style Import. To get more control over style import, turn this option on and click the Style Mapping button. When you do this, InDesign displays the Style Mapping dialog box (see Figure 3-47).

Beware the Fast Save. It's hard to resist the impulse to turn on the Allow Fast Saves option in Word's Options dialog box. It sounds like a good idea, but in this case, it isn't. The Word file format is very complicated, and using this option sometimes produces files that import filters can't read. Heck, when you turn this option on, Word sometimes writes files that *Word* can't read. Stop it before it kills again!

Text-Only Import Options

Text-only files often arrive full of extra characters—usually spaces and carriage returns added to change the appearance of text on screen. The options in the Text Import Options dialog box help you do some of the clean-up for you (see Figure 3-48).

Character Set. If you're seeing odd characters in the text files you import, it might be that the character set of the computer used to create the files is not the same character set as the one in use by your copy of InDesign. As you import a text file, you can choose a character set that matches the character set of the text file.

FIGURE 3-48
Text Import Options

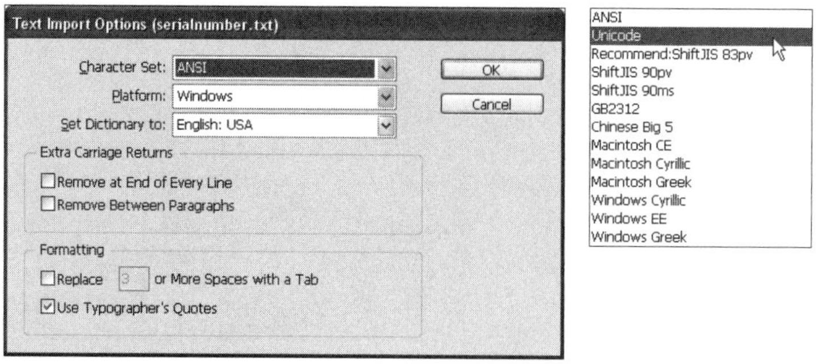

Platform. Windows and the Mac OS use different character sets and also use different ways of ending a paragraph. If you're using Windows and know the file came from the Mac OS—or vice versa—choose the appropriate platform from this pop-up menu.

Set Dictionary To. Use this pop-up menu to apply a default spelling and hyphenation dictionary to the incoming text.

Extra Carriage Returns. The people who prepare the text files for you want to help. They really do. That's why they entered all of those carriage returns (to force a page break). They are trying to do some of the work so that you don't have to. The only trouble, of course, is that they usually make a mess that you're left to fix. InDesign's Text Import filter can solve many of the problems your co-workers create. The options in the Extra Carriage Returns section of the Text Import Options dialog box help you clean up the extra carriage returns.

Use Typographer's Quotes. We recommend turning on the Use Typographer's Quotes option so that InDesign converts the straight quotes to proper typographic quotation marks and apostrophes.

Extra Spaces. Why do people enter extra spaces in text? Usually, they're trying to indicate to you, their trusted typesetter, that they want to enter some amount of horizontal space. In other words, a tab. InDesign can replace some number of spaces in the incoming text file with tabs—just enter a value for the number of contiguous space characters you want replaced. Note that this approach often enters multiple tab characters in the story, but that problem is easily cleaned up using Find and Change.

Excel Import Options

Use the options in the Excel Import Options dialog box to specify the range of cells you want to import and the formatting applied to those cells (see Figure 3-49). See Chapter 6, "Where Text Meets Graphics,"

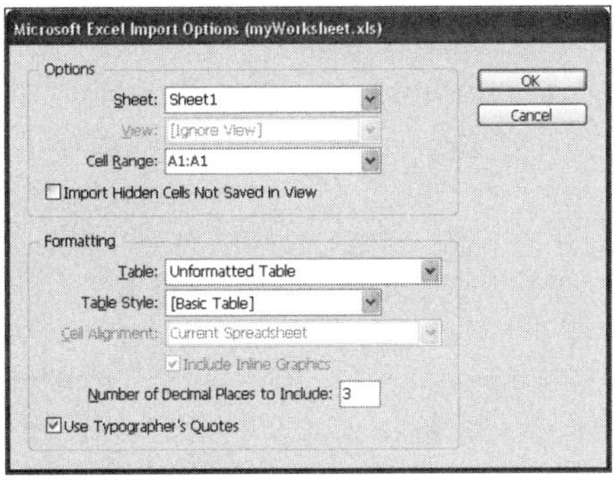

FIGURE 3-49
Excel Import Options

for more on what you can do with tables. Remember that InDesign can only import Excel tables, not charts. If you need to import a graphic chart from Excel, you should probably export it as a PDF file (and possibly even open that PDF in Illustrator to fine-tune it before saving and importing into InDesign).

View, Sheet, and Cell Range. Use these options to define which custom view, worksheet, and range of cells you want. By default, the Cell Range field selects cells of the worksheet you've selected.

Import Hidden Cells Not Saved in View. Turn this option on to import any hidden cells in the Excel file.

Table. By default, InDesign tries to match as much of Excel's table formatting as possible. If you'd prefer to handle formatting your table in InDesign, choose Unformatted Table. You can also import the table as tab-delimited text by choosing Unformatted Text.

Cell Alignment. How do you want InDesign to align the text from the cells you're importing? The default setting is Current Spreadsheet, which tells InDesign to copy the alignment from Excel.

Import Inline Graphics. Turn this option on to include any inline graphics in the spreadsheet. As with importing graphics embedded in Word/RTF files, this can be useful or dangerous, depending on the graphics and on your printing process. Again, we think it's best to save the graphics as separate files, in a high-quality graphics format, and then place them in InDesign (see Chapter 7, "Importing and Exporting," for more on file formats).

Decimal Places. You can choose the number of decimal places you want to use in the imported cells. The cell might show 3.1415926, but if you specify three decimal places, 3.142 will appear in the table.

Use Typographer's Quotes. Unless there's a good reason to stick with straight quote marks in your Excel data, turn on the Use Typographer's Quotes to get curly quotes.

Tagged Text Import Options

InDesign's Tagged Text import filter gives you a great way to get formatted text from any application that can create a text-only file. When you import a tagged text file, you can set some import options (see Figure 3-50). For more on creating tagged text files, see "Working with InDesign Tagged Text," later in this chapter.

FIGURE 3-50
Tagged Text Import Options

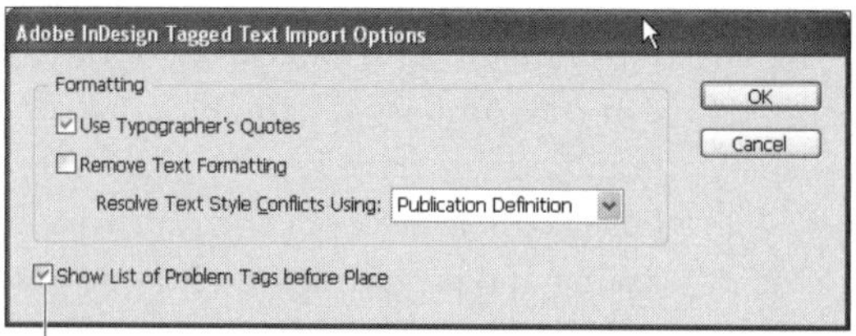

Turn this option on...

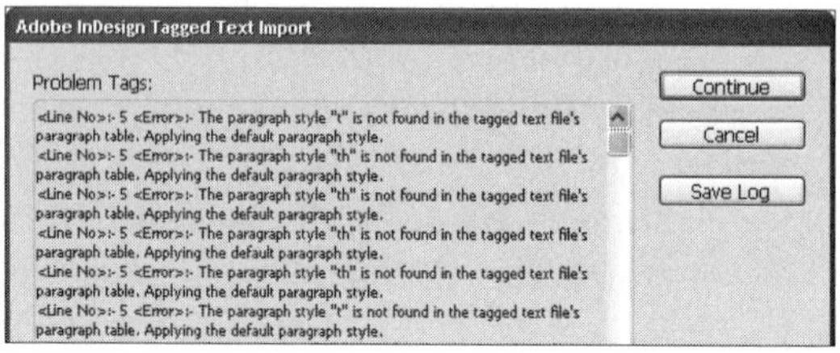

...and InDesign will list any errors it finds in your tagged text file. It will also list a number of things that aren't errors, but might be good to know about.

Use Typographer's Quotes. At this point, we're going to assume you know what it does.

Remove Text Formatting. Just because someone gave you a tagged text file doesn't mean you can't strip out the styles and import simple text. To do this, turn on the Remove Text Formatting option.

Remove Text Style Conflicts Using. If the name of an incoming style (character or paragraph) matches a style that exists in the publication, which style definition should InDesign use? Choose the Publication Definition option to apply the formatting defined by your document, or Tagged File Definition to import the style defined in the tagged text file. When you choose the latter method, InDesign adds the style to the publication and appends the word "copy" to the style's name. This does not affect the formatting of any text in the publication.

Show List of Problem Tags Before Place. If you're not getting the formatting you expect from your tagged text files, turn this option on to have InDesign display a list of errors. If InDesign does find errors, you can choose to place the file, or to cancel the place operation. You can write the error list to a text file by clicking the Save Log button.

Importing and Exporting Buzzword Files

Buzzword is an Acrobat.com service. A Buzzword document is a word processing file that's stored on the web, in an Acrobat.com workspace. If this still isn't clear, go to *www.acrobat.com*, and click Sign Up to create a free account (or sign in if you already have an Acrobat.com or Adobe ID account). Then click Create New Buzzword Document under Actions.

Importing a Buzzword document into InDesign is similar to importing Word or RTF files. Follow these steps:

1. Choose Place from Buzzword from the File menu.

2. If you haven't signed in, click Sign In, and sign in.

3. Turn on Show Import Options if you want control the import settings, then locate and double-click a Buzzword document.

The options that appear are the same options you get when you import a Word or RTF file—including options for mapping paragraph styles. Unfortunately, Buzzword doesn't have styles yet (or at least not when we were writing this book). Until Buzzword includes styles, we won't know how useful this workflow will be.

You can also export a story from InDesign and upload it as a Buzzword document, which you can share with others. Click in the story you want to export and choose Buzzword from the "Export for" submenu on the File menu.

Text Files and File Linking

Just as you can choose to link or embed graphics files, you can choose to link or embed text files. By default, InDesign embeds text files—to maintain a link to the files, turn on the Create Links When Placing Text and Spreadsheet Files option in the Text Preferences dialog box.

Linking to text files sounds cool, but watch out: Updating the file is the same as re-importing it, so you will lose any edits or formatting you've applied in InDesign. We recommend that you embed your text files. To do this, turn this preference off. If you have already imported the file, you can break the link—select the file name in the Links panel and choose Embed File from the panel menu.

Exporting Text

Now and then you need to get your text back out of an InDesign publication and back into some other program. You can export the text in a variety of text formats. To export a story, follow these steps.

1. Select the story you want to export (click the Type tool in the story) and choose Text from the Export submenu of the File menu (or press Command-E/Ctrl-E).

2. Choose an export format for the text from the Format pop-up menu. Note that some of the items in this pop-up menu, like EPS or PDF, don't export your story; they export the whole page (or document). To export the text, choose Text Only (which will export the text without any formatting), Rich Text Format (RTF), or Adobe InDesign Tagged Text.

3. Specify a name and location for the file.

4. Click the Save button to export the story.

Editing Text

Once you've entered or imported text, chances are good you're going to have to change it. InDesign includes most common word processing features, such as the ability to move the cursor through text using keyboard shortcuts, check the spelling of text, or find and change text and formatting.

Moving the Cursor Through Text

When we're entering text, one of the last things we want to do is take our hands away from the keyboard. We don't want to have to use the mouse to move the text cursor or select text. That's why we like to use keyboard shortcuts to move the cursor and select text—they keep our hands where they belong: on the keyboard.

InDesign comes with a fairly complete set of keyboard shortcuts, as shown in Table 3-5. Note that some of the shortcuts have several keys associated with them—pick the combination that works best for you. You can always change the shortcuts by choosing Keyboard Shortcuts from the Edit menu.

Whatever keyboard shortcuts you use, remember that you can typically add Shift to them to select text as you move. For example, Command-End/Ctrl-End jumps to the end of a story, so adding Shift to that will select the text to the end of the story.

To move the cursor:	Press
Right one character	Right arrow, Keypad 6
Left one character	Left arrow, Keypad 4
Right one word	Command-Right arrow Ctrl-Right arrow, Ctrl-Keypad 6
Left one word	Command-Left arrow Ctrl-Left arrow, Ctrl-Keypad 4
Up one line	Up arrow, Keypad 8
Down one line	Down arrow, Keypad 2
Up one paragraph	Command-Up arrow Ctrl-Up arrow, Ctrl-Keypad 8
Down one paragraph	Command-Down arrow Ctrl-Down arrow, Ctrl-Keypad 2
End of line	End, Keypad 1
Start of line	Home, Keypad 7
Start of story	Command-Home/Ctrl-Home, Keypad 7
End of story	Command-End/Ctrl-End, Keypad 1

We like the shortcuts on the numeric keypad, even though it takes our right hand away from the "home row." To use the keypad shortcuts, turn Num Lock off.

Mouse clicks. Of course, if you do happen to have one hand on the mouse already, you can use various combinations of clicks to select text. *Which* clicks, exactly depends on your preferences settings. Double-clicking always selects a word. If you've turned on the Triple Click to Select a Line option in the Type Preferences dialog box, triple-clicking selects a single line (not a sentence), and quadruple-clicking selects a whole paragraph; if that option is off, triple-clicking selects a paragraph and quadruple-clicking selects the entire story.

The Keyboard Dance. Selecting text in InDesign—whether you're in a story window or a document window—is in most ways the same as any other program. There is one difference, however, which drives us crazy. When you select text using keyboard shortcuts, InDesign remembers where the cursor was when you started—but it only remembers as long as you hold the modifier keys down. This is a subtle thing, and much more difficult to explain than to show.

Here's an example. You place the text cursor at the beginning of this paragraph and then Command-Shift-Down Arrow/Ctrl-Shift-Down Arrow to select the whole paragraph. Suddenly, you realize that you don't want to select the last character (the paragraph return character), so you press Shift-Left Arrow to deselect it. What happens next depends on whether or not you raised your hand from the keyboard. If you keep the Shift key down between the two shortcuts, InDesign will deselect the last character (which is what you want). If you let go of the keyboard before pressing Shift-Left Arrow, then InDesign sees this as a whole new selection and *adds* one character to the *left* of the paragraph (the last character in the previous paragraph) to your selection (which is *never* what you want).

At that point, getting the selection you want requires you to extend the selection to the right (perhaps by pressing Shift-Right Arrow) and then deselect the characters (Shift-Left Arrow, twice). This what we call doing the keyboard dance. It's so bad that we sometimes take our fingers off the keyboard and use the mouse.

Showing and Hiding "Invisibles"

Choose Show Hidden Characters from the Type menu (or press Command-Option-I/Ctrl-Alt-I) to display the carriage returns, tabs, spaces, and other invisible characters in the text (see Figure 3-51).

FIGURE 3-51
Showing Hidden Characters

Space   End of story

TimeTravelTickets#

I·Comici·Gelosi¶

Em space — 1568-1604 » Italy/France¶

virtu, fama ed honor ne f'er gelosi¶

Tab — The·most·famous·commedia·troupe·ever!¬

Carriage return

Line end

Dragging and Dropping Text

You can move text from place to place using drag and drop. By default, drag and drop text editing is turned on for the Story Editor view and turned off for layout view. To change these settings, use the options in the Type panel of the Preferences dialog box. To use drag and drop text editing (see Figure 3-52), follow these steps.

1. Select some text, then hold the cursor over the text until the drag and drop icon appears.

2. Drag the text to a new location (to copy the text, hold down Option/Alt as you drag). You can drag to the same story, to another story, to a text frame in another window or document. As you drag, InDesign displays a vertical bar to show you the destination. To insert the text without copying its formatting, hold down Shift before you drop the text—the text will take

FIGURE 3-52
**Drag and Drop
Text Editing**

The King of Elfland's Daughter, by Lord Dunsany (pen name of Edward John Moreton Drax Plunkett, 18ᵗʰ Baron Dunsany). G.P.Putnam & Sons Ltd., London, 1924. Cloth Hardcover.	Lord Dunsany () influenced H. P. Lovecraft, Clark Ashton Smith, and other fantasy authors.

Select some text, then move the cursor over the selection. If drag and drop text editing is active, you'll see the drag and drop icon.

The King of Elfland's Daughter, by Lord Dunsany (pen name of Edward John Moreton Drax Plunkett, 18ᵗʰ Baron Dunsany). G.P.Putnam & Sons Ltd., London, 1924. Cloth Hardcover.	Lord Dunsany () influenced H. P. Lovecraft, Clark Ashton Smith, and other fantasy authors.

Drag the text to a new location. As you drag, InDesign displays a vertical bar to show the destination of the text.

The King of Elfland's Daughter, by Lord Dunsany (, 18ᵗʰ Baron Dunsany). G.P.Putnam & Sons Ltd., London, 1924. Cloth Hardcover.	Lord Dunsany (pen name of Edward John Moreton Drax Plunkett) influenced H. P. Lovecraft, Clark Ashton Smith, and other fantasy authors.

Stop dragging and release the mouse button, and InDesign moves the text to the location of the vertical bar.

If you hold down Option as you drag text...

The King of Elfland's Daughter, by Lord Dunsany (pen name of Edward John Moreton Drax Plunkett, 18ᵗʰ Baron Dunsany). G.P.Putnam & Sons Ltd., London, 1924. Cloth Hardcover.	Lord Dunsany (pen name of Edward John Moreton Drax Plunkett) influenced H. P. Lovecraft, Clark Ashton Smith, and other fantasy authors.

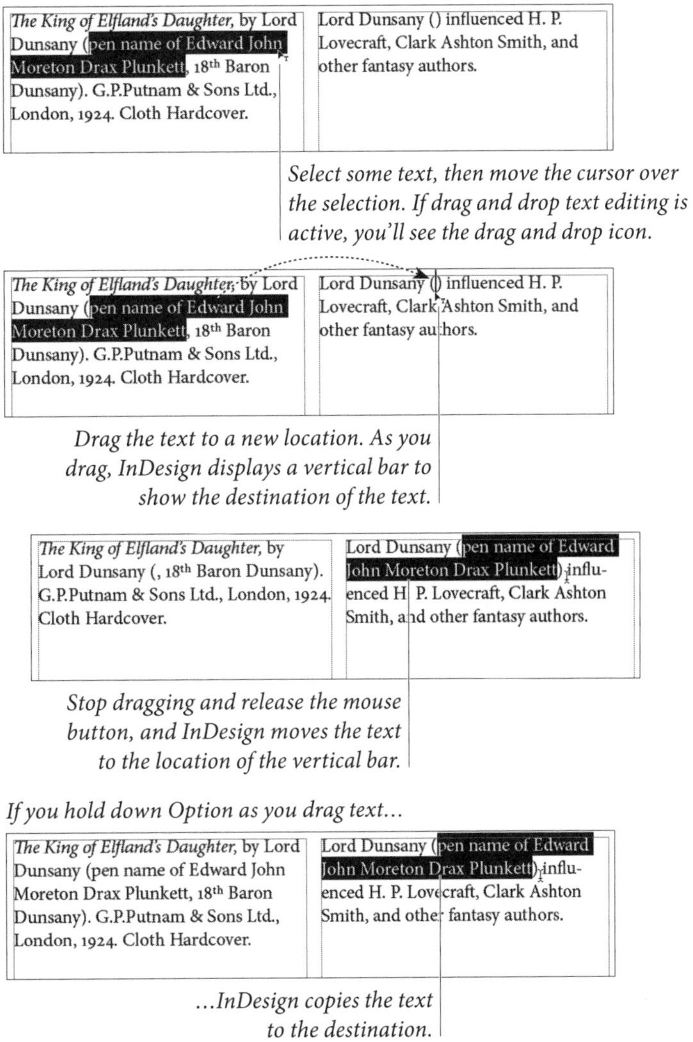

You can also hold down Shift as you drag to move or copy the text without copying its formatting.

...InDesign copies the text to the destination.

on the formatting of the surrounding text. To create a new text frame as you drop the text, hold down Command/Ctrl as you drag the selection.

3. Release the mouse button to drop the text.

Story Editor

Reading and editing text on-screen is never any fun, and it's even worse when it's set in 8-point Garamond Extra Condensed Light, all caps, and reversed out of a dark background. Eyestrain is one of the occupational hazards of graphic design, and tiny, tinted text will usually require two of your preferred pain reliever. Sure, you can zoom in to read it more easily, but then you have to scroll around to see all the text. Is there a way to view your text in a sane, responsible manner? There is—it's called the Story Editor.

Story Editor opens the text of a story in a story window (as opposed to a layout window—we discussed the window types in Chapter 1, "Workspace"). To open a story window, select some text or a text frame and choose Edit in Story Editor from the Edit menu (or just press Command-Y/Ctrl-Y).

A story window displays your story in a single column of readable text, ignoring font, size, color, indents, and most other formatting (see Figure 3-53). The text in the story window won't have the same line breaks as in the document window.

The Story Editor displays the text content of notes, tracked changes, and table cells, but inline graphics are shown as icons.

When you open or select a story window, some InDesign features are unavailable. For example, almost every tool in the Tool panel becomes grayed out. You can still use all the text-related features: apply paragraph and character styles, change text formatting, and so on. However, most of the formatting you can apply doesn't appear in the story window (though you can see it in the document window if it's visible in the background). The only formatting that Story Editor does display are the bold and italic versions of fonts and small caps—though it can also list the paragraph style for each paragraph in a column along the left side of the window (that's an option).

Multiple Windows

You can have as many story windows open as you want. If you select three text frames in the publication and press Command-Y/Ctrl-Y, InDesign opens each story in its own window. Story windows appear at the bottom of the Window menu. To move from one window to the next, press Command-F6/Ctrl-F6, or Command-'.

As you edit in a story window, InDesign doesn't change the view in the layout window, so the layout window might be displaying page 3 of a long story while you're making changes to page 23 in a story window. If you click the layout window, it comes to the front and you'll see that the text cursor can be in one place in one window and somewhere else in another window. Pressing Command-Y/Ctrl-Y while you're in a story window switches to the layout window containing the text, updates the layout window view to display the text you're editing, *and* matches the cursor position and/or text selection.

The New Window feature (in the Arrange submenu, under the Window menu) works on Story Editor windows, too. That means you

FIGURE 3-53
Story Editor

Clicking the paragraph style name will not select the paragraph, as it does in PageMaker.

The vertical depth in the left column is in inches, mm, points, or whatever the measurement system is

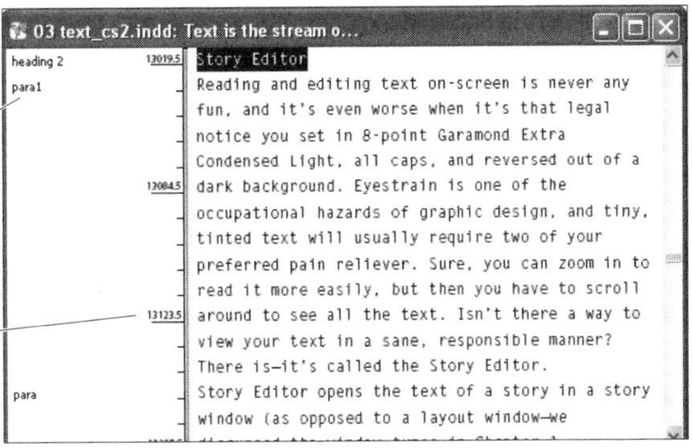

> **03 text_cs2.indd: Text is the stream o...**
>
> heading 2   120|19.5 Story Editor
> para1   Reading and editing text on-screen is never any
>   fun, and it's even worse when it's that legal
>   notice you set in 8-point Garamond Extra
>   Condensed Light, all caps, and reversed out of a
>   130|84.5 dark background. Eyestrain is one of the
>   occupational hazards of graphic design, and tiny,
>   tinted text will usually require two of your
>   preferred pain reliever. Sure, you can zoom in to
>   read it more easily, but then you have to scroll
>   131|23.5 around to see all the text. Isn't there a way to
>   view your text in a sane, responsible manner?
>   There is—it's called the Story Editor.
>   Story Editor opens the text of a story in a story
> para   window (as opposed to a layout window—we

can have two or more story windows open on the same story, each looking at a different chunk of text. This is helpful when you need to refer to text in one part of the story while editing another.

Footnotes in the Story Editor

The Story Editor displays footnotes as an icon—click the icon to expand and edit the footnote (see Figure 3-54). You can also choose to expand all footnotes by choosing Expand All Footnotes from the Story Editor submenu of the View menu, or hide them all by choosing Collapse All Footnotes.

Story Editor Options

The Story Editor is designed to be utilitarian, not pretty. You can spruce it up a bit by changing settings in the Story Editor Preferences dialog box (see Figure 3-55).

Text Display Options. You can select any font and size you want, though it behooves you to pick something as readable as possible (David likes 16-point Georgia). You can also choose line spacing (*a.k.a.*, leading), the text color, whether text should be anti-aliased, and a background color for your story windows. The Theme pop-up

FIGURE 3-54
Story Editor and Footnotes

Footnote marker.

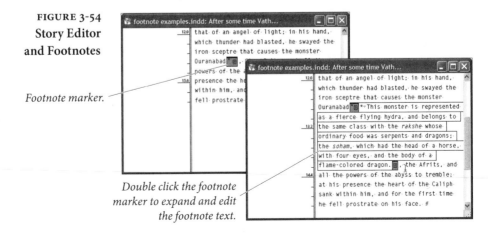

Double click the footnote marker to expand and edit the footnote text.

FIGURE 3-55
Story Editor
Display Preferences

*We trust that you will use
these settings responsibly.*

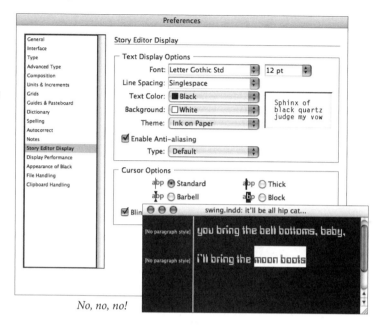

No, no, no!

menu offers several text color and background color combinations, but you don't have to use these. These settings have no effect on the printed appearance of your text; they're just for the story windows.

Cursor Options. We've never met anyone who wanted to use anything other than the normal, thin cursor (called Standard here). But you can choose Thick, Barbell, or Block. (The Block option really complements the "DOS look" described above.) And if a blinking cursor drives you mad, turn off the Blink option.

Paragraph styles column. Use this control to change the size of the paragraph style column (the column on the left in a story window).

Track Changes

InDesign now includes an editing tool that's been available in InCopy for years. When you turn on Track Changes, the Story Editor displays markup highlighting for text that's been added, deleted, and moved (see Figure 3-56). Changes are not reflected in the layout view, and the change markups cannot be printed or exported.

In a typical workflow, the author sends the publication to an editor. The editor turns on Track Changes, edits the text, and sends the publication back to the author. The author then uses the Track Changes panel to accept or reject the changes.

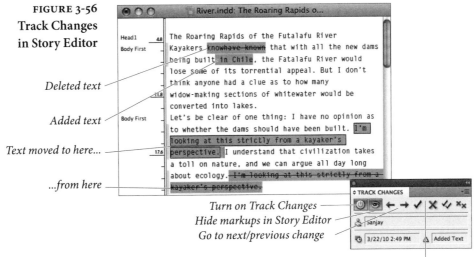

FIGURE 3-56
**Track Changes
in Story Editor**

Deleted text

Added text

Text moved to here...

...from here

Turn on Track Changes
Hide markups in Story Editor
Go to next/previous change

Accept or reject changes

Track Changes must be turned on for InDesign to create markups. If you edit text with Track Changes turned off, there is no way to view the changes after the fact.

▶ To display the Track Changes panel, choose Track Changes from the Editorial submenu of the Window menu.

▶ Click Enable Track Changes in Current Story to let InDesign keep track of changes. Turn this option off and then on again, and change tracking resumes with all changes highlighted.

Most of the Track Changes options you'll need to use are right there at the top of the Track Changes panel. There are a few additional options in the panel menu, such as Enable Track Changes in All Stories and Accept Change, Find Next.

You might enjoy being able to reject changes based on commenter. Bob once received a lot of odd comments when a reviewer used InCopy to test procedures from an InDesign user guide.

If you need to track changes frequently, you'll want to assign keyboard shortcuts to the commands you use most often.

Notes

You can attach notes to text in an InDesign story. The Notes panel is the key to managing notes (see Figure 3-57). Notes provide a great way to add comments or other information to text—especially when you're working with editors (even if they use InCopy). Notes can be

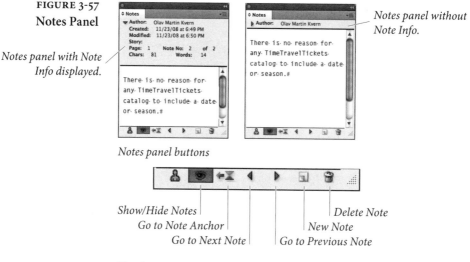

FIGURE 3-57
Notes Panel

Notes panel with Note Info displayed.

Notes panel without Note Info.

Notes panel buttons

Show/Hide Notes
Go to Note Anchor
Go to Next Note
Delete Note
New Note
Go to Previous Note

The Go to Next Note and Go to Previous Note buttons will not become active until you click the Type tool in a story that contains notes.

created, edited, converted to text, or deleted, and can be viewed in the Story Editor or the Notes panel. You won't be able to see your notes in the Layout view, though you will be able to see the note anchor when you click the Show/Hide Notes button in the Notes panel.

Notes take on the current "user color," which is based on the user name. To change the current user name or user color, choose User from the File menu and enter a new name and user color.

You can use the Notes panel to jump from one note to another note using the Go to Next Note or Go to Previous Note buttons.

Creating Notes   To create a note, do any of the following (see Figure 3-58).

▶ Click the Type tool in text at the location at which you want to insert the note, display the Notes panel, and then choose New Note from the Notes panel menu (or click the New Note button).

▶ Select the Note tool and click it in text. The Notes panel appears.

▶ Choose New Note from the Notes menu. InDesign displays the Notes panel.

▶ Select a range of text, then choose Convert to Note from the Notes menu (or from the Notes panel menu).

After creating a note using any of the first three approaches shown above, you can type the text of your note in the Notes panel.

FIGURE 3-58
Adding a Note

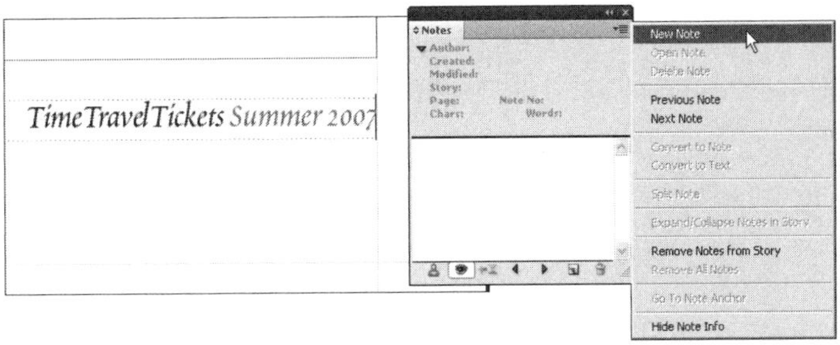

Click the Type tool in text, then choose New Note from the Notes panel menu.

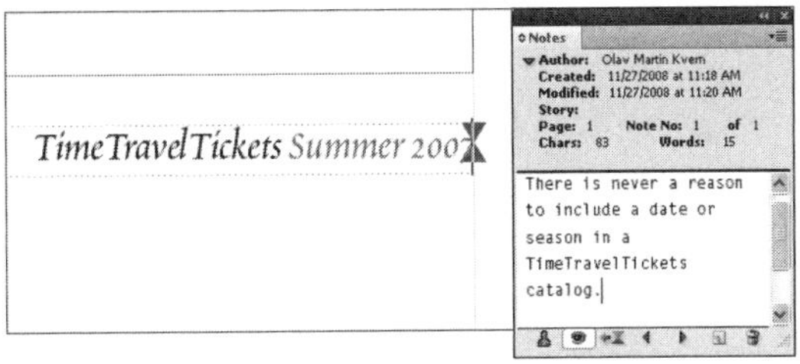

InDesign adds a note at the location of the cursor. You'll be able to see the note anchor in layout view. (If you can't see the note anchor, click the Show/Hide Notes button at the bottom of the panel.)

Enter text in the Notes panel.

Editing Notes

To view the content of the note, either select the note and display the Notes panel, or open the story in the Story Editor. Choose Expand/Collapse Notes in Story to display the notes if they are not already visible.

Deleting Notes

To delete an individual note, place the cursor immediately after it and press Delete/Backspace. To delete the note from the Notes panel, navigate to the note and then click the Delete Note button at the bottom of the panel. To delete all notes in a story, choose Remove Notes from Story from the Notes menu or the Notes panel menu.

Converting Notes to Text

To convert a note to text, select the note (or the note anchor, in layout view) and choose Convert to Text from the Notes menu. Alternatively, you can navigate to the note using the Notes panel, then choose Convert to Text from the panel menu. Text can be also be copied out of a note and pasted into normal text.

Using Adobe InCopy

We don't ordinarily talk about buying additional programs in this book, but we need to make a quick exception for Adobe InCopy, a word processor that is designed to work with InDesign documents—sort of a Story Editor on steroids. While it's not part of the Creative Suite, it's well worth buying if you work with text heavy publications, especially if you're collaborating with other people.

With InCopy you can write or edit stories using all of the text-formatting features available in InDesign, using the same paragraph and character styles, with the knowledge that what you set in InCopy will appear the same in InDesign. InCopy lets you see your stories in story mode (like Story Editor), layout mode (as though you're seeing the layout in InDesign, but can only edit the story), or galley mode (like story, but you actually see the line breaks).

Checking Spelling

Toward the end of a project, we always fall prey to the delusion that everything, every last word, on all of our pages, is misspelled. We find ourselves staring blearily at relatively simple words. Is "dog" really spelled "D-O-G?" In our typical pre-deadline panic, we don't know. Everything looks wrong.

InDesign can check the spelling of any text in an InDesign text frame, and can also catch duplicated words ("the the") and possible capitalization errors. InDesign uses the language dictionary or dictionaries associated with your text to perform the spelling check.

To check spelling, follow these steps (see Figure 3-59).

1. Press Command-I/Ctrl-I (or choose Check Spelling from the Edit menu). InDesign starts to check the spelling of the current selection, story, or document (depending on the current selection) and displays the Check Spelling panel when it finds a suspect word. You can leave the panel open while editing text.

2. At this point, you can define the scope of the spelling check using the Search pop-up menu. Note that InDesign can check the spelling of all of the open publications, if you want, or you can restrict the spell check to the current story, or—if you have one or more words highlighted—even just to the selected words.

3. Whenever InDesign finds a suspect word, you can:

   ▶ Skip the word without making any change. To do this, click the Skip button. To have InDesign ignore every occurrence of the word, click the Ignore All button.

   ▶ Replace the word with one of the suggestions. Select the suggestion, and InDesign enters the suggested word in the Change To field. Click the Change button to replace the selected word with the suggestion. Click the Change

FIGURE 3-59
Checking Spelling

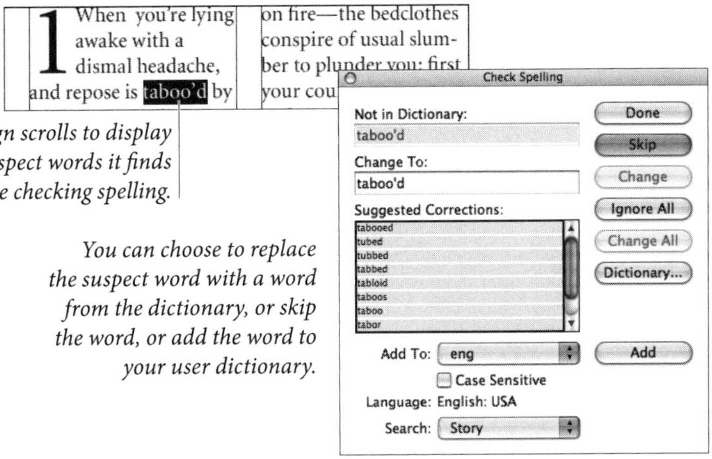

> 1 When you're lying awake with a dismal headache, and repose is taboo'd by
> on fire—the bedclothes conspire of usual slumber to plunder you: first your cou

Check Spelling

Not in Dictionary:
taboo'd

Change To:
taboo'd

Suggested Corrections:
tabooed
tubed
tubbed
tabbed
tabloid
taboos
taboo
tabor

Add To: eng

☐ Case Sensitive

Language: English: USA

Search: Story

Done
Skip
Change
Ignore All
Change All
Dictionary...

Add

InDesign scrolls to display any suspect words it finds while checking spelling.

You can choose to replace the suspect word with a word from the dictionary, or skip the word, or add the word to your user dictionary.

All button to replace every instance of the selected text with the text in the Change To field.

▶ Enter replacement text in the Change To field. Click the Change button to replace the selected word with the text you've entered, or click the Change All button to replace every instance of the selected text.

▶ Add the word to the user dictionary. This is a good thing to do with technical terms and names that appear frequently in your publications. For more on entering words in the dictionary, see "Adding Words to the User Dictionary."

After you've taken any of the above actions, InDesign continues with the spelling check.

4. When you've finished checking the spelling of the publication (or publications), you can click the Done button to close the Check Spelling panel.

Adding Words to the User Dictionary

We use lots of words in our publications that aren't found in the InDesign dictionary. Even quite common, household words such as "Kvern," "Blatner," and "Bringhurst" will provoke an angry query from the spelling checker. You can allay InDesign's fears by entering these words in a separate dictionary, the "user dictionary." When InDesign can't find a word in its dictionary, it consults the user dictionary. If a word appears in both the standard dictionary (which can't be edited) and the user dictionary, InDesign favors the word in the user dictionary.

You can add a word to the user dictionary in two ways: from within the Check Spelling panel or from the Dictionary panel. When you're checking your document's spelling and a "misspelled" word pops up, you can simply click the Add button. To add or remove items from your user dictionary, you can open the Dictionary panel by choosing Dictionary from the Spelling submenu of the Edit menu (see Figure 3-60). You can edit the dictionary while checking spelling.

1. Enter the word you want to add in the Word field of the Dictionary panel, if necessary (if you're in the middle of a spelling check, InDesign enters the unknown term in the field).

2. Click the Hyphenate button when you want to view the word's hyphenation points (see Chapter 4, "Type"). InDesign displays the proposed hyphenation points in the word.

    Hyphenation points are ranked—the best break is a single tilde ("~"), the next best point is two tildes ("~~"), and the least good is three tildes ("~~~"). You can enter hyphenation points in words you're adding to the user dictionary, or change the hyphenation points of words already in the user dictionary.

    If you do not want InDesign to hyphenate the word, enter a tilde before the first character of the word.

3. Choose either the user dictionary or your document's name from the Target pop-up menu. Generally, you'll want to add words to the user dictionary which can be used by all your documents. However, if you choose your current file, then the word will only appear spelled correctly in that document, and no others. This might come in handy if you're building an annual report for a medical company and you don't want to add "fluoxetine" to your general user dictionary.

4. Click the Add button to add the word to the user dictionary.

Removing Words From the User Dictionary

Once you add a word to your user dictionary you can remove it: Just choose Dictionary from the Spelling submenu of the Edit menu, select the word you want to remove, and click the Remove button. But you can also tell InDesign to remove a word from the regular dictionary by adding it to the Removed Words list.

1. Open the Dictionary panel and choose a target. (If you choose your user dictionary, the change will affect all your documents; if you choose just the open document from the Target pop-up menu, the word is only removed from this document.)

FIGURE 3-60
**Adding a Word to the
User Dictionary**

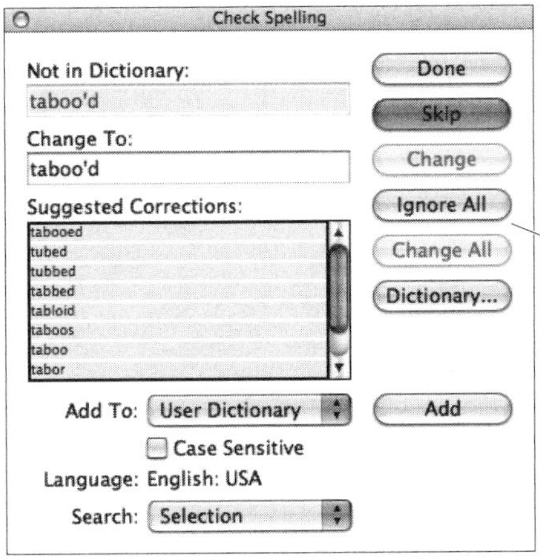

*Click the Hyphenate
button or enter tildes (~)
to indicate hyphenation
points.*

*Click the Add button
to add the word to the
dictionary.*

2. Select Removed Words from the Dictionary List pop-up menu.

3. Type the word in the Word field (if you're in the middle of checking your document's spelling, it should show up here automatically).

4. Click the Add button. This *adds* the word to the list of words that should be *removed*.

At this point, the word will appear as incorrect when you check its spelling. Later, if you want to take it off the "removed" list, you can open the Dictionary dialog box, select the word, and click Remove.

Dynamic Spelling. You can also check the spelling of text without going to the Check Spelling dialog box. To do this, turn on Dynamic Spelling (using either the Enable Dynamic Spelling option in the Spelling Preferences dialog box or the corresponding option on the Spelling submenu of the Edit menu). After you do this, InDesign will mark suspect words in your document using the colors you assigned in the Preferences dialog box. If you're working with a long document, it can take some time for InDesign to apply the highlight.

You can use the Context menu to change suspect words to any of a list of likely replacements, add the word to the dictionary, or direct InDesign to ignore the word (see Figure 3-61).

Autocorrect. If you enter a lot of text using InDesign, and you habitually type "hte," for "the," (or "pargraph," for "paragraph," as Ole does), you'll love the autocorrect feature (see Figure 3-62). As you type, autocorrect will change the text you've typed to fix common typing errors. You can also use Autocorrect to change capitalization

FIGURE 3-61
Dynamic Spelling

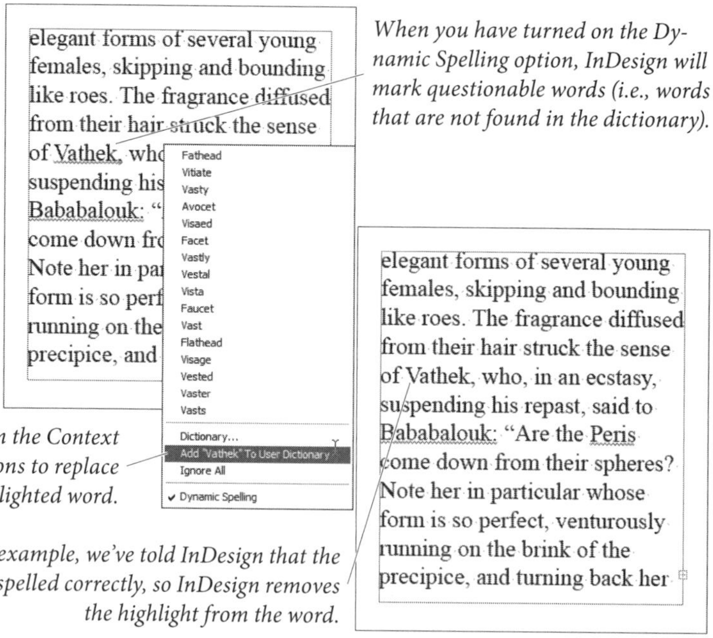

When you have turned on the Dynamic Spelling option, InDesign will mark questionable words (i.e., words that are not found in the dictionary).

To deal with one of the marked words, click the Type tool inside the word and then display the Context menu.

Choose one of the actions from the Context menu. Select one of the suggestions to replace the highlighted word.

In this example, we've told InDesign that the word is spelled correctly, so InDesign removes the highlight from the word.

FIGURE 3-62
Autocorrect

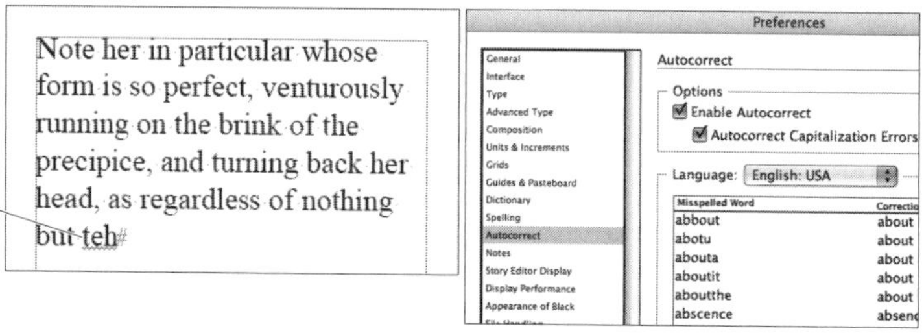

When the Autocorrect feature is on, InDesign will correct misspelled words as you type.

errors ("Indesign" to "InDesign," for example). Autocorrect has no effect on text you have already entered.

To turn this feature on or off, use the Enable Autocorrect option in the Autocorrect Preferences dialog box, or choose Autocorrect from the Spelling submenu of the Edit menu. To have Autocorrect catch errors of capitalization, turn on the Autocorrect Capitalization Errors option.

As you can see by looking at the Autocorrect Preferences dialog box, InDesign has a large list of common misspelled words and their corresponding corrections.

To add the error, click the Add button. InDesign displays the Add to Autocorrect List dialog box. Enter the typo in the Misspelled Word field, and enter the correct text in the Correction Field. Click the OK button, and InDesign adds the error to the Autocorrect list.

To remove a word from the list, select the word and click the Remove button. To edit a word in the list, click the Edit button.

Footnotes

InDesign CS2 introduced the ability to add footnotes to text, a capability requested by InDesign users[1] since version 1.0. InDesign's footnotes don't do everything that one could possibly want in such a feature, but they're able to handle a broad range of footnote needs.

What are the limitations? One drawback is that you're limited to one footnote numbering style in a document. If your publications feature one footnote numbering style for body text, and another style for sidebars, you'll have to take care of one of the footnote styles manually (as you have in previous versions).

The other significant (in our opinion) limitation is that the width of the footnote text is based on the width of the column containing the footnote reference marker.

In addition, footnote text is not affected by text wrap, and you cannot add footnotes to footnote text or text in a table.

Finally, footnotes go to the bottom of the column, which is not necessarily the bottom of the page. This means that if we want to add a graphic between the footnote reference and the footnote text, we'd have to resort to text wrap or an inline graphic just to fool the footnote into landing at the bottom of the page.

When we say "footnote reference marker," we mean the number or symbol that appears in the body text. When we say "footnote text," we're referring to the text that appears at the bottom of the column. These two parts make up a "footnote."

Creating a Footnote

To create a footnote, follow these steps (see Figure 3-63).

1. Set the cursor at the point at which you want to add the footnote.

2. Choose Insert Footnote from the Context menu (or the Type menu). When you do this, InDesign inserts a footnote marker (a number or symbol) and positions the text cursor in the footnote text. The footnote text is usually at the bottom of the column containing the marker, but can appear elsewhere in some cases.

3. Enter the text for the footnote.

When you are done editing the footnote text, you can return to the footnote marker (in the body text) by choosing Go to Footnote Reference from the Context menu.

To select all of the text in a footnote, press Command-A/Ctrl-A Editing footnote text is something like editing text in a table cell.

---

[1] Though we have never found a use for them, ourselves.

FIGURE 3-63
Creating a Footnote

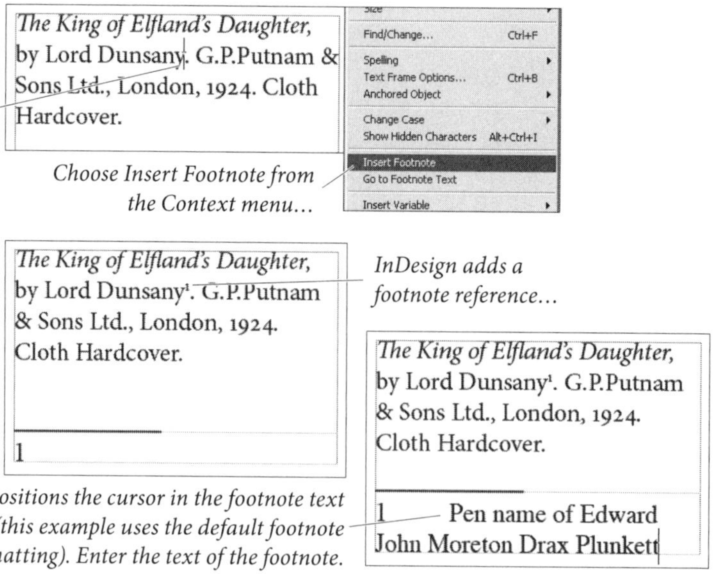
The King of Elfland's Daughter, by Lord Dunsany. G.P.Putnam & Sons Ltd., London, 1924. Cloth Hardcover.
Find/Change... Ctrl+F
Spelling
Text Frame Options... Ctrl+B
Anchored Object
Change Case
Show Hidden Characters Alt+Ctrl+I
Insert Footnote
Go to Footnote Text
Insert Variable
The King of Elfland's Daughter, by Lord Dunsany[1]. G.P.Putnam & Sons Ltd., London, 1924. Cloth Hardcover.
1
The King of Elfland's Daughter, by Lord Dunsany[1]. G.P.Putnam & Sons Ltd., London, 1924. Cloth Hardcover.
1 Pen name of Edward John Moreton Drax Plunkett

Position the cursor in text.

Choose Insert Footnote from the Context menu...

InDesign adds a footnote reference...

...and positions the cursor in the footnote text area (this example uses the default footnote formatting). Enter the text of the footnote.

If you happen to delete the footnote number in the footnote text, you can reinsert it by choosing Footnote Number from the Insert Special Character submenu of the Context menu.

To delete a footnote, delete the footnote marker.

Footnote Options

To control the appearance and behavior of the footnotes in a document, choose Document Footnote Options from the Type menu. The Footnote Options dialog box appears (see Figure 3-64).

Numbering Style. Choose the numbering style you want to use.

Start At. Use this option to set the starting number for the footnotes in each story in the document. If you're continuing footnote numbering from another document, this option comes in handy.

Restart Numbering Every. You can choose to have footnote numbering restart every page, spread, or section.

Show Prefix/Suffix In. "Prefix" and "suffix," in this case, refer to characters that can be placed before or after the figure number. These characters can appear in the footnote reference, the footnote text, or in both places (see Figure 3-65). You can also enter the character(s) you want to use, or choose a predefined character from a list.

Character Style. This option specifies the character style applied to the figure reference number.

FIGURE 3-64
Footnote Options

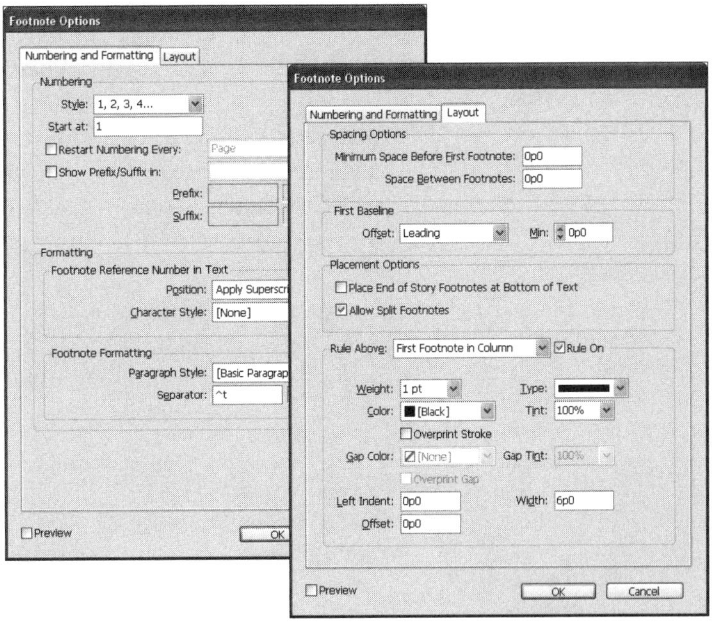

Position. Sets the position of the figure number reference character. You can choose subscript, superscript, or normal position.

Paragraph Style. Choose the paragraph style you want to apply to the footnote text.

Separator. Defines the character between the figure number and the body of the footnote text.

Minimum Space Before First Footnote. Use this option to specify the minimum amount of space between the first footnote in a column and the bottom of the text in the column.

FIGURE 3-65
Footnote Prefix/Suffix

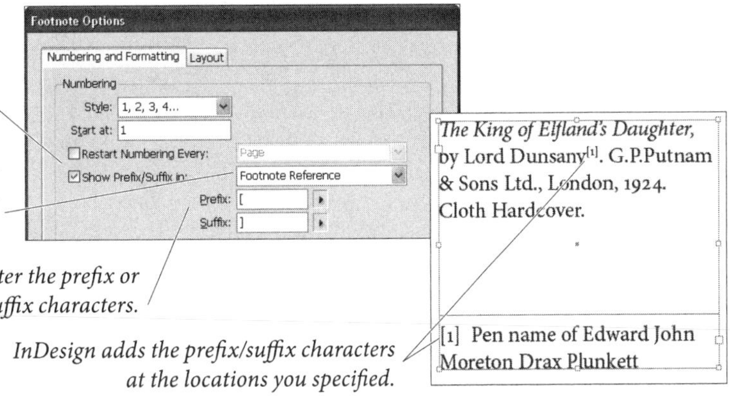

Turn the Show Prefix/Suffix option on.

Set the location(s) at which the prefix/suffix should appear.

Select or enter the prefix or suffix characters.

InDesign adds the prefix/suffix characters at the locations you specified.

The King of Elfland's Daughter, by Lord Dunsany[1]. G.P.Putnam & Sons Ltd., London, 1924. Cloth Hardcover.

[1] Pen name of Edward John Moreton Drax Plunkett

Space Between Footnotes. How much vertical space do you want to insert between footnotes? Enter it here.

First Baseline Offset. This option is very similar to the corresponding option in the Text Frame Options dialog box—it controls the method used to calculate the position of the first baseline of text in a footnote (see the discussion of first baseline offsets earlier in the chapter).

Place End of Story Footnotes at Bottom of Text. Turn this option on, and InDesign will place the footnotes at the end of the story immediately after the end of the text, rather than at the bottom of the last text column (see Figure 3-66).

Allow Split Footnotes. When this option is true, InDesign will split footnotes across columns and pages. When it's false, InDesign will attempt to fit all footnotes into the column containing the footnote (see Figure 3-67). If it's not possible to fit the footnote in that column, InDesign will push the footnote text to the last column in the frame. If that won't work, InDesign will attempt to push the reference and the footnote to the next column capable of holding them both.

FIGURE 3-66
Placing Footnotes at the End of a Story

How should InDesign handle the last footnote or group of footnotes in a story? That's the point of the Place End of Story Footnotes at Bottom of Text option.

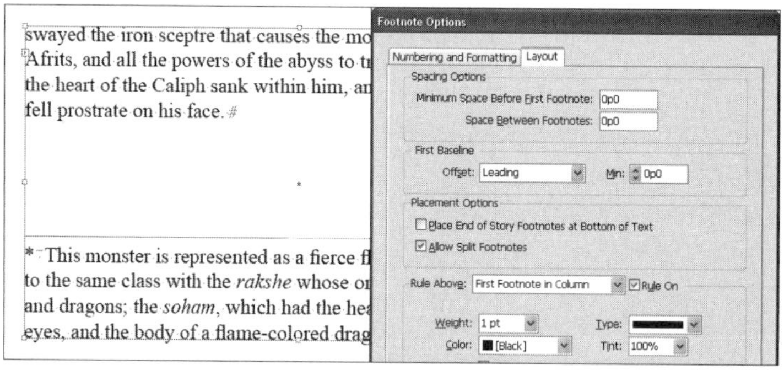

Footnotes at the bottom of the last text frame (option off).

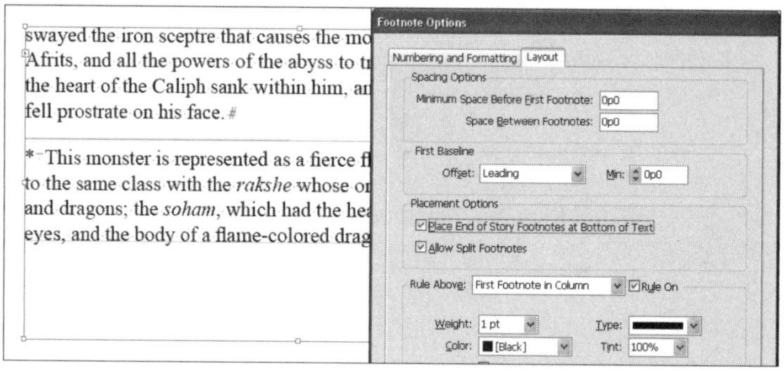

Footnotes at the bottom of the text at the end of the story (option on).

FIGURE 3-67
Splitting Footnotes
(or Not)

When you turn the Allow Split Footnotes option on, InDesign will split footnote text among columns (depending on the length of the footnote text and the location of the footnote reference marker).

Turn the Allow Split Footnotes option off, and InDesign will push the footnote (both the marker and the footnote text) to the next column capable of containing it. With this option off, long footnotes and short columns can easily result in overset text.

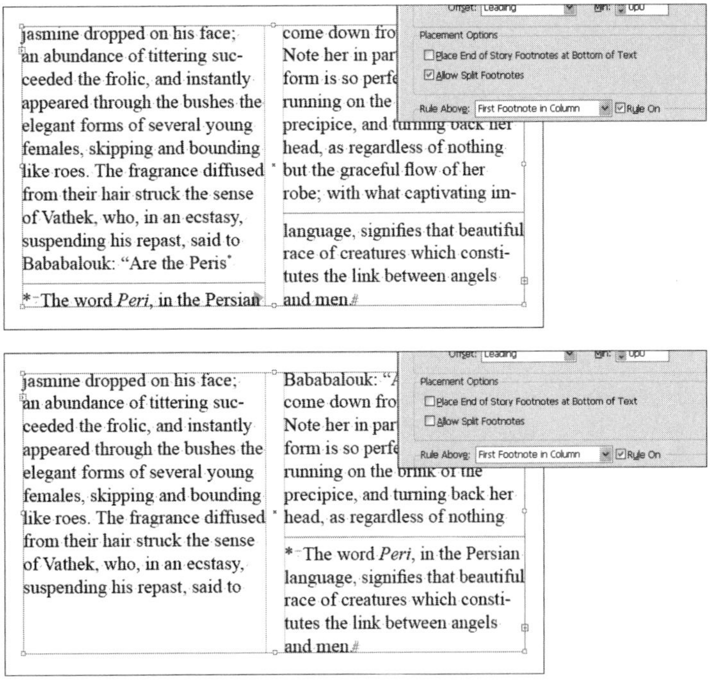

Rule Above. To add a dividing line above the footnote text, turn on the Rule Above option. Most of the controls in this section correspond to paragraph rule options (see Chapter 4, "Type" for more on paragraph rules), but some of them are specific to footnotes.

Choose First Footnote in Column from the pop-up menu to control the settings for the rule above the top of the first footnote only; choose Continued Footnotes to specify the formatting of the rules above all subsequent footnote sections, including footnotes continued in other columns.

The width of a paragraph rule can be set by either the width of the text or the width of the column, but the width of a footnote rule is determined by the value in the Width field.

Endnotes   InDesign doesn't have an Endnotes feature, but there's a workaround solution that involves numbered lists and cross-references. See the article Bob wrote at *http://tinyurl.com/yczhgxr* for details.

Conditional Text

If you publish multiple versions of a document—multiple languages, or any other time the text of the document changes from version to version—you should look at InDesign's conditional text feature.

Ole, for example, publishes (for Adobe) a number of documents related to InDesign scripting. Most of the body copy is the same from version to version, but the script examples vary. In some editions, the examples are written in AppleScript; in others, the scripting language is JavaScript; and another version features VBScript. To keep from having to maintain the different versions as separate documents, Ole uses conditional text.

Conditional text has two components: the conditions themselves, and the text you've marked using the conditions. You work with conditional text using the Conditional Text panel (see Figure 3-68). To display the panel, choose Conditional Text from the Text and Type submenu of the Window menu.

Creating Conditions

To create a condition, follow these steps (see Figure 3-69).

1. Display the Conditional Text panel, if it's not already visible.

2. Click the New Condition button at the bottom of the panel, or choose New Condition from the panel menu. InDesign displays the New Condition dialog box.

3. Enter a name for the condition, then specify the format of the condition indicator using the Method, Appearance, and Color pop-up menus.

4. Click OK to close the dialog box.

Applying Conditions

The process of applying a condition is pretty much the same as applying any other formatting—select some text, then click the condition or conditions in the Conditional Text panel that you want to apply to the text (see Figure 3-70). To remove the condition, select the text and click the condition again (or apply the Unconditional condition).

Creating Condition Sets

A condition set is a group of conditions that can be shown or hidden at the same time. When you apply a condition set, InDesign changes the visibility of all conditions as specified in the set. It's quicker than clicking them one by one. To create a condition set, follow these steps.

1. Display the Conditional Text panel, if it's not already visible. Choose Show Options from the panel menu if the Set pop-up menu is not already visible.

2. Change the visibility of the conditions using the first (left-most) column in the panel list. Make the conditions you want to include in the set visible; hide the others.

FIGURE 3-68
Conditional Text Panel

Click this column to show or hide a condition (when you see the eye icon, the condition is visible).

A check in this column shows the condition(s) applied to the selected text.

Double-click a condition to edit its definition.

Choose Show/Hide Options to display or hide the Set pop-up menu.

You can control the way that InDesign displays the condition indicators using the pop-up menu.

You can load conditions and condition sets from other documents.

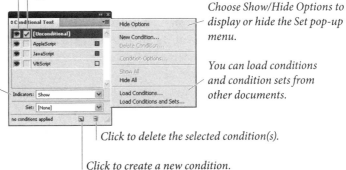

Click to delete the selected condition(s).

Click to create a new condition.

FIGURE 3-69
Creating a Condition

Choose New Condition from the panel menu...

Define the appearance of the condition using the controls in the Indicator section.

FIGURE 3-70
Applying a Condition

Select some text.

Click the condition you want to apply.

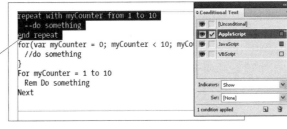

InDesign applies the condition to the text. (We've deselected the text so that you can see the condition indicator.)

3. Choose Create New Set from the Set pop-up menu. InDesign displays the New Condition dialog box.

4. Enter a name for the condition set and click the OK button. InDesign adds the condition set to the Set pop-up menu.

When you want to apply the condition set, choose it from the Set pop-up menu. InDesign will set the visibility of all conditions based on the stored settings in the condition set.

Find and Change

Economists and productivity experts keep telling us that personal computers have not lived up to their promise of increased productivity. Workers, they say, are no more productive than they were before the microcomputer revolution.

They are, of course, wrong—or maybe they've never worked as typists or typesetters. Since the advent of word processing and desktop publishing software, we "text workers" have been enjoying a productivity increase that is nothing short of mind boggling. Although we're not sure "enjoying" is quite the right word.

One of the key innovations of the text processing revolution is the ability to find text in a document and, if necessary, to change it to something else—and all in an automated fashion. It doesn't matter what you call it—"find and change" or "search and replace," it's a kind of text-manipulation tool we didn't have in the "good ol' days."

Find and change is all about pattern recognition. Most of what we do in InDesign (or in life, for that matter) is repetitive. We work our way through text, selecting each occurrence of "f f i" and changing it to "ffi" (the ligature). Or we select each bullet character and replace it with a character from Zapf Dingbats. In each case, we're searching for one pattern in our text and replacing it with another.

Finding and changing text is all about working with strings. A *string* is any range of text—a single character, a word, or a phrase. Strings can also contain special, non-printing characters, such as tab characters, em spaces, or carriage returns.

InDesign has three different ways to find and change text, which we'll call Text, GREP, and Glyph. These search methods correspond to the tabs you see in the Find/Change dialog box (see Figure 3-78). The Object tab in the Find/Change dialog box is for finding and changing formatting applied to page items (rectangles, ellipses, and text frames, for example), and is discussed in Chapter 5, "Drawing."

▶ **Text.** Find and change text strings and text formatting. Includes the ability to search for a limited set of "wildcard" characters.

▶ **GREP.** Find and change text and formatting using regular expressions. Regular expressions give you a way to use much more sophisticated patterns in your searches.

▶ **Glyph.** Find and change individual glyphs.

In addition to the different search methods, there are at least four different ways to perform a search-and-replace operation.

▶ Search for text and replace it with different text.

▶ Search for formatting and replace it with other formatting.

▶ Search for text and apply formatting to it.

▶ Search for formatting, and replace it with text.

FIGURE 3-71
Find/Change dialog box

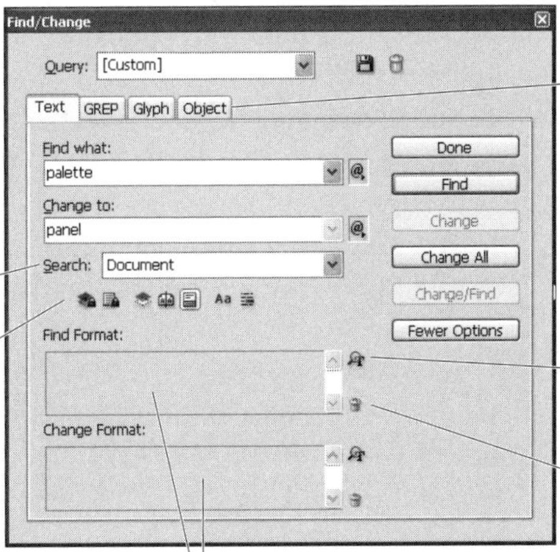

Find/change range.

Find/change options.

Click the tabs to display the options for the different find/change types.

Specify Attributes to Find button

Clear Specified Attributes button

Find/change formatting options. If you do not see these controls, click the More Options button.

Find/Change Options   All three text search methods have a set of options in common. You can turn these options on or off using the little icon buttons in the Find/Change dialog box (see Figure 3-72).

Include Locked Layers (Find Only). InDesign will not change text on locked layers, but you can find it by turning this option on. To change text on a locked layer, unlock the layer or move the text to another layer.

FIGURE 3-72
Find/Change Options

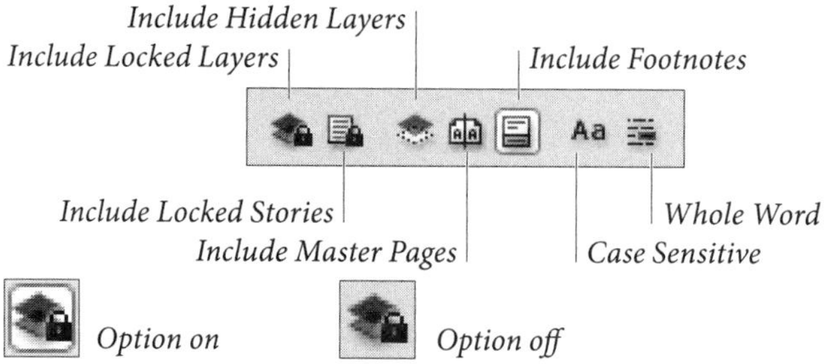

Include Hidden Layers
Include Locked Layers   *Include Footnotes*

Include Locked Stories
Include Master Pages   *Whole Word*
                                           Case Sensitive

Option on   *Option off*

Include Locked Stories (Find Only). A locked story is a story that has been checked out using InCopy. To find text in these stories, turn this option on.

Include Hidden Layers. Turn this option on to find and change text on hidden layers. InDesign will display a block highlight when it finds text on a hidden layer, but it won't show the text itself.

Include Master Pages. To find and change text in text frames on master spreads, turn this option on.

Include Footnotes. To find and change text in footnotes, turn this option on.

Text Search Method Options

In addition to the above options, the Text search method provides two additional options: Whole Word and Case Sensitive.

Whole Word. Turn on the Whole Word option when you want to find only exact matches for the text you entered in the Find What field (if you've entered "dog" and want to find only that word, and not "dogged" or "underdog").

Case Sensitive. Turn on the Case Sensitive option to find only text with the same capitalization as the word you entered (this way, you'll find "dog," but not "Dog").

Find/Change Ranges

All three text search methods give you a way to define the range of text you want to search. Choose one of the options on the Search pop-up menu to set the range of the search: Story, To End of Story, Document, or All Documents. Story always begins the search from the beginning of the story, while To End of Story only searches from the current text cursor position onward. All Documents means every currently open document; this is helpful when you need to find something that may appear in multiple chapters of a book

Finding Text   The options in the Text panel of Find/Change provide basic text search capabilities. This is where you want to go when you need to search for one word and replace it with another. Nothing fancy.

If you need to find some text, follow these steps (see Figure 3-73).

1. Open the Find/Change dialog box (press Command-F/Ctrl-F). Click the Text tab if you need to display the Text panel.

2. Enter the string you want to find in the Find What field.

3. Set the range of the search using the Search pop-up menu.

4. Set find/change options (particularly the Case Sensitive and Whole Word options) as necessary.

FIGURE 3-73
Finding Text

Enter the text you want to search for. Enter metacharacters (if necessary) using the pop-up menu (or simply type them into the Find What field).

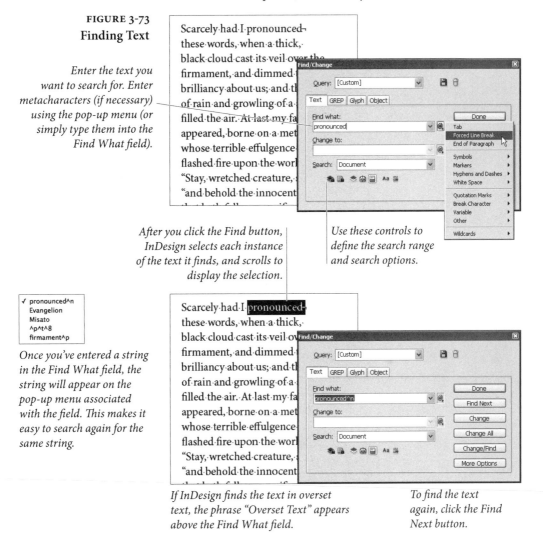

After you click the Find button, InDesign selects each instance of the text it finds, and scrolls to display the selection.

Use these controls to define the search range and search options.

Once you've entered a string in the Find What field, the string will appear on the pop-up menu associated with the field. This makes it easy to search again for the same string.

If InDesign finds the text in overset text, the phrase "Overset Text" appears above the Find What field.

To find the text again, click the Find Next button.

5. Click the Find button. InDesign finds an occurrence of the string you entered in the Find What field and displays it in the publication window, turning pages and scrolling to display the text, if necessary. You can click the Find Next button to find the next occurrence of the text in the specified search range until, eventually, you'll return to the first instance InDesign found.

About metacharacters. You can't enter invisible characters—such as tab characters, line-end characters, or carriage returns—in the Find What or Change To fields. To get around this, you enter codes—known as "metacharacters"—representing those characters. There's no need for a cheat sheet for these characters—they appear on the pop-up menus attached to the Find What and Change To fields.

To enter a metacharacter in the Find What or Change To fields, you can either enter it directly (if you know the code) or choose it from the pop-up menus associated with the fields.

Wildcard Metacharacters

Suppose you need to find all of the part numbers in a document. The part numbers start with the string "IN" and are followed by four letters, a hyphen, and four numbers. How can you find all of the strings?

Use InDesign's "wildcard" metacharacters—these give you a way to find patterns containing unspecified characters. Again, these characters appear on the pop-up menu associated with the Find What field. To match any single character, type "^?" in the Find What field. Enter "^9" to find any single digit, or "^$" to find any single letter.

To find all of the part numbers in the example, you'd enter "IN^$^$^$-^9^9^9^9" in the Find What field. Note that using wildcard metacharacters also helps you avoid finding the strings you don't want to find—if, in our example, we'd used the wildcard-laden string "IN^?^?^?^?^?^?^?^?^?" we'd run the risk of finding the word "INdubitable," which appears in our imaginary catalog many times, rather than the part numbers.

Be careful—entering these wildcard characters in the Change To field results in text being replaced by the metacharacter codes themselves, which is almost certainly *not* what you want. That's why the wildcards don't appear on the Change To field's pop-up menu.

This is the kind of find/change operation that the GREP search method is good at. Take a look at "Using GREP," later in this chapter.

Replacing Text

To replace one text string with another, you enter text in both the Find What and Change To fields of the Find/Change dialog box (see Figure 3-74). Once you've done this, you have two choices:

FIGURE 3-74
Replacing Text

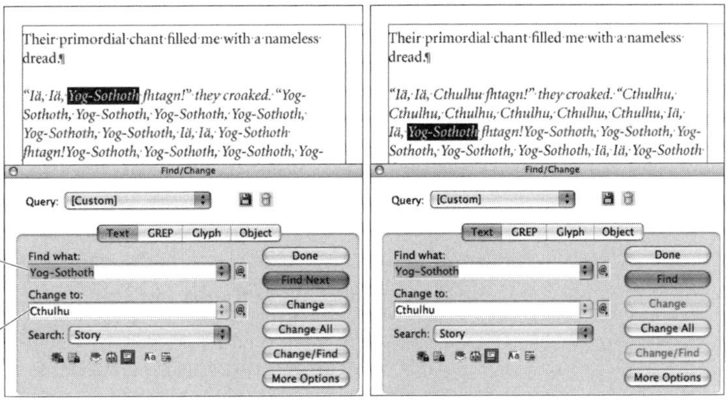

Enter the text you want to find in the Find What field.

Enter the replacement text in the Change To field.

Click the Find button to find the first instance of the text...

...then click the Change button to replace the found text with the text in the Change To field...

...or click the Change/Find button to change the text and then find the next occurrence. Or click the Change All button to change all occurrences.

▶ You can choose to have InDesign replace all instances of the string in the Find What field with the string you entered in the Change To field throughout the search range by clicking the Change All button.

▶ You can find each occurrence of the string in the specified search range and decide to replace it or not. To do this, click the Find button, view the found text, and then click the Find Next, Change, or Change/Find button. The Find Next button moves on to the next instance of the string *without* making any changes; the Change button replaces the selected text with the contents of the Change To field, and waits to see what you'll do next. The Change/Find button replaces the string, then finds the next instance and waits.

The Case Sensitive option also determines the case of the replacement characters. When this option is turned off, InDesign pays attention to the capitalization of the word: If the word it finds is capitalized, it will replace it with a capitalized word, even if the word you typed in the Change To field was in all lowercase.

Text Find/Change Keyboard Shortcuts

If you're a hardcore Find/Change fiend, you're going to want use keyboard shortcuts whenever possible. When you use keyboard shortcuts, you can find and change text without having to have the Find/Change dialog box visible.

Here are a few shortcuts we find useful; you can, of course, change them (to do this, select Keyboard Shortcuts from the Edit menu and look in the Text and Tables Product Area).

▶ You can load the Find What field by selecting one or more characters in a story and pressing Shift-F1.

▶ You can load the Replace With field by selecting some text and pressing Command-F2/Ctrl-F2.

▶ You can find the next occurrence of the most recent search by pressing either Shift-F2.

▶ Once you've found some text, you can replace it (using the current settings) by pressing Command-F3/Ctrl-F3. To replace the text and find the next occurrence of the find text, press Shift-F3.

Finding and Changing Formatting Attributes

What do you do when you want to find all of the occurrences of the word "Zucchini" formatted as 10-point Helvetica bold? It's easy—use the Find Format Settings and Change Format Settings controls at the bottom of the Find/Change dialog box (if you can't see these settings, it's because you need to expand your Find/Change dialog box—click the More Options button, and InDesign expands the panel to display these options).

To choose the formatting attributes you want to find, click the Specify Formatting to Find button. InDesign displays the Find Format Settings dialog box (see Figure 3-75).

The eleven panels of the Find Format Settings dialog box give you the ability to specify almost any formatting that can be applied to text in InDesign. Navigate through the panels until you find the formatting options you want, then use them to specify the formatting you want to find. When you're done, click the OK button to close the dialog box. InDesign displays a list of the options you've chosen in the field in the Find Format section of the Find/Change dialog box.

Note that when you first open the Find Format Settings dialog box, all the pop-up menus and fields are blank. Let's say you select a format—such as 6-point text—and then change your mind; you can simply select the field and press Delete to make it blank again. This comes in handy when searching for fonts. If you select the font Palatino, the styles field automatically changes to "Roman," which means InDesign will *only* search for the characters that use the Roman font style and won't find italic or bold text in that font. However, if you delete "Roman" from that field, the program searches for all cases of Palatino, no matter what the style.

To set up the formatting options you want to apply to any text you find, click the Specify Formatting to Change button. This displays the Change Format Settings dialog box, which is identical in all but name to the Find Format Settings dialog box. Use the Change

FIGURE 3-75
Find and Change Formatting Attributes

In this example, we want to replace the Myriad Pro text with a different font.

If you can't see the Find Format and Change Format areas in the panel, click the More Options button (which then becomes the Fewer Options button) to display Find/Change formatting options.

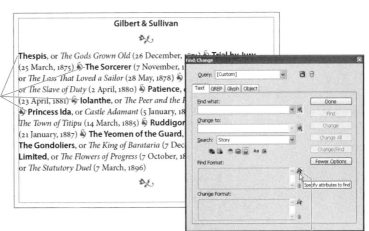

Click the Specify Attributes to Find button to display the Find Format Settings dialog box.

Use the panels of the Find Format Settings dialog box to specify the formatting you want to find.

The Find Format Settings and Change Format Settings dialog boxes contain the same set of panels and options.

Click the Specify Attributes to Change button, then use the Change Format Settings dialog box to specify the formatting you want to apply.

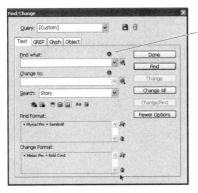

When you've specified formatting, InDesign displays an alert icon.

When you're ready to change text, click the Change All button, or click Find Next to step through the find/change process.

InDesign changes the formatting, finding and changing the font and style you specified.

GILBERT & SULLIVAN

Thespis, or *The Gods Grown Old* (26 December, 1871) ❧ **Trial by Jury**, (25 March, 1875) ❧ **The Sorcerer** (7 November, 1877) ❧ **H.M.S. Pinafore**, or *The Lass That Loved a Sailor* (28 May, 1878) ❧ **The Pirates of Penzance**, or *The Slave of Duty* (2 April, 1880) ❧ **Patience**, or *Bunthorne's Bride* (23 April, 1881) ❧ **Iolanthe**, or *The Peer and the Peri* (25 November, 1882) ❧ **Princess Ida**, or *Castle Adamant* (5 January, 1884) ❧ **The Mikado**, or *The Town of Titipu* (14 March, 1885) ❧ **Ruddigore**, or *The Witch's Curse* (21 January, 1887) ❧ **The Yeomen of the Guard**, (3 October, 1888) ❧ **The Gondoliers**, or *The King of Barataria* (7 December, 1889) ❧ **Utopia, Limited**, or *The Flowers of Progress* (7 October, 1893) ❧ **The Grand Duke**, or *The Statutory Duel* (7 March, 1896)

Format Settings dialog box to specify the formatting you want to apply, then return to the Find/Change dialog box. InDesign displays the formatting you've chosen in the field in the Change Format Settings section.

When you've specified formatting in the Find Format Settings section, InDesign displays an icon above the Find What field. When you enter formatting in the Change Format Settings section, InDesign displays the icon above the Change To field.

To clear the formatting you've set in either the Find Format Settings or the Change Format Settings dialog boxes, click the Clear button in the corresponding section of the Find/Change dialog box.

Once you've specified the formatting you want to find and/or change, you can use the Find/Change dialog box in the same manner as you would when finding/changing text strings.

Note that when you have specified formatting in the Find Format Settings or Change Format Settings dialog boxes, you can:

▶ Leave the contents of the Find What and Change To fields empty. When you do this, InDesign searches for any instances of the formatting you've specified in the Find Format Settings dialog box, and replaces it with the formatting you've entered in the Change Format Settings dialog box.

▶ Enter text in both the Find What and Change To fields. In this case, InDesign searches for an instance of the string you entered in the Find What field that has the formatting specified in the Find Format Settings dialog box, and replaces the text it finds with the string you entered in the Change To field. InDesign applies the formatting from the Change Format Settings dialog box to the replacement text.

▶ Enter text in only the Find What field and leave the Change To field blank. When you do this, InDesign searches for the string you entered in the Find What field (and any formatting you've specified in the Find Format Settings dialog box), and changes the formatting of the found text to the formatting specified in the Change Format Settings dialog box (but does not change the text string itself).

▶ Enter text only in the Change To field and leave the Find What field blank. In this case, InDesign searches for the formatting you set in the Find Format Settings dialog box, and replaces any text it finds with the string you entered in the Change To field (including any formatting you've specified in the Change Format

Settings dialog box). While you aren't likely to use this method (it's pretty strange), it's nice to know it's available.

Replacing Text with the Clipboard

Lurking near the bottom of the options on the Other submenu on the pop-up menu associated with the Change To field are a pair of menu items: Clipboard Contents, Formatted, and Clipboard Contents, Unformatted. They're obscure, but they're really useful. If you enter these metacharacters in the Change To field, you're telling InDesign to paste the current contents of the Clipboard wherever it finds the text you've asked it to find. Anything you can copy—including objects—you can paste over the text you find (see Figure 3-76).

FIGURE 3-76
Replace with Clipboard

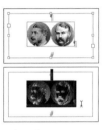

Select the text you want to copy (including inline graphics, as in this example) and copy it to the Clipboard.

In this example we're searching for a bullet character, which we enter in the Find What field as ^8.

Enter ^c in the Change To field of the Find/Change dialog box.

Click the Change All button, and InDesign will insert the contents of the Clipboard wherecver it finds the text.

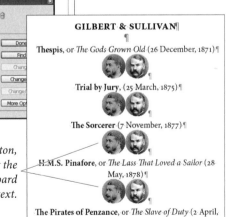

Finding Text by Its Unicode Value

You know what Unicode code point (or ID, or value) you want to search for, but you can't figure out how to enter it in the Find What field? If you're only looking for a single character, you can skip ahead to "Finding and Changing Glyphs," later in this chapter. But if you need to combine your Unicode character with other text, InDesign has a shortcut that's made for what you want to do.

In the Find What field, enter the Unicode value you want to find inside angle brackets, in the form *<number>*, where *number* is the Unicode code point. When you search, InDesign will treat this as the Unicode character you're looking for.

Note, however, that some characters *share* Unicode values. For example, some fonts (such as Minion Pro) list a number of different characters as Unicode 2022, a bullet. If you want to find a specific character in characters defined in this fashion, you'll have to use the Glyph find/change method.

Goodbye, Paragraph!   We frequently work with word processing documents containing notes written to us by other people—you know, things like, "Ole, this section still needs work." We don't want to see that paragraph in the printed version of the piece (and we have, believe us!), so we tag these paragraphs with a paragraph style named "Comment."

When we're laying out the publication, we remove all of the paragraphs tagged with this style name. Do we hunt through the text, laboriously selecting each paragraph and pressing the Delete key? No way—we use an unexpected and probably unintended feature of InDesign's Find/Change dialog box. Here's the easy way to delete paragraphs tagged with a particular style.

1. Press Command-F/Ctrl-F to display the Find/Change dialog box.

2. Leave the Find What and Change To fields empty. Choose a search range from the Search pop-up menu to define the scope of the find/change operation.

3. Click the Clear Specified Attributes buttons in both the Find Format and Change Format areas, if necessary. Then click the Specify Attributes to Find button to open the Find Format Settings dialog box.

4. Select the Style Options panel, if it's not already visible. Choose the paragraph style you want to annihilate from the Paragraph Style pop-up menu, then close the Find Format Settings dialog box by pressing OK.

5. Click the Change All button. InDesign deletes every paragraph tagged with the paragraph style from the search range.

Finding and Changing Text with GREP   There are a variety of different opinions on what the term "GREP" means, where it came from, and how it should be capitalized. We're not even going to try to unravel it all—but we can tell you that it's a way of finding and changing text using regular expressions. Regular expressions are something like the wildcard metacharacters we discussed earlier in this chapter, but they're far more powerful.

Again, it's all about patterns of text characters—and regular expressions, or GREP, give you a very deep and rich set of tools for constructing and transforming patterns. We'll admit at the outset that we cannot cover GREP in depth. There are books longer than this one that do nothing more than explore regular expressions. But we'll take a shot at providing a glimpse of what you can do with this great feature.

Table 3-7 shows the most common GREP metacharacters. GREP supports a number of metacharacters for those familiar with using GREP in a Posix environment, as shown in Table 3-9.

Because GREP uses a number of relatively common characters as part of its system for defining a regular expression, you need to have some way of entering those characters. You do this by "escaping" them, generally by adding a backslash character before the character, as shown in Table 3-8. You do not need to escape characters when they appear inside a character class ([...]).

Finding and Changing Text Using GREP

To find and change text using GREP regular expressions, follow these steps (see Figure 3-77). We'll explain what the regular expression does in Table 3-9.

1. Open the Find/Change dialog box (press Command-F/Ctrl-F). Click the GREP tab to display the GREP panel.

2. Enter the GREP string you want to find in the Find What field. You can type the string, or you can use the pop-up menu associated with the field to build a regular expression.

3. Enter the replacement string in the Change To field. Again, you can use the pop-up menu associated with the field to enter metacharacters. Note that when you use GREP, you can use wildcard characters in the Change To field—something you can't do in a normal text find/change operation.

4. Set the range of the search using the Search pop-up menu.

5. Set any find or change formatting attributes, if necessary.

6. Click the Find button. InDesign finds an occurrence of the regular expression you entered in the Find What field and displays the matching text in the publication window, turning pages and scrolling to display the text, if necessary.

TABLE 3-6
GREP Metacharacters

To match:	Enter:
Start of word	\<
End of word	\>
Word boundary	\b
Start of paragraph	^
End of paragraph	$
End of story	\Z
Zero or one time	?
Zero or more times	*
One or more times	+
Zero or one time (shortest match)	??
Zero or more times (shortest match)	*?
One or more times (shortest match)	+?
Marking subexpression	()
Non-marking subexpression	(?:)
Character set	[]
Or	|
Positive lookbehind	(?<=)
Negative lookbehind	(?<!)
Positive lookahead	(?=)
Negative lookahead	(?!)
Case insensitive on	(?i)
Case insensitive off	(?-i)
Multiline on	(?m)
Mulitline off	(?-m)
Single-line on	(?s)
Single-line off	(?-s)

7. Click the Change button to change the text to the regular expression you entered in the Change To field.

8. At this point, you can continue finding and changing text by clicking the Find Next, Change, or Change and Find buttons, or click the Change All button to apply your changes to all of the matching text in the specified range.

TABLE 3-7
Posix Metacharacters for GREP

Posix Expression	Matches:
[[:alnum:]]	Same as Any Character
[[:alpha:]]	Same as Any Letter
[[:digit:]]	Same as Any Number
[[:lower:]]	Same as Any Lowercase Character
[[:punct:]]	Any punctuation
[[:space:]]	Same as White Space
[[:upper:]]	Same as Any Uppercase Character
[[:word:]]	Same as Any Word
[[:xdigit:]]	Matches any hexadecimal digit character (1234567890ABCDEF)
[[=a=]]	Matches any alternate of the character you enter between the equals signs. In this example you would find A, a, AÂ, â, and ä.

TABLE 3-8
Escaping Special Characters

Character:	Character name:	Enter:
\	Backslash	\\
(	Open parenthesis	\(
)	Close parenthesis	\)
{	Open brace	\{
}	Close brace	\}
[	Open bracket	\[
]	Close bracket	\]
.	Period	\.

Marking Subexpressions

One of the coolest things about finding and changing text using GREP is that you can use *marking subexpressions*—a way of slicing, dicing, and rearranging the text you've found. Marking subexpressions can take a part of the text you've found and use it in the replacement text. The best way to show what this means is to present a couple of examples.

Re-ordering names. Imagine that you have to take a list of names that have been typed in "last name, first name" order and convert them to "first name last name" order. This kind of operation is impossible to do using the Text search method, but it's easy with GREP and marking subexpressions (see Figure 3-78).

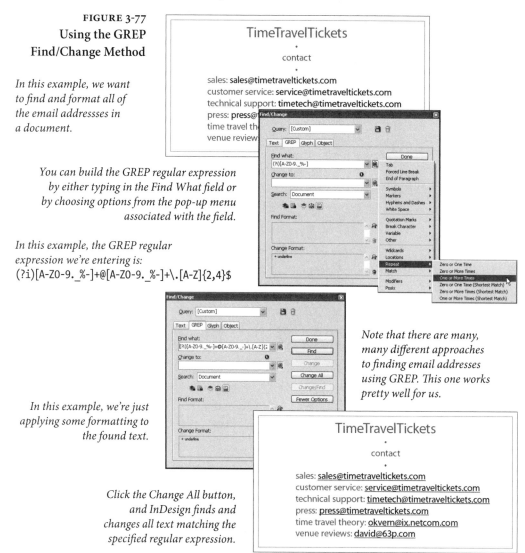

FIGURE 3-77
**Using the GREP
Find/Change Method**

*In this example, we want
to find and format all of
the email addressses in
a document.*

*You can build the GREP regular expression
by either typing in the Find What field or
by choosing options from the pop-up menu
associated with the field.*

*In this example, the GREP regular
expression we're entering is:*
(?i)[A-ZO-9._%-]+@[A-ZO-9._%-]+\.[A-Z]{2,4}$

*Note that there are many,
many different approaches
to finding email addresses
using GREP. This one works
pretty well for us.*

*In this example, we're just
applying some formatting to
the found text.*

*Click the Change All button,
and InDesign finds and
changes all text matching the
specified regular expression.*

Formatting text between tags. Imagine that you're working with
an author who consistently marks bold and italic text with simple
HTML-style formatting tags: "<i>" for italic and "<b>" for bold.
Luckily, they're quite consistent about marking the end of the formatting using "</i>" and "</i>". How can you find the text between
the formatting tags, format it, and, at the same time, remove the tags?

In this example, we'll use a marking subexpression to capture the
text between the tags, and we'll replace the text with the captured
text, excluding the tags (see Figure 3-79). Using regular expressions
to find text *between* some arbitrary beginning and ending text is one
of the great things about the GREP find/change method.

TABLE 3-9
What's Going on in the
GREP Example?

GREP Expression:	What it does:
(?i)	Makes the find/change case-insensitive
[A-Z0-9._%-]	Matches the specified character range: from A to Z, from 0 to 9, and the characters "._%-"
+	Matches the character range one or more times
@	Matches a literal ampersand
[A-Z0-9._%-]	Matches the specified character range: from A to Z, from 0 to 9, and the the characters "._%-"
+	Matches the character range one or more times
/.	Matches a literal period character
[A-Z]	Matches the character range A-Z
{2,4}	Matches a two to four letter string (.com, .org, .edu)
$	Matches the end of the word

Simple Searches Made Better with GREP

By now, every desktop publisher is familiar with the drill: place a word processing file, then find and change all of the little annoyances that make a mess of text. Double spaces. Multiple tabs. Space before punctuation. For years, we've used the standard text find/change features (what you see in the Text panel of the Find/Change dialog box) to do this—but this often means that we have to run through the search multiple times to get all of the instances of the offending text. Take double spaces as an example: we search, search, and then search again until InDesign tells us no more instances have been found.

GREP offers us a better way to deal with this type of search. Rather than finding and changing the text multiple times, we can take care of it all in a single pass. Table 3-10 shows a few of our favorite text cleanup operations. Note that we use $1 in some cases to avoid deleting a return character and, potentially, paragraph formatting.

Learning More about GREP

We don't have the space here to cover GREP in all its glory. Peter Kahrel has written an excellent tutorial on using GREP in InDesign that is available as a downloadable PDF from O'Reilly—that would probably be the best place to start learning about GREP.

Another O'Reilly book, *Mastering Regular Expressions*, by Jeffrey E. F. Friedl, is a fairly complete tour of GREP. It does not specifically

FIGURE 3-78
Re-Ordering
Names with GREP

Parentheses mark parts of the found text. In this example, the GREP regular expression we're entering in the Find What field is:

^(.+),\s(.+)$

$2

$1

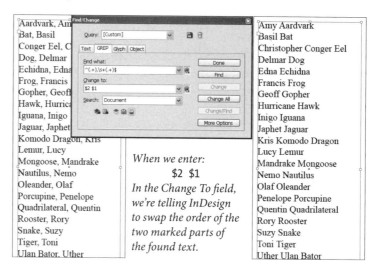

When we enter:

$2 $1

In the Change To field, we're telling InDesign to swap the order of the two marked parts of the found text.

talk about GREP in InDesign, but it's a great place to learn more about the inner details of how regular expressions do their work.

For more information on either or both of the above titles, you can go to *www.indesignsecrets.com/grep/*.

Ole likes a regular expression development and debugging tool called "RegexBuddy," by JGSoft. It's Windows-only, and a demo version is available from *www.regexbuddy.com*.

Finding and Changing Glyphs

We've talked about the wonder of Unicode and OpenType fonts, or, at least, we *will* talk about them in Chapter 4, "Type." There are lots of good things to say about a system that makes publishing in just about any language or character set much easier than it used to be, and provides great typesetting features at the same time.

But you've probably noticed that there are some things that the combination of Unicode, OpenType, and InDesign don't handle very well. By "noticed," of course, we mean that you've spent time yelling at your screen when a specific character can't be found, or can't be entered, or displays the "dreaded pinkness" of glyph substitution.

Take, for example, the font we use for this book, Minion Pro. Minion Pro has a number of ornamental characters we're very fond of—the only trouble is that they're all considered bullet characters by InDesign. Which leads to a problem: There is simply no way to enter the replacement character in the Change To field of the Text panel of the Find/Change dialog box. If you try to copy the character into the field, you'll get ^8 (or Unicode <2022>), a normal bullet. You can't even use the Unicode value you can find from your operating system to refer to the correct character.

FIGURE 3-79
Formatting Tags with GREP

Parentheses mark parts of the found text. In this example, the GREP regular expression we're entering in the Find What field is:

(.+?)
This captures the text between the tags as $1.

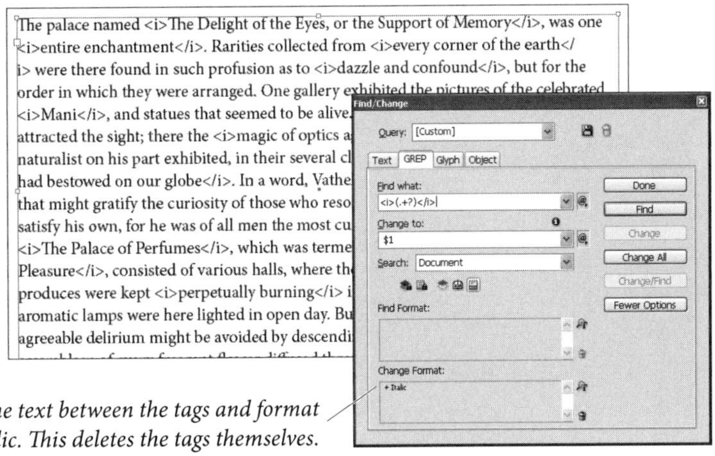

The palace named <i>The Delight of the Eyes, or the Support of Memory</i>, was one <i>entire enchantment</i>. Rarities collected from <i>every corner of the earth</i> were there found in such profusion as to <i>dazzle and confound</i>, but for the order in which they were arranged. One gallery exhibited the pictures of the celebrated <i>Mani</i>, and statues that seemed to be alive, attracted the sight; there the <i>magic of optics a... naturalist on his part exhibited, in their several cl... had bestowed on our globe</i>. In a word, Vathe... that might gratify the curiosity of those who reso... satisfy his own, for he was of all men the most cu... <i>The Palace of Perfumes</i>, which was terme... Pleasure</i>, consisted of various halls, where the... produces were kept <i>perpetually burning</i> i... aromatic lamps were here lighted in open day. Bu... agreeable delirium might be avoided by descendi...

[Find/Change dialog box]
Query: [Custom]
Text | GREP | Glyph | Object
Find what: <i>(.+?)</i>
Change to: $1
Search: Document
Find Format:
Change Format: + Italic
Done / Find / Change / Change All / Change/Find / Fewer Options

Replace the text between the tags and format it as italic. This deletes the tags themselves.

InDesign replaces applies the formatting and removes the tags themselves.

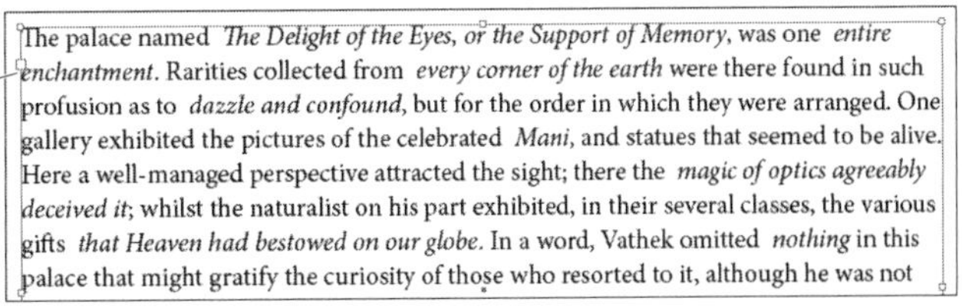

The palace named The Delight of the Eyes, or the Support of Memory, *was one* entire enchantment. *Rarities collected from* every corner of the earth *were there found in such profusion as to* dazzle and confound, *but for the order in which they were arranged. One gallery exhibited the pictures of the celebrated* Mani, *and statues that seemed to be alive. Here a well-managed perspective attracted the sight; there the* magic of optics agreeably deceived it; *whilst the naturalist on his part exhibited, in their several classes, the various gifts* that Heaven had bestowed on our globe. *In a word, Vathek omitted* nothing *in this palace that might gratify the curiosity of those who resorted to it, although he was not*

TABLE 3-10
Simple Searches Made Better with GREP

Task:	Find What:	Change To:
Replace runs of spaces with single space	\s+	<space>
Replace multiple returns with single return	(\r)+	$1
Remove empty paragraphs	^\r	
Remove spaces before a return	\s+(\r)	$1
Remove spaces before specified punctuation	\s([.?!;:,])	$1
Remove spaces at end of story	\s+\Z	

Instead of screaming in frustration, you can use the controls in the third panel of the Find/Change dialog box, Glyph. The Glyph find and change method can only find one character at a time, but it does this single job very well (see Figure 3-80).

1. Open the Find/Change dialog box (press Command-F/Ctrl-F). Click the Glyph tab to display the Glyph panel.

2. Choose the font, font style, and glyph you want to find. You can enter the Unicode/Glyph ID if you know it, but it's usually better to choose a glyph from the Glyph pop-up menu (which is really something like a miniature version of the Glyphs panel).

3. Choose the font, font style, and glyph you want to change to.

4. Set the range of the search using the Search pop-up menu.

5. Click the Find button. InDesign finds an occurrence of the character you specified and displays the matching text in the document window, turning pages and scrolling to display the character, if necessary.

6. Click the Change button to change the glyph.

7. At this point, you can continue finding and changing text by clicking the Find Next, Change, or Change and Find buttons, or click the Change All button to apply your changes to all of the matching text in the specified range.

Saving Queries

If you have a find/change operation that you use often, you should save it. To do this, click the Save Query button in the Find/Change dialog box—it looks like a floppy disk—a computer storage medium some of us can still remember.

Enter a name for the query in the Save Query dialog box, then click the OK button to save the query. Once you've done this, the name of the query will appear on the Query pop-up menu in the Find/Change dialog box, and you can recall all of the settings of that particular find/change operation by choosing the menu item.

Working with InDesign Tagged Text

One of the most useful features of InDesign is rarely mentioned in the marketing materials. It's not the typesetting features, nor is it the ability to place native Photoshop and Illustrator files. We think those are great features, but they're not it.

What is this mystery feature? It's the ability to save and read tagged text. To explain why this is so important, we've got to explain a little bit about what tags are.

The Land That WYSIWYG Forgot

Tags have been around for a long time. Before desktop publishing appeared, the world of typesetting was ruled by dedicated type-setting systems. As we set type on these machines, we didn't see

FIGURE 3-80
**Finding and
Changing Glyphs**

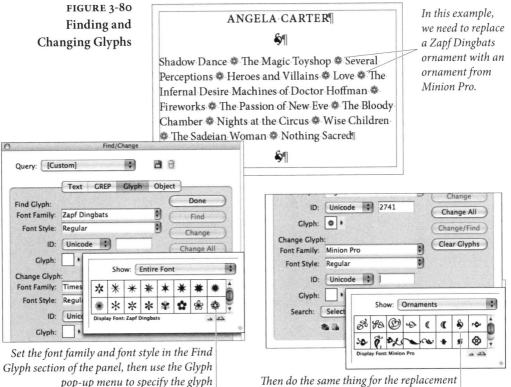

*In this example,
we need to replace
a Zapf Dingbats
ornament with an
ornament from
Minion Pro.*

*Set the font family and font style in the Find
Glyph section of the panel, then use the Glyph
pop-up menu to specify the glyph
you want to find.*

*Then do the same thing for the replacement
glyph in the Change Glyph section of the panel.*

*InDesign replaces
the glyph you're
looking for with
the replacement
glyph.*

anything that looked like the type we were setting. Instead, we saw
the text of our newspapers, books, and magazines surrounded (and
sometimes obscured) by cryptic symbols: typesetting tags and codes.

To see what these symbols meant, we had to print the file. Only
then would we see our type with its formatting applied.

Then came the Macintosh, PageMaker, the LaserWriter, and
WYSIWYG (What you See Is What You Get) publishing. This revolution made it easier for more people to set type—in part because it
freed us from having to learn and use the obscure codes and tags

of the dedicated typesetting systems. These days, modern desktop publishing programs are better typesetting systems than anything we had in the old days—and you can see what you're doing.

Why Bother with Tags?

Why should you mess with tags in this day and age? It turns out that they can make some jobs easier, and sometimes they can make it possible to do things that wouldn't be practical to do using menus, dialog boxes, and the Character and Paragraph panels.

The tagged text export filter takes formatted InDesign text and turns it into tags in a text file. The tagged text import filter reads tags and turns them into formatted ("WYSIWYG") text. InDesign's tagged text export filter is the only text export filter that doesn't change the appearance of the text you're exporting.

Here are some of the reasons you might want to use tags:

▶ If you work with people who use text editors (instead of full-featured word processors), they cannot apply formatting such as bold or italic or paragraph styles.

▶ Any application that can save files in text-only format can be used to create formatted text for use in InDesign. This means that your catalog clients can use FileMaker database to mark up their text—Visual Basic, Microsoft Excel, and Microsoft Access are other obvious choices. It might even help your old uncle who lives in a cave and uses nothing but EDLIN.

▶ You can store frequently used formatted text as tagged text files. It's far quicker to place a tagged text file than it is to open another InDesign publication and copy/paste the text you want.

Getting Started with Tagged Text

To learn how tags work, the best thing to do is export some formatted text from InDesign (select the story, choose Export from the File menu, and change the Format pop-up menu to InDesign Tagged Text) and then use a text editor to look at the file.

While it is possible to open these tagged text files in a word processor like Microsoft Word, those programs often assume that because there are tags in the file, it must be HTML (so you either get errors or things get really weird). That's why text editors (such as Windows Notepad or BBEdit) are better—they just deal with plain text and never try to format anything.

The "official word" on tagged text is the Tagged Text.pdf file, which you'll find on the web at *http://bit.ly/bExJT3*. This guide includes basic instructions and a list of most of the tags you can use.

One thing that's implied by the tagged text documentation, but not explicitly stated, is that you can enter any character using its Unicode value. To do that, use the form "<0xnnnn>", where *nnnn* is the hexadecimal form of the code (as seen in the Glyphs panel).

What Tags Can Contain

InDesign's tags can specify basic character formatting (such as font, point size, color, or baseline shift), paragraph formatting (such as indents, tabs, and paragraph space before and after), and styles (both paragraph styles and character styles). Any formatting that can be applied to text can be applied using tags. Even tables can be exported or imported as tagged text. (That means you can program your database to export fully formatted InDesign tables.)

Tag Structure

InDesign tags are always surrounded by open (<) and close (>) angle brackets (which most of us also know as "greater than" and "less than" symbols). The first characters in a tagged text file must state the character encoding (ASCII, ANSI, UNICODE, BIG5, or SJIS), followed by the platform (MAC or WIN). So the typical Windows tagged text file begins with <ASCII-WIN>, and the Macintosh version begins with <ASCII-MAC>. If InDesign doesn't see one of these tags at the start of the file, InDesign won't interpret the tags, and all the tags show up as part of your text. Here are a few more details.

▶ Any characters you enter outside a tag will appear as characters in the imported text.

▶ Enter an empty tag to return the formatting affected by the tag to its default state. For example:

```
Baseline <cBaselineShift:3>Shift<cBaselineShift:> text following
should be back to normal.
```

Paragraph Style Tags

If you're a long-time PageMaker user, you may have worked with PageMaker's style tags to apply paragraph formatting to text files. InDesign's tagged text format is different than PageMaker's, but you can create a "minimalist" tagged text file that's almost as easy to work with as PageMaker's paragraph style tags. Here's the header for an example tagged text file:

```
<ASCII-WIN>
<DefineParaStyle:heading><DefineParaStyle:subhead><DefineParaStyle:
para>
<ColorTable:=<Black:COLOR:CMYK:Process:0,0,0,1>>
```

Note that the paragraph style definitions in this tagged text file do not contain any formatting—our assumption is that you'll set up corresponding paragraph styles in your publication. Then all you need to do is paste the appropriate header at the top of a text file, and then enter the paragraph style tags for each paragraph. If, when preparing a file for import into PageMaker, you entered "<heading>" then enter "<ParaStyle:heading>" for InDesign.

Here's an example (very simple) text file marked up with Page-Maker paragraph tags:

```
<heading 1>TimeTravelTickets
<subhead>Travel through time to experience the greatest artistic
performances in history!
<para>We are pleased to announce our Summer, 2007 series.
```

Here's the same text, marked up with InDesign tags:

```
<ASCII-WIN>
<DefineParaStyle:heading><DefineParaStyle:subhead><DefineParaStyle:
para>
<ParaStyle:heading>TimeTravelTickets
<ParaStyle:subhead>Travel through time to experience the greatest
artistic performances in history!
<ParaStyle:para>We are pleased to announce our Summer, 2007 series.
```

A few things to note about converting PageMaker paragraph style tags to InDesign tagged text:

▶ While you do not need to include the `<DefineParagraphStyle>` tags in the heading of the file, it's a good idea to do so. If you don't, and then import the tagged text file into a document that does not contain the styles referred to in the tagged text file, InDesign will not associate the paragraphs with the style.

▶ While PageMaker paragraph style tags don't require that you tag each paragraph, you should tag each paragraph in the InDesign version of the file.

After Words

In academic circles, debate continues on whether we're born with the ability to understand language, or whether it's something we're taught. We don't know the answer, and, most of the time, we don't even know which side of the argument we want to be on. What we do know is that language is the most important technology humans have developed.

In this chapter, we've shown how to get words into InDesign, how to organize them in your publications, and how to get them out again. Next stop—typesetting with InDesign!

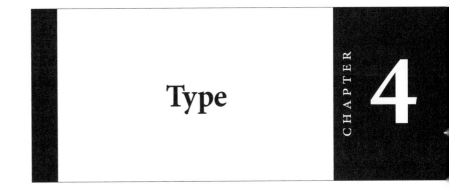

Type

Ole's tale: "Late night. The pale glow from the monochrome monitor of my Compugraphic phototypesetter. The smell of the office standard 'French Vanilla' coffee—warming, now, for several hours and resembling nothing so much as battery acid. The gentle snoring of one of the staff writers, who is curled up in the warmth of the unit that holds the filmstrips containing the fonts I'm using to set his story.

"These are the things I think of when I hear the word 'typesetting'—they're memories from my job at Seattle's free rock and roll newspaper *The Rocket*, circa 1982. Desktop publishing didn't exist yet, and digital (as opposed to photo) typesetting systems—with their WYSIWYG displays—were rare. The codes and characters I saw on my screen wouldn't look anything like type until they were printed, one character at a time, on a strip of photographic film and developed. I could set just about any kind of type using that machine, provided the characters would fit on a piece of film not more than seven inches wide, and provided I didn't need to use characters from more than six fonts."

When desktop publishing appeared, we found that it couldn't do everything Ole could do with his Compugraphic—but that being able to see what our type would look like *before we printed it* more than made up for any deficiencies. These days, page layout programs are far more capable than Ole's trusty EditWriter. Does that mean, however, that there's no more room for improvement? For surprising new features? Is typesetting "done"?

Not a chance—InDesign offers a number of improvements and surprises in the area of typesetting. It's an evolutionary product—not a revolutionary one, but, on its release, InDesign became the best desktop typesetting program, and raised the bar for its competition.

In this chapter, we'll walk through InDesign's typesetting features. We'll start with character formatting (font, point size, kerning, and baseline shift are examples of character formatting), move on to paragraph formatting (indents, tabs, space above and below, and composition), and then dive into formatting using character and paragraph styles. Along the way, there may be a joke or two.

Selecting and Formatting Text

Generally, when you want to change the formatting of some text, you have to select it with the Type tool. However, there are two caveats to this statement. First, because paragraph formatting (which we'll discuss later) always applies to an entire paragraph, you don't have to select every character in the paragraph before applying it.

Second (and more interesting) is that you can apply text formatting to text frames you've selected using the Selection tool or the Direct Selection tool. When you do this, InDesign applies the formatting to all of the text in the text frame, including any overset text. InDesign won't let you use this method to apply formatting to text frames that are linked to other text frames. Tired of using the Type tool to select and format every photo caption on a page? Use the Selection tool to select them all and apply your formatting—it's easier, and it's quicker (see Figure 4-1).

FIGURE 4-1
Formatting the Text in Text Frames

Use the Selection tool to select the text frames you want to format...

...and apply formatting. InDesign applies the formatting to all of the text in the text frames. That's all there is to it.

In this example, we changed character attributes (font, font style, and leading) and paragraph attributes (alignment).

The ability to apply formatting with the Selection tools is very powerful, but it's also slightly dangerous. Let's say you set a single character to Zapf Dingbats somewhere in your text frame. If you select the text frame using the Selection tool and then apply a new font, every character—including that dingbat—gets changed.

The only warnings that InDesign gives you that some of the text in the selected text frame uses a different font are: the Font field in the Character panel is blank, and the Font submenu (under the Type menu) has hyphens next to each font.

Character Formatting

Character formatting controls the appearance of the individual letters in your publication. Font, type size, color, and leading are all aspects of character formatting. (Longtime QuarkXPress users won't think of leading as a character format, but we'll cover that next.)

We refer to all formatting that can be applied to a selected range of text as "character" formatting, and refer to formatting that InDesign applies at the paragraph level as "paragraph" formatting. Tab settings, indents, paragraph rules, space above, and space after are examples of paragraph formatting. There are areas of overlap in these definitions. Leading, for example, is really a property that applies to an entire *line* of text (InDesign uses only the largest leading value in a line), but we'll call it "character" formatting, nonetheless, because you can apply it to individual characters.

In addition to these distinctions, InDesign's paragraph styles can include character formatting, but apply to entire paragraphs. See "Styles," later in this chapter.

Character Formatting Controls

InDesign's character formatting controls are found in both the Character panel and the Control panel (see Figure 4-2). The controls in the panels are substantially the same, so we'll discuss them once.

To display the Character panel and shift the focus to the panel's Font field, press Command-T/Ctrl-T. If the panel is already visible, InDesign hides it; you may need to press it twice.

To display the Control panel, press Command-Option-6/Ctrl-Alt-6. If the panel is already open, but is displaying the paragraph controls, press Command-Option-7/Ctrl-Alt-7.

Font Family and Font

Selecting a font in InDesign is a little bit different than selecting a font in most other page layout programs. To InDesign, fonts are categorized as font "families," and each family is made up of one or

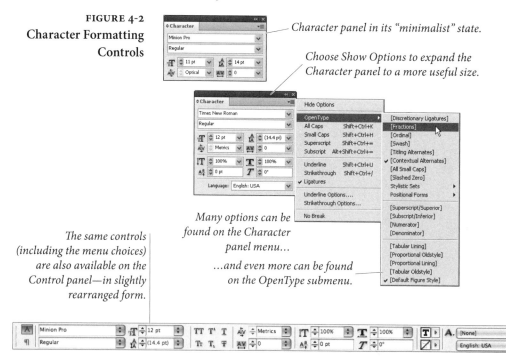

FIGURE 4-2
Character Formatting
Controls

Character panel in its "minimalist" state.

Choose Show Options to expand the
Character panel to a more useful size.

Many options can be
found on the Character
panel menu...

...and even more can be found
on the OpenType submenu.

The same controls
(including the menu choices)
are also available on the
Control panel—in slightly
rearranged form.

more type styles. A font family is a set of typefaces designed to have
a common "look." A "font," then, is specified by its font family and
type style. In this book, we've used the font family Minion Pro, and
the type style Regular for the body text—so the font of the body text
is "Minion Pro Regular."

InDesign's user interface for selecting fonts mirrors this approach.
When you choose a font from the Font submenu of the Type menu,
you must select both the font family and a specific type style.

Note that InDesign does not have "type styles" in the same way
that other programs do—it makes no assumption that the selected
font family has a "bold" or "italic" member, and will never *generate*
a fake bold or italic version. If you don't have a font for a particular
type style, you won't see it on the Type Styles menu (see Figure 4-3).

To select a font family or type style, you can type into the appropriate field—you don't have to use the menu. As you type the name
of a font family or type style, InDesign will display the available font
or fonts that match the characters you typed. For instance you can
type "T" and it will guess "Tekton" (if you have that font installed);
if you meant "Times" then you may have to type "Ti" or even "Tim".
Note that you can also press the up and down arrow keys, which is
especially helpful in the Style field to move from Regular to Bold to
Italic, and so on.

FIGURE 4-3
Selecting a Font

On the Mac OS, you can choose the family and style from the Font pop-up menu in a single step.

Select a font family...

...and then select a type style. InDesign will not generate fake bold or italic type styles.

The number of type styles available varies from family to family.

Font Style Keyboard Shortcuts. Although InDesign won't generate a bold or italic weight, you can type Command-Shift-B/Ctrl-Shift-B to make your text bold and Command-Shift-I/Ctrl-Shift-I to make it italic. If a font doesn't have a bold or italic version, InDesign will not change the text.

Symbols and Dingbats. Sometimes, when you change to a symbol font (such as Zapf Dingbats), you may encounter font substitution (the dreaded pink highlight). This can happen because InDesign is attempting to map the character from one font to another. To avoid this problem, hold down Shift as you apply the font.

Duplicate Font Names. Some folks have more than one font with the same name on their systems—such as a TrueType and a PostScript version of Times Roman. While most programs just pick one (and you never know which you're getting), InDesign displays both fonts, including either T1 or TT in parentheses after the font name.

Size   You can change the size of text by entering the point size you want in the Size field of the Character or Control panel, or choose a point size from the attached pop-up menu (see Figure 4-4). If you type the size, you can specify it in .001-point increments. After you've entered the size you want, apply the change by pressing Return/Enter or by pressing Tab to move to another field.

Size Adjustment Keyboard Shortcuts. You can increase the size of selected type by pressing Command-Shift->/Ctrl-Shift->, or decrease the size by pressing Command-Shift-</Ctrl-Shift-<. The amount that InDesign increases or decreases the point size when you use these shortcuts depends on the value in the Size/Leading field in the Units & Increments Preferences dialog box.

FIGURE 4-4
Point Size

*Click the "nudge"
buttons, or...*

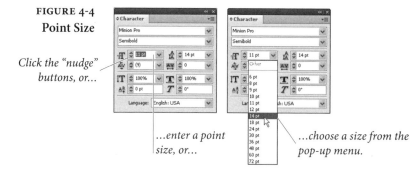

*...enter a point
size, or...*

*...choose a size from the
pop-up menu.*

To increase or decrease the size of the selected text by five times the value entered in the Size/Leading field, you can add the Option or Alt key: Command-Option-Shift->/Ctrl-Alt-Shift->, or Command-Option-Shift-</Ctrl-Alt-Shift-<.

Scaling Text by Scaling the Frame. You can scale text by scaling the frame itself. To do this, select the text frame with the Selection tool, then hold down the Command/Ctrl key and drag a corner or side handle. Hold down Command-Shift/Ctrl-Shift as you drag to scale proportionally (a good thing, as far as text is concerned).

Leading   Text characters—usually—sit on an imaginary line, the *baseline*. *Leading* (pronounced "ledding") is the vertical distance from the baseline of one line of text to the next text baseline. When you hear "10 on 12" or see "10/12", it means "10-point text on 12-point leading." In InDesign, leading is measured from the baseline of a line of text to the baseline of the line of text above (see Figure 4-5). When you increase the leading in a line, you push that line farther from the line above it, and farther down from the top of the text frame.

In InDesign—as in PageMaker—leading is an attribute of individual characters, but the largest leading value in a line predominates (see Figure 4-6). This differs from QuarkXPress, where leading is a paragraph attribute (although if you use QuarkXPress's relative leading mode, the largest leading in a line predominates).

For those of us who came to desktop publishing from typesetting, the idea of leading being a character attribute seems more natural than QuarkXPress' method of setting it at the paragraph level. Fortunately, InDesign lets you have it both ways: When you turn on the Apply Leading to Entire Paragraphs option in the Type pane of the Preferences dialog box, the program automatically sets the leading of every character in a paragraph to the same value. QuarkXPress users will probably want to turn this option on.

FIGURE 4-5
Leading

For
Character
Minion Pro
Semibold
10 pt
13 pt
Optical
0
100%
100%
0 pt
0°
Language: English: USA

Leading is the distance from the baseline of one line to the baseline of the line above it.

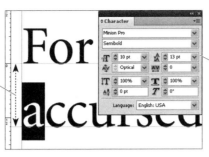

You set the leading of selected characters using the Leading control—enter a value, click the arrows, or choose a value from the pop-up menu. You can also choose Auto from the pop-up menu to base the leading on the point size of the text.

FIGURE 4-6
The Largest Leading in a Line Wins

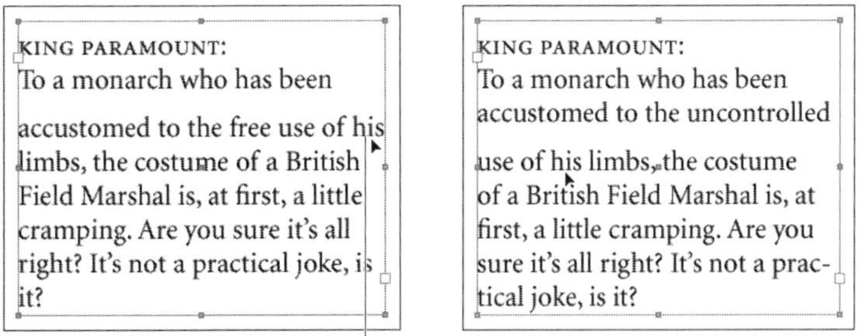

KING PARAMOUNT:
To a monarch who has been
accustomed to the free use of his
limbs, the costume of a British
Field Marshal is, at first, a little
cramping. Are you sure it's all
right? It's not a practical joke, is
it?
KING PARAMOUNT:
To a monarch who has been
accustomed to the uncontrolled
use of his limbs, the costume
of a British Field Marshal is, at
first, a little cramping. Are you
sure it's all right? It's not a practical joke, is it?

This word has a larger leading value than the other characters in the line.

When the word moves to another line (due, in this example, to a change in the text), the larger leading is applied to that line.

However, this preference only affects paragraphs that you change *after* you set it. For instance, you could have it on most of the time, then turn it off in order to vary the leading of lines within a paragraph—something you sometimes have to do to optically balance display copy—and then turn the preference back on again.

How to Avoid Wacky Leading. The main disadvantage of making leading a character attribute (when the Apply Leading to Entire Paragraphs option is turned off) is that it requires a bit more vigilance on your part than the "leading-as-a-paragraph-attribute" approach taken by QuarkXPress and most word processors. Most of the time, leading values should be the same for all of the characters in the paragraph. If, as you apply leading amounts, you fail to select all of the characters in a paragraph, you'll get leading that varies from line to line—which, most of the time, is a typesetting mistake.

You can also get this effect if you leave your paragraph's leading set to the default Auto leading, which always sets the leading to some percentage (usually 120%) of the text size—or, more specifically, some percentage of the largest character on a line. This is true even when Apply to Entire Paragraph is turned on. We strongly urge you not to use Auto leading (except for inline frames and graphics, as discussed in Chapter 6, "Where Text Meets Graphics").

If you've seen paragraphs where the leading of the last line of the paragraph is clearly different from that of the lines above it, you know exactly what we're talking about (see Figure 4-7).

It's simple—the carriage return, that sneaky invisible character, can have a different leading value than the other lines in the paragraph. When the person formatting the text selected the paragraph, they failed to select the carriage return. To avoid this, make sure you select the entire paragraph before applying formatting. Better yet, apply a paragraph style. When you apply a paragraph style, InDesign applies the character formatting specified in the style—including leading—to every character in the paragraph.

Leading Shortcuts. You can decrease the leading of selected type by pressing Option-Up arrow/Alt-Up arrow, or increase the size by pressing Option-Down arrow/Alt-Down arrow. (Yes, this does seem counterintuitive; think of it as pushing the line up or down.) The amount that InDesign increases or decreases the leading depends on the value you entered in the Size/Leading field in the Units & Increments Preferences dialog box (for more on units and increments, see Chapter 1, "Workspace").

To decrease the leading of the selected text by five times the value in the Size/Leading field, press Command-Option-Up arrow/Ctrl-Alt-Up arrow. To increase the leading by the same amount, press Command-Option-Down arrow/Ctrl-Alt-Down arrow.

FIGURE 4-7
**That Crazy
Carriage Return**

*In this example, the carriage
return character carries an
Auto leading value and point
size left over from previous
paragraph formatting (the
leading of the rest of the text
in the paragraph is
13 points).*

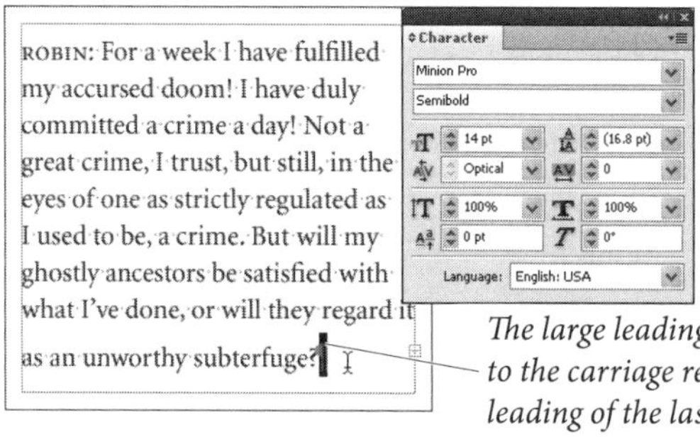

*To avoid this problem,
select the entire paragraph
before applying character
formatting—this selects the
carriage return character.*

*The large leading value applied
to the carriage return distorts the
leading of the last line of text.*

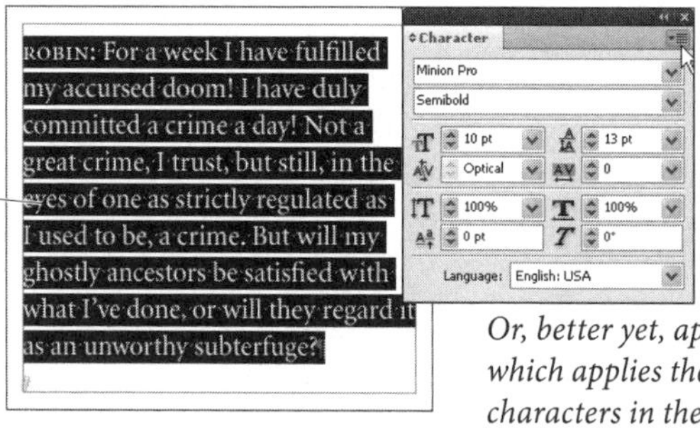

*Or, better yet, apply a paragraph style,
which applies the same leading to all
characters in the paragraph.*

Leading Techniques. Here are a few tips for adjusting leading.

▶ Increase leading as you increase line length (the column width). Solid leading (such as 12 point text on 12 points leading) produces almost unreadable text for all but the narrowest of lines.

▶ Use extra leading for sans serif or bold type.

▶ Fonts with a small x-height (the height of the lowercase "x" in relation to the height of the capital letters) can often use a smaller leading value than those with a large x-height.

▶ Decrease leading as point size increases. Large display or headline type needs less leading than body copy. You can often get by with solid leading or less—just make certain that the descenders of one line don't bump into the ascenders of the line below.

Kerning

The goal of kerning—the adjustment of the space between characters—is to achieve even spacing. InDesign offers both pair kerning (the adjustment of the space between adjacent characters) and tracking (or "range kerning")—the adjustment of all of the inter-character spaces in a series of characters.

For each space between any pair of characters in a publication, InDesign applies the total of the pair kerning and tracking values (so if you set kerning to 50 and tracking to –50, you will not see any change in the composition of the text).

InDesign adjusts kerning using units equal to one-thousandth of an em. An *em* is equal in width to the size of the type—for instance, in 18 point text, an em is 18 points wide, and so each unit in the kerning or tracking fields equals $^{18}/_{1,000}$ point (about .00025 inch). You can enter values from –1000 (minus one em) to 10000 (plus 10 ems) in the Kerning and Tracking fields.

Manual Kerning

To adjust spacing between a pair of characters, move the text insertion point between the characters and apply manual kerning (see Figure 4-8). Use any of the following techniques.

▶ Enter a value in the Kerning field of the Character panel or Control panel. If the kerning field already contains a value entered by one of the automatic kerning methods (see below), you can replace the value by typing over it, or add to or subtract from it (by typing a "+" or "-" between the value and the amount you want to add or subtract).

FIGURE 4-8
Kerning Text

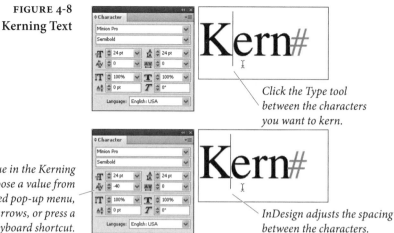

Click the Type tool between the characters you want to kern.

Enter a value in the Kerning field, or choose a value from the associated pop-up menu, or click the arrows, or press a kerning keyboard shortcut.

InDesign adjusts the spacing between the characters.

▶ Click the arrow buttons attached to the Kerning field. Click the up button to increase the kerning amount by the value you entered in the Kerning field in the Units & Increments Preferences dialog box, or click the down button to decrease kerning by the same amount.

▶ Press a keyboard shortcut (see Table 4-1).

To remove all kerning and tracking from the selected text, press Command-Option-Q/Ctrl-Alt-Q (this sets tracking to zero and sets the kerning method to Metrics).

You can't apply pair kerning when you have a range of text selected—if you try, InDesign displays an error message. When you want to apply a kerning value to a range of text, use Tracking.

Automatic Kerning

InDesign offers two automatic kerning methods: pair kerning based on kerning pairs found in the font itself (choose Metrics from the Kerning pop-up menu), and kerning based on the outlines of the characters (choose Optical). To see the difference between the two methods take a look at Figure 4-9.

▶ **Metrics.** When you turn on the Metrics automatic kerning method, InDesign reads the kerning pairs built into the font by the font's designer (or publisher). These kerning pairs cover—or attempt to cover—the most common letter combinations (in English, anyway), and there are usually about 128 pairs defined in a typical font.

You'd think that using the kerning pairs defined in the font would be the perfect way to apply automatic kerning to your text. Who, after all, knows the spacing peculiarities of a given font

TABLE 4-1
Kerning Keyboard
Shortcuts

To change kerning by:	Press:
$+^{20}/_{1,000}$ em*	Option-Right arrow/ Alt-Right arrow
$-^{20}/_{1,000}$ em*	Option-Left arrow/Alt-Left arrow
$+^{100}/_{1,000}$ em**	Command-Option-Right arrow/ Ctrl-Alt-Right arrow
$-^{100}/_{1,000}$ em**	Command-Option-Left arrow/ Ctrl-Alt-Left arrow
Reset Kerning	Command-Option-Q/ Ctrl-Alt-Q

* This is the default value in the Kerning field of the Units &
Increments Preferences dialog box.

** Or five times the default kerning amount.

FIGURE 4-9
Automatic
Kerning Methods

*Choose Optical or
Metrics from the
Kerning pop-up menu.*

Automatic kerning using the Metric method.

Automatic kerning using the Optical method.

better than its designer? Would that this were true! In reality,
very few fonts contain well-thought-out kerning pairs (often,
pair kerning tables are simply *copied* from one font to another),
and the number of kerning pairs defined per font is inadequate
(a really well-kerned font might contain several *thousand* pairs,
tweaked specifically for the characters in that typeface).

We really need a better method—a method that can adjust
the spacing between *every* character pair, while taking into
account the peculiarities of the character shapes for a particular
font. We also need a kerning method that can automatically
adjust the spacing between characters of different fonts. With
InDesign's Optical kerning method, we get both.

▶ **Optical.** The Optical kerning method considers the composed
shapes of the characters and applies kerning to even out spacing
differences between characters.

In general, the kerning applied by InDesign when you use the Optical kerning method looks looser than that applied by the Metrics kerning method. That's okay—once you've accomplished even spacing, you can always track the text to tighten or loosen its overall appearance. Because tracking applies the same kerning value to all of the text in the selection, in addition to any pair kerning, the even spacing applied by the Optical kerning method is maintained.

Viewing Automatic Kerning Amounts. As you move your cursor through the text, you'll be able to see the kerning values applied to the text in the Kerning field of the Character panel or Control panel. Kerning values specified by Optical kerning or Metrics kerning are displayed surrounded by parentheses; manual kerning values you've entered are not (see Figure 4-10).

FIGURE 4-10
How You Can Tell It's
Automatic Kerning

InDesign displays automatic kerning amounts in parentheses.

Changing Word Spacing. It's not entirely true that you can't apply kerning when more than one character is selected. You can select a range of text and select Metrics, Optical, or 0 (zero) from the pop-up menu attached to the Kerning field.

If you want to increase the spacing between words but don't want to change the letterspacing of a range of text, press Command-Option-\ or Ctrl-Alt-\ (backslash) to add the base kerning increment (as defined by the value in the Kerning field in the Units & Increments Preferences dialog box) after each space character in the range. Hold down Shift as you press this shortcut, and InDesign adds kerning by five times the base kerning amount. To decrease word spacing, press Command-Option-Delete/Ctrl-Alt-Backspace (add the Shift key to the shortcuts to multiply the effect by five).

This keystroke works simply by changing the kerning after each space character. You can always go back and change the kerning, or use Find/Change to remove it.

Tracking   Tracking, in InDesign, applies the same kerning value to every character in a selected range of text (see Figure 4-11). When you change the tracking of some text, InDesign applies the tracking in addition

FIGURE 4-11

Tracking

Select a range of text.

Enter a new value in the Tracking field.

InDesign changes the spacing of the selected text.

to any kerning values applied to the text (regardless of the method—manual or automatic—used to enter the pair kerning). Note that this is the same as the definition of tracking used by QuarkXPress, and is different from the definition used by PageMaker. In PageMaker, tracking also applies kerning, but the amount varies depending on the point size of the selected text and the tracking table in use. In PageMaker, InDesign's tracking would be called "range kerning."

Just as you cannot apply kerning using the Kerning field when you have multiple characters selected, you can't change the Tracking field when the text insertion point is between two characters—you have to have one or more characters selected. (Actually, you *can* change it, but it doesn't do anything.)

Note that the default keyboard shortcuts for tracking are exactly the same as those for kerning; which one you get depends on whether or not you have a range of text selected.

Tracking Tips. The following are a few of our favorite tracking tips.

▶ If you're setting text in all capitals or the small caps style, add 20 or 50 units of tracking to the text. Do not add tracking to the last character of the last word in the text, as that will affect the amount of space after the word, too.

▶ Printing white text on a black background often requires a little extra tracking, too. That's because the negative (black) space makes the white characters seem closer together.

▶ Larger type needs to be tracked more tightly (with negative tracking values). Often, the larger the tighter, though there are aesthetic limits to this rule. Advertising headline copy will often be tracked until the characters just "kiss."

▶ A condensed typeface (such as Futura Condensed) can usually do with a little tighter tracking. Sometimes we'll apply a setting as small as -10 to a text block to make it hold together better.

▶ When you're setting justified text and you get bad line breaks, or if you have an extra word by itself at the end of a paragraph, you can track the whole paragraph plus or minus one or two units without it being too apparent. Sometimes that's just enough to fix these problems.

Horizontal and Vertical Scaling

Enter a value in the Horizontal Scaling field or the Vertical Scaling field (or both) to change the size of the selected text (see Figure 4-12). When the values you enter in these fields are not equal, you're creating fake "expanded" or "condensed" type. We say "fake" because true expanded or condensed characters must be drawn by a type designer—when you simply scale the type, the thick and thin strokes of the characters become distorted. Entering values in these fields does not affect the point size of the type.

FIGURE 4-12
Squashing and Stretching Type

Select some text.

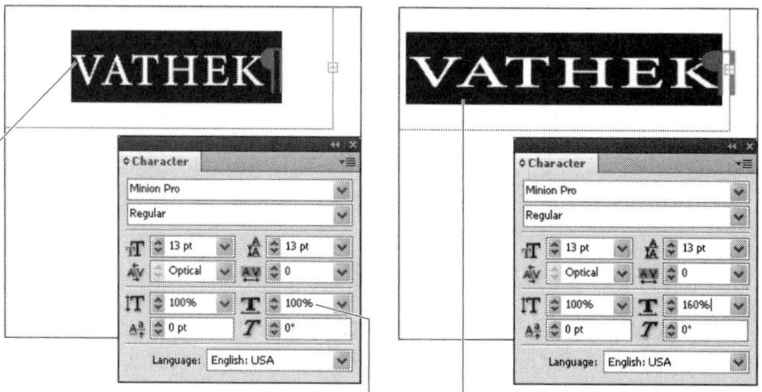

Enter a scaling value in the Horizontal Scaling field (and/or Vertical Scaling field).

InDesign squashes or stretches the characters of the selected text.

Baseline Shift

Sometimes, you need to raise the baseline of a character or characters above the baseline of the surrounding text (or lower it below the baseline). In pre-DTP typesetting, we would accomplish this by decreasing or increasing the leading applied to the character. However, that won't work in modern programs—remember, in InDesign the largest leading in the line predominates. Instead, use the Baseline Shift field in the Character panel or Control panel (see Figure 4-13).

Enter an amount in the Baseline Shift field to shift the baseline of the selected text by that amount. As you'd expect, positive values move the selected text up from the baseline; negative values move the selected text down from the baseline.

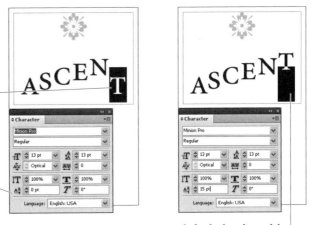

FIGURE 4-13
Baseline Shift

Select the character or characters you want to shift...

...then enter a baseline shift distance in the Baseline Shift field (positive values move the baseline up; negative values move it down).

InDesign shifts the baseline of the selected character or characters.

While it's tempting to use Baseline Shift to adjust numbers in formulae, registered trademark symbols, and so on, it's better to use the Superscript or Subscript features.

Baseline Shift Keyboard Shortcuts. To apply baseline shift using your keyboard, select some text and press Option-Shift-Up arrow/Alt-Shift-Up arrow to move the baseline of the text up two points—or whatever value you've entered in the Baseline Shift field of the Units & Increments Preferences dialog box, or Option-Shift-Down arrow/Alt-Shift-Down arrow to shift it down by the same distance.

To shift the baseline of the selected text *up* by a distance equal to five times the value you entered in the Units & Increments Preferences dialog box, press Command-Option-Shift-Up arrow/Ctrl-Alt-Shift-Up arrow. To shift the baseline down by the same amount, press Command-Option-Shift-Down arrow/Ctrl-Alt-Shift-Down arrow.

Skewing

When you apply skewing to a range of characters, InDesign slants the vertical axis of the type by the angle you enter here (see Figure 4-14). You can enter from –85 degrees to 85 degrees. Positive skew values slant the type to the right; negative values slant it to the left.

This might be useful as a special text effect, but you shouldn't count on it to provide an "italic" version of a font family that lacks a true italic type style. Why? Because there's more to an italic font than simple slanting of the characters (see Figure 4-15).

Language

The language you choose for a range of text determines the dictionary InDesign uses to hyphenate and check the spelling of the text (see Figure 4-16). Because language is a character-level attribute, you

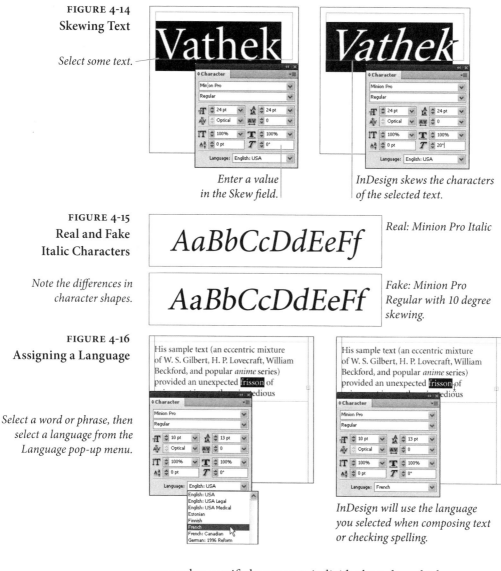

FIGURE 4-14
Skewing Text

Select some text.

Enter a value in the Skew field.

InDesign skews the characters of the selected text.

FIGURE 4-15
Real and Fake Italic Characters

Real: Minion Pro Italic

Note the differences in character shapes.

Fake: Minion Pro Regular with 10 degree skewing.

FIGURE 4-16
Assigning a Language

Select a word or phrase, then select a language from the Language pop-up menu.

InDesign will use the language you selected when composing text or checking spelling.

can apply a specific language to individual words—which means you can tell InDesign to stop flagging "frisson" or "gemütlichkeit" as misspelled words, if you want. The only languages that show up in the Language pop-up menu in the Character panel or Control panel are those for which you have a dictionary installed. If the language you're looking for isn't in this list, then you can use the InDesign installer to install that dictionary for you.

Case Options   You can change the case of selected characters to All Caps or Small Caps by choosing All Caps or Small Caps from the Character panel menu (see Figure 4-17). InDesign does not replace the characters

FIGURE 4-17
All Caps and
Small Caps

These two options work the same way; we'll demonstrate small caps.

Select some text…

…then choose Small Caps from the Character panel or Control panel menu

If you're using an OpenType font (as in this example), InDesign displays the small caps version of the selected characters (if the OpenType font contains small caps alternate characters).

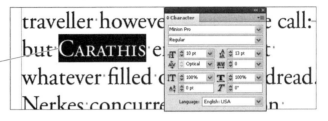

If you're using a PostScript Type 1 or TrueType font, InDesign displays scaled, capitalized versions of the selected characters.

Adobe Garamond Pro (OpenType)
THESE ARE TRUE SMALL CAPS

Adobe Garamond (PostScript Type 1)
THESE ARE NOT TRUE SMALL CAPS

If you're using a PostScript Type 1 font, don't use the Small Caps character formatting option; instead, change the font of the text to an "expert set."

themselves; it simply changes they way they look and print. To InDesign's spelling checker or Find and Change features, the text is exactly as it was entered—not the way it appears on your screen.

When you choose Small Caps from the Character panel menu (or press Command-Shift-H/Ctrl-Shift-H), InDesign examines the font used to format the selected text. If the font is an OpenType font, and if the font contains a set of true small caps characters, InDesign uses true small caps. InDesign is also smart enough to do this if you have a non-OpenType font that has an "Expert" version. If the font is not an OpenType font, doesn't have an Expert font available, or doesn't contain small caps characters, InDesign scales regular uppercase characters down to 70 percent (or whatever value you entered in the Small Cap field of the Type pane of the Preferences dialog box, as described in Chapter 1, "Workspace").

Changing Case   In addition to being able to temporarily change the case of characters using the case options, you can have InDesign change the case of the characters by typing new characters for you using the Change Case submenu (which you'll find on the Type menu and on the context menu when text is selected).

To change the case of selected characters, choose an option: Uppercase, Lowercase, Title Case, or Sentence Case. Uppercase and Lowercase are self-explanatory. Sentence Case capitalizes the first letter of each sentence. Title Case is very simpleminded: it capitalizes the first character of each word in the selection, even if the word is "the," "and," or another preposition or article (see Figure 4-18).

FIGURE 4-18
Changing Case

Select some text.

Choose a case conversion option from the Change Case submenu (on the Type menu or the context menu).

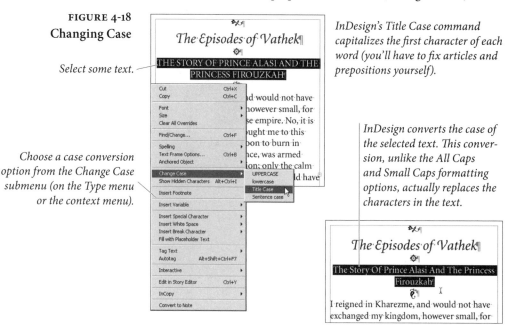

InDesign's Title Case command capitalizes the first character of each word (you'll have to fix articles and prepositions yourself).

InDesign converts the case of the selected text. This conversion, unlike the All Caps and Small Caps formatting options, actually replaces the characters in the text.

Underline   When you choose Underline from the Character panel menu, click the Underline button in the Control panel, or press Command-Shift-U/Ctrl-Shift-U, InDesign applies an underline to the selected text (see Figure 4-19).

To customize the underline, select Underline Options from the Character panel menu or the Control panel menu to display the Underline Options dialog box, where you'll find controls for setting the thickness, offset, color, and stroke style of the underscore. You can't save these settings as a style or preset, but you can build them into the definition of a character style.

Breaking at Spaces. InDesign's underline also includes any spaces in the selection. Some designs require that underlines break at spaces in the text. You could laboriously select each space and turn off the underline attribute, by why not use Find/Change to do the work for you? Find a space in the selection with the Underline attribute, then replace it with a space with Underline turned off.

FIGURE 4-19
Underline

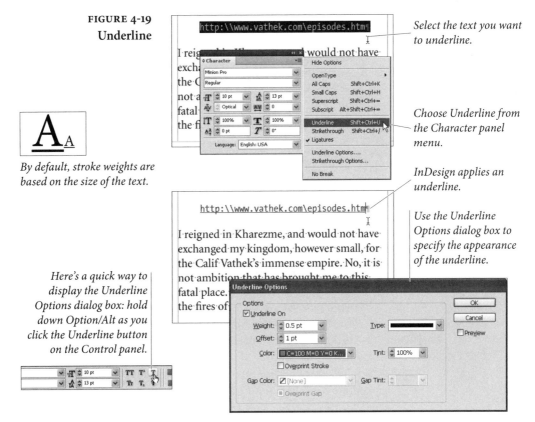

Select the text you want to underline.

Choose Underline from the Character panel menu.

InDesign applies an underline.

Use the Underline Options dialog box to specify the appearance of the underline.

By default, stroke weights are based on the size of the text.

Here's a quick way to display the Underline Options dialog box: hold down Option/Alt as you click the Underline button on the Control panel.

Breaking Underlines at Descenders. We said that there was no way to break underlines at descenders—but there is an inelegant work-around: apply a white stroke to the characters. The stroke will overlap the underline. You can use Find/Change to search for characters with descenders (such as the "j" or the "y") and use the Format button in the Change To area to give them a stroke.

Highlighting Text. Want to make some text look as if it's been highlighted with a felt "highlight" marker? You can simulate the effect using a custom underline (see Figure 4-20). Make your underline larger than the text it's supposed to cover and apply a negative offset so that it moves up to cover the text. Be sure to change the color of the underscore to yellow or pink or something that will contrast with the text its highlighting. Note that the color actually falls behind the text, but the effect will be as though the highlight was drawn over it.

You can also create interesting highlight effects by mixing a custom underline with a custom strikethrough. For instance, you could make a line appear above and below some text, sort of like putting the text in a stripe.

FIGURE 4-20
**Creating a
"Highlight" Effect**

As a valued TimeTravelTickets customer, we thought you'd like to be the first to know that we're having a massive End-of-Year sale! Here's your chance to add a special concert or recital to your time travel plans! All TimeTravelTi... price!

Highlight effect (imagine that it's bright yellow).

Underline Options

Options
☑ Underline On
  Weight: ⬍ 14 pt ▾   Type: ▬▬▬▬▬ ▾
  Offset: ⬍ -4 pt ▾
  Color: ▨ C=0 M=0 Y=100 K... ▾   Tint: ⬍ 100% ▾
  ☐ Overprint Stroke
  Gap Color: ☑ [None] ▾   Gap Tint: ⬍ ▾
  ☐ Overprint Gap

OK
Cancel
☐ Preview

Positive offset values move the underscore rule down from the text baseline; negative offset values move it up.

Strikethrough   When you choose Strikethrough from the Character panel menu (or click the Strikethrough button in the Control panel or press Command-Shift-?/Ctrl-Shift-?), InDesign applies the strikethrough text effect to the selected text (see Figure 4-21). To remove the Strikethrough text effect, select the feature or press the keystroke again.

The strikethrough style isn't particularly consistent; it changes its thickness and distance from the baseline depending on the font. However, you can control the strikethrough style by selecting Strikethrough Options from the Character or Control panel menu. The options here are very similar to those in the Underline Options dialog box: You can adjust the thickness, color, offset (from the baseline), and style of the line. If you're applying a colored strikethrough

FIGURE 4-21
Strikethrough

By default, the stroke weight of the Strikethrough effect varies based on the size of the text.

ery unruly passion; only the calm uable feelings of friendship could nd entrance there; but LustLove its own shape would have been r

| A | Minion Pro ▾ | ⬍T 10 pt ▾ | TT T¹ T   ▤ ▤ ▤ ▤ |
| ¶ | Regular ▾ | ⬍A 13 pt ▾ | Tr T₁ T̶   ▤ ▤ ▤ ▤ |

Select some text...

...then choose Strikethrough from the Character panel menu or Option/Alt-click the Strikethrough button on the Control panel.

You can use the Strikethrough Options dialog box to to specify the appearance and position of the strikethrough rule.

To display the Strikethrough Options dialog box, hold down Option/Alt as you click the Strikethrough button in the Control panel, or choose Strikethrough Options from the Control panel menu.

Strikethrough Options

Options
☑ Strikethrough On
  Weight: ⬍ 12 pt ▾   Type: ▬▬▬▬▬ ▾
  Offset: ⬍ 3 pt ▾
  Color: ▨ C=15 M=100 Y=1... ▾   Tint: ⬍ 100% ▾
  ☐ Overprint Stroke
  Gap Color: ☑ [None] ▾   Gap Tint: ⬍ ▾
  ☐ Overprint Gap

OK
Cancel
☐ Preview

on top of black text, you may want to set it to overprint so that it won't knock out a fine white line—which would be difficult to register on press. If so, make sure you like the result by turning on Overprint Preview (from the View menu).

Ligatures   Some character combinations are just trouble—from a typesetting standpoint, at least. In particular, when you combine the lowercase "f" character with "f," "i," or "l," the tops of the characters run into each other. To compensate for this, type designers usually provide ligatures—special characters in the font that are "tied" ("ligature" means "tie") together.

When you choose Ligatures from the Character panel's menu, InDesign replaces some of the character combinations in the selected range of text with the corresponding ligatures (see Figure 4-22).

If the font you've selected is not an OpenType font, InDesign replaces only the "fl" and "fi" character combinations. In Windows, InDesign uses these ligature characters if they're available in the font (and they are, for most PostScript Type 1 fonts), even though they are not part of the Windows character set—that is, there is usually no way to type them. If the font you've selected is an OpenType font, InDesign makes the ligature substitutions are suggested by the font.

OpenType fonts can also feature other sorts of ligatures—for more on this topic, see "OpenType Fonts," later in this chapter.

Superscript   While you can always create superscript or subscript characters (for
and Subscript   use in fractions or exponential notation) by changing the point size and baseline shift of selected characters, InDesign provides a shortcut: the Superscript and Subscript text effects (see Figure 4-23).

When you select Superscript or Subscript from the Character panel menu, InDesign scales the selected text and shifts its baseline. (You can also press Command-Shift-=/Ctrl-Shift-= for superscript or

FIGURE 4-22
Ligatures

Select some text and then choose Ligatures from the Character panel menu.

If you're using an OpenType font, InDesign uses additional ligatures defined in the font. In this example, InDesign applies the "ffi" and "ffl" ligatures.

Ligatures off
Adobe Garamond Pro (OpenType)
file difficult reflect affliction

Adobe Garamond (PostScript Type 1)
file difficult reflect affliction

Ligatures on
Adobe Garamond Pro (OpenType)
file difficult reflect affliction

Adobe Garamond (PostScript Type 1)
file difficult reflect affliction

FIGURE 4-23
**Superscript and
Subscript**

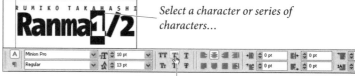

Select a character or series of
characters…

…choose Superscript from the
Character panel menu or click the
Superscript button in the Control panel.

InDesign scales the
text and shifts its
baseline…

*Tip: To display the Advanced
Type pane of the Preferences
dialog box, hold down
Option/Alt and click the
Superscript or Subscript
button in the Control panel.*

…according to the
values you entered in
the Advanced Type
pane of the dialog box.

Command-Option-Shift-=/Ctrl-Alt-Shift-= for subscript.) InDesign
calculates the scaling and baseline shift by multiplying the current
text size and leading by the values you've set in the Size fields in the
Advanced Type pane of the Preferences dialog box (see "Text Preferences" in Chapter 1, "Workspace").

If you are using an OpenType font that has true Superscript and
Subscript characters, use Superscript/Superior and Subscript/Infe-
rior options in the OpenType submenu (see below).

No Break   This one is really easy to explain: To prevent a range of text from
breaking across lines, select the text and turn on the No Break option
in the Character or Control panel menu.

OpenType Fonts

We've mentioned OpenType fonts a few times in the chapter so far;
however, we should probably take a moment to discuss them. The
OpenType font specification was created jointly by Microsoft and
Adobe as a way to represent a font with only a single file on both
Macintosh and Windows (so you can move the font cross-platform).
The characters are encoded using the international standard Unicode, so each font can have hundreds, or even thousands of different
characters—even the very large character sets in non-Roman languages such as Japanese.

InDesign can perform special tricks with OpenType fonts, such as replacing characters with swashes, or adding ligatures for character pairs such as ct and ffi.

Most of the special OpenType typesetting features in InDesign are hidden in the OpenType submenu in the Character or Control panel's menu (see Figure 4-24). If a font doesn't support one of these features, it appears in the menu within square brackets ("[Swash]").

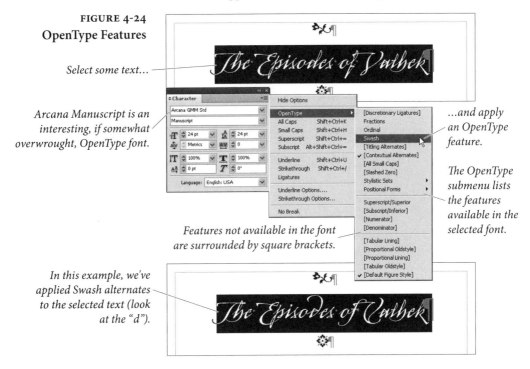

FIGURE 4-24
OpenType Features

Select some text...

Arcana Manuscript is an interesting, if somewhat overwrought, OpenType font.

Features not available in the font are surrounded by square brackets.

...and apply an OpenType feature.

The OpenType submenu lists the features available in the selected font.

In this example, we've applied Swash alternates to the selected text (look at the "d").

Alternate Characters   The OpenType features work by replacing one or more glyphs with another single glyph. "fi" and "fl" ligatures that we discussed earlier are a great example of this, but they're only the beginning.

Discretionary Ligatures. Font designers love making ligatures, but they recognize that users won't want to use more esoteric ligatures (such as "ct" or "st") in everyday text. If you select some text and turn on the Discretionary Ligatures feature, InDesign uses these lesser-known ligatures (if they're available in the font). We usually turn this off except when we're trying to make something look "old fashioned," or when using a script typeface (such as Bickham Script Pro).

Fractions. Changing fake fractions (such as $^1/_2$) to real fractions (½) has long been a thorn in the side of anyone laying out cookbooks or construction manuals. Fortunately, you can now just turn on the Fractions feature and anything that looks like a fraction will convert to the proper character automatically.

In some OpenType typefaces, only very basic fractions such as ½ and ¼ are converted. Other typefaces support those plus some extended fractions, such as ⅔ and ⅝. Some fonts support arbitrary fractions such as $355/113$. It depends on the design of the font.

Don't turn on the Fractions feature for all your text because InDesign often assumes that *all* your numbers and much of your punctuation are part of fractions and turns them into numerators.

Ordinal. "First," "second," and "third" are all examples of ordinal numbers. InDesign can automatically set the "st", "nd", and "rd" (or the "o" and "a" in Spanish) to superscript when you turn Ordinal on in the OpenType submenu. "3rd," for example, becomes "3rd".

Swash. When you need to give a character a little more flair, select it and turn on the Swash feature. Swashes are typically used at the beginning or ending of words or sentences. You can see if a particular OpenType font has any swash characters by opening the Glyph panel and looking for Swash in the Show pop-up menu; some fonts (such as Adobe Caslon Pro) have swashes in their italic styles only.

Titling Alternates. Some OpenType fonts have special "titling" characters that are designed for all-uppercase type set at large sizes.

Contextual Alternates. Some OpenType fonts—mostly the script faces—have contextual ligatures and connecting alternates, which are very similar to ligatures. When you turn on Contextual Alternates, the result looks more like handwriting because the alternate characters connect to each other.

All Small Caps. When you turn on the Small Caps feature (which we described in "Case Options," earlier), InDesign leaves uppercase characters alone. All Small Caps, however, forces uppercase letters to appear as lowercase small caps. This is useful when formatting acronyms such as DOS, NASA, or IBM.

Slashed Zero. The problem with the number 0 is that it looks much like the letter O in some fonts. Some folks like to differentiate the two by using a slashed zero (Ø) in place of a zero. When you turn on the Slashed Zero OpenType style, every zero appears with a slash automatically.

Stylistic Sets. A few fonts go beyond offering a swash or contextual alternate here and there, and provide whole sets of alternates that each give a slightly different feel to the face as a whole. For example, you might like Thomas Phinney's Hypatia Sans Pro, but realize that you don't like the font's double-loop "g". No problem: Turn on stylistic set number four and the character changes throughout the selection (see Figure 4-25). You can enable more than one stylistic set at a time; select it once to turn it on, select it again to turn it off.

FIGURE 4-25
Stylistic Sets

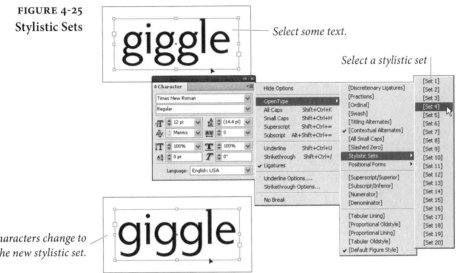

Select some text.

Select a stylistic set

The characters change to
the new stylistic set.

Positional Forms. In some languages, characters change depending on their position in a word—for example, in Hebrew, the "mem" character changes from מ to ם when its at the end of a word.

InDesign uses the General positional form—which uses the normal glyph. If you choose Automatic Form, InDesign changes the character depending on its position in the word. You can override the form by choosing Initial, Medial, Final, or Isolated Form. It's hard to find a font in which this feature does much of anything.

Raised and Lowered Characters

Typesetting a treatise on Einstein's theory of relativity? If so, you'll be mighty happy about InDesign's ability to use true superscripts and subscripts instead of the faked scaled versions that you get with the Superscript and Subscript features in the Character panel's menu. You have four choices in the OpenType submenu (each one is mutually exclusive of the others):

▶ Superscript/Superior

▶ Subscript/Inferior

► Numerator

► Denominator

However, note that most OpenType fonts only have a small set of characters designed to be superscript or subscript, so you can't set any and all characters you want in these styles. For example, if you set the word "turkey" to Superscript/Superior style, only every other character changes. In some cases you'll get the same result when you choose Denominator or Subscript/Inferior.

Formatting Numerals

We like "old style" numerals (you know, the kind with descenders: 1234567890) better than full-height "lining figures" (1234567890), and we've always gotten them by changing the font of the characters to an "expert" version of whatever font we were using (if one was available). So we were very happy to see that there are four different ways InDesign can format numerals: Proportional Oldstyle, Tabular Oldstyle, Proportional Lining, Tabular Lining (see Figure 4-26).

Tabular Lining works well for financial tables (such as those found in an annual report), because numbers have equal widths and align from one line to the next. If you choose Tabular Oldstyle from the OpenType submenu, the numerals line up, but InDesign uses old style characters. Proportional Lining numerals are all the same height, but vary in width. David prefers this style for everything other than tables, especially when interspersing numbers and upper-case characters. Ole would rather use Proportional Oldstyle, which uses old style figures of varying widths.

FIGURE 4-26
Old Style

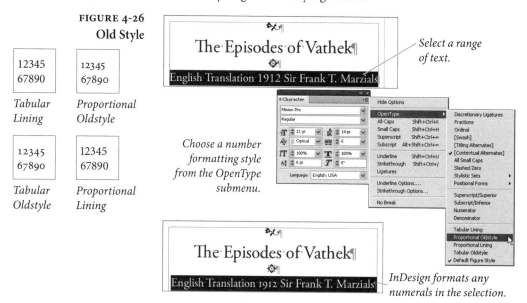

12345
67890

*Tabular
Lining*

12345
67890

*Proportional
Oldstyle*

12345
67890

*Tabular
Oldstyle*

12345
67890

*Proportional
Lining*

*Select a range
of text.*

*Choose a number
formatting style
from the OpenType
submenu.*

*InDesign formats any
numerals in the selection.*

The last OpenType numeral formatting option is Default Figure Style, which applies the figure style defined as the default by the type designer (so the effect varies from font to font).

Find Font

The Find Font dialog box (choose Find Font from the Type menu) displays a list of every font that appears somewhere on a document page—including on master pages and in linked PDF or EPS graphics (see Figure 4-27). It does not list fonts that are defined in paragraph or character styles that aren't actually applied to text. If you click the More Info button, the dialog box displays more information about each font you select, including the pages where the font is used, which styles include this font, how many text characters appear in this font, and the version of the font. (There is often more than one version of the same font, each with its own number, just like other software.) Note that showing More Info can slow down the Find Font dialog box significantly, so we often leave this closed.

If you're not sure where a font is living on your hard drive, the Find Font dialog comes to the rescue: Not only is the path to the font listed in More Info, but you can click Reveal in Finder (or Reveal in Explorer in Windows) to open the folder that contains the font.

Replacing Fonts. It's a good idea to visit Find Font every now and again, and especially before finishing your job. We often find rogue fonts sneaking in to documents when we import or copy and paste text from Word or some other document. For example, as we type this, we checked and found that Times New Roman is in this document

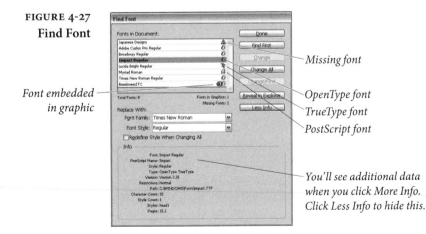

FIGURE 4-27
Find Font

Font embedded in graphic

Missing font

OpenType font
TrueType font
PostScript font

You'll see additional data when you click More Info. Click Less Info to hide this.

for some reason. More Info tells us that it's applied to 36 characters on two different pages. Fortunately, the rest of the Find Font dialog box acts like the Find/Change dialog box, so we can quickly rid ourselves of this aberration.

To replace that incorrectly-styled text, select the font from the list and click Change, Change All, or Change/Find.

If you believe the errant font is actually inside a character or paragraph style definition, then turn on the Redefine Style When Changing All option *before* you click Change All. Otherwise, you'll change the font on your pages, but the font will still be lurking inside the style, just waiting to surprise you again when you least expect it.

By the way, sometimes you'll find that Find Font lists a font as being used in your document but Find Next won't find it, and More Info tells you that there are zero characters that have this font applied to it. This happens when the font is applied only to automatic bullets or numbering (see "Bullets and Numbering," later in this chapter). Find Font will also tell you a font exists when it really doesn't if you have an empty frame that used to contain text in that font—just another good reason not to leave empty frames lying around.

Filling and Stroking Characters

InDesign can fill or stroke text as it can any other path. Once you've selected text, you can set the fill color, stroke color, stroke weight, stroke type, and stroke alignment (see Figure 4-28). The Control panel includes Fill and Stroke boxes for easy color swatch selection.

You can apply gradients to the fill and stroke of the type without converting the type to outlines. However, while gradients are easy to apply, it's not always easy to get the effect you're looking for, because gradients are based on the bounds of the text frame. If you want to change the gradient, select the text and drag the Gradient Swatch tool over it. (See Chapter 5, "Drawing," for more on gradients.)

Paragraph Formatting

What makes a paragraph a paragraph? InDesign's definition is simple—a paragraph is any string of characters that ends with a carriage return. When you apply paragraph formatting, the formatting applies to all of the characters in the paragraph. Paragraph alignment, indents, tabs, spacing, and hyphenation settings are all examples of paragraph formatting.

FIGURE 4-28
Character Fill and Stroke

Select an unlinked text frame using the Selection tool, then click the Formatting Affects Text button.

You can also click the Formatting Affects Text button in the Swatches panel.

Format the text using any of the fill and stroke formatting tools. In this example, we used the Swatches panel to apply a tint to the fill and stroke of the text, and then used the Stroke panel to set the stroke weight.

You can also select characters using the Type tool, then apply a fill and/or stroke to the text using the same controls you use to apply a fill or stroke to any path.

You can control the stroke alignment of the stroke. This stroke is center aligned; the one to the right is aligned to the outside of the stroke.

Note that the fill retains the shape of the character as you increase stroke weight. This works because InDesign strokes the characters and then fills them.

You don't have to select all of the text in a paragraph to apply paragraph formatting—all you need to do is click the Type tool in the paragraph. To select more than one paragraph, drag the cursor through the paragraphs you want to format. The selection doesn't have to include all of the text, it only has to *touch* each paragraph.

If what you're trying to do, however, is apply character formatting (such as font or point size) to all of the characters in the paragraph, you should quadruple-click (or triple-click, if you've turned off the Triple Click to Select a Line option in the Type panel of the Preferences dialog box) the paragraph with the Type tool—that way, you'll select all of the characters, including the carriage return character. (Note that you can force a line break without creating a new paragraph—called a "soft return"—by typing Shift-Return/Shift-Enter.)

You can find all of InDesign's paragraph formatting features in the Paragraph panel. To display the Paragraph panel, press Command-Option-T/Ctrl-Alt-T. These features are duplicated in the Control panel—if the Control panel is displaying character formatting, then click the panel's Paragraph Formatting Controls button or press Command-Option-7/Ctrl-Alt-7 to switch to paragraph formatting.

Alignment   Click the alignment buttons at the top of the Paragraph panel or in the Control panel to set the alignment of the selected paragraphs (see Figure 4-29).

InDesign supports the usual set of paragraph alignments—left aligned (also known as "rag right"), right aligned (also known as "rag left"), centered, and justified, but also adds a couple of variations on the justified alignment you might not be familiar with.

In addition to the standard "justified" alignment, which treats the last line of the paragraph as if it were left aligned, InDesign offers the force justified, right justified, and center justified alignments. These each tell InDesign to treat the last line of the paragraph differently. When you force justify the text, the last line is spread out all the way to the right margin, even if it's only a single word. In some cases, when the Paragraph Composer is turned on (see "Multi-line Composition," later in this chapter), turning on force justify actually reflows the paragraph significantly.

Right justified and center justified treat the last line as right aligned and center aligned, respectively. In the old days of typesetting, these alignments were known as "quad right" and "quad center."

Finally, the Align Towards Spine and Align Away from Spine options. The former aligns the text to the spine and leaves the outside of the text ragged; the latter does the opposite.

FIGURE 4-29
Paragraph Alignment

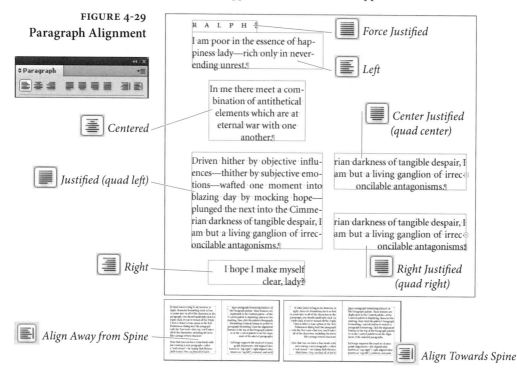

Indents   Paragraphs can be indented using the Left Indent and Right Indent fields in the Paragraph or Control panel (see Figure 4-30). You can enter values from zero (0) to 720 picas in these fields, but you can't enter negative numbers to make the edges of the paragraph "hang" outside the edges of the column or text frame.

Note that the left and right indents are always added to the text inset, as specified in the Text Frame Options dialog box. If you have a left inset of 6 points and a left indent of 12 points, then the left edge of the paragraph will sit 18 points from the edge of the frame.

There are also two special indents, called First Line Left Indent and Last Line Right Indent. The first applies to the first line of the paragraph alone—the value you enter in the First Line Left Indent field sets the distance between the first line indent and the left indent. The First Line indent may be positive or negative, but cannot be a negative number greater than the left indent (see Figure 4-31). You should *never* create an indent by typing five spaces at the beginning of a paragraph to indent; instead, use First Line indent.

How large your First Line indent should be depends on your design and on the typeface you're working with. Typically, the larger the x-height of the font, the larger first-line indent you should use. Book designers often use a one- or two-em indent, so in an 11-point type, the indent might be 11 or 22 points.

The Last Line Right Indent lets you set the position for the last line of text in a paragraph. The most common use for this is to apply a large Right Indent and then a negative Last Line Right Indent (so that the last line sticks out past the rest of the paragraph, as in many

FIGURE 4-30
Paragraph Indents

Left indent

Right indent

FIGURE 4-31
First Line Indent

Don't use tab characters to apply a first line indent...

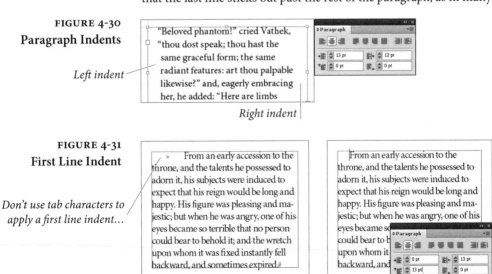

...use the First Line Indent field.

menu designs). Another use might be to set the position of the final line when using Justify All Lines (forced justification).

To change an indent value, select a paragraph and then do one of the following things:

▶ Display the Paragraph or Control panel, then enter a value in the First Line Left Indent, Left Indent, Right Indent, and/or the Last Line Right Indent fields (see Figure 4-32).

▶ Display the Tabs panel (press Command-Shift-T/Ctrl-Shift-T), and drag one of the indent icons (see Figure 4-33).

FIGURE 4-32
Setting an Indent

Click the Type tool in the paragraph you want to format.

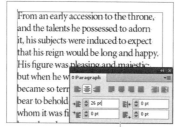

Enter values in the Left, Right, First, or Last fields.

InDesign applies the indents you've specified.

FIGURE 4-33
Indents on the Tabs Panel

First Line indent

Left indent

Right indent

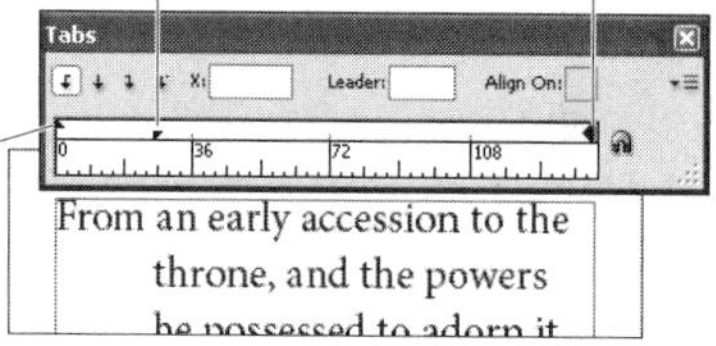

Creating a Hanging Indent

A hanging indent is one in which the first line of a paragraph "sticks out" to the left of the rest of the paragraph—often used in numbered or bulleted lists. Use hanging indents, rather than breaking and indenting each line using carriage returns and tabs—you'll thank yourself for it later, when you need to edit the text or change the width of the text block.

There are two basic methods for creating a hanging indent. First, you can apply a positive Left Indent and a negative First Line Left Indent with either the Tabs panel (see Figure 4-34) or the Paragraph or Control panel. Either way, there's no need to set a tab stop because InDesign assumes the left indent is the first tab stop.

Here's another way to create a hanging indent: Type the text you want to "hang," followed by a tab character. With the text cursor immediately after the tab character, press Command-\ or Ctrl-\ (backslash). This is the keyboard shortcut for the Indent to Here

FIGURE 4-34
Setting a
Hanging Indent

Click the Type tool in a
paragraph, then press
Command-Shift-T/
Ctrl-Shift-T to display
the Tabs panel.

Hold down Shift and drag the Left indent icon to the
right of the First Line indent marker.

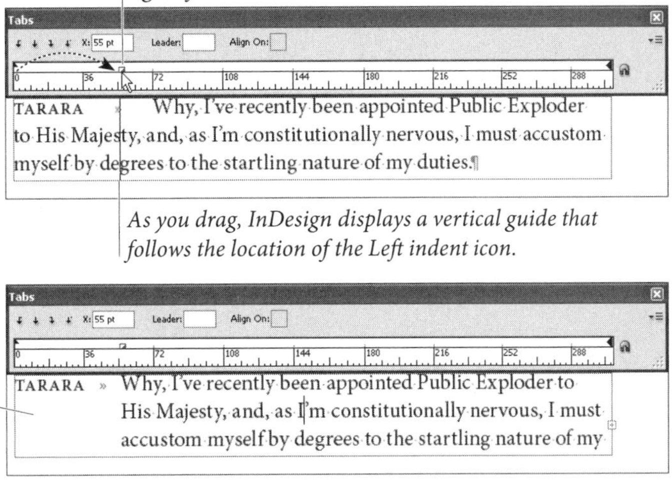

As you drag, InDesign displays a vertical guide that
follows the location of the Left indent icon.

Stop dragging, and InDesign
applies a hanging indent to
the selected paragraph.

character (you can also get this character from the Other submenu in the Insert Special Character submenu, in either the Type menu or the context menu). This invisible character causes the rest of the lines in a paragraph to indent to this place. If you want to delete it, you can place the cursor after it (since it's invisible and has no width, you might have to use the arrow keys to position it) and then press Delete.

While the Indent to Here character is easy to type, we like using the negative First Line indent trick more because we can use it in a paragraph style.

Tabs   Tabs come to desktop typesetting from typewriters, by way of word processing (with a stopover along the way at the Linotype machine). They solve a problem that didn't exist in hand-set metal type—namely, how do you position characters at precise locations in a line of type when you can't simply slide them into place with your finger?

There are two methods of controlling the horizontal position of text in a line. First, you can use space characters—word spaces, thin spaces, en spaces, and em spaces. This method places characters at *relative* positions in the line—where they appear depends on the width of the spaces and of the other characters in the line. Tabs, by contrast, provide *absolute* position on the line—a tab stop set at 6 picas will remain at that position, regardless of the content of the line.

Before we go any further, we'd better make sure we're using the same terminology. *Tab stops* are formatting attributes of paragraphs. *Tab characters* are what InDesign enters in a line of text when you press the Tab key. Tab characters push text around in a line; tab stops determine the effect of the tab characters. Each tab stop has a position (relative to the left edge of the text frame), an alignment (which specifies the composition of the text following a tab character), and, potentially, a leader (a tab leader is a series of repeated characters spanning the distance from beginning of the tab character to the beginning of the following text). Put tab stops and tab characters together, and you get *tabs*, the feature.

A Little Tab Dogma. Look. We try to be reasonable. We try not to insist that everyone work the way that we do, or that our way of doing things is necessarily the best way (in fact, we sometimes know it's not). But tabs are different—if you don't do it our way, you'll be causing yourself needless pain. Let's review the rules:

▶ Use tabs, not spaces, to move text to a specific position in a line.

▶ Use a First Line indent, not a tab, when you want to indent the first line of a paragraph.

▶ Do not force lines to break by entering tab characters (or multiple tab characters) at the end of a line! If you do, you'll find tab characters creeping back into the text as editing changes force text recomposition. To break a line without entering a carriage return, use the "soft return" (press Shift-Return/Shift-Enter).

▶ Don't use multiple tab characters when you can use a single tab character and an appropriately positioned tab stop. While there are some cases where you'll have to break this rule, putting two or more tab characters in a row should be the exception.

Types of Tab Stops InDesign features four types of tab stops (see Figure 4-35).

Left, Right, and Centered Tab Stops. InDesign's left, right, and centered tab stops are the same as the basic tab stops you'll find in any word processor.

▶ Left tab stops push text following a tab character to a specific horizontal location in a column, and then align the text to the left of the tab stop position.

▶ Right tab stops push text to a location and then align the text to the right of the tab stop position.

▶ Centered tab stops center a line of text at the point at which you've set the tab stop.

FIGURE 4-35
Tab Stop Alignment

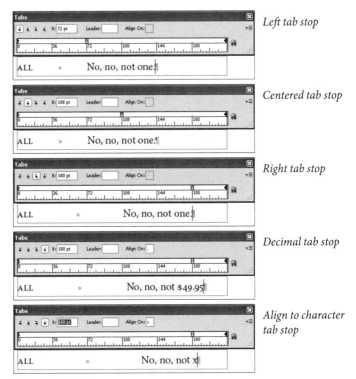

Left tab stop

Centered tab stop

Right tab stop

Decimal tab stop

Align to character tab stop

Decimal Tab Stops. Decimal tab stops push text following a tab character so that any decimal point you've entered in the text aligns with the point at which you set the tab stop.

Actually, the Decimal tab stop is an "align to any character you want" tab stop. Type the character you're trying to align in the Align On field of the Tabs panel. For example, lets say you have a column of item numbers, some with asterisks. You can make the asterisks hang out to the right by typing an asterisk character in the Align On field. If the Align On character doesn't appear in the paragraph, InDesign treats the decimal tab stop as a right tab stop.

Setting Tab Stops

To set a tab stop, follow these steps (see Figure 4-36).

1. If you haven't already entered tab characters in the text, enter them.

2. Select the paragraph(s) you want to format.

3. Display the Tabs panel (press Command-Shift-T/Ctrl-Shift-T), then click the Magnet button to snap the Tabs panel into position at the top of the text frame (if possible).

FIGURE 4-36
Setting a Tab Stop

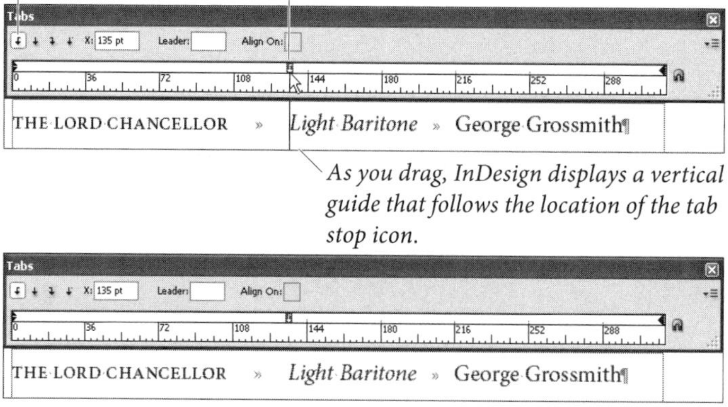

Click a tab stop button.

Drag the tab stop into position on the tab ruler.

As you drag, InDesign displays a vertical guide that follows the location of the tab stop icon.

When the tab stop icon is in position, stop dragging.

4. Click in the tab ruler and drag. As you drag, the X field shows you the position of the tab icon (relative to the left edge of the text frame). Then click one of the tab stop alignment buttons to determine the type of the tab stop.

You can also add a tab stop at a specific location on the tab ruler. To do this, enter the position you want in the X field in the Tabs panel and then press Enter. InDesign adds the tab stop.

Removing Tab Stops. To remove a tab stop, drag the tab stop icon off the tab ruler. Note that this doesn't remove any tab characters you've typed in your text, though it does make them behave differently (because you've taken away their tab stop).

Editing Tab Stops. To change a tab stop's position, drag the tab stop on the tab ruler. Alternatively, you can select the tab stop (click on it), then enter a new value in the x field or give it a leader. Don't forget that if you want to move the tab stop by a specific amount, you can add a + or – character after the value that appears in the x field and then type the amount you want to move it ("+14mm").

To change a tab stop's alignment (from left to decimal, for instance), select the tab stop on the tab ruler and then click the tab stop button corresponding to the alignment you want. Or you can Option/Alt-click on the tab stop to cycle through the alignment types.

Repeating Tab Stops. To create a series of tab stops spaced an equal distance apart, select a tab stop on the tab ruler and choose Repeat Tab from the Tabs panel menu (see Figure 4-37). InDesign repeats the tab across the width of the current column. The distance between

FIGURE 4-37
Repeating a Tab Stop

*Select the tab stop icon you
want to repeat...*

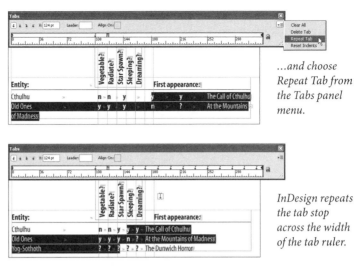

*...and choose
Repeat Tab from
the Tabs panel
menu.*

*InDesign repeats
the tab stop
across the width
of the tab ruler.*

the new tab stops is equal to the distance between the tab stop you selected and the previous tab stop (or indent) in the column. InDesign also deletes all the tab stops that were already to the right of the tab stop you clicked (which can be frustrating if you've placed tab stops there and weren't expecting them to disappear).

Working with Tab Leaders. A tab leader is a series of repeated characters that fill the area taken up by the tab character (see Figure 4-38). The most common tab leader character is a period—think of all of the "dot" leaders you've seen in tables of contents.

Characters in a tab leader are not spaced in the same fashion as other characters—if they were, the characters in tab leaders on successive lines would not align with each other. That would be ugly. Instead, characters in a tab leader are monospaced—positioned as if on an invisible grid. This means you'll see different amounts of space between the last character of text preceding a tab leader and the first tab leader. It's a small price to pay.

FIGURE 4-38
Applying a Tab Leader

Select some text.

*...and InDesign applies
a tab leader to the
selected tab stop.*

*Select a tab stop and enter the character or characters
you want to use for the tab leader in the Leader field.
Press Return/Enter...*

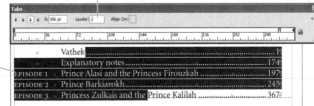

In InDesign, you can format the characters in a tab leader by selecting the tab character and applying formatting, just as you would any other character. For instance, dotted tab leaders typically look like a bunch of periods. To make them look more like traditional dot leaders, add a space after the period (in the Leader field), then select the tab character and reduce its size slightly.

Right-aligned Tabs. Setting a tab stop precisely at the right margin can be a bother; it's an even bigger bother when your art director says, "make that column narrower." Instead of using tab stops, try using a right-aligned tab character, which you can enter by pressing Shift-Tab (or add with the Insert Special Character submenu in the Type menu). The text that follows the right-aligned tab character always aligns with the right margin, even when you change the right indent or the width of the text frame.

The right aligned tab picks up the tab leader settings from the last tab stop in the line.

Adding Space Before and After Paragraphs

When you want to add extra space between paragraphs, don't use carriage returns (not even one). If you do, you're certain to end up with unwanted carriage returns at the tops of text frames when text recomposes due to editing or formatting changes. Instead of typing carriage returns, use the Space Before and Space After fields in the Paragraph or Control panel. When you add space using these controls, InDesign removes the space when the paragraph falls at the top of a text frame (see Figure 4-39). If you need to add space before a paragraph at the top of a text frame, use First Baseline offset (see Chapter 3, "Text").

In addition, adding an exact amount of space is easier when you use the Paragraph or Control panel. Want to add four picas of vertical space above the paragraph? Enter it in the Space Before field. There's no need to guess how many carriage returns it would take to make up that vertical distance.

Align to Grid

When you have more than one column of text on a page, it's important that the baselines of the text line up across the columns. The leading should be consistent with an underlying "leading grid"—an invisible set of rules for where the baselines of text should lay. Many designers even work with leading grids on pages with a single column.

Unfortunately, in most page designs, you'll find elements that have to have leading values that differ from the leading applied to the body text. Inline graphics, paragraph rules, and headings are all examples of the sort of elements we're talking about. When one of

FIGURE 4-39
**Space Before
and Space After**

*If you try to use
carriage returns to
add vertical space...*

*...you'll often
end up with
carriage
returns at the
top of a text
column.*

*To avoid this problem,
use paragraph space
before (or after).*

*If a paragraph
falls at the top
of a text frame,
InDesign does
not apply the
paragraph
space above.*

*Select some paragraphs, then
enter a value in the Space
Above (or Space Below) field.*

these elements appears in a column of text, the leading of the lines in that column gets thrown off.

You need to compensate for leading variations inside a column of text. "Leading creep," the misalignment of baselines in adjacent text columns, is one of the hallmarks of amateur typesetting.

While you could adjust the space above and below such intrusions, there's an easier way: use InDesign's Align to Baseline Grid. Select a paragraph and click the Align to Baseline Grid button in the Paragraph panel, and InDesign forces the baselines of the lines in the paragraph onto the baseline grid (see Figure 4-40). You can change the leading and position of the document baseline grid in the Grids pane of the Preferences dialog box. To see this grid, select Show Baseline Grid from the Grids & Guides submenu, under the View menu.

Frame-based Baseline Grids. The baseline grid can also be calculated for individual text frames. To activate a custom baseline grid, select the text frame and press Command-B/Ctrl-B to display the Text Frame Options dialog box. Click the Baseline Options tab, and then turn on the Use Custom Baseline Grid option. Use the controls to set up your custom baseline grid (see Figure 4-41). When you specify a custom grid, the Align to Grid option aligns the text baselines with the baseline grid applied to the text frame, rather than to the document baseline grid.

FIGURE 4-40
Align to Grid

This is all very pretty...

...but it throws the leading of the following paragraph off of the leading grid.

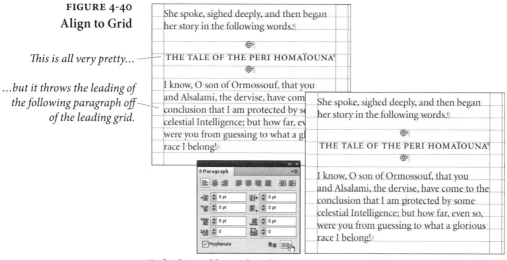

To fix this problem, select the paragraph and click the Align Baseline to Grid button.

InDesign snaps the baselines of the text in the paragraph to the baseline grid.

FIGURE 4-41
Custom Basline Grid

To set up a custom baseline grid for a text frame, select the frame, then open the Text Frame Options dialog box. Click the Baseline Options tab, then turn on the Use Custom Baseline Grid option.

Set up your custom grid using these controls.

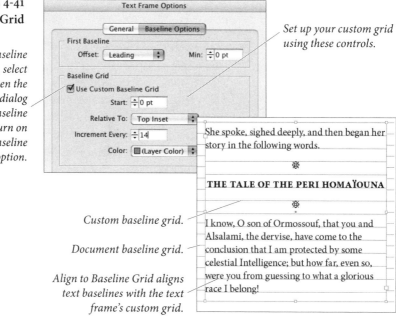

Custom baseline grid.

Document baseline grid.

Align to Baseline Grid aligns text baselines with the text frame's custom grid.

Why We Rarely Use Align to Baseline. While there's no doubt that a careful study and practice of baseline grids can make your documents better looking, we rarely use the Align to Baseline Grid feature. The reason: you can get the same result by making sure your leading, Space Before, and Space After always add up to an even multiple of the leading value.

For example, if your body text has 15-point leading, then make sure your headings also have 15- or 30-point leading. If you use Space Before or Space After, make sure those values are set to a multiple of 15, such as: 15, 30, or 45 points. Finally, snap the tops of your frame to the baseline grid and set the First Baseline setting to Leading, and you can't go wrong.

Only Align First Line to Grid. Often, sidebars in magazines or newsletters are set in a different font and leading than the main body text, and they're placed in their own text frame. You can make the first baseline of that sidebar align with the leading grid by using the Only Align First Line to Grid feature. This forces the first line of a selected paragraph to snap to the baseline grid, but then leaves the rest of the paragraph alone. To align the first baseline of a paragraph to the baseline grid, first align the whole paragraph to the baseline grid and then choose Only Align First Line to Grid from the Paragraph or Control panel menu.

Drop Caps

Drop caps are a paragraph-level attribute in InDesign (as they are in QuarkXPress). To apply a drop cap to a paragraph, enter a value in the Number of Lines field of the Paragraph or Control panel (this sets both the baseline shift and the point size of the drop cap). To apply the drop cap formatting to more than one character, enter a number in the Number of Characters field. InDesign enlarges the characters you specified and shifts their baseline down according to the value you entered in the Number of Lines field (see Figure 4-42).

FIGURE 4-42
Drop Caps

Select a paragraph.

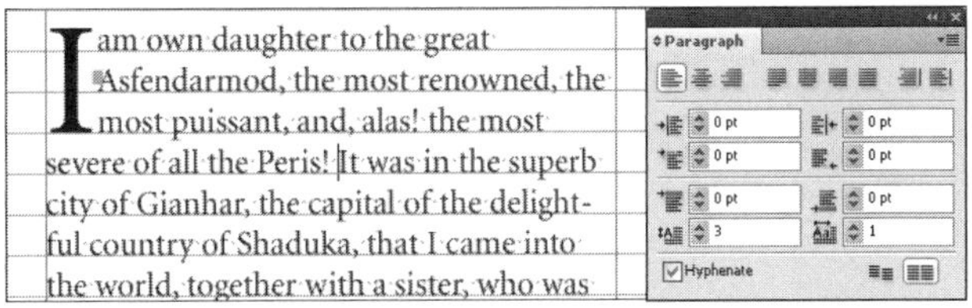

Enter the number of lines you want to
"drop" the initial character(s).

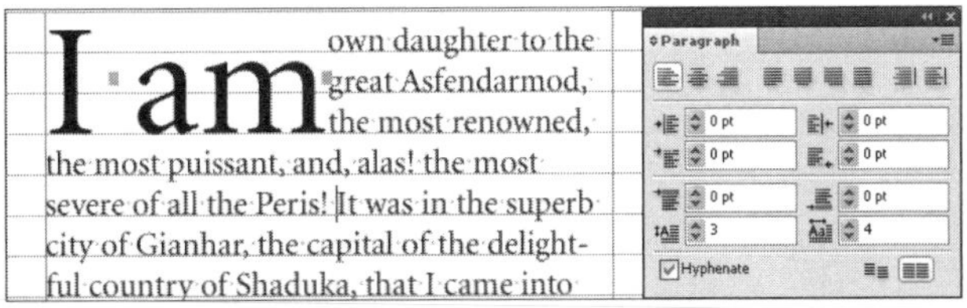

Enter the number of characters you want to
apply the drop cap format to, if necessary.

You can also make an initial cap that drops down *and* raises up by selecting the drop cap character (or characters) and increasing the point size. To add or remove space between the drop cap and the characters that follow it, place the cursor after the drop cap and adjust the Kerning value (see "Kerning," earlier in this chapter). The only good way to get your text to follow the shape of a drop cap is to convert the character to an outline and either place that outline as frame outside the text frame or as an anchored frame with text wrap.

If you find yourself often applying character formatting to your drop caps—changing size, font, color, *etc.*—then you should create a new character style that reflects that formatting, choose Drop Caps and Nested Styles from the Control panel menu (or press Command-Option-R/Ctrl-Alt-R), and choose your character style from the Character Style pop-up menu. Of course, you can also define this as part of your paragraph style (see "Styles," later in this chapter).

The Drop Caps and Nested Styles dialog box also offers two other drop cap options: Align Left Edge and Scale Descenders. The former moves the drop cap so that its left edge is placed exactly at the left edge of the left indent—this tends to be more important with very large drop caps. The latter only takes effect when the drop cap has a descender (for example, the letter "Q" or a lower-case "p"); the whole drop cap is cleverly scaled so that the descender avoids the line below.

Type in the Margin. In InDesign, the edges of text frames are usually inviolable (apart from the adjustments applied by optical margin alignment). There's no margin release (anybody still remember typewriters?), no handy command for moving one line a bit over the edge. Or is there? Instead of a single-character drop cap, specify a two-character drop cap. Add a space to the left of the first character in the paragraph—if your paragraph is justified, this should be a space that doesn't get wider, such as an en space (Command-Shift-N/Ctrl-Shift-N). Place the cursor between the space and the drop cap and apply negative kerning until the left edge of the character moves outside of the text frame. Note, also, that using optical margin alignment may provide the effect you're looking for without all of the extra work.

Nested Styles   When we look at the formatting in our documents, we see patterns. In this book, for example, a paragraph containing a run-in heading starts with our "run-in heading" character style and then reverts to the formatting of our body text. A period separates the heading from the body text. To apply this formatting, we have to select the first sentence and apply the character style. Wouldn't it be nice if we could tell our page-layout application to apply that pattern for us?

With InDesign's nested styles, we can do just that. Nested styles give you a way to automatically apply character formatting to portions of a paragraph—the first character, the first sentence, or just the third word. Nested styles rely on you first creating a character style; we discuss how to do this later in this chapter. You might want to skip forward, read that section, and then return to this explanation.

Nested styles are perfect for automatically applying a style to a drop cap, a run-in heading (where the first sentence is styled differently from the rest of the paragraph), or any structured paragraph. Catalogs, for example, often have structured paragraphs—such as a paragraph that contains an item number followed by a title, followed by a description, followed by a price. With nested styles, you can tell InDesign to apply a different character style to each element.

You can apply a nested style as local formatting, but it's generally better to define a nested style as part of a paragraph style. To apply a nested style to one or more selected paragraphs in a story, choose Drop Caps and Nested Styles from the Paragraph or Control panel menu (or press Command-Option-R/Ctrl-Alt-R). We'll discuss how to define a paragraph style later in this chapter.

The Drop Caps and Nested Styles dialog box contains two sections: formatting for drop caps and formatting for paragraphs.

Drop Caps. Earlier in this chapter, we discussed the process of applying a drop cap to paragraph—the Drop Caps section of this dialog box is an alternate way to do the same thing.

Many designs specify that the first line of text following a drop cap be formatted a particular way—small caps are quite commonly used. With nested styles, you can accomplish this easily by adding a forced line break, as shown in Figure 4-43.

FIGURE 4-43
Drop Caps and Nested Styles

By including the drop cap as part of the paragraph's nested style definition, we can automatically apply a character style to the drop cap (which is a good thing to do, in any case).

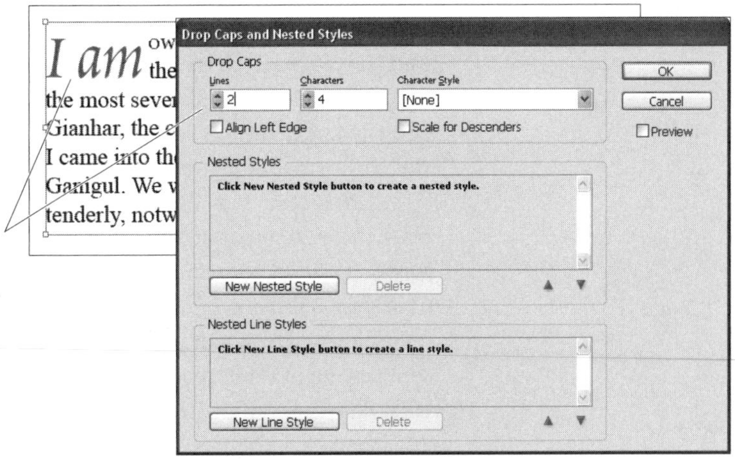

Nested Styles. The Nested Styles section is where you build a set of rules for InDesign to follow while formatting a paragraph. Here's how you make a nested style (see Figure 4-44).

1. Display the Drop Cap and Nested Style dialog box (choose Drop Caps and Nested Styles from the Paragraph panel menu or the Control panel menu). Click the New Nested Style button.

2. Select the character style you want to apply from the first pop-up menu. Of course, you have to have defined at least one character style for this to work.

3. To activate the second option, click the word "through." Select either "up to" or "through" from this pop-up menu. Choose "through" if you want to apply the style up to *and including* a given character, or "up to" to apply the style to the text but *not* to the delimiting character.

4. Click the setting in the third column to change it from "1" to some other number, if necessary. If you want to apply your character style "up to the third word," for example, you would change this number to "3."

5. Click the last column to activate the pop-up menu, then enter a delimiter character (or choose one from the pop-up menu). To apply the style up to the first en space in the paragraph, for example, choose En Spaces from the pop-up menu. You can enter any character you want into this field—including many of the find/change metacharacters.

6. If you want another style to follow the one you just made, start at Step 1 again. You can also repeat one or more rules by choosing Repeat from the first pop-up menu, creating a loop.

End Nested Style Here. What if you want to apply a character style to some portion of your paragraph, but there's no obvious "stopping point" you can target? For example, each paragraph may require the style up to a different point. No problem: Just choose End Nested Style Character from the last pop-up menu in Step 5, above. Then place the text cursor at that point in the paragraph and choose End Nested Style Here from the Other submenu in the Insert Special Character submenu (under the Type or context menu). This is an invisible character, so it won't reflow your text. If a paragraph doesn't contain one of these special characters, InDesign applies the character style you specify to the entire paragraph.

FIGURE 4-44
Nested Styles

This text needs to be formatted.

We've created character styles to assist us in formatting the text.

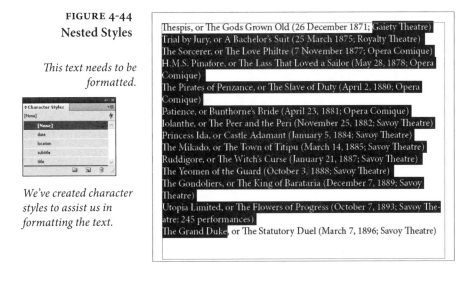

Thespis, or The Gods Grown Old (26 December 1871; Gaiety Theatre)
Trial by Jury, or A Bachelor's Suit (25 March 1875; Royalty Theatre)
The Sorcerer, or The Love Philtre (7 November 1877; Opera Comique)
H.M.S. Pinafore, or The Lass That Loved a Sailor (May 28, 1878; Opera Comique)
The Pirates of Penzance, or The Slave of Duty (April 2, 1880; Opera Comique)
Patience, or Bunthorne's Bride (April 23, 1881; Opera Comique)
Iolanthe, or The Peer and the Peri (November 25, 1882; Savoy Theatre)
Princess Ida, or Castle Adamant (January 5, 1884; Savoy Theatre)
The Mikado, or The Town of Titipu (March 14, 1885; Savoy Theatre)
Ruddigore, or The Witch's Curse (January 21, 1887; Savoy Theatre)
The Yeomen of the Guard (October 3, 1888; Savoy Theatre)
The Gondoliers, or The King of Barataria (December 7, 1889; Savoy Theatre)
Utopia Limited, or The Flowers of Progress (October 7, 1893; Savoy Theatre; 245 performances)
The Grand Duke, or The Statutory Duel (March 7, 1896; Savoy Theatre)

We apologize, in advance, for the complexity of this illustration (which continues on the next page). We can't help it—this stuff is nothing short of magical.

We want to format the text according to the following rules:

1. Apply the "title" style to the text up to the comma.
2. Leave the comma and "or" in the paragraph's default style.
3. Format the subtitle (the text up to the open parenthesis).
4. Format the open parenthesis character using the paragraph's default style.

Example line — Thespis, or The Gods Grown Old (26 December 1871; Gaiety Theatre)¶

5. Format the date (the text up to the semicolon).
6. Format the semicolon character using the paragraph's default style.
7. Apply the "location" character style to the theater name.
8. Format the close parenthesis character using the paragraph's default style.

Rather than work our way through the text and apply character styles manually, we choose Drop Caps and Nested Styles (from the Paragraph panel or the Control panel menu).

InDesign displays the Drop Cap and Nested Styles dialog box.

Click the New Nested Style button. InDesign creates a new nested style. Choose a character style from the first pop-up menu (you can also create a new character style, if necessary).

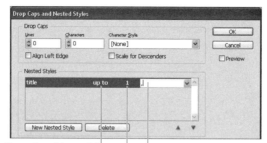

FIGURE 4-44
**Applying Nested Styles
(continued)**

*The following pop-up menus
set the length of the text
style range.*

Choose "up to" or "through"
from this pop-up menu.
Enter the number of
delimiter characters.

Enter a delimiter character (or
choose one of the preset delimiters
from the pop-up menu).

*Following the title, we want
to leave the comma and
the word "or" in the default
character formatting for the
paragraph. Click New Nested
Style and leave the Style
pop-up menu set to "[None]".*

*We entered a
space here.*

*At this point, we're ready to
set up the formatting for the
subtitle. The character at the
end of the subtitle text is an
open parenthesis, so we enter
that character and set the
range to "up to."*

*We create a further six
character styles to cover all
of the rules we've defined.
When we're done, we have
formatted all of the text. No
selecting, no clicking, and
no keyboard shortcuts. This
process takes far longer to
explain than it does to do.*

*It's even better when you
make the nested styles
part of a paragraph style,
as we'll demonstrate
later in this chapter.*

THESPIS, or *The Gods Grown Old* (26 December 1871; Gaiety Theatre)
TRIAL BY JURY, or *A Bachelor's Suit* (25 March 1875; Royalty Theatre)
THE SORCERER, or *The Love Philtre* (7 November 1877; Opera Comique)
H.M.S. PINAFORE, or *The Lass That Loved a Sailor* (May 28, 1878; Opera
Comique)
THE PIRATES OF PENZANCE, or *The Slave of Duty* (April 2, 1880; Opera
Comique)
PATIENCE, or *Bunthorne's Bride* (April 23, 1881; Opera Comique)
IOLANTHE, or *The Peer and the Peri* (November 25, 1882; Savoy Theatre)
PRINCESS IDA, or *Castl*
THE MIKADO, or *The To*
RUDDIGORE, or *The Wi*
THE YEOMEN OF THE G
THE GONDOLIERS, or *T*
Theatre)
UTOPIA LIMITED, or *Th*
Theatre; 245 performan
THE GRAND DUKE, or *T*

Repeating Nested Styles

Nested styles have a special setting, which appears on the Character Style pop-up menu in the Drop Caps and Nested Styles dialog box: the Repeat option. You can use this option to repeat some or all of the sequence of nested styles you've entered, as shown in Figure 4-45. Nested styles appearing below the Repeat nested style are ignored.

FIGURE 4-45
Repeating a Nested Style

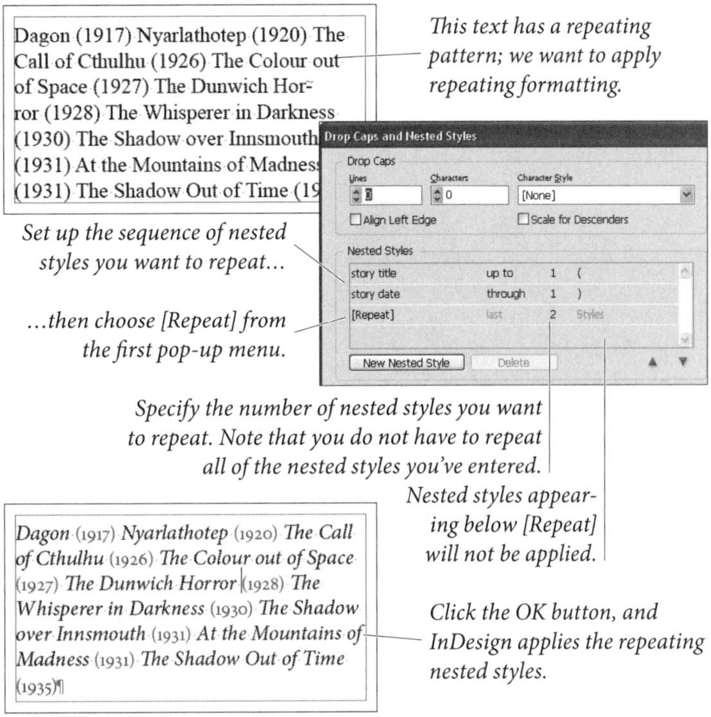

Dagon (1917) Nyarlathotep (1920) The Call of Cthulhu (1926) The Colour out of Space (1927) The Dunwich Horror (1928) The Whisperer in Darkness (1930) The Shadow over Innsmouth (1931) At the Mountains of Madness (1931) The Shadow Out of Time (19

This text has a repeating pattern; we want to apply repeating formatting.

Drop Caps and Nested Styles

Drop Caps
Lines   Characters   Character Style
0   0   [None]

☐ Align Left Edge   ☐ Scale for Descenders

Nested Styles
story title   up to   1   (
story date   through   1   )
[Repeat]   last   2   Styles

New Nested Style   Delete   ▲ ▼

Set up the sequence of nested styles you want to repeat...

...then choose [Repeat] from the first pop-up menu.

Specify the number of nested styles you want to repeat. Note that you do not have to repeat all of the nested styles you've entered.

Nested styles appearing below [Repeat] will not be applied.

Dagon (1917) Nyarlathotep (1920) The Call of Cthulhu (1926) The Colour out of Space (1927) The Dunwich Horror (1928) The Whisperer in Darkness (1930) The Shadow over Innsmouth (1931) At the Mountains of Madness (1931) The Shadow Out of Time (1935)¶

Click the OK button, and InDesign applies the repeating nested styles.

Nested Line Styles

Nested line styles are a special case of a nested style. In a nested line style, the end of a line defines the end of the style. Nested line styles are particularly useful when you want to apply special formatting to the first line of a paragraph, or repeat sequences of line formatting through a paragraph.

To create a nested line style, follow these steps (see Figure 4-46).

1. Select some text, then choose Drop Caps and Nested Styles from the Paragraph panel menu (or from the Control panel menu). InDesign displays the Drop Caps and Nested Styles dialog box.

2. Use the controls in the Nested Line Styles section of the dialog box to specify the character style and number of lines for the nested line style. Like nested styles, nested line styles can repeat.

3. Click the OK button to close the dialog and apply the nested line style(s).

FIGURE 4-46
Nested Line Styles

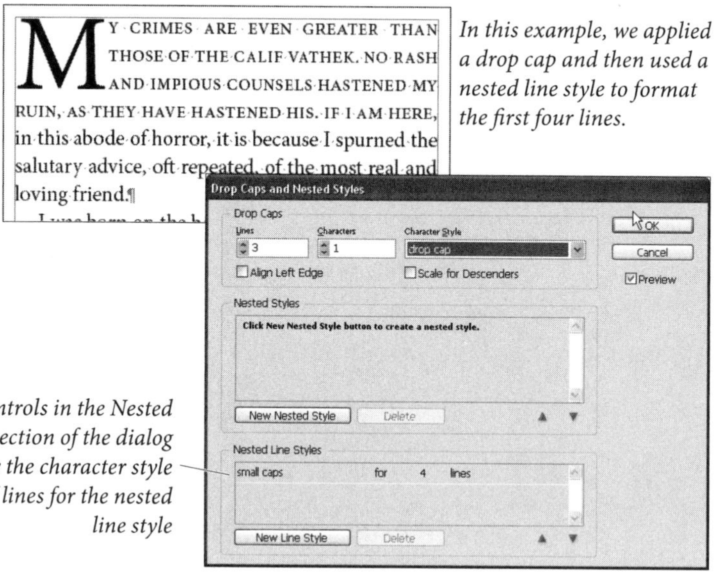

In this example, we applied a drop cap and then used a nested line style to format the first four lines.

Use the controls in the Nested Line Styles section of the dialog box to specify the character style and number of lines for the nested line style

Nested GREP Styles

While nested styles make use of ordered sequences of special characters and other text, GREP styles can apply a character style to any text that matches a GREP expression—in any location, repetition, or order in a paragraph. This feature is brilliant, and we think that your basic set of paragraph styles will probably acquire a number of nested GREP styles as soon as you fully understand what it does.

To create a GREP style, follow the steps below (see Figure 4-47).

1. Select some text, then choose GREP Styles from the Paragraph panel menu (or from the Control panel menu). InDesign displays the GREP Styles dialog box. It's a good idea to turn on the Preview option—that way, you can see the effect of your GREP style as you construct it.

2. Click the New Grep Style button. InDesign adds a new GREP style.

3. Select a character style from the Apply Style pop-up menu.

4. Enter the GREP expression in the To Text field. As in the GREP panel of the Find/Change dialog box, you can build the GREP expression using the associated pop-up menu. Even if you have Preview turned on, however, InDesign will not apply the GREP expression until you press Return.

5. Click the OK button to close the dialog box and apply the GREP style.

To delete a GREP style, select the style and click the Delete button.

FIGURE 4-47
GREP Styles

InDesign's GREP styles can add automatic GREP searches to your paragraphs. This paragraph contains two GREP styles: one converts acronyms or other words typed in ALL CAPS to small caps using the character style "small caps," the other applies the character style "email" to any email address it finds in the paragraph, such as okvern@ix.netcom.c... You may want to add G... your basic set of paragr...

Before GREP styles.

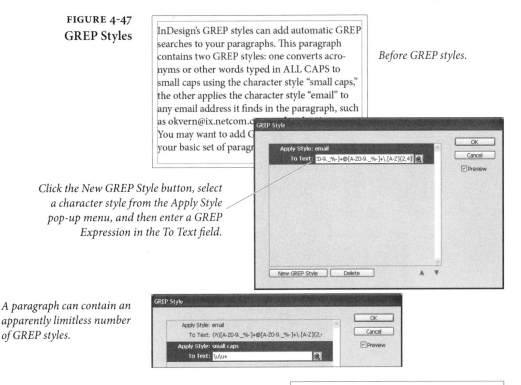

Click the New GREP Style button, select a character style from the Apply Style pop-up menu, and then enter a GREP Expression in the To Text field.

A paragraph can contain an apparently limitless number of GREP styles.

In this example, our GREP styles have formatted words typed in all caps as Open Type All Small Caps, and applied a character style with an underline to the email addresses in the text. No manual formatting was used.

InDesign's GREP styles can add automatic GREP searches to your paragraphs. This paragraph contains two GREP styles: one converts acronyms or other words typed in ALL CAPS to small caps using the character style "small caps," the other applies the character style "email" to any email address it finds in the paragraph, such as okvern@ix.netcom.com or david@63p.com. You may want to add GREP styles like these to your basic set of paragraph styles.

Multi-Line Composition

Composition—the method our desktop publishing program uses to fit text into a line—isn't glamorous. It's not going to be the focus of any glossy magazine advertisement. In fact, most people never consciously notice good or bad composition. We are convinced, however, that readers perceive the difference between well spaced and poorly spaced text. Good spacing not only improves readability, it also conveys an aura of quality to the publication or organization. In short, it's worth caring about.

There are four basic ways to fit text onto a line:

▶ Controlling the spacing between the letters.

▶ Controlling the spacing between the words.

▶ Adjusting the size of the characters themselves.

▶ Breaking the words at line endings by hyphenating.

If you're serious about type, you already know that a large part of your typesetting time is spent fixing bad line breaks and lines with poor word and letter spacing. In our experience, fully one third of our typesetting and production time in QuarkXPress or other programs is spent "walking the lines"—fixing spacing problems.

Other desktop publishing programs use a "single line composer" to compose lines of text. As the program arranges the characters on each line, it only considers the spacing of that line, which means that adjacent lines may have dramatically different spacing. The greater the variation of letter and word spacing among lines in a paragraph, the harder it is to read (and the less appealing it is to look at).

InDesign, however, has both a single-line composer and a multi-line composer, which can examine an entire paragraph at a time.

How does it work? The multi-line composer (called Adobe Paragraph Composer) creates a list of possible line break points in the lines it examines. It then ranks the different sets of possible break points, considering the effect of each break point on spacing and hyphenation. Finally, it chooses the best of the alternatives. You'd think that this would take a lot of time—but it doesn't. When you use the default settings, you get composition speed that's equal to that of a single-line composition system, and you get better-looking text (see Figure 4-48).

Multi-line composition takes some getting used to because characters *preceding* the cursor will sometimes *move* as you enter or edit text—something you won't see in most other programs. You really can't be certain of the position of the line breaks in a paragraph until you've entered the last word in the paragraph. Luckily, it doesn't take long to adjust to this behavior—especially when the results are so much better than what you're accustomed to.

In some rare cases you might want or need to turn the Adobe Paragraph Composer off and exercise manual control over the line breaks in a paragraph—when lines absolutely must break a particular way. Also, single-line composition is faster than multi-line, so if quality isn't an issue, you might consider turning it off.

Multi-line composition is on by default; to use the single-line composition method, select a paragraph and choose Adobe Single-line Composer from the Paragraph or Control panel menu (or in the Justification dialog box). To turn multi-line composition back on again for the paragraph, choose Adobe Paragraph Composer.

FIGURE 4-48
**Multi-Line
Composition**

*Note the extreme variation
in word and letter spacing
from line to line in the text
composed using the Single-
line composer.*

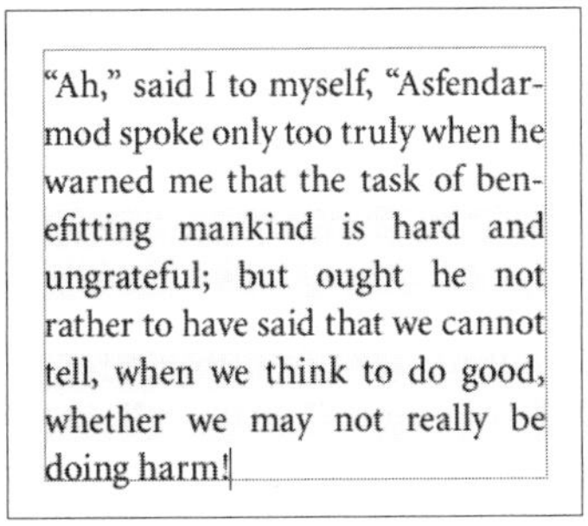

"Ah," said I to myself, "Asfendarmod spoke only too truly when he
warned me that the task of ben-
efitting mankind is hard and
ungrateful; but ought he not
rather to have said that we cannot
tell, when we think to do good,
whether we may not really be
doing harm!

"Ah," said I to myself, "Asfendarmod spoke only too truly when he
warned me that the task of benefit-
ting mankind is hard and ungrateful; but ought he not rather to have
said that we cannot tell, when we
think to do good, whether we may
not really be doing harm!

Single-line Composer. 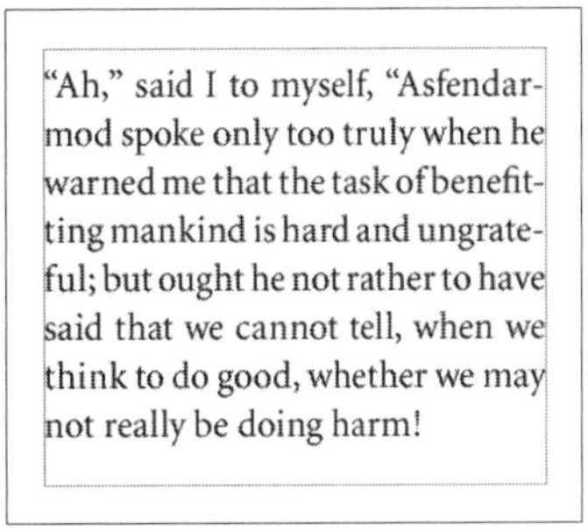   *Paragraph Composer*

Hyphenation Controls

If you're tired of having your favorite page layout program hyphenate the word "image" after the "m," you'll like InDesign's hyphenation controls. To set the hyphenation options for a paragraph, choose Hyphenation from the Paragraph or Control panel's menu. InDesign displays the Hyphenation dialog box (see Figure 4-49). QuarkXPress users are used to having both hyphenation and justification settings in one dialog box; in InDesign they're broken into two. Also, in QuarkXPress, you have to make and save an H&J setting first, and then apply it to a paragraph. In InDesign, you select a paragraph and change its hyphenation and justification settings.

The first checkbox in the Hyphenation Settings dialog box, simply labeled Hyphenate, controls whether the selected paragraph or paragraphs will be hyphenated. This is identical to turning on and off the Hyphenate checkbox in the Paragraph panel. Then there are seven other controls that determine the hyphenation rules.

Words with at Least. You can direct InDesign's hyphenation system to leave short words alone using the Words with at Least option. If you don't want short words to break, you can set this to 5 or higher.

After First. The value you enter here sets the minimum size, in characters, of the word fragment preceding a hyphen. Many typesetters dislike two-letter fragments, so they increase this value to three.

FIGURE 4-49
**Hyphenation Settings
Dialog Box**

Hyphenation Settings

☑ Hyphenate

Words with at Least: ⬍ 7   letters

After First: ⬍ 3   letters

Before Last: ⬍ 3   letters

Hyphen Limit: ⬍ 2   hyphens

Hyphenation Zone: ⬍ 36 pt

Better Spacing   Fewer Hyphens

☑ Hyphenate Capitalized Words   ☑ Hyphenate Last Word

☐ Hyphenate Across Column

OK

Cancel

☐ Preview

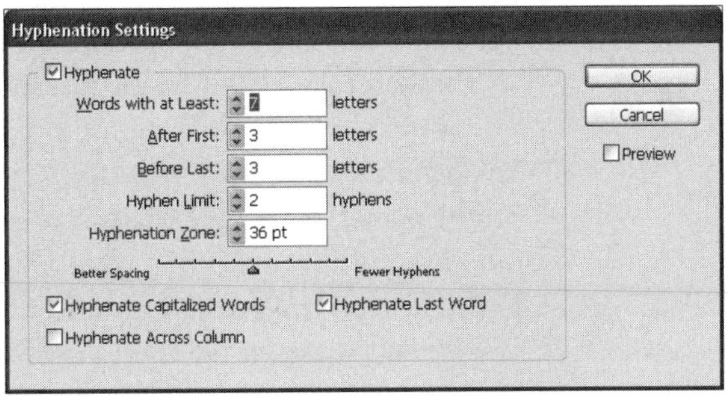

Before Last. The value you enter here sets the minimum size, in characters, of the word fragment following a hyphen. Some people don't mind if the "ly" in "truly" sits all by itself on a line. You care about type, so you set this to at least three.

Hyphen Limit. You can limit the number of consecutive hyphens you'll allow to appear at the left edge of a column of text using the Hyphen Limit field. Enter a value greater than one to allow consecutive hyphens.

Hyphenation Zone. Another way to limit the number of hyphens in a paragraph is the Hyphenation Zone setting. The idea is that there is an invisible zone along the right margin of each paragraph. If InDesign is trying to break a word at the end of a line, it looks to see where the hyphenation zone is. If the word *before* the potentially hyphenated word falls inside the zone, then InDesign just gives up and pushes the word onto the next line (without hyphenating it). If the previous word does not fall into the zone, then InDesign will hyphenate the word.

That's the concept, at least. As it turns out, InDesign's composition algorithms are complex enough that the hyphenation zone is often overridden by other factors, especially when using the Paragraph Composer. In addition, the Hyphenation Zone setting doesn't have any effect at all on justified text. In general, for non-justified text, larger amounts mean fewer hyphens but more variation in line lengths ("rag").

Hyphenation Slider. Someone, somewhere must have complained that InDesign's hyphenation controls weren't flexible enough, because those wacky engineers at Adobe have added the Hyphenation Slider to the Hyphenation Settings dialog box. We're sure there's a lot of math behind what this slider is doing, but all you really need to know is that you can move the slider back and forth between Better Spacing and Fewer Hyphens to get a more pleasing appearance (turn on preview to see the effect of the slider).

This control is called "Nigel" because it goes all the way to eleven.

Hyphenate Capitalized Words. To prevent capitalized words (i.e., proper names) from hyphenating, turn off this option.

Hyphenate Last Words. We pride ourselves on having open minds and strong stomachs, but there are few things more nauseating than the last word of a paragraph being hyphenated, leaving a little runt on the last line. We won't say that it's impossible to avoid it entirely, but you should at least turn off the Hyphenate Last Words checkbox, so that it won't happen automatically.

Hyphenate Across Columns. Our generous, kind, and patient publisher asks little from us (besides the best book we can muster), but they do ask one thing: Please don't allow words to hyphenate from one page to another. In older editions, we had to proof each page manually. Now we simply turn off the Hyphenate Across Columns checkbox in our body text paragraph style. Note that this stops hyphenation across all columns, even from one column in a multi-column text frame to the next. By the way, we have seen this control fail, so it appears that InDesign considers it a request rather than a rule; it tries not to hyphenate across a column, but it will if it thinks it needs to.

Discretionary Hyphens. There's another way to control hyphenation: Use a discretionary hyphen character. When you type a discretionary hyphen (Command-Shift-hyphen/Ctrl-Shift-hyphen) in a word, you're telling InDesign that you wouldn't mind if the word hyphenates here. This doesn't force the program to hyphenate the word at that point; it just gives it the option. This is much better than typing a regular hyphen because if (or when) your text reflows, you won't be stuck with hyphens littered in the middles of your paragraphs—the discretionary hyphen "disappears" when it's not needed. Another way to get a discretionary hyphen is to use the Insert Special Character submenu (in the Type menu or the context-sensitive menu).

By the way, longtime QuarkXPress users know that in that program you can place a discretionary hyphen before a word to make it not break. That's also true in InDesign, but, if you want a word (or phrase) not to hyphenate, select the text and turn on the No Break option in the Character panel's menu. If it's a word that you think should never be hyphenated, or should always be hyphenated differently than InDesign thinks, you can add it to your user dictionary (see "Adding Words to the User Dictionary" in Chapter 3, "Text").

Controlling Word and Letter Spacing

When InDesign composes the text in your publications, it does so by following the spacing rules you've laid down using the controls in the Justification dialog box (choose Justification from the Paragraph panel menu or press Command-Option-Shift-J/Ctrl-Alt-Shift-J to display the dialog box; see Figure 4-50). Contrary to popular opinion, this dialog box controls all text composition, not only that of justified text.

FIGURE 4-50
Justification Dialog Box

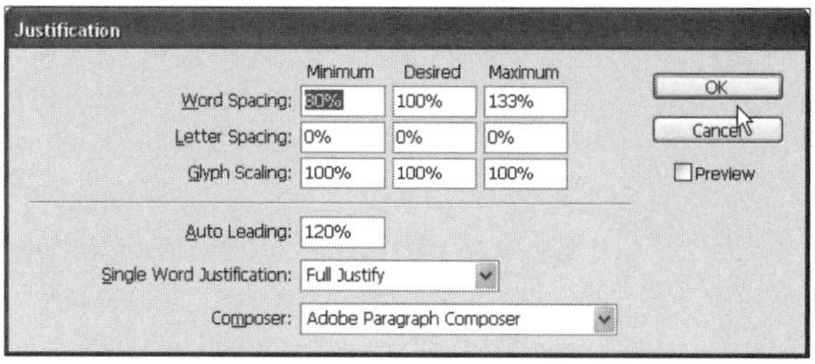

This dialog box offers six controls: Word Spacing, Letter Spacing, Glyph Scaling, Auto Leading, Single Word Justification, and Composer. The important thing to remember is that you will never find a set of spacing values that will work for all fonts, point sizes, and line lengths. The text itself plays a role: spacing settings that work for one author may not work for another, even when the typesetting specifications are the same. You have to experiment to discover the settings that work best for you and your publications.

InDesign's default settings give you a reasonable starting point. The spacing values encourage wide word spacing over narrow word spacing, and attempt to discourage letter spacing.

Word Spacing. You can adjust the amount of space InDesign places between words by changing the Minimum, Desired, and Maximum percentages. In non-justified text, only the Desired value matters. In InDesign, the values in the word spacing fields are *percentages of* the standard word space (the width of the space is defined by the font's designer, and is stored in the font). The defaults tend to encourage wide word spacing over narrow word spacing in justified text.

Letter Spacing. You can adjust the amount of space the program places between each character in your paragraphs by changing the Minimum, Desired, and Maximum percentages. Again, in text that isn't justified, only the Desired value makes a difference. Note that these percentages represent the *amount of variation* from a standard spacing unit—the "spaceband" defined in the font. By default, the percentages are all set to zero, which discourages letter spacing.

Glyph Scaling. When you enter anything other than 100% in any of the Glyph Scaling fields, you give InDesign permission to scale the characters in the paragraph to make them fit. Ole and David disagree on usefulness of this feature. Ole is not a type purist, but he does not see the point in distorting character shapes when other, better options are available. Why take the risk? David, on the other hand insists that no one can see the difference when you allow InDesign to scale glyphs by plus or minus one percent (and sometimes even two). Ole thinks that this is something like thinking that it's not committing a crime if no one catches you.

Both authors agree that glyph scaling might come in handy if you have exhausted *every other available option* to get a line to fit. What you do is, of course, up to you and your conscience.

Auto Leading. The Auto Leading feature is easy: This controls how InDesign calculates the leading of characters that have a leading of Auto (see "Leading," earlier in this chapter, for why we almost never use Auto leading). This control is here, rather than in one of the Preferences dialog boxes, because the base autoleading percentage is a property of individual paragraphs (unlike QuarkXPress, where the autoleading percentage is set at the document level).

Single Word Justification. What do you want InDesign to do when a word in the middle of a paragraph is so long (or a column so narrow) that only that one word fits on the line? If the line isn't justified, it's no big deal. But if the line is justified, do you want InDesign to add letterspacing to spread the word out across the line? Or make it flush left, flush right, or centered? That's what the Single Word Justification pop-up menu controls.

Composer. Earlier in this chapter, we discussed the Paragraph Composer and how it's different from the Single Line composer. Here's one more place you can specify which InDesign should use.

Balance Ragged Lines   Sometimes headlines or headings are way out of balance—and we don't just mean the political slant. We mean that the lines are of wildly varying length. The first line fills the column; the second line contains a single short word. This is, at best, unsightly; at worst, it makes the text hard to read.

InDesign's Balance Ragged Lines feature can help you make the line widths in a paragraph more even. To do this, choose Balance Ragged Lines from the Paragraph panel or Control panel menu. (Note that this feature only works on non-justified paragraphs.) Take a look at Figure 4-51 to see the effect of Balance Ragged Lines.

If the last line of the paragraph is significantly narrower than the other lines, the program breaks the text so that the last line is wider.

Balance Ragged Lines generally produces an inverted pyramid shape—that is, the first line is longer than the second line, the third line is shorter than the second line, and so on. This matches Ole's expectations, but is the opposite of what David expects.

FIGURE 4-51
Balancing Ragged Lines

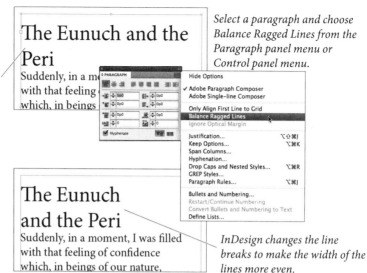

The lines of this heading are of very different widths.

Select a paragraph and choose Balance Ragged Lines from the Paragraph panel menu or Control panel menu.

Since Balance Ragged Lines is a paragraph-level attribute, it can be made part of a paragraph style.

InDesign changes the line breaks to make the width of the lines more even.

Highlighting Typographic Problems

InDesign can "flag" text composition problems—cases where the program has had to break your rules for composing text, or where substituted fonts appear in your publication. Open the Preferences dialog box, choose the Composition pane, then turn on the options in the Highlight section of the Composition Preferences dialog box. Lines in which InDesign has had to violate composition rules you've established (using the Justification and Keep Options dialog boxes) are highlighted in yellow; substituted fonts are highlighted in pink (see Figure 4-52). We usually work with these turned on so we can quickly identify "problem" lines.

Paragraph Keep Options

A *widow* is the last line of a paragraph that winds up all by itself at the top of a column or page. An *orphan* is the first line of a paragraph that lands all by itself at the bottom of a column or page. Widows and orphans are the bane of a typesetter's existence.

Designers sometimes also refer to the single-word last line of a paragraph as either a widow or an orphan. To avoid the confusion, we often just use the word *runt*.

All typographic widows and orphans are bad, but certain kinds are really bad—for example, a widow line that consists of only one word, or even the last part of a hyphenated word. Another related typographic horror is the heading that stands alone with its following paragraph on the next page.

Fortunately, InDesign has a set of controls that can easily prevent widows and orphans from sneaking into your document. These controls—along with a setting that lets you force a paragraph to begin at a particular place—live in the Keep Options dialog box, which you

FIGURE 4-52
Highlighting Loose and Tight Lines

When you turn on the H&J Violations option...

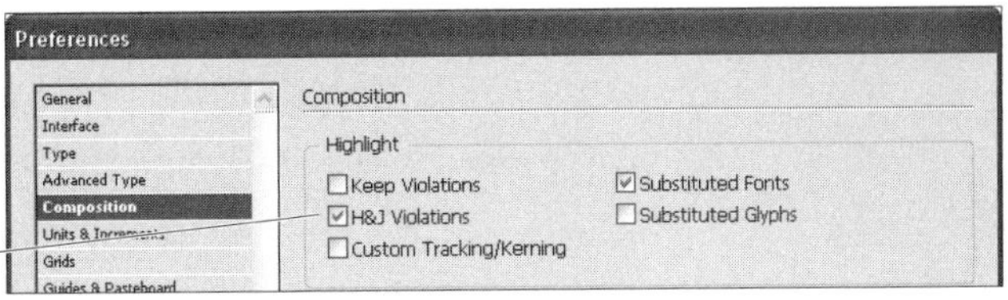

...InDesign highlights lines that break the spacing ranges you set in the Justification dialog box.

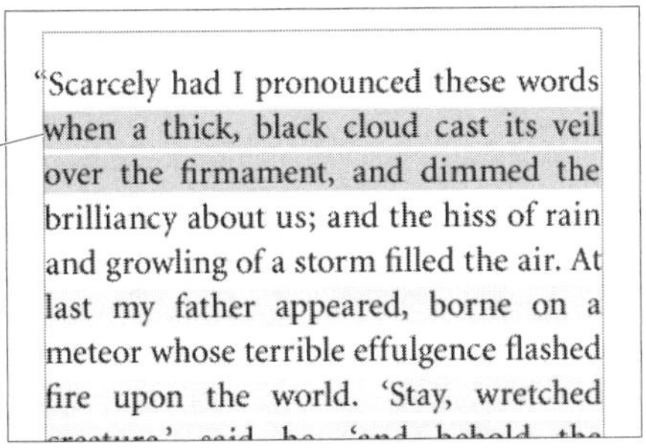

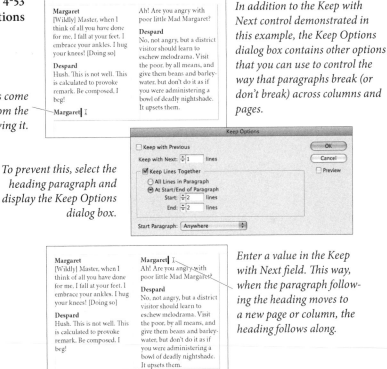

"Scarcely had I pronounced these words when a thick, black cloud cast its veil over the firmament, and dimmed the brilliancy about us; and the hiss of rain and growling of a storm filled the air. At last my father appeared, borne on a meteor whose terrible effulgence flashed fire upon the world. 'Stay, wretched

InDesign uses three shades of yellow to highlight loose or tight lines—darker shades indicate more severe spacing problems.

can find by selecting Keep Options from the Paragraph panel's menu, or by pressing Command-Option-K/Ctrl-Alt-K (see Figure 4-53). There are four parts to this dialog box: Keep with Previous, Keep with Next, Keep Lines Together, and Start Paragraph.

FIGURE 4-53
Keep Options

This heading has come "unstuck" from the paragraph following it.

To prevent this, select the heading paragraph and display the Keep Options dialog box.

In addition to the Keep with Next control demonstrated in this example, the Keep Options dialog box contains other options that you can use to control the way that paragraphs break (or don't break) across columns and pages.

Enter a value in the Keep with Next field. This way, when the paragraph following the heading moves to a new page or column, the heading follows along.

Keep with Previous. The Keep with Previous option keeps the top line of the paragraph with the previous paragraph, such as when you're adding notes below only some entries in a list.

Keep with Next. The Keep with Next Lines feature helps you ensure that headings and the paragraphs that follow them are kept together. If the paragraph is pushed onto a new column, a new page, or below an obstructing object, the heading follows. It's rare that we need to type more than 1 in the Lines field.

Keep Lines Together. The Keep Lines Together feature is the primary control over widows and orphans. When you turn on the Keep Lines Together checkbox and choose All Lines in Paragraph, InDesign won't break the paragraph across column or pages.

You can control the number of lines that should be kept together at the beginning and end of the paragraph by choosing At Start/End of Paragraph. The value you type in the Start field determines the minimum number of lines that InDesign allows at the beginning of a paragraph. For example, a Start value of 2 means that if at least two lines of that paragraph cannot be placed on the page, then the entire paragraph is pushed over to the next page. The value specified in the End field determines the minimum number of lines that InDesign lets fall alone at the top of a column or after an obstruction. Setting both Start and End to 2 means you'll never get a widow or orphan.

Start Paragraph. Use the options on the Start Paragraph pop-up menu to force a column or page break before your selected paragraph. For example, if you always want a particular paragraph to sit at the top of a page, select the paragraph and choose On Next Page from the Start Paragraph pop-up menu.

Note that you can also get a similar effect by choosing an item from the Insert Break Character submenu in the Type menu. The Start Paragraph feature is better, however, because you can use it in a definition of a paragraph style (see "Styles," later in this chapter).

Bullets and Numbering

As the human attention span has grown shorter under the stresses of modern life, lists of one sort or another have come to dominate our texts. Abraham Lincoln could spend several days delivering a single perfect paragraph to an informed audience; we must convey the same information in an executive summary that takes no more than nanoseconds to parse. InDesign aids and abets this diminution of the human intellect by providing the Bullets and Numbering feature, which provides:

▶ Bullets.

▶ Numbering.

Bullets and Numbering is a paragraph level attribute that applies a bullet character or a numeral to the start of the paragraph. Applying a bullet is straightforward; numbering is a bit more complicated.

Applying Bullets The simplest way to apply bullets to a selection of paragraphs is to click the Bulleted List button in the Paragraph view of the Control panel (or choose Apply Bullets from the Bulleted & Numbered Lists submenu of the Type menu). Follow the steps below, and you can control the formatting, and position of the bullets (see Figure 4-54):

1. Select a range of text.

2. Choose Bullets and Numbering from the Paragraph panel or Control panel menu. You can also Option/Alt-click the Bulleted List button in the Paragraph view of the Control panel. InDesign displays the Bullets and Numbering dialog box.

3. Choose Bullets from the List Type pop-up menu.

4. Pick from among the choices in the Bullet Character section, which works very much like the Glyphs panel described earlier in this chapter—the dialog contains a short list of characters, but you can click the Add button to choose characters from any of the available fonts and add them then to the list.

5. If you want the bullet to be followed by a tab, leave the Text After field set to ^t. If you'd prefer the bullet followed by something else (such as an en space), you can type it in that field or pick from the flyout menu to the right of the field.

6. You can apply formatting to the bullet character in the Character Style pop-up menu (assuming you have defined a style).

7. Adjust the position of the bullet in the Bullet or Number Position section. The Left Indent and First Line Indent fields control the indents for the entire paragraph (overriding any other indents you've set). To hang the bullet in the margin, you'd want a positive Left Indent and a negative First Line Indent.

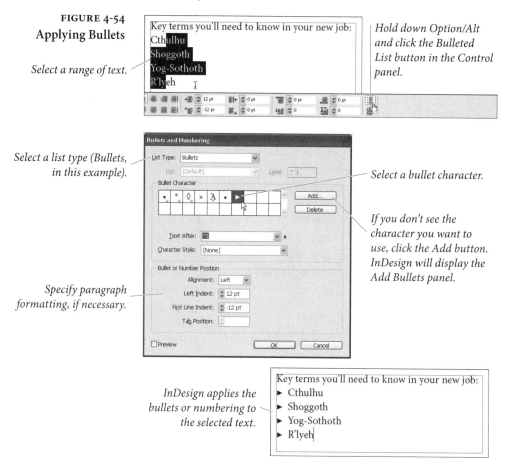

FIGURE 4-54
Applying Bullets

Select a range of text.

Hold down Option/Alt and click the Bulleted List button in the Control panel.

Select a list type (Bullets, in this example).

Select a bullet character.

If you don't see the character you want to use, click the Add button. InDesign will display the Add Bullets panel.

Specify paragraph formatting, if necessary.

InDesign applies the bullets or numbering to the selected text.

If the First Line Indent is set to zero and your Text After is set to a tab character, the position of the text after the bullet is defined by the first tab stop. If you've assigned tab stops already, you can ignore this.

The Alignment pop-up menu lets you control the position of the bullet at the beginning of the paragraph—Left, Right, or Centered—but it only works when your Left Indent is large enough to allow the character to move (InDesign won't allow the bullet to fall outside the text frame).

8. Once you've got the inserted characters to look the way you want them to (turn on the Preview option), click the OK button to apply the list formatting to the selected paragraphs.

Default Bullets. If you choose a custom bullet character with the Add button in the Bullets and Numbering dialog box, InDesign remembers that bullet in the currently-open document. If you need that same bullet character in other documents, you can add it to the list of default bullets:

1. Close all documents in InDesign.

2. Open the Bullets and Numbering dialog box.

3. Set the Type pop-up menu to Bullets.

4. Use the Add button to add your desired bullet character.

5. If you want this character to be the default bullet (the one InDesign gives you if you don't specify any other), select it.

6. Set the Type pop-up menu back to None and then click OK.

Applying Numbering   When Adobe first implemented the automatic numbering feature, we complained that it was anemic and useless. They responded in the next version by adding so many features that its now not only extremely useful but also somewhat overwhelming to use. Fortunately, it's all logical if you take it step by step and understand which parts of the Bullets and Numbering dialog box you can ignore.

The simplest way to apply numbering to one or more selected paragraphs is to click the Numbered List button in the Control panel (when it's in paragraph mode), or choose Apply Numbers from the Bulleted & Numbered Lists submenu, under the Type menu. This gives you a basic numbered list, starting at 1.

Continuing Numbering. Let's say you have five paragraphs, but the third paragraph shouldn't be numbered (that is, the section numbered "2" has two paragraphs). The fastest way to accomplish this is to select all five paragraphs, turn on numbering, then select just the third paragraph and turn numbering off.

Alternately, you could assign numbering to the first two paragraphs and then number the last two paragraphs (which will start at "1" again). Then place the cursor in the fourth paragraph (which is currently numbered "1") and choose Continue Numbering from either the Context menu or the Bulleted & Numbered Lists submenu, under the Type menu.

Formatting Numbers. The default formatting applied to automatic numbers is dull as rocks: the number—set in the same font, size, color, and styling as the first character of the paragraph—followed by a tab. In order to spice up your numbering, select Bullets and Numbering from the Control panel menu (or Option/Alt-click the Numbered

List button in the Control panel). When the List Type pop-up menu is set to Numbers, you can adjust the following settings in the Numbering Style section of the dialog box (see Figure 4-55).

▶ **Format.** You can choose from among normal numerals (such as 1, 2, 3, *etc.*), Roman numerals (I, II, III, *etc.*), or alphabet characters (a, b, c, *etc.*) from the Format pop-up menu. Choose None to omit the number entirely, though it's rare that you'd want to.

▶ **Number.** You can control how the number appears by typing codes into the Number field. The default value, ^#.^t, means type the current number for this list, followed by a period, then followed by a tab. You don't have to remember the codes—you can use the pop-up menu associated with the field. If you do use a tab character, it has to be the last code in this field.

FIGURE 4-55
Applying Numbering

Select a range of text.

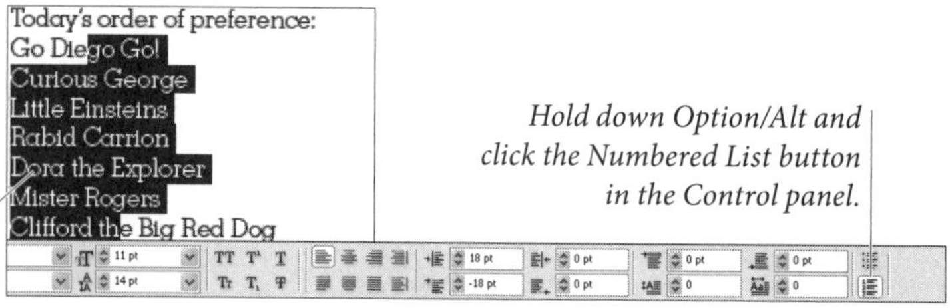

Hold down Option/Alt and click the Numbered List button in the Control panel.

InDesign displays the Bullets and Numbering dialog box.

Select a character style for the numbers, if necessary.

Here we've set up a hanging indent.

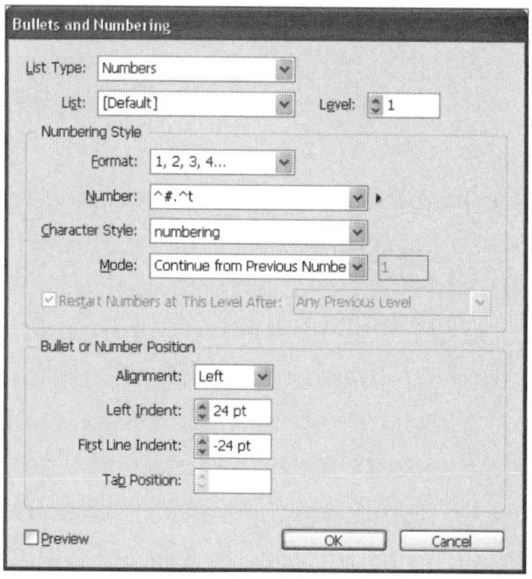

You can ignore List and Level at first.

Choose a number format.

Enter the characters you want to appear around the number.

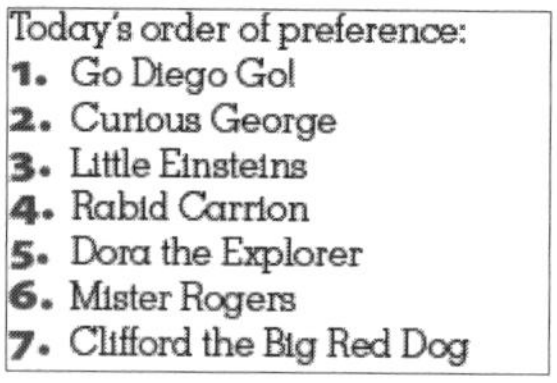

The list, numbered

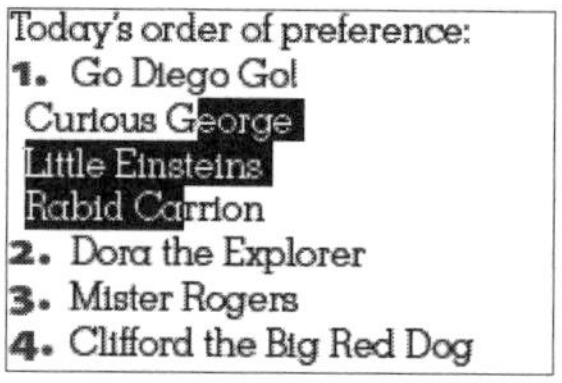

Turning off numbering for a few paragraphs renumbers the list.

You can type pretty much anything in the Number field. For example, you could type Item No. ^#^_ which means type "Item No." followed by a space, then the number, then an en dash.

▶ **Character Style.** InDesign applies the character style you choose from this pop-up menu to everything in the Number field.

▶ **Mode.** Use this pop-up menu to specify whether the list should Continue from Previous Number or Start At a specific number.

Positioning Numbers. You can adjust the position of your number in the same ways we discussed positioning bullets. You can make the right edge of the numbers align by choosing Right from the Alignment pop-up menu and setting the Left Indent to a positive number.

Multi-Level Numbering. What if you need a sub-list? For example, after number 4, you might have 4a, 4b, 4c, and so on. Or in a long technical document, you might have sections numbered 1.1.1, then 1.1.2, then 1.1.3, then 1.2.1, and so on. To pull off this kind of numbering, you need to assign levels in the Bullets and Numbering dialog box, then—optionally—adjust the Number field's codes (see Figure 4-56).

This can get confusing, so let's focus on that 4a, 4b, 4c example. After you select the paragraphs you want to affect (in this case, the three paragraphs after paragraph 4), open the dialog box and change the Level field to 2. This defines a sub-list inside the main numbered list. Now choose the lower-case alphabet from the Format pop-up menu and change the Number field to ^1^#.^t (which means "type the most recent level 1 number, then the current number in this sub-list, then a period and a tab"). You may also want to adjust the Left Indent in the Position section so that the sub-list is further indented.

Creating Named Lists. Numbering isn't just for a few paragraphs in a single story. You can create far more complex kinds of numbered lists that continue across multiple text frames, or even across multiple documents in a book. You can also have multiple numbered lists in parallel, for example, figure numbering and table numbering. The key to all these tricks is to define named lists. (InDesign just calls these "lists," but we call them "named lists" to avoid confusion with the generic "lists" that we've been discussing.)

You can define a named list by choosing Define Lists from the Bulleted & Numbered Lists submenu (under the Type menu) and then clicking the New button in the Define Lists dialog box. Or, if you already have the Bullets and Numbering dialog box open, you

FIGURE 4-56
Multi-Level Numbering

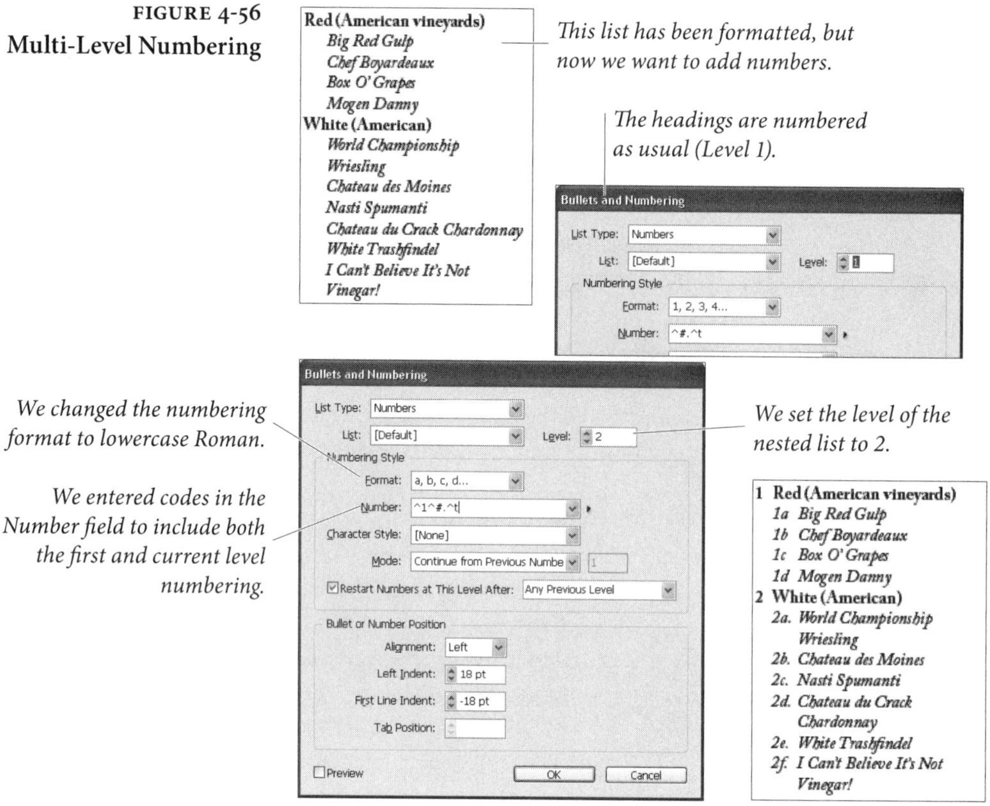

This list has been formatted, but now we want to add numbers.

The headings are numbered as usual (Level 1).

We changed the numbering format to lowercase Roman.

We entered codes in the Number field to include both the first and current level numbering.

We set the level of the nested list to 2.

can choose New List from the List pop-up menu. In either case, you get the New List dialog box, in which you can type the list's name and choose whether you want this numbered list to continue across multiple stories (that is, across more than one unthreaded text frame) and/or across more than one document in a book (see Figure 4-57).

Once you have a named list defined, you can assign it to a paragraph by choosing it from the List pop-up menu in the Bullets and Numbering dialog box.

However, the order in which paragraphs are numbered may be confusing to you. Here are the rules:

▸ In general, numbering follows page order. For example, if you have an unthreaded text frame on page 1 and another on page 2, InDesign will number paragraphs on page 1 first—just as you'd expect.

▸ If you have more than one frame on a page (and those frames aren't threaded), numbering in the frames is based on the order in which the frames were created—not the order on which they appear on the page.

FIGURE 4-57
Named Lists

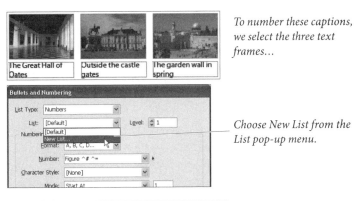

To number these captions, we select the three text frames...

...and apply numbering. Because the text frames are not threaded together, we need to create a new named list to keep our figure numbering straight.

Choose New List from the List pop-up menu.

InDesign displays the New List dialog box.

Enter a name for the list, and turn on Continue Numbers Across Stories.

Back in the Bullets and Numbering dialog box, we changed the Format and set Mode to Continue from Previous Number.

Remember that each frame on a page is numbered in the order it was created—not its position on the page!

Each caption is automatically numbered... or, um, "lettered."

▶ All the numbers in a single story (including multiple threaded text frames) are numbered at the same time—starting with the first frame in the thread—even if they're on different pages. For example, if you have a story that jumps from page 1 to page 5, and you have an unthreaded text frame on page 2, the numbered paragraphs on page 5 would be smaller than those on page 2 because InDesign is numbering the threaded story first.

　　Even stranger, if for some reason that story was instead threaded from page 5 to page 1, the numbering would start on page 2, then continue on page 5, then end on page 1.

▶ Paragraphs inside anchored text frames are numbered along with the story they're in. Let's say you're numbering your figures and some of your figure numbers are anchored inside a text story that spans from page 1 to 100—but one figure number is sitting in an unthreaded, unanchored text frame on page 2.

InDesign will number all 100 pages, including anchored frames, before it gets around to numbering page 2.

This means that you should either keep all your text frames anchored or keep them unanchored—mixing and matching will cause you heartache.

If you want a numbered list to continue from one document to the next in a book panel, your named list has to be present in all the documents—fortunately, the book panel's Synchronize feature can copy named lists for you (see Chapter 8, "Long Documents").

Removing Bullets and Numbering

To remove bullets or numbering, select the paragraphs in question and then click once on the Bulleted List or Numbered List button in the Control panel (whichever is currently highlighted). Alternately, you could choose Remove Bullets or Remove Numbering from the Bulleted & Numbered Lists submenu, under the Type menu. Or you could display the Bullets and Numbering dialog box and choose None from the List Type pop-up menu. Whichever you choose, the bullets and numbers are gone, baby, gone.

Converting Bullets and Numbers to Normal Text

To change the characters inserted by the Bullets and Numbering feature to normal text (*i.e.*, text you can select with the Type tool and format using InDesign's typesetting features), select the paragraphs and choose Convert Numbering to Text or Convert Bullets to Text from the Context menu. You can also find this command in the Paragraph panel menu, the Control panel menu, and the Bulleted & Numbered Lists submenu, under the Type menu. If you select a range of text that contains both bulleted and numbered paragraphs, choose Convert Bullets and Numbering to Text.

Bullets and Numbering in Paragraph Styles

We've been talking about applying numbering or bullets directly to paragraphs as local formatting, but in the real world we'd virtually never do this. Instead, we'd first create a paragraph style that includes the bullet or numbering, and then apply that paragraph style to the paragraphs in question. We talk about styles below, but suffice it to say that we often work with two or three paragraph styles for each type of list. For example, in this book, we use a "numbered list" style that includes both numbering and a little Space After; and we use a "numbered list first" (which we apply to the first item in the list) that is based on "numbered list" but also includes a little Space Before. Plus, we use a "numbered list last" (which we apply to the last item in the list), which includes a little Space After.

Styles

When you think about the text in your publication, chances are good you're thinking of each paragraph as being a representative of a particular kind of text. You're thinking, "That's a headline, that's a subhead, and that's a photo caption." Chances are also good that you're thinking of those paragraphs as having certain formatting attributes: font, size, leading, and indents.

That's what text styles do—they bundle all those attributes together so you can apply them to text with a single click. But there's more—if you then change your mind about the formatting, you can edit the style, and all the text with that style applied to it (that is, "tagged" with the style) is reformatted automatically.

Once you've created a text style for a specific kind of text, you'll never have to claw your way through the Character panel or Paragraph panel again. Unless, of course, you want to apply a local formatting override to your styled text, which you're always free to do.

Global versus Local Formatting. We've been using the term "local formatting." What are we talking about? The key to understanding text styles is understanding the difference between style-based formatting and local formatting.

Local formatting is what you get when you select text and apply formatting directly, using the Character panel or the choices on the Type menu. When you apply formatting using text styles, on the other hand, you're applying "global" formatting (that is, formatting specified by the selected style).

If local formatting has been applied to text that has had a paragraph style applied to it, you'll see a "+" after the style name in the Paragraph Styles panel when the text is selected (see Figure 4-58).

Plus What? When you see that the text you've selected in a styled paragraph contains a local override, how can you tell what that local override is? If you have tool tips turned on, you can move the cursor over the style name, and InDesign will display a list of the

FIGURE 4-58
Styles and
Local Overrides

The selected text contains
local formatting...

...so InDesign displays a
"+" next to the style name.

local overrides. Alternatively, you can choose New Paragraph Style from the Paragraph Styles panel menu. Look at the list of attributes in the Style Settings list at the bottom of the panel—it'll say "<stylename> + next: Same Style +" (where "<stylename>" is the name of the style applied to the paragraph) and a list of formatting. The items in the list are the local formatting. Click Cancel (or press Command-period/Esc) to close this dialog box without creating a new style.

Incorrect Style Order. Paragraph and character styles should appear in alphabetical order in their respective panels. Sometimes, though, the panels get confused and list them in a near-random order (probably the order in which you created the styles, which is silly). If that happens, just choose Sort by Name from the panel menu.

Styles Are More than Formatting. When you apply a style to a paragraph (which we call "tagging" a paragraph with a style), you're doing more than just applying the formatting defined by the style. You're telling InDesign what the paragraph is—not just what it looks like, but what role it has to play in your publication. Is the paragraph important? Is it an insignificant legal notice in type that's intentionally too small to read? The style says it all.

The most important thing to remember when you're creating and applying styles is that tagging a paragraph with a style creates a link between the paragraph and all other paragraphs tagged with that style, and between the paragraph and the definition of the style. Change the style's definition, and watch the formatting and behavior of the paragraphs tagged with that style change to match.

Character Styles

By now, most of us are used to the idea of paragraph styles, which give us a way to apply multiple paragraph formatting attributes to an entire paragraph with a single action. (If you're not familiar with paragraph styles, we discuss them in the next section.) Character styles are just like paragraph styles, except that they can be applied to ranges of text smaller than an entire paragraph (and, obviously, they lack paragraph formatting features, such as alignment). Applying a character style to a text selection establishes a link between that text and the definition of the style—edit the style, and the formatting of the text changes.

Use character styles for any character formatting you apply over and over again. Run-in headings, drop caps, and special ornamental characters are all good candidates for character styles. Each time you use a character style, you're saving yourself several seconds you would have spent fiddling with settings in the Character panel or the

Type menu. It might not seem like much, but saving a few seconds several hundred times a day can add up.

Creating Character Styles. The easiest way to create a character style is to build it "by example" (see Figure 4-59).

1. Select some text that has the formatting you want.

2. Hold down Option/Alt and click the Create New Style button at the bottom of the Character Styles panel (or select New Character Style from the Character Styles panel menu). InDesign displays the New Character Style dialog box.

3. At this point, if you want to create a relationship between this style and another character style, you can choose that style from the Based On pop-up menu (see "Creating Parent-Child Style Relationships," later in this chapter).

FIGURE 4-59
Creating a
Character Style

To create a new character style, select a range of text that has the formatting you want...

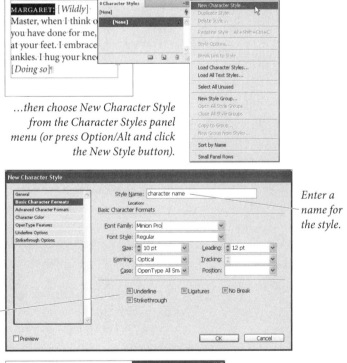

...then choose New Character Style from the Character Styles panel menu (or press Option/Alt and click the New Style button).

InDesign defines a new character style based on the formatting of the selected text.

Enter a name for the style.

Note that InDesign does not define character formatting attributes that are the same as the default formatting of the surrounding text.

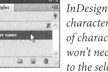

InDesign adds the new character style to the list of character styles, but it won't necessarily apply it to the selected text for you.

4. Now give your style a name. You can also assign a keyboard shortcut to the character style—the key used must use a modifier key (Command, Ctrl, or Shift and a number key from the numeric keypad; NumLock must be on to define the shortcut).

When you create a character style, InDesign won't automatically apply the style to the text you selected in Step 1 unless you turn on the Apply Style to Selection checkbox in the General pane of the New Character Style dialog box. If you neglect to turn on this helpful checkbox, you'll have to apply the style to the selected text manually.

QuarkXPress Users Beware: In QuarkXPress, a character style always defines *all* the character formatting of the text—font, color, size, and other attributes. InDesign's character styles, however, are defined by *differences* between the character formatting of the selected text and the default character formatting of the surrounding text. In InDesign you can create a character style which, when applied to text, changes only its size and color, but retains all other underlying formatting.

This is actually a good thing—it means you can create character styles that affect some, but not all, of the attributes of a selection. It's different from the way that almost every other application defines character styles, and it takes some getting used to.

Character Style Tips. Here are a few things to keep in mind when defining character styles in InDesign.

▶   If you're building a character style based on example text (as we suggested earlier), InDesign only picks up the formatting differences between the text you've selected and the paragraph style applied to the paragraph. For example, if the underlying paragraph style uses the font Minion Pro Italic, and the text you've selected uses the same font, the Font attribute of the character style will not be defined automatically. If you want the font to be part of the character style definition, you can add it once you have the New Character Style dialog box open (select the font from the Font Family pop-up menu in the Basic Character Formats pane).

▶   If you want your character style to be defined by *every* attribute of your text selection, you can use the CreateCharacterStyle script (see Chapter 12, "Scripting," for more on the example scripts that come with InDesign). Or you can create the character style from scratch (not from example text), specifying the font, size, color, leading, and all other formatting.

▶ Clicking the New Style button in the Character Styles panel creates a new character style based on whatever style was selected in the panel. It doesn't open a dialog box.

▶ If you want to "undefine" an attribute in a character style, select and delete the current value (see Figure 4-60).

FIGURE 4-60
Undefining Attributes

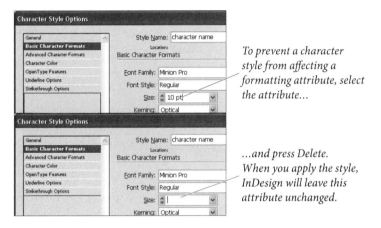

To prevent a character style from affecting a formatting attribute, select the attribute...

...and press Delete. When you apply the style, InDesign will leave this attribute unchanged.

Applying Character Styles. To apply a character style, select some text and do any one of the following things (see Figure 4-61).

▶ Click the character style name in the Character Styles panel.

▶ Press the keyboard shortcut you assigned to the character style.

▶ Point at the style name in the Character Styles panel and choose Apply from the context menu.

▶ Press Command-Enter/Ctrl Enter to display the Quick Apply panel, type the name of the style, and then press Enter.

Again, applying a character style changes only those attributes that are defined in the style. This can cause grave confusion and hair-pulling if you're used to the way QuarkXPress does it. If you apply a character style that applies only the underline type style and color, for example—InDesign leaves all other character formatting as is.

To remove a character style from a text selection, click None in the Character Styles panel—this reverts the text back to the underlying formatting of the paragraph style. If you want to remove the character style and leave the formatting alone (convert it to local formatting), choose Break Link to Style from the panel menu. This is

FIGURE 4-61
Applying a
Character Style

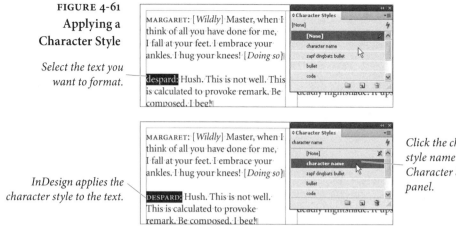

*Select the text you
want to format.*

*InDesign applies the
character style to the text.*

*Click the character
style name in the
Character Styles
panel.*

sometimes useful when you want some text to be formatted using the formatting of a given character style, but you don't want it linked to that style (because you know the style definition might change).

Editing Character Styles. The great thing about styles is that you can always change them later, and those changes ripple throughout your document. To edit a character style, you can use any or all of the following approaches—all of them display the Character Style Options dialog box, which you can use to change the attributes of the style.

▶ Hold down Command-Option-Shift/Ctrl-Alt-Shift and double-click the style name in the Character Styles panel.

▶ Point at the style you want to edit in the Character Styles panel and choose Edit from the context menu.

▶ Select the style and choose Style Options from the Character Styles panel menu.

▶ Double-click the style name in the Character Styles panel.

The first two approaches above do not apply the style; the latter two apply the style to the selected text, or to the document default formatting when no text is selected. Be aware of this difference as you go to edit a style—otherwise, you run the risk of accidentally applying the character style.

Redefining Character Styles. Editing a character style through the Character Style Options dialog box works fine, but is kind of boring. For quick changes, try this: Find some text tagged with the character style you want to redefine, then apply local formatting to it (change it to the way you want the style to be defined). A "+" will appear next to the character style name in the Character Styles panel. Next, without deselecting the text, press Command-Option-Shift-C/Ctrl-Alt-Shift-C. InDesign automatically redefines the character style based on the selected text (see Figure 4-62).

Alternatively, you can select the text and choose Redefine Style from the Character Styles panel menu. Or you could point at the style name in the panel and choose Redefine from the context menu. But the keyboard shortcut is more fun.

FIGURE 4-62
Redefining a
Character Style

Apply local formatting to an instance of the character style you want to redefine…

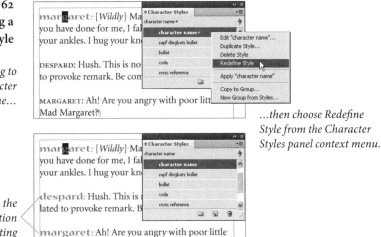

…then choose Redefine Style from the Character Styles panel context menu.

InDesign updates the character style's definition based on the formatting of the selected text.

Deleting character styles. To remove a character style, press Command-Shift-A/Ctrl-Shift-A to deselect everything (do this so that you don't accidentally apply the character style to text), then select the character style and choose Delete Style from the Character Styles panel menu (or click the Delete Style button in the panel).

InDesign displays the Delete Character Style dialog box, where you can select a replacement style (including no style). If you choose another character style, InDesign applies that character style to the text that had been formatted with the deleted style. If you choose no style, the text formatted with the style using the character style doesn't change appearance—it becomes local formatting.

Paragraph Styles   Paragraph styles encapsulate all text formatting—both paragraph formatting and character formatting.

Basic Style. If you look at the Paragraph Styles panel, you'll always see a "Basic Paragraph" style. This is something like Word's (infamous) "Normal" style, and provides a kind of default style for all text.

We tend not to use this style, or base any other style on it, because we've found it can cause problems as we move text from document to document. In a nutshell: If you have defined Basic Paragraph Style one way, then you copy a paragraph tagged with that style to a new document, the text formatting changes because InDesign applies the new document's Basic Paragraph Style definition. That's usually not what you were hoping for.

Creating Paragraph Styles. The easiest way (in our opinion) to create a text style is to format an example paragraph using local formatting, then create a new style based on that paragraph (see Figure 4-63).

1. Select a formatted paragraph.

2. Display the Paragraph Styles panel, if it's not already visible (press Command/Ctrl-F11).

3. Choose New Paragraph Style from the Paragraph Style pop-up menu in the Control panel, or from the Paragraph Styles panel menu (or Option/Alt-click the New Style button) to open the New Paragraph Style dialog box.

4. Enter a name for the style in the Style Name field. You could leave the name set to the default, but we think it's better to enter a descriptive name—"heading 1" is quite a bit easier to remember than "Paragraph Style 6."

5. You can also assign a Next Style (see "Next Styles" later in this chapter) and a keyboard shortcut to the style—the shortcut must use a modifier key (Shift, Command/Ctrl, Option/Alt, or some combination of the above) and a number key from the numeric keypad (NumLock must be on to define the shortcut).

6. Turn on the Apply Style to Selection checkbox in the General pane of the New Paragraph Style dialog box. (Otherwise, the style won't be applied to the paragraph your text cursor is in.)

7. Click the OK button.

The style definition includes all the character and paragraph formatting applied to the first character in the selected "example" text.

If you work by the hour, you can also define a paragraph style from scratch, rather than basing your style on an example:

1. Choose "New Style" from the Paragraph Styles panel menu. InDesign displays the New Style dialog box.

FIGURE 4-63
Defining a
Paragraph Style

*Select a paragraph that has the
formatting attributes you want.*

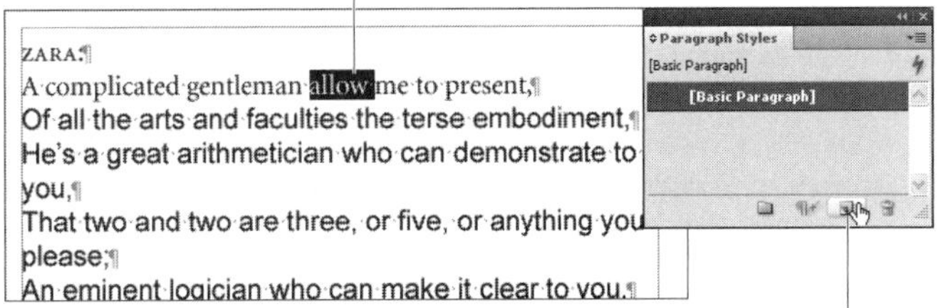

*Click the New Style button (or choose New Paragraph
Style from the Paragraph Styles panel menu).*

*InDesign creates a new style
and adds it to the list of
styles in the Paragraph Styles
panel.*

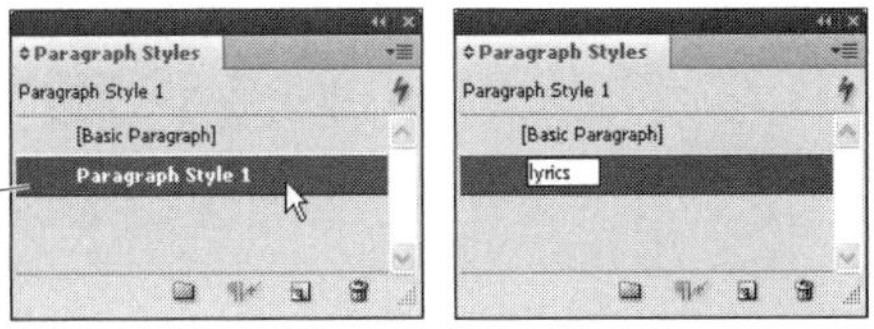

*At this point, you can enter
a name for the style, or edit
the style definition.*

2. Work your way through the dialog box, setting the options as
    you want them for your new style. When everything looks the
    way you want it to, press Return/Enter to close the dialog box.

Creating a style this way is a little bit more awkward than simply
basing a style on an example paragraph, but some people prefer it.
We've met at least one person who likes setting tabs "without all that
pesky text in the way."

Applying Paragraph Styles. To apply a paragraph style, select a paragraph or series of paragraphs (remember, you don't have to select
the entire paragraph to apply paragraph formatting) and click a style
name in the Paragraph Styles panel (see Figure 4-64). Alternatively,
if you've defined a keyboard shortcut for the paragraph style, you can
press the shortcut.

When you simply click a paragraph style to apply it, InDesign
retains all the local formatting, so italic text remains italic. The one
exception to this rule is when every character in the paragraph has
local formatting—that stuff always gets removed.

To remove all local formatting as you apply a paragraph style,
hold down Option/Alt as you click the paragraph style name. Any
formatting applied using character styles is retained.

To remove all local formatting and remove formatting applied by
character styles, hold down Option-Shift/Alt-Shift as you click the
paragraph style name.

FIGURE 4-64
**Applying a
Paragraph Style**

*Select the paragraphs you
want to format (remember,
you don't need to select
the entire paragraph).*

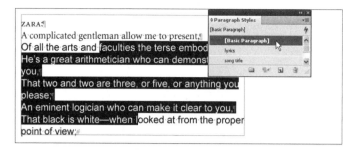

*Click a style name in the
Paragraph Styles panel,
or use the Context menu.
InDesign applies the
paragraph style to the
selected paragraphs.*

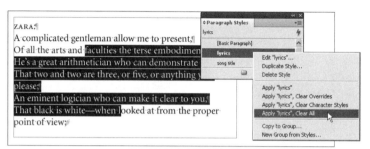

Alternatively, you can use the Context menu in the Paragraph Styles panel to control which local formatting overrides you want to clear and/or keep.

To remove all local formatting (not including character styles) after you've applied a style, click the Clear Override button at the bottom of the Paragraph Styles panel. To remove all local character formatting, hold down Command/Ctrl as you click the button; to remove paragraph formatting, hold down Command-Shift/Ctrl-Shift as you click.

To remove a paragraph style from a text selection, choose Break Link to Style from the Paragraph Styles panel menu. Note that this does not change the formatting or the look of the selected paragraphs—it simply applies the formatting applied by the paragraph style as local formatting. As we said in the "Character Styles" section, you can think of this as breaking the link between the paragraph and the style definition.

Editing Paragraph Styles. To edit a paragraph style, you can use any or all of the following approaches—all of them display the Paragraph Style Options dialog box, which you can use to change the attributes of the paragraph style.

▶ Hold down Command-Option-Shift/Ctrl-Alt-Shift and double-click the paragraph style name in the Paragraph Styles panel.

▶ Point at the style you want to edit in the Paragraph Styles panel and choose Edit from the context menu.

▶ Select the style and choose Style Options from the Paragraph Styles panel menu.

▶ Double-click the style name in the Paragraph Styles panel.

The first two approaches above do not apply the style; the latter two apply the style to the selected text, or to the document default formatting when no text is selected. Be aware of this difference as you go to edit a style—accidentally setting the default font for a document to a style featuring hot pink dingbats can be a frustrating and embarrassing experience.

Redefining Paragraph Styles. The easiest way to *create* a paragraph style is to base the style on the formatting of an example paragraph. The easiest way to update the style definition? Do the same!

First, pick any paragraph tagged with the style you want to change, and apply local formatting to it (a "+" will appear next to the style name in the Paragraph Styles panel). Then choose Redefine Style from the Paragraph Styles panel menu (or press Command-Option-Shift-R/Ctrl-Alt-Shift-R, or use the Context menu). InDesign will redefine the style based on the selected text (see Figure 4-65).

Next Style. If you're typing in InDesign, and the paragraph you're in is tagged with the "Heading" style, you probably don't want the

FIGURE 4-65
Redefining a
Paragraph Style

Change the formatting of an example paragraph tagged with the paragraph style you want to change. A "+" appears next to the style name in the Paragraph Styles panel.

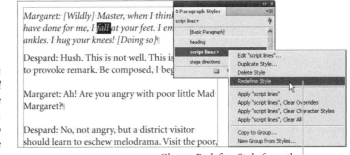

Choose Redefine Style from the Paragraph Styles panel menu.

InDesign updates all instances of the style with the formatting of the selected paragraph.

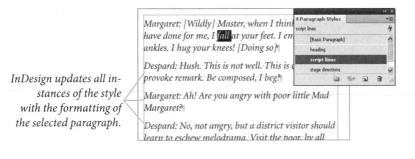

next paragraph to be tagged with "Heading" too, right? You can force InDesign to automatically change the subsequent paragraph style with the Next Style pop-up menu in the New Paragraph Style or Paragraph Style Options dialog box (see Figure 4-66). For example, if you want the subsequent paragraph to be "BodyText," then choose "BodyText" from the Next Style pop-up menu.

Note that this only works if the insertion point is at the end of a paragraph when you press Return/Enter. If the insertion point is anywhere else, you'll simply break that paragraph in two, and both new paragraphs will have the same style as the original one.

Using Next Style on Existing Text. What if you want to apply a sequence of paragraph styles to text you've already entered or imported? Select the range of text you want to format, then point at the first paragraph style you want to apply. Choose Apply *style name*

FIGURE 4-66
Next Style

In this example, we have set the Next Style option for each paragraph style to automatically apply the paragraph style we want when we press Return/Enter.

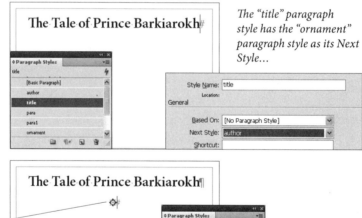

The "title" paragraph style has the "ornament" paragraph style as its Next Style…

…which means that, when we press Return/Enter, InDesign switches to that style.

The "ornament" style, in turn, has the paragraph style named "author" as its next style, so pressing Return/Enter as we type text switches to the "author" style.

When we enter text following the "author" paragraph style, InDesign applies the "para1" style, which includes drop cap formatting.

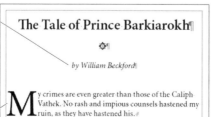

All of these paragraph style assignments take place as we type, so we don't have to reach for the Paragraph Styles panel.

Then Next Style from the context menu (where *style name* is the name of the style you want to apply). InDesign applies the sequence of paragraph styles (see Figure 4-67).

Selecting Unused Paragraph Styles. Choose Select All Unused from the Paragraph Styles panel menu to select all paragraph styles that are not applied to any text in the publication. Typically, the only reason you'd want to do this is to delete them all.

Deleting Paragraph Styles. To remove a paragraph style from your document, first deselect everything (press Command-Shift-A/Ctrl-Shift-A), then select the style name in the Paragraph Styles panel and choose Delete Styles from the panel's menu (or click the Delete Style button at the bottom of the panel). InDesign deletes the style.

InDesign gives you a choice of how to handle paragraphs already tagged with that style. You can choose No Paragraph Style to convert the formatting applied by the style to local formatting, or you can choose to apply another style. If you want to replace one style with another without deleting the original style, use the Find/Change dialog box (see Chapter 3, "Text").

FIGURE 4-67
Applying
Sequential Styles

Select the text you want to format. The first paragraph selected should be the start of the "chain" of styles you want to apply.

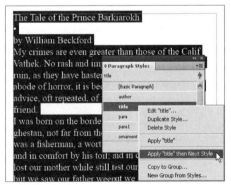

Choose Apply style name *Then Next Style from the Context menu (where* style name *is the name of the style).*

InDesign applies the styles, formatting each paragraph as specified by the Next Style setting of each style.

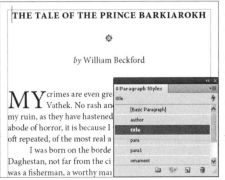

Note: You can also apply sequential styles by selecting a text frame with the Selection tool. When you do this, InDesign applies "next style" formatting to all of the text in the story, beginning with the first paragraph in the story.

Paragraph Styles and Nested Styles

As we mentioned in the discussion earlier in this chapter, nested styles really come into their own when combined with paragraph styles. Remember all of the work we did to set up the nested styles in our example? Now imagine putting all of that formatting power into a paragraph style. Imagine applying it with a single mouse click. Again, we think this stuff is very cool (see Figure 4-68).

FIGURE 4-68

Adding Nested Styles to a Paragraph Style

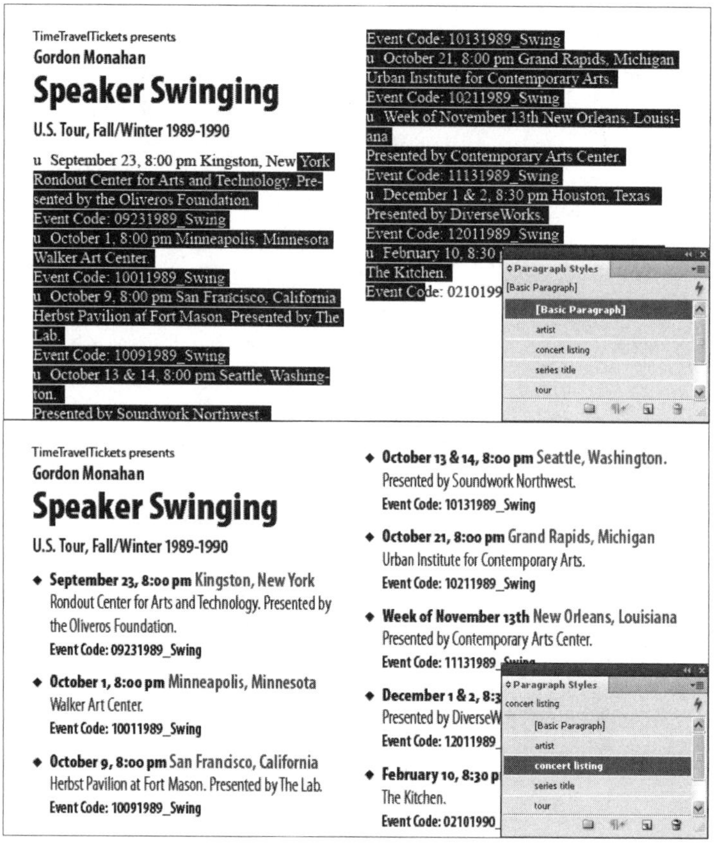

This raw text has been dumped into the document from a spreadsheet or database. Formatting a catalog full of this text would be very tedious, even if you used nested styles as local formatting.

If you add the nested style definitions to a paragraph style, however, you can apply massive amounts of formatting with a single mouse click, as we've done here.

Creating Parent-Child Style Relationships

One powerful feature of InDesign's character and paragraph styles is the ability to base one style on another, also called parent-child relationships (see Figure 4-69). You can base a style on another one by choosing a style from the Based On pop-up menu in either the New Paragraph Style or the Paragraph Style Options dialog box (this works for either character or paragraph styles).

In this book, there are body text styles for paragraphs that follow headings, paragraphs that are in lists, and so on—but they're all based on one "parent" paragraph style. If we need to make the text size a half-point smaller, we could edit the parent style and the change would ripple throughout the book.

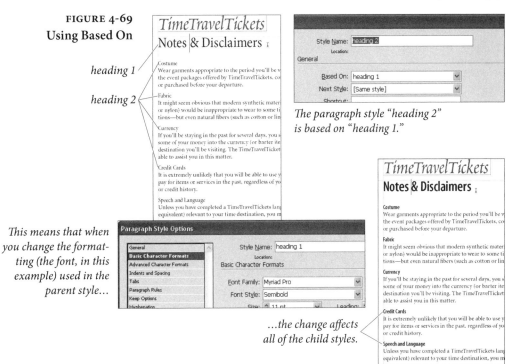

FIGURE 4-69
Using Based On

heading 1

heading 2

*The paragraph style "heading 2"
is based on "heading 1."*

*This means that when
you change the format-
ting (the font, in this
example) used in the
parent style...*

*...the change affects
all of the child styles.*

When one style is based on another, InDesign keeps track of the differences between the base style (the "parent") and the style based on it (the "child"). When you change the definition of the parent style, the changes will affect all of the attributes in the child style that are the same as the same attributes in the parent style.

Reset to Base. By the way, if your text cursor is in a paragraph when you create a new style, that paragraph's style becomes the "based on" style and any local formatting applied to the paragraph appears as the differences in the new style. If you don't want the local format-ting, click the Reset to Base button. If you don't want your new style to be based on anything, make sure the Based On pop-up menu is set to No Paragraph Style.

Style Groups

Style Groups are a way to organize your paragraph and character styles. (They work with object styles and table styles, too, but that's not what we're talking about in this chapter.) Each style group is a folder into which you can put one or more styles. You can even nest one style group into another to create style hierarchies.

To create a style group, click the New Style Group button at the bottom of the Paragraph Styles or Character Styles panel (or choose the feature of the same name from the panel's menu). If you already know which of your styles you want in your group, you can add them while creating the group by first selecting them first (see Figure 4-70).

Once you've created a style group, you can move any style into it by dragging the style name in the panel into the group. It's very similar to working with folders in your operating system.

One of the coolest things about style groups is that you can have the same-named styles in more than one group. For example, you might make a "bodytext" paragraph style in a group called "Business Section" and another, differently-styled "bodytext" style in a group called "Entertainment Section". We're not saying you have to create templates like this, but it can be useful in certain situations.

To copy one or more selected styles to another group, choose Copy to Group from the panel menu, or Option/Alt-drag them over another folder.

What's Wrong with Style Groups? At first, style groups sound great, especially if you have dozens of styles in your document. But you need to be careful with them. First, if do have same-named styles

FIGURE 4-70
Creating Style Groups

To make a new style group with already-created styles, select the styles you want to include and choose New Group from Styles.

InDesign displays the New Style Group dialog box. Enter a name for the group.

InDesign moves the styles into the style group.

You can duplicate styles from one group to another by holding down Option/Alt as you drag them from in the panel.

Quick Apply shows you both style name and style group.

with different definitions, it can be confusing *which* bodytext or *which* heading you're applying. This calls for eternal vigilance. It helps if you apply styles with Quick Apply, because the Quick Apply window displays both the style name and what style group its in.

The big problems appear if you need to export your documents as RTF (rich text format) for someone who is editing in Microsoft Word. Style groups will cause huge headaches because on export InDesign changes the style names (it adds the style group name). This isn't so bad except that when you reimport the RTF file, it's not smart enough to remap the style names back to the document's styles, so you end up with all your styles duplicated. It's horrible. We hope that Adobe will release a patch to fix this problem by the time you read this, but we're not holding our breath. Of course, in the meantime, it's a good excuse to get your editors to use InCopy instead.

Copying Styles from Other Publications

One of the great things about character and paragraph styles is that you can use them to unify standard formatting across a range of publications—the chapters of this book, for example. While you can't define a "master" style sheet and have all publications get their style definitions from it (as you can in FrameMaker), you can easily copy styles from one InDesign publication to another.

▶ To copy character styles from another publication, choose Load Character Styles from the Character Styles panel menu. InDesign displays the Open a File dialog box. Locate and select the InDesign publication file containing the styles you want and click the Open button. InDesign copies the character styles from that publication into the current document.

▶ To copy paragraph styles from one publication to another choose Load Paragraph Styles from the Paragraph Styles panel menu.

▶ To import both character and paragraph styles from another publication, choose Load All Text Styles from the panel menu of the Character Styles panel or the Paragraph Styles panel.

When you import styles that have the same name as styles that already exist in the publication, InDesign overrides the attributes of the existing styles with the attributes of the incoming styles.

You can also move styles by copying text tagged with the styles you want from one publication and pasting it into another document (or dragging a text frame from one document into another). If the styles do not exist in the document you've pasted the text into, InDesign adds them. If the styles already exist, InDesign overrides the style definitions in the incoming text with the style definitions of the existing styles.

You can also synchronize style sheets among all the documents in a book when you use the Book panel, which we talk about in Chapter 8, "Long Documents."

Styles from imported text files. When you import a Microsoft Word or RTF file that includes paragraph or character styles that don't exist in the InDesign publication, those styles get added to the Character Styles and Paragraph Styles panels. You can always tell one of these styles from those created in InDesign because the panels display a little gray floppy disk icon next to the style name.

Libraries of Styles. One of our favorite uses for libraries (see "Library panel" in Chapter 1, "Workspace") is to save paragraph and character styles that we use in multiple documents. In a small text frame, we type a few words (usually the name of the style) and then apply one or more styles to them. Then we drag the text frame into a library (select Library from the New submenu, under the File menu, if you haven't already made one) and double-click on the library thumbnail to give it a name and description. Later, when we need that style in some other document, we can open the library file, drag that text frame into our document, and then delete the text frame—the styles remain. Of course, this works with libraries of color swatches, too.

Optical Margin Alignment

Ever since Gutenberg set out to print his Bible, typesetters have looked for ways to "balance" the edges of columns of text—particularly lines ending or beginning with punctuation. Because the eye doesn't "see" punctuation, it can sometimes appear that the left or right edges of some columns of type (especially justified type) are misaligned. Some other programs compensate for this problem by using a "hanging punctuation" feature, which pushes certain punctuation characters outside the text column. But there's more to making the edges of a column look even than just punctuation. Some characters can create a "ragged" look all by themselves—think of a "W," at the beginning of a line, for example.

When you select an InDesign story (with either the Selection or the Type tool) and turn on the Optical Margin Alignment option in the Story panel (choose Story from the Type menu to display the Story panel), the program balances the edges of the columns based on the appearance of *all* of the characters at the beginning or end of the lines in the column. This adjustment makes the columns appear more even—even though it sometimes means that characters are extending *beyond* the edges of the column (see Figure 4-71).

The amount that InDesign "hangs" a character outside the text column depends on the setting you enter in the Base Size field of the Story panel (that's the field with the icon that looks like it would make a drop cap). In general, you should enter the point size of your body text in this field.

Unfortunately, it turns out that many designers don't like the look of Optical Margin Alignment. It's not that the feature is flawed; it's that designers (especially younger folks) have become so accustomed to their type lining up with a particular guide or ruler that they think it's wrong to have type inside or outside that (non-printing) line. Nevertheless, we encourage you to try turning it on and seeing how your readers like it—we think they'll find the text easier to read.

Ignore Optical Margin. Even if you do like Optical Margin Alignment, there's a good chance that you'll occasionally find a paragraph

FIGURE 4-71
Optical Margin
Alignment

"Scarcely had I pronounced these words when a thick, black cloud cast its veil over the firmament, and dimmed the brilliancy about us; and the hiss of rain and growling of a storm filled the air. At last my father appeared, borne on a meteor whose terrible effulgence flashed fire upon the world. 'Stay, wretched creature,' said he, 'and victim that hath barbarous envy!'

Story
☐ Optical Margin Alignment
12 pt

Optical Margin Alignment off

"Scarcely had I pronounced these words when a thick, black cloud cast its veil over the firmament, and dimmed the brilliancy about us; and the hiss of rain and growling of a storm filled the air. At last my father appeared, borne on a meteor whose terrible effulgence flashed fire upon the world. 'Stay, wretched creature,' said he, 'and victim that hath barbarous envy!'

Story
☑ Optical Margin Alignment
12 pt

Optical Margin Alignment on

In this close-up view, you can clearly see the way that InDesign adjusts the characters at the edge of the text column.

Punctuation is positioned outside the column.

Some characters hang outside the column...

...others are moved farther inside the column.

or two that you wish it wouldn't apply to. For example, monospaced code listings should not be optically aligned—that defeats the purpose of using a monospaced font. Fortunately, you have the option to turn off Optical Margin Alignment on a paragraph by paragraph basis or in a paragraph style.

To turn it off for one or more selected paragraphs, choose Ignore Optical Margin from the Control panel or Paragraph panel menu. To disable it in a paragraph style, turn on the Ignore Optical Margin checkbox in the Indents and Spacing pane of the Paragraph Style Options dialog box.

An Old Typesetter Never...

Late night. The sound of the espresso machine in the kitchen about to reach critical mass and melt down, destroying the office and civilization as we know it. The office is different, the equipment and the coffee are better, but we still seem to be up late at night setting type.

And, to tell you the truth, we're not sure we would have it any other way.

Drawing

You can use InDesign's drawing tools to draw almost anything—from straight lines and boxes to incredibly complex freeform shapes.

The drawing tools can be divided into three types: the Rectangle, Polygon, Oval, and Line tools are for drawing basic shapes; the Pencil, Smooth, Eraser, Pen, Add Point, Delete Point, and Convert Point tools draw or edit more complex paths (see Figure 5-1). The Scissors tool gives you a way of cutting paths.

Some of the path drawing tools (the Rectangle, Oval, and Polygon tools) have counterparts that draw frames (the Rectangular Frame, Oval Frame, and Polygonal Frame tools). The only thing different about these tools is that the "frame" versions draw paths whose content type has been set to "Graphic." That's it.

In this book, we'll use the default variant of the tool to refer to both tools—when we say "the Rectangle tool," we're referring to both the Rectangle tool and the Rectangular Frame tool.

Which path drawing tools should you use? Don't worry too much about it—the basic shapes can be converted into freeform paths, and the freeform drawing tools can be used to draw basic shapes.

The paths you draw in InDesign are made up of points, and the points are joined to each other by line segments (see Figure 5-2). A path is just like a connect-the-dots puzzle. Connect all the dots together in the right order, and you've made a picture. Because points along a path have an order, or winding, you can think of each point as a milepost along the path. Or as a sign saying, "Now go this way."

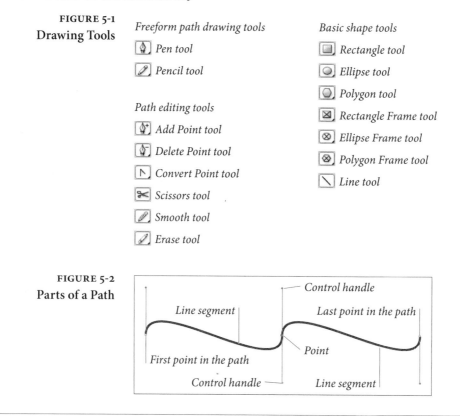

FIGURE 5-1
Drawing Tools

Freeform path drawing tools
- Pen tool
- Pencil tool

Path editing tools
- Add Point tool
- Delete Point tool
- Convert Point tool
- Scissors tool
- Smooth tool
- Erase tool

Basic shape tools
- Rectangle tool
- Ellipse tool
- Polygon tool
- Rectangle Frame tool
- Ellipse Frame tool
- Polygon Frame tool
- Line tool

FIGURE 5-2
Parts of a Path

Control handle

Line segment

Last point in the path

First point in the path

Point

Control handle

Line segment

Drawing Basic Shapes

The operation of the basic shapes tools (the Rectangle, Polygon, Ellipse, and Line tools, and their frame-drawing counterparts) is straightforward: drag the tool and get a path of the corresponding shape. If you want to draw a frame, you can either use the frame-drawing variant of the tool, or draw the path and then convert it to a frame.

To draw a rectangle, oval, polygon, or line, follow the steps below.

1. Select the appropriate tool from the Tools panel.

   To specify the type of polygon you'll be drawing, double-click the Polygon tool and choose the shape you want in the Polygon Settings dialog box before you start drawing.

2. Position the cursor where you want one corner of the shape, then drag. InDesign draws a path, starting where you first held down the mouse button.

   To draw squares or circles, hold down Shift as you drag the Rectangle tool or Ellipse tool. When you hold down Shift as you drag, the Polygon tool produces equilateral polygons. Holding down Shift as you drag the Line tool constrains the angle of the line to 45-degree tangents from the point at which you started dragging.

Hold down Option to draw a basic shape from its center.

Press the arrow keys while dragging to create a grid of shapes. For details, see "Grid Mode" in Chapter 9, "Transforming."

3. When the basic shape is the size and shape you want it to be, stop dragging and release the mouse button.

You can also create rectangles and ellipses by specifying their width and height (see Figure 5-3).

1. Select the Rectangle tool or the Ellipse tool from the Tools panel.

2. Position the cursor where you want to place one corner of the basic shape, or hold down Option/Alt and position the cursor where you want to place the center point of the shape.

3. Click. InDesign displays the Rectangle dialog box (if you've selected the Rectangle tool) or the Ellipse dialog box (if you've selected the Ellipse tool).

4. Enter values in the Width and Height fields, then click the OK button.

FIGURE 5-3
Adding a Basic Shape "by the Numbers"

You can control the origin of the basic shape by selecting a point on the Control panel's Proxy before you click.

Select a basic shape tool, then click on the page or pasteboard.

InDesign displays a dialog box (Rectangle, Polygon, or Ellipse). Enter the dimensions you want and click the OK button.

InDesign creates a basic shape using the dimensions you entered.

Points and Paths

Why is it that the most important things in life are often the most difficult to learn? Drawing by manipulating Bezier paths—the geometric construct used to represent path shapes in most of today's vector drawing programs—is one of those difficult things. When we first encountered Bezier curves, the process of drawing by placing points and manipulating control handles struck us as alien, as nothing like drawing at all. Then we started to catch on.

In many ways, we had been drawing lines from the point of view of everything *but* the line; in a Bezier-path-drawing program such as InDesign, we draw lines from the point of view of the line itself. This is neither better nor worse; it's just different and takes time to get used to. If you've just glanced at the Pen tool and are feeling confused, we urge you to stick with it. Start thinking like a line.

Thinking Like a Line

Imagine that, through the action of some mysterious potion or errant cosmic ray, you've been reduced in size so that you're a little smaller than one of the dots in a connect-the-dots puzzle. For added detail and color, imagine that the puzzle appears in a *Highlights for Children* magazine in a dentist's office.

The only way out is to complete the puzzle. As you walk, a line extends behind you. As you reach each dot in the puzzle, a sign tells you where you are in the puzzle and the route you must take to get to the next dot in the path.

Get the idea? The dots in the puzzle are points. The route you walk from one point to another, as instructed by the signs at each point, is a line segment. Each series of connected dots is a path. As you walk from one dot to another, you're thinking like a line.

Each point—from the first point in the path to the last—carries with it some information about the line segments that attach it to the previous and next points along the path.

Paths and their formatting (fill and stroke) attributes are different things. Even if the fill and stroke applied to the path is "None" or the stroke weight is 0 there's still a path there.

When you select a point, the point "fills in," becoming a solid square. Unselected points on the path are shown as hollow squares.

Winding

Paths have a direction, also known as "winding" (as in "winding a clock"). Path direction generally corresponds to the order in which you placed the points on the path (see Figure 5-4). In our connect-the-dots puzzle, path direction tells us the order in which we should connect the dots.

To reverse the direction of a path, select the path and choose Reverse Path from the Paths submenu of the Object menu. InDesign

FIGURE 5-4
Path Direction,
or "Winding"

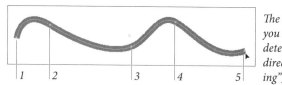

1 2   3 4   5

The order in which you create points determines the direction (or "winding") of the path.

reverses the direction of the path. You can also reverse the direction of a selected path using the Reverse Path path operation, as discussed in "Path Operations," later in this chapter.

Point Types

Points on an InDesign path are either *corner points* or *curve points*. Each type of point has its own special properties.

▶ A curve point adds a curved line segment between the current point and the preceding and following points along the path. Curve points have two control handles extended from them, and moving one control handle affects the position of the other control handle. One control handle affects the curve of the line segment following the curve point on the path; the other affects the curve of the line segment preceding the curve point. Curve points are typically used to add smooth curves to a path (see Figure 5-5).

▶ A corner point adds a straight line segment between the current point and the preceding point on the path (see Figure 5-6). Corner points are typically used to create paths containing straight line segments.

Which point type should you use? Any type of point can be turned into any other type of point, and anything you can do with one kind of point can be done with the other kind of point. Given these two points (so to speak), you can use the kinds of points and drawing tools you're happiest with and achieve exactly the results you want. There is no "best way" to draw with InDesign's Pen tool, but it helps to understand how the method you choose works.

FIGURE 5-5
Curve Points

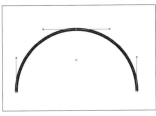

Curve points curve the line segments attached to the point. All of the points in this example are curve points.

FIGURE 5-6
Corner Points

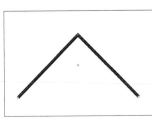

Corner points, by default, apply no curve to the line segments attached to the point. All of the points in this example are corner points.

Control Handles   You control the curvature of the line segments before and after each point using the point's control handles. Points can have up to two control handles attached to them. By default, new corner points have none and curve points have two. Note that each line segment has up to two control handles defining its curve—the "outgoing" control handle attached to the point defining the start of the line segment and the "incoming" control handle attached to the next point.

If you retract the control handle (by dragging it inside the point), the control handle has no effect on the curvature of the path. This doesn't necessarily mean that the line segment is a straight line, however—a control handle on the point at the other end of the line segment might also have an effect on the curve of the line segment.

The control handles attached to a corner point can be adjusted independently, while changing the angle of one control handle of a curve point changes the angle of the other control handle (see Figure 5-7). This difference, in our opinion, makes corner points more useful than curve points—you can do anything with a corner point you could do with a curve point.

FIGURE 5-7
Curve Points vs.
Corner Points

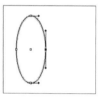

When you adjust one control handle on a curve point, InDesign adjusts the other control handle, as well.

To adjust the curvature of a line segment without changing the curve of the following line segment, use a corner point.

To convert a point from one point type to another, click the point using the Convert Point tool. If you click a curve point, this retracts both control handles. To convert a curve point to a corner point while leaving one of its control handles in place, drag the other control handle using the Convert Point tool (see Figure 5-8).

Drawing Paths with the Pencil Tool

The quickest way to create a freeform path on an InDesign page is to use the Pencil tool. Click the Pencil tool in the Tools panel (or press N), then drag the Pencil tool on the page. As you drag, InDesign creates a path that follows the cursor, automatically placing corner and curve points as it does so (see Figure 5-9).

FIGURE 5-8
Converting from One Point Type to Another

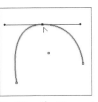 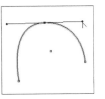 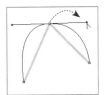

Position the Convert Point tool over a curve point...

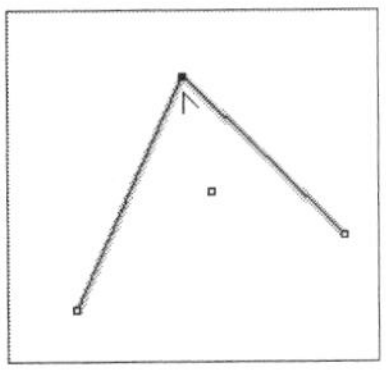

...and click. InDesign converts the curve point to a corner point.

To convert a corner point to a curve point, drag the Convert Point tool over the point.

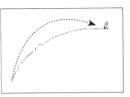

To convert a curve point to a corner point, drag one of the control handles using the Convert Point tool.

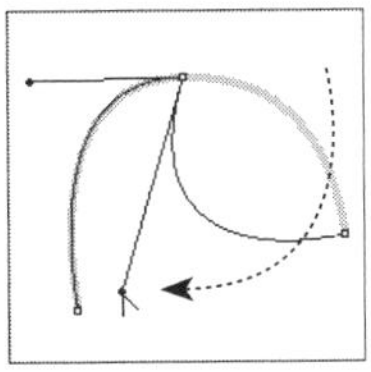

InDesign converts the curve point to a corner point. As you drag the control handle...

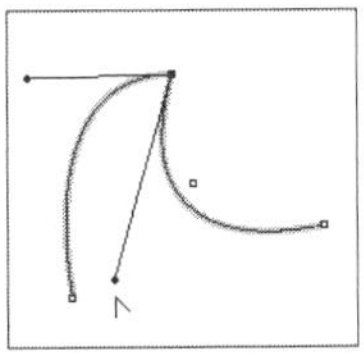

...InDesign adjusts the curve of the corresponding line segment, but leaves the other line segment unchanged.

FIGURE 5-9
Drawing with the Pencil Tool

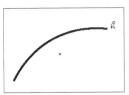

Drag the Pencil tool on the page or pasteboard.

As you drag the Pencil tool, InDesign positions curve and corner points. the path looks the way you want it to, stop dragging.

Drawing Paths with the Pen Tool

You use the Pen tool and its variants (the Remove Point, Add Point, and Convert Point tools)—to create and edit paths.

When you *click* the Pen tool on a page, InDesign places a corner point. *Drag* the Pen tool, and InDesign places a curve point where you started dragging—you determine the length of the control handles (and, therefore, the shape of the curve) by dragging as you place the curve point (see Figure 5-10).

To curve the line segment following a *corner* point, place the corner point, position the Pen tool above the point (this switches to the Convert Point tool), and then drag. As you drag, InDesign extends a control handle from the point (see Figure 5-11).

FIGURE 5-10
Placing Curve
and Corner Points

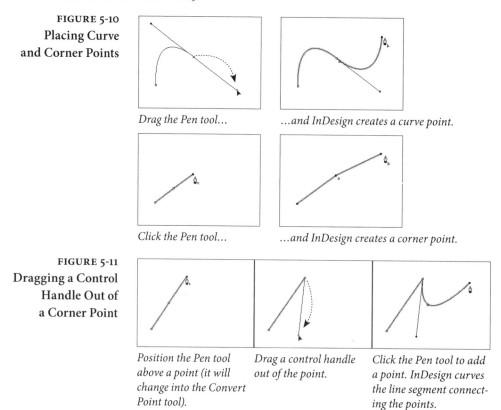

Drag the Pen tool...

...and InDesign creates a curve point.

Click the Pen tool...

...and InDesign creates a corner point.

FIGURE 5-11
Dragging a Control
Handle Out of
a Corner Point

Position the Pen tool
above a point (it will
change into the Convert
Point tool).

Drag a control handle
out of the point.

Click the Pen tool to add
a point. InDesign curves
the line segment connect-
ing the points.

The odd thing about using the Pen tool this way is that you don't see the effect of the curve manipulation until you've placed the next point. This makes sense in that you don't need a control handle for a line segment that doesn't yet exist, but it can be quite a brain-twister.

To convert a curve point you've just placed to a corner point, position the Pen tool above the point (to switch to the Convert Point tool) and then click the point. InDesign converts the point to a corner point and retracts the point's control handles.

You can change the position of points: select the point with the Direct Selection tool, then drag the point to a new location.

Drawing Techniques

Now that you know all about the elements that make up paths, let's talk about how you actually use them.

Path Drawing Tips   When you're drawing paths, don't forget that you can change the path after you've drawn it. We've often seen people delete entire paths and start over because they misplaced the last point on the path. Go ahead and place points in the wrong places; you can always change the position of any point. Also, keep these facts in mind:

▶ You can always add points to or subtract points from the path.

▶ You can change tools while drawing a path.

▶ You can split the path using the Scissors tool.

It's also best to create paths using as few points as you can—but it's not required. We've noticed that people who have just started working with Bezier drawing tools often use more points than are needed to create their paths. Over time, they learn one of the basic rules of vector drawing: Any curve can be described by two points and their associated control handles. No more, no less.

Manipulating Control Handles

The aspect of drawing in InDesign that's toughest to understand and master is the care, feeding, and manipulation of control handles. These handles are fundamental to drawing curved lines, so you'd better learn how to work with them.

To adjust the curve of a line segment, use the Direct Selection tool to select a point attached to the line segment. The control handles attached to that point—and to the points that come before and after the selected point on the path—appear. If you don't see control handles attached to the point you selected, the curvature of the line segment is controlled by the points at the other end of the line segments. Position the cursor over one of the control handles and drag. The curve of the line segment changes as you drag. When the curve looks the way you want it to, stop dragging (see Figure 5-12).

To retract (delete) a control handle, drag the handle inside the point it's attached to.

You can also adjust the curve of a curved line segment by dragging the segment itself. To do this, select the line segment (click the line segment with the Direct Selection tool, or drag a selection rectangle over part of the line segment) and then drag. As you drag, InDesign adjusts the curve of the line segment (see Figure 5-13).

FIGURE 5-12
Adjusting Curve Points

Select a point using the Direct Selection tool.

Drag the control handle attached to the point to a new location.

InDesign curves the line segment.

FIGURE 5-13
Another Way to
Adjust the Curve of
a Line Segment

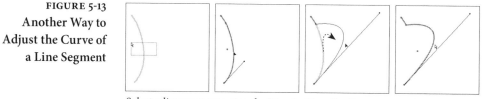

Select a line segment using the Direct Selection tool (drag a selection rectangle over the line segment).

Drag the line segment. As you drag, InDesign adjusts the curve of the line segment.

Adding Points to a Path

To add a point to an existing line segment, select the path, switch to the Pen tool, and then click the Pen tool on the line segment. InDesign adds a point to the path. You don't need to select the Add Point tool—InDesign will switch to it when you move the Pen tool above a line segment.

Removing Points from a Path

To remove a point from a path, select the path, switch to the Pen tool, and then click the Pen tool on the point. InDesign removes the point from the path.

Selecting and Moving Points

If you've gotten this far, you probably know how to select points, but here are a few rules to keep in mind.

▶ To select a point, click it with the Direct Selection tool, or drag a selection rectangle around it (using the same tool).

▶ You can select more than one point at a time. To do this, hold down Shift as you click the Direct Selection tool on each point, or use the Direct Selection tool to drag a selection rectangle around the points you want to select.

▶ To select all of the points on a path, hold down Option/Alt as you click the Direct Selection tool on the path.

▶ You can select points on paths inside groups or compound paths by using the Direct Selection tool.

▶ When you move a point, the control handles associated with that point also move, maintaining their positions relative to the point. This means that the curves of the line segments attached to the point change, unless you're also moving the points on the other end of the incoming and outgoing line segments.

▶ To move a straight line segment and its associated points, select the line segment with the Direct Selection tool and drag.

**Opening and
Closing Paths**

Paths can be open or closed (see Figure 5-14). An open path has no line segment between the beginning and ending points on the path. You don't have to close a path to add contents (text or a graphic) or apply a fill to the path.

To close an open path, select the path, select the Pen tool, and then click the Pen tool on the first or last point on the path (it doesn't matter which). Click the Pen tool again on the other end point. InDesign closes the path (see Figure 5-15).

Another way to close an open path is to use the Close Path path operation, as discussed in "Path Operations," later in this chapter.

To open a closed path, select the Direct Selection tool and click the line segment between two points on the path (you can also drag a selection rectangle over the line segment). Press Delete, and InDesign removes the line segment, opening the path between the points on either side of the line segment (see Figure 5-16).

To open a path *without* removing a line segment, select the Scissors tool and click the path. Click on a point to split the path at that point, or click a line segment to split the path at that location (see Figure 5-17).

The point closest to the start of the path (following the path's winding) becomes the point farther to the back, and the point farthest from the start of the path is on top of it.

Another way to open a closed path is to use the Close Path path operation, as discussed in "Path Operations," later in this chapter.

**FIGURE 5-14
Open and Closed Paths**

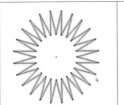  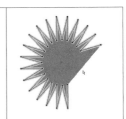

Closed path.   *Open path.*   *A path does not have to
                                              be closed to have a fill.*

**FIGURE 5-15
Closing an Open Path**

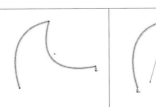 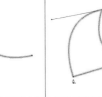

*Move the Pen tool over
an end point of an open
path.*

*Click the Pen tool, then
move it over the other
end point on the path.*

*Click on the end point.
InDesign closes the path.*

FIGURE 5-16
**Opening a Closed Path
by Deleting a
Line Segment**

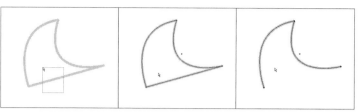

Select the Direct Selection tool, then drag a
selection rectangle over a line segment.

Press the Delete key to
delete the line segment.

FIGURE 5-17
Opening a Closed Path

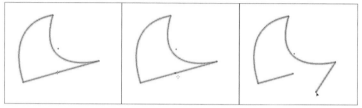

Click a line segment or
point with the Scissors
tool.

InDesign opens the path. You can drag the path's
end points apart, if necessary.

Joining Open Paths

To join two open paths, follow these steps (see Figure 5-18).

1. Position the Pen tool above the start or end point of one of the
   open paths (you don't need to select a path). InDesign changes
   the cursor to show that it's ready to add a point to the path.

2. Click the Pen tool, then position the cursor over the start or end
   point of the second path. InDesign changes the cursor to show
   that it's ready to connect the current path to the point.

3. Click the Pen tool. InDesign joins the two paths.

4. Repeat this process for the other two end points to close the path.

Alternatively, you can select two paths and choose Join from the
Paths submenu of the Object menu. InDesign will join the nearest
points of the two paths (with straight line segments).

FIGURE 5-18
Joining Two Open Paths

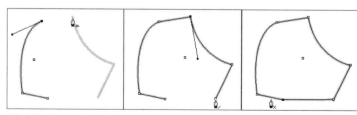

Click the Pen tool on the
end point of one open
path, then click an end
point on the other path.

To close the path, click
one of the remaining
end points.

Click the other end point
to close the path.

Compound Paths

In the old days, not only did Ole have to walk miles to school in freezing cold weather, but he also had to work his way through an impossibly difficult series of steps to create holes inside closed paths. This did nothing to improve his already gloomy outlook on life.

These days, creating holes in paths is easier—just make them into compound paths. Compound paths are made of two or more paths (which must be unlocked, ungrouped, and closed) that have been joined using the Make Compound Paths option on the Paths submenu of the Object menu. Areas between the two paths, or areas where the paths overlap, are transparent. The following steps show you how to make a torus, or "doughnut" shape (see Figure 5-19).

1. Select the Ellipse tool from the Tools panel.

2. Draw two ovals, one on top of the other.

3. Fill the ovals with a basic fill.

4. Select both ovals.

5. Press Command-8/Ctrl-8 to join the two ovals.

If you decide you don't want the paths to be compound paths, you can change them back into individual paths. To do this, select the compound path and then choose Release Compound Path from the Paths submenu of the Object menu.

FIGURE 5-19
Creating a Compound Path

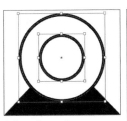

Select the paths you want to turn into a compound path.

Choose Make Compound Path from the Paths submenu of the Object menu.

InDesign creates a compound path from the selected objects (this makes a hole where the shapes overlap).

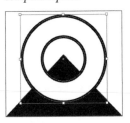

This example shows a compound path that we've used as a container for an image.

When you join paths with different lines and fills, the compound path takes on the stroke and fill attributes of the path that's the farthest to the back.

Editing Compound Paths

You can subselect the individual points that make up a compound path in the same way that you subselect objects inside a group—select the Direct Selection tool and click on the point. Once a point is selected, you can alter its position (see Figure 5-20).

FIGURE 5-20
Editing a Compound Path

 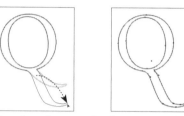

Use the Direct Selection tool to select some points.

Transform (move, scale, shear, or rotate) the points. In this example, we've dragged the points to a new location.

Splitting Compound Paths

To convert a compound path back into two or more normal paths, select the compound path and choose Release Compound Path from the Paths submenu of the Object menu (or press Command-Option-8/Ctrl-Alt-8). InDesign converts the compound path into its component paths. Note that the paths do not return to their original formatting when you do this.

Compound Paths and Even-Odd Fill

If you're familiar with Illustrator or other drawing programs, you're probably used to having two options for filling paths. These options go by different names in different applications, but they're usually known as the "Even Odd Fill Rule" and the "Zero Winding Fill Rule." These rules control the way the application fills a path that intersects itself, or the way the interior areas of a compound path are filled.

If you've pasted paths from these applications into InDesign, or if you've drawn a self-intersecting path in InDesign, you've probably discovered that InDesign supports the Zero Winding Fill Rule, but not the Even Odd Fill Rule.

What the heck are we talking about? It's much easier to show than it is to describe (see Figure 5-21).

What can you do when you want the even/odd fill? Do you have to leave InDesign, create the path in a drawing program, and then import the path as a graphic?

This question drove Ole to the brink of madness before he discovered that you can simulate the effect of the Even Odd Fill Rule

FIGURE 5-21
Fill Rules

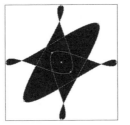

Self-intersecting path filled using the Zero Winding Fill Rule (InDesign).

Self-intersecting path filled using the Even Odd Fill Rule (Illustrator).

using compound paths and the Add path operation (we'll discuss path operations later in this chapter). See Figure 5-22.

1. Select the self-intersecting path.

2. Copy the path, then use Paste In Place (Command-Option-Shift-V/Ctrl-Alt-Shift-V) to create a duplicate of the object exactly on top of the original object.

3. Select both items and click the Add button on the Pathfinder panel (Intersect will also work). InDesign creates a compound path and fills it exactly as the original path would look if it had been filled using the Even Odd Fill Rule.

FIGURE 5-22
Simulating the Effect of the Even Odd Fill Rule

Select the path, then copy the path and paste the copy on top of the original using Paste In Place.

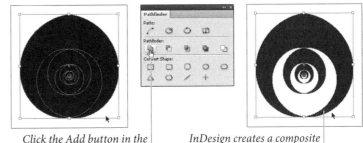

Click the Add button in the PathFinder panel.

InDesign creates a composite path that is filled using the Even Odd Fill Rule.

Smoothing Paths

You like using the Pencil tool. But your mouse hand isn't perfectly steady. Or the jerk you share office space with can't resist the urge to bump your arm while you're drawing. Either way, you need a way to smooth the path you've drawn in InDesign. Are you doomed to an after-hours workout with the Pen tool? Not with the Smooth tool on your side. This handy gadget can help you smooth out the rough patches in your InDesign paths.

To use the Smooth tool, select the tool from the Tools panel (it's usually hiding under the Pencil tool). Or select the Pencil tool and hold down Option/Alt to change the Pencil tool to the Smooth tool. Drag the tool along the path you want to smooth (see Figure 5-23). As you drag, InDesign adjusts the control handles and point positions on the path (sometimes deleting points as you drag).

To control the operation of the Smooth tool, double-click the Smooth tool in the Tools panel. InDesign displays the Smooth Tool Preferences dialog box (see Figure 5-24). The Fidelity slider controls the distance, in screen pixels, that the "smoothed" path can vary from the path of the Smooth tool (higher values equal more adjustment and greater variation from the existing path). The Smoothness slider controls the amount of change applied to the path (higher values equal greater smoothing).

FIGURE 5-23
Smoothing a Path

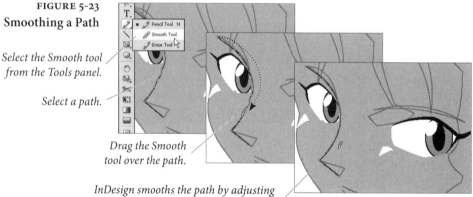

Select the Smooth tool from the Tools panel.

Select a path.

Drag the Smooth tool over the path.

InDesign smooths the path by adjusting control handles, moving points on the path, and deleting points.

FIGURE 5-24
Smooth Tool Preferences

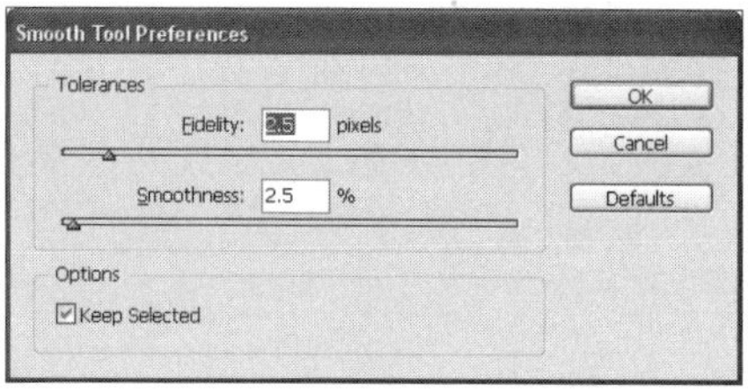

Erasing Paths

Imagine that you want to remove an arbitrary section of a path, and that the beginning and end of the section do not correspond to existing points on the path. To do this, select the Erase tool from the Tools panel, then drag the tool over the area of the path you want to delete (see Figure 5-25).

Erasing Part of a Path

Select the Erase tool from the Tools panel, then select a path.

Drag the Erase tool over the parts of the path you want to erase.

When you drag the Erase tool over a line segment on a closed path, InDesign opens the path. When you drag over an open path, it gets split into two paths.

Path Operations

Path operations—which is what we call the commands represented by buttons on the Pathfinder panel—create paths from other paths, or change the shape of paths in some predefined way. The first row of buttons in the Pathfinder panel make it easy to create complex shapes by combining simple geometric shapes, and to create shapes that would be very difficult to draw using the Pen tool.

The Convert Shape operations provide a number of "utility" functions for working with paths. Why did they end up in the same panel with the Pathfinder path operations they have little or nothing in common with? Think carefully before you answer. Do you *really* want *another* panel?

The Pathfinder path operations work with the area(s) of intersection between two or more objects. These path operations can merge objects, or create new objects, or remove the area of one object from another object.

Many people have gotten the impression that the path operations are "advanced" drawing techniques. "I can't draw," they say, "so I have no use for them. It's hard enough just using the Pen tool."

Nothing could be farther from the truth—if you *can* draw, the path operations are a nice addition to your toolbox, but if you *can't* draw, or can't draw with the Pen tool, InDesign's path operations can quickly become your best friend. Think about it—even David can draw just about anything using rectangles, ellipses, and the occasional polygon. By using path operations, you can do the same, without ending up with stacks of overlapping shapes on your pages.

Applying Pathfinder Path Operations To apply any of the Pathfinder path operations, select two or more paths, display the Pathfinder panel, and click the button corresponding to the path operation you want to apply (see Figure 5-26).

We'll cover what each of the path operations does, but first, a few ground rules:

▶ **Original shapes are deleted.** Path operations often consume the selected shapes and create a new shape. This shape is often a compound path. To retain the original shapes, you'll need to duplicate them before applying the path effect.

▶ **Stacking order matters.** Most of the path operations affect either the foreground or background object in some predefined way. If you try a path operation and don't get the result you expect, undo, then shuffle the order of the objects (using Bring to Front, Send to Back, Bring Forward, and Send Backward from the Arrange submenu of the Object menu) and try again.

▶ **Formatting changes.** In general, the fill, stroke, and other attributes of the foreground object define the formatting of the resulting object. The exception is the Subtract path operation, where the background object defines the formatting of the result.

▶ **Path operations and text frames.** When you apply a path operation to a text frame, the shape of the frame is affected—not the text in the frame.

▶ **Alternatives to clipping paths.** You can sometimes use path operations to avoid clipping paths and nested objects, which can result in faster printing.

▶ **Watch out for path contents.** Performing path operations on objects that contain other objects—such as imported graphics—sometimes deletes the path content.

Add The Add path operation creates a new path that has the outline of the selected objects, removing the area of intersection and any interior paths from the new object. If the original paths are composite paths, any interior paths will be retained unless they intersect each other or fall within the area of intersection of the shapes.

Subtract When you want to use one path to cut a hole in another, use the Subtract path operation. It's like a cookie cutter—the foreground object cuts a hole in the background object. The resulting object takes on the fill and stroke of the background object.

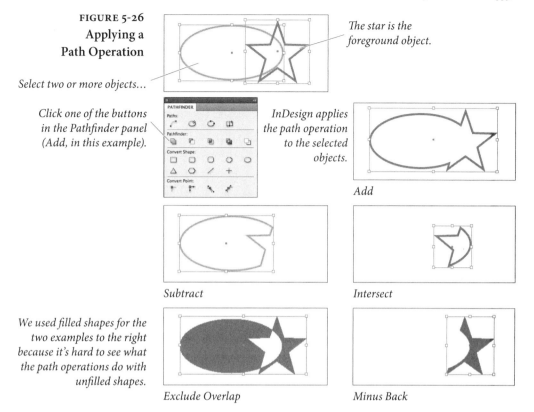

FIGURE 5-26
Applying a
Path Operation

Select two or more objects...

*The star is the
foreground object.*

*Click one of the buttons
in the Pathfinder panel
(Add, in this example).*

*InDesign applies
the path operation
to the selected
objects.*

Add

Subtract

Intersect

*We used filled shapes for the
two examples to the right
because it's hard to see what
the path operations do with
unfilled shapes.*

Exclude Overlap

Minus Back

Intersect   The Intersect path operation creates a new object that is the shape of the area of intersection of the objects in the selection. Intersect will display an error message if the objects do not share a common area of intersection.

As we've noted, path operations consume the selected objects. There are various ways to retain the original objects, but the quickest by far is to apply the path effect, copy the resulting path, undo (which restores the original paths), and then press Command-Option-Shift-V/Ctrl-Alt-Shift-V to paste in place. This trick is particularly useful when used with Intersect.

Exclude Overlap   The Exclude Overlap path operation creates a compound path from the selected objects, leaving any areas of intersection unfilled.

Minus Back   The Minus Back path operation is the opposite of the Subtract path operation. When you click the Minus Back button in the Pathfinder panel, InDesign uses the background object to cut a hole in the foreground object. The resulting object takes on the formatting attributes of the foreground object.

Applying Convert Shape Operations

To apply any of the Convert Shape operations, select an object and click one of the buttons in the Pathfinder panel.

- ▶ **Convert to Rectangle.** Converts the object to a rectangle.

- ▶ **Convert to Rounded-Corner Rectangle.** Converts the object to a rectangle and applies the Rounded corner option.

- ▶ **Convert to Beveled-Corner Rectangle.** Converts the object to a rectangle and applies the Bevel corner option.

- ▶ **Convert to Inverse-Rounded-Corner Rectangle.** Converts the object to a rectangle and applies the Inverse Rounded corner option (using the current corner radius setting).

- ▶ **Convert to Ellipse.** Converts the object to an ellipse. If you have a square selected, the resulting ellipse will be a circle.

- ▶ **Convert to Triangle.** Converts the object to a triangle.

- ▶ **Convert to Polygon.** Converts the object to a polygon, using the current settings in the Polygon Settings dialog box. This means that you can easily change one polygon into another.

- ▶ **Convert to Line.** Converts the object to a line.

- ▶ **Convert to Vertical or Horizontal Line.** Converts the object to a vertical or horizontal line.

- ▶ **Open Path.** Opens a closed path. Note that this operation does not remove the last line segment in the path—it simply opens the path at the first/last point in the path.

- ▶ **Close Path.** Closes an open path.

- ▶ **Reverse Path.** Reverses the selected path.

Applying Convert Point Operations

To apply any of the Convert Path operations, direct-select one or more points, and click one of the buttons in the Pathfinder panel.

- ▶ **Plain.** Removes direction lines from the selected points and makes a V shape.

- ▶ **Corner.** Changes points to have direction lines that can move independently of each other.

- ▶ **Smooth.** Changes the selected points to a continuous curve that can have direction lines of unequal lengths.

- ▶ **Symmetrical.** Changes the selected points to a continuous curve with direction lines of equal length.

Corner Options

Corner options can change that way corner points are drawn. Use this feature to add rounded corners to rectangles and squares.

You can curve one or more corners of a frame just by dragging the corner itself. Select a rectangular frame and click the yellow box. Four yellow diamonds appear on the selected frame, indicating Live Corners mode (see Figure 5-27).

Drag any diamond to adjust all four corners together.

Shift-drag a diamond to adjust a single corner. Option/Alt-click a diamond to cycle through the various corner effects. Drag a diamond towards the middle of the frame to change the effect's radius. To stop editing corners, click anywhere outside the selected frame.

If you don't want the yellow box to appear when you select a frame, choose Hide Live Corners from the Extras submenu on the View menu.

FIGURE 5-27
Live Corners

To add corner effects manually, click the yellow box...   *...and drag the handles.*

You can also apply corner effects by choosing a shape and size from the Corner Options widgets in the Control panel or using the Corner Options dialog box, which lets you apply different effects to each corner (see Figure 5-28).

To apply a corner option using a dialog box, select the page item and choose Corner Options from the Object menu. InDesign displays the Corner Options dialog box. To apply a different corner to each corner of a rectangle, click the chain icon in the middle of the dialog box so that it becomes a broken link icon. Choose the size and effect you want for each corner. InDesign changes the corners of the path based on the corner options you selected.

To remove corner effects, select the object and choose None from the Corner Options pop-up menu in the Control panel.

FIGURE 5-28
Corner Options

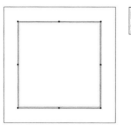
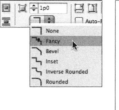

Select a path...

...and choose a corner size and effect from pop-up menu in the Control panel.

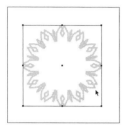

InDesign's corner options can be applied to any corner point. Try them with polygons for interesting geometric shapes.

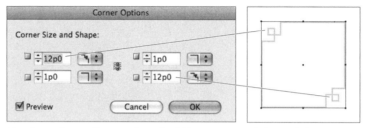

Or, choose Corner Options from the Object menu, and choose different corner settings for different corners.

InDesign's corner options

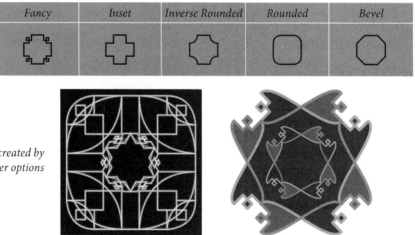

Fancy	Inset	Inverse Rounded	Rounded	Bevel

Shapes created by overlapping corner options

Strokes

Once you've created a path, you'll probably want to give the path some specific stroke weight, color, or other property. The process of applying formatting to a path is often called "stroking a path," and we refer to a path's appearance as its "stroke." Strokes specify what the outline of the path *looks like*.

To define a stroke for a path, select the path, then display the Stroke panel by pressing Command-F10/F10 (see Figure 5-29). Use the Type pop-up menu to choose the type of stroke you want to use—solid, dashed, or any of the "scotch" (i.e., multi-stroke) types.

You can define custom dashed, striped, or dotted stroke styles. We'll talk more about stroke styles later in the chapter.

Weight   You can enter a line weight for the stroke of the selected path using the Weight field, or you can choose a predefined line weight from the pop-up menu associated with the field. To remove a stroke from a path, enter zero in the Weight field.

Historical Note: In the old days of desktop publishing, some programs created hairlines using the PostScript statement "0 setlinewidth," which generates a one-pixel wide stroke on a 300-dpi laser printer. This worked pretty well—you'd get a stroke that was approximately the width of a hairline (between .2 and .25 points). When imagesetters appeared, however, this approach led to strokes that were $1/1200^{\text{th}}$ of an inch wide or even smaller—stroke weights too fine

FIGURE 5-29
Stroke Panel

Default stroke types

Solid

Thick-Thick

Thick-Thin

Thick-Thin-Thick

Thin-Thick

Thin-Thick-Thin

Thin-Thin

Dashed (3 and 2)

Dashed (4 and 4)

Left Slant Hash

Right Slant Hash

Straight Hash

Dotted

Wavy

White Diamond

Japanese Dots

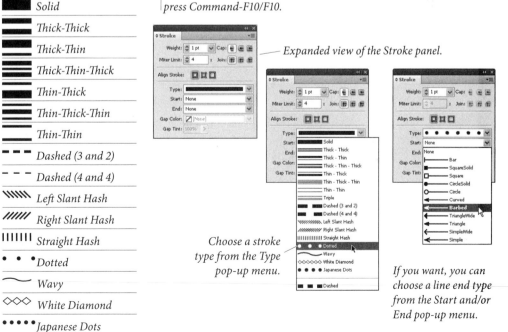

To display the Stroke panel, press Command-F10/F10.

To expand the "minimalist" Stroke panel, choose Show Options from the Stroke panel menu (or double-click the panel tab).

Expanded view of the Stroke panel.

Choose a stroke type from the Type pop-up menu.

If you want, you can choose a line end type from the Start and/or End pop-up menu.

to be printed on most presses. So, we grizzled graybeards advised all of our younger cohorts to avoid entering zero for the weight of a stroke. In InDesign, at least, it doesn't matter—entering zero won't result in a "0 setlinewidth" stroke.

Stroke Alignment   The three buttons in the Align Stroke section of the Stroke panel control the way that the stroke is positioned relative to the path. The options are Align Stroke to Center, Align Stroke to Inside, and Align Stroke to Outside, and they do just what they say (see Figure 5-30).

If you're using the Align Stroke to Inside option and increase the stroke weight of the border of an ad in a magazine layout, InDesign keeps the stroke inside the area the advertiser is actually paying for.

When you use Align Stroke to Outside, InDesign will add the stroke to the outside of the path; Align Stroke to Center adds the stroke evenly around the path.

FIGURE 5-30
Stroke Alignment
Options

Align Stroke to Center distributes the stroke evenly around the path.

Align Stroke to Inside adds the stroke to the inside of the path.

Align Stroke to Outside adds the stroke to the outside of the path.

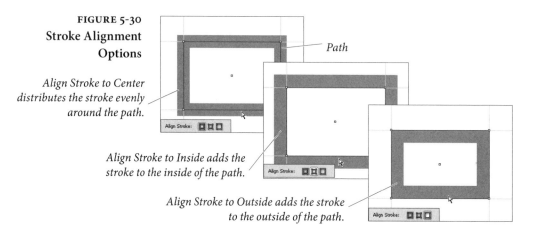

Path

Cap   Select one of the Cap options to determine the shape of the end of the stroke (see Figure 5-31). The Cap option you choose has no visible effect on a closed path.

Join   The Join option sets the appearance of corners—the place where two line segments in a path meet in a corner point (see Figure 5-32).

Miter Limit   When paths go around corners, weird things can happen. Asked to corner too sharply, the stroke skids out of control, creating spiky elbows that increase the effective stroke weight of a path's corners. The value you enter in the Miter Limit field sets the distance, as a multiple of the stroke weight, that you'll allow the corner to extend before InDesign applies a beveled join to the corner (see Figure 5-33).

FIGURE 5-31
Cap Options

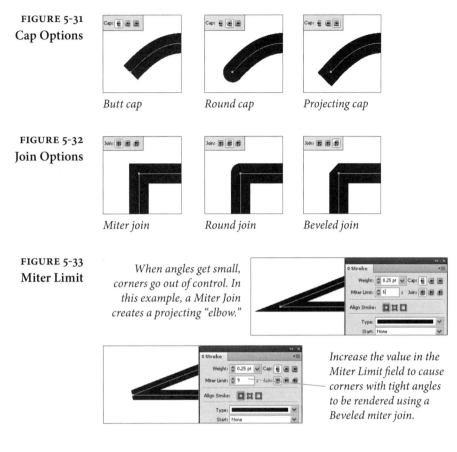

Butt cap   *Round cap*   *Projecting cap*

FIGURE 5-32
Join Options

Miter join   *Round join*   *Beveled join*

FIGURE 5-33
Miter Limit

When angles get small, corners go out of control. In this example, a Miter Join creates a projecting "elbow."

Increase the value in the Miter Limit field to cause corners with tight angles to be rendered using a Beveled miter join.

If, for example, you enter "2" in the Miter Limit field, InDesign will flatten corners when the stroke weight of the corner is equal to or greater than two times the weight of the stroke.

The Miter Limit field is only available when you're using the Miter Join option, and applies only to corner points.

Dash   For a dashed line, choose Dashed from the Type pop-up menu, and use the Dash and Gap fields that appear at the bottom of the Stroke panel to set the appearance of the dashed stroke (see Figure 5-34).

Creating Layered Strokes   We've heard a number of people complain that InDesign doesn't include their favorite "fancy" rules—if you can't find what you're looking for on the Type menu in the Stroke panel, and you can't create the stroke you want using stroke styles (discussed later in this chapter), you can make your own. To create a simple multi-stroke effect, follow these steps (see Figure 5-35).

1. Select a path.

FIGURE 5-34
Applying a
Dashed Stroke

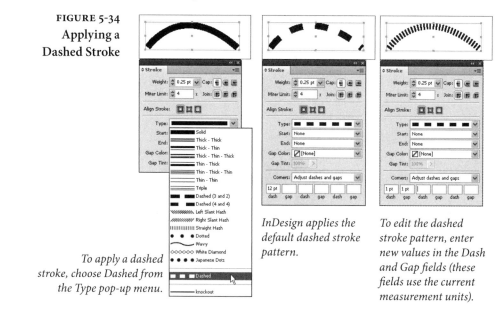

To apply a dashed
stroke, choose Dashed from
the Type pop-up menu.

InDesign applies the
default dashed stroke
pattern.

To edit the dashed
stroke pattern, enter
new values in the Dash
and Gap fields (these
fields use the current
measurement units).

FIGURE 5-35
Creating a
Complex Stroke by
Stacking Paths

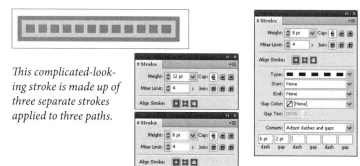

This complicated-look-
ing stroke is made up of
three separate strokes
applied to three paths.

2. Clone the path (press Command-C/Ctrl-C to copy the path,
   then press Command-Option-Shift-V/Ctrl-Alt-Shift-V. InDesign
   creates a copy of the selected path on top of the original path).

3. Change the stroke weight, stroke type, or color of the copy
   of the path.

4. Select the original path and the clone and group them (note that
   you can't make them a compound path, as that would apply one
   of the two strokes to both paths and would undo your multi-
   stroke effect).

Arrowheads   You can add arrowheads or tailfeathers to any open path you want
by choosing an arrowhead from the Start and End pop-up menus at

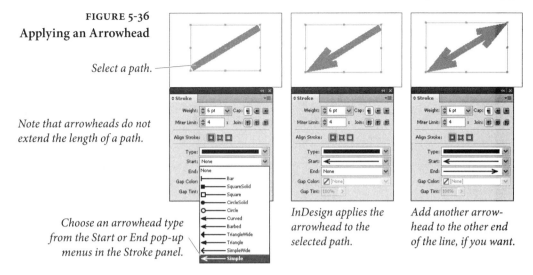

FIGURE 5-36
Applying an Arrowhead

Select a path.

Note that arrowheads do not extend the length of a path.

Choose an arrowhead type from the Start or End pop-up menus in the Stroke panel.

InDesign applies the arrowhead to the selected path.

Add another arrowhead to the other end of the line, if you want.

the bottom of the Stroke panel. The Start pop-up menu applies to the first point in the path (according to the direction of the path); the End pop-up menu applies to the last point in the path. You don't have to make choices from both of the pop-up menus (see Figure 5-36).

To swap the arrowheads on the beginning and end of a path, select the path using the Direct Selection tool and choose Reverse Path from the Paths submenu of the Object menu (see Figure 5-37).

Overprint

You won't find this basic stroke option in the Stroke panel, so stop looking. Instead, it's in the Attributes panel (choose Attributes from the Window menu). Checking the Overprint Stroke option makes the stroke overprint (rather than knock out of) whatever's behind it. This might not seem like much, but if you're creating color publications, you'll find it's one of the most important features in InDesign (see Chapter 10, "Color").

Gap Color and Gap Tint

When you choose a dotted, dashed, or striped stroke, InDesign displays the Gap Color and the Gap Tint pop-up menus at the bottom of the Stroke panel (see Figure 5-38). Use these controls to specify the color and tint of the "blank" areas in the stroke.

Corner Adjustment

When you apply a dotted or dashed stroke to a page item, InDesign displays the Corners pop-up menu at the bottom of the Stroke panel. The options on this menu control the way that InDesign draws the stroke as it crosses points on the path (see Figure 5-39).

When you choose Adjust Dashes, InDesign will change the length of the dashes in the path so that a dash appears centered on each point in the path. Choose Adjust Gaps, and InDesign will change

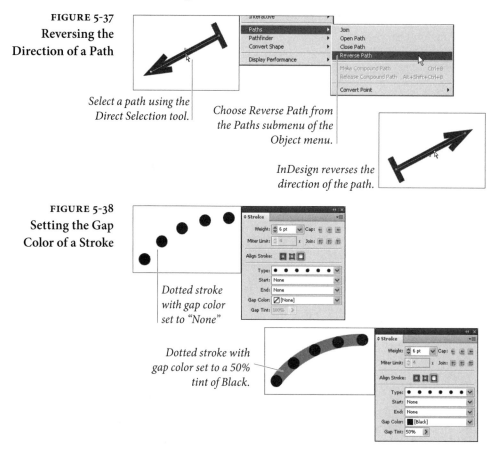

FIGURE 5-37
Reversing the
Direction of a Path

*Select a path using the
Direct Selection tool.*

*Choose Reverse Path from
the Paths submenu of the
Object menu.*

*InDesign reverses the
direction of the path.*

FIGURE 5-38
Setting the Gap
Color of a Stroke

*Dotted stroke
with gap color
set to "None"*

*Dotted stroke with
gap color set to a 50%
tint of Black.*

the length of the dashes in the path to accomplish the same effect. As you'd expect, choosing Adjust Dashes and Gaps changes the length of both dashes and gaps in the dash pattern, and choosing None does not adjust the position of dashes in the pattern at all.

Why adjust the dashes and/or gaps in a dash pattern? If you don't, you can easily end up with gaps at the corners of paths. It's particularly noticeable when you apply dashed strokes to rectangles.

Editing Strokes   Once you've applied a stroke to a particular path, you can change the stroke using any of the following methods. Again, there's no "right" way to edit a stroke—which method is best and quickest depends on how you work and which panels you have open at the time you want to change the stroke.

▶ Display the Stroke panel, then make changes in the panel.

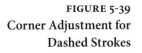

**FIGURE 5-39
Corner Adjustment for
Dashed Strokes**

*If you don't adjust the
dashed stroke pattern, you
run the risk of unsightly gaps
at the corners of the shape.*

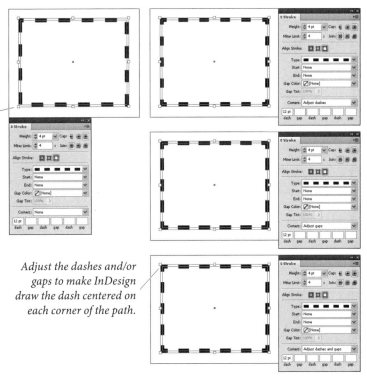

*Adjust the dashes and/or
gaps to make InDesign
draw the dash centered on
each corner of the path.*

▶ Click the Stroke selector in the Color panel, then click a color in
the panel (see Chapter 10, "Color," for more on applying colors
using the Color panel).

▶ Use the Stroke button at the bottom of the Toolbox to apply or
remove colors and gradients from the path.

▶ Select the path, then choose a new stroke weight from the Stroke
Weight submenu of the Context menu.

▶ Use the Eyedropper tool to pick up the stroke of a path and apply
that formatting to another path.

Removing Strokes   To quickly remove a stroke from a path, do one of the following.

▶ Select the path, click the Stroke selector, then click None.

▶ Select the path, display the Swatches panel, click the Stroke
selector at the top of the panel, and then click the None swatch.

▶ Enter 0 in the Weight field of the Stroke panel.

Stroke Styles

If you've looked through the default strokes and haven't seen the stroke pattern you're looking for, you can probably create it using InDesign's stroke styles. This is provided that the stroke you're looking for is dashed, dotted, or striped—InDesign does not yet support strokes made up of arbitrary shapes. If you need a special skull and crossbones stroke for your pirate/goth/metal newsletter, you'll have to create it from scratch (using text paths, as shown in Chapter 6, "Where Text Meets Graphics").

To create a stroke style, follow these steps (see Figure 5-40).

1. Choose Stroke Styles from the Stroke panel menu. InDesign displays the Stroke Styles dialog box.

2. Click the New button to create a new stroke style. If you want to base your new stroke style on an existing style, select the style from the list of stroke styles before you click the button. InDesign displays the New Stroke Style dialog box.

3. Enter a name for the stroke style. Choose a stroke style type (Dash, Dotted, or Stripe) from the Type pop-up menu.

4. Set the options for the stroke style. The available options vary depending on the type of stroke style you selected.

   For each type, InDesign displays a preview of the stroke style with an associated Preview Weight field. As you would expect, changing the stroke weight using this field affects only the preview image of the stroke—the stroke style does not include the stroke weight.

   In each of the stroke style types, the Pattern Length field controls the length of the pattern in the stroke style.

   Dash. Drag the cursor in the area below the ruler to set the length of the dashes in the stroke style, or enter values in the Start or Length fields. To make more than one dash in the pattern, click in the white area and drag. To remove a dash, point at the black area and drag it away from the ruler.

   You can also set the line cap and the way that InDesign handles the dash pattern around corners. These options work in exactly the same way as their counterparts in the Stroke panel, as discussed previously in this chapter.

   Dotted. When you choose Dotted from the Type pop-up menu, you can add dots to the pattern by clicking below the ruler, or by entering a value in the Center field. Either way, you're

FIGURE 5-40
Defining a Stroke Style

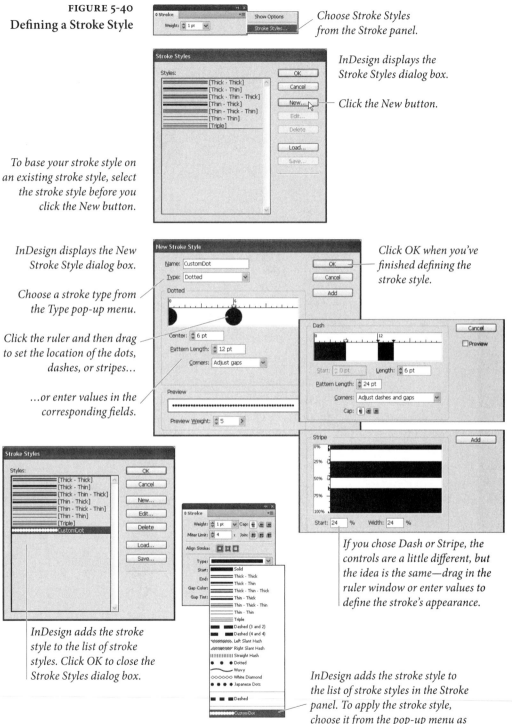

Choose Stroke Styles from the Stroke panel.

InDesign displays the Stroke Styles dialog box.

Click the New button.

To base your stroke style on an existing stroke style, select the stroke style before you click the New button.

InDesign displays the New Stroke Style dialog box.

Choose a stroke type from the Type pop-up menu.

Click the ruler and then drag to set the location of the dots, dashes, or stripes...

...or enter values in the corresponding fields.

Click OK when you've finished defining the stroke style.

If you chose Dash or Stripe, the controls are a little different, but the idea is the same—drag in the ruler window or enter values to define the stroke's appearance.

InDesign adds the stroke style to the list of stroke styles. Click OK to close the Stroke Styles dialog box.

InDesign adds the stroke style to the list of stroke styles in the Stroke panel. To apply the stroke style, choose it from the pop-up menu as you would any of the default strokes.

controlling the location of the center of the dot relative to the pattern length. You cannot scale the width or height of the dot—it's always a circle whose width is determined by the stroke weight. (If you're looking for an oval dot, use a dashed stroke with a rounded line cap.)

The options on the Corners pop-up menu control the way that dots are adjusted around corners in paths you've applied the dotted stroke style to. Choose None for no adjustment, or choose Adjust Gaps to have InDesign increase or decrease the gap between dots to make dots appear at each point on the path. Note that adjusting the gaps results in uneven spacing between dots on a path, but is probably less distracting than having dots "miss" the corners of a path (particularly on a rectangle).

To remove a dot, drag the dot out of the ruler window.

Stripe. Specify the way that the stripes fill the width of the path by dragging the cursor to the right of the ruler or by entering values in the Start and Width fields. To add a new stripe, drag the cursor in a white area. To remove a stripe, drag the stripe out of the ruler window.

Stroke styles exist inside a document; creating a stroke style in a specific document does not add that stroke style to any other documents. You can copy stroke styles from one document to another. You can save and load stroke styles, and you can add stroke styles to all new documents. To add a stroke style to all new documents, create or load the stroke style when no documents are open.

Applying Stroke Styles

You apply stroke styles just as you would apply any of the default stroke types: select an object, then choose the stroke style from the Type pop-up menu in the Stroke panel.

Editing Stroke Styles

To edit a stroke style, choose Stroke Styles from the Stroke panel pop-up menu, select the style from the list of styles in the Stroke Styles dialog box, and click the Edit button. InDesign displays the Edit Stroke Style dialog box.

Make changes to the stroke style definition and close the dialog box, and InDesign will change the appearance of all of the objects you've applied the stroke style to.

Deleting Stroke Styles

To delete a stroke style, choose Stroke Styles from the Stroke panel pop-up menu, select the style from the list of styles in the Stroke Styles dialog box, and click the Delete button.

When you delete a stroke style, InDesign will display a dialog box asking which stroke style you want to use to replace the stroke style you're deleting. Choose a stroke style from the pop-up menu and click the OK button, and InDesign will replace all occurrences of the deleted style with the stroke style you've selected.

Saving Stroke Styles

To save the stroke styles in your document to a stroke styles file, choose Stroke Styles from the Stroke panel pop-up menu, select the styles you want to save from the list of styles in the Stroke Styles dialog box, and click the Save button. InDesign displays a standard file dialog box where you can choose a location and enter a file name for the saved stroke styles file. Saved InDesign stroke style documents have the file extension ".inst".

Loading Stroke Styles

To load stroke styles from a saved stroke styles file, choose Stroke Styles from the Stroke panel menu to display the Stroke Styles dialog box, then click the Load button. InDesign displays a standard file dialog box. Locate and select the file you want to load stroke styles from and click OK to load the styles into the current document.

To copy a single stroke style from one document to another, select an object formatted with the stroke style, copy it, and then paste it into another document. InDesign will bring the stroke style along with the object, and you can then delete the object.

Fills

Just as strokes determine what the *outside* of a path looks like, fills specify the appearance of the *inside* of a path. Fills can make the inside of a path a solid color, or a linear or radial gradient. Any path you create can be filled, including open paths.

To apply a fill, select a path and do one of the following:

▶ Click the Fill button on the Control panel, and then click the color swatch.

▶ Click the Fill selector at the top of the Swatches panel, then click a color swatch (see Figure 5-41).

▶ Click the Fill selector at the bottom of the Tools panel, then click the Apply Color button (or press comma). This applies the most recently selected color or swatch (see Figure 5-42).

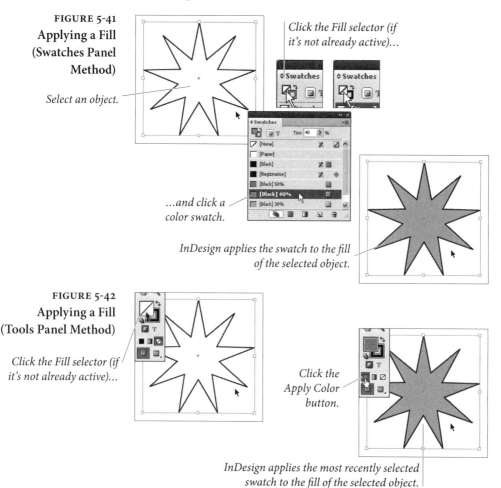

FIGURE 5-41
Applying a Fill
(Swatches Panel Method)

Select an object.

Click the Fill selector (if it's not already active)...

...and click a color swatch.

InDesign applies the swatch to the fill of the selected object.

FIGURE 5-42
Applying a Fill (Tools Panel Method)

Click the Fill selector (if it's not already active)...

Click the Apply Color button.

InDesign applies the most recently selected swatch to the fill of the selected object.

▶ Drag a swatch out of the Swatches panel or Color panel and drop it on a path, either selected or unselected.

▶ Click the Fill selector in the Color panel, then define a color in the panel.

▶ Select the Eyedropper tool. Click an object formatted with the fill you want, then click object to apply the fill.

Removing Fills   To quickly remove a fill from a path, do one of the following:

▶ Click the None swatch in the Fill pop-up menu on the Control panel.

▶ Click the Fill selector in the Tools panel, then click the None button (or, better yet, press /).

▶ Click the Fill button in the Color panel and then click the None swatch.

▶ Click the Fill button at the bottom of the Toolbox, then click the None swatch in the Swatches panel.

Gradients

A "gradient" is a type of fill or stroke that creates a graduation from one color to another—an effect also known as a "fountain," "blend," or "vignette." InDesign offers two types of gradients: "Linear" and "Radial." For either type of gradient fill, you can set the colors used in the gradient, the rate at which one color blends into another, and the colors used in the gradient (gradients can contain two or more colors). For Linear gradients, you can set the angle that the graduation is to follow.

Linear gradients create a smooth color transition (or series of transitions) from one end of a path to another; Radial gradients create a graduation from the center of a path to its edges. Gradients applied to paths are calculated relative to the geometric bounds of the path; gradients applied to text characters use the geometric bounding box of the text frame containing the text (not the individual characters themselves).

Applying Gradients
To apply a gradient to a path, follow these steps (see Figure 5-43).

1. Select the path using the Selection tool or the Direct Selection tool, or select text using the Text tool or Path Text tool.

2. Do one of the following.

    ▶ Click the Fill or Stroke selector in the Tools panel (to specify which part of the path you want to apply the gradient to). Click the Apply Gradient button at the bottom of the Tools panel.

    ▶ Display the Gradient panel (choose Gradient from the Window menu), and then click the gradient ramp.

    ▶ Click an existing gradient swatch in the Swatches panel (press F5 to display the Swatches panel). You can also drag the gradient swatch out of the Swatches panel and drop it on a path (the path doesn't have to be selected).

*Click the Fill or
Stroke selector...*

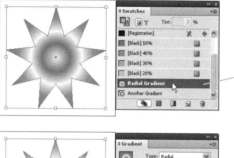

*...then click the Apply
Gradient button...*

*InDesign applies the
current default gradient.*

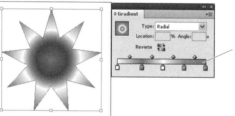

*...or select an object,
then click a gradient
swatch in the Swatches
panel...*

*...or display the
Gradient panel and
click the gradient
ramp...*

▸ Select the Eyedropper tool and click an object formatted with a gradient, then click the tool again on the selected path.

▸ Select the Gradient tool and drag the tool inside the path.

Gradient Controls

When you create or edit a gradient, you work with InDesign's gradient controls: the gradient ramp, gradient stop icons, and center point icons. What the heck are we talking about? See Figure 5-44.

**Creating a
Gradient Swatch**

In our opinion, the best way to apply gradients is to use the Swatches panel. Just as applying a color from the Swatches panel establishes a link between the color swatch and the object you've applied it to, so applying a gradient swatch links the swatch and the objects you've formatted with it. This means that you can edit the definition of the gradient swatch and update the formatting of all of the objects you've applied the swatch to.

FIGURE 5-44
Gradient Controls

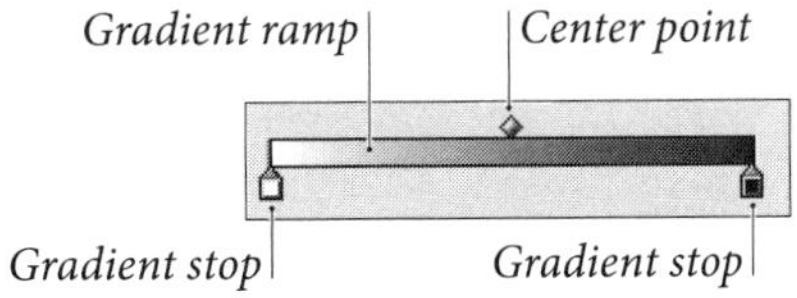

Gradient ramp | | *Center point*

Gradient stop | *Gradient stop* |

Unselected gradient stop

Selected gradient stop

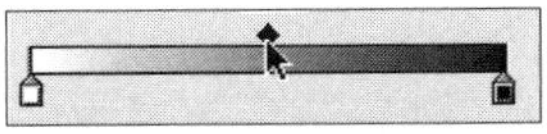

To change the position of a center point, select it...

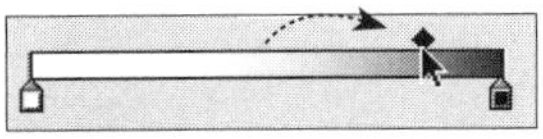

...and then drag it to a new location on the gradient ramp.

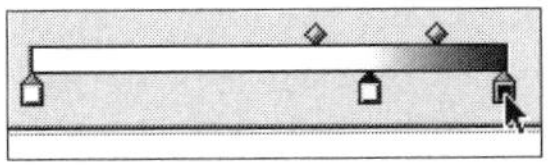

To change the position of a gradient stop, select it...

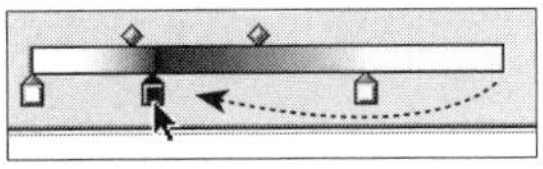

...and then drag it to a new location on the gradient ramp.

To add a new gradient stop, position the cursor below the gradient ramp...

...and click.

To remove a gradient stop, select it...

...and then drag it away from the gradient ramp.

To create a gradient swatch, follow these steps (see Figure 5-45).

1. Select an object that has the gradient you want (optional).

2. Display the Swatches panel, if it's not already visible, then choose New Gradient Swatch from the Swatches panel menu. If you selected an object in Step 1, InDesign picks up the attributes of the gradient applied to the object and displays them in this dialog box. If you did not select an object, the controls in the dialog box reflect the document's current default gradient.

3. Specify the colors and gradient stop positions for the gradient, if necessary.

4. Enter a name for the gradient swatch.

5. Click the OK button to save the gradient swatch. InDesign adds the gradient swatch to the list of swatches in the Swatches panel.

FIGURE 5-45
**Creating a
Gradient Swatch**

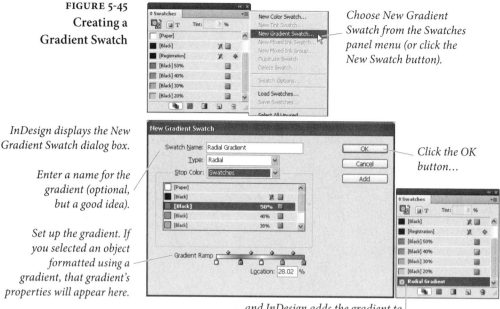

*Choose New Gradient
Swatch from the Swatches
panel menu (or click the
New Swatch button).*

*InDesign displays the New
Gradient Swatch dialog box.*

*Enter a name for the
gradient (optional,
but a good idea).*

*Set up the gradient. If
you selected an object
formatted using a
gradient, that gradient's
properties will appear here.*

*Click the OK
button…*

*…and InDesign adds the gradient to
the list of available swatches.*

**Using the
Gradient Panel**

You can also apply and edit gradients using the Gradient panel (see Figure 5-46). Like the New Gradient Swatch and Gradient Options dialog boxes, the Gradient panel contains a gradient ramp, with center points above the ramp and gradient stops below.

To apply a gradient, select a path, display the Gradient panel, then click the gradient ramp. InDesign applies the gradient object.

To edit a gradient applied to a path, select the path, then display the Gradient panel (if it's not already visible). InDesign loads the gradient applied to the path into the Gradient panel. Adjust the gradient stop positions, add gradient stops, or change the position of center points or colors, and InDesign applies the changes to the path.

Editing Gradients

To edit the color, gradient type, or angle of a gradient you've applied to an object, select the object and then display the Gradient panel. You can use any of the following techniques to change the gradient.

▶ Drag a gradient stop to a new position on the gradient ramp.

▶ Select the stop and enter a new value in the Location field.

▶ Add a new gradient stop by clicking below the gradient ramp.

▶ Change the position of the center point by dragging it above the gradient ramp. Or you can select the center point and enter a new value in the Location field.

FIGURE 5-46
Using the
Gradient Panel

FIGURE 5-46
Using the
Gradient Panel

You use the Gradient panel to edit the gradient applied to an object. You could, as shown in this example, change the location of the center point between two gradient stops.

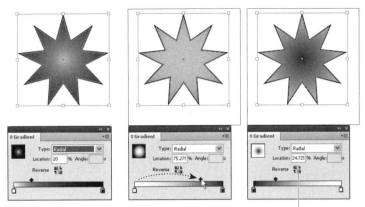

One thing that the Gradient panel has that you won't find elsewhere—the Reverse button, which reverses the direction of the gradient.

▶ Remove a stop by dragging it away from the gradient ramp.

▶ Reverse the gradient ramp by clicking the Reverse button.

▶ Change the angle of a linear gradient by entering a new value in the Angle field.

▶ Change the color of a gradient stop using the Swatches panel. To do this, select the stop, then hold down Option/Alt and click a color swatch in the Swatches panel (see Figure 5-47).

FIGURE 5-47
Getting a Swatch Color into a Gradient Stop

It's something every InDesign user has done at least once—you select a gradient stop, then click a color swatch in the Swatches panel, expecting to apply the color to the gradient stop. Instead, InDesign fills (or strokes) the path with the color. How the heck do you get a swatch color into a gradient stop?

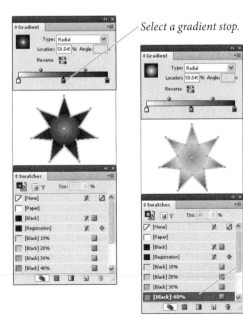

Select a gradient stop.

Hold down Option/ Alt and click the color swatch in the Swatches panel. InDesign assigns the color to the gradient stop.

FIGURE 5-48

Applying a Gradient to Multiple Objects

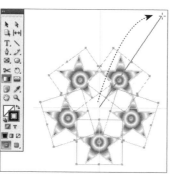

Select a series of paths. In this example, each path has been formatted using a radial gradient fill. Position the Gradient tool over the point at which you want to place the center point (for a radial gradient) or start (for a linear gradient), and then drag the tool.

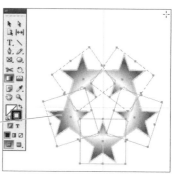

InDesign applies a single gradient to the selected paths.

▶ Change the color of a gradient stop to an unnamed color. To do this, select the gradient stop, then display the Color panel. Specify a color. As you change color values in the Color panel, InDesign changes the color applied to the gradient stop.

▶ Change the gradient type using the Type pop-up menu.

Applying a Gradient to Multiple Paths

To apply a gradient to more than one path, select the paths (which need not already have gradients applied to their fills or strokes), then drag the Gradient tool. The point at which you start dragging defines the starting point of the gradient (see Figure 5-48).

Transparency

Hands down, InDesign's sexiest feature is its transparency effects. These include drop shadows, feathering, support for transparency inside Photoshop and Illustrator graphics, changing an object's opacity or blending mode… the list goes on. But before we go any further with this wild transparency talk, we just need to be clear about something: PostScript's basic drawing model does not allow for transparency. Period.

So how does InDesign print transparent objects to a PostScript printer? Simple: it cheats. When the time comes to print, InDesign uses clipping paths to create the illusion of transparency and/or rasterizes the transparent objects and sends the printer separated image data. All of this takes place in the background—InDesign does not change the objects in your document. Instead, it changes the way that the objects are sent to the printer.

The way that InDesign sends the transparent objects to the printer is defined by the Transparency Flattener settings for the spread containing the objects. Flattener settings are described in Chapter 11, "Printing." As a rule of thumb, however, transparent objects make documents somewhat harder to print.

This brings us to our patented "With Power Comes Responsibility" speech. It's very easy to come up with combinations of transparent objects and flattener settings that create a document that can slow a printer to a crawl, or to produce files that take up enormous amounts of space on your hard drive.

This doesn't mean that you should avoid using transparency. That would be silly, given that there's sometimes no other way to create a specific creative effect. It's just that you must bear in mind that using the feature comes at a cost, and that you need to weigh the potential risks (slower printing, no printing) against the benefit (a cool layout).

If you're familiar with Photoshop's approach to transparency, you'll find InDesign's a bit different: In Photoshop, transparency is an attribute of layers; in InDesign, transparency is an attribute of individual page items—or elements of a page item. For example, you can set the opacity of the fill separately from its stroke, or give the text inside a frame an effect separate from the frame itself.

Adobe PDF Print Engine. PDF files (since Acrobat 5) support transparency. So if you're printing to a device that can understand transparency in a PDF file, then you don't have to worry about transparency flattening. For example, RIPs based on Adobe's PDF Print Engine can print native PDF files with transparency without first converting them to PostScript. No PostScript, no problem!

However, if you export an EPS or Acrobat 4 PDF file, or print or create a PDF file from the Print dialog box, then flattening kicks in.

Applying Transparency   To apply transparency to a page item, work your way through the following steps (see Figure 5-49).

1. Select a page item with the Selection or Direct Selection tool.

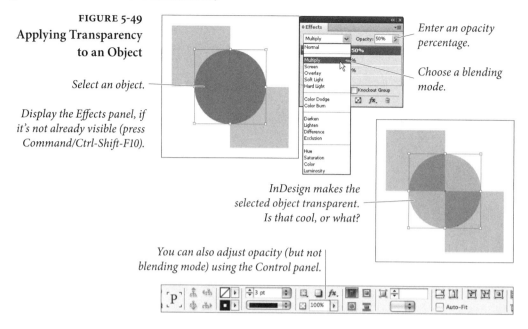

FIGURE 5-49
Applying Transparency to an Object

Select an object.

Display the Effects panel, if it's not already visible (press Command/Ctrl-Shift-F10).

Enter an opacity percentage.

Choose a blending mode.

InDesign makes the selected object transparent. Is that cool, or what?

You can also adjust opacity (but not blending mode) using the Control panel.

2. Display the Effects panel, if it's not already visible (choose Effects from the Window menu).

3. Click on the aspect of the page item you want to affect: Stroke, Fill, Text (which applies to the text inside a text frame), or Object (which affects all these facets at once).

4. Choose an option from the Blending Mode pop-up menu, if necessary.

5. Enter a value in the Opacity field (or drag the associated slider).

Blending Modes   The transparency blending modes define the way that the colors in the transparent objects interact with objects that fall behind them.

When you apply transparency, InDesign calculates the resulting color based on each color component of the foreground and background colors. For two overlapping process colors, for example, the effect of the blending mode will almost certainly differ for each of the four inks. When we say that a blending mode behaves in a particular way for a specific gray percentage value, we mean the percentage of a color component.

The effect of a blending mode is dependent on the current color management settings and the Transparency Blend Space (in the Edit menu). The ink values of the colors in a stack of transparent objects, for example, will never exceed the maximum ink coverage for the

current color management profile. (For the sake of your press opera-
tor's sanity, don't try to prove us wrong.)

The following notes provide a quick description of the most
useful of the blending modes. In these descriptions, the term "foreground color" refers to the color applied to the front-most object;
"background color" refers to the color of the background object, and
"resulting color" is the color you see where the two objects intersect.

Normal. The Normal blending mode adds the foreground color to
the background color. If the foreground color is black, and the opacity percentage is 10%, then 10% black is added to the background
color to produce the resulting color. The Normal blending mode at
100% opacity turns transparency off.

Multiply. The Multiply blending mode always results in a darker
color. The one exception is when the foreground color is white or
Paper color, in which case this blending mode has no effect at all.
Multiply is very similar to overprinting one object over another (see
Chapter 10, "Color," for more on overprinting), or overlapping lines
when drawing with felt pens. We think the Multiply blend mode is
the best choice for drop shadows (see below).

Screen. This blending mode almost always produces a resulting color
that is lighter than the background color (unless the foreground
color is black, which has no effect in this mode). The best real-world
definition of this blending mode comes from Adobe's Russell Brown:
Screen is like projecting two slides on the same screen. The result is
always lighter than either of the two sources. If the background color
is black or white, the background color remains unchanged.

Overlay. The Overlay blending mode compares the foreground and
background colors, accentuating highlights and shadows in each by
lightening light colors and darkening dark colors. If either the foreground or background color is 50-percent gray, then this mode has
no effect. Overlay increases color contrast and can get out of hand
quickly; we usually reduce the Opacity slider to temper the effect.

Soft Light. While most people describe the Soft Light blending
mode as shining a soft spotlight on the background color, we like to
think of this mode in terms of playing with semi-translucent colored
acetate. Soft Light has no effect if the background color is black or
white, but it subtly enhances any other color, making darker colors

(in either the foreground or background) a little darker and lighter colors a little lighter.

Hard Light. The Hard Light mode is something like two blending modes in one: If the foreground color is lighter than 50-percent gray, the Hard Light mode lightens the background color similar to the Screen mode; if the foreground color is darker than 50-percent gray, it darkens it using a method similar to the Multiply mode.

Color Dodge and Color Burn. Color Dodge both lightens and slightly colorizes with the foreground color. Color Burn colorizes while darkening the background. We find it's hard to predict the result with either of these, especially because you'll see radically different effects depending on whether your Transparency Blend Space is set to RGB or CMYK.

Darken. The resulting color is equal to the darker of the foreground and background colors.

Lighten. The resulting color is equal to the lighter of the foreground and background colors.

Hue. The Hue blending mode creates a new color by blending the color of the foreground object with the luminance (brightness) and saturation of the background. Putting a black object set to Hue over a colored object simply desaturates the background colors.

Saturation. The Saturation mode creates a new color by blending the foreground color's saturation and the hue (color) with luminance values of the background color.

Color. The Color mode is slightly different from the Hue mode; it combines the color and the saturation of the foreground color with the luminance of the background color. Placing a solid color set to Color over an image colorizes the image, like a fake duotone.

Luminosity. Luminosity creates a new color by blending the brightness of the foreground color with the hue and saturation of the background color.

Transparency Options   So what about those options at the bottom of the Effects panel? The meaning of the terms "Isolate Blending" and "Knockout Group" is hardly self evident. Both options apply only to groups.

FIGURE 5-50
Isolate Blending

The selected group contains three circles. Each circle is filled with Black, set to 50% transparency, and uses the Multiply blending mode.

The triangle is outside and behind the group.

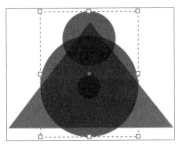

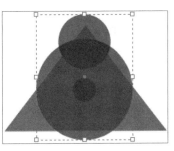

With Isolate Blending turned off, the foreground colors blend with the background colors according to their blending modes.

Turn Isolate Blending on, and InDesign changes the way that the foreground colors interact with the background colors.

FIGURE 5-51
Knockout Group

The selected group contains three circles. Each circle is filled with Black, set to 50% transparency, and uses the Multiply blending mode.

The triangle is outside and behind the group.

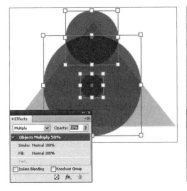

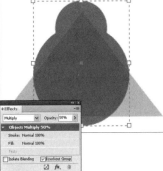

With Knockout Group turned off, the objects inside the group affect each other.

After we group the objects together, we turn on Knockout Group. The objects in the group become opaque to each other, but are still transparent to any background objects.

Isolate Blending. When you turn on the Isolate Blending option, and objects in the group you've selected use blending modes other than the Normal blending mode, InDesign changes the way that the object in the group interacts with objects behind the group. Regardless of the blending mode you've assigned to the group objects, InDesign treats them as if the Normal blending mode were assigned. *Inside* the group, blending modes behave as you specified (see Figure 5-50).

Knockout Group. When you select a group containing transparent objects and turn on the Knockout Group option, InDesign makes the objects in the group opaque to each other (see Figure 5-51). In other words, the option should really be named "Knockout Objects Inside the Group," but there's not room in the panel. Objects *outside* the group are treated according to the state of the Isolate Blending

FIGURE 5-52
Applying Transparency
to a Group

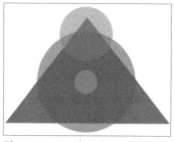

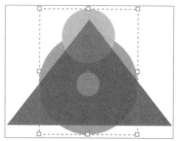

Three ungrouped circles, each filled with a different tint of Black and set to 50% transparency (with the Normal blend mode).

Here the three circles have no transparency. Instead, they've been grouped and the 50% transparency has been applied to the group.

option (see above). And yes, it is possible to have both Isolate Blending and Knockout Group turned on.

Groups and
Transparency

There's a difference between applying transparency to a group and applying transparency to the objects inside a group (see Figure 5-52). When you apply transparency to a group, InDesign will override the transparency settings for any objects in the group that have no transparency applied to them, but leaves transparent objects unchanged.

Unfortunately, any transparency settings applied to a group are lost if or when you ungroup the objects.

Transparency Effects

What is it about drop shadows, bevels, and glows? Does everyone want their page items to appear as if they are the highly mobile space battleship *Nadesico*, floating defiantly above the page? We're not sure, but we do know that these ubiquitous two-dimensional impersonations of three-dimensional space are something no graphic designer will leave home without—at least until clients stop asking for them.

Fortunately, InDesign lets you apply all of these effects to page items (text, frames, imported images, and so on), plus a half-dozen more, including Satin, Inner Shadow, and three different kinds of feathering. You can find them hiding in the Effects panel, the Effects submenu (under the Context menu or the Object menu), or the Effects pop-up menu in the Control panel.

Moreover, you can apply each of InDesign's effects to an entire object or just its stroke, fill, or—in the case of a text frame—text. For example, you could apply a Bevel and Emboss effect to a frame's fill color and a drop shadow to the text inside that frame.

FIGURE 5-53
Transparency Effects

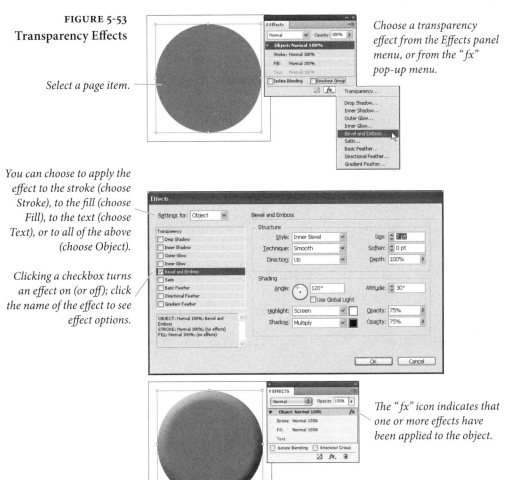

Select a page item.

Choose a transparency effect from the Effects panel menu, or from the "fx" pop-up menu.

You can choose to apply the effect to the stroke (choose Stroke), to the fill (choose Fill), to the text (choose Text), or to all of the above (choose Object).

Clicking a checkbox turns an effect on (or off); click the name of the effect to see effect options.

The "fx" icon indicates that one or more effects have been applied to the object.

Once again, we find ourselves wanting to shout out, "with power comes responsibility." Just because you can apply effects to everything in sight doesn't mean you should. Remember that overuse of effects can cause blindness and itchy palms.

Here's how to apply an effect to an object (see Figure 5-53):

1. Select an object with the Selection or Direct Selection tool. (To apply an effect to an image separate from its frame, click on the image itself with the Direct Selection tool.)

2. In either the Effects panel or the Control panel, choose what aspect of the object you want to affect: Stroke, Fill, Text, or Object (to apply the effect to the whole enchilada).

3. Choose the effect you want from either the Effects ("fx") pop-up menu in the Effects panel or Control panel, or from the Effects submenu (in the Object or Context menu). Alternately, you can simply double-click on the Object, Stroke, Fill, or Text section of the Effect panel that you chose in Step 2.

4. You can adjust the settings for that effect in the Effects dialog box. You can also add more than one effect to the object's stroke, fill, or text by clicking on the checkboxes and panes along the left edge of the dialog box, and by choosing from the "Settings for" pop-up menu.

5. Turn on the Preview checkbox to see the effect while the dialog box is still open, or click OK to accept the changes.

Note that if you apply an effect to the whole object, and it's a text frame with a fill of None, InDesign applies the effect to the text inside the frame. Give the frame an opaque fill to affect the frame itself.

Drop Shadows   The most popular (by far) transparency effect in InDesign's arsenal is the drop shadow. It's so common that Adobe even added a Drop Shadow button in the Control panel. Just select an object and click the button and a default drop shadow is applied (see "Setting Defaults," later in this section).

Alternately, you can use the Effects dialog box to control the shadow's position, color, transparency, noise, and size (see Figure 5-54). Most of the controls are self-explanatory, but here are some things to keep in mind.

▶ The Mode pop-up menu sets the transparency blending mode for the drop shadow. We've described all of the useful blending modes in the section on Transparency, above. The Multiply blending mode works well with drop shadows.

▶ You can define the color of the drop shadow by clicking on the small color swatch to the right of the Mode pop-up menu. The Opacity field defines the darkest part of the shadow.

▶ You can control the position of the shadow in two ways: Either by adjusting the Angle and Distance fields or by changing the X Offset and Y Offset fields. If you want all your drop shadows to have the same angle, turn on the Use Global Light checkbox. Later, to change the global light setting, just change it anywhere in the Effects dialog box, or choose Global Light from the Effect panel menu.

FIGURE 5-54

Applying a Drop Shadow

Display performance settings have a big effect on the way that InDesign displays drop shadows, but not on how they print; that's up to the transparency flattener.

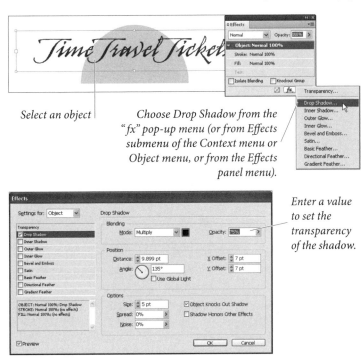

Select an object

Choose Drop Shadow from the "fx" pop-up menu (or from Effects submenu of the Context menu or Object menu, or from the Effects panel menu).

Typical Display

High Quality Display

Enter a value to set the transparency of the shadow.

Click the OK button, and InDesign applies the drop shadow.

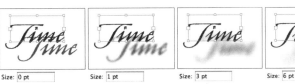

FIGURE 5-55

Size and Spread

Size: 0 pt   Size: 1 pt   Size: 3 pt   Size: 6 pt

Enter a value in the Size field to control the diffusion of the drop shadow. Entering zero produces a hard-edged (but still bitmapped) shadow.

Entering a large Size value would make the shadow disappear altogether for this 24-point example text.

Increasing the Spread value makes the shadow more dense.

Size: 3 pt   Size: 3 pt   Size: 6 pt
Spread: 10%   Spread: 40%   Spread: 70%

FIGURE 5-56
Shadow Noise

▶ A hard-edged shadow is probably not what you were looking for—what you need is a way to soften the edges of the shadow so that it looks more realistic. That's exactly what the Size field does (see Figure 5-55).

▶ The Spread field controls the intensity of the shadow. Technically, it controls how far out from the center of the shadow the darkest portion of the shadow will sit. Choosing 50 percent means the darkest area of the shadow takes up half the size of the shadow.

▶ If you want a more realistic shadow (instead of a mathematically pure one), bump up the Noise field a little bit—just 4 or 5 percent noise makes a huge difference (see Figure 5-56). Noise values above 30 or 40 percent are mostly good for special grunge effects.

▶ If your object is partially transparent, you'll be able to see your drop shadow underneath it. If that doesn't appeal to you, turn on the Object Knocks Out Shadow checkbox—this ensures that the drop shadow is removed from behind the object itself.

▶ If you've used other effects on your object—such as a Directional Feather that blurs out one side of the shape—you can control whether or not the drop shadow will apply to the object itself (as though there were no other effects applied) or the object plus the effect. If you want the latter, turn on the Shadow Honors Other Effects checkbox.

Inner Shadow   The Inner Shadow effect is identical to the Drop Shadow effect except that the shadow is drawn inside the object rather than outside of it. The result looks like the object is set behind the rest of the page. Note that the Effects dialog box settings contains a field labeled Choke; it

FIGURE 5-57
Inner Shadow

Original text frame   *Inner Shadow*

**FIGURE 5-58
Outer and Inner Glow**

*Outer Glow (blending mode: Screen)   Inner Glow (blending mode:
applied to the text*   Multiply) applied to text and fill*

**FIGURE 5-59
Bevel and Emboss**

Outer Bevel (Direction: Up)   *Outer Bevel (Direction: Down)*

*Here the effect is applied to
both the Text and the Fill.*

Inner Bevel (Direction: Up)   *Inner Bevel (Direction: Down)*

Emboss (Direction: Up)   *Emboss (Direction: Down)*

Pillow Emboss (Direction: Up)   *Pillow Emboss (Direction: Down)*

does essentially the same thing as Spread: It controls the position of the darkest part of the shadow (see Figure 5-57).

Outer and Inner Glow

In early versions of InDesign, we used to make glows around objects by making a drop shadow with the horizontal and vertical offset set to zero. It's easier to just use the Outer Glow feature (see Figure 5-58).

InDesign also offers an Inner Glow effect which sets the glow inside the object rather than around it, while retaining a sharp vector edge.

Bevel and Emboss   For the ultimate in faux three-dimensionality, consider applying the Bevel and Emboss effect to an object (see Figure 5-59). InDesign offers four types of effect in the Style pop-up menu: Inner Bevel, Outer Bevel, Emboss, and Pillow Emboss. The last three in this list affect the area around the object, and in fact look pretty dumb unless your object is sitting on top of some other object or image. Inner Bevel can stand on its own if need be.

Satin   The Satin effect is supposed to make your objects look as though wrapped in satin. While the equivalent feature in Photoshop can result in a cool look, the implementation in InDesign leaves much to be desired and we usually just ignore it. The one time it seems to create interesting effects is when applied to colored text. The reason: It needs a complex-shaped object to create a complex shaped texture.

Feathering   The usual definition of feathering goes something like this: "feathering softens the edges of page items." This isn't really quite true. A better description is that feathering blends an object to transparency. Since you cannot currently include transparency in a normal gradient swatch, feathering is extremely useful.

InDesign has three types of feathering: Basic Feather, Directional Feather, and Gradient Feather.

Basic Feather. The Basic Feather effect is identical to the feature called "Feathering" in earlier versions of InDesign. It applies the same feather (fade to transparency) on all sides of an object. Basic Feather offers four basic settings:

▶ Width sets the distance from the edges of the object at which the feathering will take effect (see Figure 5-60).

▶ Choke controls how far in the fully transparent portion of the feather area will sit. Choosing 50 percent means the transparent area takes up half the size of the feather (based on Width).

▶ The options on the Corners pop-up menu control the appearance of the feathering effect as it approaches sharp corners at the edges of the object (see Figure 5-61). When you choose Sharp, the feathering effect follows the outline of the path as closely as possible. When you choose Rounded, InDesign rounds the edges of the feather effect as it nears sharp corners. The Diffused

FIGURE 5-60
Basic Feather

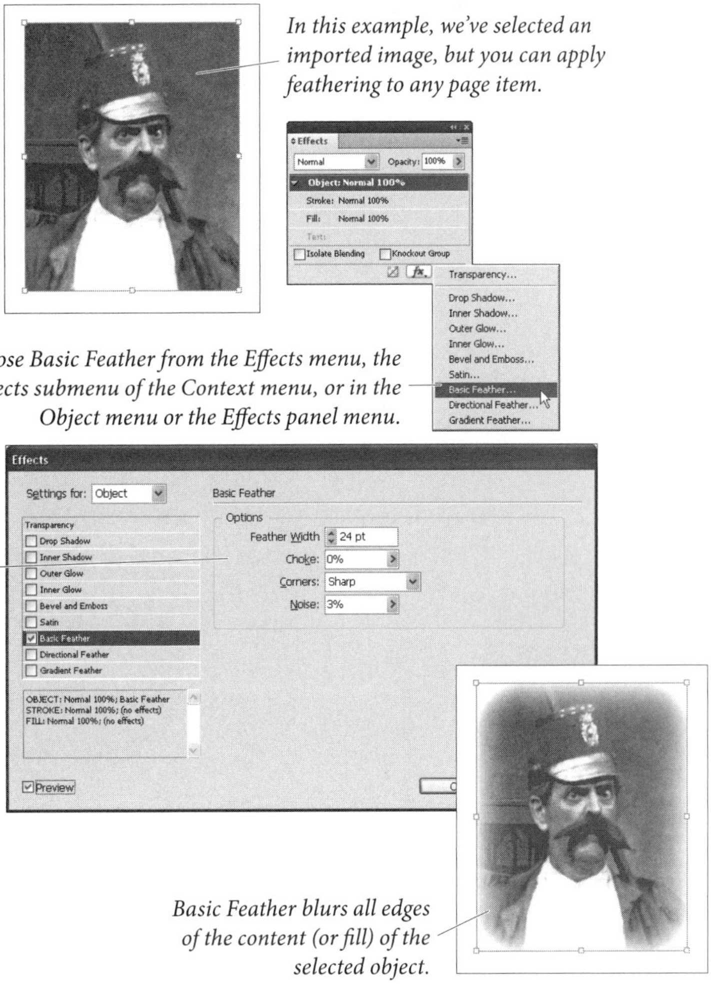

In this example, we've selected an imported image, but you can apply feathering to any page item.

Choose Basic Feather from the Effects menu, the Effects submenu of the Context menu, or in the Object menu or the Effects panel menu.

Use these controls to set up the basic feather effect.

Basic Feather blurs all edges of the content (or fill) of the selected object.

option provides a general fade from opaque to transparent, based on the geometric center of the object, rather than on the shape of the path (as is the case for the Sharp and Rounded options). This is similar to the feathering effect in Illustrator.

▶ Adding a little Noise to your feather (such as four or five percent) makes the effect significantly more realistic, especially if you're blending an object into a photographic background.

Directional Feather. What if you want a feather to appear on one side of a shape—such as an image that fades out to transparency along its bottom edge? That's when the Directional Feather effect comes in handy, letting you adjust how much feathering you want on

FIGURE 5-61
Feather Corner Options

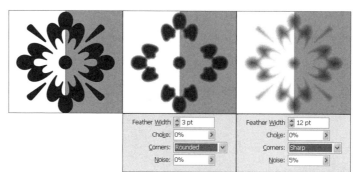

The edges of the Diffused corner option fade from opaque to transparent.

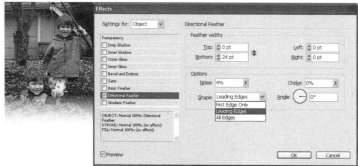

FIGURE 5-62
Directional Feather

Directional Feather is a great way to fade an image or object to transparency.

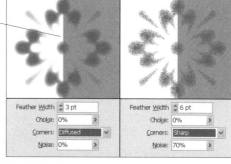

These three objects have 9 points of Directional Feather applied to their Right side.

First Edge Only   Leading Edges   All Edges

each side of your object. It offers some of the same settings as Basic Feather—such as Noise and Choke—but has three of its own options:

FIGURE 5-63
Gradient Feather

To apply an effect to an image inside a frame (but not to the frame or stroke itself), first select the image with the Direct Selection tool.

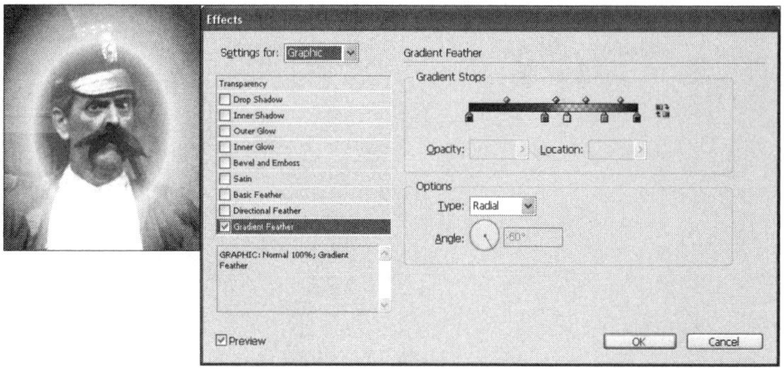

▶ **Feather widths.** To adjust the size of the feathering along the Top, Bottom, Left, and Right edges of your object independently, make sure you turn off the little chain button.

▶ **Shape.** The Shape pop-up menu lets you control what portion of your object gets feathered: First Edge Only, Leading Edges, or All Edges. In a rectangle, these all look the same. But in a non-rectangular shape, the choice makes a huge difference (see Figure 5-62).

▶ **Angle.** The Angle determines what InDesign considers to be "top," "right," and so on. Set this to 45 degrees and the feather is rotated so that the Top Feather width is actually referring to the object's upper-left corner. Rotate it 180 degrees and "top" becomes "bottom," and so on.

Gradient Feather. The Gradient Feather effect is like using a linear or radial gradient as a transparency mask—you can set a start point, end point, and transparency "stop points" anywhere else along the gradient. To set the opacity at a point along the gradient, click the stop point and choose an Opacity value (see Figure 5-63).

You can create a new stop point by clicking under the gradient bar; you can adjust the midpoint between two stops by dragging the diamond shaped icon along the top of the bar. You can specify a Linear or Radial gradient from the Type pop-up menu. And of course if it's a Linear gradient, you can rotate it in the Angle field.

Curiously, Adobe forgot to add a Noise field in this type of feather, so these blends are often too squeaky clean.

Making Blurry Text   If you try applying a feather to some text or any other object on your page in order to make it "ghostly" or "blurry" you'll be sorely disappointed. Instead, try this trick that our friend Matt Phillips taught us:

FIGURE 5-64
Blurry Objects

*The original text frame
on top of a gray frame*

*The text colored Paper,
set to Multiply, and given
a drop shadow that isn't
knocked out by the object.*

Fill your object (or text) with the Paper color, set the blending mode to Multiply (which makes the Paper color disappear), and apply a drop shadow effect. Make sure that you turn off the Object Knocks Out Shadow checkbox in the Effects dialog box (see Figure 5-64).

This technique sometimes looks odd on screen when the object is sitting on a paper background, instead of on top of another object. Turn on Overprint Preview from the View menu, or export as PDF, or print, it should look great.

Copying Effects

You've spent 20 minutes getting your effects to look just right, but now you need to apply the same effects to another object. Here's a cool way to copy effects from one object to another on the same spread: Select the object that has the effects you want, then drag the little "fx" icon from the Effects panel and drop it on another object.

You can also drag the "fx" icon from one item in the Effects panel to another. If you applied a drop shadow to Object but intended to only apply it to Text, you can drag the icon down to Text.

If you're going to be using the same effects throughout your document, use object styles (see Chapter 6, "Where Text Meets Graphics").

**Editing or
Removing Effects**

To remove an effect, open the Effects dialog box and turn off the checkbox next to the effect. To remove all the effects quickly, choose Clear Effects from the Effects panel menu. To remove all the effects and any opacity or blending modes applied to your selected object, choose Clear Transparency from the same menu.

Drawing Conclusions

Earlier in this chapter, we noted that we found the process of creating a path using Bezier drawing tools confusing, at first. After extensive research involving a tabloid newspaper and far too much coffee, we discovered that drawing itself is nothing less than an extraterrestrial plot, forced on us in classical antiquity by evil space gods, to some cosmic purpose which we cannot—as yet—reveal.

Where Text Meets Graphics

Ole laments, "I haven't looked at the PageMaker 3.0 documentation recently. I don't have to—it is forever burned into my memory.

"A feature of that manual's design was a rule drawn below a particular, and very common, heading. I know this, because I was one of the four people who put those rules there. For every one of those headings, one of us had to zoom in, measure from the baseline of the text in the heading, position a ruler guide, and then draw a rule. When the position of the heading changed, as it often did, we had to zoom in again, measure again, and move or redraw the rules.

"I still dream about it."

The solution to Ole's nightmare lies in associating a graphic with text, which lies in the shadowy realm where text meets graphics—a Twilight Zone, something like a Bermuda Triangle of page layout—where the boundary between text and graphics blurs, frays, or becomes thin.

In this strange dimension, text characters can be bound to paths, or become paths, graphics can be embedded in text and behave as if they were text characters, and nothing, nothing is what it seems.

In spite of the repeated warnings of our scientific colleagues, we must, for the sake of humanity, tell what we have discovered in this alien landscape.

Paragraph Rules

Paragraph rules are the solution to the problem implicit in Ole's above reminiscence. Paragraph rules (or "lines") can be part of your paragraph's formatting (or, better yet, part of a paragraph style definition), and follow your paragraph wherever it happens to go.

Applying Paragraph Rules

To apply a paragraph rule, follow these steps (see Figure 6-1):

1. Select the paragraph (remember, you don't need to highlight the entire paragraph—all you need to do is click the Type tool somewhere inside the paragraph).

2. Choose Paragraph Rules from the Paragraph panel menu (or press Command-Option-J/Ctrl-Alt-J). InDesign displays the Paragraph Rules dialog box.

3. Choose the type of paragraph rule (Rule Above or Rule Below) from the Rule Type pop-up menu, then turn on the Rule On option.

4. Set the rule options you want using the controls in the panel. If you turn on the Preview option, you can watch InDesign apply the paragraph rule to the paragraph as you adjust the settings.

5. Click OK to apply the paragraph rule settings to the selected paragraph, or click Cancel to close the dialog box without applying the rule.

Ground Rules for Paragraph Rules

Paragraphs can have up to two rules attached to them. The position of one rule set relative to the baseline of the first line of text in a paragraph (InDesign calls this the "Rule Above"); the position of the other line is relative to the baseline of the last line of the paragraph (the "Rule Below"). Note that these rule positions specify only the starting point of the rule—by manipulating the rule width, it's easy to create a rule below that extends far above the baseline, or a rule above that extends far below the baseline of the last line.

You can't select or manipulate paragraph rules using the Selection tool or the Direct Selection tool. Everyone tries this at least once.

Weight and Style. Paragraph rules, like any other paths you can draw in InDesign, can be up to 1000 points wide, and the stroke width can be specified in .001-point increments. Like other paths you can use dotted, dashed, or multi-line (striped) strokes, including custom stroke styles you've created.

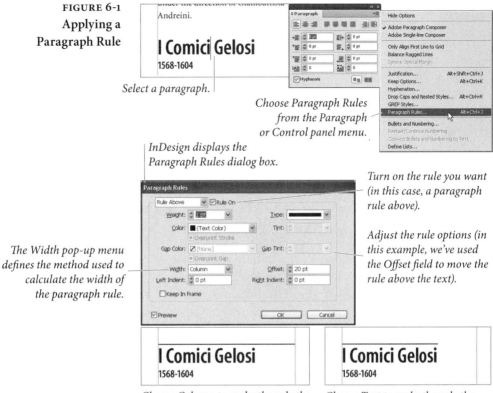

FIGURE 6-1

Applying a Paragraph Rule

Select a paragraph.

Choose Paragraph Rules from the Paragraph or Control panel menu.

InDesign displays the Paragraph Rules dialog box.

The Width pop-up menu defines the method used to calculate the width of the paragraph rule.

Turn on the rule you want (in this case, a paragraph rule above).

Adjust the rule options (in this example, we've used the Offset field to move the rule above the text).

Choose Column to make the rule the width of the column containing the paragraph.

Choose Text to make the rule the width of the text in the first line of the paragraph.

Position. A Rule Above grows *up* (that is, toward the top of the text frame) from the position you specify in the Offset field in the Paragraph Rules dialog box. A Rule Below grows *down* (toward the bottom of the text frame) as you increase its stroke weight. InDesign draws paragraph rules *behind* the text in the text frame.

Ordinarily, the position of a rule has no effect on the vertical spacing of text. If you want to make room above a paragraph for a paragraph rule above, or below a paragraph for a rule below, you should probably use Space Before and Space After.

If a rule is above the first paragraph of a text frame or below the last frame, it normally just sticks out—that is, InDesign allows these rules to sit outside the frame. However, if you turn on the Keep in Frame checkbox, InDesign forces rules to stay inside the frame and moves the text inside the frame instead. (The one exception is when First Baseline Offset is set to Fixed; in that case, Keep in Frame appears to be ignored.)

Width. You can base the width of a paragraph rule on the width of the text column or on the width of the text in the first (for paragraph rules above) or last (for rules below) line of the paragraph. Paragraph rules can also be indented from either the width of the column or the width of the text—the value you enter in the Left Indent and Right Indent fields of the Paragraph Rules dialog box determines the indent distance. You can even make paragraph rules extend beyond the width of the text or column by entering negative numbers in the Left Indent and Right Indent fields.

Tinting Paragraphs

When you want to put a tint behind a paragraph (which you might want to do for a sidebar, a line in a table, or for a note or warning paragraph in your text), consider creating the effect with paragraph rules—provided, of course, that your paragraph isn't taller than 1000 points or so (the maximum paragraph rule width) and the paragraph fits inside a single text frame or text column. (When you want to put a tint behind a character, word, or line, however, you'll be better off using custom strikethrough rules and/or underlines.)

To use a paragraph rule to add a tint behind a paragraph, follow these steps (see Figure 6-2).

1. Calculate the height of the paragraph by adding up the leading of the lines in the paragraph.

FIGURE 6-2
**Placing a Tint Behind
a Paragraph**

Select a paragraph.

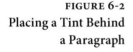

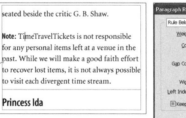

*Display the Paragraph Rules dialog box
and add a rule below.*

*Make the stroke weight of the rule at least equal to
the sum of the leading of the lines in the paragraph.*

Move the rule up or down by entering values in the Offset field (we usually start with the stroke weight, then add or subtract smaller values to fine-tune the rule position).

2. Select the paragraph, then use the Paragraph Rules dialog box to apply a paragraph rule below. Use the Weight field to set the stroke width of the rule to at least the height of the paragraph.

3. Use the Color pop-up menu to set the color of the rule.

4. Enter a value in the Offset field to move the paragraph rule up or down behind the paragraph (remember, a negative value in the Offset field moves a paragraph rule below toward the top of the paragraph).

5. When the paragraph rule looks the way you want it to, click the OK button to apply it to the selected paragraph.

There are all kinds of paragraph rule tricks. Figure 6-3 shows a method of adding a tint behind a hanging heading.

By the way, when you work with a paragraph rule that extends beyond the boundaries of a text frame, InDesign sometimes forgets to redraw the rule as you edit text in the frame. To see the rule or rules again, press Shift-F5 to redraw the screen.

FIGURE 6-3
Hanging Headings
and Paragraph Rules

Set the text color of the heading to "Paper."

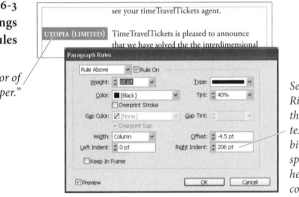

Set the value in the Right Indent field to the width of the body text column (plus a bit, if you want some space between the heading and the body copy).

Two Rules Above   What can you do when your design calls for two rules above your paragraph? A common design specification calls for two rules above a heading: a thin rule the width of the column and a thick rule the width of the text in the heading. How can you accomplish this? It's easy, as shown in the following steps (see Figure 6-4).

1. Select a paragraph.

2. For the rule below, choose Column from the Width pop-up menu, then enter a negative value in the Offset field to position the rule above the tops of the characters in the first line (this will be something like the sum of the leading in the paragraph). Set the line weight to a hairline (.25 points) or so.

FIGURE 6-4
Thick/Thin Rule Above

For the paragraph Rule Above...

...choose Text from the Width pop-up menu...

For the paragraph Rule Below (which we're going to place above the paragraph—don't get confused)...

...enter a thin stroke weight (such as a hairline)...

...choose Column from the Width pop-up menu...

When you change the text in the first line, InDesign changes the width of the thicker rule.

...enter a thick stroke weight...

...and set the offset to the leading value minus the stroke weight.

...and set the offset to the leading value of all of the lines in the paragraph (there's only one in this example).

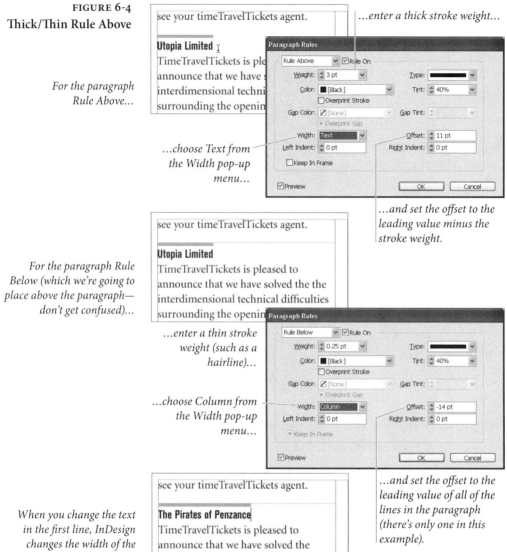

3. For the rule above, choose Text from the Width pop-up menu, then set the stroke weight of the paragraph rule to something thicker than the stroke weight of the rule below (4 points, for example). Set the value in the Offset field so that the top edge of the rule above touches the bottom of the rule below.

When you need to attach more than two rules above or below a paragraph, enter extra carriage returns before or after the paragraph, then apply paragraph rules to the resulting "blank" paragraphs.

Tables

Tables are a great way to present information that falls naturally into a set sequence of categories. InDesign can create and edit tables, or import tables from Word, Excel, or XML. This feature isn't perfect, but it's more than good enough to alleviate most of the pain of working with tables in a layout.

Table Anatomy

Tables are a matrix; a grid made up of *rows* (horizontal subdivisions) and *columns* (vertical subdivisions). The area defined by the intersection of a given row and column is called a *cell*. InDesign has a complete vocabulary of terms for the various parts of rows, columns, and cells, which we've attempted to explain in Figure 6-5.

Understanding InDesign Tables

Now that we've got the terminology out of the way, but before we dive into the details of working with tables in InDesign, there are a few conceptual points we'd like to make, as follows.

▶ Tables exist inside text frames. There is no "Table tool"—you create a text frame and then add a table to it, or convert text in the text frame to a table.

▶ A table acts like a single character (albeit a potentially *very large* one). Another way to look at a table is to think of it as a special

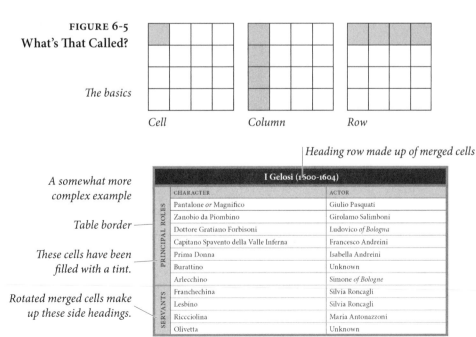

FIGURE 6-5
What's That Called?

The basics

Cell   Column   Row

Heading row made up of merged cells

A somewhat more complex example

Table border

These cells have been filled with a tint.

Rotated merged cells make up these side headings.

I Gelosi (1500-1604)	
CHARACTER	ACTOR
Pantalone *or* Magnifico	Giulio Pasquati
Zanobio da Piombino	Girolamo Salimboni
Dottore Gratiano Forbisoni	Ludovico *of Bologna*
Capitano Spavento della Valle Inferna	Francesco Andreini
Prima Donna	Isabella Andreini
Burattino	Unknown
Arlecchino	Simone *of Bologne*
Franchechina	Silvia Roncagli
Lesbino	Silvia Roncagli
Riccciolina	Maria Antonazzoni
Olivetta	Unknown

PRINCIPAL ROLES / SERVANTS

type of inline frame. Like a character, a table changes position as you add or delete text preceding it in its parent story; like an inline frame, you can't apply character formatting (point size, font, or leading) to the character containing the table.

▶ Like text, tables can flow from column to column, text frame to text frame, and from page to page. Table header and footer rows can automatically repeat when the table breaks across multiple text objects. An individual table row cannot be broken from one text frame to another or from one column to another.

▶ Table cells are something akin to text frames: they can contain text, which can contain inline graphics, text frames, or tables. Any and all of InDesign's typesetting features can be used on the text in a table cell, including character and paragraph styles, indents, tab stops, and character formatting.

▶ Tables are not only for formatting tabular data—they're also useful for a number of other things. Want to put a box around a paragraph? Convert the paragraph to a single-cell table. Want to compose paragraphs "side by side"? Use a two-column table.

Creating a Table

There are (at least) four ways to create a table.

▶ **"From scratch."** Click the Type tool inside a text frame, then choose Insert Table from the Table menu. In the Insert Table dialog box, enter the number of rows and columns you want and click OK. InDesign creates the table (see Figure 6-6).

   Once you've created a table using this approach, you can add text or graphics to the table the same way you would add text to any text frame—click the Type tool inside a cell, then enter text, or paste text or graphics, or place text or graphics into the cell.

▶ **Converting Text to a Table.** To turn a range of text into a table, select the text and choose Convert Text to Table from the Table menu. In the Convert Text to Table dialog box, select the delimiter characters you want to use, and specify the number of columns, if necessary. InDesign will only display this field when it cannot determine the number of columns in the table, given the specified delimiter characters. Click OK, and InDesign converts the selected text to a table, using the delimiter characters to split the text into table rows and columns (see Figure 6-7).

FIGURE 6-6
Creating a Table
"From Scratch"

Click the Type tool in a text frame, then choose Insert Table from the Table menu (or press Command-Option-Shift-T/Ctrl-Alt-Shift-T).

InDesign displays the Insert Table dialog box. Enter the number of rows and columns you want and click OK.

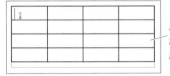

InDesign inserts the table into the text frame.

▶ **Importing a Table.** Another way to create a table is to import a table you've saved in a Word, Excel, or RTF document. There's no trick to this—select a file containing a table in the Place Document dialog box and place it, just as you'd place any other type of file. If there is a table in the document, InDesign will convert it to an InDesign table as you flow the text onto a page.

▶ **Pasting a table.** You can also copy and paste tables from Word and Excel—just select the table, then copy, return to InDesign, and paste. However, this only works if you first change the Paste option in the Clipboard Handling pane of the Preferences dialog box to All Information. The default setting (Text Only) tells InDesign to paste the data as text, with tabs between columns.

In theory, you can also copy tables from HTML pages displayed in a web browser. However, not all HTML tables seem to convert, nor are the results identical from browser to browser. It won't work unless your browser copies the table to the system clipboard as RTF. (David cannot get this to work at all.)

When you create a table, InDesign sets the width of the table to the width of the text frame. But you're not limited to that width—InDesign tables can be narrower or wider than their containing text frame. As you'd expect, tables take on the alignment of the paragraph containing them (though the text inside the table can be of any alignment). To change the position of the table in (or relative to) the text frame, change the paragraph alignment.

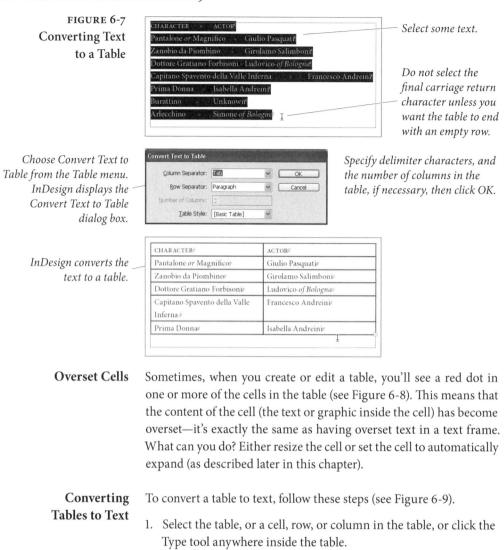

FIGURE 6-7
Converting Text to a Table

Select some text.

Do not select the final carriage return character unless you want the table to end with an empty row.

Choose Convert Text to Table from the Table menu. InDesign displays the Convert Text to Table dialog box.

Specify delimiter characters, and the number of columns in the table, if necessary, then click OK.

InDesign converts the text to a table.

Overset Cells

Sometimes, when you create or edit a table, you'll see a red dot in one or more of the cells in the table (see Figure 6-8). This means that the content of the cell (the text or graphic inside the cell) has become overset—it's exactly the same as having overset text in a text frame. What can you do? Either resize the cell or set the cell to automatically expand (as described later in this chapter).

Converting Tables to Text

To convert a table to text, follow these steps (see Figure 6-9).

1. Select the table, or a cell, row, or column in the table, or click the Type tool anywhere inside the table.

2. Choose Convert Table to Text from the Table menu. InDesign displays the Convert Table to Text dialog box.

3. Enter the delimiter characters you want to use, if necessary, then click the OK button. InDesign converts the table to text.

FIGURE 6-8
Overset Cell

The dot (you have to imagine it in red) indicates that the cell content is overset.

Editing Tables

Once you've created a table, you can't just sit and *admire* it (as tempting as that might be for longtime page layout users); you've got to *do something* with it.

Before we talk about that, though, we'd better lay down a few ground rules about cells, rows, and columns.

- A column is always the width of the widest cell in the column. When you change the width of a cell, you're really changing the width of the column containing the cell.
- A row is always the height of the tallest cell in the row. Just as changing the width of a cell changes the width of a column, so altering the height of a cell changes the height of a row.
- In spite of the above restrictions, you can create tables containing cells that are wider than their parent columns or taller than their parent rows. You do this by merging cells, which we'll discuss later, in "Merging Cells."

Selecting and Editing Table Items

To select elements in a table, or to edit a table's content (text, rows, or columns), click the Type tool in one of the cells of the table. This activates InDesign's table tools. Once you've done this, you can enter

FIGURE 6-9
Converting a Table to Text

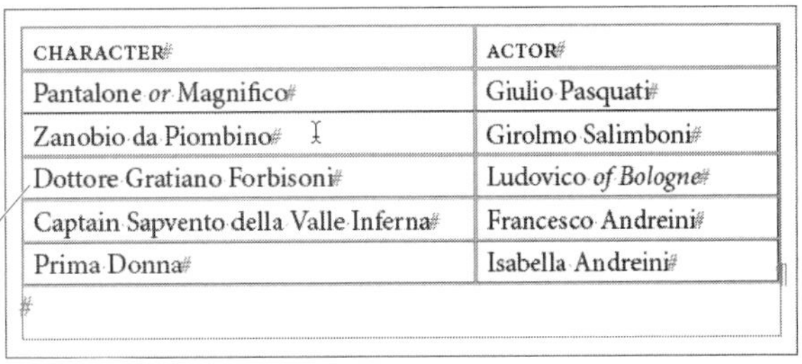
CHARACTER
ACTOR
Pantalone or Magnifico
Giulio Pasquati
Zanobio da Piombino
Girolmo Salimboni
Dottore Gratiano Forbisoni
Ludovico of Bologne
Captain Sapvento della Valle Inferna
Francesco Andreini
Prima Donna
Isabella Andreini

Select a table, row, column, or cell, or click the Type tool inside a cell in the table you want to convert.

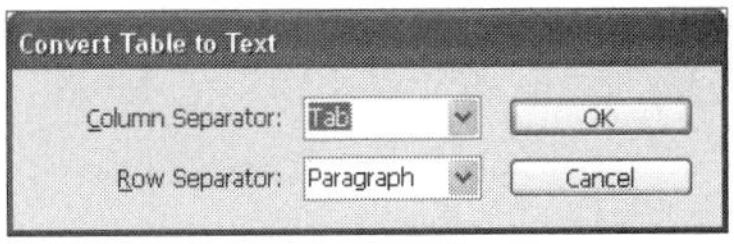
Convert Table to Text
Column Separator: Tab
Row Separator: Paragraph
OK
Cancel

Choose Convert Table to Text from the Table menu. InDesign displays the Convert Table to Text dialog box.

Specify delimiter characters, if necessary, then click OK.

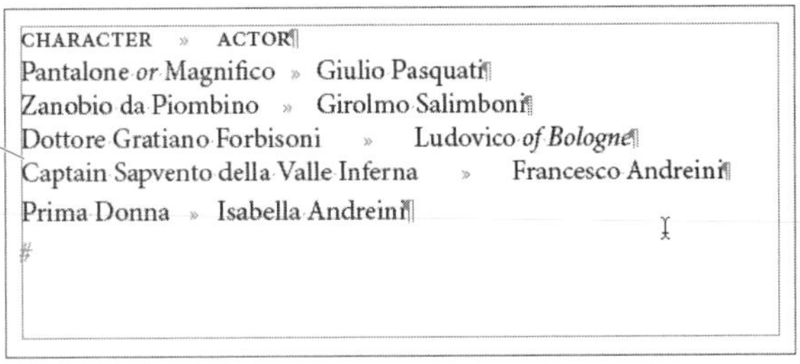
CHARACTER » ACTOR
Pantalone or Magnifico » Giulio Pasquati
Zanobio da Piombino » Girolmo Salimboni
Dottore Gratiano Forbisoni » Ludovico of Bologne
Captain Sapvento della Valle Inferna » Francesco Andreini
Prima Donna » Isabella Andreini

InDesign converts the table to text, separating the rows and columns with the delimiter characters you specified.

and edit text in the cell, paste or place text or graphics in the cell, or even create another table inside the cell.

It's easy to tell when you're in this mode, because the cursor changes shape as you position it above cell, row, column, and table boundaries. What do these different cursors mean? What can you do with these tools? To find out, take a look at Table 6-1.

In addition, the Context menu changes to display options related to working with tables (see Figure 6-10).

To select a range of cells, drag the text cursor through them. You cannot select non-contiguous cells. Note that dragging the cursor through multiple cells selects *all* of the text in the cells, regardless of the starting or ending position of the cursor.

To select a row, position the cursor above the left edge of the first cell in the row, then click; for a column, move the cursor above the top of the first cell in the column, then click (see Figure 6-11).

You select text inside a table cell using the same methods you use to select text in a text frame: Use the Type tool.

Entering Tab Characters

How the heck can you enter a tab character in a table cell? When you press Tab, InDesign moves the cursor to the next cell in the table (see "Table Shortcuts," later in this chapter). If the cursor is in the last cell of the table, pressing Tab creates a new table row. Either way, you don't get the character you're looking for.

To enter a tab character, choose Tab from the Other submenu in the Insert Special Character submenu of the Context menu (or, if you're using the Mac OS, press Option-Tab).

Pasting Data Into Tables

You can paste data into a table, but before you choose Paste from the Edit menu (or press Command-V/Ctrl-V) pay attention to what's selected. If the text cursor is flashing inside a cell when you paste, InDesign pastes all the data into that one cell. If you select the cell itself (press Esc to toggle between selecting what's inside the cell and the cell itself), and if the data you're pasting has tabs or carriage returns in it, InDesign maps the clipboard data across more than one cell. If you need to update the data from an Excel document that you've turned into an InDesign table, you can copy the cells in Excel, switch to InDesign, select one or more cells in your table, and paste.

Placing a Graphic in a Table Cell

You place a graphic in a table cell in exactly the same fashion as you insert a graphic in text: click the Type tool in a cell, or select some text inside a cell, then place a file or paste a graphic you copied to the Clipboard earlier (see Figure 6-12). Note that you must select text or

TABLE 6-1
Table Editing Cursors

When you see:	Your cursor is:	And you can:
↘	Above the top-left corner of the table	Click to select the table.
→	Above the left edge of a row	Click to select the row.
↓	Above the top of a column	Click to select the column.
↔	Above the right or left edge of a cell	Drag to resize the column containing the cell.
↕	Above the top or bottom of a cell	Drag to resize the row containing the cell.

FIGURE 6-10
Context Menu Options for Working with Tables

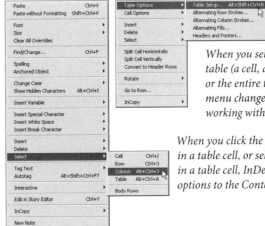

When you select an item in a table (a cell, a row, a column, or the entire table), the Context menu changes to offer options for working with the selected item.

When you click the Type tool in a table cell, or select text in a table cell, InDesign adds options to the Context menu.

FIGURE 6-11
Selecting Rows and Columns

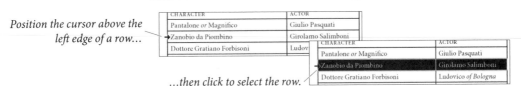

Position the cursor above the top of a column...

...then click to select the column.

Position the cursor above the left edge of a row...

...then click to select the row.

FIGURE 6-12
**Placing a Graphic
in a Cell**

*Click the Type tool
inside a table cell.*

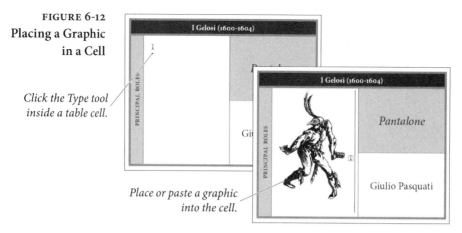

*Place or paste a graphic
into the cell.*

have an active text insertion point; selecting the cell itself will not get the graphic into the cell.

If you want the graphic to fill the entire cell, make sure the Cell Insets values are set to zero and the Clip Contents to Cell checkbox is turned on in the Cell Options dialog box (see "Formatting Tables," later in this chapter).

**Table Controls in the
Control Panel**

Some of the controls in the Table panel can also be found in the Control panel. You won't see these controls unless you select a table item—a cell, a row, a column, or a table—when you select text in a table, the Control panel displays text formatting options.

In most of the table-related illustrations in this chapter, we'll show the Table panel, rather than the Control panel, because the Control panel's width makes it difficult to fit into our page layout. This doesn't mean that we prefer the Table panel—in fact, we use the Control panel whenever the options we need are available there.

**Adding Table Headers
and Footers**

InDesign tables can include header and footer rows, which can repeat as the table breaks across text frames, text columns, or pages. You can add header and footer rows when you create the table, or you can add them to existing tables, or you can convert table body rows to header or footer rows.

▸ If you're using the Insert Table command to create a table, you can use the Header Rows and Footer Rows fields in the Insert Table dialog box to specify the number of header or footer rows as you create the table.

▸ If you want to add header and/or footer rows to an existing table, select a cell in the table (or a row, or a column, or the table itself) and choose Headers and Footers from the Table Options sub-

FIGURE 6-13
Adding a Header Row

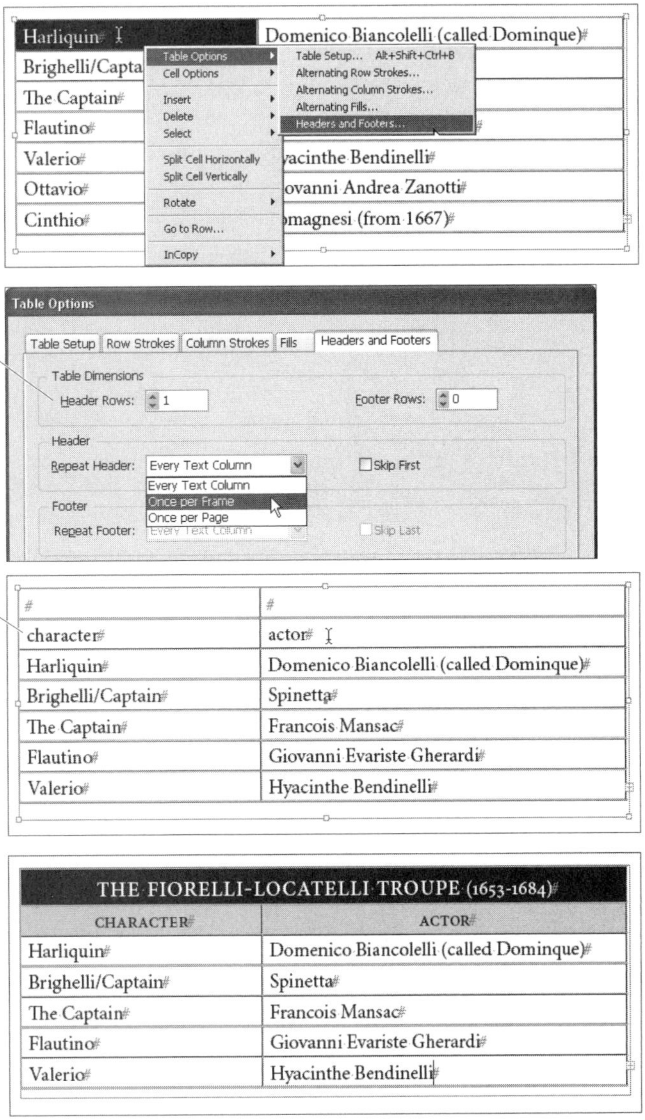

Select a cell, then choose Headers and Footers from the Table Options submenu of the Context menu.

Harliquin#	Domenico Biancolelli (called Dominque)#
Brighelli/Capta	
The Captain#	
Flautino#	
Valerio#	acinthe Bendinelli#
Ottavio#	ovanni Andrea Zanotti#
Cinthio#	magnesi (from 1667)#

Table Options
- Table Setup... Alt+Shift+Ctrl+B
- Alternating Row Strokes...
- Alternating Column Strokes...
- Alternating Fills...
- Headers and Footers...

Cell Options

Insert
Delete
Select

Split Cell Horizontally
Split Cell Vertically

Rotate

Go to Row...

InCopy

Enter the number of header rows you want, then define the rate at which the rows should repeat.

Click OK to apply the header rows.

Table Options

Table Setup | Row Strokes | Column Strokes | Fills | Headers and Footers

Table Dimensions

Header Rows: 1   Footer Rows: 0

Header

Repeat Header: Every Text Column   ☐ Skip First

Every Text Column
Once per Frame
Once per Page

Footer

Repeat Footer: Every Text Column   ☐ Skip Last

InDesign adds the header rows. Enter the header text.

#	#
character#	actor#
Harliquin#	Domenico Biancolelli (called Dominque)#
Brighelli/Captain#	Spinetta#
The Captain#	Francois Mansac#
Flautino#	Giovanni Evariste Gherardi#
Valerio#	Hyacinthe Bendinelli#

Format the header rows. In this example, we've merged the cells of the first header row.

THE FIORELLI-LOCATELLI TROUPE (1653-1684)#	
CHARACTER#	ACTOR#
Harliquin#	Domenico Biancolelli (called Dominque)#
Brighelli/Captain#	Spinetta#
The Captain#	Francois Mansac#
Flautino#	Giovanni Evariste Gherardi#
Valerio#	Hyacinthe Bendinelli#

menu of the Context menu. InDesign displays the Headers and Footers panel of the Table Options dialog box. Enter the number of header and/or footer rows you want, specify the repeat properties of the header/footer rows, and click OK (see Figure 6-13).

▶ To convert an existing row to a header row, select the row (it must be the first row in the table) and choose Convert to Header Rows from the Context menu (see Figure 6-14). To convert multiple table body rows to header rows, select the rows—the first row in the table must be included in the selection (if it's not, the

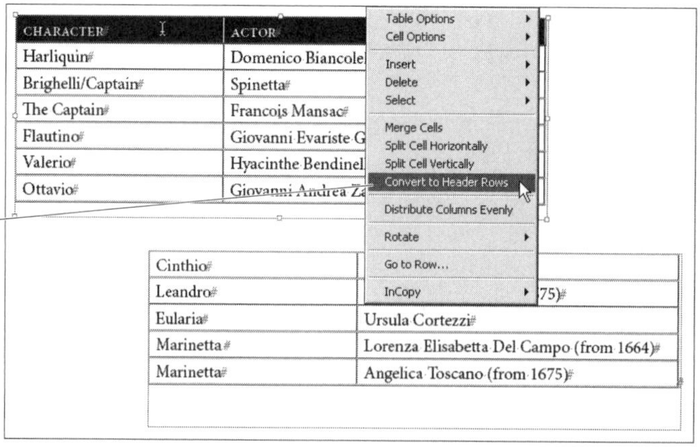

FIGURE 6-14
**Converting a
Table Body Row into a
Header Row**

*Select the first row in the
table, then choose Convert
to Header Rows from the
Context menu.*

option won't appear on the Context menu). Converting a row to
a footer row works the same way—select the last row in the table
and choose Convert to Footer Rows from the Context menu.

**Editing Header and
Footer Rows**

The first header and footer rows can be edited just as you'd edit any
other row—the only difference is that the changes that you make are
applied to all instances of the header or footer throughout the table.
Subsequent header/footer rows, however, will defy your efforts to get
the cursor into them (InDesign coyly displays a lock icon when you
move the cursor over the row).

InDesign provides a pair of shortcuts, however, that will take you
back to the first header or footer row—Edit Header and Edit Footer
on the Context menu.

**Changing the
Size of a Table**

To resize a table by dragging, follow these steps (see Figure 6-15).

1. Click the Type tool inside the table.

2. Move the cursor over the left or right edge of the table (to change
   the table's width), or over the top or bottom of the table (to
   change its height). Position the cursor above the lower-right
   corner of the table to resize the width and height of the table.

3. Drag the cursor to resize the table. Or—better—hold down Shift
   as you drag to resize all the rows or columns an equal amount.

When you resize the table by dragging the lower-right corner
of the table, or when you hold down Shift as you drag, InDesign
applies the changes in size equally to all of the cells in the table. If
you drag the sides of the table without holding down Shift, InDesign

FIGURE 6-15
Resizing a Table

*Note that this table
is wider than its
text frame.*

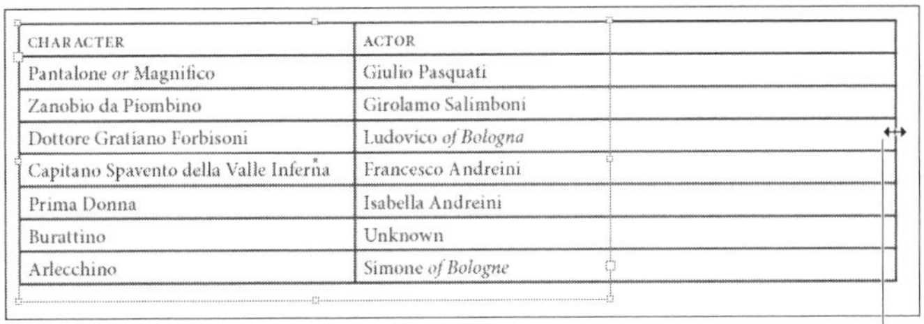

Position the cursor over one side of the table...

*...and drag. InDesign resizes
the table. To resize the table
proportionally, hold down
Shift as you drag.*

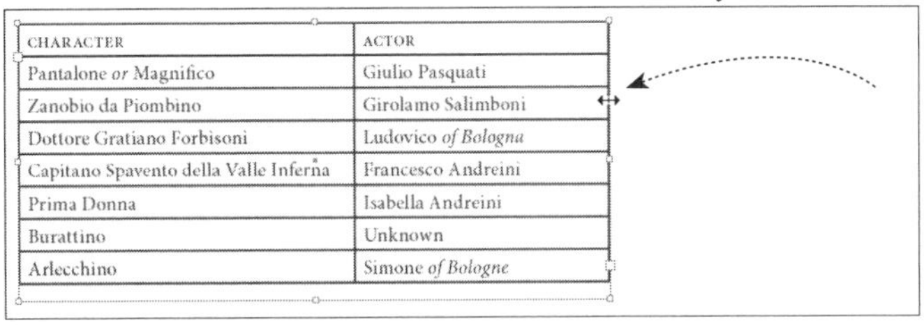

FIGURE 6-16
**Distributing
Columns Evenly**

*Select the columns you want
to make equal in width. In
this example, we've selected
the entire table.*

*Choose Distribute Columns Evenly
from the Context menu or Table menu.*

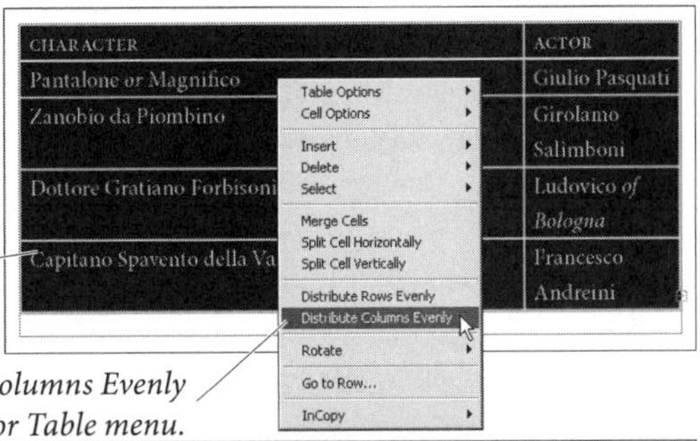

*InDesign makes the
selected columns
equal in width.*

only changes the row or column nearest the edge you're dragging. Resizing the table this way does not scale the text in the table.

What? You've resized the table and now want all of the columns to be the same width? Don't start dragging columns around. Instead, select the table and choose Distribute Columns Evenly from the Table panel menu or Table menu (see Figure 6-16). If you've changed the height of the table and want to make all of the rows in the table the same height, select the table and choose Distribute Rows Evenly (again, from the Table menu or from the Table panel menu).

FIGURE 6-17
**Changing Row
Height by Dragging**

FIGURE 6-17
**Changing Row
Height by Dragging**

*Position the cursor
above a cell border.*

*Drag the cursor up or
down to resize the row.*

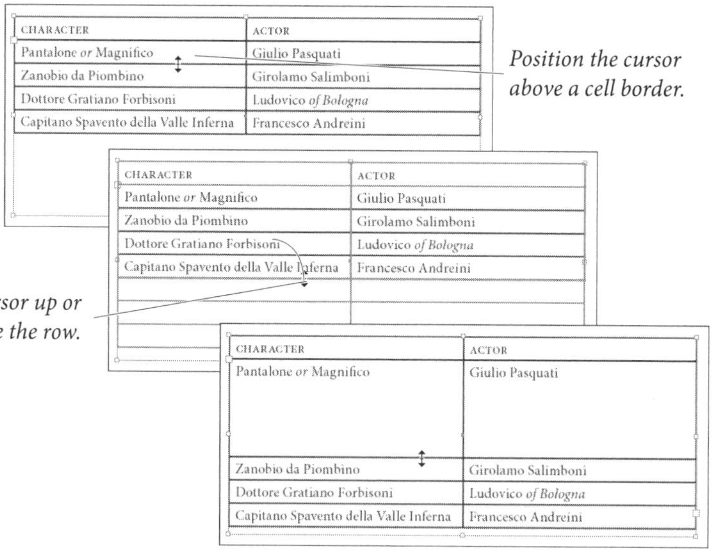

**Changing the Size of
Rows and Columns**

To change the height of a row or the width of a column by dragging, follow these steps (see Figure 6-17).

1. Click the Type tool inside a cell.

2. Move the cursor over the top or bottom of the cell to change the height of the row containing the cell, or over the left or right of the cell to change the column width.

3. Drag the cursor up or down to resize a row, or right or left to resize a column.

To change the height of a row or the width of a column using the Table panel, click the Type tool inside a cell, and adjust the values in the Row Height and Column Width field (see Figure 6-18).

FIGURE 6-18
**Changing Column
Width Using the
Table Panel**

*Select a column (or
any cell in a column)...*

*...then enter a new value
in the Column Width field.
Press Return/Enter to apply
the new column width.*

FIGURE 6-19
Changing Column Width Using the Cell Options Dialog Box

Select a column (or any cell in a column)...

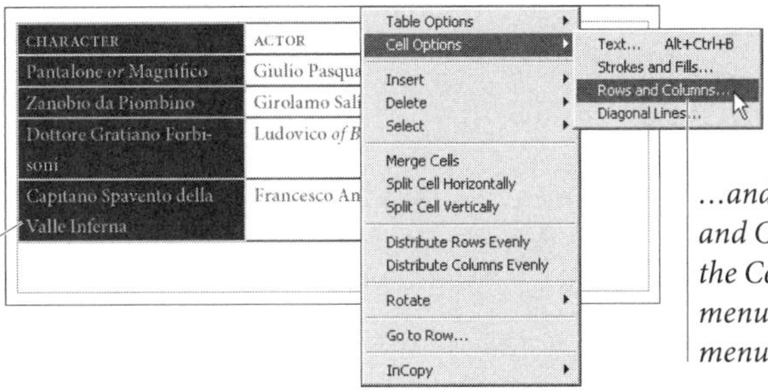

...and choose Rows and Columns from the Cell Options submenu of the Context menu.

To change the height of a row or the width of a column using the Cell Options dialog box follow these steps (see Figure 6-19).

1. Select a cell, a row, a column, or the entire table.
2. Choose Rows and Columns from the Cell Options submenu of the Context menu (or from the Table menu).
3. Enter a value in the Row Height field or the Column Width field to change the width of a column.

Adding Rows Or Columns

If you're entering text in a table, and have reached the cell of the last row, you can add a row by simply pressing Tab—InDesign assumes that this means that you want to add a row to the table. If you need to add rows inside an existing table, it's a little bit more complicated.

To add a row or a series of rows to a table, follow these steps (see Figure 6-20).

1. Click the Type tool in a cell in a row that is above or below the point at which you want to add the new rows.
2. Choose Row from the Insert submenu of the Table or Context menu. InDesign displays the Insert Row(s) dialog box.

FIGURE 6-20
Adding Rows

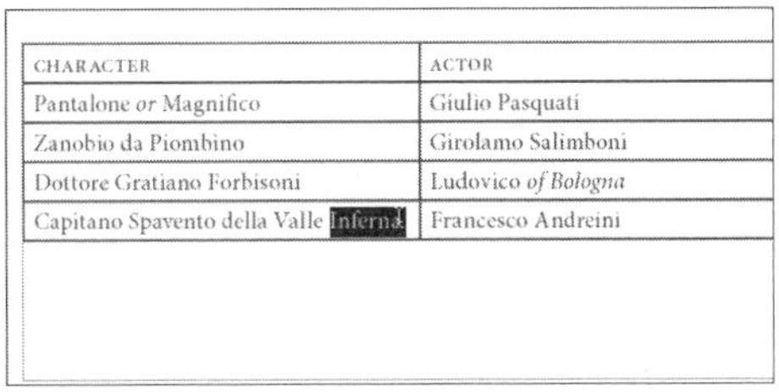

Click the Type tool in a cell, then choose Row from the Insert submenu of the Context menu.

InDesign displays the Insert Rows dialog box.

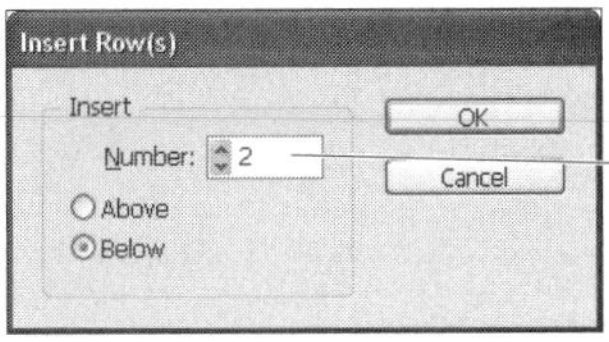

Enter the number of rows you want to add to the table, and specify whether you want them added above or below the selected row. Click the OK button to add the row or rows.

3. Enter the number of Rows you want to add in the Number field, and choose the Above or Below option to tell InDesign where to put the rows (relative to the selected row).

4. Click the OK button. InDesign adds the empty rows.

To add a column or a series of columns to a table, follow these steps (see Figure 6-21).

1. Click the Type tool in a cell in a column that is adjacent to the point at which you want to add the new columns.

2. Choose Column from the Insert submenu of the Context menu. InDesign displays the Insert Column(s) dialog box.

3. Enter the number of Columns you want to add in the Number field, then choose the Left or Right option to tell InDesign where to put the rows (relative to the selected row).

4. Click the OK button. InDesign adds the empty columns.

You can also add a row or column by dragging. To do so, follow these steps (see Figure 6-22).

1. Click the Type tool in a cell.

2. To add a column, position the cursor over the left or right side of the cell; to add a row, position it above the top or bottom.

3. Hold down the mouse button, then press Option/Alt and drag. InDesign adds a row or column to the table.

FIGURE 6-21
Adding a Column

Click the Type tool in a cell (or select text in a cell), then Choose Column from the Insert submenu of the Context menu.

InDesign displays the Insert Columns dialog box.

Enter the number of columns you want to add, and specify the location (to the right or left of the selected column) at which you want to add them.

InDesign adds the columns to the table.

FIGURE 6-22
Adding a Column
by Dragging

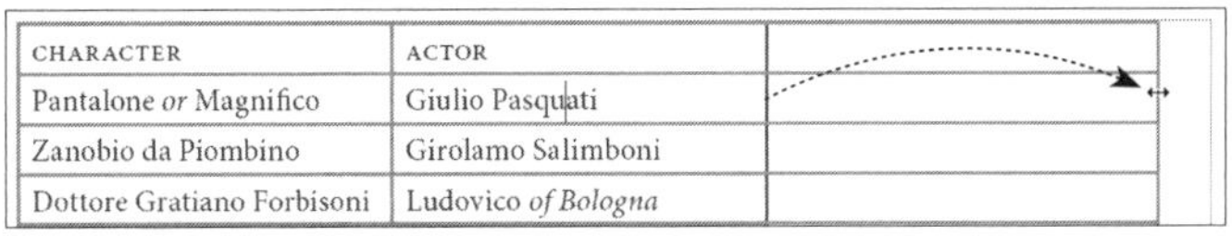

CHARACTER	ACTOR	
Pantalone *or* Magnifico	Giulio Pasquati	
Zanobio da Piombino	Girolamo Salimboni	
Dottore Gratiano Forbisoni	Ludovico *of Bologna*	

Position the cursor over a column edge. Hold down the
mouse button, then press Option/Alt and drag.

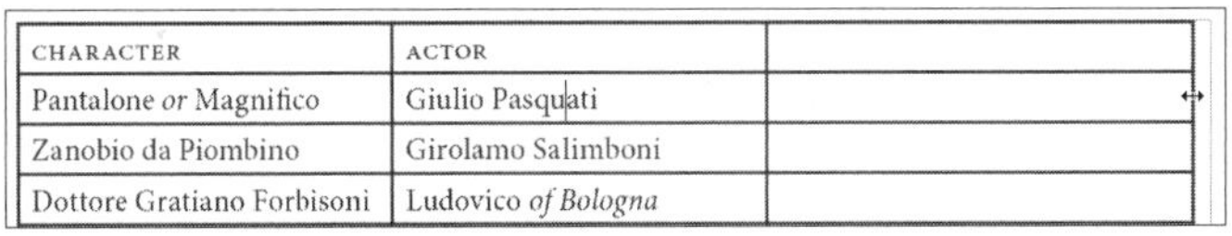

Stop dragging, and InDesign
adds a column to the table.

CHARACTER	ACTOR	
Pantalone *or* Magnifico	Giulio Pasquati	
Zanobio da Piombino	Girolamo Salimboni	
Dottore Gratiano Forbisoni	Ludovico *of Bologna*	

To add a row to a table using the Table panel, follow these steps (see Figure 6-23).

1. Click the Type tool in a cell.

2. Display the Table panel (press Shift-F9[1]), then change the value displayed in the Rows field or the Columns field.

When you add a row using this technique, the new row appears below the row you selected; when you add a column, the new column appears to the right of the selected column.

Deleting Rows,
Columns, and Tables

To delete a single row, click the Type tool in a cell in the row, then choose Row from the Delete submenu of the Context menu. There's no need to select the row or cell. To delete more than one row, select at least one cell in each row you want to delete, then choose Row from the Delete submenu of the Context menu.

To delete a single column, click the Type tool in a cell in the column, then choose Column from the Delete submenu of the Table or Context menu. To delete more than one column, select a cell in each column you want to delete, then choose Column from the Delete submenu of the Context menu.

To delete a table, click the Type tool in any cell in the table, and then choose Table from the Delete submenu of the Table menu or the Context menu. InDesign deletes the entire table containing the cell,.

You can use the Type tool to select the character containing the table (though it can be a very *large* character, it's still a single character), or place the cursor after the table in the story, and press Delete.

---

[1] In Mac OS X, you may need to open System Preferences, choose Keyboard & Mouse or Dashboard & Exposé to disable this shortcut before it will work properly in InDesign.

FIGURE 6-23
Adding a Row Using
the Table Panel

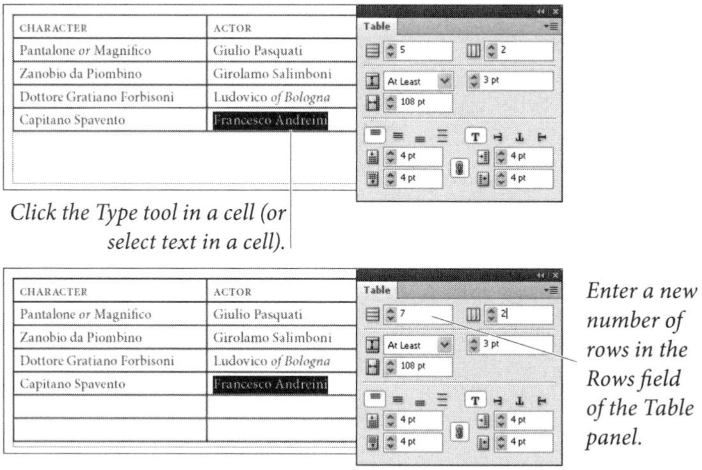

*Click the Type tool in a cell (or
select text in a cell).*

*Enter a new
number of
rows in the
Rows field
of the Table
panel.*

FIGURE 6-24
Deleting a Column
Using the Table Panel

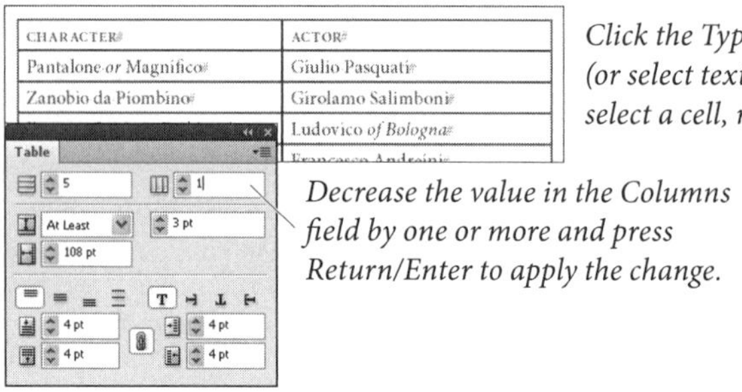

*Click the Type tool in a cell
(or select text in a cell, or
select a cell, row, or table).*

*Decrease the value in the Columns
field by one or more and press
Return/Enter to apply the change.*

To delete rows or columns using the Table panel, follow these
steps (see Figure 6-24).

1. Click the Type tool in a cell.

2. Display the Table panel (press Shift-F9) if it isn't already visible,
    then reduce the value in either the Rows field or the Columns
    field. InDesign asks if you're certain you want to remove the
    row(s). You are certain, so click the OK button.

**Merging and
Unmerging
Table Cells**

To merge a series of selected table cells into a single cell, select the
cells and choose Merge Cells from the Context menu or Table menu
(see Figure 6-25). The text and graphics in the selected cells are placed
in the new merged cell.

To unmerge a cell that has been created by merging cells, select
the cell and choose Unmerge Cells from the Context menu or Table
menu. Unmerging a merged cell is different from splitting the cell,
which only divides the cell in half along its horizontal or vertical axis.
Unmerging a cell actually returns the cells in the merged cell to their
original geometry, though it does not restore their original content.

FIGURE 6-25
Merging Cells

Select a range of cells.

Choose Merge Cells from the Context menu (or Table menu).

InDesign merges the cells. Any content in the merged cells is retained in the new cell.

Splitting Table Cells

To split a cell, select the cell and choose Split Cell Horizontally or Split Cell Vertically from the Context menu (see Figure 6-26).

Rotating Table Cells

Cells in an InDesign table can be rotated in 90-degree increments (see Figure 6-27). To rotate a cell, select the cell and then choose one of the options (0, 90, 180, 270) on the Rotate submenu of the Context menu (or click the corresponding button in the Table panel).

Using a Table to Create a Box Around a Paragraph

Sometimes, you need to place a box around a paragraph—you often see this formatting used to set off notes and warnings in technical manuals.

We know of other methods for accomplishing this (involving paragraph rules and inline frames)—but the best way to put a box around a paragraph is to convert the paragraph to a single-cell table. We do not know if single-cell tables can reproduce by fission, as other single-cell animals can, but they're certainly useful nonetheless.

To convert a paragraph to a single-cell table, select all of the text in the paragraph up to, but not including, the return at the end of the paragraph. Then choose Convert Text to Table from the Table menu (see Figure 6-28). Apply whatever formatting you want to the fill and stroke of the table's single cell.

FIGURE 6-26
Splitting a Cell

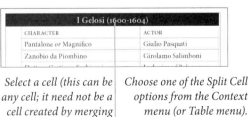

Select a cell (this can be any cell; it need not be a cell created by merging other cells).

Choose one of the Split Cell options from the Context menu (or Table menu).

InDesign splits the cell into two cells.

FIGURE 6-27
Rotating a Cell

Select a cell. —

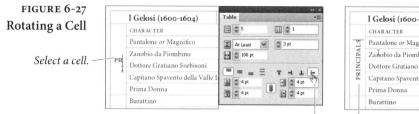

Click one of the rotation options in the Table panel (or choose one from the Context menu).

InDesign rotates the content of the cell.

FIGURE 6-28
Placing a Box Around a Paragraph

seated beside the critic G. B. Shaw.¶

Note: TimeTravelTickets is not responsible for any personal items left at a venue in the past. While we will make a good faith effort to recover lost items, it is not always possible to visit each divergent time stream.¶

Princess Ida¶

Select the text of the paragraph, leaving the return character unselected, then choose Convert Text to Table from the Table menu.

Convert Text to Table

Column Separator: Tab
Row Separator: Paragraph
Number of Columns:
Table Style: [Basic Table]

OK
Cancel

InDesign displays the Convert Text to Table dialog box. Click the OK button.

InDesign creates a table containing a single cell.

seated beside the critic G. B. Shaw.¶

Note: TimeTravelTickets is not responsible for any personal items left at a venue in the past. While we will make a good faith effort to recover lost items, it is not always possible to visit each divergent time stream.¶

seated beside the critic G. B. Shaw.¶

Note: TimeTravelTickets is not responsible for any personal items left at a venue in the past. While we will make a good faith effort to recover lost items, it is not always possible to visit each divergent time stream.¶

Princess Ida¶

Apply formatting to the table.

Table Shortcuts

As you might expect, InDesign has a number of keyboard shortcuts related to working with tables (see Table 6-2).

By default, some cool shortcuts have no key assigned to them. Go to Row, in particular, is worth its weight in gold when working with long tables. You can find it and other very helpful table shortcuts by choosing Keyboard Shortcuts from the Edit menu, then choosing Tables Menu from the Product area pop-up menu.

	Function	Shortcut
TABLE 6-2 **Table Shortcuts in** **the Default set**	Text Options	Command-Option-B/Ctrl-Alt-B*
	Delete Column	Shift-Backspace*
	Delete Row	Command-Backspace/ Ctrl-Backspace*
	Insert Table	Command-Shift-Option-T/ Ctrl-Alt-Shift-T
	Insert Column	Command-Option-9/Ctrl-Alt-9*
	Insert Row	Command-9/Ctrl-9*
	Next Cell	Tab
	Previous Cell	Shift-Tab
	Select Cell	Command-/(slash)/ Ctrl-/ (slash) or Esc*
	Select Column	Command-Option-3/Ctrl-Alt-3*
	Select Row	Command-3/Ctrl-3*
	Select Table	Command-Option-A/Ctrl-Alt-A
	Table Setup	Command-Option-B/Ctrl-Alt-B*

* This command is only active when you have an active text
insertion point in a text frame or table cell.

Formatting Tables

Earlier, we mentioned that table cells are similar to InDesign text frames—and we now want to point out that that similarity extends to the realm of formatting, as well. Table cells can be filled using any fill you could apply to a frame, and can use all of the strokes in InDesign's Stroke panel (including custom stroke styles).

To format table cells, however, you don't (usually) use the same controls you use to format page items. Instead, you use a set of table formatting controls, most of which you'll find in the Table Options dialog box (press Command-Option-Shift-B/Ctrl-Alt-Shift-B) and Cell Options dialog box (press Command-Option-B/Ctrl-Alt-B).

Table Cell
Strokes and Fills

Before we start talking about table formatting, it's important that you understand that applying a stroke to a column is exactly the same as applying a stroke to the left and right edges of all of the cells in that column. There are not separate stroke properties for rows and columns. If you change the stroke property of a column, the strokes on the corresponding cell borders in the column also change. The same is true for table border strokes—these properties apply to the outside edges of the cells at the top, right, bottom, and left edges of the table.

Applying Strokes to Cells. InDesign offers a number of different ways to set the fill or stroke of a cell. You can set the stroke weight using the Stroke panel, or the Strokes and Fills panel of the Cell Options dialog box, or from the table controls in the Control panel. You can set the fill of a cell using the Swatches panel, the Color panel, or the Strokes and Fills panel of the Cell Options dialog box. This is not a complete listing of the different methods you can use to format cells, but we think you get the idea.

When you want to apply a stroke to all of the borders of a cell or cells, follow these steps (see Figure 6-29).

1. Select a range of cells.

2. Display the Stroke panel or display the Strokes and Fills panel of the Cell Options dialog box (choose Strokes and Fills from the Cell Options submenu of the Context menu), or display the Control panel.

FIGURE 6-29

Applying a Stroke to All Cell Borders

Click the Type tool in the table, then press Command-Option-A/Ctrl-Alt-A (or choose Table from the Select submenu of the Context menu) to select the table.

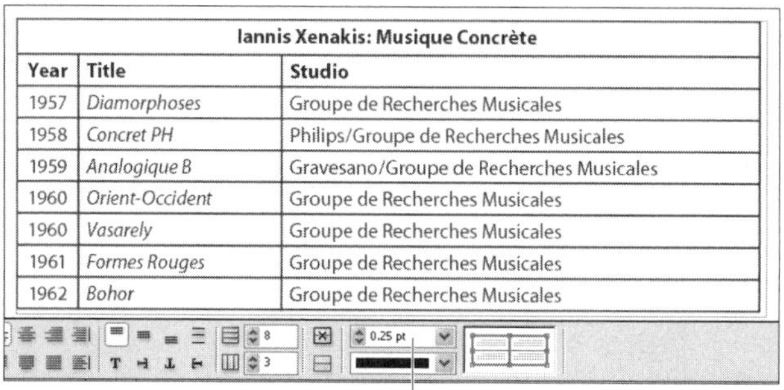

Iannis Xenakis: Musique Concrète		
Year	Title	Studio
1957	Diamorphoses	Groupe de Recherches Musicales
1958	Concret PH	Philips/Groupe de Recherches Musicales
1959	Analogique B	Gravesano/Groupe de Recherches Musicales
1960	Orient-Occident	Groupe de Recherches Musicales
1960	Vasarely	Groupe de Recherches Musicales
1961	Formes Rouges	Groupe de Recherches Musicales
1962	Bohor	Groupe de Recherches Musicales

Enter a stroke weight in the Weight field of the Control panel, or choose a stroke weight from the associated pop-up menu.

You can apply any stroke style to the stroke of a table cell, including dashed and striped strokes you've defined.

InDesign applies the stroke to the cell borders of the table.

Iannis Xenakis: Musique Concrète		
Year	Title	Studio
1957	Diamorphoses	Groupe de Recherches Musicales
1958	Concret PH	Philips/Groupe de Recherches Musicales
1959	Analogique B	Gravesano/Groupe de Recherches Musicales
1960	Orient-Occident	Groupe de Recherches Musicales
1960	Vasarely	Groupe de Recherches Musicales
1961	Formes Rouges	Groupe de Recherches Musicales
1962	Bohor	Groupe de Recherches Musicales

FIGURE 6-30
Cell Proxy

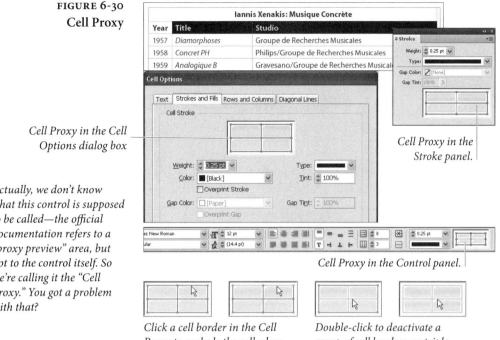

Cell Proxy in the Cell Options dialog box

Cell Proxy in the Stroke panel.

Actually, we don't know what this control is supposed to be called—the official documentation refers to a "proxy preview" area, but not to the control itself. So we're calling it the "Cell Proxy." You got a problem with that?

Cell Proxy in the Control panel.

Click a cell border in the Cell Proxy to exclude the cell edges from formatting. Click again to activate the cell border.

Double-click to deactivate a group of cell borders, or triple-click to deactivate all cell borders.

3. Enter a stroke weight in the Weight field and press Return/Enter (or otherwise apply the new value).

4. Apply a stroke color. If you're applying the stroke using the Stroke panel or the Control panel, you can use the Swatches panel, the Color panel, the Gradient panel, or any of the other color controls. If you're using the Strokes and Fills panel of the Cell Options dialog box, you can use the Color pop-up menu.

Each border of a cell in an InDesign table can have a different stroke. Note, however, that cells share borders with adjacent cells. Applying a stroke to the right border of a cell affects the left border of the next cell in the row.

The Cell Proxy (in the Strokes panel of the Cell Options dialog box, or in the Control panel or Stroke panel) is the way that you tell InDesign which border you want to work with (see Figure 6-30). Just as the Proxy in the Transform panel "stands in" for the current selection, the Cell Proxy represents the selected cell or cell range.

When the borders in the Cell Proxy are highlighted (in light blue), changes you make to the stroke color or stroke weight will affect the corresponding cell borders. To prevent formatting from affecting a

FIGURE 6-31

**Applying a Stroke to
Selected Cell Borders**

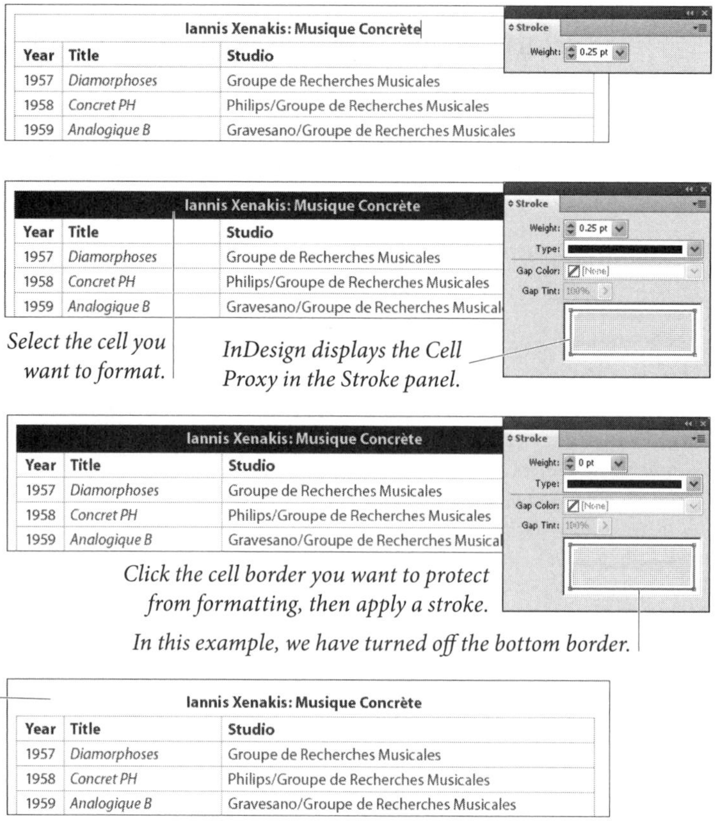

*In this example, we want to
remove the strokes around
the outside edges (top, left,
and right) of the first row in
the table, but we don't want
to remove the stroke at the
bottom of the row. To do
this, we use the Cell Proxy
in the Stroke panel.*

*Select the cell you
want to format.*

*InDesign displays the Cell
Proxy in the Stroke panel.*

*When you click a border in
the Cell Proxy, it changes
from blue to gray (which
is hard to represent in this
book!)*

*Click the cell border you want to protect
from formatting, then apply a stroke.*

In this example, we have turned off the bottom border.

*The top, left, and right
borders of the first row have
been set to zero point strokes,
but the bottom border of
the row retains its original
stroke weight.*

cell border, click the corresponding active border in the Cell Proxy.
To make an inactive border active again, click it again.

If you want to apply a stroke to some, but not all, of the borders of
a cell, follow these steps (see Figure 6-31).

1. Select the cell or range of cells you want to format.

2. Display the Stroke panel or display the Strokes and Fills panel of
    the Cell Options dialog box (choose Strokes and Fills from the
    Cell Options submenu of the Context menu).

3. Use the Cell Proxy to select the cell borders you want to format.

4. Apply stroke formatting using the Strokes and Fills panel of the
    Cell Options dialog box, or the Stroke or Swatches panels.

Applying Fills to Cells. To apply a fill to a cell, follow these steps (see
Figure 6-32).

1. Select a cell or a range of cells.

FIGURE 6-32
**Applying a Fill to a Cell
(Dialog Box Method)**

*Select a cell or
series of cells.*

*Choose Strokes and Fills from the Cell
Options submenu of the Context or Table
menu. InDesign displays the Strokes and
fills panel of the Cell Options dialog box.*

*Specify fill options
in the Strokes and
Fills panel of the Cell
Options dialog box.*

*InDesign applies the fill to
the selected cells.*

FIGURE 6-33
**Applying a Fill to a Cell
(Panel Method)**

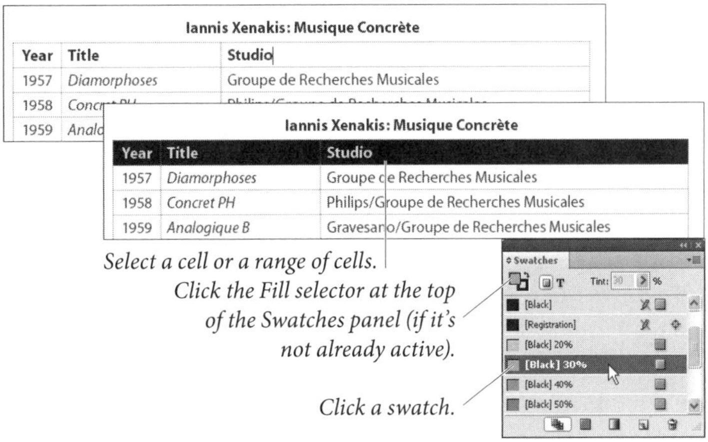

Select a cell or a range of cells.
*Click the Fill selector at the top
of the Swatches panel (if it's
not already active).*

Click a swatch.

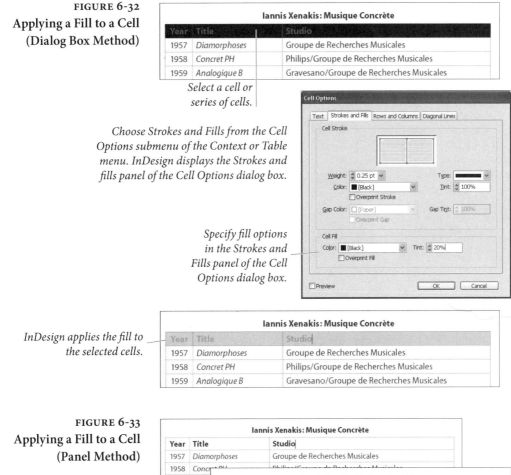

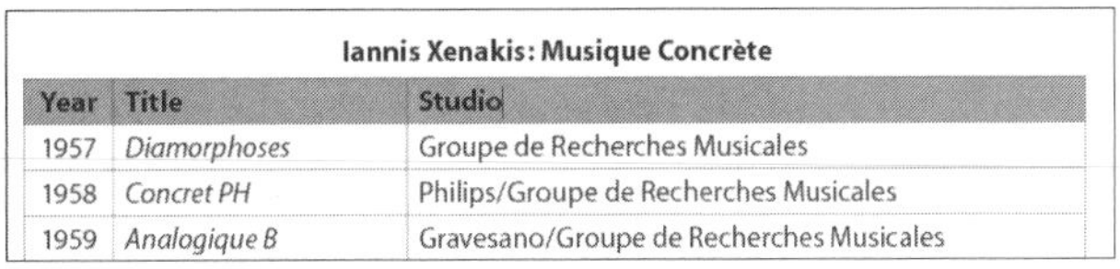

InDesign applies the fill to the selected cells.

*InDesign positions the start
and end of the gradient (in
this example, the center
point of a radial gradient)
based on the width and
height of the entire table—
not the width of the cell itself.*

*Display the Gradient panel
and click the Gradient Ramp
to apply a gradient fill.*

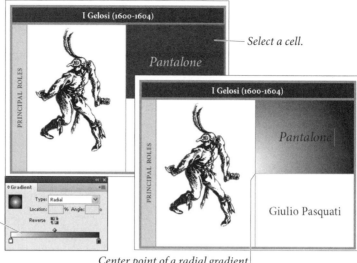

Select a cell.

Center point of a radial gradient
applied to the cell.

2. Display the Strokes and Fills panel of the Cell Options dialog box (to display this panel, choose Strokes and Fills from the Cell Options submenu of the Context or Table menu).

3. Choose a color swatch from the Color pop-up menu, and enter a tint value in the Tint field, if necessary. Note that you can also set the fill to overprint using the Overprint option.

4. Click the OK button to close the dialog box and apply the fill.

Alternatively, you can apply a fill to a cell using the Swatches panel or Color panel (see Figure 6-33).

1. Select a cell or range of cells.

2. Click the Fill selector at the top of the Swatches panel or Color panel to make it active (if it's not already active).

3. Click the swatch (if you're using the Swatches panel) or color (if you're using the Color panel) to apply it to the cell.

Applying Gradients to Table Cells. You can apply a gradient to the fill and stroke of a cell, but the results might not be what you'd expect (see Figure 6-34).

1. Select the cells.

2. Display the Gradient panel, if it's not already visible.

FIGURE 6-35
Applying Diagonal Lines to a Cell

Select a cell, then choose Diagonal Lines from the Cell Options submenu of the Context or Table menu.

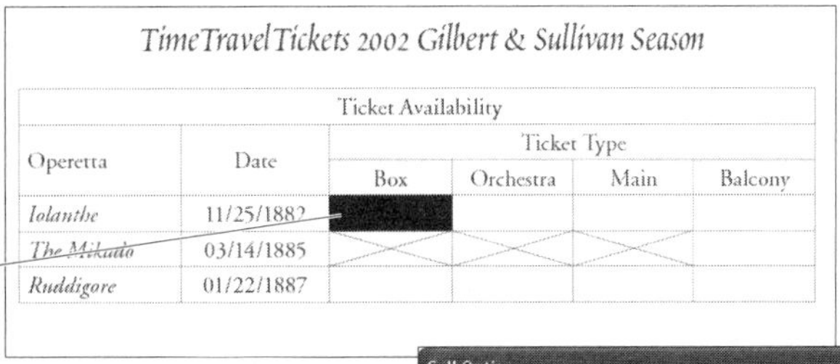

InDesign displays the Diagonal Lines panel of the Cell Options dialog box.

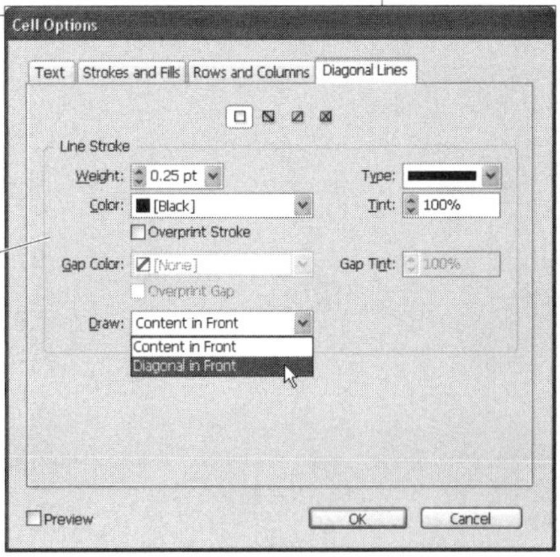

In this example table, a diagonal line in a cell indicates that the seats in that section are no longer available. TimeTravelTickets has run out of box seats for the November 25, 1882, premiere of "Iolanthe," so we have to apply diagonal lines to the corresponding cell.

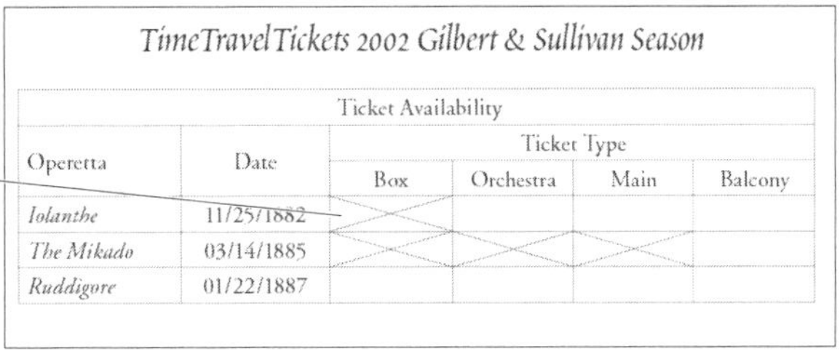

Use the controls to specify the formatting of the diagonal lines.

InDesign applies the diagonal lines to the cell.

3. Click in the Gradient Ramp to apply a gradient to the selected cells. Adjust the gradient settings to define the type, color, and angle of the gradient (as discussed in Chapter 5, "Drawing").

   Note that the gradient is based on the width and height of the table, rather than on the selected cell or cells. This may or may not give you the effect you're looking for. To gain more control over the start/end points of the gradient, create and fill a rectangle, then paste the rectangle into the cell.

Applying Diagonal Lines. To apply diagonal lines to a cell, use the options in the Diagonal Lines panel of the Cell Options dialog box (see Figure 6-35).

1. Select a cell, row, column, or table (table border strokes apply to the entire table, so you need only select part of the table).

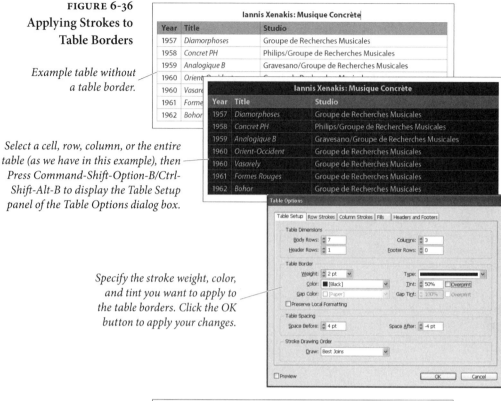

FIGURE 6-36

**Applying Strokes to
Table Borders**

*Example table without
a table border.*

*Select a cell, row, column, or the entire
table (as we have in this example), then
Press Command-Shift-Option-B/Ctrl-
Shift-Alt-B to display the Table Setup
panel of the Table Options dialog box.*

*Specify the stroke weight, color,
and tint you want to apply to
the table borders. Click the OK
button to apply your changes.*

*InDesign applies the stroke
to the outside borders of
the cells at the outside (left,
right, top, or bottom)
of the table.*

2. Display the Diagonal Lines panel of the Cell Options dialog box (choose Diagonal Lines from the Cell Options submenu of the Context menu).

3. Turn on one of the diagonal lines options. Choose a stroke weight, stroke type, color, and tint. If you want the diagonal lines to overprint, turn on the Overprint option. If you want the diagonal lines to appear in front of the table, turn on the Draw in Front option.

4. Click the OK button to apply the diagonal lines.

Formatting Table Borders. To apply a stroke to the edges of a table, use the options in the Table Border section of the Table Setup panel of the Table Options dialog box (see Figure 6-36). Note that applying a border to a table is the same as applying borders to the outside edges of each of cells on each side of the table—but it's a lot faster.

1. Select a cell, row, column, or table (table border strokes apply to the entire table, so you need only select part of the table).

2. Display the Table Setup panel of the Table Options dialog box (press Command-Option-Shift-B/Ctrl-Alt-Shift-B).

3. Choose a stroke weight, stroke type, color, and tint. If you want the stroke to overprint, turn on the Overprint option.

4. If you want to prevent the table border formatting from overriding formatting you've applied to the cells in the table (i.e., any formatting other than the default table formatting), turn on the Preserve Local Formatting option.

Applying Alternating Fills and Strokes. The options in the Row Strokes, Column Strokes, and Fills panels of the Table Options dialog box provide a way for you to vary the formatting of rows and columns in a table according to a predefined pattern. Shading table rows or columns is often a more visually pleasing way to format a table than using strokes (this depends on the design of the piece in which the table appears).

All of these panels work the same way—you select a pattern from the Alternating Pattern pop-up menu, and then you specify the formatting applied by that pattern. If the pattern you chose is None, InDesign doesn't alternate the corresponding fill or stroke properties in the table. Otherwise, InDesign applies one of two formats to the rows and columns in the table. Formatting you apply using alternating fills or strokes overrides any cell formatting you've already applied to the cells in the table (it has no effect on text formatting).

To apply an alternating fill or stroke pattern to a table, follow these steps (see Figure 6-37).

1. Select a cell, row, column, or table (this formatting applies to the entire table, so do whatever is easiest for you).

2. Display the panel of the Table Options dialog box that corresponds to the attribute you want to work with (i.e., Row Strokes, Column Strokes, or Fills). Turn on the Preview option—it can help you understand the effect of the formatting options.

FIGURE 6-37
Applying Alternating Fills

Select a cell, row, column, or table, then choose Alternating Fills from the Table Options submenu of the Context or Table menu.

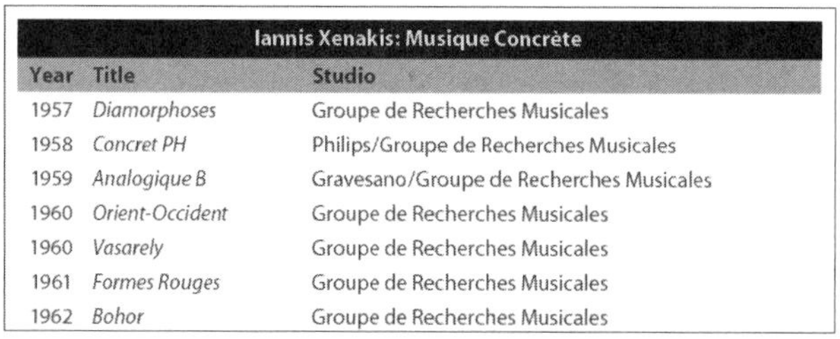

Iannis Xenakis: Musique Concrète		
Year	Title	Studio
1957	*Diamorphoses*	Groupe de Recherches Musicales
1958	*Concret PH*	Philips/Groupe de Recherches Musicales
1959	*Analogique B*	Gravesano/Groupe de Recherches Musicales
1960	*Orient-Occident*	Groupe de Recherches Musicales
1960	*Vasarely*	Groupe de Recherches Musicales
1961	*Formes Rouges*	Groupe de Recherches Musicales
1962	*Bohor*	Groupe de Recherches Musicales

Select a pattern from the Alternating Pattern pop-up menu, then specify the formatting you want to apply.

Note that we've directed our alternating pattern to skip the first two rows in the table (to avoid the table header row and title).

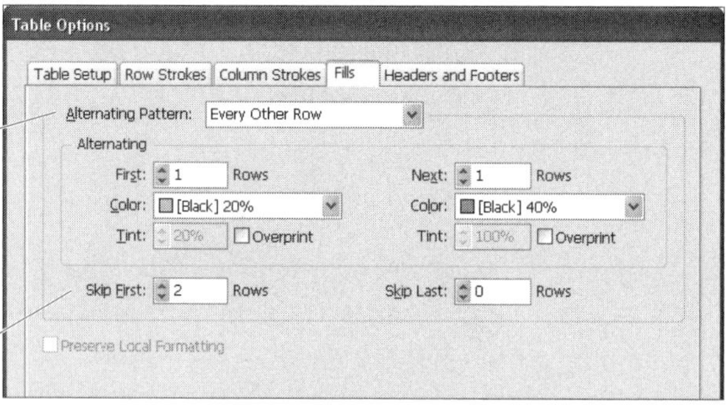

InDesign applies the alternating fill pattern to the rows in the table.

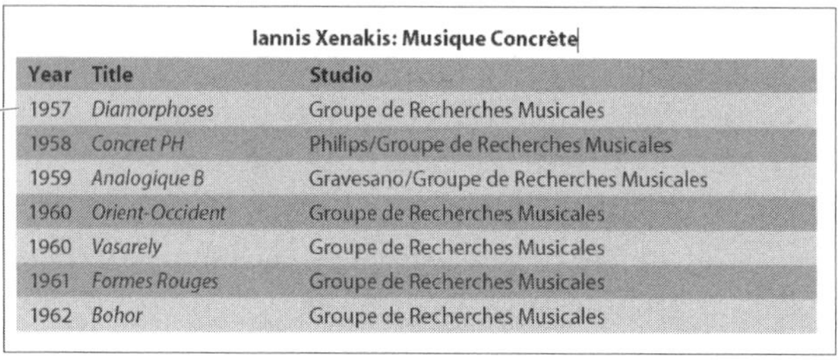

Iannis Xenakis: Musique Concrète		
Year	Title	Studio
1957	*Diamorphoses*	Groupe de Recherches Musicales
1958	*Concret PH*	Philips/Groupe de Recherches Musicales
1959	*Analogique B*	Gravesano/Groupe de Recherches Musicales
1960	*Orient-Occident*	Groupe de Recherches Musicales
1960	*Vasarely*	Groupe de Recherches Musicales
1961	*Formes Rouges*	Groupe de Recherches Musicales
1962	*Bohor*	Groupe de Recherches Musicales

3. Choose an option from the Alternating Pattern pop-up menu.
4. Choose a color for the alternating pattern (until you do this, you probably won't see any changes to the table, even if you have turned on the Preview option).
5. If you want the alternating pattern to ignore rows at the beginning or end of the table (for alternating row strokes) or at the left or right edges of the column (if you're working with alternating column strokes), enter the number of cells in the Skip First and Skip Last fields.

It should be clear you can create quite complex alternating formatting using these options. The only real way to learn how the different alternating formatting features work is to experiment with the settings. Create an example table, open the Table Options dialog box, turn on the Preview option, and play!

Table and Cell Styles

The problem with formatting tables is that it just takes far too long, especially when you have a bunch of tables in a document. That's where table styles come in handy! Table styles—like their cousins paragraph styles and object styles—are a way to collect a bunch of formatting together and give it a single name. InDesign offers both table styles (for table-wide formatting) and cell styles (for formatting that affects a single cell).

The Basic Table Style. Every new document comes with one table style called Basic. The problem is that if you redefine Basic and use it

FIGURE 6-38
Defining Cell Styles

Hold down Option/Alt and click the New Cell Style button to force the New Cell Style dialog box to open.

Work your way through the panels in the Cell Style Options dialog box to define a new cell style.

Just as in a Character style, blank fields are ignored when the cell style is applied.

Click the OK button to close the dialog box, and InDesign adds a new cell style.

To apply a cell style, place the cursor in the cell and click in the Cell Styles panel.

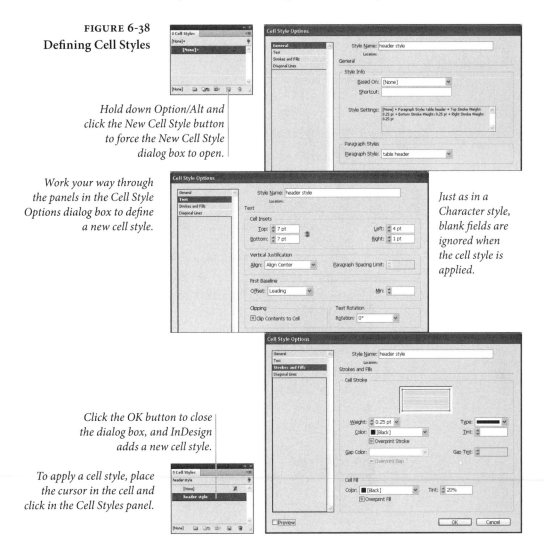

in your document, and then later copy one of these tables and paste it into a different document, your table will change in appearance. Because of that, we recommend you create your own styles instead of using Basic.

Defining Cell Styles

While it's tempting to jump in and discuss table styles, it's typically better to define your cell styles first because you'll use them in your table style definition. To define a new cell style, follow these steps (see Figure 6-38):

1. Choose New Cell Style from the Cell Style panel menu or Option/Alt-click on the New Cell Style button in the panel.

2. In the General pane of the New Cell Style dialog box, give the style a name and—if you want—a keyboard shortcut. (Shortcuts have to be based on the keys on a numeric keypad.) If you've already created a cell style, you can base your new one on it so that it takes on all the same formatting.

   The coolest feature in the General pane is the Paragraph Style pop-up menu. If you choose a paragraph style here, it will automatically apply to any text inside the cell.

3. The next three panes—Text, Strokes and Fills, and Diagonal Lines—are virtually identical to same-named panes in the Cell Options dialog box, so there's no reason to repeat ourselves. For more information, see those sections earlier in this chapter.

   The important thing to note about these panes, however, is that—like character styles—all the controls are blank until you set them. A blank field or pop-up menu (or a dash in a checkbox) means "ignore this formatting" so it won't be applied when the cell is styled. For example, if you leave the Cell Fill Color pop-up menu blank, then your cell style will not override the cell fill color already applied to the cell in the table.

If your cursor is currently inside a formatted cell when you create a new cell style, the current formatting appears in the New Cell Style dialog box automatically. That's often the fastest way to define a cell style. However, InDesign won't apply the cell style for you after you click OK—you still have to do that with a click in the Cell Styles panel.

Defining Table Styles

Once you've defined the cell styles you need, it's time to build your table style. To define a table style, follow these steps (see Figure 6-39):

1. Choose New Table Style from the Table Style panel menu or Option/Alt-click on the New Cell Style button in the panel.

FIGURE 6-39
Defining a Table Style

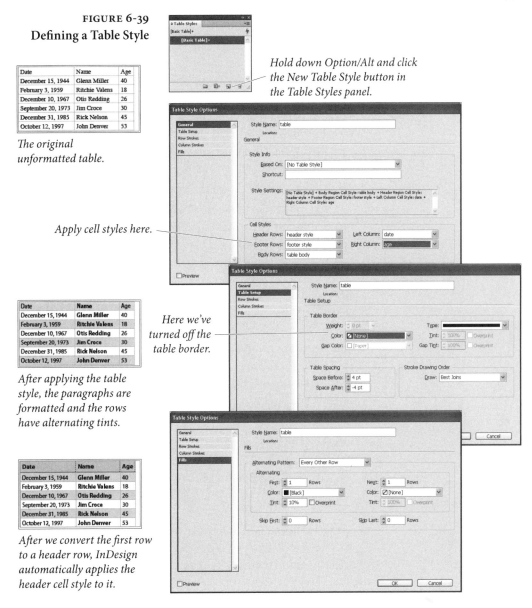

Hold down Option/Alt and click the New Table Style button in the Table Styles panel.

The original unformatted table.

Apply cell styles here.

After applying the table style, the paragraphs are formatted and the rows have alternating tints.

Here we've turned off the table border.

After we convert the first row to a header row, InDesign automatically applies the header cell style to it.

2. In the General pane of the New Table Style dialog box, give the style a name and—if you want—a keyboard shortcut based on the numeric keypad keys. If you want to base the table style on another table style, choose it from the Based On dialog box. We recommend not basing new styles on the Basic Table style, as it makes it too easy for tables to get messed up when copying them to a new document.

You can have InDesign automatically apply cell styles to areas of your table by choosing from the Cell Styles pop-up menus. For example, if you have created a cell style to describe the look of all the cells in your table (not including a header row), choose that style from the Body Rows pop-up menu. You can specify different cell styles for Body Rows, Header Rows, Footer Rows, and the cells in the Left Column and Right Column.

Remember that each of these cell styles can apply its own paragraph style to the text inside those cells, too. That's how you apply paragraph styles throughout a table by using a table style.

3. The next four panes of the New Table Style dialog box—Table Setup, Row Strokes, Column Strokes, and Fills—are nearly identical to the similarly-named panes in the Table Options dialog box, so go read about those earlier in the chapter.

However, some features are conspicuously absent in the table style definition, notably anything that has to do with the structure of the table: Table Dimensions, Headers, and Footers. Table styles cannot control these aspects of a table. That can be quite frustrating at times. For example, if you import an Excel or Word table and apply a table style to it, there's no way for the style to tell the table that the first row should be a header row. Instead, you have to manually use Convert Rows to Header. That can get tiresome with a lot of tables.

4. When you're done specifying the look at feel of the table, click OK. InDesign won't apply the style to a currently selected table; you have to click on the style name in the panel.

Applying Table and Cell Styles. As mentioned above, you can apply a table or cell style by—gasp!—placing the cursor in the table or cell (or selecting more than one cell) and clicking on the style name in the Table Styles or Cell Styles panel. Unfortunately, we don't see any way to apply a table style when placing a Word or Excel document.

You can also apply a table style to a table when you first create it with the Insert Table or Convert Text to Table features (both dialogs sport a Table style pop-up menu from which to choose a style).

Redefining Styles. You can change the definition of your table or cell styles at any time by selecting the style in the panel and choosing Style Options from the panel menu (or, better, from the Context menu). You can also change the formatting on your document page, then select the table or cell and choose Redefine Style from the Table Styles or Cell Styles panel menu. When you change a table or cell style definition, the new formatting is immediately reflected throughout your document.

Clearing Overrides. Just because you've applied a table or cell style doesn't mean you can't override that with further local formatting. When you do apply local formatting on top of a cell or table, you'll see the familiar plus (+) sign next to the style name, indicating there's additional formatting here. You can see what that formatting is by hovering the cursor over the style name.

To remove the local formatting, you can Option/Alt click on the style name in the Table Styles or Cell Styles panel. If you want to remove both local formatting applied to a table as well as any cell styles that were applied, Option-Shift/Alt-Shift-click on a table style.

FIGURE 6-40
Loading Table Styles

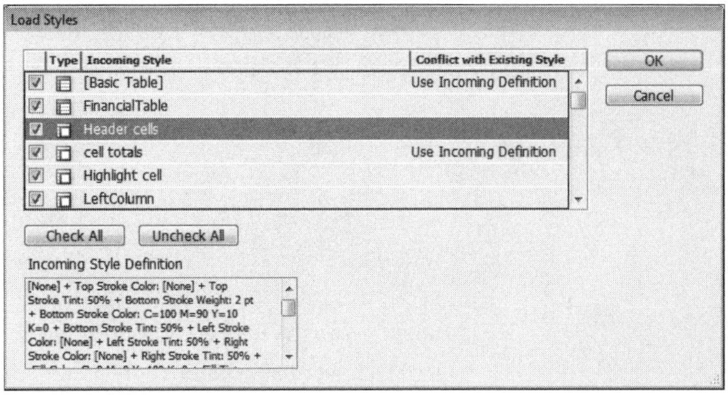

Another way to remove styles is to choose Clear Overrides from the Table Styles or Cell Styles panel menu (or click the Clear Overrides button at the bottom of the panel)—this is the same as Option/Alt-clicking. When it comes to cell styles, you have a final option in the panel menu (and panel button): Clear Attributes Not Defined by Style. The difference is subtle: Clear Overrides only removes the local formatting that overrides the cell style definition. Clear Attributes Not Defined by Style will clear all local formatting, even if it had nothing to do with the cell style's definition.

If you want to remove the cell style entirely, select the cell (or cells) and click [None] in the Cell Styles panel.

Sorting Styles. If you don't like the order in which styles appear in the Table Styles or Cell Styles panel, you can rearrange them in two ways: You can choose Sort by Name from the panel menu or you can drag each style up or down to the position you want it.

Loading Styles. You can copy the cell styles or table styles from another InDesign document by choosing Load Table Styles or Load Table and Cell Styles from the Table Styles or Cell Styles panel menu. When you do this, InDesign asks which styles you want, and—if some of the incoming styles have the same names as styles in your current document, what you want to do about it (see Figure 6-40).

Style Groups. You can group your table and cell styles together into groups (or folders, or sets, or whatever you want to call them) using the same techniques as grouping in the Paragraph Styles panel or elsewhere. First, make a style group by clicking the New Style Group button at the bottom of the Table Styles or Cell Styles panel, then drag your styles into the group. Alternately, you can select one or more styles and choose New Group from Styles from the panel menu.

If you want the same-named style in more than one group, select that style and choose Copy to Group from the panel menu.

Text Wrap

Any independent object in an InDesign publication can have a text wrap—a boundary that repels text—applied to it. Wrapping text around an object is something like the opposite of flowing text inside a text frame. When you flow text inside a frame, you want text to stay inside a path; when you apply a text wrap, you want to keep it out. To set the text wrap for an object, follow these steps (see Figure 6-41).

1. Select an object—any frame or group—on an InDesign page.

2. Display the Text Wrap panel, if it's not already visible (press Command-Option-W/Ctrl-Alt-W).

3. Click one of the Text Wrap buttons in the Text Wrap panel. InDesign displays the text wrap boundary around the selected object, and pushes any text falling inside the text wrap boundary to the outside of the boundary. If you applied the text wrap to a text frame, the text in that frame is unaffected by the text wrap boundary.

4. Set the text wrap offset distances using the Top, Left, Bottom, and Right fields in the Text Wrap panel. If you want the text wrap to be the same on all four sides, make sure the Link icon is enabled in the middle of the panel. However, if you've selected anything other than a rectangular frame, you'll only be able to adjust a single field (the Left field) to set the offset distance.

FIGURE 6-41

Text Wrap

To wrap text around an object, select the object and then click one of the text wrap options in the Text Wrap panel (we've listed the "official" name of the text wrap type below each example).

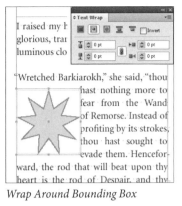

No Text Wrap

Wrap Around Bounding Box

Wrap Around Object Shape

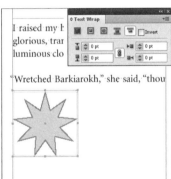

Jump Object

When you choose one of the rectangular text wrap options (Wrap Around Bounding Box, Jump Object, or Jump to Next Column), you can adjust the offset values for the top, right, left, and bottom independently. If you choose Wrap Around Object Shape, you can only enter a single offset value that applies to all sides of the text wrap.

Jump to Next Column

The Jump Object text wrap option causes text in any column touching the text wrap boundary to jump over the text wrap—it's as if the wrap extends to the width of the column. The Jump to Next Column text wrap option pushes any text in the column below the top of the text wrap boundary to the top of the next column.

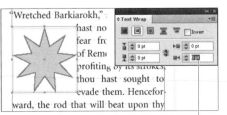

Enter a value in one of the offset fields...

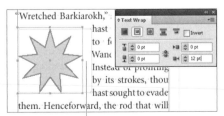

...and InDesign changes the offset for the corresponding side.

FIGURE 6-42
**Contour Text
Wrap Options**

*This image includes a path
saved in Photoshop.*

*If you don't see the bottom
half of the panel, choose
More Options from the
panel menu.*

*When you first apply a
contour text wrap, InDesign
bases the text wrap on the
image bounding box.*

*To base the text wrap
contour on the saved path,
choose Photoshop Path
from the Type pop-up
menu...*

*...and then choose the path name
from the Path pop-up menu.
InDesign sets the text wrap contour
to the shape of the path.*

FIGURE 6-43
Inverted Text Wrap

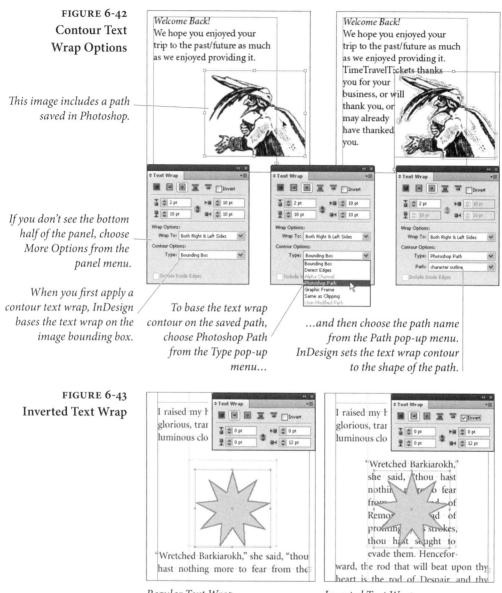

Regular Text Wrap

Inverted Text Wrap

Note that when it comes to inline or anchored objects (objects that are anchored to a position in a text story), text wrap doesn't always play by the same rules. We cover that in more detail in "Inline Frames and Anchored Objects," later in this chapter.

Contour Options   When you choose the Wrap Around Object text wrap type, and have an imported graphic selected, InDesign adds a new section to the bottom of the Text Wrap panel (if you don't see it, choose Show

FIGURE 6-44
Editing a Text Wrap

The text wrap boundary appears in a tint (we think it's 50 percent) of the selection color of the layer containing the object—this can make it difficult to see.

You can also use the Pen tool to add points, delete points, or change the control handles of points of a text wrap boundary.

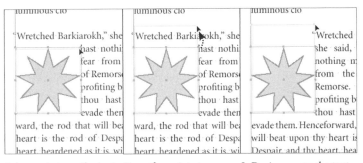

Select points on the text wrap boundary just as you would select points on any path.

Drag the points to a new location.

InDesign wraps the text around the edited text wrap boundary.

Options from the Text wrap panel menu). You can create the text wrap contour from paths or an alpha channel stored in a graphic, or detect the edges of objects in an image (see Figure 6-42). It's very similar to the clipping path options.

Ignoring Text Wrap

As we pointed out in the "Composition Preferences" section of Chapter 1, "Workspace," many people aren't used to the fact that applying text wrap to an object affects the text below *and* above that object in the stacking order. Fortunately, you can make individual text frames immune to text wrap: Select the frame, choose Text Frame Options from the Object menu (or press Command/Ctrl-B) and turn on the Ignore Text Wrap checkbox.

FIGURE 6-45
Choose a Wrap To Option

The default Wrap To setting (Both Right & Left Sides) leaves something to be desired.

Choosing Right Side or Largest Area from the Wrap To pop-up menu forces the text to flow on only one side of the object.

Inverted Text Wrap InDesign can apply an inverted text wrap to an object, which causes text to wrap to the inside of the text wrap (see Figure 6-43). We find this very helpful when... well, actually, almost never. But it's nice to have options.

Editing a Text Wrap The text wrap boundary is a path, and can be edited and adjusted just as you'd change the shape of any path in InDesign (see Figure 6-44). You can draw new line segments using the Pen tool, or change the location of path points using the Direct Selection tool.

Master Page Text Wrap In CS2 and earlier, items on the master page that had text wrap would not affect document page items unless they were overridden. Now there's a choice: By default, a master page object does affect text wrap on document pages, but if you don't want it to, you can select the object on the master page and choose Apply to Master Page Only from the Text Wrap panel menu.

Wrap To Options When you apply text wrap to an object that is narrower than the column of text, the text will typically flow on both the left and the right sides of it—useful in a few instances, ugly in most. You can control where you want the text to flow by choosing from the Wrap To pop-up menu in the Text Wrap panel (see Figure 6-45). If you want it to work like QuarkXPress, choose Largest Area.

Converting Text to Outlines

When you work in graphic design, you frequently need to alter character shapes for logos or packaging designs. For years, we dreamed about the ability to turn type into paths (or "outlines") we could edit. Finally, applications such as FreeHand and Illustrator added the feature. And, as you'd expect in a modern page layout program, InDesign has it.

You can convert characters from just about any font (including TrueType, PostScript Type 1, and OpenType fonts) for which you have the printer (outline) font.

Once you've converted the characters into outlines, you lose all text editing capabilities, but you gain the ability to paste things inside the character outline, to use the path as a frame, and to change the shapes of the characters themselves.

To convert characters of text into paths, follow these steps (see Figure 6-46).

FIGURE 6-46
**Converting Text
to Outlines**

*Select a text frame
with the Selection tool…*

*…and choose Create Outlines from
the Type menu. InDesign converts
the characters in the selected text
frame into a compound path.*

*To see the individual paths and points, select the
compound path using the Direct Selection tool.*

FIGURE 6-47
**Working with
Character Outlines**

*Select the compound path
containing the character
outlines and choose Release
Compound Path from the
Paths submenu.*

*InDesign converts the
compound path into
normal paths.*

*The same formatting (fill and
stroke) is applied to all of the
resulting paths—even the paths
that create the hollow areas
inside characters.*

*To put the characters back together again,
use the Direct Selection tool to select the path
representing the hollow area or areas of a
character and choose Reverse Path from the
Paths submenu of the Object menu.*

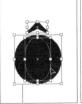

*Select the other path or paths in the character
and choose Make Compound Paths from the
Paths submenu of the Object menu.*

*InDesign joins the
paths, restoring the
interior space.*

1. Select the text you want to convert. You can select text using
   either the Type tool, or select the text frame using the Selection
   tool or the Direct Selection tool.

2. Choose Create Outlines from the Type menu (or press
   Command-Shift-O/Ctrl-Shift-O). InDesign converts the
   characters into paths. If you selected the characters using the
   Type tool, InDesign positions the paths on the current line as an
   inline graphic; if you selected the text frame using the Selection

tool or the Direct Selection tool, InDesign joins the resulting outlines into a compound path.

When you convert individual characters containing interior space (such as "P" or "O") into paths, InDesign turns them into composite paths (see "Compound Paths" in Chapter 5, "Drawing"). This is handy. Not only are multiple-part characters (such as i, é, and ü) treated as single paths, but characters with interior paths (such as O, P, A, and D) are transparent where they should be, and fill properly.

You can always make the characters into normal (not composite) paths. To do this, select the character and choose Release Compound Path from the Paths submenu of the Object menu (see Figure 6-47).

If Your Characters Won't Convert

If you weren't able to convert the text into paths, make sure that you have the outline (printer) fonts and that they're somewhere InDesign can find them. If you don't have the outline fonts, InDesign won't be able to convert your text into paths.

Also, note that some text elements don't convert to paths at all. For example, paragraph rules (Rule Above or Rule Below) and automatic bullets or numbers.

Inline Frames and Anchored Objects

It was the Dark Age of page layout. The flame of classical desktop publishing knowledge flickered but dimly, kept barely alive by devoted acolytes in isolated monasteries. Pestilence and famine stalked the narrow aisles between our unheated cubicles. And, almost worst of all, page layout programs could not paste graphics into text. Producing publications featuring graphics "anchored" to a specific piece of text was a nightmare. It went something like this. Scroll. Zoom in. Measure. Pull a guide down from a ruler. Select a graphic. Drag the graphic until it snaps to the guide. Sigh heavily. Repeat.

These days, we embed graphics in lines of text whenever the graphics have a defined relationship to the text. You know what we we're talking about—illustrations that should appear immediately after a paragraph (think of the screen shots in a manual), or icons "hanging" to the left of a column of text, or graphic symbols in a line of text. If you anchor the graphics in the text, they'll follow the text as it flows through the text blocks or text frames containing the story.

Really early versions of InDesign offered only "inline frames," but now you can create inline frames, above line frames, and anchored objects, too.

▶ An inline frame sits in the text position where it's placed, though you can adjust its vertical offset (how far up or down it sits from the baseline of the text around it). For example, you might want to put graphic in the middle of a line of text.

▶ An above line frame sits between the line you placed it on and the line above it. InDesign adds space between the lines to make room for the object, ignoring leading or other spacing you've set. We usually call these inline frames, even though they're technically different.

▶ An anchored object can be placed anywhere on your page, even outside the text frame.

Using inline frames does more than just "stick" a frame to a particular location in a story—it also makes it easier for you to control the space between the graphic and the text. Complicated spacing arrangements that would be difficult (and involve lots of measuring and moving) without inline frames become easy to implement using leading, tabs, indents, and paragraph space above and below.

FIGURE 6-48
Creating an
Inline Frame

1. Select the object (graphic frame, text frame, or group) you want to embed in the text and cut or copy it to the Clipboard.

3. Paste the object into the text. At this point, you can select the object using the Selection tool (or select object contents using the Direct Selection tool) and adjust the object's vertical position relative to the line of text.

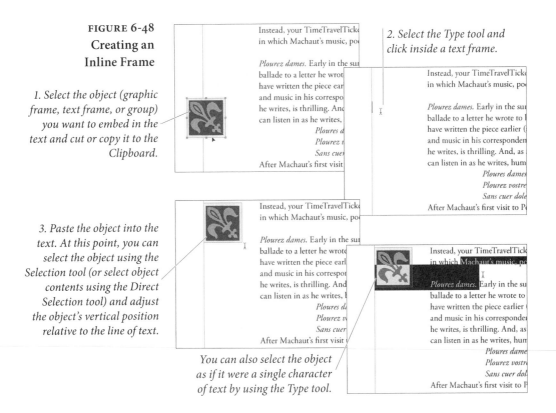

2. Select the Type tool and click inside a text frame.

You can also select the object as if it were a single character of text by using the Type tool.

What can you anchor? Even though we keep saying "frames," you can actually anchor any kind of object into a text frame. You can use graphic frames, text frames, lines, and groups as well, opening up new ways to solve old problems and adding capabilities that are entirely new. You can even create inline frames or anchored objects using frames that contain other frames or other inline frames.

What can't you do to anchored objects? Despite an impressive array of cool things you can do with inline frames and anchored objects, there are still a few things you can't do. For example, you can't link (or "thread") an inline or anchored text frame to another text frame. You also cannot see what's inside them when you're in Story Editor mode (or Galley or Story mode in InCopy). The latter is especially annoying. In fact, we're typing this in Story Editor right now and can't see the heading in the next paragraph because it's already anchored. Just another good reason to buy a another monitor so that you can have Story Editor and the document layout visible at the same time.

Creating an Inline Frame

You can use any of the following methods to create an inline frame (see Figure 6-48).

▶ Paste a frame or group into text.

▶ Place a graphic when you have an active text insertion point.

▶ Position the text cursor where you want the inline frame and choose Insert from the Anchored Object submenu (under the Object menu or the context menu). Then choose Inline or Above Line from the Position pop-up menu. We virtually never use the Insert Anchored Object feature, but it's nice to know it's there. Instead, we usually paste an existing object, or place a file.

▶ Use the Type tool to select a character or a range of characters and choose Convert to Outlines from the Type menu. InDesign creates a path for each character in the selection and embeds the paths, as a compound path, in the text.

InDesign treats each inline frame as a single character of text. When you view the text in Story Editor, you can see the "anchor marker" (a little anchor symbol) in the text.

You can select an inline frame using the Type tool and adjust its leading and baseline shift using the Character panel. You can adjust the horizontal distance between the inline frame and the other characters on the line using kerning or tracking—you can even kern text

FIGURE 6-49
**Adjusting the Position
of an Inline Frame**

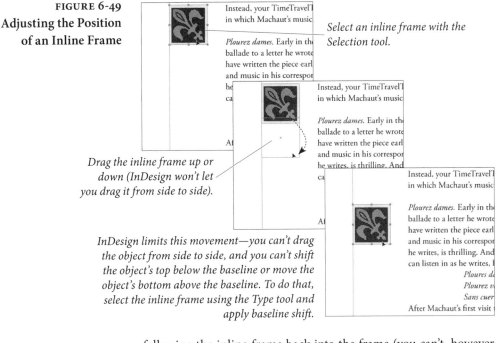

Select an inline frame with the
Selection tool.

Drag the inline frame up or
down (InDesign won't let
you drag it from side to side).

InDesign limits this movement—you can't drag
the object from side to side, and you can't shift
the object's top below the baseline or move the
object's bottom above the baseline. To do that,
select the inline frame using the Type tool and
apply baseline shift.

following the inline frame back into the frame (you can't, however, kern the frame back into characters preceding it on a line).

You can select an inline frame using either selection tool, and you can edit the shape of the inline frame using the path drawing tools. You can also drag an inline frame up or down in the text frame using either of the selection tools (see Figure 6-49), or you can apply a baseline shift to the character containing the inline frame.

Another way to adjust the vertical offset of a selected inline object is to choose Options from the Anchored Objects submenu (under the Object menu or the context menu) and change the Y Offset value. This is a particularly good way to get the offset back to zero if you have accidentally nudged it up or down.

**Inline Frames
and Leading**

When you insert an inline frame into a text frame, InDesign gives it the leading value of the surrounding text. If you're using "auto" leading, and if the inline frame is taller than the height of the text, InDesign pushes the line down to prevent the inline frame from overlapping the lines above it. If you're using a fixed leading value, you'll see the inline frame overlap the text. By default, InDesign positions the bottom of the inline frame at the baseline of text.

This works perfectly for us—when the inline frame shares a line with other text, we usually want the leading of the line to stay the same as the other lines in the paragraph—and we can get this effect using fixed leading values. When we place an inline frame in a paragraph by itself, however, we usually want the height of the paragraph to equal the height of the inline frame—and we can get that effect by using "auto" leading for the paragraph.

The rules are a little different when an inline frame falls on the first line of text in a text frame. In that case, the position of the baseline of the inline frame is controlled by the First Baseline option in the Text Frame Options dialog box.

If the height of the inline frame is greater than the height of the characters in the line (and it usually is), choosing "Ascent" positions the top of the inline frame at the top of the text frame. This pushes the first line down to accommodate the height of the inline frame. If you adjust the vertical position of the inline frame, the position of the first line of text moves up or down. The same thing happens when you choose "Cap Height" (note that these two settings produce different results for text, but are the same for inline frames).

When you choose "Leading" InDesign positions the baseline of the first line of text according to the largest leading value in the line. If you're using a fixed leading value, and you've set the leading of the inline frame to the leading of the surrounding text, the position of the baseline of the first line of text won't change, regardless of what you do with the inline frame.

FIGURE 6-50
Inline Frames and "Auto" Leading

Height of inline graphic: 56 points (4 × 14)

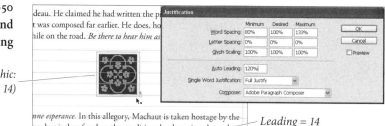

Leading = 14

In this example, the leading of the paragraph containing the inline frame is set to "Auto," and the Auto Leading value is set to 120 percent, which means that the lines following the graphic do not align to the 14-point baseline grid.

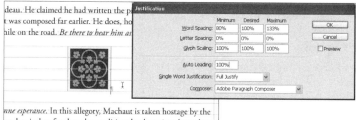

Set the Auto Leading value to 100 percent, and InDesign makes the vertical space occupied by the inline frame equal to the height of the frame.

We always use the "Baseline" option for our first baseline position, and we always set the leading of a graphic that shares a line with text characters to the leading of those characters. This way, we always know where the first baseline of text will fall, and we don't have to worry that changes to the shape, size, or baseline position of the inline frame will mess up the leading.

The only time we use "auto" leading is when we're working with a paragraph that contains only an inline frame. The only trouble is that we want the vertical distance taken up by the paragraph to be exactly equal to the height of the inline frame—no more, no less. By default, InDesign's "auto" leading value is equal to 120% of the point size of the type (or, in this case, the height of the inline frame). How can we get the base "auto" leading percentage down to 100%?

The percentage used to calculate "auto" leading, as it turns out, is a paragraph-level attribute. To view or adjust this percentage, choose Justification from the Paragraph panel's menu. InDesign displays the Justification dialog box. Enter 100 in the Auto Leading field and click OK to close the dialog box (see Figure 6-50). Once you've done this, the leading of the paragraph will equal the height of the inline frame. If you want, you can add this to a paragraph style definition.

Creating Hanging Side Heads

If there's one thing that inline frames make easier, it's hanging side heads. You know—the headings that appear to the left of a column of text (like the one to the left of this paragraph). In InDesign, you can create a hanging side head that follows a paragraph of text as it flows through a publication—no more dragging the headings to a new position when text reflows. You use a hanging indent and an inline frame, as shown in the following steps (see Figure 6-51).

1. Create a hanging indent. To do this, set a left indent that's the width of the "companion column" you want to the left of the paragraph, then set a negative first line indent equal to the width of the left indent. Place a tab stop at the left indent.

2. Enter a tab character before the first character of the paragraph. This pushes the text to the left indent.

3. Paste a text frame before the tab character you just entered. Adjust the position of the inline text frame, if necessary.

4. Enter the heading's text in the inline text frame.

5. Format the heading.

That's all there is to it—you now have a hanging side head that will follow the paragraph anywhere it goes. This same technique can

FIGURE 6-51

FIGURE 6-51
Creating a
Hanging Side Head

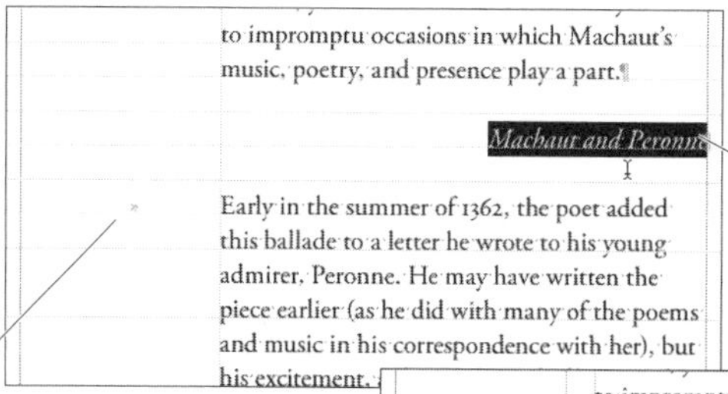

This paragraph has a negative first line indent to accommodate the heading, and I've already entered a tab character before the first line of the paragraph.

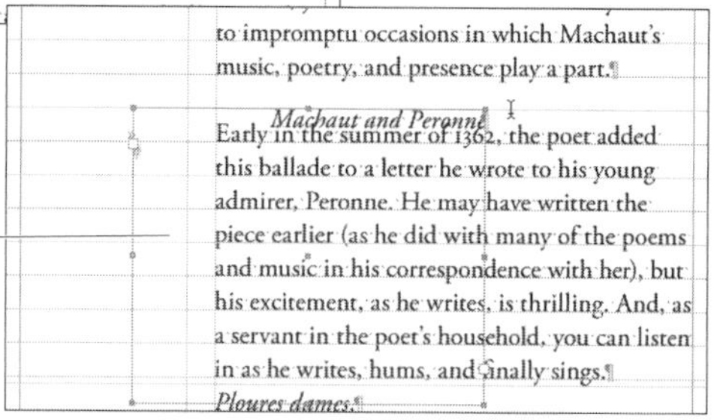

Use the Type tool to select the text you want to format as a hanging side head.

Cut or copy the heading to the Clipboard, then press Command-Shift-A/ Ctrl-Shift-A (to deselect all), and then paste. InDesign places the text from the Clipboard in a new text frame.

Adjust the size of the text frame, if necessary.

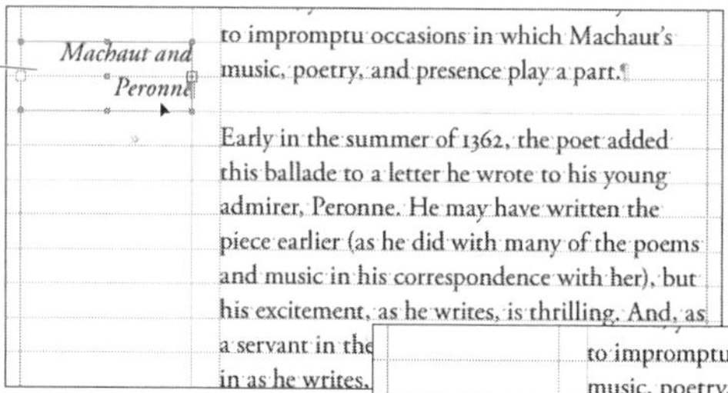

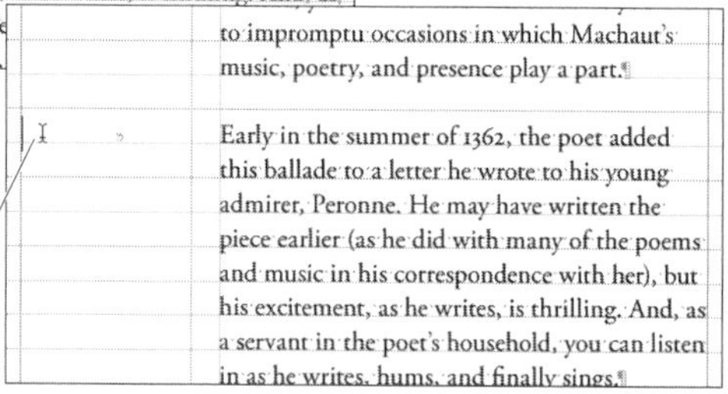

Cut or copy the text frame to the Clipboard, then click the Type tool in the text (before the tab character) and paste the text frame from the Clipboard.

Adjust the size and/or position of the inline text frame until it looks the way you want it to.

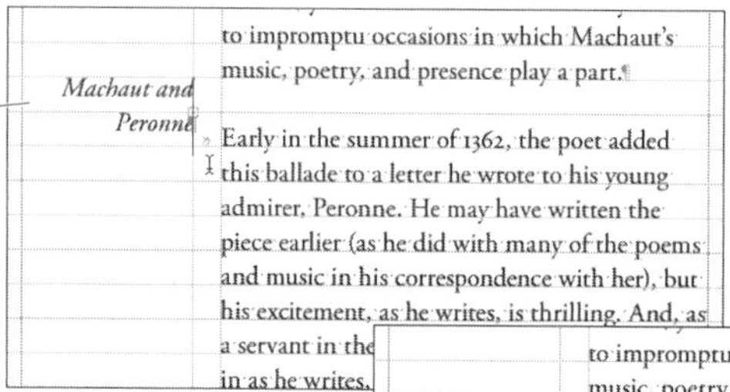

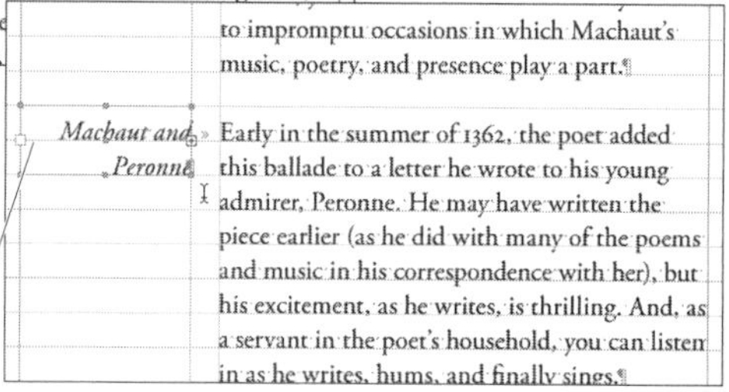

You've created a hanging side head that will move with the paragraph of body text as that paragraph moves in response to editing or layout changes.

be used to position graphics frames, and is handy when you need to "hang" an icon or a vertical rule to the left of a particular paragraph.

Of course, you can accomplish the same thing with an anchored object—which can actually sit in the margin outside the text frame (see "Creating an Anchored Object," later in this chapter). But some people find inline frames easier to work with.

Selecting and Removing Inline and Anchored Objects

As we mentioned earlier, you can select an inline or anchored object using the Type tool (the object behaves as if it were a single character in the story) or the Selection tool or Direct Selection tool. If you use the Type tool, you can select more than one inline or anchored object at a time (to control their position in the Anchored Object Options dialog box). Using either method, you can delete the object by pressing Delete.

To "unanchor" an inline frame or anchored object, select it using the Selection tool, then cut and paste. If it's an anchored object, you

FIGURE 6-52
Creating an Above Line Object

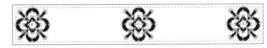

Select a graphic.

Paste the graphic into the first line of the paragraph, and it will appear as an inline object.

Choose Options from the Anchored Object submenu in the Object or Context menu. InDesign displays the Anchored Object Options dialog box.

Turn on the Above Line option, then select an alignment and enter the space before and space after distances you want.

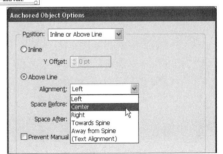

Here's the final anchored object, with space above and below added.

can also select Release from the Anchored Object submenu (on the Object menu or context menu). Release doesn't work for inline or above line objects.

Creating Above Line Objects

Above line objects are much like paragraph rules, but you can use any object (or group of objects), to create a wider range of effects. For example, you might use an imported graphic as a rule above a paragraph. You can make an above line object in one of two ways.

▶ Choose Insert from the Anchored Object submenu (from the Object menu or the context menu), and then choose Above Line.

▶ Create an inline frame as we described earlier in this section. Then select it using either the Selection tool or the Type tool (the latter is especially helpful when you want to convert a number of inline frames to above line objects at the same time) and choose Options from the Anchored Object submenu. When the Anchored Object Options dialog box appears, turn on the Above Line option.

Once you create an above line object, you can use the Anchored Object Options dialog box to control where the object will appear in the space between the current line and the line before it (see Figure 6-52). The Alignment pop-up menu lets you choose Left, Center, Right, Toward Spine, Away from Spine, and Text Alignment. The last item simply means use the same alignment as the horizontal alignment of the paragraph the above line object is sitting in (left, center, or right).

You can also adjust the space before or after the object. Increasing these values adds vertical space around the above line object. You can also use negative values for Space Before and Space After (up to the height of the object itself), which will cause the object to overlap the preceding or following line. InDesign changes the Space Before and Space After values whenever you drag the object up or down. (As you'd expect, you won't be able to drag the object if you have turned on the Prevent Manual Positioning option or if you have enabled Lock on the Object menu. Turning either of these features on enables the other.)

Creating Anchored Objects

Unlike inline frames and above line objects, anchored objects can appear anywhere on the page or spread containing their text anchor. Just like above line objects, you can create an anchored object using either the Insert Anchored Object dialog box or by creating an inline

FIGURE 6-53
Creating an
Anchored Object

*Paste the frame into a text frame,
just as you would to create an
inline frame.*

*Open the Anchored Object
Options dialog box and turn
on the Preview checkbox.
The object will appear to
the left of the text frame by
default. Click OK.*

*Drag the object to a new
location and turn on text
wrap. The object will remain
positioned in relation to
the frame and the anchor
marker in the story.*

object and then converting it to an anchored object by copying and
pasting (see Figure 6-53).

1. Select the inline object by clicking on it with the Selection tool or
    by dragging over it with the Type tool.

2. Choose Options from the Anchored Object submenu (under the
    Object menu or the context menu).

3. Choose Custom from the Position pop-up menu at the top of
    the Anchored Object Options dialog box. The dialog box now
    offers a dizzying array of options. Don't panic. All will be
    explained below.

4. To manually position the object on the page, just click OK (to
    close the dialog box). You can then move the object with the
    Selection tool to wherever you want it.

At this point, the anchored object acts as if it is tethered to the
anchor marker As the text reflows, the object moves, too. To be more
precise, the horizontal location of the anchored object remains fixed

relative to the text frame (it only moves when the text frame moves or when the anchor marker moves into a different frame), but its vertical location moves with the line of text itself (the line containing the anchor marker). With these default settings, the anchored object will also stay within the top and bottom boundaries of the text frame—you can't drag it above or below the frame.

But the default settings are only the beginning. Let's look at what else you can do in the Anchored Object Options dialog box.

Relative to Spine. If you want to position an anchored object precisely (as opposed to just dragging it somewhere), the first decision you need to make is whether to turn on the Relative to Spine option. When this option is on, InDesign positions the object differently depending on whether it sits on a left hand (verso) or on a right hand (recto) page. This option is similar to the Align Toward Spine and Align Away from Spine paragraph alignment feature, and is useful when you want an object to appear in the outside or inside margin of a page.

Anchored Object. The next step is to tell InDesign what part of the anchored object you're positioning. When Relative to Spine is off, you'll see a single Reference Point proxy from which you can choose a corner, side, or center point. If you choose the lower-right corner of this proxy, you're telling InDesign to position the lower-right corner of the anchored object at a particular place on the page. (We'll get to where it'll be positioned in a moment.)

If you've turned on the Relative to Spine checkbox, you'll see two proxies in the Reference Point section. When you choose a point on one proxy, it'll be mirrored on the other. What InDesign is trying to tell you is that you're no longer choosing the left or right sides of the anchored object, but rather the inside (toward spine) or outside (away from spine) sides. Click the lower-right corner point of the left Reference Point proxy, and you're telling InDesign that you want the lower-inside corner to be positioned at a particular place on the page.

Turn on the Preview checkbox! You will likely go insane if you try to figure out all these controls without it. With the Preview checkbox turned on, you can see the effect of each change you make.

Anchored Position. The final step to positioning an anchored object is in some ways the most complex: Telling InDesign where you want the object to appear on the page using the Anchored Position section of the Anchored Object Options dialog box. We find that it helps to learn to "read" the dialog box (see Figure 6-54).

FIGURE 6-54
"Reading" the Anchored
Options Dialog Box

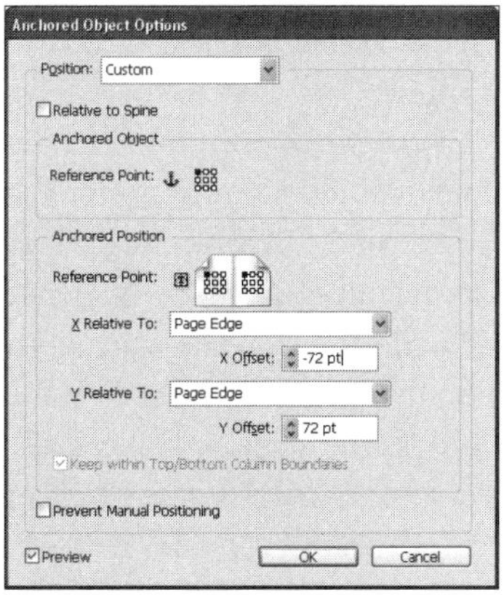

The upper left corner of the anchored object is placed 72 points in from the upper left corner of the page.

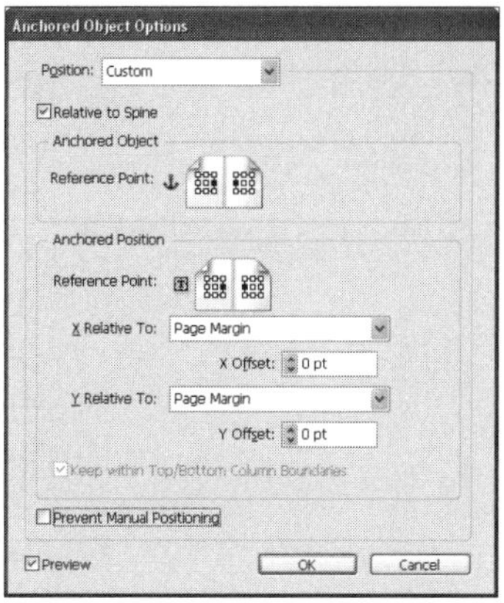

The inside center edge of the object sits halfway down the page and against the inside margin.

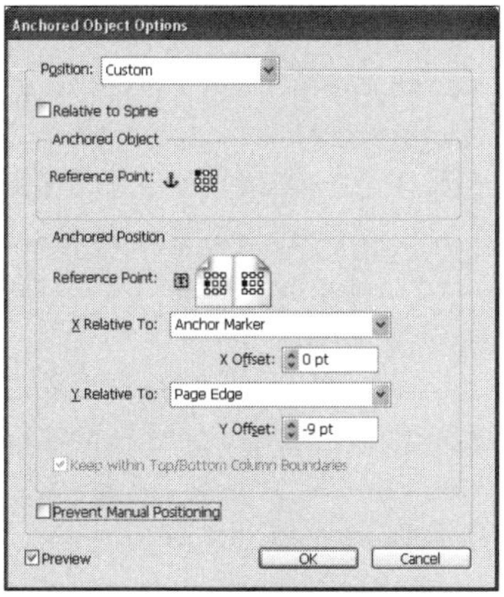

The object is centered around the anchor marker and raised 9 points. As the marker moves, so does the object.

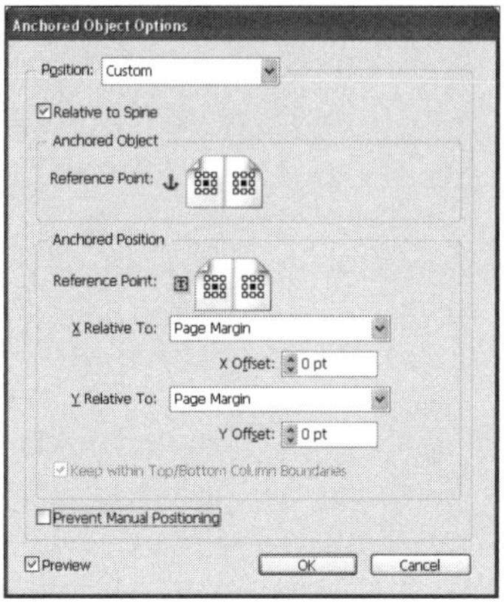

The object is always placed at the center of the page.

The Reference Point control in this section (note to Adobe: Please don't give two different settings the same label) makes no sense until you look at the X Relative To and Y Relative To sections, so skip it for a moment. The X Relative To pop-up menu sets the horizontal position of the anchored object. You can choose Anchor Marker, Column Edge, Text Frame, Page Margin, or Page Edge.

If you click the left point in the Reference Point proxy (the one in the Anchored Position section) the default setting of Text Frame means, "position the anchored object relative to the left side of the current text frame." If you select the right point of the Reference Point proxy, it means "position the anchored object relative to the right side of the current text frame." If you have turned on the Relative to Spine checkbox, these mean, "relative to the outside/inside of the text frame."

The Y Relative To pop-up menu determines the vertical position of the anchored object. Your options are: Line (Baseline, Cap Height, or Top of Leading), Column Edge, Text Frame, Page Margin, or Page Edge. The default setting is "Line (Baseline)," which means, "position the anchored object on the page so that it aligns with the baseline of the line that includes the anchor marker." As the line shifts up or down, so does the anchored object.

When you choose one of the Line options from the pop-up menu, the Reference Point proxy limits your choices to left, center, or right. The reason is obvious: There is no "upper left" corner of the anchor marker's baseline. However, if you choose a Y Relative To setting having to do with the frame, column, or page, the Reference Point proxy changes to allow you to choose more points (upper left corner of the page, lower left corner of the page, and so on).

You can also specify X Offset or Y Offset values in order to precisely position the anchored object. If you select the right-center point of the Reference Point proxy and select Page Edge from the X Relative To pop-up menu, and then type 20 mm in the X Offset field, what you're saying is, "Place the anchored object 20 mm from the right edge of the page." You can enter negative numbers for all kinds of positioning tricks (such as putting an object on the page *opposite* the page containing the anchor marker).

The last control in the Anchored Position section is the Keep within Top/Bottom Column Bounds. (It'll be grayed out unless you have chosen one of the Line options from the Y Relative To pop-up menu.) The idea here is that if the line containing the anchor marker gets too close to the top or bottom of the text frame, the anchored object might extend past the frame's top or bottom edge. If you don't want this to happen, turn this option on.

Prevent Manual Positioning. As we noted earlier, turning on the Prevent Manual Positioning checkbox is exactly the same as choosing Lock from the Object menu. It's just a good way to ensure that your anchored objects don't get accidentally moved.

Seeing Markers. Once you've set up an anchored object, you may not remember where, exactly, the anchor marker is located. Choose Show Hidden Characters from the Type menu, and you'll see a little anchor marker symbol in the story—it's a light blue yen character (¥). Similarly, if you open Story Editor, you can see a black anchor symbol at that location. But perhaps the most useful indicator appears when

FIGURE 6-55
Wrapping Around an
Anchored Drop Cap

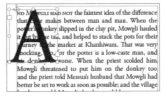

*The original paragraph
with a drop cap*

*Cut the drop cap, remove the drop cap
formatting from the paragraph, and
then paste the drop cap into a new text
frame. Choose Fit Frame to Content,
then use the Selection tool to cut the
drop cap frame and paste it into the line
before the paragraph.*

*Choose Wrap Around Bounding Box in
the Text Wrap panel, increase the wrap
a few points (so you can see them) and
then use the Direct Selection tool to create a custom wrap.*

you choose Show Text Threads from the View menu—select the text
frame or the anchored object with the Selection tool and you'll see a
dashed line connecting the two.

**Text Wrap and Inline
and Anchored Objects**

You can wrap text around inline or anchored objects. This feature
comes with three big caveats. First, only the story in which the object
is anchored is affected. Text in other frames ignores anchored objects.
Second, if you anchor an object inside a table cell, text wrap is completely ignored. Finally, only the lines *following* the line containing
an anchored object are affected by the object's text wrap. The line
containing the anchored object ignores the text wrap.

Drop Cap Wrap. One of the most frustrating aspects of drop caps
is that there is no way to tell InDesign to wrap the subsequent text
around them. You can fake it by putting the drop cap character in a
separate text frame, or by converting the character to outlines, but
then the drop cap wouldn't travel with the text, right?

Enter inline frames. As David first documented in his book with
Anne-Marie Concepción, *Adobe InDesign Breakthroughs*, you can
place a drop cap character in a separate frame, paste it at the end of
the paragraph *before* the paragraph in which it's supposed to appear
(you can put the frame in a blank paragraph when the drop cap
appears at the beginning of the story), and then adjust the text wrap

FIGURE 6-56
Hanging Side Heads as
Anchored Objects

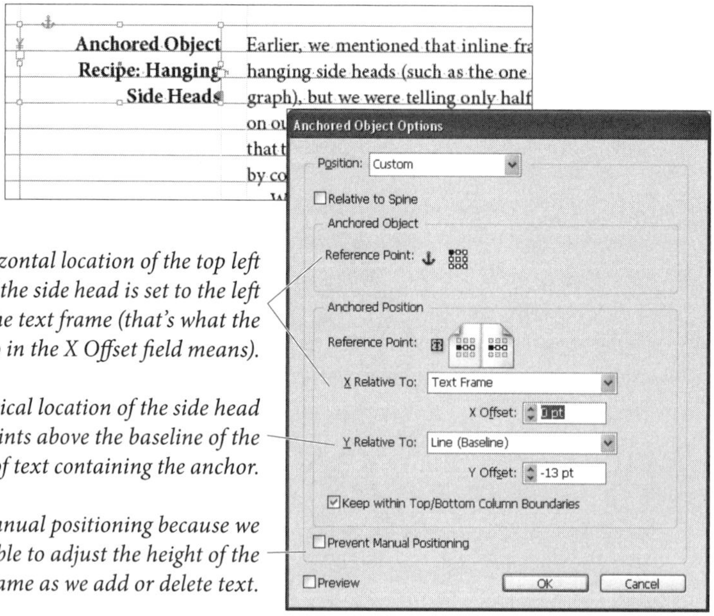

The horizontal location of the top left corner of the side head is set to the left edge of the text frame (that's what the zero in the X Offset field means).

The vertical location of the side head is 13 points above the baseline of the line of text containing the anchor.

We allow manual positioning because we need to be able to adjust the height of the frame as we add or delete text.

boundaries with the Direct Selection tool to get the effect you want (see Figure 6-55).

Ole notes that this is a heck of a lot of work to go through to achieve a design effect that is both ugly and makes your text harder to read (as varying the starting position of successive text lines always does). Further, he notes in his irritating, pedantic fashion, there's a reason that the drop caps in beautiful old books always place the ornamental drop cap in a rectangular frame—to avoid this very temptation.

Anchored Object Recipe: Hanging Side Heads

Earlier, we mentioned that inline frames are the best way to create hanging side heads (such as the one loitering to the left of this paragraph), but we were telling only half of the story. By experimenting on ourselves (as any good pair of mad scientists should), we've found that the best approach to hanging side heads is to create inline frames by copying, pasting, and then converting them to anchored objects.

We did this because we found that changes in InDesign between CS and CS2 made it much more difficult to control the vertical position of inline frames—which, in turn, made managing our hanging side heads a bit of a challenge. The good news is that anchored objects offer a level of precision that inline frames just can't match. We found a set of anchored object settings that worked well with our hanging side heads, and then created a script to apply the changes to our chapters.

We set up the hanging side heads—most of which were already inline graphics—as shown in Figure 6-56. The horizontal location of the top left corner of the hanging side head is set to the left edge of the text frame, and the vertical location is 13 points above the baseline of the line of text containing the anchor (our leading grid is based on 13 point increments).

We want the frame to remain within the vertical bounds of the text frame, and we allow manual positioning (because we need to be able to adjust the height of the frame as we add or delete text).

Object Styles

The sidebars in your magazine have a twenty percent cyan fill and a soft drop shadow. How many thousand times must you apply that same fill and shadow before you go mad and throw someone else's computer out the window? (You wouldn't throw your own out the window; your favorite games are there.) One solution would be to keep an example object in a library (see Chapter 1, "Workspace") or a snippet (see Chapter 7, "Import and Export"). A more flexible and powerful solution is to create an object style.

Object styles are just like paragraph and character styles, except that they apply to objects instead of text. An object style is basically just a bunch of object formatting with a name. You can apply that style to a frame or path on your page and all the appropriate formatting is applied. If you later change the definition of the style, the change immediately ripples through to all the objects tagged with that style.

Creating Object Styles

To create an object style, hold down Option/Alt and click the New Object Style button at the bottom of the Object Styles panel (press Command-F7/Ctrl-F7 to display the panel if it is not already visible). If you have an object selected, the new object style takes on the formatting attributes of the object. If you don't have anything selected on the page, then the object style takes on the default formatting of the document, and you will have to define the style from scratch. We strongly urge you to use the "create style by example" approach, as shown in Figure 6-57.

The New Object Style dialog box consists of 10 panels (count 'em!), including Fill, Stroke, Transparency, and Anchored Object Options. You can turn the checkbox next to each panel on or off. On means "apply this formatting as part of the style." Off means "ignore this formatting." That is, if you turn off the Fill checkbox, it doesn't mean that the fill should be set to None; it means that this object style has no effect on the fill of objects.

FIGURE 6-57
Creating an
Object Style

1. Select an object that has the formatting attributes you want to assign to the object style.

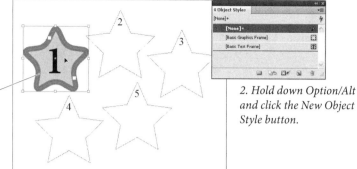

2. Hold down Option/Alt and click the New Object Style button.

3. Make any changes you want in the panels of the New Object Style dialog box.

Turn off sections to prevent the style from affecting the corresponding object properties.

You can also apply transparency effects to Object, Fill, Stroke, or Text inside an object style.

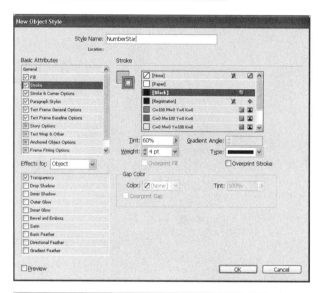

4. Click OK, and InDesign adds the new object style to the list of available styles.

5. Select an object or objects and apply the style, and you'll see that the formatting attributes of the original object are applied to the selected objects.

In this example, we associated a paragraph style and text frame baseline offset with the object style, so the text was affected, too.

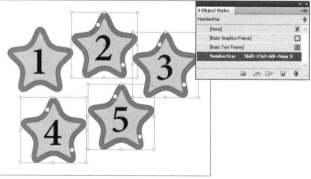

You can create one object style that applies only a specific text wrap to an object, and a different style that applies only a stroke and a drop shadow. If you draw a frame and apply the first style, only the text wrap would be applied. Then you can apply the second style, changing only the stroke and drop shadow. At this point, the object is tagged with the second style, not the first, which means that if you redefine the first object style, this object will not be updated.

Note that you can press Tab to jump to the list of panels, and then press the up and down arrow keys on your keyboard to move among them. You can also Option/Alt-click on a checkbox to toggle the other categories: Option/Alt-click on an "on" checkbox to turn all the others off, and vice versa.

Style Settings. At the bottom of the General panel of the New Object Style dialog box is a list of Style Settings. You can use this as a summary of settings the object style will apply. But to be honest, we never use this. It's just easier to use the shortcuts to flip through each panel. If you do use it, you should Option/Alt-click on the little triangles so that they fully expand. (Otherwise, you have to click over and over again, which is annoying.)

Keyboard Shortcuts. You can assign a keyboard shortcut to an object style in the General panel. Like keyboard shortcuts for paragraph styles and character styles, the shortcut must use the numeric keypad keys (make sure that Num Lock is on), not normal numbers, characters, or function keys.

Basing One Object Style on Another. You can also choose another object style from the Based On pop-up menu in the General panel to create a "parent/child" relationship between styles. If you change the definition of the based on ("parent") style, that change is passed along to this style, too—provided that the child style didn't already override the parent style's formatting.

To clear the formatting in an object style that differs from its parent style, click the Reset to Base button. This makes the attributes of the style identical to those of the parent style.

FIGURE 6-58
Setting a Default
Object Style

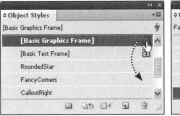

Drag the default icon (for either the graphics frame or text frame) to a new object style.

The object style you drop the icon on becomes the default object style for the corresponding frame type.

The Default Styles   Every new document you create contains three initial object styles: None, Basic Graphics Frame, and Basic Text Frame. (They're listed in the panel with brackets so you know that they're special and can't be deleted.) When you create a path or an empty frame (one with an "X" through it), the None style is applied—that is, no style at all. When you make a text or graphics frame, the relevant style is applied. You can redefine these styles (see "Editing Object Styles," later in this section), and once you create new object styles, you can even tell InDesign to use those as your defaults instead.

For example, you might need to create a bunch of similarly-formatted text frames. You could change the Default Text Frame Style to one with the appropriate formatting, draw the frames, and then restore the original settings to the default style. To change the default text frame style, choose a style from the Default Text Frame Style submenu in the Object Styles panel menu. (Or the Default Graphics Frame Style submenu to change that default.)

Actually, it's even easier than that: See the little icons to the right of the default styles in the panel? Just drag one of them to the style you want to set as the default (see Figure 6-58). Alternatively, you can deselect everything and then select a style. In general, this sets the default graphics frame style; but when you have the Type tool selected, this sets the default text frame style.

Applying Object Styles   You can apply an object style in any of several ways.

▶ Select an object or series of objects and click the object style name in the Object Styles panel (or choose it from the object style pop-up menu in the Control panel).

▶ Drag an object style name from the Object Styles panel and drop it on an object (the object need not be selected).

▶ Select an object, then press Command-Return/Ctrl-Enter to invoke the Quick Apply feature, and then type a few characters of the style name (see "Quick Apply," later in this chapter).

Note that if you have a lot of object styles, you can rearrange them in the panel by dragging them up or down. To reset them to alphabetical order, choose Sort by Name from the panel menu.

Clearing Local Formatting. Just as you can apply local text formatting to text over a paragraph or character style, you can apply local object formatting over an object style. You might apply an object style that fills a frame with cyan, and then manually override that to make the frame yellow. To remove all of the local overrides, click the

Clear Overrides button in the Object Styles panel (or choosing the feature of the same name from the panel menu). Or you can Option/Alt-click on the style name to reset it and remove all overrides.

There's another "clear" button in the panel: Clear Attributes Not Defined by Style. Clicking this button (or choosing it from the panel menu) is the same as applying the None object style and then reapplying the style. InDesign sets all the object formatting that isn't described in the style definition (all of the panels without checkmarks next to them) to equal what you'd get with the None style.

Breaking the Link. As we mentioned earlier, applying an object style creates a link between the object and the style. To convert the formatting applied by the object style to local formatting and break the link between the object and the style, choose Break Link to Style from the Object Styles panel menu. The object's appearance won't change, but future changes to the style definition have no effect on the object.

Editing Object Styles

There are a whole mess o' ways to edit an object style.

▶ Double-click the style name in the Object Styles panel. If an object is selected on the page when you do this, the style will be applied to it.

▶ Right-click (or Control-click until you come to your senses and buy a two-button mouse) the style name in the Object Styles panel and choose Edit. This has the advantage of not applying the style to any selected objects.

▶ Select an object that has the style applied to it and then choose Style Options from the object style pop-up menu in the Control panel (this pop-up menu sits to the left of pop-up menu that lists the object styles).

▶ Press Command-Return/Ctrl-Enter to bring up Quick Apply, type enough of the style name so that it is highlighted, and then press Command-Return/Ctrl-Enter again.

▶ Change the formatting of an object that is already tagged with the style, and then choose Redefine Style from the Object Styles panel menu. This updates the style definition to match the current formatting of the selected object.

Deleting Object Styles

To delete an object style, select the style in the Object Styles panel and click the Delete Style button, or drag the style name on top of the button. If the style is in use (if any objects are tagged with it),

InDesign asks you which style it should apply in its place. If you choose None, you also have the option to Preserve Formatting. When this checkbox is on, objects that were tagged with the style will still appear the same, but all the formatting will be converted to local formatting. If you turn off Preserve Formatting, the objects will be completely cleared of formatting: no fill, stroke, and so on.

Importing Object Styles

How can you move your carefully-constructed object styles from one document to another? One easy way is to copy any object tagged with the style and then paste it into the target document—the style comes with it and you can then delete the object if you want.

If you want to import a bunch of styles, it may be easier to choose Load Object Styles from the Object Style panel menu. InDesign asks you to select another InDesign document, and then asks you which object styles you want to import from it. If there are object styles that have the same name in the two documents, you have a choice whether to use the incoming definition or to rename the style.

Placing Text on a Path

InDesign can place text *on* a path, as well as place text *inside* a path (which is what a text frame is, after all). Once you've added text to a path, you can select the text just as you would select any other text—select the Type tool and drag it through the characters you want to select, or click the Type tool in the text and use keyboard shortcuts. To select the path, use the Selection tool or Direct Selection tool.

To attach text to a path, follow these steps (see Figure 6-59).

1. Select the Path Type tool.

2. Move the tool over a path. The cursor changes to indicate that InDesign is ready to place text on the path.

3. Click the tool on the path. InDesign places the cursor on the path. The position of the cursor depends on the document's default paragraph alignment (if the default alignment is left, for example, the cursor will appear at the start of the path). Instead of clicking, you can drag the tool along the path to define the area of the path you want to fill with text.

   If InDesign cannot fit all of the text onto the path, the extra text is stored as overset text.

4. Add text to the path just as you would add text to a text frame—by typing, pasting text from the Clipboard, or import-

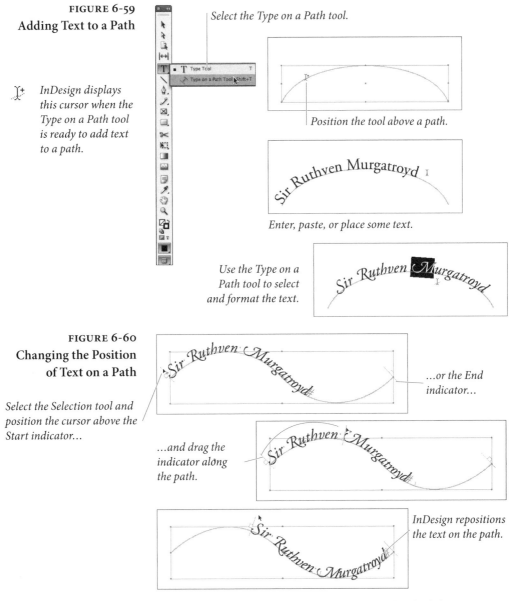

FIGURE 6-59
Adding Text to a Path

InDesign displays this cursor when the Type on a Path tool is ready to add text to a path.

Select the Type on a Path tool.

Position the tool above a path.

Enter, paste, or place some text.

Use the Type on a Path tool to select and format the text.

FIGURE 6-60
Changing the Position of Text on a Path

Select the Selection tool and position the cursor above the Start indicator...

...or the End indicator...

...and drag the indicator along the path.

InDesign repositions the text on the path.

ing text from a text file. This creates a new kind of object—not a text frame, not a path, but a blending of the two we'll refer to as a "path text object" from here on out.

Once you've attached text to a path, you can change its position on the path by dragging the Start Indicator or the End Indicator (see Figure 6-60), or change its orientation relative to the path using the Center/Flip Direction Indicator (see Figure 6-61).

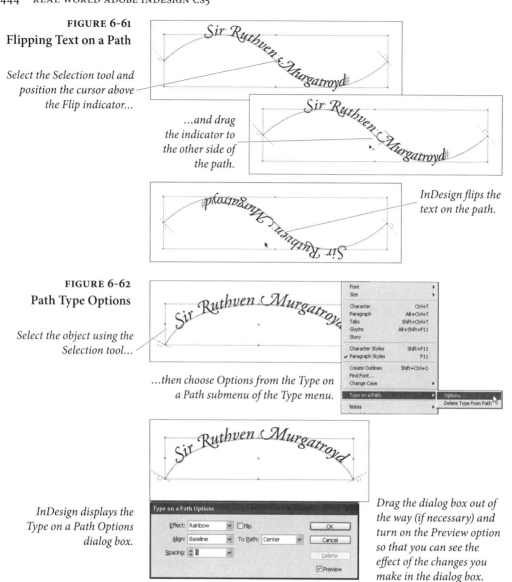

FIGURE 6-61
Flipping Text on a Path

*Select the Selection tool and
position the cursor above
the Flip indicator...*

*...and drag
the indicator to
the other side of
the path.*

*InDesign flips the
text on the path.*

FIGURE 6-62
Path Type Options

*Select the object using the
Selection tool...*

*...then choose Options from the Type on
a Path submenu of the Type menu.*

*InDesign displays the
Type on a Path Options
dialog box.*

*Drag the dialog box out of
the way (if necessary) and
turn on the Preview option
so that you can see the
effect of the changes you
make in the dialog box.*

Like text frames, path text objects feature an in port and an out port you can use to link the text to other text containers (text frames or other text path objects). You can even link text from a path text object to the interior of the path text object. InDesign does not apply paragraph rules to text in path text objects.

Type on a Path Options   You can control both the baseline position of text on a path and the relationship of the text to the shape of the path. To do this, select

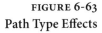

FIGURE 6-63
Path Type Effects

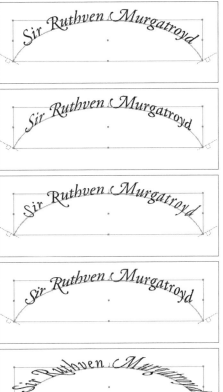

Rainbow rotates the characters around the path.

Skew skews the horizontal axis of each character to match the angle of the path, but leaves the vertical axis of the character unchanged.

3D Ribbon skews the vertical axis of each character to match the angle of the path, but leaves the character's horizontal axis unchanged.

Stair Step moves the characters along the path, but does not skew or rotate the characters to match the path.

Gravity is a combination of Rainbow and Skew—it rotates the characters around the path and skews the horizontal axis of each character.

a path text object (or some of the text on a path) and then choose Options from the Type on a Path submenu of the Type menu (or Context menu). InDesign displays the Type on a Path Options dialog box (see Figure 6-62).

Effect. Do the character shapes distort in some way, or do they remain unchanged? That's the question you're answering when you make a choice from the Effect pop-up menu (see Figure 6-63). What, exactly, do these oddly named options do?

▶ Rainbow rotates the center point of each baseline to match the angle of the path at the location of the character.

▶ Skew skews the horizontal axis of the character to match the angle of the path at the location of the character, but leaves the vertical axis of the character unchanged.

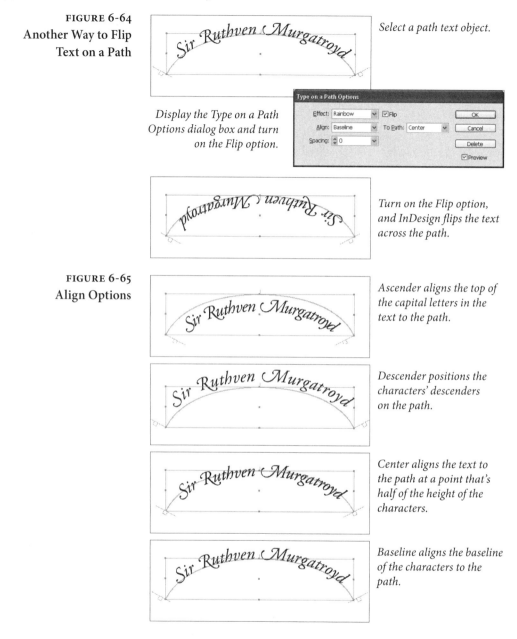

FIGURE 6-64
Another Way to Flip
Text on a Path

Select a path text object.

Display the Type on a Path Options dialog box and turn on the Flip option.

Turn on the Flip option, and InDesign flips the text across the path.

FIGURE 6-65
Align Options

Ascender aligns the top of the capital letters in the text to the path.

Descender positions the characters' descenders on the path.

Center aligns the text to the path at a point that's half of the height of the characters.

Baseline aligns the baseline of the characters to the path.

▸ 3D Ribbon skews the vertical axis of each character to match the angle of the path at the location of the character, but leaves the character's horizontal axis unchanged.

▸ Stair Step aligns the center point of each character's baseline to match the angle of the path at the location of the character, but does not rotate the character.

FIGURE 6-66
To Path Options

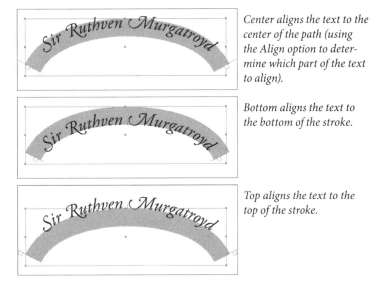

Center aligns the text to the center of the path (using the Align option to determine which part of the text to align).

Bottom aligns the text to the bottom of the stroke.

Top aligns the text to the top of the stroke.

▶ Gravity rotates the center of the baseline of each character to match the angle of the path at the character, skews the horizontal axis of the character to match that angle, and skews the vertical axis of each character around the geometric center point of the path.

Flip. You've probably noticed that path text follows the direction of the path—the first character of the text typically appears at (or, if you've dragged the Path Type tool, nearest) the first point in the path. Given this, you'd think that you could select the path and choose Reverse Path from the Options menu to make the text read from the opposite end of the path. But you can't (not without first removing

FIGURE 6-67
Spacing

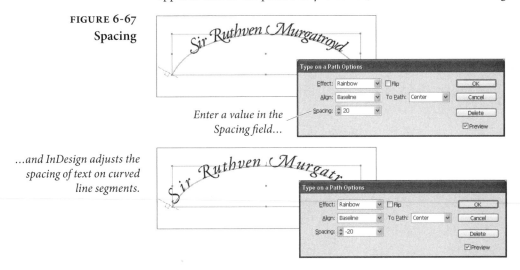

Enter a value in the Spacing field...

...and InDesign adjusts the spacing of text on curved line segments.

the text from the path, anyway). To do what you're trying to do, turn on the Flip option (see Figure 6-64).

Align. These options control the way the text aligns to the path itself. Choose Ascender to align the top of the capital letters in the text (more or less) to the path, or choose Descender to position the bottoms of the characters on the path. Choose Center to align the text to the path at a point that's half of the height of the capital characters in the font, or choose Baseline to align the baseline of the characters to the path (see Figure 6-65).

To Path. The options on the To Path pop-up menu control the way that the text aligns to the *stroke* of the path. Choose Top to place the alignment point (whatever it was you chose from the Align pop-up menu) of the text at the top of the stroke; or Bottom to place it at the bottom of the stroke; or Center to align the alignment point of the text with the center of the path (see Figure 6-66). For more precise control of the text position, use baseline shift.

Spacing. The Spacing field (and attached pop-up menu) control the spacing of text around curves in the path. Enter a value (in points) in this field to tighten or loosen character spacing around curves (see Figure 6-67). Note that this setting has no effect on the kerning or tracking of text on straight line segments.

Removing Type from a Path

To remove the text from a path type object and convert the object back into a "normal" path, you need to do more than simply delete the text characters. If you do this, the object remains a path type object. Instead, select the path (or some of the text on the path) and choose Delete Type on a Path from the Type on a Path submenu (of the Type menu or Context menu).

Quick Apply

There are some InDesign features that make a huge difference in the way that we work, but seem, in some ways, very small. They don't take long to describe, and, once you're used to them, you barely have to think about them. Take unlimited undo, for example—it's hard to imagine doing without it, but you hardly notice it. It just works. The same is true for the Quick Apply feature, which feels to us as if it's become part of our autonomous nervous systems (see Figure 6-68).

Quick Apply gives you a way to apply character, paragraph, object, table, or cell styles. It also lets you select menu items, run scripts, and insert text variables. So what? You can already do all these things with panels, keyboard shortcuts, and the menus themselves. The trouble is that these methods *cost something*. Panels use up precious screen real estate. Keyboard shortcuts are limited by available keys and by our overstressed memories. And using menus to do anything expends a precious commodity—human patience.

Quick Apply takes up no space on screen when it's not in use, requires that you remember only one shortcut, and doesn't require you to drag a cursor around.

Press Command-Return/Ctrl-Enter to display the Quick Apply window. This window (which acts like a floating pane) normally appears in the center of your screen, but you can drag it anywhere you want and it'll show up there the next time you open it.

The Quick Apply window displays different information depending on what is selected; if you have an object selected, it will display things like menu items, object styles, and paragraph styles. If your cursor is in text, it won't show you object styles.

FIGURE 6-68
Quick Apply

1. Select an object and press Command-Return/ Ctrl-Enter.

2. InDesign displays the Quick Apply panel.

3. Start typing. As you type, InDesign matches the characters you type with style names. You can press the up or down arrow keys to select from the list.

4. When you see that InDesign has selected the style you want to apply, press Return/Enter.

5. InDesign hides Quick Apply and applies the style to the selection (in this case, we've applied a paragraph style to a text frame).

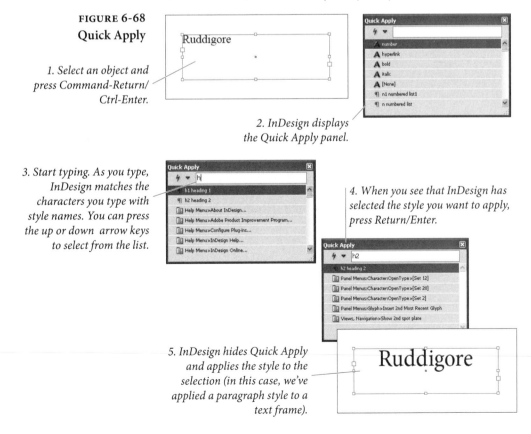

FIGURE 6-69
Customizing
Quick Apply

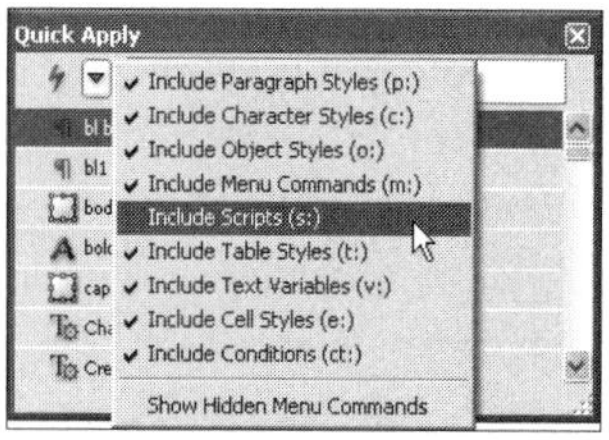

You can control which items are listed in the Quick Apply panel using the panel menu. By choosing Include Scripts, we can run scripts using Quick Apply.

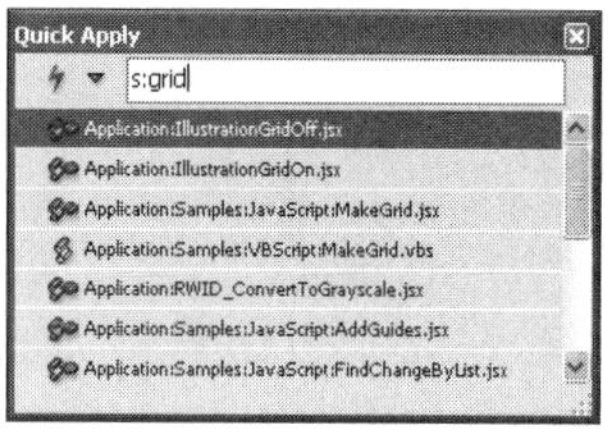

You can also limit the items in the list by using codes. Here, the list is limited to scripts (s:) that are similar to "grid." (Why does InDesign display all of the scripts that contain the character "G"? We have no idea.)

Once the Quick Apply window is open, type a few letters of the style, variable, or feature name. InDesign displays a list of all near matches. For example, if you type "place", InDesign displays "Edit menu > Paste in Place," "File Menu > Place," and any paragraph styles that might have the word "place" in them. You can use the up and down arrow keys to scroll through the list. Once the style or feature you want is selected, you can:

▶ Press Return/Enter to apply the style to the selection. This closes the Quick Apply panel; to apply the style and leave the panel open, press Shift-Return/Shift-Enter.

▶ Press Command-Return/Ctrl-Enter to edit a selected paragraph, character, table, cell, or object style.

▶ Press Option-Return/Alt-Enter to apply the style and override any local formatting. (If you're applying a paragraph style and want to override all formatting, including character styles, press Option-Shift-Return/Alt-Shift-Enter.)

▶ Press Escape to close the panel without applying a style.

Quick Apply is very clever in how it matches what you type to the list of available style names. For example, if you have a style named "Heading 3" you can just type "h3" or even just "3" (if you have more than one style with the number three in it, they'll all appear).

Customizing Quick Apply. The only problem with the Quick Apply window is that it often offers too many styles, variables, or menu items to choose from. Fortunately, you can add or remove items from its list by selecting from the panel menu (see Figure 6-69). For example, if you never want to see menu items in the Quick Apply list, then select Include Menu Items from the panel menu to turn off its checkmark. If you want Quick Apply to include all your scripts, select Include Scripts.

You can also filter the items by typing a code at the beginning of the Quick Apply text. For example, you can type "p:note" to limit the search to paragraph styles that have the word "note" in them. Similarly, typing "c:" at the beginning limits to character styles, "m:" limits to menu commands, and so on. The panel menu displays the codes next in case you can't remember them.

Figure Captions

A caption is text that describes an image or a table, such as "Figure 3-7: Cowboy Dance." A live caption contains a text variable that displays the metadata associated with the image, such as the image name or description. If the image metadata changes, or if the text frame containing the live caption is associated with a different image, the live caption is updated accordingly. Like a live caption, a static caption can also be generated from image metadata, but a static caption is "dead"—it's not updated automatically.

A key point about live captions is that the text frame containing the caption must touch (or be very close to) the graphic or be grouped with the graphic for the feature to work. If this isn't the case, the caption won't be updated if the graphic changes.

Create a Caption from an Existing Image

If you've already placed an image, you can generate a caption—live or static—for that image. Before creating the caption, specify settings in the Caption Setup dialog box. Choose Caption Setup from the Captions submenu on the Object menu (see Figure 6-70).

After you've changed the settings in the Caption Setup dialog box, select an image. Choose Captions from the Object menu, and then choose either Generate Static Caption or Generate Live Caption. You can also Command-click or right-click an image and choose an option from the Captions submenu (see Figure 6-71).

The text frame is created based on the settings in the Caption Setup dialog box, where you can set these options:

Text Before / Text After. Type text that you want to appear before or after the metadata. For example, if the metadata you specify is the author's name, you could make the Text Before "Photograph by: " If you want to use a running caption (such as Figure 1.1, Figure 1.2,

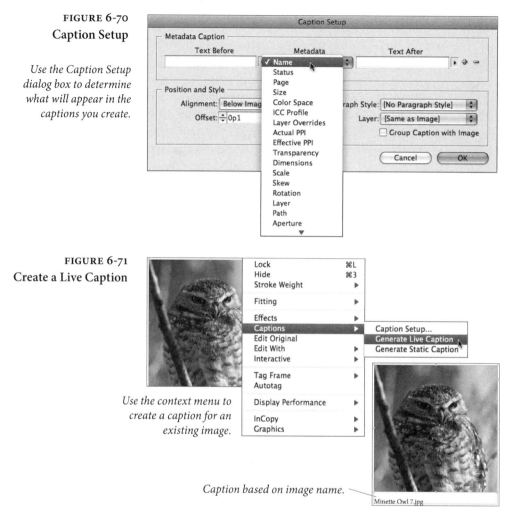

FIGURE 6-70
Caption Setup

Use the Caption Setup dialog box to determine what will appear in the captions you create.

FIGURE 6-71
Create a Live Caption

Use the context menu to create a caption for an existing image.

Caption based on image name.

etc.), don't use Text Before. Instead, use the Paragraph Style option for running captions. For details on creating caption variables, see "Text Variables" in Chapter 3, "Text."

Metadata. Choose the metadata option from the list. Common options include Name, Author, Description, Copyright, and Creation Date.

You can add multiple metadata items to the caption. Click the plus icon to add more metadata items. Each metadata item is displayed on a different line in the caption text frame.

Many of the Metadata options are identical to the settings that appear when you choose File Info from the File menu. One exception is the Folder options, which let you display each level of the pathname.

Alignment. Tell InDesign where to place the caption in relation to the image when you generate a caption based on a placed image.

Offset. Specify how far apart the caption text frame will be from the image. InDesign applies a text frame inset on the side where the caption text frame is placed.

Paragraph Style. Specify a paragraph style to apply to the caption text. If you want the caption to include automatic numbering, include the numbering in the paragraph style. See "Bullets and Numbering" in Chapter 4, "Type."

Layer. Specify which layer the caption belongs to. This is especially useful if you want text to appear on one layer and images on another.

Group Caption With Image. Group the image frame and caption text frame. Grouping the caption and image is especially useful if you want to move the text frame further away from the image but still have it associated with the image.

Create Static Captions When Placing Images

When you're placing images, notice the Create Static Captions option in the Place dialog box. Selecting this option lets you create caption text frame whenever you place an image. After you click or drag to place the image, the cursor is loaded, and then you click or drag to place the caption text frame (see Figure 6-72). The appearance of the caption is based on the Caption Setup dialog box settings.

If you place multiple files, a caption text frame is loaded for each image. For example, suppose you select three images in the Place dialog box. If Create Static Captions is selected, six objects are loaded in the place gun—three images and three text frames containing captions. You then place the first image, then the caption for that image, and so on. If you use the arrow keys to place a grid of images, the text captions are part of the grid, which usually isn't what you want.

FIGURE 6-72
Create Static Caption While Placing Image

Select Create Static Captions in the Place dialog box...

...and then use the loaded cursor to place the caption after you place the image.

If you select multiple pages to place from a PDF or InDesign document, all the pages are loaded first, and then all the captions for those pages are loaded last. Use this as a nifty trick to place multiple pages from a PDF or artboards from an Illustrator file.

Create a Caption Text Variable

You can define a text variable that specifies the metadata you want to capture. Metadata can include the image's name, description, author, creation date, or any of the settings that appear when you choose File Info from the File menu in Photoshop.

Caption Messages

The text frame containing a caption text variable may display the following messages:

<No intersecting link>. If the text frame containing the caption variable says there is no intersecting link, it most likely means you need to move the text frame next to the image frame (or group it with the image). It could also mean the image was pasted into the document rather than placed. Live captions work only with placed images.

<Multiple intersecting links>. The text frame touches more than one text frame.

<No data from link>. The metadata field is blank for that image. Open the image in Photoshop or Illustrator, choose File Info from the File menu, and then fill in the metadata fields.

Alternate Reality

What wonders—or horrors—exist in this weird place, where the boundary between text and graphics breaks down? Where magic works, and previously immutable laws of physics no longer apply? We have been there, reader, and, as it turns out, we have discovered new and useful techniques that can be put to immediate use in the "normal" world.

Importing and Exporting

Someday you'll need to do something that's beyond the drawing and typesetting capabilities of InDesign. You'll need to edit large amounts of text, adjust bitmap images, render 3-D objects, or create Web pages. Other applications do these things better than InDesign does. But you can add the files you create in other applications to your InDesign publication. And you can export InDesign pages for use in other page-layout and drawing programs.

That's what this chapter is all about: importing files from disk, controlling the way that they appear in your document, and exporting your document (or pieces of it). For the most part, our discussion of importing focuses on graphics because we cover importing text in Chapter 3, "Text."

Importing

InDesign offers three ways to bring files from other applications into your publications. Here are your options:

▶ **Place the file.** The Place feature (in the File menu) is the most common method for getting files onto your pages. When you place one or more files, InDesign creates a link to the file on disk. In the case of graphics, InDesign stores only a low-resolution, "proxy" (or "preview") image in the publication. When you print, InDesign uses the high-resolution version of the graphic from the file on your disk. You can link to text files, or not, depending on the setting of the Create Links when Placing Text and Spreadsheet Files option in File Handling preferences.

▶ **Copy and paste.** The most obvious, simplest, and *least* reliable method of getting information from another application is to copy it out of the application and paste it into InDesign. While this technique can work reasonably well for small amounts of text, it can spell disaster for graphics and images created in other programs. We don't mean to imply that you should *never* use copy and paste, just that you should approach it with caution.

A good reason to use copy and paste, however, appears when you're working with Illustrator: When you copy paths out of this program and paste them into InDesign, you get editable InDesign paths. Actually, this only works if you have turned on the AICB setting in Illustrator's Preferences dialog box.

▶ **Drag and drop.** As we mentioned in Chapter 2, "Page Layout," you can drag objects out of one InDesign publication and drop them into another. You can drag files from your desktop and drop them into your InDesign publication window. This is essentially the same as importing the files using the Place command (except that you won't be able to set import options for the files). Even better, dragging from the desktop is a great way to import more than one file at a time (you can even drag a whole folder full of images into your document, if you want).

You can also drag one or more images from Adobe Bridge or Mini Bridge into your InDesign page to import them.

Or you can drag objects from some other programs and drop them into InDesign. This, in general, is the same as copying and pasting, and comes with the same cautions.

Note that you can also open QuarkXPress and PageMaker files—that's covered in Chapter 2, "Page Layout."

Placing Anything

To get a graphic file into an InDesign publication, follow these steps (see Figure 7-1).

1. Before you leap to the Place command on the File menu, take a second to think about where you want the graphic to appear.

   ▶ Do you want the graphic to fill an existing frame? If so, select the frame.

   ▶ Do you want the graphic to appear as an inline frame in a text frame? If so, select the Text tool and click it inside the text frame.

   ▶ Do you want to place the graphic in a new frame? If so, press Command-Shift-A/Ctrl-Shift-A to deselect everything before placing the graphic.

2. Press Command-D/Ctrl-D (or choose Place from the File menu). The Place dialog box appears.

3. Locate and select one or more files. You can control certain import options for some file formats. To view the available import options, turn on the Show Import Options checkbox.

4. If you have a frame selected, and want to place the file inside the frame, make sure you turn on the Replace Selected Item checkbox. If you don't want to replace the selection (perhaps you forgot to deselect all before selecting Place), turn this option off.

5. Click the Open button. If you turned on the Show Import Options checkbox, InDesign displays the Import Options dialog box, which looks slightly different depending on the file type you've selected. In many cases, the options are grayed out because they aren't relevant (the clipping path option is grayed out when there is no clipping path embedded in the file, for example). Make any changes you want (or can) in this dialog box and then click the OK button (we discuss the import options for each file type in "Working with Images," later in this chapter).

What happens after you click OK depends on the choice you made in Step 1. If you had a frame selected, and turned on the Replace Selected Item option, the graphic appears inside that frame. If you had an active text insertion point in a text frame, and if you turned on the Replace Selected Item option, InDesign places the graphic into the text frame (at the location of the cursor) as an inline graphic.

FIGURE 7-1

Placing a Graphic Without First Making a Frame

Choose Place from the File menu (or press Command-D/ Ctrl-D). InDesign displays the Place dialog box. Locate and select a file, then click the Open button.

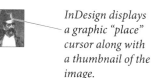

InDesign displays a graphic "place" cursor along with a thumbnail of the image.

Click the graphic place icon on the page or pasteboard.

InDesign places the graphic on the page, creating a frame that is exactly the size of the graphic.

When you position the place icon near a ruler guide or grid line, InDesign changes the appearance of the place icon to show that clicking or dragging the icon will "snap" the incoming graphic to the guide or grid.

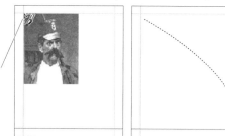

If you drag the place icon as you place a graphic…
…InDesign places the graphic inside a frame that's the width and height you define by dragging, scaling the image proportionally to fit the frame

When you position the place icon over an existing frame, InDesign changes the appearance of the icon to indicate that clicking the icon will place the file inside the frame.

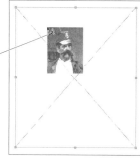

You can also click the place icon on an existing frame…

…to place the graphic inside the frame.

The Place Icon If you deselected everything before placing, or if you turned off the Replace Selected Item option, InDesign displays the place icon (some folks call this the "place gun"). Click the place icon on a page or on the pasteboard, and InDesign imports the file you selected and positions the upper-left corner of the file at the point at which you clicked the place icon.

Instead of clicking, you can *drag* the place icon. This produces a frame that's the width and height you define by dragging. The frame is constrained to the height/width ratio of the image and the final image fits the frame size exactly. If you don't like the proportional constraint, hold the Shift key down while dragging.

To place the graphic inside an existing, empty frame, click the place icon in the frame. This frame doesn't have to be a graphic frame, and it doesn't have to be selected.

To place the graphic inside a frame that already has an image in it, hold down Option/Alt while clicking with the place cursor. This is the same as first selecting that frame and turning on the Replace Selected Item in the Place dialog box, but is useful when you have forgotten to select the frame first, or when you need to replace multiple graphics (see "Placing Multiple Files," below).

If you accidentally placed the graphic inside a frame, don't panic. Remember that Command-Z/Ctrl-Z will "undo" the action and display the place icon again, ready to place the graphic somewhere else. At this point, you can cancel the Place operation by pressing Command-Z/Ctrl-Z again, or by clicking the place icon on any tool in the Tools panel.

Placing Multiple Files   If you need to import two or more images or text files at the same time, why bother opening the Place dialog box multiple times? Instead, the Place dialog box lets you select more than one item in a folder at a time and import them all at once. To select more than one item in the dialog box, Shift-click (to select contiguous items) or Command/Ctrl-click (to select discontiguous files).

Be careful about the state of the Show Import Options checkbox in the Place dialog box. If it's turned on when you click Open, you'll be rewarded with an Import Options dialog box for each file you've imported—kind of a pain if you're importing 20 images.

After you click Open (or click OK in the Import Options dialog box), InDesign loads all the files into the place cursor, showing you a thumbnail of the first one along with a number that shows the total number of files loaded. You can rotate through the loaded files by pressing the left or right (or up and down) arrows on your keyboard. If you decide you want to "throw away" one of the files (remove it from the Place cursor), press Esc.

Of course, you can also import a bunch of images at the same time by dragging them all in from Adobe Bridge, Adobe Mini Bridge, the Mac OS Finder, or Windows Explorer. In that case, InDesign also loads all the files into a Place cursor.

Once the place cursor is loaded with multiple files, you can:

▶ Click in an empty frame to place the current image there.

▶ Click where there are no frames to create a frame and import the image.

▶ Option/Alt click on a frame that contains an image to replace it.

Contact Sheets   Here's one more option you have when you have more than one image loaded in the Place cursor: You can Command-Shift-click/ Ctrl-Shift-click to create a "contact sheet" grid the size of your page (you typically would want to click in the upper-left corner of the page). Or, after you begin dragging, press the arrow keys to change the size of the grid. Use the up and right arrow keys to increase the number of rows and columns, respectively.

To adjust the space between columns or rows, hold down Command-Shift/Ctrl-Shift while pressing the arrow keys (and still dragging). The Page Up and Page Down keys also adjust the spacing.

If you select the Create Static Captions option in the Place dialog box when placing multiple files, captions are placed in the same grid as the images.

About Graphic File Formats

InDesign can import a range of graphic file formats, including Adobe Illustrator (AI) and Adobe Photoshop (PSD) formats, TIFF images, JPEG images, GIF images, and EPS files. It can even import other InDesign files themselves as graphics. From InDesign's point of view, there are certain limitations and advantages to each.

There are three fundamental graphics file format types:

▶ Bitmap (or "raster") files store pictures as matrices (rows and columns) of squares known as pixels, with each pixel having a particular gray or color value (also known as a gray depth, color depth, or bit depth). Bitmap files are typically created by image editing programs such as Adobe Photoshop. TIFF, JPEG, BMP, and GIF are all bitmap graphic file formats.

▶ Vector files contain sets of instructions for drawing graphic objects—typically geometric shapes, such as lines, ellipses, polygons, rectangles, and arcs. The drawing instructions say, "Start this line at this point and draw to that point"; or, "This is a polygon made up of these line segments."

▶ Hybrids can contain both vector and bitmap graphics. Adobe Illustrator, PDF, EPS, and WMF (Windows metafile) formats are all examples of metafiles. (Adobe Photoshop files look like hybrids, as they can also contain a combination of vector and raster graphics, but InDesign rasterizes any visible Photoshop vector data so we don't count it as a true hybrid.) Metafiles don't have to contain *both* vector and bitmap objects. Often these file contain only an image, or only vector artwork.

Which File Format to Use? We could talk about the pros and cons of various graphic file formats all day, but deciding which file format to use comes down to two things: what works in your workflow and which features you need.

Before we launch into which formats you should use, let's first talk about a few formats we think you should *not* use: PICT, WMF, BMP. The process of printing any of these on a PostScript printer isn't perfect, which means that what you see on your screen may not be what you get from your printer.

We also discourage using EPS and DCS files, unless you have a very good reason to do so, which is rare. Most people who think they need to use these formats are surprised to learn that AI, PDF, or PSD are better formats (see below).

Vector and Hybrid Artwork. Vector artwork is pretty straightforward. We usually import Adobe Illustrator files as native AI files, because they're essentially PDF files. Note that you must enable the Create PDF Compatible File checkbox when saving an AI file, or else InDesign can't read it—technically, InDesign is reading the PDF inside the AI file. We save vector graphics from other programs (such as FreeHand) as PDF or EPS.

We tend to avoid EPS when we can for a couple of reasons. First, PDF files can be viewed and edited by a wider array of programs. It can also support transparency and works beautifully with InDesign. In general, while EPS will always be with us, it's an old, crotchety format that we avoid at social gatherings.

Raster Artwork. When it comes to saving bitmapped images from Photoshop, you have to be careful, because Photoshop files can contain so much more than simple image data. A Photoshop file can contain images, layers, transparency, vector artwork, and text objects. The native Photoshop (PSD) format is the closest thing to a one-size-fits-all solution, so we tend to save in that format and import the PSD directly into InDesign. However, PSD has its limitations.

InDesign can read spot colors, duotones, and transparency from PSD files, but it can't read vector or text layers. Well, it *can* read them, but the vector or text layers become rasterized (turned into a bitmap). Instead, we recommend saving as PDF when you have vector or text layers. However, for technical reasons we barely understand, Photoshop won't let you save a file that has both spot color channels and background transparency as a PDF file. Also, InDesign can't handle PSD files when they're in Photoshop's Multichannel mode—you'll have to use DCS files for that.

If all this has your head spinning, check out Table 7-1, which Matt Phillips (an Adobe software engineer extraordinaire) created.

Other options for raster images include TIFF and JPEG (sometimes shortened to JPG). TIFF has a long and venerable history, and we still use it quite often (virtually all the images in this book were saved in the TIFF format). It supports images with layers and even transparency, though—like PSD—it does not support vector objects. The cool thing about TIFF is that you can save a layered, transparent image as a TIFF and InDesign will honor the transparency, but you can also import it into a program like Microsoft Word and it appears as though you had flattened it.

Photoshop can save TIFF files using LZW, Zip, or JPEG compression. Few programs other than InDesign can read Zip or JPEG TIFFs, but if you're just using Photoshop and InDesign, you should definitely give Zip-compressed TIFFs a try. Often, using Zip compression in a layered Photoshop file for both the image data and the layer data makes a file smaller than a flattened, non-compressed TIFF. And Zip is a lossless compression scheme, so no image data will be lost.

We don't use JPEG-compressed TIFF files, because it's just plain weird. If we want more file size compression, we'll save the file in the regular JPEG file format. The JPEG file format does not support layers or transparency, but it has the benefit of using a lossy compression scheme—your image degrades each time you save it, but it can compress far more than the Zip or LZW "lossless" schemes. Most images saved using Maximum quality JPEG compression are virtually indistinguishable from TIFF or PSD images, unless they have very high-contrast, sharp edges, such as solid colored text on top of a solid colored background.

Layered vs. Flattened. How do you want to deal with layered or 16-bit Photoshop files? InDesign can read layered 8-bit and 16-bit images in the PSD and TIFF file formats, and 32-bit HDR images in the PSD file format. However, InDesign can turn on and off layers (make them visible or not) in layered PSD or PDF files, but not layered TIFF files (see "Object Layer Options," later in this chapter).

TABLE 7-1
Matt's Matrix

Vectors	Spots	Transparency	PDF	PSD	DCS	EPS
No	No	No	✓	✓	✓	✓
No	No	Yes	✓	✓	•	•
No	Yes	No	✓	✓[1]	✓	•
No	Yes	Yes	•	✓[1]	•	•
Yes	No	No	✓	•	✓[2]	✓
Yes	No	Yes	✓	•	•	•
Yes	Yes	No	✓	•	✓[2]	•
Yes	Yes	Yes	•	•	•	•

[1] Except in Multichannel mode

[2] Works as long as you print separations from InDesign and the DCS file is not affected by transparency on the page.

But just because you can import these files into InDesign doesn't mean you should. Sometimes it's better to flatten or downsample the image. The decision really comes down to file size. If you have a hundred images and each one is 100 MB when layered or 10 MB when flattened, then it's probably better to flatten before saving—just for the sake of drive space or network speed. (Tip: If the file has a transparent background, then use Photoshop's Merge Visible feature rather than Flatten Layers, because the latter always flattens to an opaque background.)

By the way, note that InDesign does not support layer blending modes inside images. For example, if you have applied the Multiply mode to a layer in Photoshop, and that layer is over a transparent area (the checkerboard background), InDesign can't multiply it into the InDesign document page. It treats it as the Normal blend mode.

Image Resolution and Scaling

It's natural to assume that a higher image resolution will provide a sharper image. However, for grayscale and color images, your image resolution should be no higher than twice the halftone screen frequency you intend to use. All higher resolutions give you are larger file sizes, longer printing times, bigger headaches, and potentially lower quality.

In fact, you can almost always get away with resolutions only 1.5 times your screen frequency. For instance, at 133 lpi your images need not be any greater than 200 pixels per inch(ppi); at 150 lpi you probably don't need more than 225 ppi images. The difference between a 300 ppi image and a 225 ppi image is more significant than you might think: A four-by-five-inch CMYK image is 6.9 Mb at 300 ppi and only 3.8 Mb at 225 ppi—about half the size. That means it takes less time to transfer across the network (to a server or to a printer), less disk space to store, faster printing times, and so on.

We like to resize and downsample images in Adobe Photoshop, and then sharpen them using Photoshop's Unsharp Masking filter (all scanned images need some sharpening if you intend to print them using halftone screens). David wrote about this process in greater detail in his books *Real World Photoshop* (co-authored with Bruce Fraser and Conrad Chavez) and *Real World Scanning and Halftones, 3rd Edition* (co-authored with Glenn Fleishman, Conrad Chavez, and Steve Roth).

Line Art   Line art images (which have only black and white pixels, saved using Photoshop's Bitmap mode) obey different rules than grayscale or color images. These monochrome (or bi-level) bitmapped images do not use halftone screening. This means that they're exempt from the resolution balancing act mentioned above, but it also means that they require higher resolutions to avoid jaggy (pixelated) edges.

If your final artwork will be printed on a desktop laser printer, you probably don't need to use resolutions greater than 600 ppi. Imagesetter output rarely requires more than 1200 ppi (though for a sheetfed art book, we might bump this up to 1500 ppi). Printing on uncoated stock requires a lower resolution because of halftone spots spreading; you can easily get away with 800 ppi for newsprint.

Scaling in InDesign   Ideally, you should import your bitmapped images at the same size as you intend to print them. Resolution changes when you change the size of the image in InDesign. For instance, doubling the size of a 300 dpi picture on your page cuts the effective resolution in half, to 150 dpi (because each pixel in the image has to be twice as wide and twice as tall as before, so fewer of them fit "per inch"). Conversely, making this graphic 25-percent smaller increases to 400 dpi. (If you really care why the resolution increases by a third instead of by 25 percent, e-mail us and we'll explain the unpleasant math.)

Graphic Display Properties

Once you import a graphic into InDesign, the quality of its onscreen appearance depends almost entirely on the Display Performance setting in the View menu. You can choose among three settings: Fast Display, Typical Display, and High Quality Display. By default, these reflect low-, medium-, and high-quality displays. However, if you hate these terms you can change each setting's meaning so that Fast is higher quality than Typical, or whatever (see "Display Performance Preferences," in Chapter 1, "Workspace").

The default settings follow these basic rules:

▶ When you choose Fast Display, InDesign grays out both vector and bitmapped images and turns off all transparency effects. The display of these gray boxes is very fast, but somewhat lacking in detail.

▶ When you choose Typical Display, InDesign uses a proxy image—either one embedded in the image or one InDesign generated when you placed the file. (InDesign always creates a proxy preview when it imports TIFF and JPEG; it's an import option for EPS files.) InDesign uses this proxy to display the graphic at all magnification levels—which means that images are going to get pretty ugly as you zoom in on them. The advantage? The screen display of proxy images is much faster than generating new previews for every magnification change. In this setting, transparency effects are visible, but only at a reasonable quality (drop shadows and feathering are displayed at low resolution, for instance).

▶ When you choose High Quality display, InDesign gets image data from the original file on your hard drive to render the best possible preview for the current screen magnification. For an EPS, it means that InDesign reinterprets the file to create a new preview (this is where those beautiful EPS previews come from). As you'd expect, either process takes more time than simply slamming a fixed-resolution preview onto the screen (which is what the Proxy option does). The anti-aliasing of vector images (so they look smooth on screen) and high-quality transparency effects is also calculation-intensive.

Remember, all of these settings affect only the way that graphics appear on screen, not in print.

Local Display Overrides

You can also vary the display quality for individual graphics. This can come in handy when you need to see more detail in one graphic than in others, or when you want to speed up the redraw of a specific slow-drawing graphic. To control the display properties of a graphic, select the graphic, and then display the context menu (hold down Control before you press the mouse button on the Macintosh; press the right mouse button in Windows). Choose one of the display

FIGURE 7-2
**Setting the Display
Resolution for a Graphic**

*InDesign displays the
graphic using the display
setting you selected.*

Fast Display   *Typical Display*   *High Quality Display*

options from the Display Performance submenu (see Figure 7-2). You can also choose from the Display Performance submenu in the Object menu if you have a bizarre aversion to context menus.

Later, after applying local display overrides to various images throughout your document, you can turn all these local overrides on and off with the Allow Object-Level Display Settings from the Display Performance submenu. As with any other feature in InDesign, you can assign a keyboard shortcut to these local override features.

Image Import Options

When you place an image, you can turn on the Import Options checkbox and use the subsequent Image Import Options dialog box to specify a number of important things about the image. The settings in this dialog box change depending on the file format of the graphic. Note that if you later drag and drop a graphic from the desktop into InDesign, the program remembers the import options from the last file you placed.

Bitmapped Images   If you are importing a bitmap image, such as a TIFF, JPEG, GIF, or native Photoshop (PSD) document, InDesign displays four options in the Image Import Options dialog box: apply a clipping path, pick an alpha channel, enable color management, and choose layer visibility (see Figure 7-3).

Apply Photoshop Clipping Path. If the image you're placing contains a clipping path, InDesign makes the Apply Photoshop Clipping Path checkbox available. When you turn this option on as you place the image, InDesign applies the clipping path to the image. If this

FIGURE 7-3
Import Options for
Bitmap Images

Turn this option on to apply the first clipping path defined in the incoming file. If you want to use a different clipping path, you can choose Clipping Path from the Object menu after placing the file.

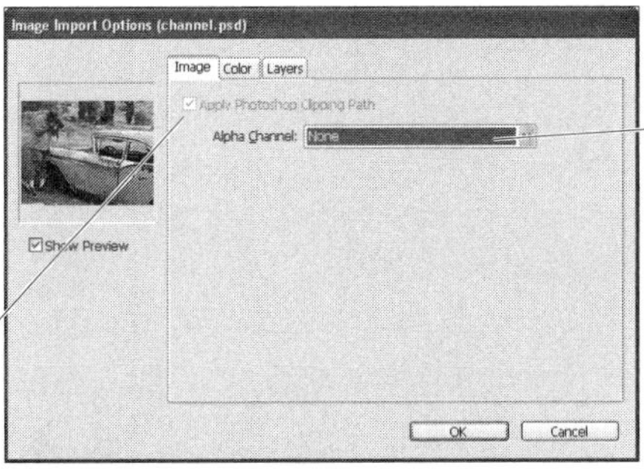

If the file contains one or more alpha channels, you can choose to apply transparency to the object using one of the alpha channels.

The options in this dialog box only become active when the file you selected contains the corresponding features.

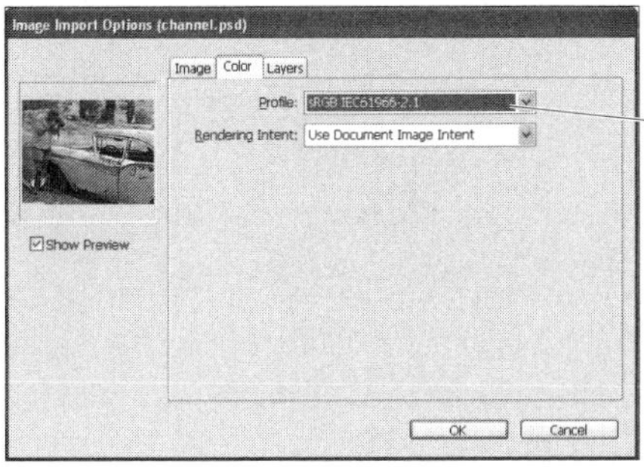

If the file has an embedded color management profile, you can choose whether to use that profile or to use some other profile.

isn't what you want, you can always change the clipping path (see "Working with Clipping Paths," later in this chapter).

If the image does not contain a clipping path, this option won't be available. You can always create a clipping path for the image in InDesign, or choose another path saved with the image as the clipping path (again, we cover this later in this chapter).

Alpha Channel. InDesign can apply transparency to an image if you have one or more alpha channels saved within the file. (An alpha channel is just any additional channel beyond the standard red, green, blue, cyan, yellow, magenta, or black channels.) For example, you could make three extra channels in Photoshop—each with a different sort of blurry vignette around the image's subject—and then choose which one you want to use in InDesign when you import the file. Unfortunately, InDesign doesn't give you any sort of visual feedback inside the Import Options dialog box, so you'd better use descriptive names for the channels. Once you have imported the image, there's no way to switch to a different transparency mask for the picture other than reimporting it and revisiting this dialog box.

Enable Color Management. When you're importing a color image, InDesign activates the options in the Color tab of the Image Import Options dialog box. Color management is a very complicated topic, and the following control descriptions do not attempt to discuss the finer points of each topic. For more on color management, see Chapter 10, "Color."

▶ **Profile.** If the image file you've selected contains a color management profile, InDesign selects Use Embedded Profile from the Profile pop-up menu. If you know that the embedded profile is not the one you want, choose a different profile from the menu.

Note that if you have chosen the Preserve Numbers (Ignore Linked Profiles) option in the CMYK Policies section of the Color Settings dialog box, InDesign acts slightly differently. Instead of displaying an embedded profile name in the Image Import Options dialog box, it will show Use Document Default, pointing out that the embedded CMYK profile is being ignored and the document profile is being used instead.

▶ **Rendering Intent.** Choose the gamut scaling method you want to use to render the colors in the image. For most photographic images, you'll probably want to choose Perceptual (Images).

Layer Visibility. When you import a Photoshop document or PDF file that contains layers, InDesign offers a third tab in the Import Options dialog box: Layers. This tab lets you turn the visibility on or off for each layer, or choose a layer comp (if you used Photoshop's Layer Comp panel to make comps). We discuss these options further in "Object Layer Options," later in this chapter.

EPS Files

When you import an EPS graphic with Import Options turned on in the Place dialog box, InDesign displays the EPS Import Options dialog box (see Figure 7-4).

Read Embedded OPI Image Links. Open Prepress Interface (OPI) is a standard for maintaining image links between desktop page layout and illustration software using dedicated color prepress systems, such as some of the systems manufactured by Kodak and Creo. When you work with an OPI system, you typically work with low-resolution proxy images as you lay out a page, and then link to high-resolution images saved on the prepress server when you print

FIGURE 7-4
**Import Options
for EPS Files**

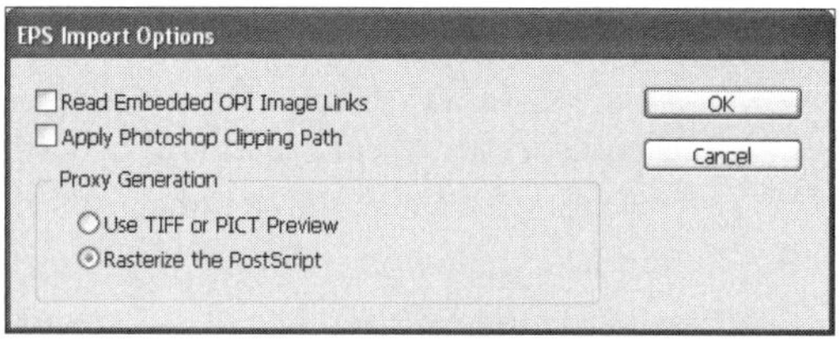

(or otherwise hand the job off). OPI concerns imported images only, and has nothing to do with vector graphics or type.

Turn this option off if the prepress system will take care of replacing any OPI images in the EPS; turn it on if you want InDesign to replace the images as you print. (In this case, InDesign itself is acting as an OPI server.) InDesign will store the OPI image information regardless of the setting of this option.

Apply Photoshop Clipping Path. Turn on this option when you want to apply the first clipping path saved in the EPS graphic. This only affects Photoshop EPS images.

Proxy Generation. EPS graphics usually contain an embedded, low-resolution preview image. However, because InDesign can interpret almost any PostScript file, you can ask it to create a new preview image for you by selecting Rasterize the PostScript in the EPS Import Options dialog box. If you want to use the file's built-in preview, select Use TIFF or PICT Preview. We think these should have been labeled, "Use Cruddy Preview" and "Make It Look Good." We almost always make it look good by selecting Rasterize the PostScript (even though it takes a little longer to import the file). On the other hand, if you need to import 250 EPS files and onscreen quality doesn't matter, then save yourself some time and use the embedded previews.

AI and PDF Files   When you import a PDF graphic or a native Illustrator (AI) file, and have turned on the Import Options checkbox in the Place dialog box, InDesign displays the Place PDF dialog box (see Figure 7-5).

Pages. PDF files can contain multiple pages (unlike EPS, which is, by definition, a single-page-per-file format), so you need some way to select the page you want to place. Similarly, if you have multiple artboards in an Illustrator document, you can choose which to import

FIGURE 7-5
Place PDF Dialog Box

The Place PDF dialog box can display a preview of the pages of the PDF you've selected.

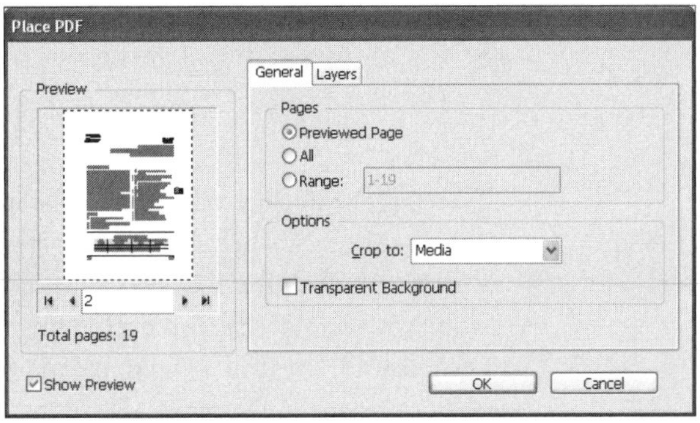

because each artboard acts like its own page. You can scroll through the pages until you find the one you want. When you place a PDF or AI file without displaying the Place PDF dialog box, InDesign places the first page in the file.

If you want to import more than one page, choose All or type in the page numbers (using commas or hyphens to denote multiple pages) in the Range field. To import the page displayed in the preview, select Previewed Page.

When you import more than one page from a PDF, InDesign loads them all in the Place cursor. It would be nice to have the option to place each page of the PDF on a different page of the InDesign document, but there isn't. That's why Ole wrote the PlaceMultipage-PDF script (see Chapter 12, "Scripting," for more on where to find scripts and how to use them.)

Crop To. Do you have to import the whole page? No—you can use this pop-up menu to define the area of the page you want to place. Choose one of the following options (depending on the PDF, some options may be unavailable).

▶ Choose Bounding Box to crop the incoming PDF graphic to an area defined by the objects on the PDF page.

▶ Choose Art to place the area defined by an art box in the PDF graphic (if no art box has been defined, this option will not be available). For a PDF exported from InDesign, the art box is the same as the Trim area (see below).

▶ Choose Crop to crop the area of the incoming PDF graphic to the crop area defined in Acrobat (using the Crop Pages dialog box). If the PDF has not had a crop area defined, this area will be the same as the Media setting (see below).

▶ Choose Trim or Bleed to import the area defined by the trim or bleed settings in the PDF.

▶ Choose Media to import the area defined by the original paper size of the PDF.

Transparent Background. Turn this option on when you want to be able to see objects behind the imported PDF or AI file, or turn it off to apply an opaque white background to the graphic. In general, we think you should leave this option turned on—if you want an opaque background, you can always apply a fill (of any color) to the frame containing the PDF graphic. If you turn this option off, on the other

FIGURE 7-6
PDF Layer Options

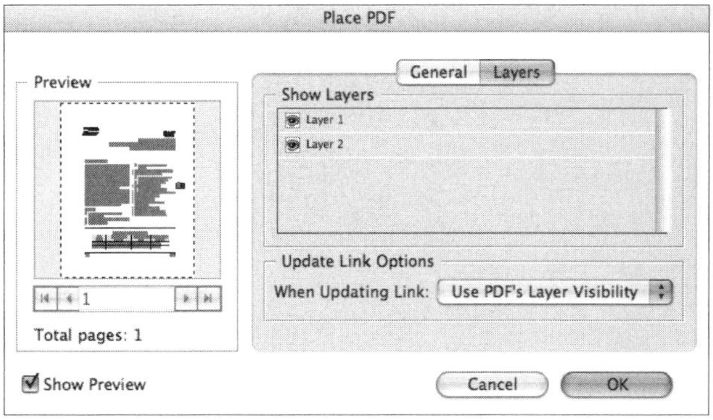

hand, the white background applied by InDesign cannot be changed by setting the fill of the frame.

Placed PDFs and Color Management. InDesign can't apply color management profiles to PDF graphics, but profiles embedded in the PDF will be used when you color separate the publication. If your PDFs require precise color matching, apply and embed the appropriate color profiles before saving the PDF for import into InDesign.

PDF Layer Options. If you're placing a PDF that includes layers (such as from Illustrator or InDesign) or an AI or INDD file, you can choose to show or hide individual layers using the Layers tab of the Place PDF dialog box (see Figure 7-6).

The options in this tab are self-explanatory except, perhaps for the When Updating Link pop-up menu. This controls what happens if, down the line, you update or relink the graphic to a newer version (see Object Layer Options," later in this chapter). Choose Keep Layer Visibility Overrides if you want to make sure the changes you make here are respected if the image gets updated.

InDesign INDD Files

You can place an InDesign file as a graphic as easily as you can place a PDF file. In fact, in most ways, a placed InDesign (INDD) file acts like a PDF file—if you select Show Import Options in the Place dialog box, you'll see virtually the same options, from which pages or layers you want, to whether to include the document's bleed or not.

Importing an INDD file can be more efficient because you don't have to first export a PDF file. This becomes even better if the source InDesign document later changes. When you place an INDD file, any images that were imported into it appear in the Links panel (which we discuss in the next section). When you use the Package feature (see Chapter 11, "Printing"), those linked images are packaged, too.

In case you were worrying: We've imported an InDesign file into an InDesign file in an InDesign file in an InDesign file—about 10 documents "deep"—and it printed and exported with no trouble. And yes, you can place an INDD file from an earlier version into an InDesign document.

Note that the LayoutZone script from *Automatication.com* can convert a portion of a spread (or a whole spread) into an external InDesign document. Even more amazing, it can convert placed InDesign documents back into editable objects. Check it out.

Linking and Embedding

In InDesign, you can choose to embed (that is, store) imported graphics in your publication, or you can choose to store them externally and link to them.

When you link to a graphic, InDesign doesn't include the graphic file in your publication, but establishes a link between the publication and the imported file. InDesign creates a low-resolution screen preview of the graphic, and uses that preview to draw the image on your page. Linking means you don't have to store two copies of the original file—one on disk, and one in your InDesign publication—thereby saving disk space.

When you print, InDesign includes data from linked graphics in the stream of PostScript sent to your printer or to disk. This means that you need to take any externally stored graphics with you when it's time to print your publication at an imagesetting service bureau.

Which method should you use? It's up to you. When you embed graphics, your publication size increases, but you don't have to keep track of the original files. When you link to externally stored graphics, your publications will take up less space on disk, but you'll have to keep track of more than one file. We generally recommend linking, partly because that is what the industry has come to expect (that's the way QuarkXPress works), and partly because we don't like our InDesign files becoming tens (or hundreds) of megabytes larger.

If you import a bitmapped image smaller than 48K, InDesign embeds a copy of the graphic in your publication. This "automatic" embedding differs from "manual" embedding—you can maintain links to automatically embedded files, but not to manually embedded graphics.

Opening Documents with Links   When you move a linked file or change its name, you break the link between the file and any InDesign publication you've placed it in.

You can also break the link when you move the publication file to another volume.

When you open a publication, InDesign looks in the folder containing the document for the linked file, and in a folder inside that folder named "Links." If InDesign finds that one or more of the files have been modified, it displays an alert asking if you want to update the links automatically. It will also tell you if one or more files on disk are missing; in that case, you must relink those files manually using the Links panel. We'll discuss that in more detail later in this section.

Note that you can tell InDesign not to check for missing or modified links (see "Links Preferences," later in this chapter).

The Links Panel

The key to InDesign's linking and embedding features is the Links panel (see Figure 7-7). To display the Links panel, press Command-Shift-D/Ctrl-Shift-D, or choose Links from the Window menu. The Links panel can show you a wide array of details about each placed image. When you first launch InDesign, the default settings display a tiny thumbnail for each image, next to its name, its location in the document (by page number), and its current status:

▶ If a graphic has been modified since its last update, you'll see a Caution icon (a yellow triangle with an exclamation mark).

▶ If a graphic is missing, you'll see the Missing link icon—it's a red circle with a question mark in it. This means that InDesign can't find the file—it's been moved or deleted (or maybe you've lost your connection to the server that holds the file).

▶ If you have embedded a graphic (see "Embedding a Graphic," later in this section), a square with two shapes in it (another square and a triangle) appears.

FIGURE 7-7
Links Panel

Press Command-Shift-D or Ctrl-Shift-D to display the Links panel.

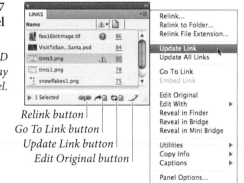

Relink button
Go To Link button
Update Link button
Edit Original button

You can change the width of each column in the Links panel by placing the cursor over the vertical bar next to the column heading and dragging. To rearrange the order of the columns, drag the header icon before or after another column header. You can also change the order in which the linked files are displayed by clicking on a header. For example, to sort by status, click on the status icon. Click again to reverse the sort order.

The Links panel can expand to include more information. Choose Panel Options in the panel menu to adjust the size of each row, decide whether thumbnails are displayed, and specify what link information should appear in the Links panel. For example, if you turn on the Scale checkbox in the Show Column column of the Panel Options dialog box, the Links panel will show the scaling percentage for each image. If the Links panel is too narrow to show the information, you can widen it by dragging the panel's edge.

If you double-click on a file in the Links panel (or select the link and click the "twisty triangle" in the lower-left corner of the panel), InDesign opens the File Info section of the panel. We usually just leave this section open.

The meaning of most of the items in the Link Info area is fairly straightforward—the Size field shows the amount of disk space taken up by the graphic, for example. However, you can ask InDesign to display some additional information to the Link Info area in the Panel Options dialog box, and a few of those "extra" rows deserve further explanation.

▶ **Link Type.** If you enable the Link Type checkbox, it will probably always display "import," indicating that you imported a graphic. Or, if you have linked to an InCopy (or other text) story, it may display "Bi-directional," pointing out that edits you make here will export as well as import. However, behind the scenes, InDesign was written so that it could link to all kinds of things—even directly to a field in a database somewhere or some data on a Web page. Those features are currently those features are only available to third-party plug-in developers.

▶ **Folder Number.** Folder 0 (zero), in InDesign parlance, means "the folder in which this linked file is saved." Folder 1 is the folder that contains Folder 0, and so on.

▶ **Story Status and Information.** There are a handful of features that relate to the status of a "story." In this case, InDesign is talking about an InCopy story—one that you have exported using Edit > InCopy > Export.

FIGURE 7-8
Updating a Link

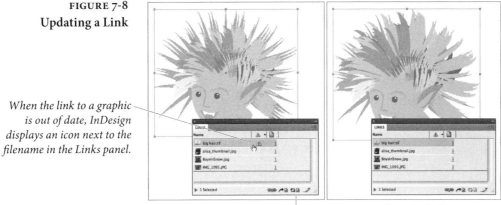

When the link to a graphic is out of date, InDesign displays an icon next to the filename in the Links panel.

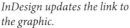

To update the link, select the filename and click the Update Link button.

InDesign updates the link to the graphic.

Updating a Link

InDesign checks the status of your graphics when you open a document or when you switch from another application back into InDesign. As soon as it notices a linked file is modified or missing, it displays an icon in the Links panel. To update the link of an imported graphic that has been modified since you last updated it or placed it, follow these steps (see Figure 7-8).

1. Display the Links panel, if it's not already visible.

2. Select the graphic you want to update (on the page), or select the corresponding link in the Links panel.

3. Choose Update Link from the Links panel menu (or click the Update Link button at the bottom of the Links panel). InDesign updates the link to the graphic file.

To update all the modified links in a publication, choose Update All Links from the panel menu, or select one of the modified images and Option/Alt-clicking the Update button.

Linking to Another File

Modified files are easy to update; *missing* files are quite another matter. To link to another file, or relink to the original file in a new location, follow these steps (see Figure 7-9).

1. Display the Links panel, if it's not already visible.

2. Select the graphic you want to update, or select the corresponding link in the Links panel.

3. Click the Relink button (or choose Relink from the Links panel menu). InDesign displays the Locate dialog box.

FIGURE 7-9
Linking to Another File

Select an imported graphic.

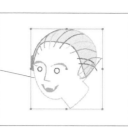

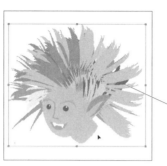

*Choose Relink from
the Links panel menu
(or click the Relink
button at the bottom
of the panel).*

*InDesign replaces the
original graphic with the
graphic file you selected.*

4. Locate and select a file.

5. Click the OK button.

If a bunch of images are listed as missing and they all exist in the same folder on disk, you can relink to them all by selecting the Search for Missing Links in This Folder checkbox in the Locate dialog box (it's on by default), or choose Relink to Folder from the panel menu.

By the way, each time you relink an image, the Locate dialog box normally displays the last folder you relinked to. If you don't like that behavior, see "Links Preferences," later in this chapter.

Multiple Instances. InDesign treats each instance of an image as a separate item in the Links panel, so if you have 20 copies of the same image, it will appear 20 times in the Links panel. However, at the top of the list of those 20 images, you'll find a "master" link of the same name. If you want to relink all the instances of an image, select that master link and then click the Relink button.

Relink All. If you have multiple missing links spanning multiple folders, you can tell InDesign you want to relink all of them by selecting one of them in the Links panel and then Option/Alt-clicking on the Relink button. In this case, you will get a series of Locate dialog boxes that you'll need to navigate.

Relinking to a Different File Type. When you manually relink an image to another image, InDesign doesn't care if the new image is the same file type or a different file type. This is especially useful if you have imported a folder full of low-resolution JPEG images for position only (FPO) and you now want to relink them all to high-res PSD files.

To do this, select the images you want to relink, then choose Relink File Extension from the Links panel menu. In the Relink File Extension dialog box, type the new file extension into the field (in this case, you'd type "psd"). For example, this would automatically relink a file called "myimage1.jpg" with "myimage1.psd".

Edit Original and Edit With

One of the most useful features in the Links panel is the Edit Original button (or choose it from the panel menu), which opens the selected graphic in an editing application. If you select a TIFF image (on the page or in the Links panel) and choose Edit Original, that image typically opens in Photoshop. We have to add the caveat "typically" because InDesign relies on the operating system to know which application to use. If the Mac OS or Windows is set to open TIFF files in Photoshop, then that's where Edit Original will take you.

To specify exactly which application you want to open the file with, you can use Edit With instead. The Edit With submenu lives inside the Edit menu, in the Links panel menu, and in the context menu (when you right-click on an image). It will, by default, show you a list of applications that the operating system believes can open the particular file. Or, you can choose Other to open the file in any other program on your computer.

Some graphics don't work well at all with Edit Original and Edit With—such as an EPS files from FreeHand or CorelDraw—because the original application isn't designed to open the exported file. Nevertheless, in most cases, Edit Original and Edit With are great ways to make quick changes. Also, if you use either of these features, when you return to InDesign, the graphic is automatically updated, so you don't have to update the link manually.

By the way, there's an even faster way to invoke Edit Original: Option/Alt-double-click on the graphic with the Selection or Direct Selection tool.

Embedding a Graphic

To store a graphic inside the publication, select the name of the graphic in the Links panel and choose Embed Link from the Links panel menu. When you embed a graphic, InDesign displays an embedded graphic icon next to the graphic's filename. Embedding a graphic has the following effects.

▶ It breaks the link to the external file, which means you won't be able to update the embedded graphic when you make changes to the original file (except by replacing the embedded graphic using the Relink command).

▶ The size of your publication file increases by the size of the graphic file. Fortunately, if you duplicate the embedded graphic, the publication does not grows again by the same amount—InDesign is smart enough to only embed one copy of it.

▶ You can't use the Edit Original command to open and edit the graphic file.

Ultimately, you shouldn't embed a graphic just because you want to take your publication to another system or to an output provider; instead, you should try using InDesign's Package features (see Chapter 11, "Printing"). However, embedding a relatively small graphic (such as a logo or a small graphic) can be very useful if you're tired of tracking the file on disk.

Unembedding a Graphic. You can link an embedded graphic by selecting it in the Links panel and choosing Unembed File from the panel menu. The program gives you a choice of linking to the original file on disk or saving the embedded file to disk and linking to it.

Link Actions   As we've shown, the Links panel menu doesn't just show you information about your linked files, but lets you manage them, too. Here are several other ways the Links panel lets you work with files.

XMP Data. If a linked image has embedded XMP data (such as data from a digital camera), you can find that information by choosing XMP File Info from the Utilities submenu in the Links panel menu (see "File Info and Metadata," later in this chapter").

Go to Link. To display any file that appears in the Links panel, select the file and click the Go To Link button. InDesign selects and displays the graphic, centered in the publication window (jumping to another spread, if necessary, to do so). This is helpful when trying to ascertain where in your document a particular image is hiding.

Reveal Linked Files on Disk. Someone hands you an InDesign file, and now you need to find one of the imported images on disk. The Link Info area shows you the path, but it's much faster just to select the image on your page, then right-click on it (or Control-click with a one-button mouse) and choose Reveal in Finder (in Mac OS) or Reveal in Explorer (in Windows) from the Context menu. Or, you could choose Reveal in Bridge, if you want to launch Adobe Bridge and view the image there. You can also find the Reveal features in the Links panel menu.

Gathering Linked Images. When it comes time to send your file to someone else (such as a print provider), you're going to need to gather up all your linked graphics in one place. The easiest way to do that is with the Package feature, which we discuss in Chapter 11, "Printing." However, you may find yourself with a need to gather only a handful of linked images—for example, to send to someone else in your workgroup. To do this, select the files in the Links panel and choose Copy Link(s) To from the Utilities submenu in the panel menu.

Copy File Path. While you can display the currently-selected image's file path in the File Info area of the Links panel, you cannot extract the path as text that you can put into a text frame. While there are scripts that allow you to do this, the easiest method is to choose Copy Full Path or Copy Platform Style Path from the Copy Info submenu in the Links panel menu. The former copies from the current user folder, using slashes; for example: "/Users/user_name/Pictures/image1.jpg". The latter uses the whole path—from the hard drive—and uses backslashes on Windows and colons on Mac OS, such as: "HardDrive:Users:user_name:Pictures:image1.jpg".

Search for Missing Links. Let's say you have opened a file and gotten a message that 50 linked images are missing. You realize that those images are on a server that you're not currently connected to, so you mount it. You can tell InDesign to "go check again" by choosing Search for Missing Links from the Utilities submenu in the Links panel menu. Note that this should also find missing links that are in any folder that you have already relinked to during the current run of InDesign (since the last time you launched the program).

Check In/Out and Versions. The Utilities submenu in the Links panel menu lists several features relating to Check In, Check Out, and so on. These are related to InCopy, and are outside the scope of this book.

Links Preferences   The File Handling pane of the Preferences dialog box lets you control several aspects of how InDesign handles linked files.

Check Links Before Opening Document. You can stop InDesign from checking the status of your linked images by turning off the Check Links Before Opening Document checkbox. This could be useful if you were working remotely on a file on a server with a slow network connection—InDesign would open the file far faster. InDesign will still check the status of the links, but it starts after opening the file, and it works in the background as you work.

Find Missing Links Before Opening Document. If InDesign finds that one or more links are missing when you open your document, it will normally attempt to locate the files on disk. It searches the Links folder, the folder the document is in, other folders relative to the current document, and in any other folders that you have pointed to with the Relink command since the last time you launched InDesign. This can be very helpful and save you a lot of time, but it can also potentially cause problems if you have several images with exactly the same name but in different folders, because InDesign might relink to an image that you did not intend. If this describes a situation you might find yourself in, then turn off the Find Missing Links Before Opening Document checkbox in Preferences. That tells InDesign to leave well enough alone and not relink automatically.

Create Links When Placing Text and Spreadsheet Files. You can link to text and spreadsheet files if you first turn on this checkbox in the Preferences dialog box. However, as we point out in "Text Files and File Linking" (in Chapter 3, "Text"), this can cause problems if you edit or format the text once it is placed in InDesign.

Preserving Dimensions. Ordinarily, when you relink to a new image, InDesign attempts to make the new image fit in the same space as the old one. This is great when you're replacing a low-resolution image with a high-resolution version; the cropping and rotation are maintained, and the scaling is adjusted appropriately. However, if you want to make sure all the image transformations stay the same, including applying the same scaling percentage, then turn off the Preserve Image Dimensions When Relinking checkbox in the File Handling pane of the Preferences dialog box.

Default Relink Folder. As we noted earlier, when you click the Relink button in the Links panel, InDesign opens the Locate dialog box. But which folder do you want this dialog box to default to?

If you choose Original Relink Folder from the Default Relink Folder pop-up menu, InDesign always points the Locate dialog box at the folder where the link currently points (that is, where the file is, or where InDesign thinks the file should be). That's how it worked in InDesign CS2 and earlier.

If, instead, you choose Most Recent Relink Folder, InDesign sends you to whichever folder you last relinked to (this is the way that CS3 worked).

Which you want depends on your workflow. Personally, we leave this set to Most Recent Relink Folder because when we're relinking, we tend to link a bunch of files to new files in the same folder.

Working with Graphic Frames

Getting used to the way that InDesign works with graphics and graphics frames can take some time—especially for users of FreeHand and PageMaker (where graphics are not obviously stored inside frames).

Selecting Frames and Graphics

You can modify the size, shape, and formatting of a graphic frame, or you can modify the frame's contents, or you can change both at once. The key to making these adjustments lies in your selection method.

▶ When you mouse over a graphics frame, the Content Grabber appears in the middle of the frame. Clicking the Content Grabber selects the contents of the frame. Dragging the Content Grabber pans the image within the frame (see Figure 7-10).

▶ When you use the Selection tool to click the frame or frame contents outside the Content Grabber, you're selecting both the frame and its contents. At this point, any changes you make using the Control panel or transformation tools affect both the

FIGURE 7-10
Frame and Its Content

Content Grabber

Image being panned

Frame

Hold the cursor over the Content Grabber...

...and drag to move the image within the frame.

frame and its contents (see Chapter 9, "Transforming"). However, resizing the frame does not resize the contents.

▶ When you click the Content Grabber using the Selection tool, or when you click inside the frame using the Direct Selection tool, you select the contents—not the frame itself. Select the graphic when you want to move the graphic within the frame, transform (rotate, scale, move, or skew) the graphic alone, or apply color to the graphic.

▶ When you double-click the image with the Direct Selection tool, you're selecting the frame only—not its contents. Select the frame when you want to edit the shape of the frame using the drawing tools, or transform (scale, rotate, skew, or move) the frame using the transformation tools or the Control panel without transforming its contents.

Resizing Imported Graphics

When you select a graphic frame with the Selection tool and drag the corner handle, InDesign resizes the frame but does not scale the graphic—unless Auto-Fit is selected, but we'll get to that later. To scale the graphic inside the frame as you scale the frame, hold down Command/Ctrl as you drag the corner handle (see Figure 7-11). Hold down Command-Shift/Ctrl-Shift as you drag to proportionally resize the frame and graphic.

FIGURE 7-11
Scaling a Graphic with the Selection Tool

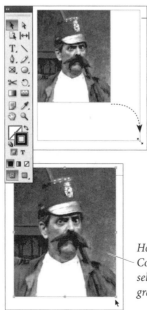

When you simply drag one of the selection handles of a frame containing a graphic, InDesign scales the frame, but does not scale the graphic.

Hold down Command/Ctrl (or better, both Command/Ctrl and Shift) as you drag a selection handle, and InDesign will scale the graphic as it scales the frame.

You can also resize both the frame and the graphic using the Scale tool or the Scale Horizontal and Scale Vertical fields in the Control panel, provided you've selected the frame using the Selection tool. Note that you can type measurements into these scaling fields. For example, if you want the frame and its image to be 10 cm across, replace the 100% in the Scale Horizontal field with 10 cm. For more information, see Chapter 9, "Transforming."

After you scale an image with the Selection tool, the scale fields in the Control panel usually revert to 100%. To see the actual scaling percentage of the image, choose it with the Direct Selection tool.

Panning a Graphic

When you "pan" a graphic, you move the graphic without moving the graphic's frame. To do this, drag the Content Grabber using the Selection tool. Or, select the graphic with the Direct Selection tool, then drag. As you drag, InDesign repositions the graphic inside the frame (see Figure 7-12). Of course, no matter what method you use, if you pan the contents too far, the graphic won't even be visible in the frame, which makes it frustrating to select again later. Select the frame and choose Center Content from the Fitting submenu (in the Object menu, or the context menu) to recover the picture.

Note that it's possible to move the graphic entirely outside the frame, off the page, and beyond the edge of the pasteboard. Don't.

FIGURE 7-12
Panning a Graphic

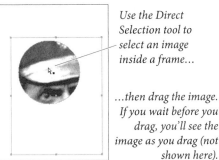

Use the Direct Selection tool to select an image inside a frame...

...then drag the image. If you wait before you drag, you'll see the image as you drag (not shown here).

Fitting Frames and Graphics

We want to point out one more scaling-related feature that involves graphic frames: Fitting. InDesign Fitting features let you automatically adjust an image's size within its frame, or the size of the frame to fit the image—either after you place an image, or upon placing it.

Fitting After Placing. You can choose each of the following from the Fitting submenu (under the Object menu or in the context menu). These commands also appear as somewhat cryptic buttons on the right side of the Control panel (see Figure 7-13).

▶ **Fit Content to Frame.** The Fit Content to Frame feature resizes the graphic to fit into the current frame size. However, unless the graphic already has the same height/width proportions as the frame, it will be stretched non-proportionally.

▶ **Fit Content Proportionally.** To ensure your image is resized with the same X and Y percentages, choose Fit Content Proportionally. The image is sized so that the entire image fits inside the frame. This often results in an empty portion of the frame.

▶ **Fill Frame Proportionally.** Choosing Fill Frame Proportionally will resize the image so that it completely fills the frame, cropping out a portion of the graphic if necessary. The upper-left corner of the resized image is placed in the upper-left corner of the frame, and whatever doesn't fit gets cropped out.

FIGURE 7-13
**Fitting Frames
and Images**

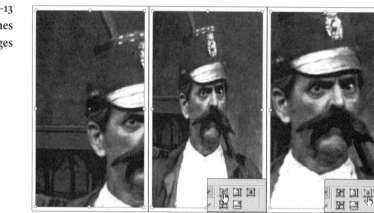

Original image   *Fit Content to Frame*   *Center Content*

Fit Frame to Content expands or contracts the frame to fit the content.

Fit Content Proportionally   *Fill Frame Proportionally*

▶ **Fit Frame to Content.** When you select Fit Frame to Content, InDesign resizes the frame to match the size of the graphic. The size or position of the graphic itself does not change.

Note that the Fit Frame to Content feature also works for text frames (as long as they're not linked to other frames). When there is only a single line of text in the frame, InDesign adjusts the height and width of the frame. When there is more than one line of text, only the height is adjusted.

You can also fit a frame to its content by double-clicking on a corner or side handle. If you double-click on a corner handle, InDesign changes both the width and height of the frame. Double-clicking on a side handle adjusts only the width or height of the frame.

▶ **Center Content.** Choose Center Content to position the center point of the graphic at the geometric center of the frame. This is especially helpful if you accidentally position an image outside of the frame boundaries (so that you can no longer see it).

Auto-Fit. If you don't like the fact that resizing a frame doesn't resize its image, turn on Auto-Fit so that you don't have to hold down the Command/Ctrl keys while resizing. If Auto-Fit is turned on when you resize the frame, the image scales automatically according to the frame's Frame Fitting settings. You can turn on Auto-Fit in the Control panel and in the Frame Fitting Options dialog box.

To remove accidental fitting settings applied when Auto-Fit is turned on, choose Clear Frame Fitting Options from the Fitting submenu on the Object menu.

FIGURE 7-14
Frame Fitting Options

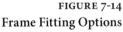

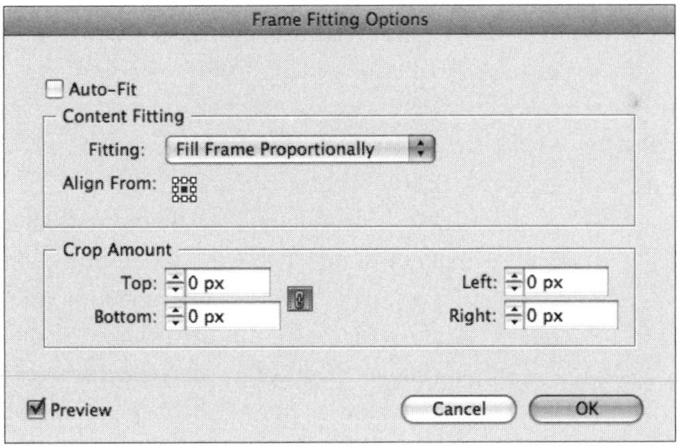

Fitting Upon Placing. If you're building a template, you may want to create empty graphic frames which will later be filled with images. If so, you can also assign fitting commands to those frames so that those images will be scaled accordingly automatically. To do this, select the frame and choose Frame Fitting Options from the Fitting submenu (under the Object menu or the Context menu). The Frame Fitting Options dialog box offers three options (see Figure 7-14).

▶ **Crop Amount.** The Crop Amount controls the amount of the image that should be cropped out, based on the original size of the image. For example, let's say you know the incoming photograph will have a 4 mm white border on all four sides. If you set the Crop Amount fields to this amount, that border will be "removed" before any of the other fitting features are applied.

▶ **Alignment.** The Reference Point proxy lets you specify how your image should map to the frame. If you choose the center point, your incoming image will be centered in the frame; if you choose the lower-right corner, the lower-right corner of the image will be placed in the lower-right corner of the frame; and so on.

▶ **Fitting on Empty Frame.** Here's where you choose one of the options we discussed above: Fit Content to Frame, Fit Content Proportionally, or Fill Frame Proportionally.

While everything about this dialog box implies that it works only on empty graphic frames, it works equally as well with frames with images already in them. It does not, however, work with text frames—too bad, as it would be cool to create a frame that automatically stretches to fit its text, or stretches the text to fit the frame.

Note that Frame Fitting Options can be applied as part of an object style definition (see Chapter 6, "Where Text Meets Graphics").

File Info and Metadata

Metadata (which literally means "data about data") isn't a new thing. Photoshop's File Info dialog box has allowed you to add metadata such as captions, copyright info, and routing or handling instructions for years. But the Adobe Creative Suite applications are beginning to incorporate metadata features more seriously now (based on the open standard XMP structure, which is based on XML, if you care). Metadata can be almost any kind of information about your file, and it travels invisibly behind the scenes with the file as it moves

FIGURE 7-15

Metadata in the
File Info dialog box

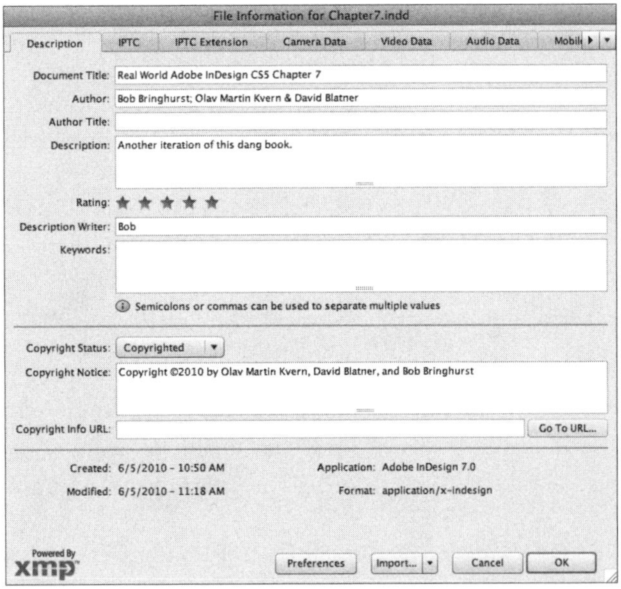

from machine to machine. We think you'll find that the more time you take to add metadata to your files now, the happier you'll be in the long run.

Adding Metadata to InDesign Files

You can add metadata to an InDesign file by selecting File Info from the File menu (see Figure 7-15). The File Info dialog box contains several panes of fields and pop-up menus, though you'll likely just use the Description pane most of the time. Some panes—such as Camera Data 1 and 2—aren't applicable to InDesign documents at all. See *Real World Photoshop* for more information on image-related metadata.

Another, less intuitive way to add metadata to InDesign documents is to use Adobe Bridge. Just select an InDesign document and choose File Info from Bridge's File menu. To apply metadata to more than one InDesign file at a time, choose the documents and use Bridge's Metadata and Keyword panels. (Beware, though—this action isn't undoable.)

Metadata in an InDesign file travels not only with the file itself, but also with PDF files exported from the document. When you export a PDF file of your InDesign document, InDesign automatically includes the metadata, too. (If you include any sort of personal or trade information in your metadata, you may need to strip it out manually with Acrobat or Bridge before sending a PDF file to someone else.)

Reading Metadata in Imported Images

Both Illustrator and Photoshop let you add metadata in the same way, which is especially useful when you're creating live captions. Besides captions, what other ways can you retrieve metadata from imported images? There are two ways to see this hidden information: After selecting an imported graphic, you can select File Info from the Info panel menu, or you can select XMP File Info from the Utilities submenu in the Links panel menu. You cannot use these methods to edit metadata. Do that in Bridge, Photoshop, or Illustrator.

You can also extract the metadata from the imported image. For example, if someone added a caption to an image from within Photoshop, you could copy that caption out and paste it into a text frame in InDesign—no more PostIt notes with captions passed from person to person! You should be able to copy this info to the Clipboard by selecting a field and pressing Command/Ctrl-C.

Searching for Metadata

Besides generating captions, an important reason to add metadata to your images and documents is so that you can search for that data later. For example, you might want to find all the InDesign documents on your hard drive that include the phrase "square the circle" in the Description field or the word "frogs" as a keyword. InDesign doesn't have a built-in way of doing these kinds of searches, but several asset management utilities do. The most obvious one is Adobe Bridge: Choose a folder, Choose Find from Bridge's Edit menu, and select from the Criteria pop-up menu.

When you find the InDesign file you're looking for, you can select it in Bridge and then choose Open with InDesign from the context menu (right-click in Windows or Control-click on the Macintosh).

By the way, if you're searching for a PDF file that contains metadata, you can also use Bridge, but Acrobat's own Search feature may be even faster. It's not obvious that the Search feature looks for file metadata, but it does. You just need to set it to look through documents on disk rather than the currently open file.

Object Layer Options

We've long loved InDesign's ability to import native Photoshop (PSD) files, layers and all. Now, our favorite page-layout program goes one step beyond by letting us turn those layers on and off (making them visible or hidden). You can control layer visibility in PSD, AI, or PDF files that contain layers. Ironically and sadly, it won't work for Photoshop's PDF files, but Adobe Illustrator's PDF files work great, as long as you turn on the Create Acrobat Layers option when making the PDF from Illustrator.

You can turn layers on or off when you first import a file into InDesign by turning on the Show Import Options checkbox in the Place dialog box (see "Image Import Options," earlier in this chapter). Or, if you have already imported the image, select it on your page and choose Object Layer Options from the Object menu (or the context menu). In either case, you're presented with the same three options (see Figure 7-16).

FIGURE 7-16
Changing
Layer Visibility

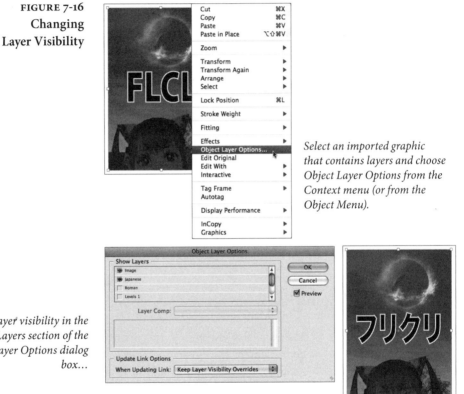

Select an imported graphic that contains layers and choose Object Layer Options from the Context menu (or from the Object Menu).

Change layer visibility in the Show Layers section of the Object Layer Options dialog box...

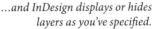

...and InDesign displays or hides layers as you've specified.

Show Layers. It's unclear whether a feature could be any simpler than this: To make a layer visible or invisible, click in the column to the left of the layer's name. If you've used layer sets in Photoshop, you can view the individual layers within those by clicking the triangle next to the layer set name. Also, you can Option/Alt-click on an eye icon to toggle all the other layers. That is, if all the other layers are visible when you do this, they'll all become hidden, and vice versa.

Layer Comps. Photoshop's Layer Comp panel lets you create "comps" of layer settings. For example, you might have one layer comp that shows layers A, B, and C; and another layer comp in which A, C, and D are visible. Or you might make a layer comp in which some of the layers have layer styles (like drop shadow or emboss) turned on, and another comp in which they're turned off. Layer comps are great when you have a lot of ideas in Photoshop but you're not sure what will look best when the image hits the page. The good news is that you can choose any of your layer comps from the Layer Comps pop-up menu. Of course, if a PSD file has no layer comps saved in it, this menu is unavailable.

Update Link Options. After you override the native layer visibility settings (what the file was saved with) with the Object Layer Options dialog box, InDesign displays a small eye icon in the Links panel next to that image's name. This helps alert you that someone did something to those layers. However, what if you go back, change the layer visibility in Photoshop or Illustrator, and then save the file again?

InDesign offers two options: If you choose Use Photoshop's Layer Visibility (or Use PDF's Layer Visibility, depending on what kind of image it is) from the When Updating Link pop-up menu, InDesign will throw out any layer visibility overrides as soon as you Relink or Update the image link. Alternately, if you choose Keep Layer Visibility Overrides, then your overrides will be maintained even after the image is modified and updated.

Working with Clipping Paths

Earlier in this chapter, we talked about InDesign's ability to use a clipping path stored in a graphic as you place the graphic—but what about creating a clipping path for a graphic that doesn't have one? First, there's nothing magical about clipping paths. In fact, you could say that every graphic you place in InDesign is inside a clipping path—its graphic frame.

A clipping path is a PostScript path, much like other Bézier lines in InDesign or Illustrator. However, a clipping path acts like a pair of scissors, cutting out an image in any shape you want. Clipping an image is actually the same as cropping it, but because InDesign makes a distinction, we will, too: The shape of a graphic frame crops the picture, but the clipping path (if there is one) clips it.

Why Use Clipping Paths?

Remember that InDesign can read transparency in imported images. Even if you don't want to use any of the transparency effects, you may want to take advantage of this feature because it means you might avoid using clipping paths altogether. Save yourself time and just make the background of the image transparent in Photoshop.

Nevertheless, some people will still want to use clipping paths. For example, clipping paths are always drawn at the resolution of the output device, so you can get very sharp edges. If you like this sharp-edged effect, use a clipping path. Also, those folks who want to avoid the transparency flattener might still want to use clipping paths. As for us, we haven't bothered with clipping paths for years.

Selecting an Existing Clipping Path

If the selected graphic contains a clipping path—or, in the case of a Photoshop image, *any* path saved in Photoshop's Paths panel—you can select the clipping path you want to apply. To do this, select the graphic or its frame, then display the Clipping Path dialog box (choose Options from the Clipping Path submenu, under the Object menu, or press Command-Option-Shift-K/Ctrl-Alt-Shift-K). Select

FIGURE 7-17
Using an Existing Clipping Path

Place a graphic containing a clipping path (in this example, we've used a Photoshop file).

Select the graphic, then press Command-Option-Shift-K/ Ctrl-Alt-Shift-K (or choose Options from the Clipping Path submenu, under the Object menu) to display the Clipping Path dialog box.

Choose Photoshop Path from the Type pop-up menu.
Choose a path from the Path menu.

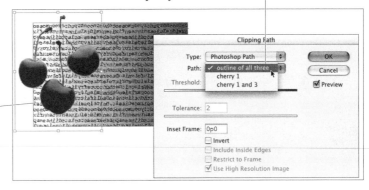

InDesign applies the first clipping path defined in the graphic. If that's not the path you wanted, choose a different one.

Photoshop Path from the Type pop-up menu. If there are multiple paths, choose one from the Path pop-up menu (see Figure 7-17).

Creating a Clipping Path

You can ask InDesign to create an "automatic" clipping path using the following steps (see Figure 7-18). However, to be honest about it, we tend to shy away from this option unless we're building a quick comp for a client or we're planning on spending some time editing the resulting path. In general, you'll just get better results making clipping paths by hand in Photoshop.

1. Select a graphic. You'll have the best luck with a graphic against a white background. In addition, it's a good idea to select the graphic using the Direct Selection tool (as opposed to selecting the frame). We know this seems odd, but bear with us.

2. Choose Options from the Clipping Path submenu, under the Object menu (or press Command-Option-Shift-K/Ctrl-Alt-Shift-K). InDesign displays the Clipping Path dialog box.

FIGURE 7-18
Creating a Clipping Path

Select a graphic, then press Command-Option-Shift-K/ Ctrl-Alt-Shift-K (or choose Options from the Clipping Path submenu, under the Object menu) to display the Clipping Path dialog box.

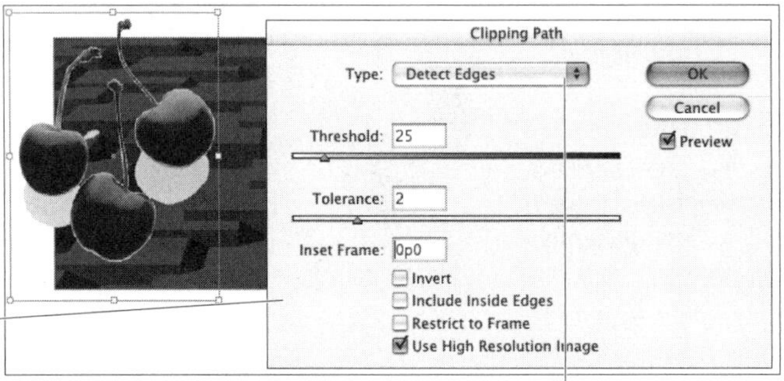

Choose Detect Edges from the Type pop-up menu.

InDesign attempts to find the edges in the graphic. Of course, InDesign does a better job of this when the graphic has a simple outline and a simple background.

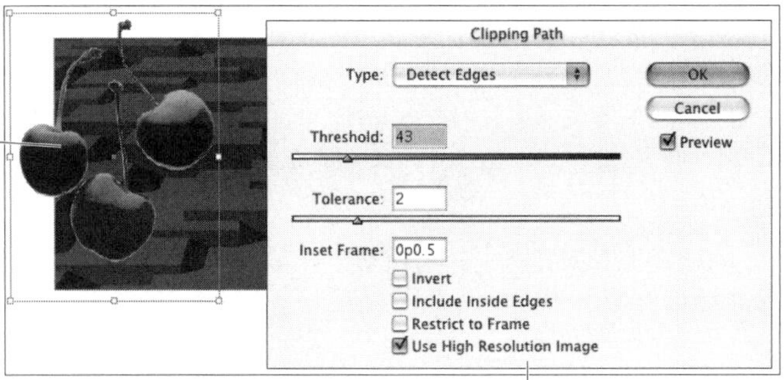

You can fine-tune the clipping path using the controls in the Clipping Path dialog box. Here, we've adjusted the Threshold and Inset Frame values to remove some off-white areas.

3. Choose Detect Edges from the Type pop-up menu. Turn on the Preview option, if it's not already on, and drag the Clipping Path dialog box out of the way so that you can see the selected image. Look at the clipping path that InDesign has built around the image. What? You can't see the clipping path? That's because you didn't select the image using the Direct Selection tool, like we told you to in Step 1. If you had, you'd be able to see the clipping path as you adjust the settings in the Clipping Path dialog box.

4. Work with the controls in the dialog box.

    ▶ Adjust the values in the Threshold and Tolerance fields (either enter values in the fields or drag the associated sliders) until the clipping path looks the way you want it to.

    ▶ Turn on Invert to turn the clipping path "inside out."

    ▶ Turn on the Include Inside Edges option to create "holes" inside the clipping path for any blank (as defined by the value you entered in the Threshold field) areas inside the graphic.

    ▶ Turn on Restrict to Frame to limit the clipping path to the boundaries of the graphic frame. (Since the image can't extend past the edges of the graphic frame anyway, this is reasonable. However, if you change your frame cropping, you'll have to rebuild your clipping path, so we leave this turned off.)

    ▶ Most of the time, you'll probably want to turn on the Use High Resolution Image option—it uses data from the image file on disk (rather than simply using the screen preview image) to create a more accurate clipping path.

    ▶ If necessary (and it usually will be), enter a value in the Inset Frame field to shrink (enter positive values) or expand (enter negative values) the clipping path. We often use a small inset value, like .5 points.

5. Once the clipping path looks the way you want it to, click the OK button.

Don't worry about making a mistake; you can always open up this dialog box again and change the values, or change the clipping path using the Direct Selection tool or the various Pen tools.

You can also create a clipping path based on an alpha channel if one has been saved in an imported image. To do this, select Alpha Channel from the Type pop-up menu. The problem is that alpha channels can have soft anti-aliased or feathered edges, and clipping paths cannot. So, InDesign has to convert soft edges into hard-edged Bézier paths using the features above. It's hardly worth the trouble.

Removing a Clipping Path

To remove a clipping path, select the image, display the Clipping Path dialog box, and choose None from the Type pop-up menu. InDesign removes the clipping path.

Convert Clipping Path to Frame

You can convert a clipping path into a frame of the same shape by selecting any image with a clipping path and choosing Convert Clipping Path to Frame from the Context menu (right-click with a two-button mouse or Control-click with a one-button mouse) or from the Clipping Path submenu. This works for all clipping paths, including clipping paths generated by the Detect Edges feature.

Applying Color to an Imported Graphic

You can't apply color to just any imported graphic—but you can apply colors to bi-level (*i.e.*, black-and-white) and grayscale images. To apply a color to an image, select the image using the Direct Selection tool, then apply a color as you normally would—probably by clicking a swatch in the Swatches panel (see Chapter 10, "Color").

If you want the image to overprint any objects behind it, select the image using the Direct Selection tool, display the Attributes panel, and then turn on the Overprint Fill option— or simply set the image to Multiply mode in the Effects panel. You can use this technique to create duotones from grayscale images you've placed in a publication.

Exporting Documents

You can export InDesign content as EPS, Print PDF, Interactive PDF, JPEG, HTML, IDML, SWF, FLA, or XML (in addition to the text export options described in Chapter 3, "Text"). We explore each of these in depth in the following sections—except SWF, FLA, and Interactive PDF, which we cover in Chapter 13. We cover XML briefly in this chapter and provide more complete coverage on the web. In most cases, the first step is to select Export from the File menu (or press Command-E/Ctrl-E).

Exporting JPEG

The best way for someone else to see a page from your document if they don't own InDesign is to export and send them a PDF file. However, a JPEG image of your document page often works as well. A JPEG file is smaller and easier to view than a PDF. A JPEG file is a bitmapped image, so whoever you send it to can't really zoom.

InDesign can export a JPEG file of any page or object in your document—you can even export a series of JPEG files for more than one page at a time. To export a JPEG file, choose Export from the File menu and pick JPEG from the Format pop-up menu.

The Export JPEG dialog box is pretty simple (see Figure 7-19). You can control which page or pages you want to export (use commas and hyphens to type ranges of pages). To export one or more objects from a page or spread, select them before choosing Export and then turn on the Selection option in the dialog box.

▶ **Quality.** The Quality pop-up menu offers a handful of choices, from Low to Maximum—the lower the quality you choose, the smaller the file will be on disk. Unfortunately, there's no way to preview the quality difference before saving the file.

▶ **Format Method.** Use the Format Method pop-up menu to choose Baseline or Progressive—we recommend Baseline unless you need people to see the image progressively appear in stages (low resolution, then higher resolution) when they view it.

FIGURE 7-19
JPEG Export Options

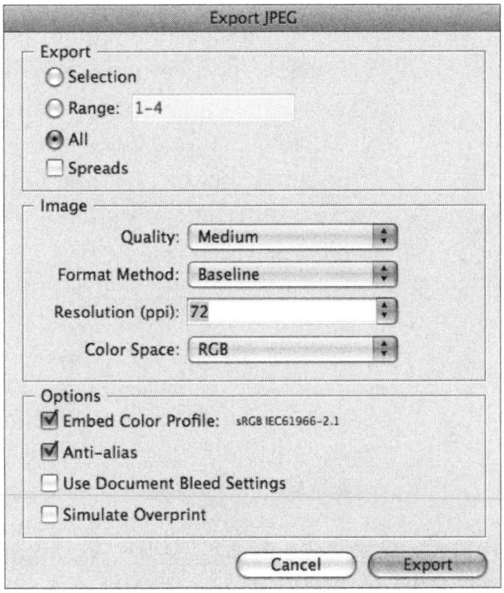

▶ **Resolution.** Early versions of InDesign could only export 72 ppi JPEG images. Now you can specify any resolution you want (up to 2400 ppi).

▶ **Color Space.** Export as CMYK, RGB, or Gray.

▶ **Embed Color Profile.** Turn on this option to embed the document's color profile in the JPEG file. Look to the right of the option to see the current profile. If you want a different profile, choose Assign Profiles from the Edit menu, and then export.

▶ **Anti-Alias.** Turn this option on to smooth out the jagged edges of text and bitmap images.

▶ **Use Document Bleed Settings.** If you turn on this option, the bleed area specified in Document Setup appears in the JPEG.

▶ **Simulate Overprint.** If you turn on this option, the JPEG file simulates the effects of overprinting spot inks with different neutral density values by converting spot colors to process colors.

Exporting EPS

Although we tend to eschew EPS when we can, there are times when it can come in handy. For example, if you have designed an ad that will be placed in a magazine produced with any version of QuarkXPress earlier than version 7. Those versions didn't handle PDF particularly well, so EPS is probably the better bet.

To export an InDesign page (or series of pages) as an EPS graphic (or series of graphics, as EPS is, by definition, a single-page-at-a-time format), choose EPS from the pop-up menu in the Export dialog box, pick a location for the file, and then click Save. The Export EPS dialog box has two tabs: General and Advanced. Here's a quick description of the options in each tab.

General. The controls in the General tab define the way that InDesign exports objects to the EPS file (see Figure 7-20).

▶ **Pages.** Which pages do you want to export? Bear in mind, as you work with the controls in this tab, that each page in the page range you specify will be exported as a separate EPS file. To export pages one, two, three, seven, and twelve, for example, enter "1-3,7,12" into the Ranges field. See "Page Ranges" in Chapter 11, "Printing," for more information. When you turn

FIGURE 7-20
**EPS Export Options,
General Tab**

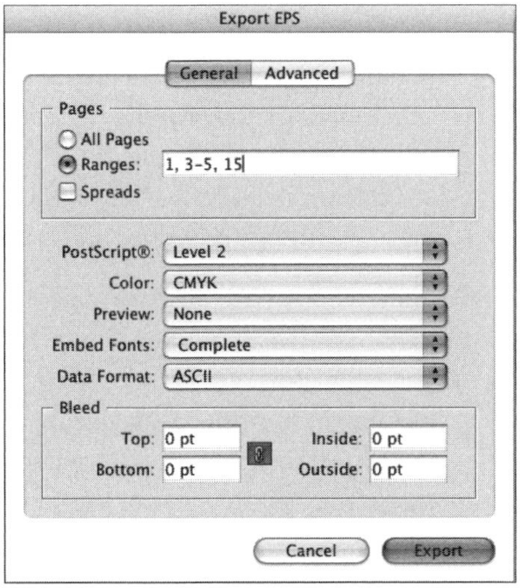

on the Spreads checkbox, InDesign exports the pages in readers spreads, just as they appear in your document window. For
instance, pages 2 and 3 are combined into one wide EPS file.

▶ **PostScript.** Choose the PostScript version of the printer you
expect to use to print the EPS. If you're sure you're printing on
a PostScript 3 printer, choose Level 3. Choose Level 2 if your
printer could be PostScript Level 2 or PostScript 3. InDesign no
longer supports PostScript Level 1 printers; a Level 2 EPS file
may or may not print on one of these old beasts.

▶ **Color.** Do you want to convert RGB images in your publication
to CMYK as you create the EPS? If so, choose CMYK from the
Color pop-up menu. The method InDesign uses for this conversion depends on the settings in the Color Settings dialog box
(see Chapter 10, "Color," for more on color management). While
it's rare that you'd need to choose Gray or RGB, these options
will convert all colors to their grayscale or RGB equivalents.

If you're using some other software to handle the EPS's color
separation, choose Leave Unchanged so that InDesign leaves
RGB and CMYK images alone during the export process.

▶ **Preview.** EPS files usually have low-resolution, built-in previews,
which applications use to display the EPS on screen; Macintosh
EPS files typically have PICT previews, Windows EPS files must
use TIFF previews. If you're re-importing the EPS file back into
an InDesign document, you can leave the Preview pop-up menu
set to None, because InDesign actually creates a preview on the
fly when you import the file. Similarly, if you're going to open

the EPS file in Photoshop (rasterizing it into a bitmapped image), Illustrator (converting it into paths), or process the EPS file with some software that doesn't require a preview image, you can leave Preview set to None. If the EPS will be used in any other program, select PICT or TIFF (the latter is more flexible because most Macintosh programs can read both PICT and TIFF).

▶ **Embed Fonts.** To make sure that the EPS contains all of the fonts you've used, choose Complete from the Embed Fonts pop-up menu. Why not do this every time? Because your EPS files can become huge, bloated, and swollen with included fonts. To reduce the size of the EPS, choose Subset to include only the characters needed to print the text in the EPS. Choose None when you don't want or need to include any fonts in the EPS.

Some fonts cannot be embedded—the font manufacturer has included information in the font that prevents embedding. When InDesign reads this information, it will not include the fonts in the EPS, regardless of the choice you make from the Embed Fonts pop-up menu. If you find you're missing a font in an EPS, return to the InDesign publication and convert all of the characters that use the missing font to outlines and then export the EPS again.

▶ **Data Format.** Choose ASCII if you expect to print the EPS on a system connected to a printer via a serial cable, or if you plan to edit the EPS using a text editor or word processor—otherwise, choose Binary to create a compressed version of the file. Binary files are smaller and therefore transmit to the printer faster, but they sometimes choke really old networks.

▶ **Bleed.** If you do not enter values in the four Bleed fields (Top, Bottom, Inside, and Outside—or Left and Right, in a non-facing-pages document), InDesign sets the edge of the EPS bounding box to the edge of the page you're exporting. Enter a value in the Bleed fields to expand the area of the page. See Chapter 11, "Printing," for more on bleeding off the edge of the page.

Advanced. The Advanced options let you control how images and transparency are handled in EPS files.

▶ **Send Data.** In most cases, you want the full resolution of your bitmapped images to be included in your EPS files (so they can later be printed properly). On occasion, however, you may want only a low-resolution version of your images in the EPS file. For example, let's say you were going to rasterize the EPS in

Photoshop in order to save it as a GIF or JPEG and place it on the Web; there's no need for the full-resolution images, so you could choose Proxy from the Send Data pop-up menu. If you're planning to print the EPS through an OPI system, and plan to replace the images, or if you're creating the EPS for onscreen viewing only, choose Proxy.

▶ **OPI Image Replacement.** Turn this option on to have InDesign perform OPI image replacement as you export the EPS. If you're exporting a page containing EPS graphics with OPI image links, you'll probably need to turn this option on (unless your EPS will later be processed by an OPI server).

▶ **Omit For OPI.** To keep InDesign from including a certain type of imported graphic file in the EPS, turn on the corresponding option in the Omit section (to omit placed TIFF images, for example, turn on the Bitmapped Images option). We discuss OPI in more detail in Chapter 11, "Printing."

▶ **Transparency Flattener.** In order for transparency effects to print on most devices, InDesign must "flatten" them. We discuss flattening and transparency flattening styles in great detail in Chapter 11, "Printing." Suffice it to say that you can choose a flattener style here, as well as tell InDesign to ignore any flattener style spread overrides that you (or someone else) may have made in the document (by turning on Ignore Spread Overrides).

▶ **Ink Manager.** The Ink Manager manages how colors trap with each other and how spot colors interact (for instance, you can use the Ink Manager to alias one spot color to another). We cover the Ink Manager in Chapter 10, "Color."

Exporting PDF for Printing

InDesign can export Adobe Acrobat Portable Document Format files (what normal people call "PDF"), which can be used for remote printing, electronic distribution, or as a graphic you can place in InDesign or other programs.

In InDesign CS5, exporting to PDF is two separate options: Adobe PDF (Print) and Adobe PDF (Interactive). We'll cover exporting to interactive PDF in Chapter 13, "Interactive Documents."

InDesign doesn't need to use the Acrobat Distiller (or the Distiller Assistant) to create PDF files. If you want to use Distiller to make

PDF files instead of creating them directly using the Export feature, use the Print dialog box to write PostScript to disk first (we discuss how to do that in Chapter 11, "Printing").

You export a PDF by selecting Export from the File menu and choosing Adobe PDF (Print) from the Format or Save as Type pop-up menu. The Export Adobe PDF dialog box contains seven panes for setting PDF export options. Remember that in all paned dialog boxes, you can jump to the second pane by pressing Command-2/Ctrl-2, the third pane with Command-3/Ctrl-3, and so on.

Above all these panes sits the Adobe PDF Preset pop-up menu, which lets you select an export preset (each of which is a collection of various export options). These styles are basically identical to those found in Illustrator and Distiller. We discuss creating your own in "Defining a PDF Export Preset," later in this chapter.

General   The General pane of the Export PDF dialog box (see Figure 7-21) is a hodge-podge of options, controlling everything from what pages get exported to whether non-printing objects should be included.

Standard (PDF/X). InDesign fully supports several important international ISO standards, including PDF/X-1a and PDF/X-3. You can select either of these from the Standard pop-up menu or the Preset menu. However, if you're going to use PDF/X, we strongly recommend you choose from the Preset menu instead of the Standard menu—otherwise, it's easy to make a PDF/X file that, while technically valid, will make the recipient of the file unhappy.

The PDF/X-1a preset is for a straight CMYK-only (or CMYK plus spot color) workflow, and is relatively popular in the United States. PDF/X-3 is used in color managed workflows, especially in Europe, because they can include RGB and Lab color data, too.

PDF/X-4 is similar to PDF/X-3, but with an important twist: While PDF/X-3 is based on the Acrobat 4 format, PDF/X-4 is based on Acrobat 5. As we point out below, Acrobat 5 (PDF 1.4) supports transparency, so it doesn't require flattening. That's why PDF/X-4 is the preferred format when printing to a printer with a PDF RIP (as opposed to a simple PostScript RIP), such as one with the Adobe PDF Print Engine.

Both of these standards aren't some weird, proprietary flavor of PDF; they're just regular PDF files that specify the sorts of things that can be included. For example, all fonts must be embedded in a PDF/X-1a file. Note that you can make a PDF/X compliant PDF file without choosing from the Standard or Preset pop-up menus; these just make it easier.

FIGURE 7-21
Export PDF Options,
General Pane

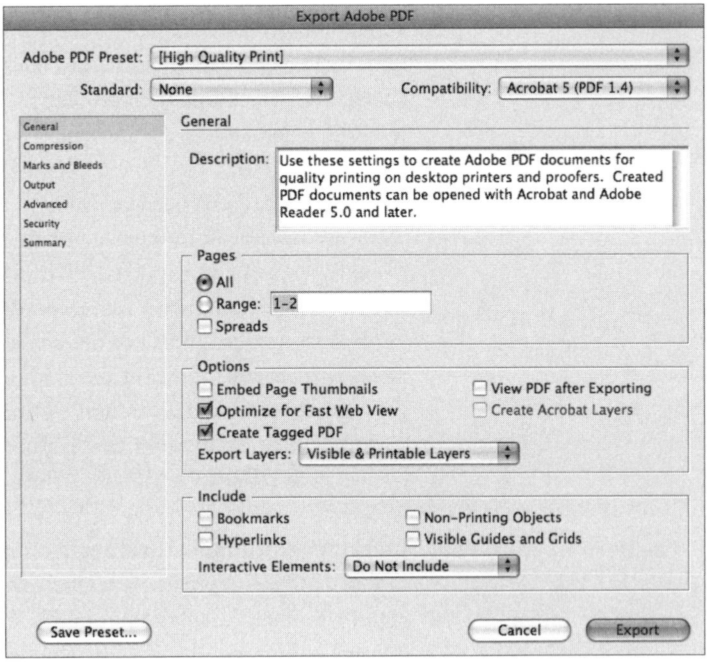

Compatibility. Who is your audience for this PDF file? Acrobat 9 has been out for a couple of years now, so we usually assume that most professionals have it but many of the general public may only have Acrobat 5 (or the free Acrobat 5 Reader). If there's any chance your recipient only has Acrobat 4, choose Acrobat 4 from the Compatibility pop-up menu. The PDF version numbering can be confusing: Version 1.3 is Acrobat 4, 1.4 is Acrobat 5, 1.5 is Acrobat 6, version 1.6 is Acrobat 7, and version 1.8 is both Acrobat 8 and Acrobat 9.

There's another reason you want to pay attention here: If you have used any transparency effects in your document, the Compatibility pop-up menu controls who does the flattening. Choosing Acrobat 4 means you want InDesign to flatten the file (see "Transparency Flattener" later in this section, and "Printing Transparency" in Chapter 11, "Printing"). Later Acrobat versions can read the unflattened transparency effects. If we're sending files to our printer, then we'd much rather send them Acrobat 6 or later PDF files.

Page Ranges. Which pages do you want to export? Just as in the General pane of the Print dialog box, you can export all document pages (click the All option) or specify individual page ranges (135-182) or noncontiguous pages (3, 7, 22) in the Range field. Note that unless you have Absolute Numbering selected in the General pane of the Preferences dialog box, you'll need to type page ranges with their actual names. For instance, if you want to export the first four pages and you're using roman numerals, you'll have to type "i-iv". If you've specified a page number prefix, like "A", you'll have to include that in the Range field, too.

Reader's Spreads. When you turn on the Spreads option, InDesign exports each spread in the page range you've specified (see above) as a single page of the exported PDF. This is called "reader's spreads" because the spread appears as it would to a reader flipping through a book or magazine. This does not create "printer spreads," which you need to print a saddle-stitched booklet. You need a separate plug-in to do that. Personally, when we want to view a PDF in reader's spreads, we don't turn on this feature; we just turn on the Facing option in Acrobat's View menu—the effect is basically the same.

Embed Page Thumbnails. Creates a preview image, or "thumbnail" of each page or spread (if you're exporting reader's spreads) you export. You can display thumbnails when you view the PDF using Acrobat or Acrobat Reader. They increase the size of the file.

Optimize for Fast Web View. The key word here is "Web." The only time you'd want to turn this on is when you're creating a document that will only be viewed on the Web. When this option is off, InDesign includes repeated objects (such as objects from master pages) as individual objects on each page of the PDF. When you choose Optimize PDF, InDesign exports a single instance of each repeated item for the entire PDF. When the item appears on a page in the PDF, InDesign includes a reference to the "master" item. This reduces the file size of the PDF without changing the appearance of the exported pages. When this option is on, InDesign also overrides the settings in the Compression pane with its own Web-appropriate settings, and restructures the file so that it can be downloaded one page at a time from a Web server rather than having to download the whole megillah.

Create Tagged PDF. Most people expect their PDF files to always appear just as they do in InDesign—each line of text ending in the same position on the page. But what if someone who is blind wants to read your document with a Braille reader? What if someone wants to see your PDF on their iPhone or other mobile device? In that case, it would be very helpful if the PDF included some "intelligence" or "accessibility" in the form of tags that—behind the scenes—declare this to be a paragraph that can reflow as necessary, that thing in the upper corner of the page to be a page number that doesn't have to appear on a mobile device, and so on.

If you predict that your PDF file might show up in a non-traditional reader, turn on the Create Tagged PDF checkbox. Obviously, there is hardly ever a need for tags in documents that are simply being printed, but they don't affect file size or export time much, so we often just leave this option turned on.

Note that inside the PDF these tags are actually written in XML, and any tags you've applied with the Tags panel (see "XML," later in this chapter) will appear in the PDF, too. This offers some interesting side effects. For example, if you create a tag named "Artifact" in the Tags panel and then apply it to a text frame, Acrobat considers the object irrelevant and not part of the text flow when reading the PDF out loud or displaying it on some mobile devices. That's perfect for text frames such as running heads and page numbers.

To be honest, in most cases, if you really want your documents to be accessible (especially to be "Section 508" compliant), you will likely need to do a lot more clean-up work on them in Acrobat Professional after exporting with tags.

View PDF after Exporting. When you turn this option on, InDesign opens the file in Acrobat after exporting the PDF.

Create Acrobat Layers. Acrobat 6 introduced the idea of hiding and showing layers within a PDF file. If you turn on the Create Acrobat Layers checkbox, all your InDesign document's layers (even hidden layers) are converted into Acrobat layers and can be controlled from within Acrobat. In a stroke of brilliance, even the page marks (like crop and registration marks) are put on their own layer. Obviously, this only works when exporting in the Acrobat 6 (PDF 1.5) format or later.

Export Layers. Normally, an object will only appear in your PDF if it's on a layer that is both visible and printable—that is, the Show Layer and Print Layer checkboxes are both enabled in the Layer Options dialog box. However, you can override this by choosing either All Layers or Visible Layers from the Export Layers pop-up menu. The former prints everything, even objects on hidden or non-printing layers. That's nice when you forget to turn on hidden layers before starting the PDF export process. The latter option prints all visible layers (whether they're "printable" or not).

Bookmarks. If you've used the table of contents feature (which we discuss in Chapter 8, "Long Documents"), you can tell InDesign to automatically build bookmarks for your PDF file based on the table of contents. Just turn on the Include Bookmarks checkbox. Or, if you used the Bookmarks panel to add custom bookmarks to your document (see Chapter 13, "Interactive Documents") you have to turn this checkbox on to actually see them in the PDF file. Again, this is a feature suitable for PDFs destined for onscreen viewing, not prepress.

Hyperlinks. You can use the Hyperlinks panel to add as many hyperlinks to your document as you want, but unless you turn on this checkbox they won't appear in your PDF file. When you turn this option on, InDesign also creates hyperlinks in your table of contents and indexes (see Chapter 8, "Long Documents," for more on these features). Of course, it's not really appropriate to include hyperlinks when sending off a PDF for high-resolution printing. See Chapter 13, "Interactive Documents," for more on hyperlinks.

Non-printing Objects. Ordinarily, nonprinting objects (items for which you've turned on the Non-printing checkbox in the Attributes panel) won't appear in exported PDF files. You can force them to export (overriding the Attributes panel) by turning on the Export Non-printing Objects checkbox in the Export PDF dialog box. Why would you do this? We bet someone can think of a good reason.

Visible Guides and Grids. If you turn on this export option, InDesign exports all visible guides (margins, ruler guides, baseline guides, and so on), which may be helpful for designers who are collaborating on a project. The only guide type that doesn't export is the document grid (even if it's visible).

Interactive Elements. If your document contains buttons, movies, or sounds and you want them to be active in the PDF document, you'll want to export using the Adobe PDF (Interactive) option. (See Chapter 13, "Interactive Documents.") If these interactive items appear in the PDF you're exporting for printing purposes, you need to decide whether you want to include or leave out the appearance of the interactive items.

If you need a printable document that also includes interactive items, you'll probably want to place the interactive items on one layer and printable substitutes on a different layer. Then show/hide these layers and export two PDF versions.

FIGURE 7-22
**Export PDF Options,
Compression Pane**

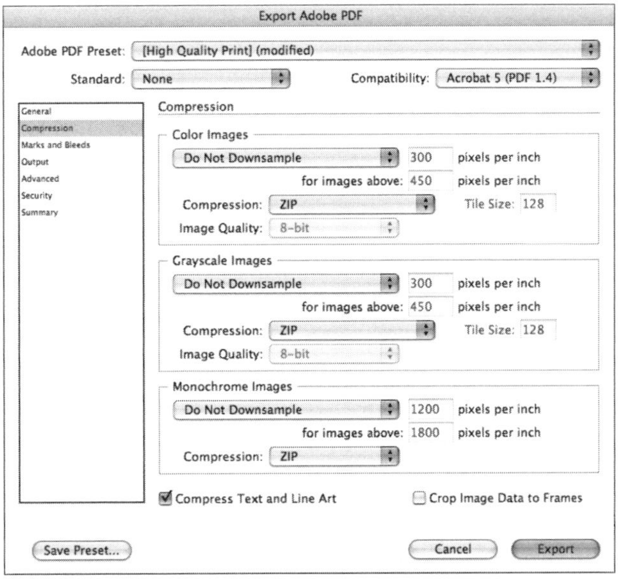

Export Adobe PDF

Adobe PDF Preset: [High Quality Print] (modified)

Standard: None   Compatibility: Acrobat 5 (PDF 1.4)

General
Compression
Marks and Bleeds
Output
Advanced
Security
Summary

Compression

Color Images
Do Not Downsample   300   pixels per inch
for images above: 450   pixels per inch
Compression: ZIP   Tile Size: 128
Image Quality: 8-bit

Grayscale Images
Do Not Downsample   300   pixels per inch
for images above: 450   pixels per inch
Compression: ZIP   Tile Size: 128
Image Quality: 8-bit

Monochrome Images
Do Not Downsample   1200   pixels per inch
for images above: 1800   pixels per inch
Compression: ZIP

☑ Compress Text and Line Art   ☐ Crop Image Data to Frames

Save Preset...   Cancel   Export

Compression

The options in the Compression pane define the compression and/ or sampling changes applied to the images in your publication as it's exported as a PDF (see Figure 7-22). Compression is almost always a good thing, but you need to choose your compression options carefully, depending on where your PDF is headed. PDFs for onscreen viewing can handle more compression, and those destined for the Web typically *need* a lot of compression to keep file sizes down. A PDF file that you're sending to a printer for high-resolution output requires very little compression, if any (unless you have to e-mail the file or it won't otherwise fit on a disk for transport).

Bitmapped images are almost always the largest part of a document, so PDF's compression techniques focus on them. InDesign has two methods of making your files smaller: lowering the resolution of the images and encoding the image data in clever ways.

Resampling. If you place a 300 ppi CMYK image into your document and scale it down 50 percent, the effective resolution is 600 ppi (because twice as many pixels fit in the same amount of space). When you export your PDF, you can ask InDesign to resample the image to a more reasonable resolution. If your final output is to a desktop inkjet printer, you rarely need more than 300 or 400 ppi. Printing on a laser printer or imagesetter (or any device that uses halftone screens, as explained earlier in this chapter) requires no more than 1.5 to 2.0 times the halftone screen frequency—a 150 lpi halftone rarely needs more than 225 ppi of data to print beautifully.

Monochrome (or bi-level) bitmapped images do not have halftone screens applied to them by the printer and, therefore, are not subject to the same rules that govern grayscale and color images. In a monochrome image, you never need more resolution than the resolution of the printer. If your final output is your 600 dpi laser printer, you certainly never need more than 600 dpi monochrome images. Imagesetter output rarely requires more than 1200 dpi (though for a sheetfed art book, we might bump this up to 1500 dpi). Printing on uncoated stock requires less resolution because of halftone spots spreading; you can easily get away with 800 dpi for newsprint.

If you're exporting a PDF for online viewing, you can get away with 72 or 96 ppi, unless you want the viewer to be able to zoom in on the image and not see pixelation.

InDesign only downsamples when exporting PDF files. That is, it throws away data to decrease image resolution (it won't add resolution). Downsampling works by turning an area of pixels into a single, larger pixel, so the method you use to get that larger pixel is crucial. When you *downsample* an image, InDesign takes the average color or gray value of all of the pixels in the area to set the color or gray value of the larger pixel. When you *subsample* an image, on the other hand, InDesign uses the color or gray value of a single pixel in the middle of the area. This means that subsampling is a much less accurate resampling method than downsampling, and shouldn't be used for anything other than proofing your document. We rarely use Average Downsampling or Subsampling; instead, the best option is Bicubic Downsampling, which provides the smoothest sampling algorithm.

Ultimately, however, we much prefer to just get the resolution right in Photoshop before placing the image, rather than relying on InDesign to downsample it. That way, we can see the result of resampling on the screen, and undo the change if necessary. Otherwise, we won't see the result until we view the PDF.

Compression. The PDF specification supports both ZIP and JPEG encoding for grayscale and color bitmapped images; and CCITT Group 3, CCITT Group 4, ZIP, and Run Length encodings for monochrome bitmapped images. In Acrobat 6 or later, you can even use JPEG 2000. It's enough to make your head spin! Which method should you use? Again, it depends on where the PDF is going and what kind of images you've got.

Scanned images generally compress better with JPEG, and synthetic images (such as screen captures that have a lot of solid colors and sharp edges) compress better with ZIP. However, JPEG compression, even at its highest quality setting, removes data from an image file (it's "lossy"). Most designers find that some JPEG compression for scanned photographs is an acceptable compromise, as it results in dramatically smaller file sizes. JPEG 2000 compresses even smaller and results in less degradation. But, ultimately, when we don't need to worry about file size, we prefer to use ZIP for everything because ZIP compression does not discard image data (it's "lossless"). You never know when you might need that image data!

If we are using JPEG, then we make a choice from the Image Quality pop-up menu: You get the best compression with Minimum quality, but who wants to look at the results? Unfortunately, the only good way to choose from among the Image Quality options is to save two or three to disk, look at them in Acrobat, and compare their file sizes.

Exporting PDF files for print is easier: We usually just choose ZIP from the Compression pop-up menu for both color and grayscale images. However, if you need to save some disk space (again, like if you're emailing the file to your output provider), it's usually reasonable to use Automatic (JPEG) compression with the Image Quality pop-up menu set to Maximum quality—the resulting JPEG images are usually indistinguishable from uncompressed images. Or, if you know that the recipient has Acrobat 6 or later, then consider using the better-quality JPEG 2000 compression.

As for monochrome image encoding, it's rare to see much of a difference among the choices (they're all lossless and provide reasonable compression). We usually use Run Length or ZIP encoding, but only because we don't like the sound of CCITT. Say it aloud a few times, and you'll see what we mean.

Compress Text and Line Art. The Compress Text and Line Art option applies to text and paths you've drawn in InDesign—we cannot think of any reason you should turn this option off.

Crop Image Data to Frames. When you turn this option on, InDesign sends only the visible parts of the images in the publication. This sounds reasonable, and can result in a much smaller file for publications that contain cropped images. But it also means you won't have access to the image data if you edit the image in the PDF. Most of the time, this isn't a problem, but you might want to turn this option off if your PDF includes images that bleed (so that you or your service provider can later increase the bleed area, if necessary).

Marks and Bleeds   In a desperate attempt at reducing the redundancy in our overly complex lives, we're going to skip a detailed analysis of the Marks and Bleeds pane of the Export PDF dialog box and instead point out that these features are exactly the same as the features in the Print dialog box (see "Marks and Bleeds" in Chapter 11, "Printing").

Output   The Output pane lets you control how color in your document is handled.

Color Conversion. Choose No Color Conversion from the Color Conversion pop-up menu if you don't want InDesign to mess with your colors and just write them into the PDF as specified. That is, RGB colors will remain RGB, and CMYK colors will stay CMYK. This is what you get with PDF/X3 or PDF/X4, because in that standard, colors are managed at print time from Acrobat.

If you do want InDesign to manage the colors, you should choose either Convert to Destination or Convert to Destination (Preserve Numbers). In either case, all RGB colors get converted to CMYK based on the CMYK profile you choose in the Destination pop-up menu. However, when you choose the "preserve numbers" option, any CMYK colors that you have specified in your InDesign document (such as colors you have applied to text or frames) are left alone—that is, they are not converted from your document CMYK profile to the destination CMYK profile. For example, this stops 100-percent black text changing to four-color CMYK text, or 100-percent cyan changing to a mix of cyan, yellow, and magenta (which was a problem in earlier versions of InDesign).

However, whether or not you choose "preserve numbers," if your CMYK image is tagged with a color profile *and* that profile was preserved when you placed it (which is typically not the case with CMYK images), it will get cross-converted to the new CMYK space. (See Chapter 10, "Color," for more on color management.)

Note that choosing CMYK does not separate spot colors to CMYK in the PDF file; if you want to do that, you should use the Ink Manager (see below).

If you have turned off color management (that is, you chose Emulate InDesign 2.0 in the Color Settings dialog box), then you have only three choices: do nothing, Convert to CMYK, or Convert to RGB. Either way, InDesign uses its internal RGB-to-CMYK conversion method (the default CMYK space is based on SWOP inks—technically, it's the default CMYK settings from Photoshop 5; the default RGB space is AdobeRGB).

Profile Inclusion Policy. When you're converting colors, you can tell InDesign whether or not to embed ICC profiles into your PDF file. In a color-managed workflow, it is important to include profiles, or else other programs (or InDesign, if you're re-importing the PDF into another InDesign document) cannot color-manage the file. However, if you are simply creating a CMYK files (such as a PDF/X1-a workflow), there is no reason to include your profiles. Also, turn this option off when exporting PDF files for the Web, since the Web isn't color managed and ICC Profiles increase file size.

Simulate Overprint. Acrobat 4 has no way to preview overprinting instructions, so if you need to use Acrobat 4 and you need to proof overprinting, you can turn on the Simulate Overprint option. Because everyone we know is using a newer version of Acrobat, we rarely have to worry about this feature. Note that Simulate Overprint should not be used for final artwork, as it radically changes your document (spot colors are changed to process colors, for instance). It's just a low-end proofing tool.

Ink Manager. Have a spot color that should be a process color? Or two different spot colors that really should be one? The Ink Manager handles these kinds of troubles (for more information, see "Ink Manager" in Chapter 10, "Color").

PDF/X. If you have chosen one of the PDF/X options in the Standards pop-up menu at the top of the dialog box, InDesign offers you the option of specifying the final output destination profile in the mysteriously named Output Intent Profile Name. Fortunately, this is almost always exactly the same as the Destination profile you chose above. You can also add a short description in the Output Condition Name field if you think anyone downstream at the printer will care (seems doubtful to us). If the profile you choose is registered somewhere (such as the International Color Consortium at *www.color. org*), you can specify a name and URL in the final two fields of this section. That information simply gets embedded in the PDF file so someone can later decode what you've done.

Advanced   There's nothing particularly "advanced" about any of the options in this pane, and while you probably won't spend much time messing with these settings, it is important to understand what they do and why you'd want to change them (see Figure 7-23).

FIGURE 7-23
Export PDF Options,
Advanced Pane

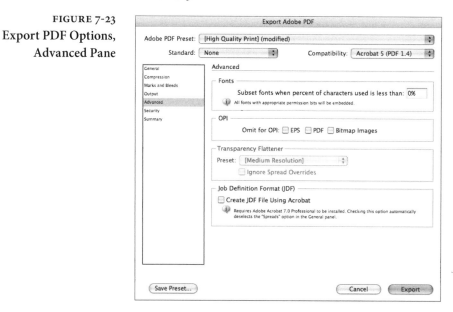

Subset Fonts. InDesign can always embed font information in exported PDF files, so it doesn't matter whether the person you give the file to has the font. The exception to this is when the font manufacturer has specified that their font should not be embedded. Many Asian fonts cannot be embedded, for instance. This is a political and legal hot-potato that we're not going to touch, other than to say that if your fonts cannot be embedded, complain to the font developer, not Adobe (or us). Or, better yet, if there isn't a lot of text in that font, convert the text to outlines before printing or exporting.

Anyway, usually the question isn't whether to embed your fonts, but rather how much of the font you want to embed. The value you enter in the Subset Fonts field sets the threshold at which InDesign includes complete fonts in the PDF you're exporting. When you "subset" a font, you include only those characters that are used on the pages you're exporting, which keeps file size down. Enter 100 to force InDesign to always save a subset of the font's characters, or enter 0 to force InDesign to include the entire font (or fonts) in the PDF. You can also enter some other percentage value to strike a balance between the two extremes, but we generally find that either we want subsets or we don't.

One reason you might not want to subset your fonts is to maximize the potential for editing the PDF later. Let's say you subset your fonts, and later need your output provider to edit the PDF (perhaps to change a typo). If they need to change "karma" to "dharma" and you haven't used the letter "d" elsewhere in the document, they can't do it (unless they have the font installed on their system).

Another reason not to use font subsetting is if you expect users on a platform other than your own to view and print your exported PDFs. We know, it's supposed to work. In our experience, it doesn't. Platform-specific character encoding and printer driver issues always seem to cause problems when we subset fonts in a PDF. At least one of the authors (Ole!) feels strongly that font subsetting should always be avoided for this reason. The small amount of (cheap!) disk space you use to embed the entire font is a small price to pay, compared to (expensive!) last-minute print production problems.

Omit for OPI. In an OPI workflow, the high-resolution image data is kept separate from your document until it's merged in at the last minute before printing. If you have an OPI server capable of processing PDF files with OPI comments, you can keep InDesign from including a certain type of imported graphic file in the PDF file by turning on the corresponding option in the Omit section (to omit placed EPS images, for example, turn on the EPS option). We discuss OPI in more detail in Chapter 11, "Printing."

Transparency Flattener. While Acrobat 5 and later can handle InDesign's transparency effects, Acrobat 4 is clueless. So if you're exporting an Acrobat 4 file, InDesign must "flatten" all transparency effects. We discuss flattening and the Transparency Flattener Style pop-up menu in great detail in Chapter 11, "Printing." Suffice it to say that you can choose a flattener style here, as well as tell InDesign to ignore any flattener style spread overrides you may have made in the document (by turning on the Ignore Spread Overrides checkbox).

Job Definition Format. The Job Definition Format (JDF) is talked about a lot, but most people don't realize that it all just comes down to adding some metadata about your document to the file (in this case, the PDF file). Adobe wants you to think that InDesign directly supports JDF, but if you turn on the Create JDF File Using Acrobat checkbox, all you really get is a regular PDF file plus a tiny JDF file in the same folder. Plus, InDesign launches Acrobat Professional (which you have to have installed to make use of this feature) and lets you use its JDF tools to fill in the details—such as who is the primary contact person for this print job, what kind of paper stock should it be printed on, and so on.

Security   Digital Rights Management (DRM) is all the rage these days. The basic issue is who gets to do what with your content? When it comes to PDF files, you have several DRM options set out in the Security pane of the Export PDF dialog box (see Figure 7-24).

In our view, most of the PDF security features are for PDFs you're exporting for online distribution (that is, the PDF is the final product of your production process), and not for prepress use. We might have our paranoid moments, but our practicality gets the better of them most of the time—and it's just not practical to lock up a PDF that's headed for printing and prepress work. Think about it—do you want your imagesetting service bureau calling you at four in the morning to ask for the password you used to lock up a PDF?

On the other hand, if you're exporting a PDF to send to a client or a printer who you don't have a close relationship with, you might want to activate some of these settings.

Passwords. You can give your PDF file two different passwords: one to limit who can open the document (Document Open Password), and one to limit who can change the security settings in the document (Permissions Password). The two passwords must be different. If you're going to turn on *any* security settings in the PDF—even if you don't require a Document Open Password—then we strongly encourage you to provide a Permissions Password (just in case you need to make changes to the PDF later).

Note that if you choose to export in Acrobat 4 (PDF 1.3) format, InDesign only uses the older 40-bit RC4 encryption, which isn't

FIGURE 7-24
**Export PDF Options,
Security Pane**

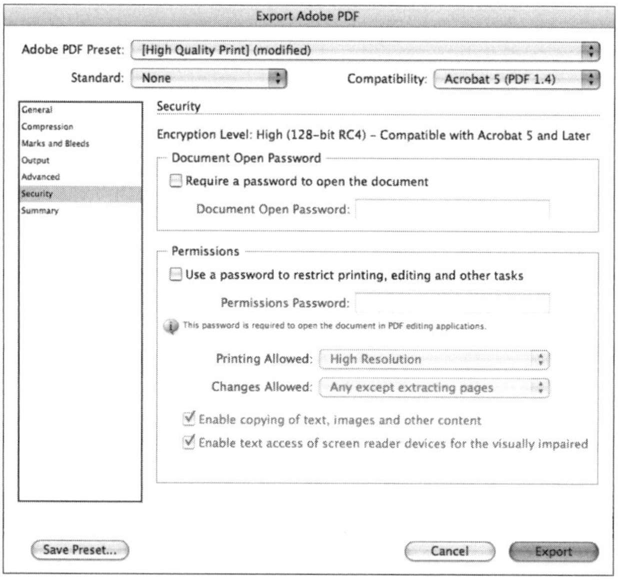

nearly as powerful as the newer 128-bit encryption—you get better encryption when you export as Acrobat 5 or later.

Permissions. The two pop-up menus and three checkboxes in the Permissions settings are self-explanatory: They let you control whether the file can be printed (or at what resolution), whether it can be altered, whether content can be copied or extracted, whether screen readers for the visually impaired should be supported, and whether your metadata should be readable by databases or search systems (see "File Info and Metadata," earlier in this chapter). These are useful if you're sending a file to a client and you don't want them to do anything but add comments, or if you're sending a file to be printed, and you want to make sure the output provider doesn't "accidentally" change anything. But the security settings can play havoc with some non-Adobe PDF readers (like Mac OS X Preview).

Summary

The last pane of the Export PDF dialog box, Summary, lists all the settings in all the tabs in one long text list. Do we ever sit and read through this? Nope; it's more time-consuming to read through this unformatted list of settings than it is to skip through each of the panes. However, it's nice that you can click the Save Summary button to save this list to disk as a text file. If you're exporting a PDF file to send to someone else, consider including this summary along with it, so that they know how you set up the dialog box (and can see whether you did anything inappropriate). You can also use this saved summary as a log of what you did to later refer to if something prints in an unexpected fashion.

Defining a PDF Export Preset

PDF export presets are like paragraph styles—they're bundles of attributes that can be applied in a single action. Almost all of the attributes in the PDF Export dialog box are included in a PDF export preset (the Ink Manager and the Security settings aren't). It's easy to create a PDF export preset; set up the Export PDF dialog box with the options the way you want them, click the Save Preset button at the bottom of the dialog box, and then give the style a name. You can then go ahead and export, or just cancel out of the Export PDF dialog box (if you just wanted to set up the preset without exporting).

InDesign also has a second method for making PDF export presets, though we find it slightly more cumbersome (see Figure 7-25).

1. Choose Define from the Adobe PDF Presets submenu, under the File menu. InDesign displays the Adobe PDF Presets dialog box with a list of the current PDF export presets.

FIGURE 7-25

Defining a PDF Export Preset

Choose Define from the Adobe PDF Presets submenu, under the File menu. InDesign displays the Adobe PDF Presets dialog box.

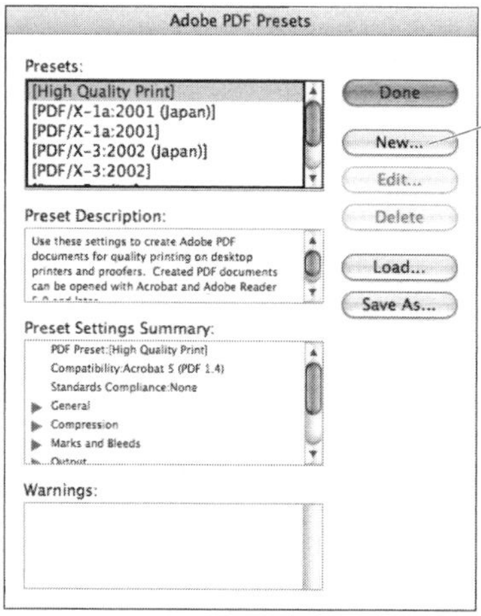

Click the New button.

2. Click the New button. InDesign displays the New PDF Export Preset dialog box, but with a few differences: there's a Name field at the top, there's no Security pane, and Ink Manager and page ranges are grayed out. Note that if you select an export preset before clicking New, this dialog box will be based on the preset you selected.

3. Enter a name for the PDF export preset in the Name field, then set up the PDF export options using the panes of the dialog box. Click the OK button when you're done. InDesign returns you to the Adobe PDF Presets dialog box and adds the new preset to the list of available presets.

To export a PDF using the settings in a PDF export preset, choose the preset name from the Adobe PDF Preset pop-up menu in the Export PDF dialog box. InDesign applies the settings of the PDF export preset to the controls in the Export PDF dialog box. You'll still need to enter a page range in the General pane—the export preset does not include that information.

Note that you can also make PDF presets in Acrobat Distiller or any other Creative Suite application. InDesign and the other Creative Suite programs share PDF presets, which makes creating consistent PDF files much easier.

Managing PDF Export Presets

You can use the Adobe PDF Presets dialog box to add, delete, rename, edit, and import or export PDF export presets.

▶ To delete a PDF export preset, select the preset name and click the Delete button. (You can't delete the default presets: High Quality Print, PDF/X-1a, PDF/X-3, PDF/X-4, Press Quality, and Smallest File Size.)

▶ To export PDF export presets, select the presets and click the Save As button. InDesign displays the Save PDF Export Presets dialog box. Specify a file name and location and click the OK button.

▶ To import a PDF export preset or set of presets, open the Adobe PDF Presets dialog box and click the Load button. InDesign displays the Load PDF Export Presets dialog box. Locate and select a file containing the saved presets and click the OK button. If the PDF export presets you're importing already exist in the publication, InDesign will create copies (InDesign appends a number—usually "1"—to the duplicate presets).

▶ To edit or rename a PDF export preset (other than the default ones), select the preset name in the Adobe PDF Presets dialog box, then click the Edit button.

InDesign Markup Language (IDML)

What if you could describe your whole InDesign document as a compact text file? That's what the InDesign Markup Language (IDML) formats is: XML representations of each and every object on every page of your document, as well as the styles, colors, margins, and all other document information. You can export an IDML file, send it to someone else, and, when they open it, InDesign creates a new file that looks exactly like the one you made. Note that IDML replaced the InDesign Interchange (INX) option available in versions before InDesign CS5.

Why would you want to do this? One reason is backward compatibility—IDML is the only way that you can "save back" from InDesign CS5 to InDesign CS4. Unfortunately, you cannot open CS5's IDML files in InDesign CS3. Instead, you'd have to open it in CS4, then export as INX to save down from there.

Another reason to use IDML is to remove corrupt data that may have snuck into your file. For example, some folks have reported that they cannot export to PDF or delete unwanted swatches in their Swatches panel. In most cases, simply exporting the document in the IDML format and then reopening it clears out the trouble.

One last reason you might want to use IDML: It's really easy to edit or even create these files, without ever using InDesign. For example, a database could be programmed to write IDML files that turn into fully-formatted InDesign documents when you open them. We talk more about that in the "XML" chapter posted on the web.

To export an IDML file, choose Export from the File menu, then select InDesign Markup (IDML) from the pop-up menu. You can open an IDML file just as you would open any other InDesign document.

Snippets

What happens when you select one or more objects on your page and drag them to the desktop? InDesign creates a snippet file with the .IDMS file name extension. A snippet is a file written in the InDesign Markup language that describes one or more objects from a page or spread. (A snippet is similar to an IDML file, which describes an entire document in XML language.)

You can also create a snippet file by dragging one or more objects into Adobe Bridge, or by selecting and exporting the objects on the page and choosing InDesign Snippet from the pop-up menu in the Export dialog box.

Snippets are great for sending InDesign objects to someone else via email, or for saving objects that you want to reuse. In fact, the Library feature (see Chapter 1, "Workspace") actually saves objects internally as snippets. Because snippets are just small XML files, you could easily place a bunch of them in a database, and then use some program to build your InDesign pages on the fly by pulling just the snippets you need from the database.

To place a snippet into your InDesign file, you can use the Place command from the File menu to place IDMS files (or INDS from previous InDesign versions), or simply drag the snippet file in from the desktop, Bridge, or Mini Bridge. If you use File > Place while the text cursor is inside a text frame, the snippet will automatically become an anchored object (as long as the snippet defines a single object or group of objects).

The position of your newly placed snippet depends on the Snippet Import setting in the File Handling pane of the Preferences dialog box: You can choose between Position at Cursor Location (wherever you drop it or click to Place it), or Position at Original Location (which remembers where it was on the page when you originally made it). If you want a snippet to always remember its location, lock the position of the objects before creating the snippet file.

Exporting HTML

Just about everyone needs to repurpose content from an InDesign document into a Web page sooner or later. Back in the ancient days, InDesign 2 could export any story as HTML. Then InDesign CS and CS2 replaced that with a featured called Package for GoLive, which was so painful to use that we have still never found anyone who used it in a real world production workflow.

The good news is that Package for GoLive is now gone. The even better news is that InDesign can now export HTML with CSS tags. But the bad news is that InDesign is still very limited in what it can do. And the even worse news is that InDesign still cannot import HTML, so this is still a one-way road.

What to expect when you're expecting. First and foremost, you should not plan on using InDesign to actually build or design Web pages. Its abilities are limited to exporting content (text and images) in a form that someone who knows about HTML and Web authoring will be able to accept and manipulate relatively easily. It's pretty clever, but you should expect that virtually every file you export from InDesign will require some cleanup.

Does that make this feature useless? Far from it! It can be an incredible time-saver as long as you know what you're getting into.

What gets exported. InDesign can export text and—optionally— placed graphics and imported SWF files. That's it. It will *not* export any page geometry (where things are on your page), path or frame information (shape, fill color, and so on of anything you draw), text or graphics on master pages (unless the frame has been overridden on a document page), effects such as drop shadows, QuickTime movies, pasted objects, or stuff on the pasteboard.

InDesign exports only hyperlinks that jump to text anchors in the same document or to web pages. Tables are also exported, but not some table formatting like cell strokes. Tables are assigned unique IDs, which is handy for reference in Dreamweaver.

However, note that all your local text formatting is stripped away. The only text "formatting" you'll get is paragraph and character styles. So if you want a word to be italic in your exported HTML, make sure you assign an italic character style to it.

Even then you won't get an HTML tag such as "<em>" because all character and paragraph styles are applied using CSS class tags. This is typically what you'd want for your character styles, but often not what you want with paragraph styles—it all depends on how your

CSS tags are defined. Fortunately, it's pretty easy to clean up these class tags in a Web authoring tool, such as Dreamweaver or even a text editor.

The thing to keep in mind here is that all text formatting in InDesign must be defined by the CSS definitions in HTML.

Exporting XHTML   You can search the Export dialog box all day, but you won't find a way to export HTML. That's because the feature lives someplace unexpected. Here's how to export an XHTML file:

1. Choose "Export for" from the File menu, and then choose Dreamweaver. Note that the name is misleading because it isn't exclusive to Adobe Dreamweaver—these files will work with any modern Web authoring tool.

2. Choose a file name and location and then click Save.

3. In the General pane of the XHTML Export Options dialog box, choose whether you want to export the entire document or only the currently-selected objects (see Figure 7-26). If you choose Selection and you have a text frame selected, InDesign exports the entire story, even if part of the story is overset or if the story threads across multiple pages.

   The General pane lets you control the order of page items. If you select Based on Page Layout, InDesign exports text and graphics on each page as they're positioned from left to right, and top to bottom. That means that if a caption is slightly to the left of its image, the caption will appear first in the HTML. If you want more control over the order of page items, select Same As XML Structure. InDesign uses the order of the tags in the XML Structure panel for the exported content. Just drag the tags in the XML Structure panel to set the XHTML Export order. If your content isn't tagged, you can choose Add Untagged Items from the Structure panel menu to generate tags for you. If you don't want any item to be included in the export, you can simply delete the tag in the XML Structure panel.

   The General pane also lets you control how paragraphs with automatic bullets or numbering should be handled. In general, you should choose Map to Ordered List for numbered lists and Map to Unordered List for bulletted paragraphs; however, if you want, you could force InDesign to convert either one to text (so the bullet or number character becomes a character in the text). You can also choose to convert numbered paragraphs using Map

FIGURE 7-26
Exporting to XHTML/
Dreamweaver

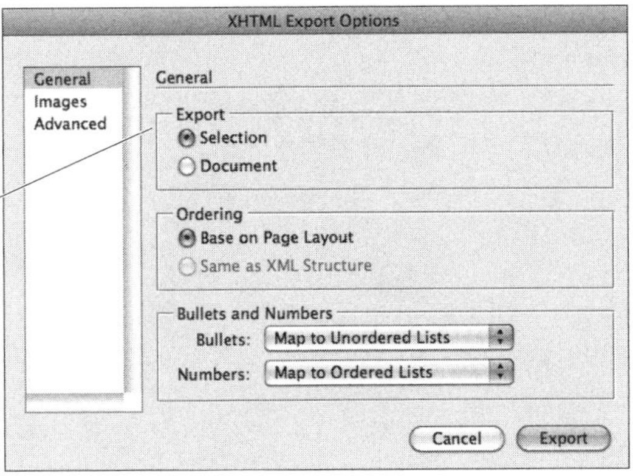

To export a single story,
or a group of images
and stories on a spread,
select them first, then
choose Selection here.

to Static Ordered List, which still applies the <ol> tag, but adds a "value" attribute to each paragraph.

By the way, don't let the "X" bother you; XHTML is simply a form of HTML with a few more strict rules.

4. The Copy Images pop-up menu in the Images pane (see Figure 7-27) lets you choose what to do with images in your document or selection. If you choose Original, InDesign copies the original linked files into an "images" folder in the same location as the HTML file—similar to what happens when you Package for output. (Actually, the folder is given a name constructed of the HTML file plus "-web-images".)

If you choose Optimized, InDesign creates a new version of the image. Unfortunately, InDesign does not have the Save for Web dialog box (as in Photoshop and Illustrator), so you have very limited options for the conversion. Turn on the Formatted checkbox to apply image cropping, scaling, rotation. However, in general, you'll get a *much* better conversion to GIF or JPEG if you use a program such as Photoshop, Fireworks, or Illustrator to optimize these images.

The third option, Link to Server Path, won't copy or convert your images at all, or even create a folder for them. Instead, it lets you specify a folder name in which the final images will be placed. For example, if you choose this and then type "images/" into the Path on Server field, InDesign assumes you are converting the images yourself and putting them in a folder called "images" in the same directory as the HTML file. Alternately, you can type a specific URL here, such as "http://mydomain.com/files/images/".

5. In the Advanced pane, choose how you would like the CSS tags to appear in your document:

FIGURE 7-27
**Exporting images
along with the HTML**

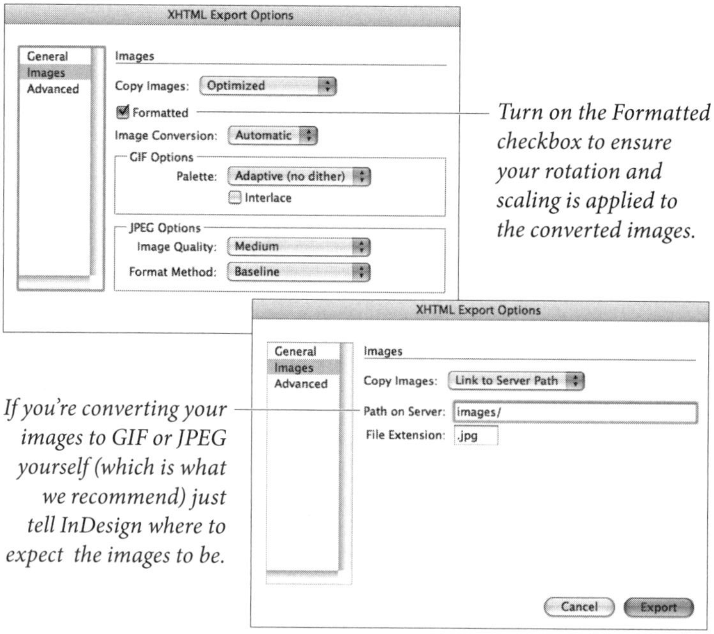

*Turn on the Formatted
checkbox to ensure
your rotation and
scaling is applied to
the converted images.*

*If you're converting your
images to GIF or JPEG
yourself (which is what
we recommend) just
tell InDesign where to
expect the images to be.*

▶ **Embedded CSS.** When exporting to XHTML, you can create
a list of CSS styles that appears in the header of the HTML
file with declarations, or attributes. If you turn on Include
Style Definitions, InDesign attempts to match the attributes
of the InDesign text formatting with CSS equivalents. If you
turn off this option, the HTML file includes empty declarations. You can edit these declarations in Dreamweaver. If
you select Preserve Local Overrides, local formatting such as
italic or bold is included.

▶ **No CSS.** If you just want your text (and optionally, graphics) without any tags, choose No CSS. You still get basic tags,
such as "<div>" and "<p>", so it's easy to import this neutral
content into any Web authoring program.

▶ **External CSS.** The last option, External CSS, lets you set up
a link to an external CSS. For example, you might type "../
styles/mycss.css" here. Most newspapers or magazines will
choose this option because they'll have a CSS file already
created for their Web site. The only problem then is that the
paragraph and character styles in the InDesign file usually
don't match the external file's CSS style names properly, so
you may have to do some clever search/replace in the final file
in order to get the style names right.

The final feature in the Advanced pane lets you include a link to an external JavaScript file in the header of the HTML file. We've never had to do this, so we're not sure why you'd want to.

6. Finally, click the Export button to save the XHTML file to disk.

Other Techniques

By the way, there is another way to get HTML out of InDesign—a method that can actually apply text formatting such as <em> to italic text, and so on. However, the trick is sort of a hack and takes a while to explain. If you're curious, you can read Anne-Marie Concepción's description here: *tinyurl.com/yr5fuo* (the actual page is at indesignsecrets.com).

David often also resorts to simply copying and pasting text from InDesign into an HTML editor, even though he loses text formatting as he does so. You could also export an RTF file from InDesign, open it in Microsoft Word, export that as HTML, and then open that file in a Web authoring tool.

EPUB (eBooks)

If you ask David what the most important technology will be in the next ten years, he'll give you the same answer he gave ten years ago: eBooks. Adobe has taken a few stabs towards producing eBook technology, and its newest version lets you create eBooks using the EPUB file format. For more information about the EPUB file format, visit *www.idpf.org*.

If your document has an elaborate design, you'll end up with a garbled EPUB unless you set up the document properly.

Some content is removed when you export to EPUB, including master page items, automatic page numbers, page breaks, generated tables of contents, and shapes created with drawing tools. Plus, some text formatting is removed. Again, format your text using styles.

Here are some other things you can do to improve the quality of the exported EPUB file:

▶ When you want a section of the eBook to start on a new page, either select the Use First Level Entries as Section Breaks option during export, or create a separate InDesign document for it and combine the documents in a book file. To export all the chapters into one EPUB file, choose Export Book For Digital Editions from the Book panel menu.

▶ To control the position of the content in the eBook, you may want to keep it simple. Set up one text frame per page in your InDesign document, link all the text frames together as a single story, and then flow all the text and graphics within that story.

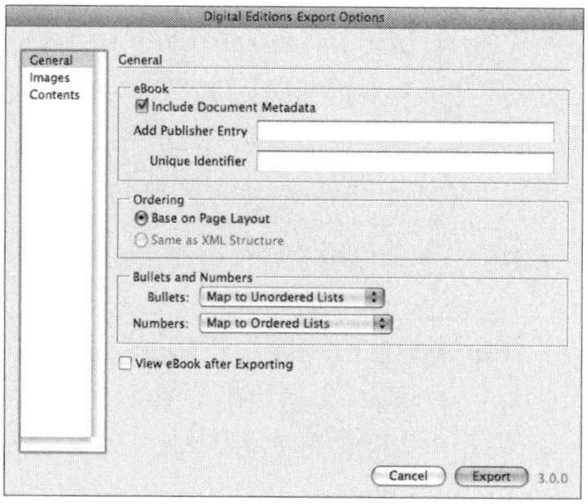

FIGURE 7-28
Export eBooks

Another option is to apply XML tags to all your content and use the Structure view to determine the order of page items. When you export, select the Same as XML Structure option.

▶ Anchor graphics and other design elements within the main body of text so that they travel with the text when it reflows.

▶ Set up a table of contents manually for the book. Insert the text for the entries and then turn each entry into a cross-reference that jumps to a specific section in the eBook. To create a TOC that functions as a navigation menu, set up a TOC style by choosing Table of Contents Styles from the Layout menu. You can then select that TOC style when you export the EPUB file.

Creating the EPUB file. First, you'll need the Digital Editions software, which you can download free at *www.adobe.com/products/ digitaleditions*.

Then, to make an .epub file, open an InDesign document and choose "Export for" from the File menu, and then choose EPUB. After you give the .epub file a name and tell InDesign where to save it, click OK and you'll see the Digital Editions Export Options dialog box (see Figure 7-28), which bears a passing resemblance to the XHTML Export Options dialog box that we've already looked at. We'll just cover the options that are different from the XHTML Export Options dialog box.

Select Include Document Metadata to export the metadata entered in the File Information dialog box. If you are exporting from a book file, make sure that the style source includes the metadata. Publisher information isn't includes in the File Information dialog box, but eBook creators wanted it, so you can specify publishing information in the Add Publisher Entry. You can also type a specific unique identifier, such as the ISBN, if you don't want it to be generated automatically.

On the Contents panel, note that you can choose two flavors of .epub: XHTML and DTBook. The latter is based on a format by the Daisy Consortium, and helps in making your content accessible for people with disabilities. You can learn more about this at *www.adobe.com/accessibility/products/indesign/.*

Select Include InDesign TOC Entries to generate a table of contents based on a TOC style that you created (the TOC style must be in the master document).

For a list of videos and how-to guides about ebooks, go to this Adobe website: *http://tinyurl.com/ycjow54.*

Data Merge

It's hard to be creative when you're faced with hundreds (or thousands) of pieces of data from a database or spreadsheet that need to be formatted. Fortunately, there are tools that can help you automate mundane formatting tasks like this, and one of them is built right into InDesign: Data Merge. Data Merge is not as powerful as other database publishing tools—such as Em Software's InData or Teacup Software's DataLinker—but it's better than doing the work by hand.

In order for Data Merge to work, you need two things: a file with all the raw, unformatted data; and an InDesign file that has template information that says where the data should go and how to format it. You'll also need the Data Merge panel, which you can find in the Utilities submenu (under the Window menu).

Setting up the Data   Virtually every database and spreadsheet program lets you export your data as a comma-delimited (.csv) or tab-delimited (.txt) file. The difference is in what's used between each field and record (or column and row, in a spreadsheet), but Data Merge can read both. Note that if you're exporting a .csv file and a single cell or field includes one or more commas (such as "Yoyodyne, Inc."), then you need to make sure that that field is surrounded by double straight quotes, or else InDesign will get confused as to which comma should be in the text and which one is a delimiter. This is one reason we almost always opt for tab-delimited files.

By the way, the first line of the data file must list the names of each field. You'll use these same names in the InDesign template.

Using variable images. You can also import images along with your text data by including the file path to each image (on your hard disk) as one of the fields. The trick is to place an "at" symbol (@) before the field's name in the *first line* of the data file (see Figure 7-29). Then, when you enter each field, specify a file path to the graphic. File paths are written differently between the Mac OS and Windows: In Windows, you need to use backslashes between folder names, while on the Mac, you use a colon.

Here's a trick to make sure you get the pathname right. Insert an image in an InDesign document. With the image selected, choose Copy Info from the Links panel menu, and then choose Copy Platform Style Path. Then paste it in your data source. Presto!

FIGURE 7-29
Setting Up the
Data File

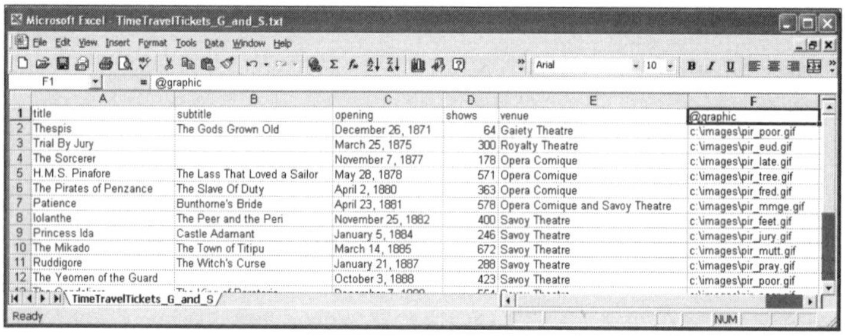

Setting up the Template

Once you have your data in a file that InDesign can import, it's time to set up a prototype (or template, or proxy, or whatever you want to call it) in InDesign (see Figure 7-30).

1. Open the Data Merge panel (choose Data Merge from the Automate submenu, under the Window menu).

2. Choose Select Data Source from the panel menu and pick the file you created on your disk. InDesign is smart enough to tell whether the text is comma-delimited or tab-delimited, but if you felt a strong need to tell it (let's say the import wasn't working properly and you wanted to check the settings), you could turn on the Show Import Options in the dialog box. If the data file isn't set up properly (for instance, if the first line in the data file ends with some extra tab characters), you'll see an error alert.

3. A list of all the data field names appears in the Data Merge panel. (This is why the first line of the data file needs to list those names.) If something looks terribly wrong, you can always select Remove Data Source from the panel menu to reset the panel.

4. Place the flashing text cursor in a text frame and click on one of the field names in the panel. InDesign inserts the field name at

FIGURE 7-30
Creating the
Data Template

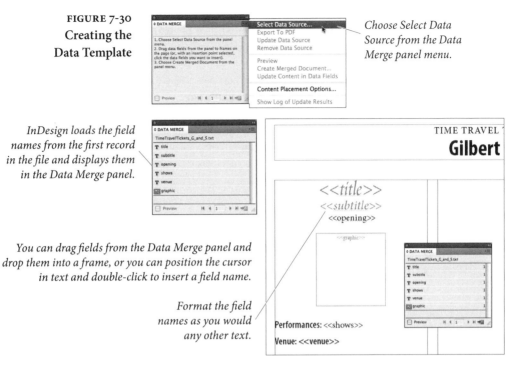

Choose Select Data Source from the Data Merge panel menu.

InDesign loads the field names from the first record in the file and displays them in the Data Merge panel.

You can drag fields from the Data Merge panel and drop them into a frame, or you can position the cursor in text and double-click to insert a field name.

Format the field names as you would any other text.

that position, surrounded by double angle brackets. (Or drag the field name on top of any frame. If the frame is empty, it becomes a text frame and the field name appears in it; if the frame has text in it, the field name is appended at the end of that text.) No, you cannot just type the field name surrounded by angle brackets—you have to use the panel. You may want to insert these in text frames on a master page; we'll explain why in just a moment.

To place an image label (something that was specified as an image path in the data file) as an inline graphic, place the text cursor where you want it and click the label in the panel. To place an image in its own frame on the page, choose an empty frame with the Selection tool before clicking on the image name in the Data Merge panel.

5. Continue adding field names until you've used all the fields you want. You do not have to use all the fields in the data source. You can put the fields in as many text frames as you want, even on more than one page of your document. You can also put text around the field names. For example, you might want to insert a <<LastName>> field, followed by a comma and a space, followed by a <<FirstName>> field, followed by a paragraph return.

6. Apply text formatting to each field name in the text frame. For example, if you want the <<company>> data to appear in bold,

just select that field name and apply the bold style or a bold character style or paragraph style.

Using a Master Page. You don't have to insert the data labels on your master page, but we usually do because it makes the final merged document more flexible. Specifically, if you need to make a change or reimport the data, you can do so from the document InDesign is about to create rather than having to go back to this original document and more or less start the import process over. However, if you do put this stuff on the master page, make sure it's on the right side of a facing page document. For example, you probably want to put it on the right-hand page of a master page spread, or else nothing will show up on page 1 (which is a right-hand page).

Merging the Data

InDesign now knows where the data is and what it's supposed to look like in your InDesign document, so it's time to merge the two. Turn on the Preview checkbox in the Data Merge panel and InDesign immediately replaces the data labels with the first record from the data file (see Figure 7-31). This way you can see if you set up the template correctly. To preview another record, click the Next Record button at the bottom of the panel, or type a record number in the text field.

When you're certain you've got everything arranged just right, it's time to choose Create Merged Document from the Data Merge panel menu (or click the button in the lower-right corner of the panel) to create a merged document (see Figure 7-32). Alternately, you can skip creating an InDesign document and create a PDF file instead by choosing Export to PDF from the panel menu.

FIGURE 7-31
Data Merge Preview

Click the Preview option at the bottom of the panel, or choose Preview from the Data Merge panel menu…

…and InDesign will display a preview layout of the first record (or any other record you specify using the controls at the bottom of the panel.

FIGURE 7-32
Doing the Data Merge

Choose Create Merged Document (or click the button at the bottom of the Data Merge panel).

InDesign displays the Create Merged Document dialog box. Set up the data merge using the controls in this dialog box and click the OK button.

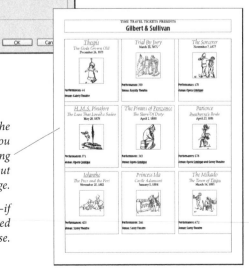

InDesign creates a new document and merges the data from the data file into the data template you created, duplicating frames and applying formatting as necessary. In this example, we chose to lay out multiple records per page.

The headline is on the master spread—if it weren't, it would have been duplicated with everything else.

Data Merge
Layout Options

InDesign then offers you a number of options in the Create Merged Document dialog box.

Records. The first tab of this dialog box lets you choose which records you want to import from the data file. You can also choose whether you want each data record to appear on its own page (choose Single Record from the Records per Document Page pop-up menu) or whether you want more than one record (like a sheet of mailing labels). We'll cover the more-than-one record choice below.

If you turn on the Generate Overset Text Report with Document Creation checkbox, InDesign will save a text file to your hard disk if the import process causes any text frames to become overset. That's handy so we generally turn it on. Similarly, we turn on the Alert When Images are Missing checkbox, because we want to know if something has gone wrong during the import process.

Multiple Record Layout. If you choose Multiple Records from the Records per Document Page pop-up menu, InDesign attempts to duplicate your page objects in a grid on your page. For example, let's say you were making name tags for several hundred people. You could create one or more text frames on your page (it doesn't matter where on the page you put them), insert the data merge labels, and then specify Multiple Records. The Create Merged Document dialog box has a Preview Multiple Record Layout checkbox that shows you what the layout will look like before you commit to the data merge procedure. It takes a little time to process, but it's well worth the wait, as you'll inevitably find you need to tweak something the first time you try it.

You can control how InDesign lays out the frames on your page in the Multiple Record Layout tab of the dialog box, including how much space you want between the rows and columns. The Margins fields here simply overrides those in the Margins and Columns dialog box. We wish we could save these settings as a preset to recall them quickly later, but no can do.

If you have laid out your initial template with more than one frame, InDesign treats them all as a single "group" that gets duplicated multiple times across the page. Also, if you have more than one page in your template file, you can't do multiple record layout (*n*-up layout) because... well, because it'll just get too confusing.

Options. The Options tab of the Create Merged Document dialog box lets you control how Data Merge handles imported images, blank lines in the data file, and large numbers of imported records. Choose a method from the Fitting pop-up menu to control what happens to images that don't match the frame size you've drawn in the template. For instance, you might want to choose Fill Frame Proportionally to get the largest image possible in the frame, but that will crop out a portion of the image if the image height/width ratio isn't the same as the frame. If you want imported images to be placed in the center of the frame rather than in the upper-left corner, turn on the Center in Frame checkbox. (Of course, if you have no images in your data file, then you can ignore both of these.)

If Link Images is disabled, InDesign embeds all the images into the document itself. When enabled, InDesign acts as though you placed the images, linking them to the file on disk.

What should InDesign do when a whole line ends up being blank? For example, let's say you're inserting someone's name on one line, their company name on the second line, and their address on the third line. If someone isn't affiliated with a company, then you'd normally end up with a blank line. However, if you turn on the Remove Blank Lines for Empty Fields checkbox, InDesign will simply delete that line from the final merged document. Note that this only works when there would be *no* text on that line—even a blank space after the text label will foil this feature.

The last option, Page Limit Per Document, lets you control how large the final document will be. InDesign will import records and keep adding pages until this limit is reached. However, if you wanted only single-page InDesign documents, you could change this number to 1. (That's a good way to max out InDesign's resources and possibly cause mayhem.)

Doing the Merge. When you're confident that all is well and you've chosen your options wisely, click OK. InDesign creates a new document based on the one you built (the template) and the settings you made. If your data merge labels were placed on the master page, they will also be on the master page of this new document, which will allow you to update the data, should the need arise.

Updating Your Data   When you first import the data source into the Data Merge panel, InDesign creates a link between the InDesign file and the .txt or .csv file—you can even see this link in the Links panel. Then, when you create the new merged document, it, too, has that link (as long as the template fields were sitting on the master page rather than the document page). That means if some of the data changes, you don't necessarily have to go back to the original and create a new merged file. Instead, you can choose Update Content in Data Fields from the

Data Merge panel menu. However, this appears to work only when the data fields appear in a single text frame—if you used more than one text frame, it gives you an error message. We think this is probably a bug.

If the names or number of fields in each record change in the data source (perhaps you decided to export from the database with more fields), you should to be able to choose Update Data Source from the panel menu. We have never gotten this to work correctly. Unfortunately, it appears that the best solution is to remove all of the data fields from your original template, choose Update Data Source (or Select Data Source again), and then reapply the data fields manually.

Ultimately, we find Data Merge very handy for small or simple jobs, but it's buggy enough and limited enough that we try not to lean too hard on it.

XML

XML is a way to mark up (or tag) information in a text file. Any application that can write text files can be used to write XML. Like HTML, XML uses tags, such as "<h1>" to mark a piece of text. Unlike HTML, XML doesn't have a limited set of predefined tags. That's what the "extensible" part of the acronym means. You're not limited to <h1>, <h2>, <p>, and so on, as you are in HTML.

About XML Workflow   The following is an outline of one approach we see for working with XML in an InDesign document.

1. Create an InDesign document. You can use empty placeholder frames, dummy text, fixed text (text you don't expect to have in the XML data file), or you can mark up an existing document.

2. Load XML tags from an XML file. This doesn't have to be the file containing your data, and it doesn't even have to be an XML file with the same structure as you'll be using. All it needs to include are the names of the elements you expect to have in the XML data you plan to import.

   Alternatively, you can create XML tags from scratch. You'll have to remember to make sure that the XML tag names match the element names for the XML files you'll be importing.

3. Apply XML tags to frames and text in your template document.

4. Map styles to XML tags using the Map Tags to Styles dialog box.

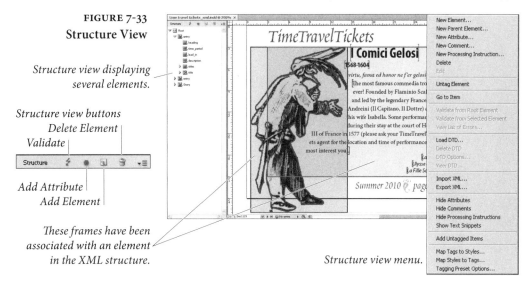

FIGURE 7-33
Structure View

Structure view displaying several elements.

Structure view buttons
Delete Element
Validate

Add Attribute
Add Element

These frames have been associated with an element in the XML structure.

Structure view menu.

5. Import XML into the document. When you do this, the data in your XML file (including any graphics specified in the XML structure) will appear in your layout.

When you import a new XML file and choose to replace the existing structure, InDesign will apply the formatting you've already applied. This makes this workflow particularly useful for setting up a document with a repeating publication schedule (newsletters, product data sheets, and so on). To make certain that new XML files match the layout, you might want to export the XML from the document to use as a template for the next iteration of the publication, or for use in a Web site or database.

You may also want to add XML tags to a document to determine the order of content on a page when you're exporting a document to HTML or EPUB format.

Inside the Structure View

Use the options in the Structure view to create XML elements and attributes, associate elements with InDesign page items or text, rearrange XML elements, and delete XML elements (see Figure 7-33).

To see a short passage of the text associated with the XML elements, choose Show Text Snippets from the Structure view menu. To see which frames are associated with XML elements, turn on the Show Tagged Frames option on the View menu. To see text that's been associated with an XML element, choose Show Tag Markers from the Structure submenu of the View menu.

FIGURE 7-34
**Tagging Frames
and Text**

Select a frame.

*Click a tag in
the Tags panel.*

*InDesign tags the frame
and adds a corresponding
element to the XML
structure of the document.
When Show Tagged Frames
is on, InDesign highlights
the frame.*

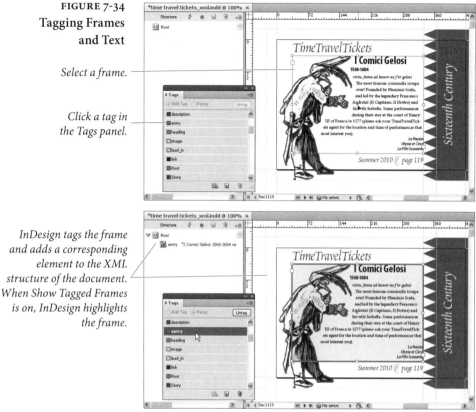

Using XML Tags   You use the Tags panel to manage XML tags, and to apply tags to frames and text. To apply a tag, select something—a frame or a range of text—and click a tag in the Tags panel (see Figure 7-34). When you apply a tag, InDesign creates an element in the XML structure.

To create an XML tag, follow these steps.

1. Display the Tags panel, if it's not already visible (choose Tags from the Utilities submenu on the Window menu).

2. Click the New Tag button at the bottom of the panel.

3. Enter a name for the tag.

Importing XML   To import XML into the structure of an InDesign document, follow these steps. If you want to import the XML into a specific XML element, select the element first.

1. Choose Import XML from the File menu.

2. Locate and select an XML file to import.

3. Turn on the Show Import Options option (most of the time, we think you'll want to have this option turned on).

4. Click the Open button. InDesign displays the XML Import Options dialog box.

5. Make any changes you need in the XML Import Options dialog box (see "XML Import Options" in the online version of this chapter).

6. Click the OK button. InDesign adds the XML data to the document.

When you import XML for the first time, the incoming XML data will appear in any page items that have been tagged with the Root XML element.

Exporting XML   Once you've created an XML structure in an InDesign document, you can export structure to an XML file. This is a good thing, because you can then use the exported XML file as a template for future files. To export XML, follow these steps.

1. If you want to export a selected element (and all of the elements it contains), select the XML element you want to export in the Structure view.

2. Choose Export from the File menu. InDesign displays the Export dialog box.

3. Choose XML from the Format pop-up menu and enter a name for the XML file.

4. Click the Save button. InDesign displays the Export XML dialog box.

5. Select an encoding for your exported XML document from the Encoding pop-up menu. If you want, you can choose to view the XML after exporting (and the browser you want to use for that purpose). If you want to export the selected element (if any), turn on the Export from Selected Element option.

6. Click the Export button to export the XML file.

Exporting Structure Tags to PDF   Acrobat PDF documents (PDF version 1.4 and above) can include eBook structure data. In essence, these are a defined set of XML tags that have a specific meaning to Acrobat.

The easiest way to tag the elements in your document with these tags is to choose the Add Untagged Items option from the Structure view menu. When you do this, InDesign automatically applies a tag named "Article" to untagged text frames and applies the tag "Figure" to untagged imported graphics.

You can create tags with these names and apply them. You can also use the tag name "Artifact" to mark page items you want to omit when the PDF is viewed on small-screen devices.

After you've applied these tags, turn on the Include eBook Tags option as you export PDF. The PDF will then be set up to reflow when displayed by the Acrobat Reader software.

Where to Learn More   Due to space constraints (we would even find a page count limit of 2,000 pages to be too confining), we moved most of the XML coverage to the web, along with other bonus material:

`http://www.peachpit.com/realworldindesigncs5`

The web version of the XML chapter includes more detailed coverage of the Structure View and Tags panel, mapping tags, creating placeholders for repeating content, XML rules, DTDs, and transforming XML with XSLT. If you're relying heavily on an XML workflow, consider getting a copy of James Maivald's *A Designer's Guide to Adobe InDesign and XML*.

The Best of All Possible Worlds

Can you get there from here? When you're working with InDesign, you can almost always export or save files in a form you can use in another program, and you can usually produce files in other programs you can import or open using InDesign.

Someday, we'll have a more complete, universal, and sophisticated file format for exchanging publications. And the streets will be paved with gold, mounted beggars will spend the day ducking winged pigs, and the Seattle Mariners will win the World Series.

Long Documents

What constitutes a long document? Die-hard denizens of the Frame-Maker universe insist that if a document isn't over a thousand pages, it's not a long document. Poster designers, on the other hand, maintain that folded flyers and newsletters qualify.

We're not sure what our definition of a "long document" is, but we think that anyone building a book, a magazine, a newspaper, a journal, or a catalog—just about any document, really, of any number of pages—can benefit from the long document features in InDesign.

There are three features in InDesign that relate directly to publishing long documents.

▶ **Books.** You can tie multiple documents together into a book, which appears in the form of a panel in InDesign. From here, you can control page numbering, printing, and synchronize document attributes as styles, colors, and master pages.

▶ **Table of Contents.** If you use paragraph styles regularly, you're going to love the Table of Contents feature, which can build a table of contents (or a list of figures, or a table of advertisers, or any number of other things) quickly and easily.

▶ **Indexes.** Building an index is a hardship we wouldn't wish on anyone (we've done enough of them ourselves), but InDesign's indexing features go a long way toward making it bearable.

Books

Even though an InDesign document can be thousands of pages long, it's best to split long documents up into smaller parts. Splitting a large project into smaller parts is generally more efficient, especially when more than one person is working on the project at the same time. The burning question is: if you break up your project into small documents, how can you ensure style consistency and proper page numbering among them? The answer is InDesign's Book feature.

In InDesign, a book is a collection of InDesign documents on your disk or network that are loosely connected with each other via the Book panel. Just because it's called a "book" doesn't mean it's not relevant for magazines, catalogs, or any other set of documents.

There are five benefits to using the Book panel.

▶ It's a good way to organize the documents in a project, and it's faster to open them using the Book panel than with File > Open.

▶ If you use automatic page numbering in your document (see "Numbering Pages" in Chapter 2, "Page Layout"), InDesign can manage the page numbering throughout the entire book.

▶ You can print, package, or export one or more documents from the Book panel using the same settings without even having the documents open.

▶ The Synchronize feature helps you ensure that styles, colors, and other settings are consistent among the documents.

▶ By associating files together as a book, you can mix page sizes and page orientations in a publication—which you can't do in a single InDesign document (without a third-party plug-in).

The more documents there are in your project, and the more pages, styles, colors, and whatnot are used in each document, the more useful the Book feature will be to you. Even if you're juggling two or three documents, it may be worth the minor inconvenience it takes to build a book.

Building a Book   To build a new book, select Book from the New submenu of the File menu. At this point, InDesign displays the New Book dialog box. Tell the program where to save your new book file (you can put it anywhere you want on your hard drive or network, but you should put it somewhere easy to find—because you'll be using it a lot).

Book files appear in InDesign as panels. When you've saved your new book, InDesign displays a new Book panel.

Adding and Removing Book Documents

To add a document to your Book panel, click the Add Document button in the panel and choose a document from your disk or network (see Figure 8-1). If no documents on the panel are selected when you add a new document, the new document is added at the end of the list. If you select a document first, the new document is added after the selected document. You can drag files directly from Windows Explorer or from the Mac OS X Finder into a book panel; this is often the fastest way to get a folder full of files into a book.

If you accidentally insert a document in the wrong place in a Book panel, don't worry—you can move a document up and down on the list. To do this, select the book document and drag it to a new location in the list (see Figure 8-2).

FIGURE 8-1

Adding a Book Document

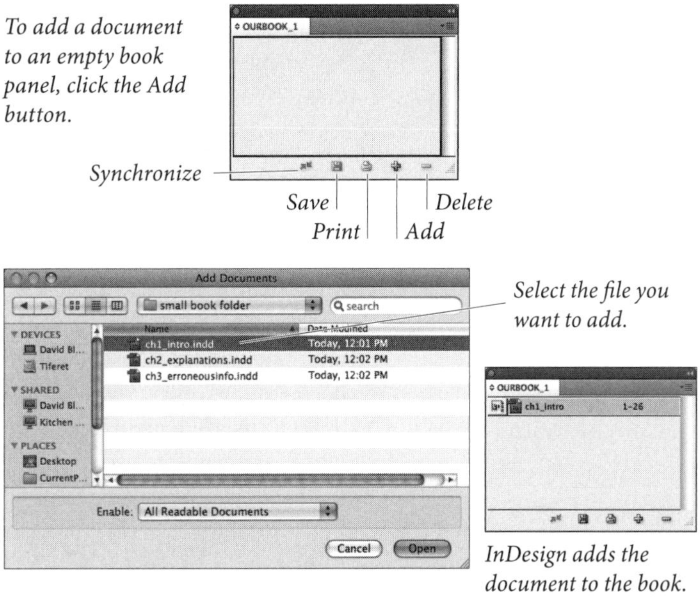

To add a document to an empty book panel, click the Add button.

Synchronize

Save | Delete

Print | Add

Select the file you want to add.

InDesign adds the document to the book.

FIGURE 8-2

Moving a Book Document

To change the position of a book document in the book list, select the document...

...and drag it up or down in the list.

Drop the document, and InDesign moves the document to a new position in the list.

Although Adobe's documentation points out that you can copy a document from one book panel to another by Option-dragging/Alt-dragging, we don't recommend this in most cases. Having the same document in more than one book can cause pagination problems and general confusion.

To remove a document from a Book panel, select the document and click the Remove Document button. If you want to remove more than one document, select the documents (use Shift for contiguous selections, or Command/Ctrl for discontinuous selections on the list) and then click the Remove Document button. Note that deleting a document from the Book panel does *not* delete the file from disk; it simply removes it from the list.

To replace a book document, select the document in the Book panel and choose Replace Document from the Book panel menu. InDesign displays the Replace Document dialog box. Locate and select the file you want to replace the document with, then click the OK button to close the dialog box and replace the document.

Converting Books from Past Versions

InDesign CS5 can open and convert books saved in previous versions of InDesign. It's pretty straightforward—just open the book. There are a couple of options that can help you—or hurt you—during the process of converting the book and the documents in the book.

▶ If, after opening the book, you choose Save Book from the Book panel menu, InDesign will over write the InDesign book file with the converted book. Unless you have a backup copy of the book file, we think that you should save the converted book to a new book file by choosing Save Book As.

▶ After you've opened and converted a book from an earlier version of InDesign, you can select the Automatic Document Conversion option from the Book panel menu. While this sounds like a great idea, it will over write every InDesign document in the book with an InDesign CS5 version of the document. Again, unless you have a backup of the previous version files, we think you should avoid this option. If you do not use this option, you'll need to save each document in the book to a new file.

Using a Book As a Navigational Tool

Because there is only a very loose connection among the various documents in the Book panel, you could use this feature as an informal database of documents. For instance, let's say you've built 15 different product data sheets and three small brochures for a client, and the client is forever updating them. Even though the documents may each use very different colors, styles, and so on, you could put them all on one Book panel and save this collection under the client's name. Next time the client calls for a quick fix, you don't have to go searching for a document; just open the Book panel and double-click the document name to open it.

However, if you do this, you probably first want to turn off the book panel's autorenumbering feature (see "Page Numbering and Sections," later in this chapter).

Editing Your Book   Once you've added documents to your Book panel, you can go about your regular routine of editing and preparing the documents. There are, as usual, a few things you should keep in mind.

▶ Whenever possible, you should open your book's documents while the Book panel is open. (The fastest way to open a document is to double-click the document name in the Book panel.) When you open and modify a document while the panel is not open, the panel isn't smart enough to update itself (see "File Status," below). If InDesign can't find your document (perhaps it's on a server that is not mounted), it'll ask you where it is.

▶ In general, if you're going to use automatic page numbering, you should let the Book panel handle your page numbering for you (see "Page Numbering and Sections," later in this section).

▶ Each time we use Save As, we change the name slightly ("mydocument1," "mydocument2," and so on), so we can always go back to an earlier version if necessary. However, note that the Book panel doesn't catch on to what you're doing; it just lists and keeps track of the original document. So every time you use Save As, you have to select the original file and select Replace Document from the Book panel's menu.

Note that you cannot Undo or use Revert to Saved for changes in the Book panels. Also, be aware that the changes you make to your Book panel, including adding, removing, and reordering documents, aren't saved until you close the panel, quit InDesign, or select Save Book from the panel's menu.

File Status   As you work with book documents, the Book panel monitors and displays the status of each document in the book. There are five possible icons in the Status column of the panel: Available, Open, Modified, Missing, or In Use (see Figure 8-3).

▶ **Available.** The normal status of a document is Available (no icon). This means that no one has the document open for editing

FIGURE 8-3
**Book Panel
Status Icons**

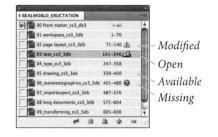

Modified
Open
Available
Missing

and that the document has not changed since the last time it was open on the computer you're using.

▶ **Open.** When you have a document open on your system, the status of that file is listed as Open (an open book icon).

▶ **Modified.** When you or anyone else who has access to the file opens and changes a document while the Book panel is not open, the status will be listed as Modified in the Book panel (triangle icon). It's easy to change the status back to Available: open the file while the Book panel is open, then close the document again. Or, even easier: select Update Numbering from the panel's menu.

▶ **Missing.** If you move a document after adding it to the Book panel, InDesign won't be able to find it, and the status is listed as Missing (red stop sign icon). To "find" a file again, double-click the chapter name in the Book panel; InDesign displays the Replace Document dialog box in which you can tell it where the document now resides.

▶ **In Use.** If someone else on your network opens one of the documents in your book via the Book panel, the Status field of the Book panel lists that chapter as in use (padlock icon).

It's important to pay attention to the Status column readings, because documents must be either Available or Open in order to synchronize, print, or renumber properly.

Books and Networks People are increasingly working on projects in groups rather than individually. Adobe anticipated this, and if you put your book file and documents on a server, more than one person can open the panel at the same time. (Only one person can open an InDesign document at a time, however.) While this isn't as powerful as a full-blown document management system, it's certainly useful if a group of people have to work on different documents in the book at the same time.

We don't like working on documents when they're on a server. It makes us nervous, and it's also really slow. Instead, we prefer to copy the file to our local hard drive, edit it at our leisure, and then return the file to the server when we're done with it.

There are two problems with this. First, the Book panel doesn't update properly. Second, other people on your network might not realize that you've got the "live" file, so make it clear to them: hide the document on the server, or put it in another folder called "work in progress" or something like that.

Synchronizing Your Book Documents

The more documents you're working with, the more likely it is that one or more of them contain settings inconsistent with the others in the book. Perhaps you decided to change a style definition in one document out of 20, and then forgot to change it in the other 19. Or perhaps your art director decided to change a Pantone color in a document and you now need to update the color in all of the other documents in the book.

Fortunately, the Synchronize Book button on the Book panel lets you ensure that items such as styles and color settings are consistent throughout the documents in a book. Here's how it works.

The Master Document

One document on the Book panel is always marked as the *master document* (by default, it's the first document you add to the panel; InDesign's documentation refers to this document as the *style source document*). The master document—which has a cryptic little icon to the left of it—is the document to which all the other documents will be synchronized. That means that if you add a new color to the master document and click the Synchronize Book button, the color will be added to all of the other documents in the book. If you add a new color to a document that is not the master document, the color won't be added when you synchronize the documents.

You can always change which document is the master document. To do that, click in the left column of the Book panel next to the document you want to set as the master document.

Synchronize

In order to synchronize your book documents, you must first select which files you want to synchronize in the Book panel; remember that you can Shift-click to select contiguous documents or use Command-click/Ctrl-click to select discontinuous documents. Or, if you want to synchronize all the files, make sure that no documents (or all documents) are selected in the panel.

▶ A style, color swatch, variable, numbered list, or master page that is defined in the master document but not in another document gets added to that other document.

▶ If a setting is named the same in both the master document and another document, the definition for that setting in the master document overrides the one in the non-master document.

▶ If a setting is not defined in the master document but exists in some other document, it's left alone. (This means you can have "local" settings that exist in one document that don't have to be copied into all the others.)

▶ By selecting Synchronize Options in the Book panel's menu, you can choose which settings will be synchronized among the documents (see Figure 8-4). However, if the master document contains table of contents styles (which we talk about later in this chapter) and you turn on the TOC Styles check box in the Synchronize Options dialog box, all the character and paragraph styles are synchronized, even if you've turned off the Character Styles and Paragraph Styles check boxes. Select Smart Match Style Groups if you have moved styles in or out of style groups (folders) and all your styles are uniquely named.

Synchronizing a document can be a time-consuming process—the more documents and the more settings, the longer it takes.

FIGURE 8-4
Synchronization
Options

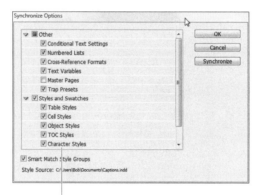

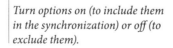

Turn options on (to include them in the synchronization) or off (to exclude them).

Page Numbering and Sections

Perhaps the most helpful aspect of the Book feature is that it keeps track of your page numbering for you and updates the page numbers when you add pages to or delete them from a document, or if you add a new document between two other documents in a book. Of course, this only works if you've placed automatic page numbers on your document pages (see "Numbering Pages" in Chapter 2).

Let's say you've got one 16-page document in your Book panel already. When you add another document, InDesign automatically sets its first page number of the new document to 17 (provided you had not already specified the first page as a section start in the Numbering and Section Options dialog box). If you later open the first document and add two pages, InDesign automatically renumbers the second document—the next time you open it, you'll see that it starts on page 19.

If, on the other hand, you use the Numbering and Section Options dialog box (you can jump to this feature quickly by double-clicking on the page numbers in the Book panel) to create a section start, the Book panel respects that. Any subsequent documents in the Book panel continue the page numbering from where the previous document's page numbering left off.

If you don't use automatic page numbers, or you have manually specified page numbers for each document in your book, you will probably tire of watching InDesign repaginate your book. Fortunately, you can turn this feature off by selecting Book Page Numbering Options from the Book panel's menu, and unchecking Automatically Update Page and Section Numbers (see Figure 8-5).

Odd Versus Even Page Numbers

When chapter 2 ends on page 45, what page number does InDesign assign to the first page of chapter 3? If you're in the book business, you probably want chapter 3 to start on page 47, because it's a right-hand page. (Olav insists on editing and/or adjusting the layout to avoid a blank left-hand page.) Catalog and magazine publishers would want the third file to begin on page 46, even though it's a left-hand page. You can specify what you want InDesign to do by choosing Book Page Numbering Options from the Book panel's menu. You've got three choices: Continue from Previous Document, Continue on Next Odd Page, and Continue on Next Even Page.

When you turn on the Insert blank page option, InDesign adds a page to fill any gaps between chapters. For example, if chapter 2 ends on page 45 and you turn on the Continue on Next Odd Page, then InDesign adds a blank page at the end of chapter 2. This page is truly blank—it's not based on any master page. If you want a running head on that page, you'll have to apply the master page yourself. (By the way, David once almost drove himself mad trying to figure out why he couldn't delete the last page from a document. The answer, of course, was that he had forgotten this feature was on.)

Chapter Numbering

If you'd like to number each document in your book, you can let InDesign handle the numbering for you using chapter numbers. To

FIGURE 8-5
Book Page
Numbering
Options

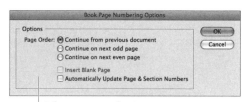

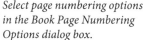

*Select page numbering options
in the Book Page Numbering
Options dialog box.*

set up chapter numbering, select the first page in the document, then choose Numbering & Section Options from the Layout menu (or from the Pages panel menu). In the Document Chapter Numbering section of the dialog box (see Figure 8-6), choose a numbering Style (such as regular numerals, roman numerals, or letters). Then choose whether you want to specify a chapter number for this book or base the number off the chapter number of the previous document in the book panel. Note that even though a single document can have multiple sections, it can have only one chapter number.

Once you have set up the Numbering & Section Options dialog box, you can "type" the chapter number in a text frame by inserting a chapter number text variable. For more information on text variables, see Chapter 3, "Text."

Note that when your chapter numbering changes (for example, if you rearrange the order of the documents in the book panel), the chapter numbers in your documents are not updated until you choose Update All Numbers or Update Chapter & Paragraph Numbers from the Update Numbering submenu in the book panel's menu. If the number on the screen in front of you still doesn't update, remember that text variables only change when you force the screen to redraw.

**Printing and
Exporting Books**

Even though we cover printing documents in Chapter 11, "Printing," we should take this opportunity to mention a few things that are specific to printing, packaging, or exporting books.

Each chapter in a book must be listed as Open, Available, or Modified on the Book panel in order for the document to print. InDesign invisibly opens each document at print or export time.

If you only want certain documents in a book to print or be exported, select them in the Book panel. Hold down the Shift to select contiguous documents, or Command/Ctrl to select non-contiguous documents. If no documents are selected, they'll all print. (Click in the blank area at the bottom of the panel to deselect all documents.)

When you're ready to print, click the Print Book button in the Book panel or select Print Book (or Print Selected Documents) from the panel's menu.

You can export your book as an Acrobat PDF file by choosing Export Book to PDF (or Export Selected Documents to PDF) from the panel's menu. If you turn on the Create Acrobat Layers checkbox when you export the PDF, InDesign merges all layers that have the same name into a single PDF layer. However, if you first deselect Merge Identically Name Layers on Export in the book panel's menu, the PDF will include individual layers for each document.

Choose Export Book to EPUB from the panel menu to export your book to EPUB format. Each document in the book starts on a new page in the eBook.

To package all the documents in the book, and their required fonts and linked graphics, choose Package Book for Print from the panel's menu. When you package a book, all the linked graphics are copied into a single Links folder. If your documents contains graphics that are unique but have the same name, InDesign is smart enough to automatically rename them.

Table of Contents

Don't get fooled into thinking the Table of Contents feature (under the Layout menu) is only for making book tables of contents. This feature lets you build collections of paragraphs that have been tagged with specific styles. For instance, if you use even two styles when you're formatting a book—one for the chapter name and another for your first-level headings—you can build a basic table of contents by collecting all the paragraphs tagged with these two styles. But if you use paragraph styles to tag your product names, you could just as easily build an index of products for a catalog. Anything you can tag with a paragraph style, you can build into a "table of contents."

This all depends entirely on your using styles. You should be using styles anyway—if you're not, you're working way too hard; refer to Chapter 4, "Type," to see why you should.

Making a Table of Contents

Making a table of contents (or a list of figures, or whatever) is easy, but it requires a methodical approach to the Table of Contents dialog box (see Figure 8-7).

1. If you only have one list (table of contents, list of figures, etc.) in your document, you can leave the Style pop-up menu set to [Default]. We'll cover table of contents styles later in this section.

2. Fill in a name for your list in the Title field. InDesign places this title at the beginning of the list, so you might want to type

FIGURE 8-6
Chapter Numbering

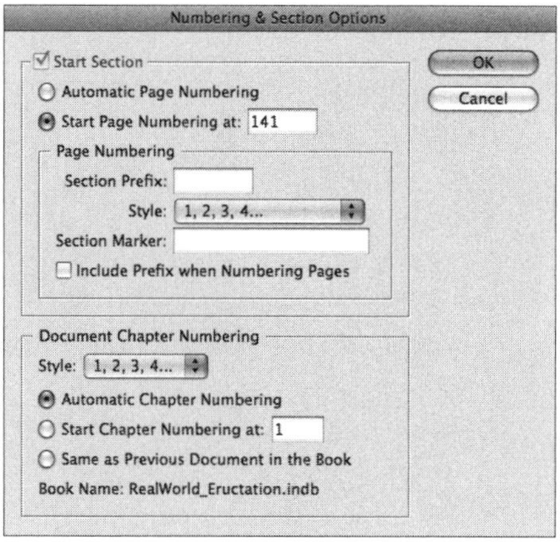

"Table of Contents" or "Advertisers" or something like that. We usually leave this field blank and later make our own title on the document page. If you do include a title, choose a paragraph style for it from the Style pop-up menu to the right of the Title field. (InDesign automatically adds a paragraph style called "TOC title" to your document when you open this dialog box, but you don't have to use that style if you don't want to.)

3. Choose the paragraph styles that you want included from the list on the right. You can click the Add button to add them to the list, but double-clicking the style names is faster. You can also select more than one style (by Command/Ctrl-clicking each one) and then click Add to add them all at once (in which case they're added alphabetically—if you want to rearrange the order, just click and drag the style names after adding them).

4. One by one, click each style in the Include Paragraph Styles list and choose a paragraph style for it from the Entry Style pop-up menu. This is helpful because you'd rarely want a heading from your document to appear in your table of contents in the actual Heading style; instead, you'd probably create a new style called "TOC-head" or something like that. If you want certain paragraphs to be indented on your final list, you should apply styles here that include indentation. InDesign adds a paragraph style called "TOC body text" to your document when you open this dialog box, but you don't have to use it—we just roll our own.

5. If your document is included in a Book panel, you can choose to include the entire book in your list by turning on the Include Book Documents check box.

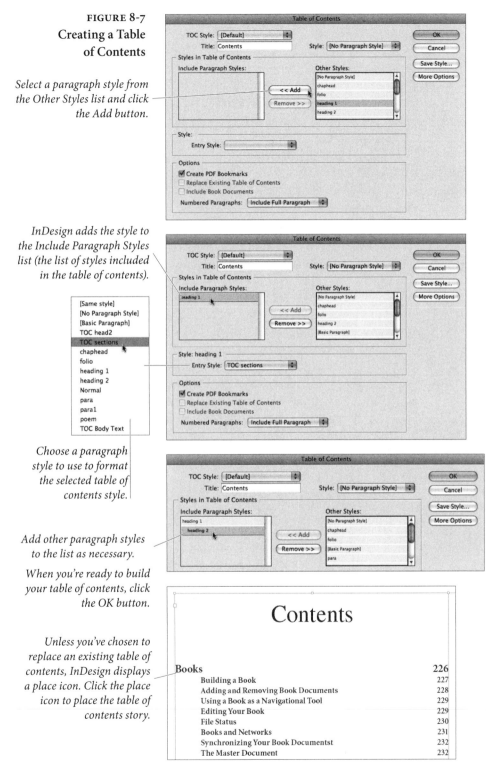

FIGURE 8-7
Creating a Table of Contents

Select a paragraph style from the Other Styles list and click the Add button.

InDesign adds the style to the Include Paragraph Styles list (the list of styles included in the table of contents).

Choose a paragraph style to use to format the selected table of contents style.

Add other paragraph styles to the list as necessary.

When you're ready to build your table of contents, click the OK button.

Unless you've chosen to replace an existing table of contents, InDesign displays a place icon. Click the place icon to place the table of contents story.

6. Finally, when you click OK, InDesign builds the table of contents (which might take a little while, especially if you have many documents in a book). When it's done, InDesign displays the text place icon, just as if you had imported a text file (see Chapter 4, "Text," if you need to know more about placing text).

More Table of Contents Options

The default Table of Contents dialog box gives you the basic controls you need for a simple table of contents, but for most lists we make we click the More Options button, which gives us more options for fine-tuning the table of contents (see Figure 8-8).

▶ **Page Number.** You may not want every entry in your table of contents to be followed by a page number. Perhaps you want page numbers after the headings, but not after the chapter titles in a book. You can control how page numbers will appear with the Page Number pop-up menu. You've got three options for numbering: After Entry, Before Entry, and None. The first two tell InDesign to include the page number (either before or after the entry), separated from the text of the paragraph by a tab character. We typically create a character style for the page numbers and select it from the Style pop-up menu to the right of the Page Number menu. This way, all the page numbers appear the same rather than appearing in the Entry Style.

▶ **Between Entry and Number.** By default, InDesign places a tab character between the entry and the page number (whether the page number is before or after the entry). However, you can change this to some other character or characters. For instance, we usually replace the ^t character (which is code for a tab) with ^y (a right-indent tab, which always sits flush on the right margin, even if you haven't placed a tab stop). If you're planning on including dot leaders between the entries and the page numbers (which you would set up in the Tabs panel), you may want to pick a character style from the Style pop-up menu. A regular dot leader looks too much like periods in a row (which is exactly what it is), so we often make a character style of 7-point text with 500 units of tracking, then apply this style to the leader.

▶ **Sort Entries in Alphabetical Order.** If you turn on the Sort Entries in Alphabetical Order option in the Table of Contents dialog box, InDesign sorts the list in alphabetical order when you build it. Whether or not you want your final list alphabetized is up to you; you probably wouldn't want it when you build

FIGURE 8-8
More Table of
Contents Options

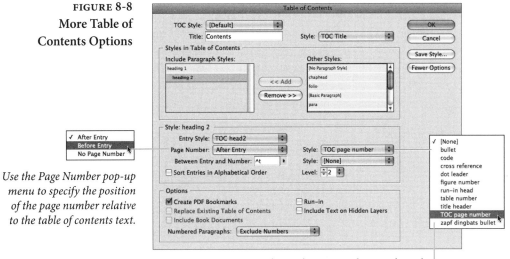

*Use the Page Number pop-up
menu to specify the position
of the page number relative
to the table of contents text.*

*You can select a character style to apply to the
page number and/or to the separator character.*

the table of contents for a book, but you might if you're creating
a list of items in a catalog.

▶ **Level.** Each paragraph style you include appears with a different
indent in the Include Paragraph Styles list. You can control how
much indent with the Level feature. This only adjusts the display
in this dialog box; it has no effect on the final list unless your
list is alphabetized—in which case, the entries are alphabetized
by level.

▶ **Run-in.** Some tables of contents, such as those found in
academic journals, are "run-in"—that is, the headings are all
in one paragraph, separated by semicolons. If you want this
sort of list, turn on this option (see Figure 8-9).

▶ **Include Text on Hidden Layers.** This option is pretty self-
explanatory. If you have multiple layers in your document, you
can choose whether to include the text on those layers even
when the layers are hidden. While it's rare that you'd turn this
on, you might do so if you have made a layer that contains key-
words or explanatory text that you want in the table of contents
but don't want in print (see the next section).

▶ **Numbered Paragraphs.** If you have used automatic paragraph
numbering in your document, you have a choice of what will
appear in the table of contents: the entire paragraph (with the
numbering), the paragraph with no number, or only the number.

Using Dummy Text for Lists

One of the things we like most about tables of contents is that they're document-wide rather than simply story-wide. That means that any text in any text frame can be included in a table of contents—even text in a nonprinting text frame. With this in mind, you can add "tags" to items on your page that don't appear in print, but do appear in your table of contents.

FIGURE 8-9
The Run-in Option

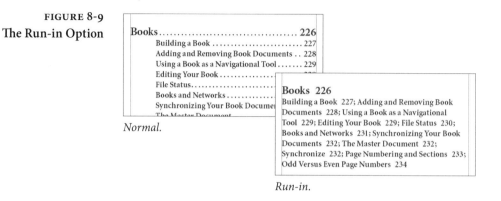

Normal.

Run-in.

One of the best uses for this trick is an advertiser index. You can place a text frame with an advertiser's name on top of an ad in your document. Set the text frame's color to None and turn on Nonprinting Object in the Attributes panel (or put the frame on a hidden layer), and it's almost as though this were a "non-object"—the text won't print, and it won't affect the ad underneath. But if that advertiser's name is tagged with a style, you can include it on a list of advertisers.

The same trick applies to building a list of pictures in a catalog, or for any other instance where what you want on the list doesn't actually appear on the page.

Building and Rebuilding Tables of Contents

There is nothing magic about the text or page numbers in your table of contents—they're just regular text and numbers. That means if you update the document on which the list is based (such as adding pages or changing the text), the entries and page numbers in the table of contents don't automatically update, and you will have to rebuild it. We find that we build and rebuild a table of contents several times for each document or book. It isn't that we're having so much fun with the feature—it's that we make mistakes.

To update a table of contents, use the Selection tool or Text tool to select the text frame containing the list, then choose Update Table of Contents from the Layout menu. Or, if you want to make a change to the Table of Contents dialog box settings, you can choose Table of Contents from the Layout menu, make the changes, turn on the Replace Existing Table of Contents check box, and click OK.

Table of Contents Styles

Everything we've said about table of contents so far is based on the idea that you have only one of these in your document. However, you can define lots of different table of contents styles in a single document—one for headings, one for figures, one for bylines, and so on. The easiest way to do this is to build various table of contents styles, which are simply saved collections of settings. Once you set up the Table of Contents dialog box just the way you want it, you can click the Save Style button to save this setup as a style (see Figure 8-10). Later, you can reload those settings by choosing your style from the TOC Style pop-up menu at the top of the dialog box.

A second way to build a "style" is to select Table of Contents Styles from the Layout menu and click New. You get a nearly identical dialog box, but when you click OK your settings are saved for use later. You can also use the Table of Contents Styles feature to delete and edit styles, or load them from other InDesign documents.

Note that if you save your table of contents style after building a table of contents in your document, InDesign isn't smart enough to match your built list to the style name. That means you can't use the Replace Existing Table of Contents feature. Instead, you'll have to delete the already-built list and replace it with a new one.

FIGURE 8-10
Creating a Table of Contents Style

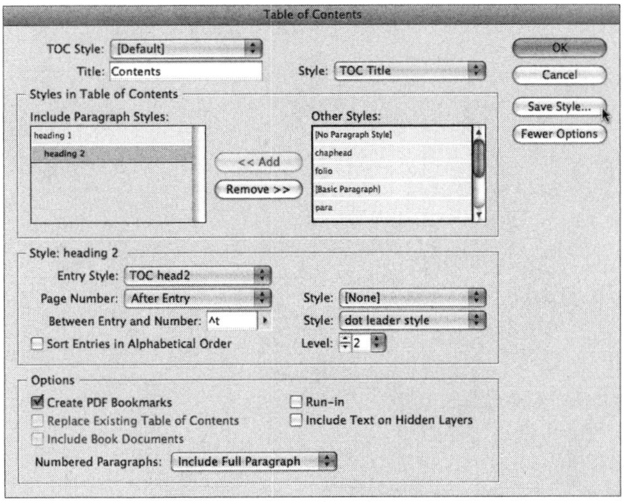

To save the current settings of the Table of Contents dialog box as a table of contents style, click the Save Style button.

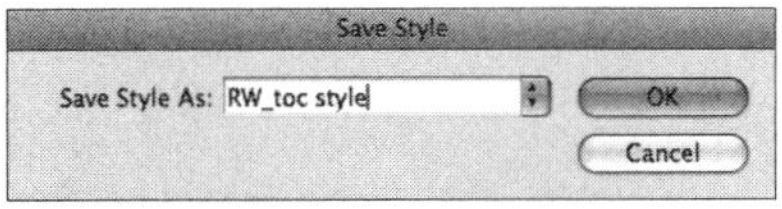

Enter a name for the style in the Save Style dialog box and click the OK button.

InDesign adds the style to the list of available styles.

Indexes (Or Indices)

Sitting down and indexing a book is—in our experience—the most painful, horrible, mind-numbing activity you could ever wish on your worst enemy. And yet, where this is the kind of task that a computer should be great at, it's actually impossible for a computer to do a good job of indexing a book by itself. A good index requires careful thought, an understanding of the subject matter, and an ability to keep the whole project in your head at all times. In short, it requires *comprehension*—a quality computer software, at this early stage of its evolution, lacks. Until recently, it also required a large stack of note cards, highlighter pens, Post-It notes, and serious medication.

Fortunately, InDesign has a built-in indexing feature, which, while it won't make the index for you, does remove the note card and highlighter requirements.

Some people ask us, "Why can't a computer build an index? InDesign should just give me a list of all the words in my document and what page they're on." Unfortunately, this is not an index; it's a concordance. A concordance records the location of *words*; an index records the location of *ideas*. There are times when a concordance can be useful, especially in catalogs. In those cases, you might want to use a plug-in such as Sonar Bookends, which can build concordances automatically and very quickly. But in general, if you're looking for an index, you're going to have to do it manually with InDesign's indexing features.

You can index a document at any time in the production cycle, but it's almost always best to wait until the text has become fixed—until no text in the document will be deleted, copied, cut, pasted, and so on. The reason: as you edit the text, you may accidentally delete index markers.

The Index panel (choose Index from the Type & Tables submenu, under the Window menu) lets you add either single words or whole phrases to the index, and it displays a list of currently indexed words and phrases (see Figure 8-11). First we're going to discuss how to add, edit, and remove index entries with the Index panel. Then we'll explore how to collect all the tagged entries and build a finished index on your document pages.

A Note to the Author Contemplating Self-Indexing. Hire a professional indexer. You simply know the material too well to create a useful index. A professional indexer will read and understand your text, and will create an index that opens it up to a wider range of possible readers than you ever could. It's what they do.

FIGURE 8-11
The Index Panel

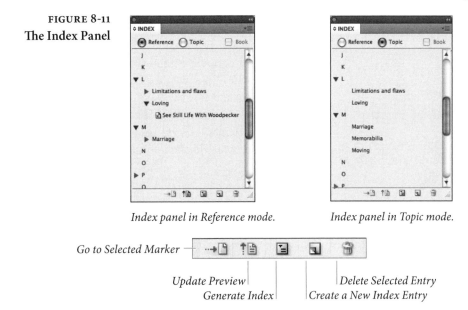

Index panel in Reference mode.   *Index panel in Topic mode.*

Go to Selected Marker ─┤

Update Preview│
Generate Index│   │Delete Selected Entry
              │Create a New Index Entry

Adding a New First-Level Index Entry

There's very little that is automatic about building an index. Again, it's not difficult, but you have to be methodical about it. Here are the steps you should go through for each new index entry. (Note that we always differentiate between a new index entry or topic and a new reference to an index entry. For example, "Pigs" might be a new entry for page 34, but when it appears again on page 59, it would simply be a new reference to your already added index entry—see "Adding a New Reference to an Entry," later in this section.)

To add an index entry, follow these steps (see Figure 8-12).

1. If the word or phrase you want indexed appears on the page, select it and click the New Entry button at the bottom of the Index panel, or select New Page Reference from the panel's menu (or better yet, just press Command-7/Ctrl-7). If the index entry isn't found on the page, place the text cursor anywhere in the text related to the topic and click the New Entry button. For example, a page may include a discussion of cows, but you want to index the word under the phrase "Farm animals." In this case, you would simply insert the cursor in the text and click New Entry (or press the keystroke).

2. In the New Page Reference dialog box, edit the entry under the Topic Levels heading, if needed. Whatever you type here will be what shows up in the index. Since we're focusing on first-level entries right now, you can just skip over the other two Topic Levels fields. (We'll discuss the finer points of second-level entries in "Adding a New Second-Level Index Entry," later.)

3. Index entries always appear in alphabetical order. However, occasionally you may not want your index entry to appear where it would normally be alphabetized. For instance, the famous "17-Mile Drive" would ordinarily be placed at the beginning of the index, before the "A"s. You can place it along with other words that begin with "S" by typing "Seventeen" in the first Sort As field of the New Page Reference dialog box. You'll probably leave this field blank most of the time.

4. The Number Style Override feature is yet one more control that you will ignore most of the time. Let's say you want the page numbers that refer to an illustration (rather than to just text on the page) to appear bold in the final index. You can build a character style to define how you want the page numbers to appear and—when you're indexing that illustration—you can turn on the Number Style Override check box and choose that character style from the pop-up menu.

5. An index entry can span a range of pages or text. If, for example, your treatise on pigs and goats spans six pages of your document, you don't want to have to make a separate index entry for each and every page. Instead, you can specify one index entry and choose a range of pages in the Type pop-up menu. There are nine page-range choices in the Type pop-up menu, plus six more cross-reference choices. We cover those last six in "Cross References (X-Refs)," later in the chapter.

   In the previous edition, an online reviewer chastised us (thereby taking food away from our hungry children) for our failure to explain in detail when and why we might use each of these index entries. We admit that we thought it was self-evident.

   We still think so. You, the indexer, know the text. Knowing the text means that you understand that a given topic covers a specific range of pages or paragraphs (you'd use the For Next # of Pages option or the For Next # of Paragraphs option), or runs from one heading to another (you'd use the To Next Use of Style option and choose the paragraph style of the heading).

   ▶ Current page, the default page range, indexes the page that includes the index marker.

   ▶ To Next Style Change tells InDesign to index from the paragraph containing the index marker to the next paragraph style change.

FIGURE 8-12
Adding an Index Entry

*In this example, we've gotten
lucky: the text we want to
add to the index is present
on the page.*

I knew only too well. I raised my head and saw
Hamaïouna, glorious, transfigured, and seated on
a luminous cloud.
    "Wretched Barkiarokh," she said, "thou hast
nothing more to fear from the Wand of Remorse.
Instead of profiting by its strokes, thou hast sought
to evade them. Henceforward, the rod that will beat
upon thy heart is the Rod of Despair, and thy heart,
hardened as it is, will be broken and crushed
throughout every moment of a frightful eternity."

Select the text...

*...and click the New Entry button
or press Command/Ctrl-7.*

*If necessary, edit the text in the
Topic Levels field (or fields).
For this example, we don't
need to edit the text.*

*Choose an indexing range
from the Type pop-up menu.*

*Turn on the Number Style
Override option if you want
to apply a specific character
style to the page number in
the index (we don't, so we left
the option unchecked).*

✓ Current Page
To Next Style Change
To Next Use of Style
To End of Story
To End of Document
To End of Section
For Next # of Paragraphs
For Next # of Pages
Suppress Page Range

See [also]
See
See also
See herein
See also herein
[Custom Cross-reference]

*If our index contained more
than this single index entry,
we'd see a list of other topics
in this field.*

*InDesign adds the page
reference to the index.*

▶ To Next Use of Style is the option we use most often. This
indexes from the paragraph containing the index marker to
the next use of a specific style, which you can choose in a
pop-up menu next to the Type pop-up menu. For instance,
let's say you've got a book about farm animals where each
animal's heading is tagged with a paragraph style called
"Heading-A." You could select the heading "Rabbit" and set
the Type to "To Next Use of Style." Then you could choose
Heading-A from the pop-up menu of styles. If the "Horse"

section starts three pages after the Rabbit section, the page range in the index will span three pages; if it starts 14 pages after, the page range will span 14 pages, and so on.

▶ To End of Story tells InDesign to index from the paragraph containing the index marker to the end of the current story. Note that InDesign assumes that the story falls on every page. If your story starts on page 1, then skips to page 9, and ends on page 12, the index will display pages 1–12, ignoring the skipped pages.

▶ To End of Document is the same as To End of Story, but it spans from the paragraph containing the index marker to the end of the file. In the example of the farm animals chapter, you could index the entire chapter by placing the cursor anywhere on the first page of the chapter, specifying an index entry labeled "Farm animals," and choosing To End of Document.

▶ To End of Section is the same as the previous two options, but the page range extends from the index marker to the end of the current section (see Chapter 2, "Page Layout").

▶ For Next # of Paragraphs works when you know exactly how many paragraphs you want indexed. Unfortunately, currently InDesign only spans to the beginning of the final paragraph, rather than the end of the paragraph—a problem if that paragraph spans two pages.

▶ For Next # of Pages indexes from the index entry marker for the number of pages you specify.

▶ Suppress Page Range. Some first-level index entries don't include page numbers at all. For instance, in the book we've been discussing, "Animals" is too broad a topic to include page numbers (every page in the book would be indexed). So you might specify Suppress Page Range for this one entry, and then follow it with 15 second-level entries, each with appropriate page numbers listed. (Again, we discuss second-level entries later.)

6. After you've chosen the scope from the Type menu, click OK and InDesign adds the index entry to the Index panel, along with the page range. If the indexed text sits on a master page or on the pasteboard, the master page label or "PB" shows up in the Index panel, but these items will not actually appear in the final index.

If you're happy with the default settings of the New Page Reference dialog box, you can streamline this process significantly by selecting a word or phrase on your page and typing Ctrl-Alt-Shift-[or Command-Option-Shift-[, which adds the selection to the index, skipping the dialog box. Or, if the selection is a proper name, press the] (right bracket) instead—that indexes the selection based on the last word in the selection (so James Joyce would show up as Joyce, James). You can control how words in a proper name show up by placing a nonbreaking space between them; for instance, if you put a nonbreaking space between "King" and "Jr.," then this keyboard shortcut will index the name under King instead of Jr.

Add and Add All   You may already have spotted the Add and Add All buttons in the New Page Reference dialog box. Clicking the Add button adds the index entry but leaves the dialog box open so that you can add more entries. This is very helpful—you frequently need to index the same text using more than one entry.

Add All searches throughout your document for every instance of the index entry and adds it automatically to the index. If you select the word "Bee" on your page and then click Add All, InDesign places another identical index entry at each instance of the word "Bee" in your file. (If you have turned on the Book option in the Index panel, InDesign also adds all instances of the index entry in other documents, too—as long as those documents are open.)

When you click Add All, InDesign uses the same scope (Type) settings for every instance of the entry text. Whether this is a great feature or a potential problem depends on the formatting of your index. If each instance of an indexed topic needs special attention (this one only showing up on this page, the next one using a To Next Use of Style scope, and so on), you should avoid this feature.

You also need to be careful with Add All because it only finds exact matches. That is, if you type "Cow" in the New Page Reference dialog box and then click Add All, InDesign won't find "Cows" or even "cows".

Cross-References (X-Refs)   As you build an index, think of all the ways that your reader might look for a topic and include those words in your index. For instance, because you're familiar with your own book, you might include an index entry called "Llamas." However, another reader might look for "Cute wool-producing animals that spit." Fortunately, InDesign lets you add cross-references in your index such as "Spitting animals. *See* Llamas" and "Wool 34–46. *See also* Llamas."

To add a cross-reference to your index, you go through the same steps as you would to add a normal index entry. The one difference is that you set the Type pop-up menu to one of the six cross-reference settings: See [also], See, See also, See herein, See also herein, and Custom Cross-Reference. When you select any of these, InDesign provides a text field in which you can enter the cross-referenced word or phrase. If you want your index entry to be "Koi. *See* Carp" you would type "Koi" in the first Topic Levels field, and type "Carp" in the Referenced field (see Figure 8-13).

▶ *See* is generally used when an index entry has no page number references, such as "Supermarket. *See* Grocery."

▶ *See also* is used when an index entry does have page references, but you also want to refer the reader to other topics, such as "Grocery 34–51. *See also* Farmer's Market."

▶ We like the *See [also]* option best, because it uses either See or See also, depending on whether you've specified page references.

▶ *See herein* is a special case in which you are cross-referencing to a second-level entry within the same entry as the cross-reference itself, and it's used more in legal indexes than anywhere else.

▶ If you choose Custom Cross-Reference, you can type any kind of cross-reference you prefer, such as "Hey dude, go look at page".

Note that if you're cross-referencing to an index entry that you've already added to your index, you can find that entry in the list of entries at the bottom of the dialog box and drag it to the Referenced field. That's certainly faster (and probably more accurate) than typing the words again.

Because no page number is involved in a cross-reference, it doesn't matter where in your document you specify it (though it must be in a text frame).

Some people prefer to put cross-references at the end of a list of second-level index entries rather than directly after the first-level entry. InDesign won't do this for you automatically, but you can fake it by creating a dummy second-level entry (see "Adding a New Second-Level Index Entry," below) and setting its Type to a cross-reference. The dummy second-level entry should just be named with "zzz" so that it automatically falls at the end of the alphabetized list of second-level entries. Later, once you build the index onto your document pages, you will have to perform a Find/Change to remove these symbols.

FIGURE 8-13
**Adding a
Cross-Reference**

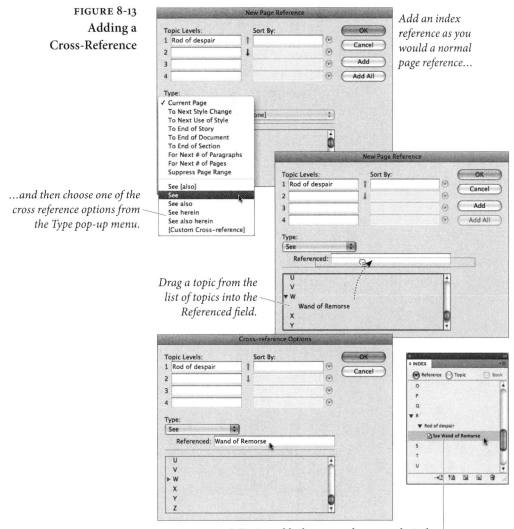

*Add an index
reference as you
would a normal
page reference...*

*...and then choose one of the
cross reference options from
the Type pop-up menu.*

*Drag a topic from the
list of topics into the
Referenced field.*

InDesign adds the cross-reference to the index.

**Adding a New
Reference to an Entry**

Once you've got an entry on your Index panel, you can easily add
more page references to it. Let's say you added the name "Farmer
Jones" to your index back on page 13 of your document. Now,
"Farmer Jones" appears again on page 51.

1. Place the cursor in the appropriate place in the text story. In this
    case, you'd probably put the cursor next to the word "Farmer"
    on page 51.

2. Click the entry in the Index panel. Here, you'd select "Farmer
    Jones."

3. Alt/Option-click the New Entry button. Make sure that the Type pop-up menu is set up according to how you want your new reference to appear, and then click OK. If you want to use the default New Page Reference dialog box settings, you can just drag the index entry on top of the New Entry button instead.

Note that while you don't necessarily have to click the entry in the Index panel in step 2 (you could just retype the entry in the New Page Reference dialog box or select it on the page), we recommend clicking because it ensures consistency. For example, if you relied on your typing ability, you might create the index entry "Chickens" and then later—meaning to type the same thing—create a new entry, "Chicken," causing two different entries to be made when you only meant to make one.

Adding a New Second-Level Index Entry

Now that you've specified first-level index entries, you can—if you wish—add second-level entries. As we mentioned earlier, second-level entries are subcategories of the first-level entries. For example, under the first-level index entry "Grape Varieties," you might find the second-level entries "Merlot," "Chardonnay," and "Syrah." You can make a second-level index entry just as you would make the first-level index entry, but with two added steps.

After you open the New Page Reference dialog box, click the down arrow button to move your index entry to the second Topic Level field. Then, double-click the first-level entry in the list at the bottom of the dialog box (which enters it in the first Topic Level field).

Once you've created a second-level entry, you can place a third-level entry under it. Similarly, you can put fourth-level entries under third-level entries.

Importing Topics

Many people prefer to index their text in Microsoft Word before placing the text in InDesign. Fortunately, InDesign can import Word's index markers, adding the index entries to the Index panel automatically. In fact, if you delete the Word file after importing it, the index topics remain in the Index panel. This is one good way to import a list of topics into the panel without having to type them manually in InDesign. Another way to import index topics is to choose Import Topics from the Index panel's menu, which lets you select any other already-indexed InDesign document.

Index entries in your panel that don't have corresponding index markers in the text won't show up in your final index. If you don't want to see these topics in your Index panel, select Hide Unused

Topics in the panel's menu to them. To view the topics you've hidden, choose Show from the panel menu.

Deleting Entries   There are several ways to delete an entry from your index.

▶ To delete an entire entry, including all its page references, select it in the Index panel and click the Delete button. Note that this also deletes all the subcategories under it and their page references, too.

▶ To delete a single page reference, you can select it in the Index panel (click the gray triangle next to the index entry to display its page references) and click the Delete button.

▶ To remove a particular page reference in your index, delete the index marker. The marker is a zero-width character, but it is a character nevertheless. To view the character, choose Show Hidden Characters from the Type menu. To delete it, put the text cursor immediately after it (you may have to use the arrow keys to accomplish this) and press Backspace/Delete.

Editing Entries   We make mistakes, so it's a good thing that InDesign gives us a way to edit our flubbed index entries. When you're editing an index entry, you have to decide whether you want to edit the entry itself or a particular page reference of the entry.

Let's say that halfway through indexing your document, you realize that the index entry "Martha Washington" should have been indexed as "Washington, Martha." You can select the entry in the Index panel and choose Topic Options from the panel's menu—or even faster, you can just double-click the entry. In this case, you'd change the first Topic Level field to "Washington, Martha," and then click OK.

One of the most common entry edits is capitalizing an entry, so the folks at Adobe snuck a Capitalize feature into the Index panel's menu. While this is nice, we wish there were a further option to change an entry to lowercase (useful for level 2 entries, which are usually set in lowercase). Maybe next version.

Editing References   You can also change the scope (type) or style of a particular page reference. For instance, let's say the reference to Martha Washington on page 47 should have spanned nine paragraphs, but you accidentally set it to Current Page instead. To fix this, click the gray triangle next to the index entry; this displays the page references for the entry.

Double-click the page reference that corresponds to the one you want to change (in this case, you'd double-click the number 47). Change the index entry options, and when done, press Return/Enter.

If you actually wanted the above reference to begin on page 48 instead of page 47, you have to select the entry, cut it to the Clipboard, and then paste it in the new location. Selecting entries can be difficult, so make use of the arrow keys and the Shift key.

Finding Entries   Know you indexed "bugs" as a second-level entry, but can't remember which first-level entry it was under? Select Find from the Index panel's menu to display the panel's Find field. After typing "bugs" into the field, you can click the down arrow to see the next instance of this entry in your panel. (Or click the up arrow to see the previous instance.)

Sorting Entries   To control which language scripts (such as Greek, Cyrillic, Japanese Kana, and so on) you want included in your index, and in what order they should appear, choose Sort Options from the Index panel menu. For example, if you have indexed special symbols (such as π), and you want those to be listed at the end of the index, select Symbols and then click the down arrow button to move it below Roman.

Building the Index   You've reached the finish line—and it's finally time to place your index on a document page so you can see it in all its glory. This is the fun part, because you can just sit back, choose Generate Index from the Index menu's panel, and let InDesign do the work of collecting the index entries and page numbers for you. There is still one more dialog box you need to pay attention to: the Generate Index dialog box (see Figure 8-14).

The Generate Index dialog box presents a (somewhat bewildering) array of choices you need to make in order to get the index of your dreams. InDesign shows you a few controls by default; you can see the others by clicking More Options. Fortunately, once you make your choices in this dialog box, InDesign will remember them the next time you build an index for this document.

Title. Fill in a name for your index in the Title field. InDesign places this title at the beginning of the list, so you might want to type "Index" or "My Indexio Grandioso" or something like that. We leave this field blank and make our own titles. If you do include a title, choose a paragraph style for it from the Style pop-up menu to the right of

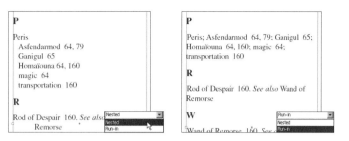

Once again, designing a readable index is as much an art as a science. Take some time to peruse other people's indexes, checking for details such as indentation (what does a first-level entry do when it's longer than one line, for example?) and punctuation.

Note that InDesign builds styles for you called "Index Level 1", "Index Level 2", and so on. If you haven't already created your own styles, then use these and adjust their definitions in the Paragraph Styles panel later.

Index Style. One of our favorite things about making indexes in InDesign is that we can apply paragraph or character styles to every index element, down to the page numbers and the cross-reference words (such as "See" or "See also"). By assigning styles, you can later make global changes to the look and feel of the index by changing the style definitions. While we often apply styles in the Section Heading and Cross-reference pop-up menus, we usually leave the Page Number and Cross-referenced Topic settings alone. It all depends on the index.

Entry Separators. Index formatting is as varied as art directors' whims—or the whims of the indexers, which tend to be even more obscure. One of the main differences revolves around the incredibly picayune art of choosing punctuation. Do you want an en dash between numbers in a page range or a hyphen? An en dash is more appropriate, but the ends of the dash bump up against some numbers. Fortunately, you can type thin spaces on each side of the en dash in the Page Range field in the Generate Index dialog box. (Actually, we never type these characters themselves; we just select them from the menu to the right of the field.)

You can change the punctuation for Following Topic, Between Entries (which only applies in run-in indexes or where there are multiple cross-references per line), Page Range, Between Page Numbers, Before Cross-reference, and Entry End (see Figure 8-16).

FIGURE 8-16
Specifying
Entry Separators

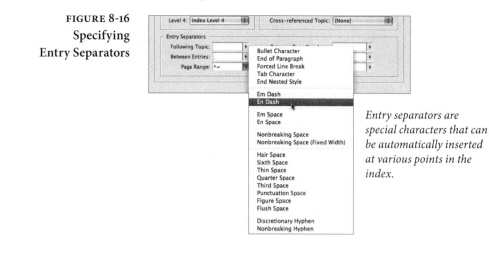

Entry separators are special characters that can be automatically inserted at various points in the index.

Putting It Together

The Book, Table of Contents, and Indexing features in InDesign go a long way toward making the process of creating long documents more bearable. Whether you're building a magazine, a book, a journal, a catalog, or even a newsletter, we're sure you'll be able to find good use for these features. Remember that a little work up front—building styles, putting documents in a Book panel, and so on—can go a long way to saving lots of time in the long run.

Transforming

In the previous chapters, we've covered the process of getting text and graphics into your InDesign publication. This chapter is all about what you can do with those elements once you've wrestled them onto your pages. The process of moving, rotating, scaling, reflecting, or shearing an object is called *transformation*.

Many of the topics in this chapter have been touched on in the preceding chapters—mainly because everything you can do in InDesign is interconnected. In the old days, software was entirely linear and modal: one had to proceed from this screen to that screen following a particular sequence of steps. These days, software is extremely non-linear and non-modal (that is, you can do things many different ways in many different orders), and, therefore, much harder to write about. It's enough to drive one mad! Your purchase of this book will make our time at the Looney Farm that much more pleasant. Thank you.

Transformation Basics

There are many ways to transform an object in InDesign. Select the object using the Selection tool, then:

▶ Drag a selection handle to scale the object (but not necessarily the contents of that object).

▶ Select a transformation tool from the Tools panel, set the center of transformation (if necessary), and drag the tool.

▶ Display the Transform panel or Control panel and enter values in the panel field corresponding to the transformation you want to apply—or choose a preset value from the pop-up menu associated with that field.

▶ Choose one of the "preset" rotation or reflection options from the Transform panel menu or Control panel menu. See "Transformation Presets," later in this chapter

▶ Double-click one of the transformation tools in the Toolbox to display the corresponding transform dialog box (double-click the Rotate tool, for example, to display the Rotation dialog box).

▶ Select the Free Transform tool, and drag the tool around the object. See "Using the Free Transform Tool," later in this chapter.

▶ Press keyboard shortcuts. See "Scaling with Keyboard Shortcuts," later in this chapter.

There's no "right" or "best" way to do transformations—you can experiment with the different methods and see which you like best. We change methods depending on the situation (and our mood).

Setting the Center of Transformation

When you select an object and then choose one of the transformation tools from the Tools panel, InDesign displays the center of transformation icon (it looks something like a small registration mark) on or around the object (see Figure 9-1). The initial position of the icon is determined by the point selected in the Proxy in the Transform panel or Control panel (by default, it's in the center).

When you scale, rotate, or shear an object, InDesign transforms the object around the center of transformation. To reposition the center of transformation icon, either drag it to a new position (with whatever transformation tool you have selected) or click a point on the Proxy in the Transform panel or Control panel.

FIGURE 9-1
**Center of
Transformation**

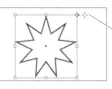

When you select an object and choose a transformation tool, InDesign displays the center of
transformation icon.

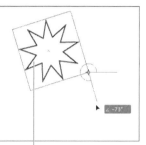

*The center of transformation icon
appears at the point selected on the
Proxy (in the Control panel or
Transform panel).*

*When you move the cursor over the
icon, InDesign changes the cursor to
show that dragging will move the icon.*

*Drag the center of
transformation icon to a
new location, if necessary.
It does not have to be on
the selected object; it can be
anywhere on the spread.*

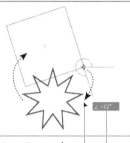

*Drag the tool to transform the object. As you drag,
InDesign transforms (in this example, rotates) the
object around the center of transformation.
If you've turned on the Show Transformation Values
option in the Interface panel of the Preferences dialog
box, InDesign displays the transformation value.*

*If Live Screen Drawing is set
to Delayed in Interface preferences, dragging quickly moves
only a rectangle representing
the object.*

**Transforming Line
Segments and Points**

To transform a point or line segment on a path, select the path or
point using the Direct Selection tool, then transform it as you would
any other object (drag it, or enter values in the X and Y fields of
the Transform panel or Control panel, or press the arrow keys, or
display the Move dialog box, or use any of the other transformation
techniques). This can produce interesting effects (see Figure 9-2).

You can also select the points and/or line segments of a path and
then copy as you transform the object by holding down the Option/
Alt key after you start dragging or clicking the Copy button in the
any of the transformation tool's dialog boxes. In this case, InDesign
splits the path at the unselected points on the path. This takes a little
getting used to, but might come in handy. If you want to transform
line segments or points of a copy of a path, copy the path first, then
apply the transformation.

**Transforming
Path Contents**

When you transform a shape that contains other objects (an image
frame with a picture in it, for example), you can control whether the
content is transformed. By default, dragging the handles of a frame
does not scale the content, but using any of the transformation tools
or using the scaling fields in the Transform panel or Control panel to

FIGURE 9-2
**Transforming
Points, Not Paths**

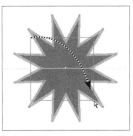

*Select some points using the
Direct Selection tool.*

*In this example, the points on
the inside of the star polygon are
selected; the outside ones aren't.*

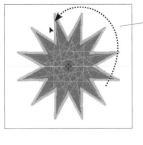

*Apply a transformation. In this exam-
ple, we've rotated the selected points.*

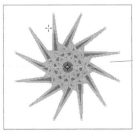

*InDesign
applies the
transforma-
tion to the
selected
points, not
to the entire
path.*

alter a frame *does* scale the content. The Width and Height fields in
the panels, by contrast, scale the frame without scaling the content.

To transform a frame without transforming its content, select the
frame with the Direct Selection tool—this way, the frame is selected
but the content is not. At this point, you can transform the object
as you normally would—the content will not be transformed (see
Figure 9-3).

FIGURE 9-3
**Transforming Path
Contents (or Not)**

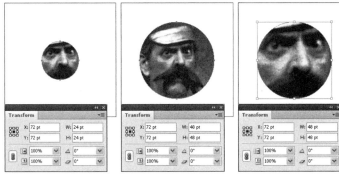

*Untransformed object.
We've selected the
frame using the Direct
Selection tool.*

*Scale the frame (we
entered 200% in the
scaling fields), and the
content will not be
scaled.*

*Here's what you'd see if
the content were scaled
in this example. Scary.*

If you're familiar with earlier versions of InDesign, you might be asking, "What happened to the Transform Content option?" Don't ask us—we'd like to have it back. We think this whole Direct Selection tool business is silly.

Apply to Content or Adjust Scaling Percentage

Transforming text frames in InDesign 1.0 was incredibly frustrating because the program would scale the frame and the text in it, but the Control, Character, and Paragraph panels would still stubbornly display the original point size. If you used the Scale tool to double the size of a text frame containing 12-point text with a two-pica indent, for example, the Point Size field in the Character panel would still show "12 pt", the Left Indent field in the Paragraph panel would show "2p", and the Transform panel would show "200%".

The same problem haunted the process of transforming groups, or transforming frames with objects in them (such as frames containing imported graphics).

Fortunately, Adobe changed this behavior in later releases. Turn on the Apply to Content option in the General panel of the Preferences dialog box, and InDesign will apply the scaling amount to the content (text, group items, or frame contents) as you scale.

With this option turned on, scaling a text frame with the Scale tool immediately applies the transformation to the text, and the Transform panel and Control panel scaling fields revert to 100%. In the example above, the text size would show "24 pt" and the indent would appear as "4p".

If you like, you can go back to the old system by turning on the Adjust Scaling Percentage option in the General panel of the Preferences dialog box (press Command/Ctrl-K, then Command/Ctrl-2). See Figure 9-4 to see what we're talking about.

In spite of the wording of these options, the scaling is always applied to the content. The only difference lies in the values (point sizes or scaling percentages) shown in the relevant panel fields.

Transforming Multiple Selected Contents

You can resize, scale, or rotate multiple objects with the Selection tool, and you don't even need to group them first. Simply select the items you want to transform, and you see a transformation bounding box around the selected items. Dragging a handle resizes the selected elements; holding down Shift resizes them proportionally. Holding down Command/Ctrl scales them. Holding down Command/Ctrl+Shift scales them proportionally. Including the Option/Alt key performs the transformations from the center of the selected objects.

FIGURE 9-4

Applying to Content vs. Adjust Scaling Percentage

When you have the Apply to Content option turned on, scaling a text frame...

...adjusts the point size of the text in the text frame and shows the correct value in any of the point size fields.

When you have the Adjust Scaling Percentage option turned on, scaling a text frame...

...adjusts the point size of the text, but continues to display the original point size in the point size fields. The current (scaled) point size appears in parentheses. Not only is this odd and of questionable utility, but it's hard to see.

FIGURE 9-5

Friendly Numbers

*Coordinates of the point correspond to the point selected on the Proxy, and are measured relative to the current zero point on the ruler.

The Control panel has all of the controls found in the Transform panel, and offers a few additional options, as well.

Vertical coordinate* | Width
Horizontal coordinate* | Height

Proxy

Horizontal scaling
Constrain Proportions
Vertical scaling | Shearing
Rotation

Most of the time, we use the Control panel, but it's much harder to show in our screen shots.

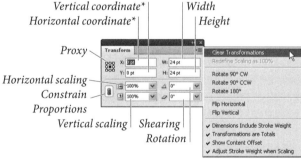

To rotate the selected items, position the mouse outside one of the corner handles of the selection box, and drag to rotate around the center of the selection.

FIGURE 9-6
The Proxy

The point you select on the Proxy also sets the center of transformation.

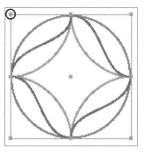

The points you see on the Proxy correspond to the selection handles you see when you select an object.

The point you select in the Proxy determines the content of the X and Y fields in the Transform panel or Control panel—select the upper-left corner (as in this example), and you'll see the coordinates of that corner of the selection.

Numbers Are Your Friends

If numbers scare you, you're going to be scared by the Transform panel and Control panel. Don't give in to math anxiety—these panels are simply too useful to avoid. The first step to taming them is to understand the controls are called, and what they can do for you (see Figure 9-5). To display the Transform panel, choose Transform from the Object and Layout submenu of the Window menu; to display the Control panel, press Command-Option-6/Ctrl-Alt-6.

The Proxy

A "proxy" is something that stands in for something (or someone) else. The Proxy in the Transform and Control panels stands in for the object or objects you've selected (see Figure 9-6). The points on the Proxy icon correspond to the selection handles InDesign displays around an object when you select it with the Selection tool (not the Direct Selection tool).

When you select a point on the Proxy, you're telling InDesign that changes you make in the panel affect that point (the X and Y fields), or are centered around that point (the Width, Height, Horizontal Scaling, Vertical Scaling, Rotation Angle, and Shear Angle fields).

Understanding Page Coordinates

An InDesign page is a two-dimensional surface; a plane. You can define the position of any point on a plane using a pair of coordinates: the horizontal location ("X") and the vertical location ("Y"). The numbers you see in the X and Y fields of InDesign's Transform and Control panels represent the horizontal and vertical distance of the selected point on the Proxy from the zero point on the rulers.

As you move farther to the right, the value in the X field increases; move the object to the left, and the value in the X field decreases. Horizontal locations to the left of the zero point are represented by negative numbers. As you move farther down on the page, the value in the Y field increases. Vertical locations above the zero point are represented by negative numbers. Note that this means that InDesign's vertical coordinate system is *upside down* relative to the two-dimensional coordinate system you learned in junior high school geometry class (see Figure 9-7).

FIGURE 9-7
Page Coordinates

InDesign's two-dimensional coordinate system. All coordinates are measured from the zero point. x represents the horizontal location of a point; y represents the vertical location.

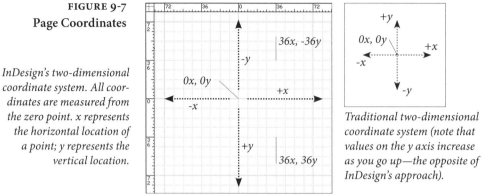

Traditional two-dimensional coordinate system (note that values on the y axis increase as you go up—the opposite of InDesign's approach).

Duplicating As You Transform

Hold down Option/Alt as you press Return/Enter to apply a change you've made to any of the Transform or Control panel fields, and InDesign copies the object and then applies the transformation to the duplicate (see Figure 9-8).

If you hold down arrow keys while dragging, you can duplicate the objects into a grid of columns and rows. See "Grid Mode" later in this chapter.

Panel Menu Options

The options in the Transform panel and Control panel control the way that transformations affect objects and their contents.

Redefine Scaling as 100%. If you had Adjust Scaling Percentage enabled in Preferences when you scaled an object, you can make the panel fields display "properly" by choosing this option.

FIGURE 9-8
Duplicating As You Transform

Enter a value in the Horizontal Scaling, Vertical Scaling, Width, or Height fields...

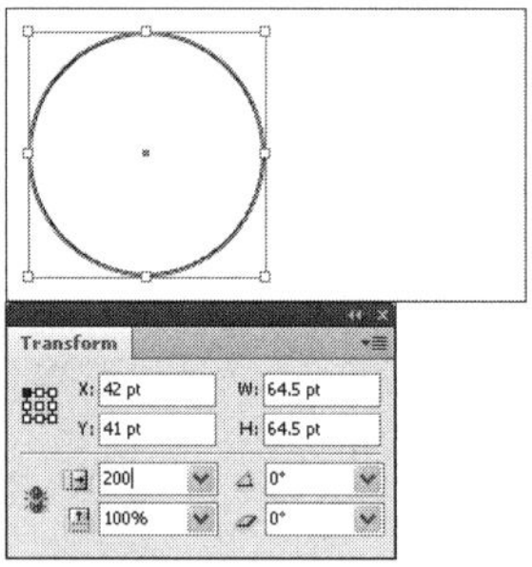

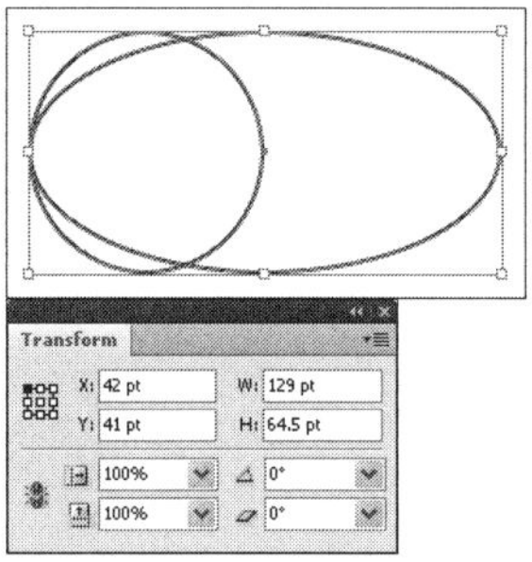

...and press Option-Return (Macintosh) or Alt-Enter (Windows). InDesign applies the transformation to a copy of the selected object.

Transformation Presets. Some transformations are so common that Adobe added the following presets to the Transform and Control panels: Rotate 180 degrees, Rotate 90 degrees clockwise, Rotate 90 degrees counter-clockwise, Flip Vertical, Flip Horizontal, Flip Both. These options are buttons in the Control panel (see Figure 9-9), or menu options in the Transform panel.

Dimensions Include Stroke Weight. What defines the dimensions of a path? Is it the geometric representation of the path itself? Or should it include the stroke weight applied to the path? We prefer to work with the geometric bounds of a path, so we turn off the Dimensions Include Stroke Weight option. You might prefer to work with the visible bounds of objects—if you do, turn this option on (it's on by default).

Transformations Are Totals. When you select an object that's contained by a frame, should the panel fields reflect the state of the selected object relative to the pasteboard, or relative to the frame containing the object? That's the question you answer by turning the Transformations are Totals option on the Transform panel or Control panel menus on or off (it's on by default). When it's on, InDesign displays the rotation, scaling percentages, and shear angle of the selection relative to the pasteboard. Turn this option off to display the information relative to the containing frame (see Figure 9-10).

FIGURE 9-9
Transformation
Preset Buttons

Rotate 90 degress clockwise | | Rotate 90 degress counterclockwise

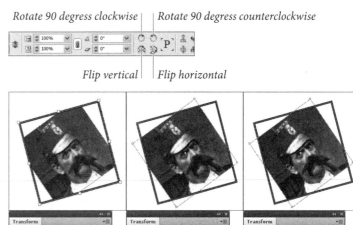

Flip vertical | Flip horizontal

FIGURE 9-10
Transformations
Are Totals

The outer frame has been rotated 15 degrees. The inner frame has been rotated by 20 degrees. The value shown in the Rotation field when you select the inner frame depends on the state of the Transformations are Totals option (on the Transform panel menu or Control panel menu)

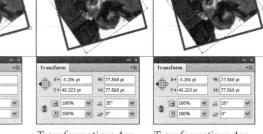

Transformations Are Totals on: 35 degrees.

Transformations Are Totals off. 20 degrees.

Show Content Offset. If you nest one object inside another, and then select that nested item with the Direct Selection tool, what should appear in the X and Y fields of the Transform panel and Control panel? By default, the Show Content Offset option is turned on in either panel menu, so the X and Y fields display the offset of the nested object from the "parent" frame.

Moving Objects

There are many ways to move objects in InDesign—select the object and then try any of the methods shown here. (To move the content of a frame without moving the frame itself, select the Direct Selection tool and click inside the frame.)

Moving Objects by Dragging

To move an object, select the object with the Selection tool or the Direct Selection tool and drag—make sure not to drag the Content Grabber or you'll move only the frame contents, often resulting in an empty frame. Hold down Option/Alt as you drag to duplicate the object.

The Live Screen Drawing option in Interface preferences determines what happens when you move an object. If Immediate is selected, the object moves when you drag. If Delayed is selected when you start dragging, you'll see only a box representing an object; however, holding down the mouse button for a moment before dragging causes the object to move as you drag it.

Moving Objects with the Transform Panel or Control Panel

When we need precision, we always move objects by entering numbers in the X and Y fields of the Transform or Control panel (see Figure 9-11). And it's not just because we're closet rocket scientists; it's because we don't trust the screen display, even at 4000 percent magnification. You shouldn't either, when it comes to making fine adjustments in your InDesign publication.

1. Select the object you want to move.

2. Display the Transform panel or Control panel.

3. Enter values in the X field (to move the object horizontally) and the Y field (to move the object vertically). If you want to move the object to an *absolute* position, enter a new value in the field; to move the object some distance *relative* to its current location, add or subtract that distance from the value in the panel field.

4. Press Return/Enter. InDesign moves the selected object.

Moving Objects with the Move Dialog Box

To move objects using the controls in the Move dialog box, follow these steps (see Figure 9-12).

1. Select an object.

2. Double-click the Selection tool (or choose Move from the Transform submenu of the Object menu).

FIGURE 9-11
FIGURE 9-11
Moving Objects Using the X and Y Fields

To move an object to a specific location on the page or pasteboard...

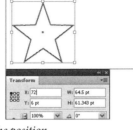

...enter the position in the X or Y field.

Move to 72

Press Return/Enter to move the object to that location.

To move an object by a certain amount, add (to move to the right or down) or subtract (to move to the left or up) the amount to the value in the X or Y field.

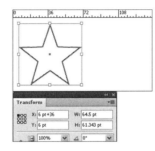

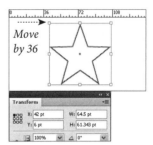

Move by 36

Press Return/Enter to move the object relative to its current position.

FIGURE 9-12
Moving Objects with the Move Dialog Box

Choose Move from the Transform submenu of the Object menu to display the Move panel (or double-click the Selection tool in the Tools panel), and InDesign will display the Move dialog box.

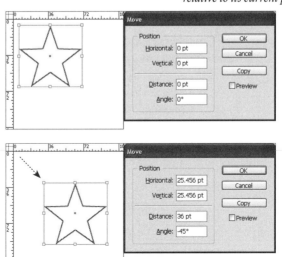

Enter values in the Move dialog box. Turn on Preview if you want to see the effect of the move.

Click the OK button, and InDesign moves the object relative to its current position.

3. Set movement options using the controls in the Move dialog box. Values here are always relative to the current position. If you want to move a frame but not its contents, turn off the Move Content option. To see the effect, turn on the Preview option.

4. Press Return/Enter to move the object, or click the Copy button to move a copy of the object.

Using the Free Transform Tool

To use the Free Transform tool to move objects, position the tool over any part of the object other than the selection handles, and the Free Transform tool works just like the Selection tool. Drag the center point, and InDesign snaps it to any active grids or guides. Hold down Option/Alt as you drag to duplicate the object as you move it.

Moving Objects by Pressing Arrow Keys

As if dragging by eye and specifying coordinates weren't enough (in terms of movement options), InDesign also sports "nudge" keys. Select an object and press one of the arrow keys, and the element moves in that direction, using the increments you set in the Cursor Key field in the Units & Increments Preferences dialog box.

To move the selected object by ten times the distance you entered in the Cursor Key field, hold down Shift as you press the arrow key. To duplicate the selection as you move it, hold down Option/Alt as you press the arrow key.

Duplicating and Moving Objects with Step and Repeat

When you want to duplicate an object and move the duplicate to a new location, or create a series of duplicates, turn to InDesign's Step and Repeat feature. Select an object, then choose Step and Repeat from the Edit menu. In the Step and Repeat dialog box, enter the number of duplicates you want in the Repeat Count field, then enter the horizontal and vertical offsets for each duplicate. Or, select the "Create as a grid" option, and specify the number of rows and columns in the grid. Click OK. See Figure 9-13.

InDesign's Duplicate command remembers the settings from the Step and Repeat dialog box. The next time you choose Duplicate, the duplicate will be offset from the original by the same distance.

Scaling

To change the size of an object, select the object and then use any of the following techniques.

► Drag the Scale tool.

FIGURE 9-13
Step and Repeat

Enter the number of duplicates you want in the Repeat Count field.

Positive values in Vertical Offset move the duplicates down the page; negative values move them up.

Positive values in Horizontal Offset move the duplicates to the right of the original; negative values move them to the left.

InDesign duplicates the object, spacing the new page items according to the values you entered.

▶ Drag a selection handle with the Selection tool or the Free Transform tool.

▶ Enter values in the fields of the Transform or Control panel or the Scale dialog box.

▶ Press a keyboard shortcut.

Scaling with the Scale Tool

When you want to scale an object until it "looks right," use the Scale tool (see Figure 9-14).

1. Select the object you want to scale.

2. Select the Scale tool from the Tools panel (or press S).

FIGURE 9-14
Scaling an Object with the Scale Tool

Select an object, move the center of transformation icon (if necessary), and then drag the Scale tool on the page or pasteboard.

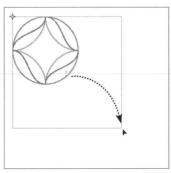

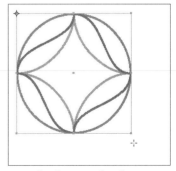

Hold down Shift to scale the object proportionally, or Option/Alt to scale a duplicate.

Once the object reaches the size you want, stop dragging.

3. Change the location of the center of transformation icon, if necessary. To do this, either drag the icon to a new location or click one of the points in the Proxy in the Transform panel.

4. Drag the Scale tool horizontally to scale the object's width, or drag vertically to scale the object's height. Dragging diagonally sizes the object's width and height. Hold down Shift as you drag to scale the object proportionally. Hold down Option/Alt as you drag to duplicate the object and scale the duplicate.

As you drag the Scale tool, InDesign displays the scaling percentages in the Horizontal Scaling and Vertical Scaling fields in the Control panel and Transform panel. If you're scaling a page item (a rectangle, ellipse, polygon, line, or frame), these fields return to 100 percent when you stop dragging. If you've selected an imported graphic with the Direct Selection tool before scaling it, the fields reflect the scaling applied to the object.

Scaling with the Selection Tool

As in almost any other drawing or page-layout application, you can change the size of objects by dragging their corner handles with the Pointer tool. As you drag, the object gets larger or smaller. Hold down Shift as you drag to resize the object proportionally.

When you scale a frame using the Selection tool, InDesign, by default, does not scale the frame's contents. To do this, hold down Command/Ctrl as you drag one of the selection handles. Or, select Auto-Fit before you start dragging.

Scaling with the Free Transform Tool

To scale an object using the Free Transform tool, follow these steps.

1. Select an object.

2. Select the Free Transform tool from the Tools panel.

3. Position the tool above a selection handle, then drag. Hold down Option/Alt to scale the object proportionally around its center point, or hold down Shift to scale proportionally.

Scaling with the Transform Panel or Control Panel

When you know you want to make an object larger or smaller by an exact percentage, or to scale the object to a specific width or height, use the Transform panel or Control panel (see Figure 9-15).

1. Select the object you want to scale.

2. Display the panel if it's not already visible.

FIGURE 9-15
**Scaling an Object Using
the Transform Panel**

*Select a point on the
Proxy, if necessary.*

*Enter a scaling percentage
in the Horizontal Scale or
Vertical Scale field, or enter
a new value in the Width or
Height field.*

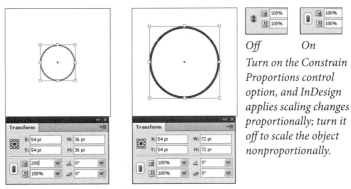

Off   *On*

*Turn on the Constrain
Proportions control
option, and InDesign
applies scaling changes
proportionally; turn it
off to scale the object
nonproportionally.*

Press Return/Enter to apply the scaling change.

3. Enter a new value in the Width or Height field (or in both fields), or enter a scaling percentage in the Horizontal Scaling field or the Vertical Scaling field.

4. Press Return/Enter to scale the object. To apply proportional scaling, hold down Command/Ctrl as you press Return/Enter, or turn on the Constrain Proportions option.

Note that the Horizontal and Vertical Scale fields operate differently than the Width and Height fields. When you enter a value in the Horizontal Scale field or Vertical Scale field, and have selected the object using the Selection tool, the scaling *is* applied to the content of the object (if any). When you use the Width or Height field, the scaling is *not* applied to the object. Bonus tip: You can enter percentages in the Width and Height fields, and you can enter measurements in the Horizontal Scale and Vertical Scale fields. Try it!

**Scaling with the
Scale Dialog Box**

To scale using the Scale dialog box, select one or more objects and follow these steps (see Figure 9-16).

1. Double-click the Scale tool (or choose Scale from the Transform submenu of the Object menu). InDesign displays the Scale dialog box.

FIGURE 9-16
**Scaling an Object Using
the Scale Dialog Box**

*Double-click the Scale
tool in the Tools panel.*

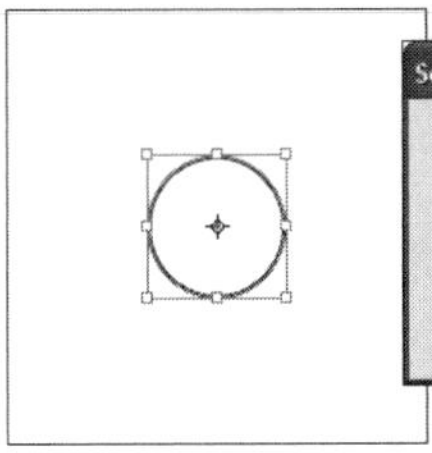

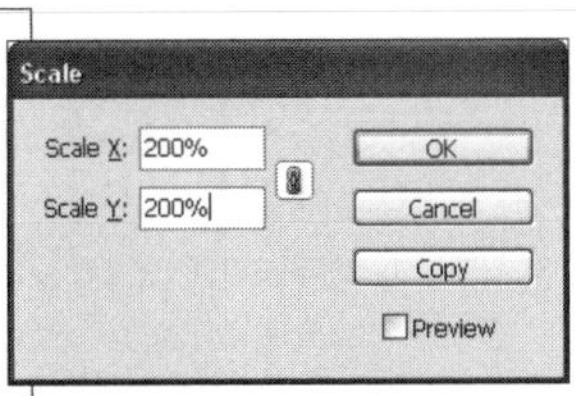

*InDesign displays the Scale
dialog box. Enter a scaling
percentage and click OK.*

*InDesign scales the
object.*

2. Set scaling options using the controls in the dialog box. To scale the object proportionally, turn on the Uniform option and enter a scaling percentage in the Scale field. To scale an object non-proportionally, turn on the Non-Uniform option, then enter scaling percentages in the Horizontal and Vertical fields. To scale the contents of a path, turn on the Scale Content option. To see the effect of the current settings, turn on the Preview option.

3. Press Return/Enter to scale the object, or click the Copy button to scale a copy of the object.

Scaling with Keyboard Shortcuts

You can also scale the selected object by pressing keyboard shortcuts. Note, however, that these changes don't appear in the scaling percentages of the Transform panel when you are scaling page items (rectangles, ellipses, polygons, lines, and text frames).

▶ Press Command-. (period)/Ctrl-. to increase the scale of the object by one percent.

▶ Press Command-, (comma)/Ctrl-, to decrease the scale by one percent.

▶ Press Command-Option-. (period)/Ctrl-Alt-. to increase the scale by five percent.

▶ Press Command-Option-, (comma)/Ctrl-Alt-, to decrease the scale by five percent.

Note that these shortcuts do exactly what they say: they scale the object relative to its *current size*, not its original size. They are the same as entering scaling percentages in the Horizontal Scale and Vertical Scale fields in the Control panel.

If you'd rather have your scaling keyboard shortcuts change the size of the object rather than the scaling percentage (as if you were entering values in the Width and Height fields of the Control panel), those shortcuts are available in the Keyboard Shortcuts dialog box..

Scaling Strokes

We often want to scale a page item without scaling its stroke. This is especially true when we're scaling frames containing images. To do this, turn off the Adjust Stroke Weight When Scaling option on the Transform Panel or Control panel menu before you scale the frame.

This option is not available when the Adjust Scaling Percentage option is turned on (in the General panel of the Preferences dialog box). Oddly, it's grayed out in the Transform panel menu, but disappears from the Control panel menu altogether.

Rotating Objects

InDesign can rotate any object on a page, in .001-degree increments. The rotation angle shown is relative to the pasteboard (where 0 degrees is horizontal) or to the frame containing the rotated object. If you rotate an object by 30 degrees, entering that value again will not change the rotation of the object. To do that, you'd need to enter "+30" following the value shown in the Rotation Angle field.

Rotating with the Rotate Tool

Follow these steps to rotate using the Rotate tool (see Figure 9-17).

1. Select the Rotate tool from the Tools panel (or press R).

2. Drag the center of transformation to the point you want to rotate around, or click a point in the Transform panel's Proxy. To rotate around the geometric center center point in the Proxy.

3. Drag the Rotate tool.

4. When the object looks the way you want it to, stop dragging.

Rotating with the Selection Tool

Follow these steps to rotate an object using the Selection tool (see Figure 9-18).

1. Select the Selection tool from the Tools panel (or press V).

2. Select the object you want to rotate. Click the Content Grabber if you want to rotate the image within the frame. Click the frame edge if you want to rotate the frame and its contents.

3. Position the tool anywhere outside the object's selection handles, then drag. InDesign rotates the object around its center point, regardless of the Proxy setting. Hold down Shift as you drag to constrain rotation to 45-degree increments.

FIGURE 9-17
Rotating an Object Using the Rotate Tool

Select the Rotate tool from the Tools panel, then move the center of transformation icon, if necessary, to set the point you want to rotate around.

Drag the Rotate tool. If you pause for a second before you drag, InDesign displays a preview of the rotated object.

FIGURE 9-18
Rotating an Object with the Selection Tool

With the Selection tool (or the Free Tranform tool), position the cursor outside one of the object's selection handles.

Drag the handle to rotate the object. Hold down Shift to rotate in 45-degree increments.

Rotating with the Free Transform Tool

To rotate an object using the Free Transform tool, follow these steps.

1. Select an object and then choose the Free Transform tool from the Tools panel (or press E).

2. Position the tool anywhere outside the object's selection handles, then drag (positioning the tool near the selection handles scales the object, so move a bit farther away). InDesign rotates the object around its center point. Hold down Shift as you drag to constrain rotation to 45-degree increments.

Rotating with the Transform Panel

To rotate an object using the Transform panel or Control panel, follow these steps (see Figure 9-19).

1. Select the object or objects you want to rotate.

2. Click a point on the Proxy to set the point you want to rotate around, if necessary.

3. Enter a new value in the Rotation Angle field. To rotate the object to a specific angle, enter that angle in the field. To rotate the object relative to its current rotation angle, add to or subtract from the value in the Rotation angle field.

    You can enter positive numbers (such as "45") or negative numbers (such as "-270") between -360 and 360 degrees. Positive rotation angles rotate the selected object counterclockwise; negative values rotate the object clockwise. You enter rotation angles in .001-degree increments.

4. Press Return/Enter to rotate the object, or Option-Return/Alt-Enter to rotate a copy of the object.

Rotating with the Rotate Dialog Box

To rotate an object using the Rotate dialog box, follow these steps (see Figure 9-20).

1. Select an object.

2. Double-click the Rotate tool to display the Rotate dialog box.

3. Enter a rotation angle in the Angle field. To see the effect of the current settings, turn on the Preview option.

4. Press Return/Enter to rotate the object, or click the Copy button to rotate a copy of the object.

Rotating Multiple Selected Objects

When you rotate more than one object (we're counting groups as single objects), the objects rotate around a single point. This point can be their joint geometric center, or around any other point you've specified. They don't all rotate around their individual center points.

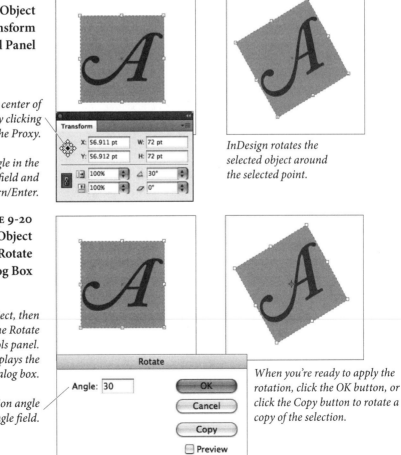

FIGURE 9-19
Rotating an Object Using the Transform Panel or Control Panel

Set the center of transformation by clicking a point on the Proxy.

Enter an angle in the Rotation field and press Return/Enter.

InDesign rotates the selected object around the selected point.

FIGURE 9-20
Rotating an Object Using the Rotate Dialog Box

Select an object, then double-click the Rotate tool in the Tools panel. InDesign displays the Rotate dialog box.

Enter a rotation angle in the Angle field.

When you're ready to apply the rotation, click the OK button, or click the Copy button to rotate a copy of the selection.

Reflecting Objects

Reflecting—or mirroring—objects in InDesign is very simple, and you can reflect, or "flip" an object over its vertical axis, its horizontal axis, or both its vertical and horizontal axes at once. That's it. There's no reflection tool, no need to enter a reflection angle anywhere.

To reflect an object, follow these steps (see Figure 9-21).

1. Select the object you want to reflect.

2. Choose Flip Vertical, Flip Horizontal, or Flip Both from the Transform panel menu. InDesign reflects the selected object.

FIGURE 9-21
Reflecting an Object

Note that reflecting an object across an angle is the same as reflecting the object across its horizontal or vertical axis and then rotating.

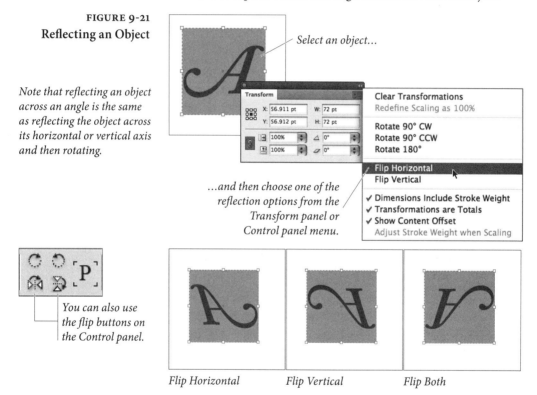

Select an object...

...and then choose one of the reflection options from the Transform panel or Control panel menu.

You can also use the flip buttons on the Control panel.

Flip Horizontal   Flip Vertical   Flip Both

Shearing Objects

Shearing (or skewing) an object makes it appear that the plane the object's resting on has been rotated away from the plane of the page. It's good for creating perspective effects—but it's not a replacement for a serious 3D rotation program (see Figure 9-22).

No amount of shearing applied to objects on an InDesign page will produce wool.

FIGURE 9-22
Shearing an Object

No shearing.   *Horizontal shearing.*   *Vertical shearing.*

Shearing with the Shear Tool

To shear an object using the Shear tool, follow the steps below (see Figure 9-23).

1. Select an object.

2. Choose the Shear tool from the Tools panel (or press O).

3. Change the location of the center of transformation icon, if necessary (you can either drag the icon to a new location, or click one of the points in the Transform panel Proxy).

4. Drag the Shear tool. As you drag the cursor, the skewing angles display in the Shearing Angle field of the Transform panel. The panel shows that vertical shearing is actually done by horizontal shearing (skewing) *and* rotating the object.

5. When the object looks the way you want it to, stop dragging.

Shearing with the Transform Panel

To shear an object using the Transform panel, follow these steps (see Figure 9-24).

1. Select the object you want to shear.

2. Display the Transform panel, if it's not already visible.

3. Click one of the points on the Transform panel Proxy. This sets the center of transformation.

FIGURE 9-23
Shearing an Object with the Shear Tool

Select an object, then drag the Shear tool. As you drag, InDesign shears the selection.

When the object looks the way you want it to, stop dragging.

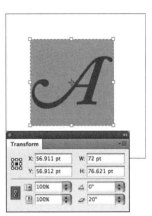

*Press Return/Enter to shear the
selection. Press Option-Return/
Alt-Enter to apply the shear to a
copy of the selection.*

4. Enter an angle in the Shear Angle field, or add or subtract a value from the current content of the field.

5. Press Return/Enter to shear the selected object.

   Typing a value in the Shear Angle field only lets you skew (horizontal shear) the object. To create a vertical shear, type the same angle into the Rotation angle field.

**Shearing with the
Shear Dialog Box**

To shear an object using the Shear dialog box, follow these steps (see Figure 9-25).

1. Select an object.

2. Double-click the Shear tool (or choose Shear from the Transform submenu of the Object menu). InDesign displays the Shear dialog box.

FIGURE 9-25
**Shearing an Object
Using the Shear
Dialog Box**

*Select an object,
then double-click the Shear
tool in the Tools panel (or
choose Shear from the
Transform submenu of
the Object menu).*

*InDesign displays the Shear
dialog box. Specify the angle
and axis you want to use.*

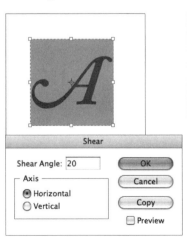

*Click the OK button, or click
the Copy button to shear a
copy of the selection.*

3. Set the shearing options using the controls in the dialog box. Enter an angle in the Shear Angle field, and pick an axis (the options are horizontal or vertical). To rotate the contents of a path, turn on the Shear Content option.

4. Press Return/Enter to shear the object, or click the Copy button to shear a copy of the object.

Repeating Transformations

The options on the Transform Again submenu of the Object menu give you a way to repeat transformations you've recently applied (see Figure 9-26). You can repeat individual transformations, or you can repeat a series of transformations. InDesign will remember a transformation until you apply a different transformation, and will keep track of any uninterrupted sequence of transformations.

FIGURE 9-26
Transform Again

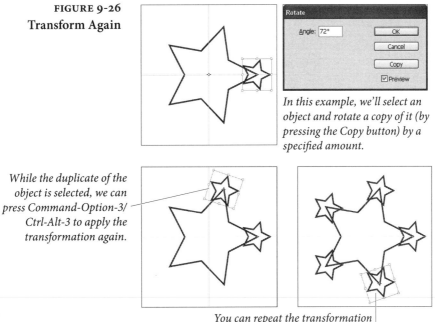

In this example, we'll select an object and rotate a copy of it (by pressing the Copy button) by a specified amount.

While the duplicate of the object is selected, we can press Command-Option-3/ Ctrl-Alt-3 to apply the transformation again.

You can repeat the transformation as many times as you like, and you can apply it to other objects.

How it works: select an object and apply a transformation, then select another object and choose one of the options from the Transform Again submenu of the Object menu or use the associated keyboard shortcut.

There are four ways to use Transform Again:

▶ **Transform Again.** Applies the most recent transformation to the selected object or objects.

▶ **Transform Again Individually.** Applies the most recent transformation to each object in the selection (see Figure 9-27).

▶ **Transform Sequence Again.** Applies the most recent series of transformations to the selected objects (see Figure 9-28).

▶ **Transform Sequence Again Individually.** Applies the most recent series of transformations to each object in the selection.

Want to make a series of objects the same size? Select one of the objects, then change its width and height. Select the other objects, and choose Transform Again Individually (see Figure 9-29). Fitting options that you apply to a frame can also be repeated using Transform again (see Figure 9-30).

FIGURE 9-27
**Transform Again
vs. Transform Again
Individually**

*After you've selected and
transformed an object...*

*...you can select other objects and
apply the same transformation.*

*In this example, Transform
Again rotates the objects
around their common
center; Transform Again
Individually rotates each
object around its own center.*

*Choose Transform Again, to
transform all of the objects
in the selection as a unit.*

*Choose Transform Again
Individually to transform each
item in the selection.*

FIGURE 9-28
**Transform
Sequence Again**

*Object created by moving
(with Copy), rotating, and
scaling the original star.*

*Repeat the sequence of trans-
formations using Transform
Sequence Again Individually.*

*Then repeat the sequence for
the other stars in the row.*

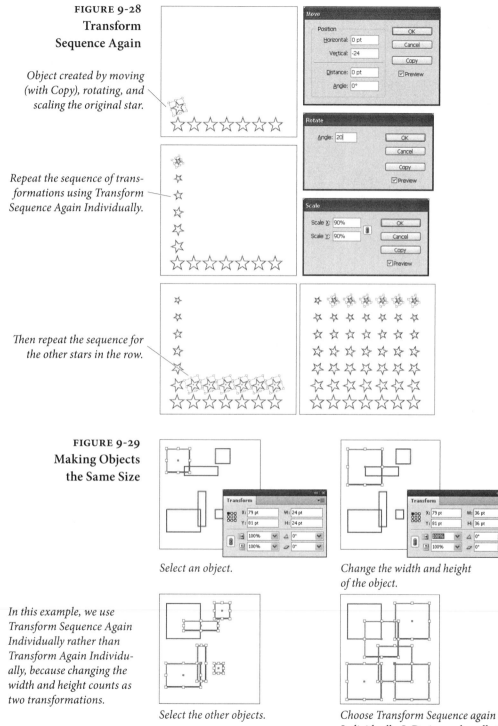

FIGURE 9-29
**Making Objects
the Same Size**

Select an object.

*Change the width and height
of the object.*

*In this example, we use
Transform Sequence Again
Individually rather than
Transform Again Individu-
ally, because changing the
width and height counts as
two transformations.*

Select the other objects.

*Choose Transform Sequence again
Individually. InDesign makes all of
the objects the same size.*

FIGURE 9-30
**Fitting and
Transform Again**

*In this example, we have a
variety of images in varying
degrees of distress.*

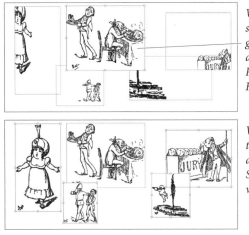

*We apply proportional
scaling to one of the
graphics, and then
apply Fit Content
Proportionally and Fit
Frame to Content.*

*We then select all of
the other graphics
and choose Transform
Sequence Again Indi-
vidually. Much better!*

Grid Mode

When you're dragging an object, you can press the arrow keys to duplicate the object into a grid. The InDesign team calls this "Grid Mode." You can use Grid Mode to create a grid of objects when you're placing multiple images, when you're creating objects, or when you're duplicating objects

In Grid Mode, use the arrow keys to change the number of rows and columns; use the Page Up and Page Down keys to change the gutter space between both rows and columns; use Command/Ctrl plus arrow keys to change the gutter space between either rows or columns.

Placing multiple graphics into a grid. After you select multiple files in the Place dialog box and click Open, start dragging, and then use the arrow keys to change the number of columns and rows of the placed images.

Drawing a grid of shapes or text frames. Select a tool that lets you draw a frame. Begin dragging. While still dragging, press the right arrow key to increase the number of columns and the up arrow key to increase the number of rows (see Figure 9-31).

When using the Polygon tool, press the Spacebar while dragging to turn on and off Grid Mode. When Grid Mode is off, pressing the arrow keys changes the star inset and number of sides rather than the number of shapes.

Duplicating objects into a grid. Use the Selection tool to select an object. Hold down Option/Alt and begin dragging. While still drag-

FIGURE 9-31
Grid Mode

 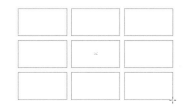

With the Rectangle tool selected,
start dragging...

...and then press the up and right
arrow keys to create a grid.

ging, release the Alt or Option key, and press the right arrow and up arrow keys to increase the number of columns and rows. Drag a rectangle to specify the size of the grid, and release the mouse button.

Here's a nifty trick. If multiple column guides appear on the current spread, InDesign automatically uses the gutter width as the amount of space between each frame in the grid. That makes it easy to place a grid of images neatly within the columns. And if you're drawing text frames, the frames are threaded automatically.

Aligning and Distributing Objects

InDesign features both object alignment and object distribution. InDesign aligns objects based on the object's bounding box, and bases the alignment on the option you've selected in the Align To pop-up menu in the Align panel. You can align objects to the selection, to the page, to the margins, or to the spread by choosing the correspondingly named menu options.

When you distribute objects you're telling InDesign to evenly arrange the selected objects. Objects can be distributed inside the area occupied by the objects, or by a specific distance.

Aligning Objects   When you've selected the objects you want to align, press Shift-F7 to display the Align panel. Click one of the alignment buttons to align the selected objects (see Figure 9-32).

If you've locked an object in the selection, InDesign doesn't move that object when you apply an alignment. If an object doesn't seem to be following the herd, unlock it by clicking the object's lock icon.

While none of the alignment or distribution options are assigned a keyboard shortcut by default, you can use the Keyboard Shortcuts dialog box to add this feature to your copy of InDesign (you'll find them in the Object Editing section).

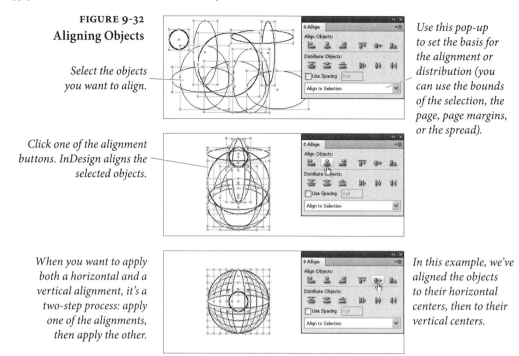

FIGURE 9-32
Aligning Objects

*Select the objects
you want to align.*

*Use this pop-up
to set the basis for
the alignment or
distribution (you
can use the bounds
of the selection, the
page, page margins,
or the spread).*

*Click one of the alignment
buttons. InDesign aligns the
selected objects.*

*When you want to apply
both a horizontal and a
vertical alignment, it's a
two-step process: apply
one of the alignments,
then apply the other.*

*In this example, we've
aligned the objects
to their horizontal
centers, then to their
vertical centers.*

Distributing Objects

Have you ever wanted to space a bunch of objects at even distances from each other (from each other's centers, at any rate) across a particular horizontal measurement? If you have, InDesign's Distribute feature should make your day. To distribute the selected objects inside the rectangle defined by the objects' bounding box, click one of the distribute buttons in the Align panel. InDesign distributes the objects as you've specified (see Figure 9-33).

To distribute (or space) the objects by a specified distance, use the Use Spacing option in either the Distribute Objects section of the Align panel or the Distribute Spacing section (see Figure 9-34).

When you click one of the buttons in the Distribute Objects section, the value you enter in the Use Spacing field sets the distance between the object sides (top, bottom, right, and left) or object centers (vertical or horizontal). If you enter 12 points, for example, and then click the Horizontal Distribute Lefts button, InDesign spaces the left edges of the objects in the selection 12 points apart.

When you use the Use Spacing option in the Distribute Spacing section, InDesign spaces the objects apart by the distance you enter in the Use Spacing field. Click the Vertical Distribute Space button to distribute the objects vertically, or click the Horizontal Distribute Space button to distribute the objects horizontally. The objects do not need to be the same shape or size.

FIGURE 9-33
Distributing Objects

*Select the objects
you want to distribute.*

*Click one of the distribution
buttons. InDesign distributes
the selected objects evenly
across the bounds of the
selection...*

*...or use the Use Spacing
field to space the corresponding object faces (top, bottom,
side, or center) by a specific
distance apart.*

FIGURE 9-34
**Distributing Space
Between Objects**

*To apply an even spacing
between objects, expand the
panel to show the Distribute
Spacing options, then click
one of the buttons. To space
the objects apart by a specific
distance, enter a value in
the Use Spacing field.*

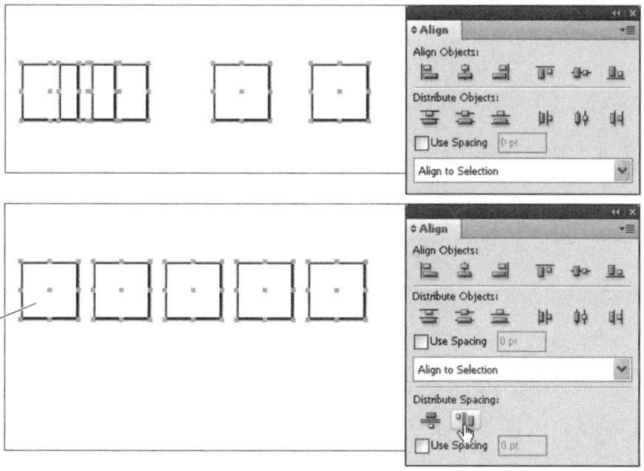

Live Distribute

When you select several objects, you can resize the space between the objects proportionally instead of resizing the actual objects. Simply start dragging a selection handle and then hold down the Spacebar while still dragging.

Using the Gap Tool

The Gap tool lets you adjust the gap size between objects (see Figure 9-35). The Gap tool is oddly counter-intuitive when you first start using it, because you're not used to working on the space between objects. Once you get used to it, you'll find it's an easy way to adjust your layout.

You can also use the Gap to resize several objects that have commonly aligned edges simultaneously, while keeping the gaps between them fixed.

FIGURE 9-35
Gap Tool

Select the Gap tool and move the cursor between objects.

Drag down to move gap and resize objects.

Command/Ctrl-drag to increase the gap without moving objects.

Command/Ctrl+Option/Alt-drag to increase the gap and move the objects.

Shift-drag to affect only the nearest objects.

Option/Alt-drag below the objects to increase the gap and move the objects.

The Gap tool ignores locked objects and master page items.

Select the Gap tool from the Tools panel (or press U), and then move the pointer between two objects. Again, you're working on the space between objects, not the objects themselves. Use modifier keys to determine how the gap is resized and which objects are affected (see Table 9-1).

Here's a tip that might help—the Gap tool doesn't have to be between objects. You can use it to change the space between objects

TABLE 9-1
Gap Tool Shortcuts

To do this:	Using the Gap tool, do this:
Move the gap and resize all objects along the gap.	Drag between two objects
Move the gap between only the two nearest objects.	Shift-drag
Resize the gap instead of moving it.	Command/Ctrl-drag
Resize the gap between only the two nearest objects.	Shift+Command/Ctrl-drag
Move the gap and objects in the same direction.	Option/Alt-drag
Move the gap and only the nearest objects in the same direction.	Shift+Option/Alt-drag
Resize the gap and move the objects.	Command/Ctrl+Option/Alt-drag
Resize the gap and move only the nearest objects.	Shift+Command/Ctrl+Option/Alt-drag

and the edge of the page. When Bob first started using the Gap tool, he couldn't figure out how to "push" a row of objects away from other objects. Then he realized he needed to move the Gap tool to the other side of the objects and "pull." It'll make sense once you start using the tool.

Locking Objects

In InDesign, you can lock an object's position—which means that you can't transform it. You can determine whether locked objects can be selected. If the Prevent Selection of Locked Objects option is turned on in General preferences, you cannot select a locked object. If it's turned off, you can select the object and copy it or change its appearance; you just can't transform it.

To lock an object, select it and press Command-L/Ctrl-L (or choose Lock from the Object menu). To unlock an object, click its lock icon (or choose Unlock All on Spread from the Object menu). You can also lock or unlock an object in the Layers panel.

Of course, another good way to lock an object is to place it on a layer and then lock the layer. An object on a locked layer is totally locked; you can't even select it.

Hiding Objects

You can hide an object if you don't want it to be printed, exported, or selected. To hide objects, choose Hide from the Object menu or use the Layers panel. Choose Show All On Spread from the Object menu to view all hidden objects

Transform Your Life!

Fuzzy caterpillars turn into moths. Clark Kent jumps into a phone booth and emerges as Superman. Werewolves stalk the moors under the full moon. Bewildered authors turn into parents. These transformations are all everyday, natural phenomena.

Make InDesign's transformation tools an integral part of how you work with the program, and you'll have their powerful, almost magical forces on your side.

Color

Color communicates, telling us things about the object bearing the color. Without color cues, we'd have a hard time guessing the ripeness of a fruit or distinguishing a poisonous mushroom from an edible one. And many animals would have a hard time figuring out when to mate, or with whom.

We associate colors with human emotions: we are green with envy; we've got the blues; we see red. Colors affect our emotions as well. Various studies suggest that we think best in a room of one color, and relax best in a room of another color.

What does all this mean? Color's important. A rule of thumb in advertising is that a color advertisement gets several times the response of a black-and-white ad. Designers of mail-order catalogs tell us that color is often cited as the reason for buying a product—and it's usually the reason a product is returned.

InDesign features a formidable array of features dedicated to creating, editing, applying, and printing colors. In addition, InDesign's color management can make what you see on your screen much closer to what you'll get when you print. Before we go any further, however, we have to talk about color printing.

Seeing Color, Printing Color

It's impossible to discuss the process of creating and using colors without first talking a little about printing and visual perception. The *visible spectrum* is the range of light wavelengths visible to the human eye. It's the job of our scanners, monitors, printers, and printing presses to reproduce the colors we see in the visible spectrum.

The range of color a device, color model, or printing method is capable of reproducing is referred to as its *color gamut*. There's no device, apart from your eye, that's capable of reproducing the range of light that your eye is capable of seeing. And even your eye isn't consistent from day to day.

Spot and Process Inks

Printing presses put ink on paper one ink at a time. Some presses have more than one printing cylinder and can print several colors of ink on a sheet of paper in one pass through the press, but each printing cylinder carries only one color of ink.

Spot-color printing is simple: your commercial printer uses inks that exactly match the color you want (or mixes inks to get the same result), then loads the press with that ink. In spot-color printing, we sometimes use "tint builds"—screens of inks printed on top of each other—to create a new color without using another ink. In process-color printing, tint builds are where it's at; we use overlapping screens of four inks (cyan, magenta, yellow, and black) to simulate part of the spectrum of visible color. If everything's gone well, the dots of the different inks are placed near each other in a pattern called a rosette.

Process-color printing can't simulate all the colors our eyes can see (notably very saturated colors, or metallic and fluorescent colors), but it can print color photographic images. Spot colors can print any color you can make with pigments, but aren't generally used to reproduce color photographic images (that's what process color printing was designed to be good at).

Color in InDesign

Now that you know all about color perception and color printing, it's time to get down to the process of specifying and applying colors in your InDesign publication.

Named and Unnamed Colors

InDesign has two basic methods for working with color: unnamed colors and color swatches. Both unnamed colors and color swatches can change the appearance of an object's fill or stroke, but swatches establish a relationship between the object and the named color swatch. Change the definition of the color swatch, and the color of all of the objects you've applied that swatch to will change as well.

Here's another way to look at it: unnamed colors are to color swatches as local text formatting is to a character style. You get the *appearance* you're looking for, but you don't get the link between the style (in this case, the color swatch) and the object.

Why do you need that link? Because people change their minds. The client's corporate color may have been Pantone 327 when you started the job, but it's now Pantone 199.

If you've used unnamed colors, there's nothing to do but claw your way through the objects in your publication, selecting and changing each affected object. If you've used named color swatches, just change the definition of the swatch, and the objects are updated.

Colors and Inks   It's worth noting that *colors* and *inks* are often two separate beasts. Sure, a spot color swatch corresponds directly to an ink you'll use to print the publication. However, most process color swatches are made up of some or all of the four process inks (cyan, magenta, yellow, and black).

When it comes time to print, the ink list (in the Output panel of the Print dialog box) displays the inks needed to print the colors you have defined in your publication. You'll always see the process inks (cyan, magenta, yellow, and black) in the ink list, whether you've defined process colors or not. If you've defined spot colors, you'll see the spot inks associated with those colors in the ink list. If you want, you can simulate your spot colors with process inks using the Ink Manager (we cover the Ink Manager later in this chapter).

Color Models   InDesign lets you define colors using any of three color models—CMYK, RGB, and LAB. Which color model should you use? That depends on how you plan to produce your publication.

Process colors. If you're working with process colors, *specify your color using the CMYK color model or a CMYK color-matching system*, or be ready for some surprises when your publication gets printed. It's always best to look at a printed sample of the process color (like those in the Trumatch or Pantone Process swatch books) and enter the values given in the sample book for the color. In other words, trust what you see on paper, not what you see on your screen.

Spot colors. You can define a spot color using any color space: RGB, LAB, CMYK, or a swatch book like a Pantone color. It really doesn't matter what the color looks like on the screen, as long as you let your output provider know what color of ink they should use. That said, if you're going to use a spot color, it's usually best to choose colors from swatch libraries (such as the Pantone libraries), which we cover later in this chapter.

Onscreen colors. If you're creating a publication for on-screen distribution (such as a SWF or interactive PDF), use the RGB color model.

Tints. If you're trying to create a tint of an existing color (process or spot). You can base your tint on a spot color or a process color, but you can't base tints on another tint. You can mix tints of spot colors with a mixed ink swatch, which we discuss later in this chapter.

Color Conversion Errors. When you convert a color from one color model to another—from RGB to CMYK, for example—a certain amount of error is introduced by the process of conversion. This is largely because the color models don't cover the same color gamut, and there is often more than one way to represent the same color in a different color space. Each time you convert the color, the rounding error is compounded: if you convert 100C 10M 50Y 0K to RGB, you'll get 0R 230G 128B—converting that RGB color back to CMYK will yield a color defined as 90C 0M 40Y 10K. Just remember: There's no "round trip" in color model conversion.

InDesign's Color Controls

InDesign's controls for working with color are found in several panels and menus. The most important panels are the Toolbox, because it contains the Fill selector and the Stroke selector, and the Swatches panel, because it contains tools for defining, editing, and applying swatches (which can be colors, gradients, or tints) to objects. The Swatches panel is also duplicated in the Control panel, where you can quickly apply a stroke or fill.

You can also use the Color panel and the Gradient panel to create and apply unnamed colors and gradients—but, as we've noted earlier, you'll be better off if you use named color swatches. If you apply a color to an object using the Color panel, there is no swatch associated with it—it's an *unnamed color*. Unnamed colors are a nightmare for output providers and co-workers because it's hard for them to figure out what colors you used if they need to troubleshoot your file. They can also be a nightmare for you if you ever need to go back to change a color. Given that everything you can do using the Color panel can be accomplished using the Swatches panel, we recommend just leaving the Color panel closed.

Fill and Stroke Selectors

At the bottom of the Tool panel and in the upper-left corner of the Swatches panel and the Color panel, you'll see the Fill selector and the Stroke selector. These aren't labeled in any way (unless you count the tool help we always turn off), but the Fill selector is the filled square on the left (here's proof that InDesign's user interface, while easy to use, is hard to write about). When you want to work with an object's fill, click the Fill selector; to work with an object's stroke, press the Stroke selector (the outlined square). InDesign shows you which selector is active by bringing it to the front.

Honestly, we rarely actually click on those squares; rather, we use these favorite shortcuts for working with the Fill and Stroke selectors.

Stroke selector active

Fill selector active

Fill text selector active

▶ Press X (this is another of those keyboard shortcuts that doesn't work when you're editing text) to toggle between the Fill selector and the Stroke selector.

▶ Press Shift-X to swap fill and stroke colors (this is the same as clicking the double-headed arrow Swap Fill and Stroke icon).

▶ Press D to apply the default fill and stroke colors to the selected object (black stroke and a "None" fill).

▶ To apply the currently selected swatch to an object's stroke or fill, click the Apply Color button (or click the swatch itself, or press comma). To remove a fill or stroke from the selected object, click the appropriate selector and then click the Apply None button (or click the None swatch in the Swatches panel, or press /). To apply the last-used gradient, click the Apply Gradient button at the bottom of the Tool panel (or press period).

Swatches Panel

The Swatches panel is InDesign's "color control center"—it's where you create, edit, and apply colors, tints, and gradients. The Swatches panel often displays a bewildering array of icons and symbols. What does it all mean? To find out, take a look at Figure 10-1.

Press Command-Option/Ctrl-Alt and click inside the Swatches panel to activate the list. Once you've done this, you can select a color by typing its name, or move up and down in the list of swatches using the arrow keys. (But note that this will change the color of any selected objects on any page. We prefer to press Command-Shift-A/Ctrl-Shift-A to deselect all objects before messing with swatches.)

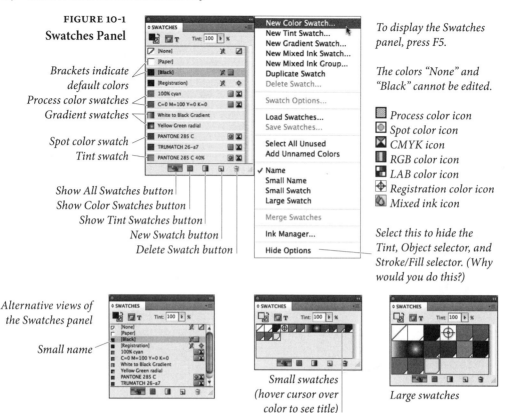

FIGURE 10-1
Swatches Panel

Brackets indicate default colors
Process color swatches
Gradient swatches
Spot color swatch
Tint swatch

Show All Swatches button
Show Color Swatches button
Show Tint Swatches button
New Swatch button
Delete Swatch button

To display the Swatches panel, press F5.

The colors "None" and "Black" cannot be edited.

Process color icon
Spot color icon
CMYK icon
RGB color icon
LAB color icon
Registration color icon
Mixed ink icon

Select this to hide the Tint, Object selector, and Stroke/Fill selector. (Why would you do this?)

Alternative views of the Swatches panel

Small name

Small swatches (hover cursor over color to see title)

Large swatches

Creating a color swatch. To create a color swatch, follow these steps (see Figure 10-2).

1. Choose New Color Swatch from the Swatches panel menu. InDesign displays the New Color Swatch dialog box, set to duplicate whatever the currently selected color is. As long as None or Paper is not selected in the Swatches panel, you can also open this dialog box by Option/Alt-clicking on the New Swatch button at the bottom of the panel.

2. Enter a name for the new color swatch (it's optional—InDesign will have filled in the Name field with a default name).

3. Define the color using the controls in the New Color Swatch dialog box.

4. Click the OK button or press Return/Enter to close the dialog box. InDesign adds the new color swatch to the list of swatches shown in the Swatches panel. Alternatively, you can click the Add button to add the swatch to the list and immediately start working on a new swatch (without closing the dialog box first).

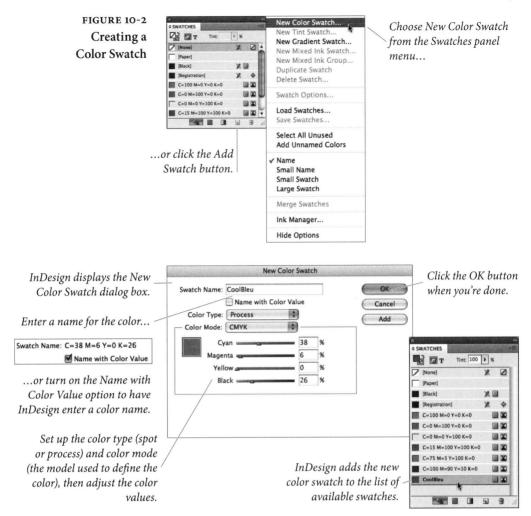

FIGURE 10-2

Creating a Color Swatch

Choose New Color Swatch from the Swatches panel menu...

...or click the Add Swatch button.

InDesign displays the New Color Swatch dialog box.

Enter a name for the color...

...or turn on the Name with Color Value option to have InDesign enter a color name.

Set up the color type (spot or process) and color mode (the model used to define the color), then adjust the color values.

Click the OK button when you're done.

InDesign adds the new color swatch to the list of available swatches.

Adding Unnamed Colors. As we said earlier, if you've used the Color panel to apply a color to an object, that color will not appear in the Swatches panel; it's an unnamed color. Fortunately, there are two ways to add unnamed colors to your Swatches panel. First, you can add unnamed colors by selecting the object colored with the unnamed color, then clicking the New Swatch button (or choose New Color Swatch from the Swatches panel menu, then click OK). InDesign adds the color applied to the object to the list of colors in the Swatches panel.

If you've created more than one unnamed color, or you're working with a document in which someone else applied unnamed colors, you can add all these colors to the Swatches panel at once by selecting Add Unnamed Colors from the panel's menu.

Adding Colors from a Swatch Library. Most of the time, we think you should add colors from swatch libraries. Why? Because your commercial printer wants you to (when they talk in their sleep, they call out Pantone numbers and common process tint builds), and because it's the quickest way to add a named color. To choose a color from a color library, follow the steps for adding a color, above, but choose a swatch library from the Color Mode menu in the New Color Swatch dialog box (see Figure 10-3). This differs from Adobe Illustrator, which forces you to open special swatch library panels.

In some cases, you can also change the Color Mode after selecting a color swatch. For example, if you need to simulate a Pantone spot color using process colors, first specify the Pantone color, then change the Color Mode pop-up menu to CMYK and the Color Type pop-up menu to Process. The CMYK values you get depend on the current status of the Use Standard Lab Values for Spots checkbox in the Ink Manager (see "Ink Manager," later in this chapter). Of course, some Pantone colors don't convert to process colors particularly well because you can't make any given hue just using process colors.

Adding Swatches from Another InDesign Publication. To add swatches stored in a different document, choose Other Library from the Color Mode menu in the New Color Swatch dialog box. InDesign displays the Open a File dialog box. Locate and select a document, then click the Open button. InDesign displays the swatches defined in that document, and you can add them to the current publication just as you'd add swatches from any swatch library.

FIGURE 10-3
Working with Swatch Libraries

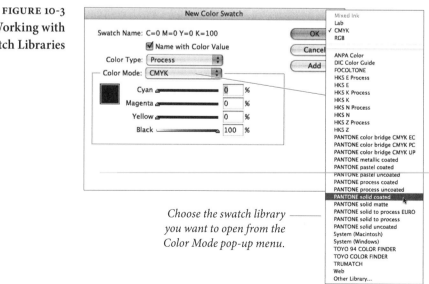

Choose the swatch library you want to open from the Color Mode pop-up menu.

You can also import color swatches from other InDesign files by choosing Load Swatches from the Swatches panel menu. Or, to save individual swatches for use in other documents or Creative Suite applications, select them in the Swatches panel and choose Save Swatches for Exchange from the panel menu. This creates an .ase file which you can load with Load Swatches.

Out of gamut warning

Out of Gamut Warning. InDesign constantly monitors the values of the colors you create, and when a color swatch definition falls outside the gamut defined by the default CMYK document profile, InDesign displays an alert icon next to the color sliders in the New Color Swatch or Swatch Options dialog box. To adjust the color definition so that it falls in the gamut of the separations profile, click the alert icon. We discuss document profiles in detail when we explore color management later in this chapter. If you choose colors from swatch libraries or using the CMYK mode, you won't see this alert.

Creating a Tint Swatch

To create a new tint swatch, follow these steps (see Figure 10-4).

1. Select a color swatch in the Swatches panel. If you select a tint swatch, the new tint will be based on the same color as the existing tint swatch—you can't create a tint based on a tint.

2. Choose New Tint Swatch from the Swatches panel menu. InDesign displays the New Tint Swatch dialog box.

3. Enter a new value in the Tint field or drag the slider.

4. Click the OK button or press Enter to close the dialog box and add the tint to the list of swatches in the Swatches panel.

If you remove a color (see "Deleting a Swatch," later in this chapter), all tint swatches based on that color will change to tints of the color you choose in the Delete Color dialog box. If, as you remove a color, you choose to convert the color to the default colors "None" or "Paper," InDesign removes all of the tints based on that color from the Swatches panel. This is also what happens when you remove a color swatch and choose Unnamed Swatch as the Delete Color option.

Creating a Gradient Swatch

To create a gradient swatch, follow these steps (see Figure 10-5).

1. Choose New Gradient Swatch from the Swatches panel menu. InDesign displays the New Gradient Swatch dialog box.

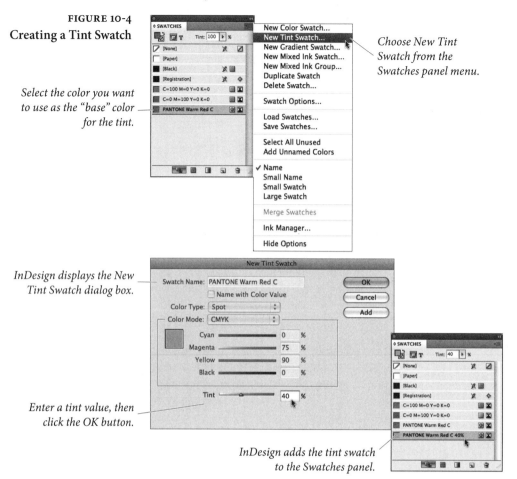

FIGURE 10-4
Creating a Tint Swatch

Select the color you want to use as the "base" color for the tint.

Choose New Tint Swatch from the Swatches panel menu.

InDesign displays the New Tint Swatch dialog box.

Enter a tint value, then click the OK button.

InDesign adds the tint swatch to the Swatches panel.

2. Enter a name for the gradient (the default name of "New Gradient Swatch" isn't particularly useful). Edit the gradient's ramp and color attributes using any or all of the following techniques.

   ► Click on one of the gradient stops to edit it. Or, to add a new gradient stop, click below the gradient ramp.

   ► To change the color of a gradient stop, select the stop, then adjust the color definition using the controls above the gradient ramp. Note that you can dial in a color or pick Swatches from the Stop Color pop-up menu (to choose a color you're already saved as a swatch). You can even pick the Paper swatch as a gradient stop color.

   ► To change the position of a gradient stop, drag it along the ramp.

FIGURE 10-5
**Creating a
Gradient Swatch**

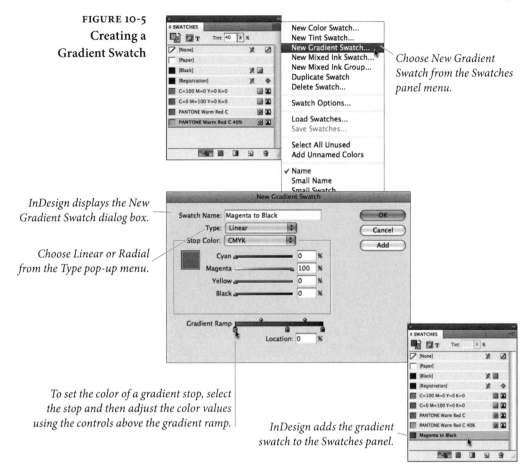

*Choose New Gradient
Swatch from the Swatches
panel menu.*

*InDesign displays the New
Gradient Swatch dialog box.*

*Choose Linear or Radial
from the Type pop-up menu.*

*To set the color of a gradient stop, select
the stop and then adjust the color values
using the controls above the gradient ramp.*

*InDesign adds the gradient
swatch to the Swatches panel.*

▸ To delete a gradient stop, drag it away from the ramp.

▸ To change the midpoint location between any two gradient
stops, drag the midpoint icon along the top of the ramp.

3. Once the gradient looks the way you want it to, click the OK
button to add the gradient swatch to the Swatches panel. You
can then apply this gradient to any object (or even text) as easily
as applying a color swatch.

You can also build a gradient swatch directly within the Gradient
panel by dragging swatches from the Color or Swatches panel on top
of the gradient bar (or on top of gradient stops). When you're done
with designing the blend, drag the preview swatch from the Gradient
panel into the Swatches panel.

Also, once you've created a gradient swatch and applied it to an
object on your page, you can fine-tune that object's gradient using
the Gradient panel—reversing the order of the blend, dragging the

gradient stops, and so on. Most importantly, the Gradient panel is where you can adjust a blend's angle. (Unfortunately, gradient angle can't be built in to a gradient swatch; you have to change that manually for each object or use an object style.)

Note that you cannot assign transparency (opacity) to a gradient stop, as you can in Illustrator. Instead, you must use the Gradient Feather effect. We hope this changes in the next version.

Mixed Ink Swatches   If you can overlay two tints of process colors to create a third color, it stands to reason that you can do the same thing with spot colors. InDesign's Mixed Ink Swatch feature helps considerably, because it lets you build a single color based on varying percentages of other colors in your Swatches panel. However, there are some issues you need to think about when mixing spot colors (also called "tint builds" or "multi-ink colors").

▸ Most spot colors are made with inks that have a different consistency than process-color inks; the more opaque the inks, the harder it is to mix varying tints of them on a page.

▸ Some inks don't tint well; for instance, metallic and fluorescent inks lose much of their special appearance unless you use a very coarse halftone.

▸ There's only one spot-color swatch book that shows what happens when you mix colors together (the Pantone Two-Color Selector), and while it's extensive, it certainly doesn't show every combination of every spot color on the market. Therefore, there's often a lot more guessing involved when you mix spot colors.

Discuss multi-ink colors with your printer before jumping in and using them. Ask them if it'll be okay to mix two particular colors on press. Perhaps they'll make a "draw-down" for you so you can see how the colors will look when they're mixed together (though this only shows you what the colors will look like when they're overprinted at 100 percent).

Making a Mixed Ink Swatch. It was painful to mix spot colors in the old days because you had to duplicate objects, apply a different color and tint to each one, and then make sure one properly overprinted the other. Now, mixing colors is as easy as one, two, three.

1. Choose New Mixed Ink Swatch from the Swatches panel menu.

2. Click in the checkbox to the left of a swatch color, then type in the percentage in the field on the right or use the color slider (see

Figure 10-6). Repeat this for each color you want included in the swatch.

3. Click OK to finish, or click Add to add this swatch and start making a new one right away.

You can even mix process colors with spot colors in this dialog box. For example, you might want to create darker shades of a spot color by mixing it with a tint of black ink.

When you print color separations, each color appears on its proper plate, just as you'd expect. However, each color in a mixed ink swatch needs a correct halftone angle, or else you'll get dot-doubling (halftone spots that overprint each other, creating muddy colors) or moiré patterns when your pages come off press. We discuss halftone angles in Chapter 11, "Printing."

FIGURE 10-6
Making a Mixed Ink Swatch

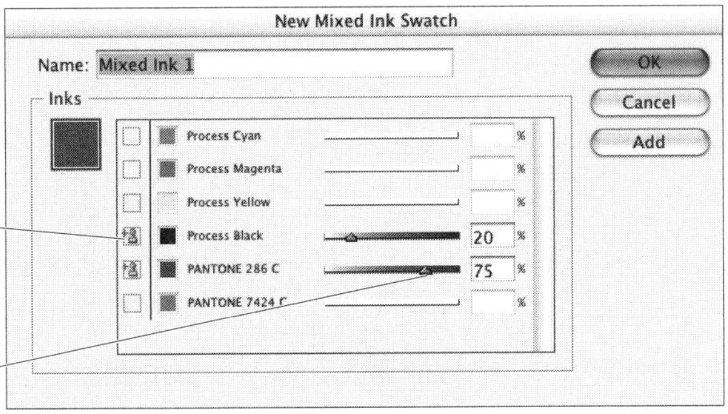

Click in this column to add an ink to the mix

Drag the sliders or enter percentages to specify the contribution of each ink to the mix

Mixed Ink Groups. Once you've got the hang of mixed ink swatches, you're going to want to use them all the time because they make two- and three-color jobs look much more interesting. However, it's a pain in the *tuchus* to make a bunch of similar mixed ink swatches. That's where mixed ink groups comes in handy. InDesign can mix two or more colors together in varying percentages for you. Unfortunately, the user interface is confusing at best. Here's how you do it.

1. Select New Mixed Ink Group from the Swatches panel menu.

2. Give the group a name (preferably something descriptive).

3. Choose which inks you want in the group by clicking in the checkbox in the left column. You must pick at least two colors, of which one must be a spot color (see Figure 10-7).

4. For each ink, pick an initial tint. For example, let's say you're trying to make darker tints of your Pantone color by adding

black. The initial value for the Pantone would be 100 percent and the initial tint for black could be 10 percent.

5. The Repeat value tells InDesign how many separate ink swatches it should build. Choosing a Repeat of 4 results in five inks: the initial swatch plus four more. Set Repeat to 0 (zero) to keep the color at the initial tint throughout the group.

6. If the Repeat value is anything other than zero, you can set how much each repeat increases in the Increment field. For instance, you might want an ink to increment by 15 percent, to get swatches of 15 percent, 30 percent, 45 percent, and 60 percent.

7. Click the Preview Swatches button to see a list of all the swatches InDesign will build when you click OK. This "preview" is pretty silly, as it just shows you a bunch of little color swatches, but at least it helps you see if you made some obvious mistake (like setting Repeat to 50 instead of 5).

8. Click OK when you're satisfied.

When you build a mixed ink swatch group, InDesign adds all the new swatches to the Swatches panel, plus a "group" swatch. You can't apply this group swatch to an object; it's just there so that you

FIGURE 10-7
Making a Mixed Ink Group

Clicking in this column turns inks on or off.

Enter the initial, repeat, and increment values for each ink.

Pay attention to this number—it's easy to end up with too many swatches.

InDesign assigns spectacularly unhelpful names to each swatch.

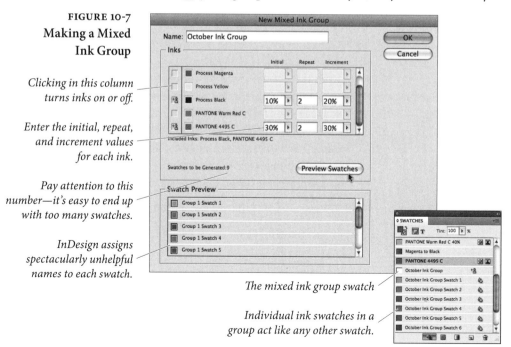

The mixed ink group swatch

Individual ink swatches in a group act like any other swatch.

can later go back and edit the group. Note that InDesign names each swatch in the group with a number (like Swatch 1, Swatch 2, and so on) rather than anything that would actually be helpful in identifying what the color is. If this annoys you as much as it annoys us, please email someone at Adobe and complain.

Editing Groups. You can edit a mixed ink group at any time by double-clicking on the group swatch in the Swatches panel (or, more slowly, clicking on it and choosing Swatch Options from the panel menu; see Figure 10-8). The Swatch Options dialog box lets you rename the group, remove inks from the group (by clicking in the left column next to the ink's name), swap one ink for another (by clicking on the ink name and picking from the pop-up menu), or convert the swatches to process color. We can't recommend converting spot colors to process colors in this way; the results may not match your expectations. And deleting colors from the list is problematic, too, because InDesign won't actually remove redundant swatches (so you usually get a bunch of swatches that are exactly the same).

You might want to swap one ink for another if, for instance, you have a monthly newsletter that uses a different Pantone color each month. If you used the mixed ink group swatches throughout your document, you'd simply need to change the ink in the group and the whole file's colors would change in one fell swoop.

Process Color Groups. Earlier, we noted that you must have one spot color in your mixed ink group. Fortunately, there's always a workaround. Let's say you just want various process-color green swatches. You could make a mixed ink group with cyan, yellow, and a spot color—but leave both the Initial and Repeat fields for the spot color set to 0 (zero). Then, after clicking OK, you could double-click on the group swatch and delete the spot color. This converts all the swatches to normal process-color color swatches. (But there's no way to make this a group again, other than the normal Undo feature.)

FIGURE 10-8
**Mixed Ink
Group Options**

*Click in this column to
turn an ink on or off.*

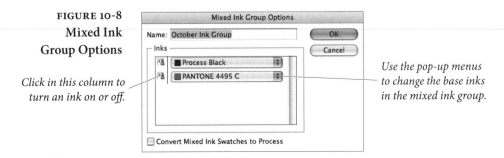

*Use the pop-up menus
to change the base inks
in the mixed ink group.*

Managing Swatches

Once you've built up an armory of color, tint, gradient, and mixed ink swatches, you need to know how best to manage them.

Changing the order of the swatches in the Swatches panel. You can change the order in which colors appear in the Swatches panel by dragging them up or down in the panel. This can be handy when you've got a long list of colors and want to position frequently used colors near the top of the panel. (Be careful to deselect all objects before playing in this panel or you may apply colors accidentally.)

Editing a Swatch. To edit a swatch, do one of the following:

▸ Double-click the swatch in the Swatches panel. (We don't use this shortcut because the first click applies the swatch to the fill or stroke of any object we've selected, or applies the swatch to the default fill or stroke if no object is selected.)

▸ Select a swatch in the Swatches panel, then choose Swatch Options from the Swatches panel menu. Again, this method applies the swatch to the selection or to the document defaults, so we tend to avoid it.

▸ Right-click (or Control-click with a one-button mouse) on a swatch and choose Swatch Options to open the swatch for editing. We always use this method, as it does not apply the swatch to the selection or to the document default fill or stroke.

After any of the above actions, InDesign displays the dialog box appropriate to the type of swatch you clicked (the Edit Color Swatch, Edit Tint Swatch, or Edit Gradient Swatch dialog box). Make changes to the swatch definition, then click the OK button to close the dialog box. InDesign updates the appearance of all the objects formatted using the swatch.

Note that if you're looking for a different shade of the same basic CMYK color, you can hold down the Shift key while dragging one of the sliders. This moves the other sliders at the same time to achieve a lighter version of the same hue.

Deleting a Swatch. To delete a swatch from a publication, follow these steps (see Figure 10-9).

1. Select the swatch in the Swatches panel (you may want to deselect all objects on the page first). To select a range of swatches, hold down Shift as you click the swatch names. To select noncontiguous swatches, hold down Command/Ctrl as

FIGURE 10-9

Deleting a Swatch

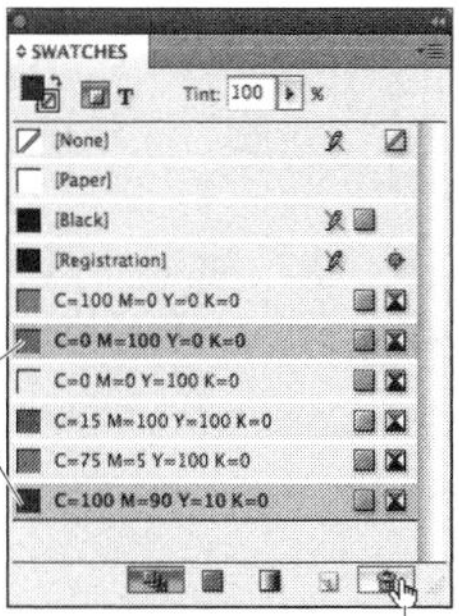

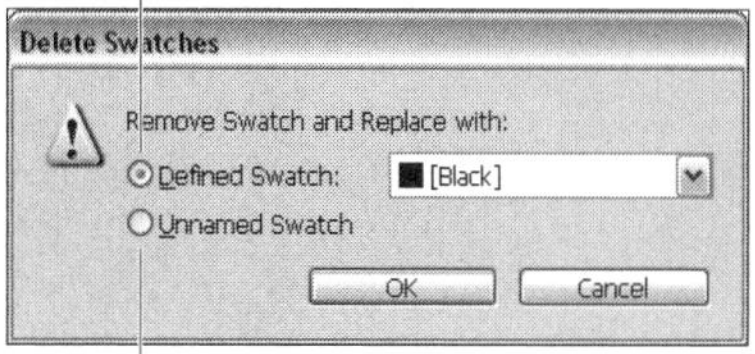

Select the swatch
(or swatches) you
want to delete.

Choose Delete Swatch from the
Swatches panel menu or click
the Delete Swatch button.

*To apply an existing swatch
to the objects colored with the
swatch you're removing, turn
on the Defined Swatch option
and choose a swatch from the
pop-up menu...*

*...or choose Unnamed Swatch
to have InDesign apply an
unnamed swatch of the same
color to the objects.*

you click the swatch names. If you want to select all the swatches that appear in the panel but aren't used anywhere in your document, choose Select All Unused from the panel menu.

2. Click the Delete Swatch button in the Swatches panel (or choose Delete Color Swatch from the panel's menu). InDesign displays the Delete Swatch dialog box.

3. If you want to replace the color you're deleting with an existing swatch, turn on the Defined Swatch option and choose the name of the swatch from the attached pop-up menu. To replace the swatch with an unnamed color (why would you want to do this?), turn on the Unnamed Swatch option.

4. Click the OK button. InDesign deletes the swatch and applies the replacement swatch (if you selected the Defined Swatch option) or an unnamed color (if you selected the Unnamed Swatch option) to all of the objects formatted using the swatch you're deleting.

As we noted earlier, when you remove a swatch that you've used as a basis for tint swatches, InDesign bases the tint swatches on the color you specified (if you selected the Defined Swatch option), or just deletes the tint swatch if you choose Unnamed Swatch, Paper, or None.

Merging Swatches. The folks at Adobe threw a rather confusing little feature into InDesign called Merge Swatches. The idea is simple: Take two or more swatches in the Swatches panel, merge them together into a single swatch, and delete the others. The problem is few people ever figure out how it works.

The key is that the *first* swatch you select will be the one that survives, the one that the other swatches will get merged into. After clicking on one swatch (make sure nothing is selected first, or else this click will apply the color to the selected object), then Command/Ctrl-click on one or more other swatches in the panel. Finally, select Merge Swatches from the Swatches panel menu. We find this helpful only when you've got a lot of swatches you want to merge together; for one or two, we usually just use Delete Swatch.

Duplicating Swatches. If you want to base a swatch on an existing swatch, select the swatch in the Swatches panel and then choose Duplicate Swatch from the panel's menu. (You can also click the New Swatch button in the Swatches panel, but that also applies the duplicate to any selected objects.) InDesign creates a copy of the swatch and assigns it a name (the default name is the name of the original swatch plus the word "copy"). Now, you can edit the swatch by right-clicking (or Control-clicking with a one-button mouse) on it.

The Color Panel and the Color Picker

Given that we've already stated that you should use the Swatches panel instead of the Color panel, you might wonder why we're bothering to write this section. Over the years, we've come to realize that our methods are not necessarily for everyone, and that some people have very different working habits from our own. For some of you, working with the Color panel and unnamed colors might be better than the process of creating named swatches—and there's nothing wrong with that.

The Color panel is always *on*—whenever you adjust the controls in the panel, you're applying them to something (either the selected object or the document's default fill and stroke formatting). For a look at the Color panel, see Figure 10-10.

The Color panel does have one thing that the Swatches panel's methods for defining colors lack: the color bar. To apply a color, drag the cursor in the Color Bar.

Color Panel Shortcuts

The Color panel has shortcuts, too.

▶   To display (or hide) the Color panel, press F6.

FIGURE 10-10
The Color Panel

Fill and stroke selectors

Click this area to apply "none."

Enter color values using the fields and sliders...

After you apply a color, a swatch appears in this area. Click it to apply the color last applied.

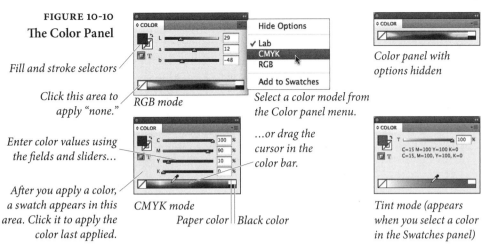

RGB mode

Select a color model from the Color panel menu.

...or drag the cursor in the color bar.

CMYK mode

Paper color | *Black color*

Color panel with options hidden

Tint mode (appears when you select a color in the Swatches panel)

▸ To change the color mode of the panel, select RGB, LAB, or CMYK from the panel menu or Context menu (right-click or Control-click). Even faster, just Shift-click on the color bar to rotate through these options. If you're using a named swatch, Shift-clicking will also offer you a tint bar of the current color.

▸ When you enter a value (or a mathematical expression) in one of the color value fields, you can hold down Command/Ctrl as you press Return/Enter to apply the same percentage change to all of the color value fields.

▸ To select a color that is similar in hue, but different in shade, hold down Shift as you drag a color value slider. This moves the other sliders in tandem (unless you're dragging the Black slider, or one of the other sliders is set to zero).

Out-of-Gamut Warning. The out-of-gamut warning also appears in the Color panel, too, when a color swatch definition falls outside the gamut defined by the default CMYK document profile. To adjust the color definition so that it falls in the gamut of the separations profile, click the alert icon. (See "Color Management," later in this chapter.) Note that as long as you are choosing colors in the CMYK mode, you won't see this alert (because they're all in gamut, by default). Also, note that you won't see this icon when you've chosen Hide Options from the panel menu.

The Color Picker

You can also choose an unnamed color or create a color swatch with the Color Picker dialog box (double-click on the fill or stroke icons at the bottom of the Tool panel). The Color Picker is a sad and pathetic attempt at providing a Photoshop-like feature in a page-layout program. We don't use it. However, if you are going to use it, there is one thing you need to know: The kind of swatch you get depends on where the text cursor is flashing in the dialog box. If you want a CMYK swatch, click in one of the CMYK number fields first.

Applying Colors and Gradients

Once you've selected an object, you can use the following techniques to apply a color, tint, or gradient to the object (see Figure 10-11).

▶ Click one of the selectors (Fill or Stroke) at the bottom of the Toolbox or in the Swatches panel, then click a color in the Swatches panel.

▶ Select an object, then choose a color from the Fill or Stroke pop-up menu in the Control panel.

▶ Click the Fill selector or the Stroke selector, then click the Apply Color button, Apply Gradient button, Apply None button, swap fill and stroke icon, or the default fill and stroke icon. Or press any of the keyboard shortcuts corresponding to the buttons (comma, period, slash, Shift-X, or D, respectively).

▶ Select an object, then adjust any of the controls in the Color panel or open the Color Picker and choose from there.

▶ Drag a color swatch out of the Swatches panel and drop it on the fill or stroke of an object.

▶ Use the Eyedropper tool to pick a color from an existing object, then click on another object to apply that color to it.

Applying Colors to Text

You can apply a fill or stroke to the characters of text in your publication. Characters of text act just like individual objects on your page, so to apply a color to text, select it with the Text tool, and apply a color using any of the techniques described above. Note that this means you can apply any color swatch, including gradients or None, to text. If you select the text block with the Selection tool, you can apply a color to all the text in the frame by first clicking the Formatting Affects Text button in the Tool, Swatches, or Color panel.

Applying Colors to Imported Graphics

You can apply colors to bi-level (black and white only) TIFFs, and grayscale TIFFs (or native Photoshop .PSD files). To apply a color to

FIGURE 10-11

Applying a Color

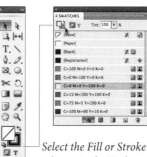

Press X to switch between the Fill selector and the Stroke selector.

These three buttons apply last-used color swatch, gradient swatch, or None.

Click the Formatting Affects Text button (it looks like a little "T") to apply a color to the text inside a frame rather than the frame itself.

Select the Fill or Stroke selector in the Tools panel or the Swatches panel (F5).

Click a color swatch in the Swatches panel.

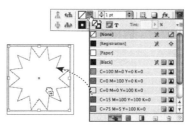

Choose a color from the Stroke or Fill widgets in the Control panel, or...

...drag a color swatch onto the object. Note that you do not need to select an object to apply a color via this method.

Press F6 to display the Color panel.

Click the cursor in the color bar, or adjust one of the color controls in the Color panel, and InDesign applies the color to the selected object.

an imported image, select the image using the Direct Selection tool, click the Fill selector in the Toolbox, and then click a color swatch. When you print, InDesign prints the image on the appropriate separation (for a spot color) or series of plates (for a process color).

Kuler

The *kuler.adobe.com* Web site is a great way to create sets of colors based on a base color, share those color sets with others, or download other people's sets. Now, the kuler technology has shown up inside InDesign in the guise of the Kuler panel, which you can find by choosing Window > Extensions > Kuler.

The coolest thing about the Kuler panel is that it's actually written in Flash—that is, the panel is actually a SWF running inside a player built into the program, and it retrieves data over the internet in real time. The least cool thing about Kuler is that it still only lets you create and manipulate RGB colors, so it's pretty much only useful when making interactive documents (such as SWF or PDFs that will be viewed on-screen). We hope that Adobe will update this feature before too long to be color managed and allow CMYK colors, but we're not holding our breath.

(To be precise, the Kuler panel *can* download color sets based on CMYK from the kuler web site—for example, if someone created a set of colors using CMYK using Illustrator and uploaded that set. But creating or editing colors using the panel always results in RGB.)

To find a set of colors that someone uploaded, click the panel's Browse tab (see Figure 10-12). Type a name in the search field, or choose a search type from the pop-up menu (for example, Highest Rated or Most Popular.) You can add the color set to the Swatches panel by clicking the Add Selected Theme to Swatches button.

To create your own color sets, or edit sets you have selected in the Browse tab, click the Create tab. To change the colors, drag the color circles, adjust the sliders, or choose a rule from the Select Rule pop-up menu. If you want to create a color theme around a color from your document, set it as the current fill or stroke color, then click the Add Current Fill (or Stroke) Color as Current Base Color button, just above the RGB color sliders.

FIGURE 10-12
The Kuler Panel

These themes (color sets) are loaded dynamically from the kuler Web site

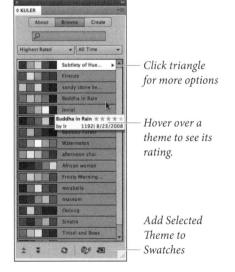
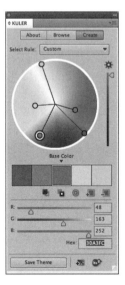

Click triangle for more options

Hover over a theme to see its rating.

Add Selected Theme to Swatches

Ink Manager

One of the most common complaints among prepress service providers is that too many publishers don't understand the difference between spot and process color inks, and they're forever creating spot color inks that need to be converted to process color at print time. If you're one of those service providers, you're going to love the Ink Manager. And if you're a designer, the Ink Manager still offers a couple of features that you'll find really helpful. The Ink Manager does three things.

▸ You can tell the Ink Manager to convert spot colors to process colors at the time of output (but it won't change the actual color swatch definitions in your document). It also gives you some control over how the colors will be converted.

▸ You can alias one spot color to another, so two (or more) different spot colors will output onto the same plate.

▸ You can tell InDesign how your inks act so that the program can trap them properly.

We'll discuss converting and aliasing spot colors here, and hold off on the trapping features until later in this chapter.

The Ink Manager appears in four different places: the Output panel of the Print dialog box, the Swatches panel menu, the Advanced panel of the Export PDF dialog box, and the Advanced panel of the Export EPS dialog box. A change made in any one of these places affects the Ink Manager in all its locations.

Converting Spot Colors

The Ink Manager dialog box lists the four process colors, plus every spot color in your document, whether or not they're actually used (see Figure 10-13). When you click in the column to the left of a spot color, the color changes to a process color (the little four-color icon appears). Click again, and it's a spot color again. As we said earlier, this does not change the color's definition; the color only changes at print or export time.

If you want to output all the spot colors in the document as process colors, turn on the All Spots to Process checkbox at the bottom of the Ink Manager dialog box.

You can control how your spot colors appear on screen (in RGB) and in print (when simulated with CMYK). By default, InDesign uses old CMYK tables built-in to the libraries. But you can get newer, more accurate simulations by turning on the Use Standard Lab

FIGURE 10-13
Ink Manager

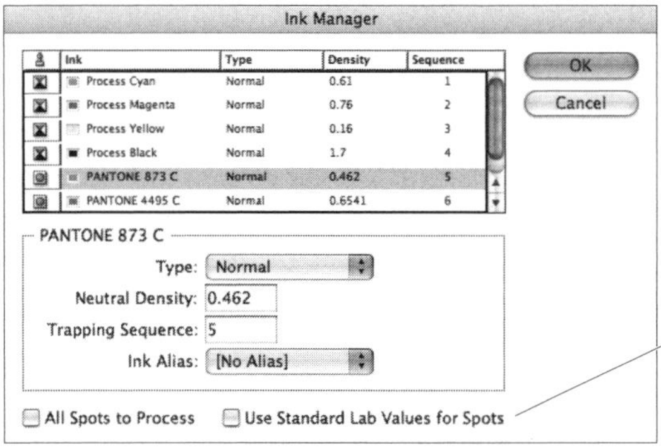

While the Lab values are more accurate, turn this off to match colors in older files.

Values for Spots checkbox. It's disabled by default to maintain consistency with legacy documents; but if you care more for quality than legacy, then turn it on and leave it on!

Aliasing Spot Colors

Let's say you create a document with two spot colors, but later find that you can only afford to print black and one spot color. You could replace one spot color with the other throughout your document by deleting one of them (see "Deleting a Swatch," earlier in this chapter). However, it's easier and more flexible to merge the two spot colors together at print time by *aliasing* one to the other.

To make an alias, select a spot color in the Ink Manager dialog box and choose a different color from the Ink Alias pop-up menu. Notice that the icon changes to the left of the color's icon (the icon, almost impossible to see without a loupe, is of an arrow pointing to a little ink well). You can still convert this color to a process color later if you want, using the techniques described above.

One of the coolest aspects of aliasing colors is that it works not only for spot colors applied to InDesign objects, but even to spot colors embedded in EPS or PDF graphics. Note that you can preview the spot color aliasing in your document by turning on both Overprint Preview and High Quality Display in the View menu.

Trapping

A "trap" is a method of overlapping abutting colored objects to compensate for the imperfect registration of printing presses. Because registration, even on good presses with good operators, can be off by a quarter point or more, abutting elements in your publication may not end up abutting perfectly when the publication is printed by your commercial printer. What happens then? The paper shows through where you don't want it to.

Do we need to tell you what happens when you take your work to a press that's badly out of register or run by turkeys? Disaster. Before this happens to you, talk with your commercial printer regarding the tolerances of their presses and/or operators. Don't ask them if they're turkeys—it's considered rude.

In the "good ol' days" printers handled all your trapping for you. Then came the "bad ol' days" when designers had to do most of it themselves. The basic method of creating manual traps involves adding additional strokes to objects and then setting those strokes to overprint using the Attributes panel.

But in the past few years, output providers have taken to doing it all "in-RIP"—this is far, far better than you trying to do it yourself. And, in many cases (especially with digital printing) no trapping may be required anyway. So check with your printer first.

If you find you do need to do some manual trapping, please download this file for more information: *http://www.indesignsecrets.com/rwid/trapping.pdf*

Color Management

When you aim at a target—and it doesn't matter whether you're aiming a rifle, a bow, a laser, or a camera—you have to make adjustments. You've got to consider the atmospheric conditions, the distance to the target, the characteristics of the target itself. Once you know what the variables are, and how they affect what you're trying to do, you've got a better chance of hitting the bullseye.

The same thing is true in color management. You need to understand the tools you have to work with, how they work together (or don't), and how they combine to produce the colors you see in the printed version of your publication.

It would be nice if we could make what we see on our screen exactly match what we'll get when we print. But we can't, for a variety of practical and physiological reasons (not to mention simple lack of time and money). That said, we must also add that we can get very close—and we can also make the relationship between the display and the printed piece more consistent and predictable.

The "device" (a printer, scanner, monitor, or printing press) is the key. Every device renders colors in a slightly different way. To adjust color in one environment so that it matches the color as seen in another environment, color management systems refer to a file containing information on the color characteristics of a device (how it displays or prints color). This file is called a "device profile."

Device profiles for scanners and printers are usually created by the manufacturers who make the hardware, though quite a few come with InDesign. You've got to make monitor profiles yourself, because every monitor is different (just as several television sets from the same manufacturer can show the same image differently). The process of creating a device profile is called "characterizing" a device.

Once a device profile has been created for a device, you've got to maintain (or "calibrate") the device so that it doesn't vary from the profile. Imagesetter operators and commercial printers calibrate their equipment regularly (or should) to match industry standards.

InDesign's color management system uses device profiles compatible with the International Color Consortium (ICC) specification. If you're on the Macintosh, you can also use device profiles provided by Apple with the system-level ColorSync color management system (these profiles are also ICC compatible).

For more on choosing device profiles, see "InDesign's Color Management Controls," later in this chapter.

For More Information

Color management is an enormous subject and we can only focus on one aspect of the big picture here: How color management works in InDesign. If any terminology in this section is confusing to you (like gamut, ICC profile, color engines, and rendering intents), we encourage you to go look at two other sources for a truly in-depth look at getting consistent color *Real World Photoshop* (which David wrote with Bruce Fraser and Conrad Chavez) and *Real World Color Management*, by Bruce Fraser, Chris Murphy, and Fred Bunting.

Do You Need Color Management?

Everyone wants consistent color from original to screen to proof print to printing press, but it's worth asking yourself whether you really need it. Managing color is not as simple as turning on a checkbox, and though it's not as hard as flying an airplane, it can still cause a fair amount of rifling through medicine cabinets trying to ease the pain in your head. You may not need to worry a lot about managing color in InDesign if you can rely on color swatch books when picking solid colors, and if you can rely on color prepress professionals to deal with your color Photoshop images.

There are other instances when it's not even worth trying to get InDesign to manage your color. For example, InDesign can't manage grayscale images or spot colors. Similarly, InDesign isn't really set up to color-manage vector art when saved as an EPS file (it can do it, but we don't recommend it). Vector art saved as PDF or native Adobe Illustrator (.ai) files should work reasonably well.

Nevertheless, we must admit that it is particularly satisfying when you work through all the issues and achieve (as close as possible) parity among your screen, inkjet printer, and final press output. Being able to rely on your screen ("soft proofing") and desktop color printer is a great boost in efficiency, too. Plus, as the world becomes increasingly reliant on direct to plate technologies, bypassing film entirely, color management systems become increasingly important to ensure quality output. And if you want to import RGB images and let InDesign do the color separation for you at print time, you'll get better results if color management is turned on.

Controlling Your Color-Viewing Environment

If it's important to you that what you see on your screen looks as much like the printed version of your publication as possible, there are a few rules you need to follow.

▶ Characterize and calibrate your monitor with a tool like the Datacolor Spyder or X-Rite's EyeOne. If color is of critical importance to you and your publications, find a system that works with your monitor, or buy a monitor with built-in color management capabilities.

▶ Control the lighting around your monitor and keep it consistent when you're working. The fluorescent lighting used in most of our office buildings is the worst possible lighting for viewing colors. Turn it off, if you can, and rely on incandescent or "full spectrum" lighting. Avoid glare and bright light if possible.

Why is lighting important? Basically, the temperature of the light affects what a color "objectively" looks like.

Printed Proofs and Swatches

Remember that, unlike the paper you'll be printing on, your screen is backlit, so it displays colors very differently from what they'll look like when printed. Therefore, any time you're working with ink, try to refer to printed samples, rather than looking at the colors on your screen.

If you're using uncoated paper, look at samples of the ink (spot color) or ink mix (process color) printed on uncoated stock. If you're using coated paper, look at examples printed on coated paper. Even better, try to find an example of the ink printed on the paper stock you're using—though these examples are much harder to find.

Pantone makes a line of swatch books showing their libraries of spot and process colors (including process color equivalents of the spot colors); they're printed on both coated and uncoated stocks, and, although they're kind of expensive, they're not as expensive as pulling a job off of a press because you didn't like the press check. They're downright cheap if you consider what they must cost to print.

If you're specifying CMYK colors, use a swatch book printed with process colors that tells you what the CMYK breakdowns are. Our favorite is the one made by Trumatch. You can also find process color books made by Pantone.

Definitely don't assume that your color inkjet or laser printers will automatically produce an accurate simulation of what the colors in your publication are going to look like when they're printed by your commercial printer. To do that, you'll have to do some work—we'll cover that in more detail later in this chapter.

InDesign's Color Management Controls

You can control how color appears in InDesign in a number of places. For example, under the Edit menu, you'll find Color Settings, Assign Profiles, and Convert to Profile. In the View menu, there's the Proof Colors feature. And the Appearance of Black pane of the Preferences dialog box also lets you manage one color (black).

Application Color Settings

The choices you make in the Color Settings dialog box form the basis for how InDesign displays and prints color (see Figure 10-14). These controls all match the similarly named features in Adobe Photoshop, though the meanings are sometimes subtly different. Note that these controls adjust future documents you create, but not already-created files—not even the currently-open document.

Settings. In a valiant effort to make color management easier, Adobe has created color management "presets" that you can pick in any of the Creative Suite applications. You can pick the same setting in all the applications to get consistent color as you move files from one program to another. (You can automate this by launching Adobe Bridge and then choosing Edit > Creative Suite Color Settings.)

If InDesign's Color Settings dialog box is set up differently than other Suite applications, you'll see a message alerting you to the fact that the Suite isn't synchronized. This isn't necessarily a bad thing—for example, we typically like seeing missing profile alerts in Photoshop but not in InDesign. (We cover alerts like this in "Color Management Policies," in a few pages.)

InDesign's color management is turned on by default. The Settings pop-up menu typically shows five presets.

FIGURE 10-14
**Color Settings
Dialog Box**

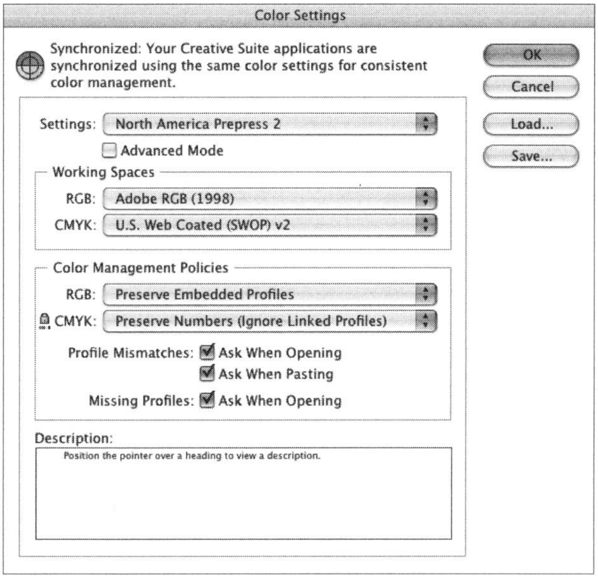

> ▸ **Emulate Adobe InDesign 2.0 CMS Off.** "Off" is misleading—there is no such thing as truly turning color management off. This setting tells InDesign to hide what it's doing from you. For example, if you import an RGB image and print color separations, InDesign will still convert the RGB to CMYK (which is one of the prime uses of color management). The result may look only adequate because InDesign is assuming your RGB image is based on the Adobe RGB profile and the CMYK ink behavior is based on the Photoshop 5 Default CMYK settings. We'd rather gnaw off our leg than use this setting.

> ▸ **Monitor Color.** This is good for... um... well, it might have some marginal use in Photoshop (if you're creating output for video perhaps), but we can't think of any reason to use it here.

> ▸ **General Purpose.** The default setting is General Purpose, which turns off most of the color management alert dialog boxes that make people nervous, uses sRGB as the default RGB space, and uses U.S. Web Coated SWOP for the default CMYK space (or Fogra or Japan Color in Europe or Asia). This is probably the best setting for most InDesign users.

> ▸ **Prepress.** It's tempting to choose North American Prepress 2 (or Europe Prepress 2 or Japan Prepress 2, depending on where you're reading this) if you're aiming for a printing press. This uses the same CMYK default, but standardizes on the Adobe RGB model for RGB colors. While we do like this for Photoshop

image editing (because it encompasses a spectrum of colors better suited for print than sRGB), it's both unnecessary and often misleading or incorrect in InDesign.

▶ **Web/Internet.** If virtually all your pages are destined for the Web, you might choose the Web/Internet preset. It uses the sRGB workspace for RGB colors (it even forces non-sRGB images to convert to sRGB), but that's appropriate for Web files.

Again, these are only defaults—not necessarily what you'll use for your documents. If you have a custom CMYK profile for a project, you can use that for your document instead (see "Changing Document Spaces," later in this chapter).

Note that you can also save your Color Settings dialog box setup by clicking Save. If you save it in the location that InDesign offers, you'll find it in the Settings pop-up menu in the future. Plus, you can use that setting in all your other Creative Suite applications, too.

Working Spaces. Perhaps the most important features of the Color Settings dialog box are the two Working Spaces pop-up menus, which control InDesign's default color profiles for RGB and CMYK colors. Remember that an RGB value doesn't mean anything because red, green, and blue phosphors are different on different devices. Cyan, magenta, yellow, and black inks can also be radically different depending on ink manufacturer, paper stock, press conditions, and so on. So RGB and CMYK colors are all just a bunch of numbers. Profiles assign color meaning to the numbers: such-and-such CMYK value *on this particular device.*

The profiles you choose from the CMYK and RGB pop-up menus are the profiles InDesign will use for any swatches you create in InDesign, and for any imported graphics that did not include a color management profile (and that you have not applied a profile to using the Image Color Settings dialog box). Also, as we'll point out in the discussion below about color policies, the default CMYK profile is also used for imported CMYK images—even those that have their own profile—when you choose the Preserve Numbers option (which you probably will).

We generally recommend using sRGB for the RGB working space rather than something like Adobe RGB. The reason: the RGB working space is applied to RGB images that have no embedded profile, and if an image has no profile, it was probably pulled off a Web site or shot with a cheap camera—in both those cases, sRGB is the safest assumption.

The choice of a CMYK working space depends entirely on your print workflow. In a perfect world, you'd have a color profile for your particular printing press or output device, with your particular paper stock, and so on. But in reality, you can typically get away with picking a generic target profile. The best target profile is probably Coated GRACoL when printing on a sheetfed press, or Web Coated Stock 2006 Grade 3 Paper (or Grade 5 Paper) when printing on a Web press. ("Web" here refers to a Web press, as opposed to a sheetfed press, and has nothing to do with the World Wide Web.)

Other "middle of the road" targets include Europe ISO Fogra27 (which David erroneously pronounces *fois gras*) and the well-used-but-pretty-mediocre U.S. Web Coated SWOP v2.

If you're looking for a particular profile that you know you've installed in the operating system correctly, but doesn't appear here, try turning on the Advanced checkbox (see "Advanced Color Settings," later in this section).

Color Management Policies. InDesign assigns the default working spaces to each new document you create while color management is on. But what should InDesign do when color management is turned on and you open a document that was created when color management was turned off (so no profile was associated with the document)? What if you open a document made by someone else who used a different working space? You can tell InDesign what to do in these cases with the Color Management Policies section of the Color Settings dialog box.

Perhaps more importantly, the Policies section also manages what happens to images that you import, which has huge implications over how they appear in print.

► **RGB.** We suggest leaving the RGB pop-up menu set to its default value (Preserve Embedded Profiles) most of the time. This means InDesign will keep track of embedded profiles in RGB images and InDesign documents that contain RGB colors—very useful if you receive RGB images or files from other people.

We can't think of any reason to set RGB to Off (which would simply ignore all profiles and stop InDesign from embedding an RGB profile in the document, causing untold horrors when it comes to getting any sort of color consistency). However, choosing Convert to Working Space could be useful on occasion, if you knew you had to open 50 InDesign documents that had simply been created with the wrong RGB profile. But watch out: Any RGB colors you created in the InDesign document will look the same, but the actual RGB numbers will likely change upon conversion.

▸ **CMYK.** The choice for the CMYK policy is not so cut and dry. Most people will want to use Preserve Numbers (Ignore Embedded Profile), but if you're serious about color management you may want to choose Preserve Embedded Profile. The first choice (Preserve Numbers) tells InDesign to use the current CMYK document profile as the profile for all your CMYK colors and imported CMYK images. For example, let's say you make a 100-percent cyan in a CMYK TIFF that uses some wacky custom CMYK profile, then you import that into your InDesign document that uses the default SWOP profile. InDesign ignores the wacky profile entirely and just assumes that the image uses SWOP. You can override this (see "Applying Device Profiles to Images," later in this chapter), but you wouldn't want to have to do that very often.

Even though Preserve Numbers (Ignore Embedded Profile) sort of defeats the greater purpose of color management, it tends to be the choice we recommend—especially when all your incoming CMYK images are created with the same profile (which is often the case).

On the other hand, if you receive CMYK images that have embedded CMYK profiles from a number of sources, you're pretty sure that the sources each used different CMYK profiles, and you need to make sure they all look good when you print or export PDF, you'll want to use Preserve Embedded Profile. This tells InDesign to keep their appearance consistent with the originals (how they looked in Photoshop, for example), even if it means changing the CMYK numbers to accomplish that. For example, that 100-percent cyan swatch might change to 95-percent cyan plus 5-percent magenta.

Again, we urge people not to set the CMYK policy to Off, as it will likely only cause you heartache down the road. (If you're frustrated with your previous experiences with color management, choose Preserve Numbers rather than Off.)

Unless you're obsessive about color management, we recommend turning off the two Profile Mismatch checkboxes, and leaving on the Missing Profiles checkbox in the Color Management Policies section. The mismatch warnings you get tend to be confusing, misleading, and annoying. But having a document with no profiles at all could cause even more trouble, so it's good to be alerted in that situation.

**Advanced
Color Settings**

While the color management options we've described are enough for many workflows, you can get even more tweaky by turning on the Advanced Mode checkbox (see Figure 10-15). First, when Advanced Mode is turned on you can select any color profile installed in your operating system for your working spaces (as opposed to only the recommended Adobe profiles). Next, you can select an alternate color management engine, adjust the default rendering intent, and choose whether or not to use black point compensation.

Engine. Color management engines (the actual software at the heart of the system that converts one color into another) are made by a variety of manufacturers. Ultimately, it's very unlikely that you would ever see a difference between any of these. Unless you have a *really* good reason to switch, you should just use the Adobe (ACE) CMS (which is also what Photoshop uses by default).

Intent. What happens when the color management system encounters a color that is outside of the gamut of the selected printing device? The color management system must change the color to one that's inside the printer's gamut. *How* it does that is the topic of the Intent pop-up menu. Intent is shorthand for *rendering intent*.

When you choose either Relative Colorimetric (which is the default) or Absolute Colorimetric, the out-of-gamut colors are moved to the nearest edge of the color gamut—also called gamut clipping—which means that differences between out-of-gamut colors can disappear (*very* red and *very, very* red both become the same in-gamut CMYK red). When this happens, you'll see an effect similar to posterization in the more saturated areas of images. The Perceptual rendering intent squeezes all the document's colors so that out-of-gamut colors are brought into the color gamut in a way that maintains a distinction between the colors. The Saturation rendering intent, on the other hand, moves all colors toward the edge of the color gamut, resulting in more saturated color.

**FIGURE 10-15
Advanced
Color Settings**

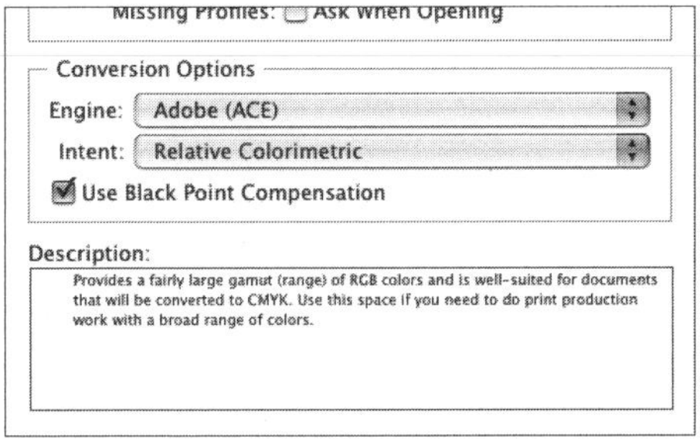

In general, Relative Colorimetric is best for solid colors and synthetic images (like images made in Illustrator or FreeHand), and Perceptual is best for scanned images. Unfortunately, InDesign uses this rendering intent both for colors built in InDesign and for imported images (unless you specifically override it, which we discuss in "Applying Device Profiles to Images," below). However, for most documents and images—especially those already in CMYK mode—Relative Colorimetric probably makes the most sense. On the other hand, if you use a lot of RGB images with saturated out-of-gamut colors, and you're trying to match these colors with swatches built in InDesign, you might want to use Perceptual instead. If you want more intense color in business graphics (such as charts and graphs), you might try choosing Saturation.

Use Black Point Compensation. The Use Black Point Compensation option, when turned on, maps the black of the source profile to the black of the target profile. We usually think of black as being "just black," but of course black on different devices appears differently (for instance, solid black on newsprint is much more gray than solid black on glossy sheetfed stock). We generally recommend leaving this turned on, ensuring that the entire dynamic range of the output device is used.

Changing Document Spaces

By default the document working space is whatever Color Settings was set to when you first created the document. If you later change Color Settings, the application's default working space will be different than your document's space; that's no big deal because InDesign always uses the document space if there is one.

What if you want to change the document working space? For example, you thought you were going to print on coated stock but later found you had to cut your budget and switch to uncoated stock? You can add or change a document's working space profiles using the Assign Profiles and the Convert to Profile features in the Edit menu.

Assign Profiles lets you tag your document with another set of RGB and/or CMYK profiles, or even remove the document profile entirely (see Figure 10-16). Changing the document profiles with Assign Profiles is like saying, "The colors in this document now mean something else, because cyan now looks like this, magenta looks like this, and so on." Accordingly, the colors on screen may change, but the actual color definitions don't.

Convert to Profile is the opposite: It actually converts the colors in your document to a new profile, changing the color definitions to maintain the look of the colors (see Figure 10-17). That means

FIGURE 10-16
Assign Profiles

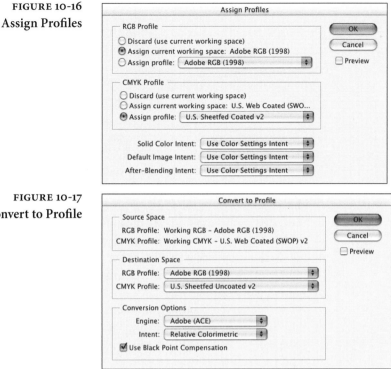

FIGURE 10-17
Convert to Profile

a 100-percent magenta will end up as something like 96-percent magenta, 6-percent yellow (or something else, depending on what profile you're converting to). We encourage you to be very careful when using Convert to Profile; it can really mess up your documents, or it can be a lifesaver if you really know what it's doing.

Note that Convert to Profile is the only good way to find out what your document space currently is (you'll find it listed at the top of the dialog box).

Applying Device Profiles to Images

When you save an image from Adobe Photoshop, by default the program embeds a color profile that describes the image's color space (see *Real World Photoshop* for more on Photoshop's behavior). InDesign recognizes that profile when you place the graphic on your page, though if the CMYK policy was set to Preserve Numbers (Ignore Linked Profiles) when you created this document, any embedded profile is ignored at this point.

However you can force InDesign to honor the embedded profile if you turn on the Show Import Options checkbox in the Place dialog box, and then click on the Color tab of the Image Import Options dialog box (see Figure 10-18). Of course, this works only with color-manageable images (that is, pretty much any reasonable format other

FIGURE 10-18
Applying a Profile
at Import

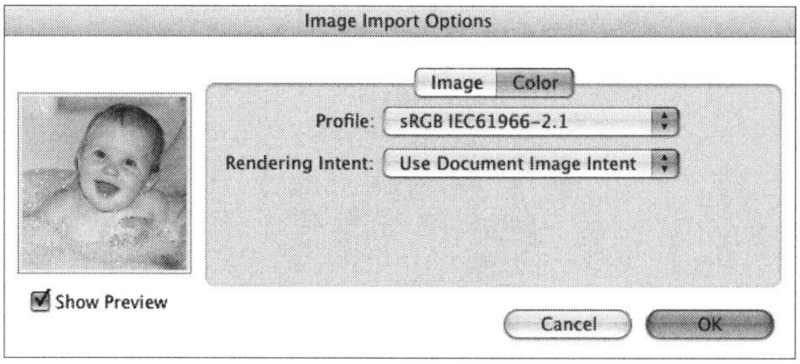

than EPS). You can choose what profile to apply, and what rendering intent to use when InDesign needs to convert the colors to a different profile space. If the Profile pop-up menu reads Use Document Profile, it means the InDesign document, not the image. To use the embedded profile instead, choose it from the pop-up menu (it should be listed at the top of the list). Note that this is like using Assign Profile in Photoshop; it doesn't change the data; it just changes the meaning of the data.

Whatever you choose upon placing the image, you can also tell InDesign which profile to use by selecting the image and choosing Image Color Settings from the Object menu.

Soft-Proofing Controls

You probably want to get some sense of what your pages are going to look like before you commit to a $50,000 print run. Increasingly, proofing is being done not on traditional color proofing systems, but rather on desktop inkjet printers and on screen. Proofing color on screen is called soft-proofing, and the quality of soft-proofing in InDesign is limited only by the accuracy of the profiles involved.

The Proof Colors command on the View menu lets you turn soft-proofing on and off. But it's in the Proof Setup submenu that you can control what the proof is showing you. Note that the settings you make in Proof Setup are specific to the window that's in the foreground, not the document itself. This means you can create several views of the same page (by choosing New Window from the Window menu) and apply different soft-proofing settings to each view, letting you see how the page will work in different output scenarios.

The three items in the Proof Setup submenu are Document CMYK, Working CMYK, and Custom. We typically just use Custom, which displays the Proof Setup dialog box (see Figure 10-19), which gives us more control over the soft-proof (though not as much as Photoshop offers). First, choose the profile of the device you're trying to emulate. Then, choose whether to preserve CMYK numbers, and whether to simulate Paper White and Ink Black.

Preserve CMYK Numbers. The Preserve CMYK Numbers checkbox lets you tell InDesign what you want done with the CMYK colors you defined in the document and CMYK images that either have no embedded profile or have an embedded profile but are using the document CMYK profile because you have set the CMYK policy to Preserve Numbers (Ignore Linked Profiles). Which you choose should depend on which you're going to pick in the Print or Export PDF dialog box (see "Color Management in Output," below).

Simulate Black/White. The two checkboxes in this section control the rendering of the document's colors from the proofing space to the monitor. When Paper White and Ink Black are turned off, InDesign does a relative colorimetric rendering, mapping the white of the proof device's paper to monitor white and the black of the device's black ink to monitor black. This isn't particularly useful; after all, for a soft-proof you're trying to see what the real paper's white and ink's blacks will look like.

Instead, we almost always turn on the Paper White checkbox (which automatically also turns on the Ink Black checkbox). This way, the monitor simulates the paper's white (which is often duller than monitor white), and you can see the compressed dynamic range of print. If you're simulating a low-dynamic-range process—like newsprint, or inkjet on uncoated paper—turning on Ink Black (or Paper White) gives you a much better idea of the actual color range you'll get in print.

FIGURE 10-19
Soft-Proofing

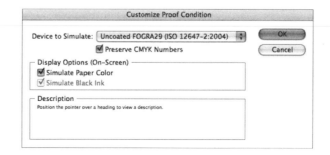

Select Custom to open the Proof Setup dialog box and specify your own output profile.

Unfortunately, the effect of simulating a compressed dynamic range is so dramatic that it feels like it ruins the document's colors. It's a good idea to put the document in Preview mode (press W while not editing text), hide your panels (press Tab), then select Proof Colors from the View menu, but before actually letting go of the mouse button, close your eyes for a few seconds. When you open your eyes, your brain can readjust its own internal white point, giving you a better sense of what the image really will look like when it comes off the printer.

It's worth noting again that you'll never get an exact match between screen and final printed output. However, like any proofing system, the key is not in getting a perfect match, but rather in getting pretty dang close, and then learning the *relationship* between screen and printed piece. The more you do this (and the more accurate your profiles are), the more accurate you'll get at predicting final color.

Color Management in Output

None of this color management stuff is relevant if you can't get your final design to print well. Fortunately, you can perform color conversions from your document space to a selected profile when you print your document or export it to PDF or EPS.

Print dialog box. The key to managing color at print time is to specify a source space and a target space in the Color Management tab of the Print dialog box (see Figure 10-20). That way, the color management engine knows where the color is coming from (what the color is supposed to look like) and where the color is going (how that device images color, so it can convert the colors properly).

► **The Source.** You have two choices for a source space in the Print section of this panel: Document (the document working space) or Proof (the profile you last chose in the Custom Proof Setup dialog box). The Proof option lets you print your file to a composite printer, like a desktop inkjet, and make it simulate the CMYK output you've been soft-proofing—that is, it gives you a hard copy of your soft-proofed document.

When you choose Proof, you can also choose whether to simulate the paper color of the final target by turning on or off the Simulate Paper Color checkbox in the Color Management section of the dialog box.

► **Who Handles the Color.** You next need to determine who is going to do the color management: InDesign or your PostScript printer. You can choose one or the other from the Color Handling pop-up menu. We virtually always choose Let InDesign

FIGURE 10-20
Color Management in
the Print Dialog Box

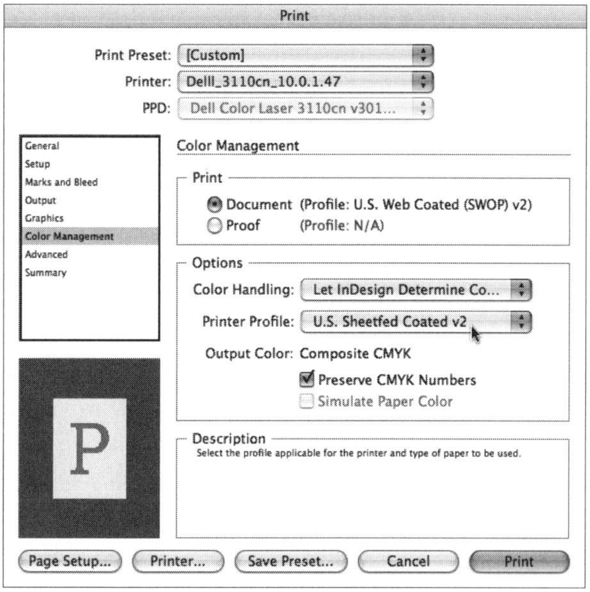

Determine Color, as we trust Adobe's color management system more than most.

On the other hand, if you don't have a good profile for your printer, or you trust your printer's PostScript RIP to provide the color management, you can choose PostScript Printer Determines Color. Of course, this only works on PostScript devices, and it only works when you've selected one of the Composite options or InRIP Separations from the Color pop-up menu in the Output tab of the Print dialog box.

▸ **The Target.** The target profiles you can choose from the Printer Profile pop-up menu (the space of the print device) depend on whether you have chosen an RGB or a CMYK space from the Color pop-up menu in the Output tab of the Print dialog box. If you're printing to an inkjet printer, you should probably choose Composite RGB and then pick the RGB profile for that device (or, if you don't have a profile, often the sRGB works well).

▸ **Preserve CMYK Numbers.** When you print, InDesign compares your target print space to the document space and the profiles applied to or embedded in graphics; if they're all the same, then it doesn't do any color conversion. Whenever the profiles differ, InDesign has to decide whether to run the colors through the color management engine to maintain visual consistency of the colors. For example, if your document CMYK setting is U.S. Web Coated (SWOP) but you choose a Newsprint output profile,

InDesign will obviously have to convert your RGB colors to the Newsprint CMYK space. But it may also convert your CMYK colors from their original space to Newsprint, too.

Converting from one CMYK space to another CMYK space is called cross-rendering, and it can be a blessing or a curse. It can really get you out of a last-minute jam if you don't have time to go back and reseparate RGB images into your new CMYK space. However, there's no way to tell InDesign to cross-render your images but not other things, so all your 100-percent black text also gets cross-rendered—resulting in four-color CMYK text—rarely what you'd expect or want.

Fortunately, you can turn on the Preserve CMYK Numbers checkbox in the Print dialog box. When this is on, InDesign won't cross-render any of your document's CMYK colors or CMYK images that either have no embedded profile or have an embedded profile but were imported with the Preserve Numbers (Ignore Linked Profiles) color policy enabled in the Color Settings dialog box. This is our best friend in the color management wars. We suggest you turn it on unless you really know what you're doing. (If the source and target profiles are the same, it's grayed out because colors aren't in danger of cross-rendering.)

Don't forget that you can have the Preserve Numbers (Ignore Linked Profiles) policy turned on and still force InDesign to cross-render a specific image by giving it a profile with the Image Color Settings dialog box that we talked about earlier. Also, don't forget that you can change your document profile before printing with Assign Profile or Convert Profile.

Export as PDF. You can tell InDesign whether to color-manage your exported PDF files in the Output tab of the Export PDF dialog box (see Figure 10-21). You have several options here.

▶ **Color Conversion.** If you don't want InDesign to convert any colors (if you want all the document and image color data left as is) then select No Color Conversion from the Color Conversion pop-up menu in the Output tab. This is what you get when you use the PDF/X3 standard because the understanding is that the color management will be handled downstream when the PDF is printed.

However, if you want InDesign color manage the file while generating the PDF, choose either Convert to Destination or Convert to Destination (Preserve Numbers). For example, if you're exporting the PDF for primarily onscreen viewing, choose Convert to Destination from the Color Conversion pop-up menu and then choose an RGB profile from the Destination pop-up menu—the sRGB profile is probably the most useful, as it purports to define the "average" monitor. This forces everything into the sRGB space.

If you're exporting for print and you want to color-manage the entire document, then choose Convert to Destination and choose your final output device in the Destination pop-up menu. However, if the Destination profile is different than your document profile, your CMYK colors will likely get cross-rendered into a different CMYK space. As we noted earlier, this is the cause of the four-color black text problem that many people had in early versions. So in most circumstances, we would recommend the Convert to Destination (Preserve Numbers) option, which leaves document colors and untagged colors alone.

► **Include Profiles.** The Profile Inclusion Policy pop-up menu lets you choose whether or not to embed various profiles in your PDF. If you choose one of the two Convert to Destination options in the Color Conversion pop-up menu, you can choose to either not embed any profiles or to embed the destination profile. If you expect your PDF to be further color managed by some other application (even to view it properly on screen), you should definitely include your profiles. But it does make a larger PDF file, so in many cases, we just leave it out.

FIGURE 10-21
**Color Management
in the Export
PDF Dialog Box**

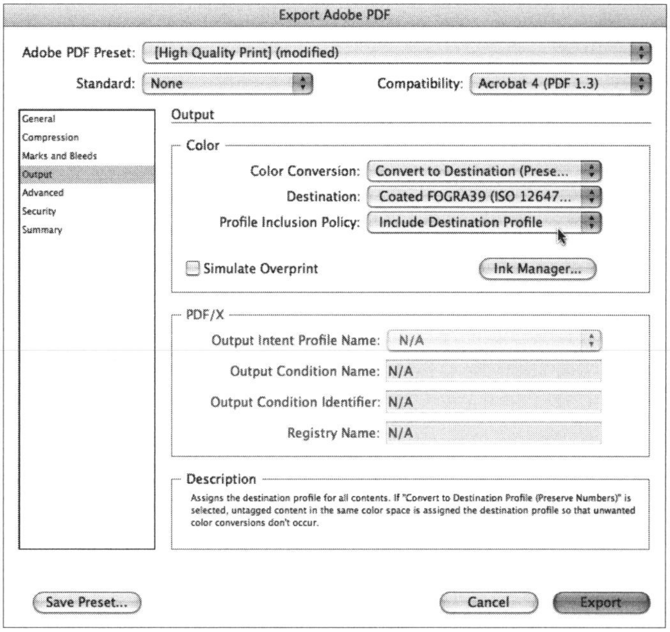

Export Adobe PDF

Adobe PDF Preset: [High Quality Print] (modified)

Standard: None   Compatibility: Acrobat 4 (PDF 1.3)

General
Compression
Marks and Bleeds
Output
Advanced
Security
Summary

Output

Color

Color Conversion: Convert to Destination (Prese...
Destination: Coated FOGRA39 (ISO 12647...
Profile Inclusion Policy: Include Destination Profile

☐ Simulate Overprint   Ink Manager...

PDF/X

Output Intent Profile Name: N/A
Output Condition Name: N/A
Output Condition Identifier: N/A
Registry Name: N/A

Description
Assigns the destination profile for all contents. If "Convert to Destination Profile (Preserve Numbers)" is selected, untagged content in the same color space is assigned the destination profile so that unwanted color conversions don't occur.

Save Preset...   Cancel   Export

If the Color Conversion pop-up menu is set to leave your colors alone (again, the assumption here is that your file will be color managed later), you have three different choices in the Profile Inclusion Policy dialog box: Include All Profiles, Include Tagged Source Profiles, and Include All RGB and Tagged Source Profiles. Of course, you can also just tell InDesign not to include any profile, but we're not sure why you'd do that.

Export as EPS. There is little color management interface in the Export EPS dialog box; when you pick RGB or CMYK from the Color pop-up menu, InDesign simply assumes your document profiles are the destination profiles, and it color-manages your document—converting all imported images (at least the ones that it can, like TIFF and .PSD files) to the document working space. You can avoid this by choosing Leave Unchanged from the Color pop-up menu.

The Color "Done"

As you work with commercial printing, always remember that you're at the mercy of a series of mechanical processes that, in many ways, haven't changed since 1900. Temperature, humidity, and ambient static electricity play large roles in the process, and the people who operate these systems are at least skilled craftspeople; at best, artists. Ask them as many questions as they'll answer, set your job up the way they want it, and then sit back and watch your job come off the press.

Printing

Printing is an ancient art, and has been invented and reinvented many times. You can print by rolling a carved cylinder over a sheet of wet clay, as the Mesopotamians did. Or you can smear a carved block of wood with ink and then press the block into a sheet of paper, as the Chinese started doing in the eighth or ninth century. With grease, water, and ink, even a slab of limestone can learn to transfer an image to paper, as Alois Senefelder of Munich found in 1798 (thereby inventing lithography).

In the fifteenth century, Gutenberg (and possibly others) came up with moveable type made of cast metal—which, in turn, transformed printing from a craft into an industry. Scribes the world over lamented the decline in the quality of written materials.

Printing—the ability to make dozens, hundreds, thousands, millions of copies of an image—flourished. For whatever reason, we humans will go to great lengths to get our pictures, text, and advertising into the hands of our willing or unwilling audience. And, in spite of the encroachments of the Web, printing is arguably still the best way to do that.

The InDesign Print Dialog Box

When you press Command-P/Ctrl-P or choose Print Book from the Book panel (see Chapter 8, "Long Documents"), InDesign displays the Print dialog box. There are so many features packed into this dialog box that Adobe had to break it up into eight different panes, each listed along the left side of the dialog box: General, Setup, Marks and Bleeds, Output, Graphics, Color Management, Advanced, and Summary (Figure 11-1).

Even if you're printing to a lowly desktop printer, it's worth at least glimpsing at each of these panes. Fortunately, you can use keyboard shortcuts to navigate among them: Command/Ctrl-Down arrow jumps to the next pane, Command/Ctrl-Up arrow jumps to the previous pane, and holding down the Command/Ctrl key while pressing a number from 1 to 8 skips to the corresponding pane number (1 for General, 2 for Setup, and so on). We'll cover each of these panes, in order, below.

Printers, PostScript Files, and PPDs

Before you go anywhere in the Print dialog box, you've got to make one or two important decisions. First, you must choose from the options on the Printer pop-up menu, which lists the printers you have installed on your computer. When you choose a printer, InDesign looks to the printer driver to see what PPD (PostScript

FIGURE 11-1
The Print Dialog Box

Hold down Command or Ctrl and press 2 to jump to the Setup panel, 3 for the third panel, and so on.

Click once or twice on the Preview to see more information about your print job.

Click Setup to open the printer driver's print options. In general, you should avoid using the printer driver dialog boxes and use InDesign's controls instead.

Printer Description) file is associated with that printer, and it displays it—grayed out—in the PPD pop-up menu. In the case of a non-PostScript device, InDesign leaves this pop-up menu blank.

If you want to print a PostScript file directly to disk rather than to a device (also called making a "PostScript dump"), choose PostScript File from the Printer pop-up menu. In this case, you must also pick the PPD file that describes your final output device or choose Device Independent. You can typically use device-independent PostScript files—also called "sep," ".ps" or "prepress" files—for output using imposition and trapping systems.

Most output providers now prefer receiving PDF files rather than PostScript files. Some companies don't even accept PostScript files anymore, except from clients that they know will create them properly (because it's difficult to make changes to your document once it's written as PostScript).

Do not create your PDF by printing PostScript to disk or by using the PDF "printer driver." Export the file as PDF, instead, as we discuss in Chapter 7, "Importing and Exporting."

Note that PPDs are not, and should not be confused with, printer drivers. Printer drivers are pieces of software that direct information from your system and applications to a hardware port—usually, your computer's printer port or network connection. PPDs work in conjunction with printer drivers to give applications information about the printer (what paper sizes are available? what's the resolution of the printer? what do the printer error messages mean?) and, on occasion, to customize the printer's operation for the application (what PostScript routine does the application use to render halftones?).

InDesign and other applications use PPDs to optimize printing for a specific printer. If you are specifying a PPD file, it's important that you choose the right one, or else your pages may not print correctly (and might not print at all). The settings you choose here determine what options you have in the rest of the Print dialog box.

By the way, if you have installed a PPD in OS X and it doesn't appear in the PPD pop-up menu, it may be a compressed PPD. Try decompressing it using StuffIt Expander first.

Printer Driver Settings   Our eagle-eyed readers will quickly find a Setup button (in Windows) or Page Setup and Printer buttons (on the Macintosh) at the bottom of the Print dialog box. These are doorways into your operating system's printer drivers. At print time, InDesign interacts with whatever printer driver you're using. However, there are very few instances when you'd need to click these buttons to change the printer driver settings. In most cases, the settings are duplicated somewhere in InDesign's Print dialog box, and it's always better to set it within this dialog box than in the driver.

However, if you know of an option in the printer driver that InDesign doesn't handle, click the appropriate button. For example, many inkjet printers require you to specify resolution, quality, and color adjustments in their own drivers.

Note that in some rare cases you may get really weird results when applying both printer driver settings and Print dialog box settings (such as trying to print color separations while, at the same time, telling the driver to print multiple document pages per printed page).

PostScript vs. PDF Print Engine vs. Non-PostScript   While InDesign can print to other printers reasonably well, you'll get the best results with Adobe's printing technologies: PostScript 3 and the PDF print engine (which is not the same thing as the PDF "printer driver").

When InDesign detects (based on the driver you're using) that your printer isn't equipped with PostScript or the PDF print engine, it grays out the features in the Print dialog box that don't work on non-PostScript/PDF devices, such as color separations and the transparency Flattener (transparency effects print fine on these devices, but you don't need the Flattener to create them; see "Printing Transparency," later in this chapter).

Print Preview   InDesign displays a preview of the way your page fits on the selected paper size in the lower-left corner of the Print dialog box. The preview provides feedback that can save you from printing pages in the wrong orientation or printing pages that won't fit on the paper.

InDesign displays additional information "behind" the preview graphic. Click once on the preview and you can see data such as the paper size, the page size, how many tiles will print (see "Tile" in "Setup," later in this chapter), and so on. Click again, and InDesign shows you how your page will print relative to the paper path through the printer.

General

The General pane of the Print dialog box contains basic printing features: which pages do you want to print, how many copies do you want, and how do you want them to come out of the printer (see Figure 11-2).

FIGURE 11-2
The General Panel
of the Print Dialog Box

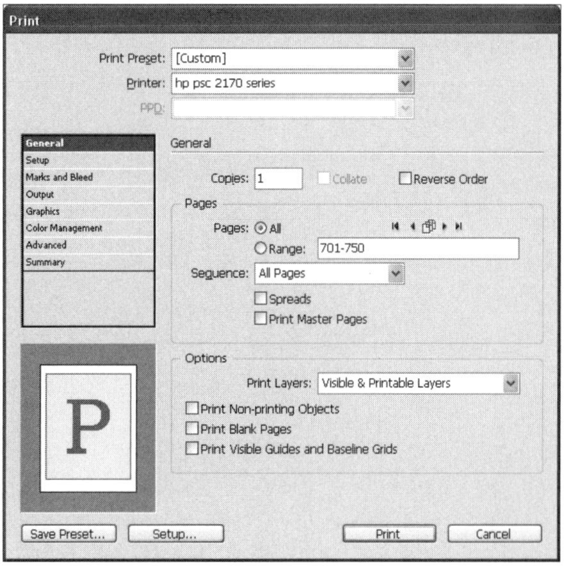

Copies   Enter the number of copies of the page you want to print in the Copies field. You can print up to 9999 copies of your publication.

Collate   When you turn on the Collate option, InDesign prints the range of pages you've specified, in order, for each copy of the publication you print. This makes for much slower printing. When you print multiple copies of a page, your printer only needs to process each page once (and then prints multiple copies of the page using the same image); when you turn on the Collate option, your printer must process each page once for every copy of the print job.

Reverse Order   When you print a multipage document, do you want the first page to come out first or last? Turning on the Reverse Order check box tells InDesign to print the last page first, then print "backwards" to the first page. You'll want to turn this on if your pages come out of the laser printer face up.

Page Ranges   Turn on the All Pages option to print all of the pages in the publication. To print a range of pages, turn on the Range option. Enter the page range in the Range field as shown in Table 11-1.

You can mix and match page ranges. To print pages one, three, six through ten, and 20, for example, you'd enter "1,3,6-10,20." The pages and ranges you specify must be in order (you couldn't, for example, print page 20 before printing page 6). Specifying "1,5,5,9" means print page 1, then two copies of page 5, and then page 9. If you

TABLE 11-1
Printing Page Ranges

To print:	Enter:	Example:
A continuous range of pages	first page - last page	12-21
Up to a specific page	- last page	-5
From a page to the end of the document	first page -	5-
Noncontiguous pages	page, page	1, 3
Mixed page ranges	page, range	-3, 6-9, 12, 15-
Pages by section	section:page	Sec1:1, Sec2:5

want to print from page 10 to the end of the document, type "10-". Or, to print from the beginning of the file up to (and including) page 10, type "-10".

If you've used the Page Numbering and Section feature, then printing specific page ranges gets even more complicated. For example, let's say your first section uses roman numerals and is 5 pages long. To print the first six pages, you type "i-6" (you can't type "1-6" because there is no page called "1"—the first page is called "i"). However, you can change this behavior: If you select Absolute Numbering in the View pop-up menu of the General pane of the Preferences dialog box, then you should type "1-6" because the range now refers to *absolute* page numbering ("the first through the sixth page").

If your document contains different page sizes, use the widgets above the Range field to specify a range containing all pages of the matching size. For example, suppose you need to print a brochure that has three different page sizes. If you select one of the covers, clicking the middle icon adds all the other pages of the same size to the range. Click the arrows to the right or left of the middle icon to cycle through spreads to print.

Note: If you've chosen Absolute Numbering from the View pop-up menu in the Page Numbering section of the General Preferences dialog box, InDesign expects you to enter absolute page numbers in the range field, rather than the number of the page as defined by the section containing the page. If page 1 of section 3 of the document is the fifteenth page in the document, you would enter "15" in the Range field (if, on the other hand, you chose Section Numbering from the View pop-up menu, you would enter "Sec3:1").

Sequence To print even and odd pages, select the All Pages option from the Sequence pop-up menu; to print even pages, select Even Pages Only;

and to print odd pages select Odd Pages Only. These choices affect all page ranges, including page ranges you've entered in the Range field. The only time we've used this pop-up menu is when we've printed double-sided documents on a laser printer (print just the odd pages, then flip the pages, put them back in the printer, and print the even pages). If you've turned on the Spreads option, these options will be unavailable.

Spreads   When you turn on the Spreads option, InDesign tries to print each spread in the publication on a single sheet of paper (or other output media). If the spread is larger than the selected paper size, you can turn on the Scale to Fit option in the Setup panel of the Print dialog box and/or change the paper orientation. This is also called "readers spreads." Note that this is not the same as printer spreads, which are a form of imposition, printing the first and last page together, and so on (see "Print Booklet" later in this chapter).

Print Master Pages   Sometimes you need to print your master pages instead of your document pages. No problem: Just turn on the Print Master Pages check box. When you do this, you cannot specify page ranges—InDesign prints all the master pages in the document.

Print Layers   InDesign normally prints all visible layers and doesn't print hidden layers or layers made non-printing in the Layer Options dialog box. However, you can override this, printing All Layers (whether visible or printable) or all Visible Layers (whether printable or not) by choosing these from this pop-up menu.

Print Non-Printing Objects   When you turn on the Print Non-printing Objects check box, InDesign prints every object on your pages, regardless of the state of the Nonprinting check box in the Attributes panel. However, this feature does not print objects that are on hidden (and therefore non-printing) layers.

Print Blank Pages   What happens when you print a three-page document that has nothing on page 2? By default, only pages 1 and 3 print out. If you want the blank page 2 to print, too, you'd better turn on the Print Blank Pages check box.

Print Visible Guides and Baseline Grids   When you turn the Print Visible Guides and Baseline Grids check box on, all visible margin guides, baseline grid guides, and page guides print out (but not the document grid). We find this particularly helpful when designing templates for others to use.

Setup

When we talk about page size, we're talking about the page size you've defined for your publication. This page size should be the same as the page size of the printed piece you intend to produce. "Paper size," on the other hand, is the size of the medium you're printing on. The Setup pane of the Print dialog box lets you specify paper size, as well as how you want the page to appear on that paper (see Figure 11-3).

Paper Size

PPDs contain information about the paper sizes that a printer can handle, and this information then shows up in the Paper Size pop-up menu. When you specify a non-PostScript printer, Paper Size changes to Defined by Driver, and you'll have to handle the paper size in the printer driver dialog box. Once again, the paper size doesn't have to be the same as your page size; if you're printing page marks (like crop marks), then the paper size will need to be larger. In the case of printers that image larger sheets of film, we usually set Paper Size to Custom, and then leave the Width and Height fields set to Auto (so InDesign figures out the proper imaging area for us).

Orientation

You can control the rotation of your page on the paper using the Orientation setting. The four choices (each rotated another 90 degrees) are indicated with tiny icons, but we find it easier to watch the preview page in the lower-left corner of the dialog box.

Offset

The Offset feature controls the placement of your document on the paper, film, or plate. The printer's default paper offset, even when set to zero, is almost always large enough so that you don't have to worry about changing the value of Offset here. However, if you need the page to image farther from the paper edge, change this value.

Gap

The Gap setting, which is really only relevant for roll-fed printers, determines the amount of blank space between each page of the document as it prints out. Some output providers that print to film like to set this to about 2p, so they can cut the pages apart more easily. In most cases, you can just ignore this setting.

Transverse

The Transverse setting is like Orientation, but is used for roll-fed imagesetters and platesetters when the Paper Size is set to Custom. When you turn on Transverse, the width of the paper is placed along the length of the imagesetter's paper roll, which can save paper or film. The best way to get a feel for the Transverse command is to click the Preview icon twice (to see the page versus the paper path), then turn on and off this check box. Of course, you have to first select an appropriate PPD.

FIGURE 11-3
**The Setup Panel
of the Print Dialog Box**

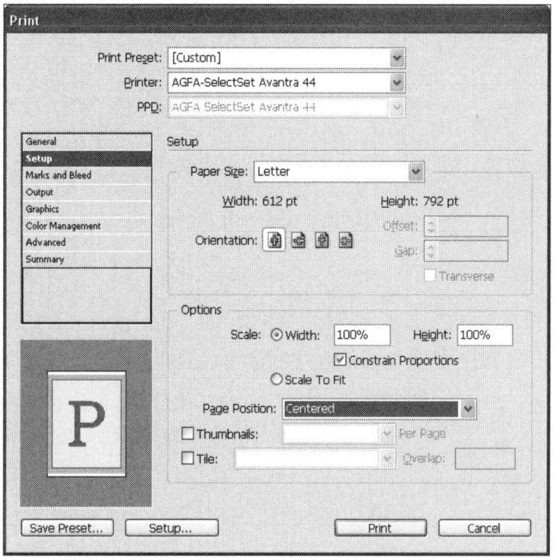

Scale
You can scale the output of your pages, from as small as one percent to as large as 1000 percent of their actual size. You can specify a scaling percentage yourself, or ask InDesign to fit the page to the size of the paper. When you use large percentages, watch the print preview to see that the enlarged page will fit on the paper you've selected.

If you're printing using a commercial printing process that distorts the printed images (flexographic printing, for example, typically stretches the axis parallel to the rotation of the printing cylinder), you can compensate for the distortion by entering different values in the Width and Height fields. To do this, turn off the Constrain Proportions option, then enter the percentages you want in the Width and Height fields. When the Constrain Proportions option is turned on, any changes you make in one field are reflected in the other.

When Scale to Fit is on, InDesign calculates the scaling percentage necessary to fit the page (plus any printer's marks you selected in the Marks and Bleeds panel of the Print dialog box) onto the selected paper size, and uses that scaling percentage when you print.

Page Position
When you select a paper size that is larger than your document, you can use the Page Position pop-up menu to define the relationship of your page to the paper. You've got four choices: Upper Left, Center Horizontally, Center Vertically, and Centered. Upper Left is the default; the other three are self-explanatory. We find this control a matter of personal preference most of the time, though it's not uncommon for the printer's internal margins (the area of the paper where the printer simply cannot lay down toner or ink) to clip off the top or left part of your page. In this case, just change the page position to Centered and try printing again.

Thumbnails   Thumbnails are great when you're trying to print out an overview of your document. For instance, you can print nine pages on a single piece of paper—three across and three down—by turning on the Thumbnails check box and then choosing 3×3 from the Per Page pop-up menu. You'll also get little page numbers next to each thumbnail. Note that on PostScript printers it takes as long to print this one sheet as it would to print all nine pages individually, so plan your time accordingly.

Tile   If your pages just won't fit on your paper, you've got to resort to tiling and (horror of horrors) tape, wax, or glue. InDesign offers three ways to tile documents—Automatic, Auto Justified, and Manual.

Automatic Tiling. When you choose this option from the Tile pop-up menu, InDesign starts the tile at the upper-left corner of the page, and prints as much of the page as it can given the paper size. Then it starts the next tile, with an overlap as specified in the Overlap field. It goes across the page, then moves down the page by the height of the paper you're printing on, and then goes across the page again.

If you click once on the page preview, InDesign tells you how many tiles will be required to print each page. If you find that it's producing *lots* of tiles per page, try reducing the overlap. If you're just tiling together a proof, a slight reduction in the scaling percentage could save you a lot of time with scissors and tape.

Auto Justified Tiling. The Auto Justified tiling option lays out the pieces of your page on the paper so that there's no extra white space to the right or underneath the page image (as you typically get with Automatic tiling). When you use this option, the Overlap field is meaningless; InDesign is actually figuring the overlap amount itself.

Manual Tiling. When you choose Manual tiling, InDesign only prints one tile per document page, using the zero point on the ruler as the upper-left corner of the tile. To print successive tiles, you have to move the zero point and print again. We find Manual tiling much more useful than Automatic tiling—have you ever tried cutting and pasting to get the halftone dots in a photograph to line up? With Manual tiling, you can ensure that items that you want to be able to proof are positioned so they're easy to see.

Note: As far as we can tell, there's no way to turn off the tiling marks InDesign adds around the edges of pages printed using Automatic tiling.

Tiling: Just Say No. Now it's time for pure, unfettered, talk-radio-style opinion. Any time anyone tells us that they plan to tile a publication, our sense of honesty and fair play forces us to ask them why they want to do that. Is it a masochistic streak they've had since childhood? A profound sense of personal inferiority? Something genetic?

If you can't find some way to print your publication without tiling, then go find a large-format printer or some other process to enlarge it to the size you want, rather than printing tiles and then trying to paste the printed tiles together. If you don't know if such a service is available in your area, do a Web search for "large format printing." Even if you have to send the publication across the country to get it blown up to the size you want, do it. Sure—these services do cost money. But what's your time—or your sanity—worth?

Marks and Bleeds

When you print your publication, you can choose to include (or exclude) a number of printer's marks—crop marks, registration marks, and other information (see Figure 11-4). The preview window displays the effect (given the current page and paper sizes) of your choice of printer's marks options, though they're usually too small to see well.

All Printer's Marks   Turn on the All Printer's Marks option when you want to print all of the printer's marks and page information. This is usually more than you need; for instance, if you don't have any objects bleeding off the page, then why bother with the Bleed Marks?

Crop Marks   Turn on the Crop Marks option to print lines outside the area of your page that define the area of the page (these are also called "trim marks"). Of course, if your paper size is not larger than your page size, InDesign won't (can't) print your crop marks. When you select Crop Marks, fold marks are printed as solid lines.

Bleed Marks   Turn on the Bleed Marks option to print lines outside the area of your page that define the area of the bleed. Like crop marks, if your paper size is not larger than your page size, InDesign won't print your bleed marks. We almost always turn this option off, even when bleeding objects off the page; in our experience, it doesn't offer any useful information, and it can cause confusion.

FIGURE 11-4
The Marks and Bleeds
Panel of the Print
Dialog Box

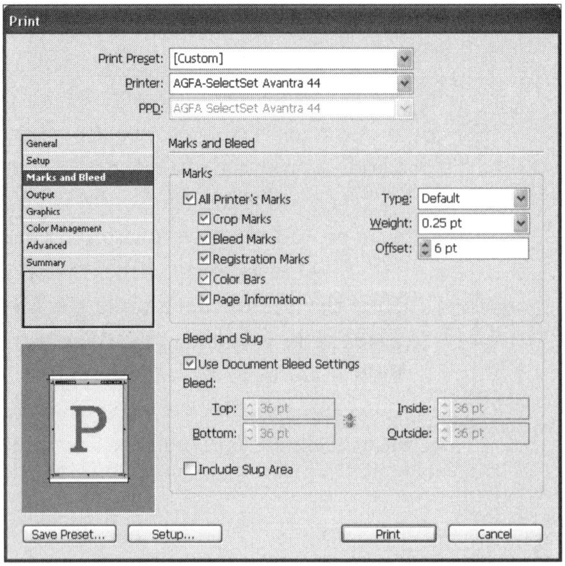

Registration Marks When you turn on the Registration Marks option, InDesign prints little targets around the edge of your page for your commercial printer to use when they're lining up, or registering, your color separations for printing. If your paper size is smaller than your page size, InDesign won't print the registration marks.

Color Bars When you turn on the Color Bars option, InDesign prints small squares of color outside the bleed area of your printed page. Your commercial printer can use these samples to adjust their press as they print the publication. It's worth checking with your printer to find out if they really want these before turning on this check box.

Page Information Turn on the Page Information option to print the file name and date of your publication on each printed page. In color separations InDesign also adds the name of the color plate. This makes it easy to tell which of several printed versions is the most current. It can also make it easier for your commercial printer to tell which pieces of film in a stack of separations go together (it's easy for you to tell, but put yourself in their shoes for a minute). We almost always leave this turned on (as long as the paper size is larger than the page size).

Type Now here's an intriguing option—a pop-up menu offering only "Default" as a choice. The idea is that developers will be able to add different printer's marks at some point. We haven't seen any yet (apart from the specialized Japanese marks in InDesign-J).

To try to spur the development of alternative printers' marks, we'll show you how to create your own printers mark customization files later in this chapter.

Weight   You can change the thickness of the page marks by choosing from among three options in the Weight pop-up menu: .125 pt, .25 pt, and .5 pt. We're pretty happy with the default weight, .25 pt.

Offset   The Offset feature determines how far from the edge of the page the page marks should sit. The default value of six points seems a little tight to us. We don't operate a two-ton paper cutter at a bindery, but if we did, we'd sure wish people increased the space between page and trim marks (and registration marks) to at least 12 points.

Bleed   The values you enter in the Bleed fields set the real boundary of the printed page. When the value in the Bleed fields is zero, InDesign neatly clips off any page elements extending beyond the edges of the page. This leaves little room for error in trimming the resulting printed pages—usually, when you want a page element to bleed off of a page, you should allow at least 24 points of bleed to compensate for inaccuracies in printing and trimming. If objects bleed off the page to the pasteboard, you must change these Bleed values in order for the object to still bleed upon printing.

Output

Do you want to print a composite version of your publication, or do you want to print separations? If you're printing separations, which inks do you want to print? Those are among the questions you answer using the Output pane of the Print dialog box (see Figure 11-5).

Composite vs. Separations   If you've only used black ink in your document, you can ignore the Output pane. However, for those of us who create color documents, the most important setting here is the Color pop-up menu, with which you can tell InDesign to print composite color or color separations. Which of these you should choose depends on your printer and the output you're trying to achieve.

Desktop inkjet printers and even many color laser printers should generally be considered RGB devices (even though they use CMYK inks), so you should choose Composite RGB to send them RGB data. If you choose Composite CMYK, InDesign converts all your RGB data (including any RGB TIFF files) into CMYK at print time. You

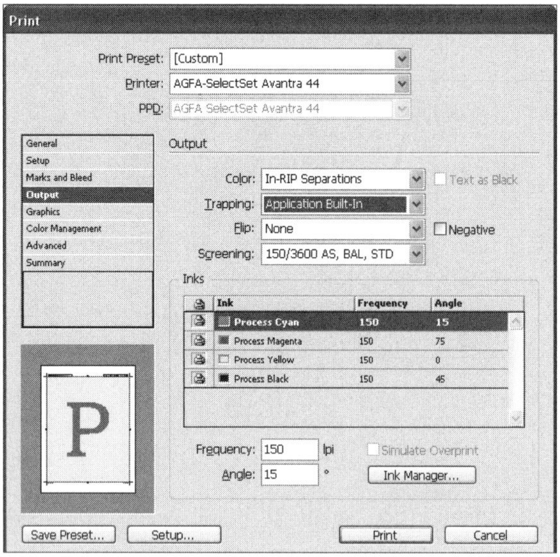

FIGURE 11-5
The Output Panel
of the Print Dialog Box

FIGURE 11-5
The Output Panel
of the Print Dialog Box

can use any of the composite choices when printing to a black-and-white desktop laser printer.

Composite CMYK is also useful for workflows in which the separations will be performed by a RIP, even if that RIP is running as software on another machine. However, in most of these instances, it makes more sense to create a PDF file, a device-independent PostScript file, or—for the adventurous—a device-dependent PostScript file using In-RIP separations, especially if you are using trapping (trapping is not supported in CMYK composite output). Choosing In-RIP Separations from the Color pop-up menu instructs InDesign to create a special type of composite CMYK file that will only print properly on a PostScript 3 output device and some newer PostScript Level 2 devices.

To tell InDesign to send the composite color information to the printer without changing it, choose Composite Leave Unchanged. If you do this, you will not be able to use Simulate Overprint.

You can also tell InDesign to separate each of your pages into four plates (or more, in the case of spot colors) by choosing Separations from the Color pop-up menu. If you select the Separations or In-RIP Separations option, InDesign activates the Inks list and its associated controls (the Flip, Frequency, Angle, Trapping settings, and so on).

Text As Black   One problem with printing proofs on a desktop laser printer is that it's sometimes difficult to read colored text because it appears as a tint. Similarly, when you want to fax a black-and-white version of your document, screened text becomes almost unreadable. When you turn on the Text as Black check box, InDesign ensures all your text appears as solid black—except for text that is already set to solid white, Paper color, or None.

Trapping

The Trapping pop-up menu controls whether InDesign applies automatic trapping to your documents. Choose one of the following trapping options from the Trapping pop-up menu:

- ▸ **Off.** Use this option if you've done all of your trapping manually (using InDesign's fills and strokes) or if you plan to separate and trap the publication using a post-processing program.

- ▸ **Application Built-In.** Choose Application Built-In when you want InDesign to trap your publication as it's sent to the printer (or to disk).

- ▸ **Adobe In-RIP.** Select this option when you want to leave trapping up to the RIP in your printer or imagesetter. This feature, which makes us rather nervous, only works on PostScript 3 and some PostScript Level 2 printers.

We cover trapping in a bit more detail in Chapter 10, "Color."

Flip and Negative

InDesign can mirror pages at print time if you choose Horizontal, Vertical, or Horizontal & Vertical from the Flip pop-up menu. Flipping an image is used for creating either wrong- or right-reading film from imagesetters, or film with emulsion side up or down. This is often handled in the imagesetter or platesetter, so be careful before you go changing this setting. The same thing goes for the Negative check box, which inverts the entire page so that everything that is set to 100-percent black becomes zero-percent black (effectively white). Never make assumptions about what your output provider wants; what you think will help might actually hinder (and cost you money in the long run).

Screening

What halftone screen frequency (in lines per inch) and screen angle do you want to use to print your publication? If you selected Composite Gray in the Color pop-up menu, you can choose either the printer's default (which is defined by the PPD you selected) or you can choose Custom and then enter your own values in the Frequency and Angle fields.

When you're printing separations, you'll see more choices on the Screening pop-up menu, and the values shown in the Frequency and Angle fields change as you select inks in the Inks list. Where the heck are these choices and values coming from? They're coming from the PPD. Every PPD contains a list of screen frequencies and screen angles optimized to avoid moiré patterns on the specific PostScript device described by the PPD. Because of the way that PostScript halftoning (or any digital halftoning, for that matter) works, a PostScript RIP cannot perfectly "hit" just any halftone screen.

On PostScript Level 1 devices, the screen angle and screen frequency you'd get would sometimes fail to match the frequency and angle you specified. This often resulted in serious output problems and severe moiré patterns. PPDs list combinations of screen angles known to be safe for a given printer at a screen frequency and angle.

While the need for these optimized screen angles has diminished somewhat with newer versions of PostScript, we strongly advise you to stick with them when you're printing separations.

To override the optimized screen settings for an ink, select the ink in the Inks list and then enter new values in the Frequency and Angle fields. Again, we don't recommend this, but you might have a very good reason for doing so that we simply haven't thought of yet (like perhaps you've lost your mind).

The optimized screen angles only cover the process inks, however. When your publication includes spot inks, InDesign sets the screen angle of every spot ink to 45 degrees.

For spot-color work—especially where you're overlaying tints of two spot colors or using duotones from Photoshop based on two spot inks—you need to specify the screen angles appropriately. Here's how to set them.

▶ If the spot inks *never* interact, set the screen angle for the inks to 45 degrees (because a 45-degree halftone screen is the least obvious to the eye).

▶ If you're creating lots of two-ink tint builds, or using duotones, you have a few choices, and two (somewhat contradictory) goals. You want both colors to print as close as possible to 45 degrees (especially the dominant, or darker, color), and you want as much separation between the angles as possible (the greater the separation between angles—45 is the maximum possible—the less patterning will be visible where the screens interact). Table 11-2 lists some options.

▶ If you're printing with two spot inks and the spot colors don't overprint any process inks, use the default screen angles for Magenta and Cyan from the optimized screen you've selected.

TABLE 11-2
Screen Angles for
Spot Color Work

Subordinate:	Dominant:	Notes:
15	45	Traditional. Only a 30-degree separation, but neither angle is very obvious on its own.
0	45	Avoids patterning. Ideally, the ink printed at zero degrees is a very light color—otherwise, the horizontal bands of halftone dots will be too obvious.
22.5	67.5	The complete compromise. Both angles are more obvious than 45 degrees, but less obvious than 0, and you get the full 45-degree separation to avoid patterning.
75	30	The dominant color screen is slightly less obvious than the subordinate screen. Full 45-degree separation.

Note that even if you set specific screen frequencies and angles for every color, you may not get what you ask for. Most imagesetters and platesetters these days strip out all screening settings and replace them with their own unless you (or your output provider) turns off this process. We've been caught by this several times, when we've chosen low-frequency screens in order to create a special effect, only to find our instructions ignored and the normal 133 lpi halftone appear. Very annoying.

Inks   When you select the Separations option, InDesign activates the Inks list. In this list, you'll see at least the four process inks (yes, they'll appear even if you aren't using process colors in your publication), plus any spot inks you've defined. When you select an ink in the Inks list, InDesign displays the halftone screen properties for that ink in the Frequency and Angle fields (see "Screening," above).

To tell InDesign not to print an ink, click the printer icon to the left of the ink name in the Inks list. You can also turn on or off all the inks by Option/Alt-clicking. Don't worry about inks that aren't used in your publication—InDesign will not generate a blank separation for them. If, for example, your publication uses only black ink and a spot ink, InDesign will not create separations for Cyan, Magenta, and Yellow, even though those inks appear in the Inks list.

Simulate Overprint   As we discussed in Chapter 10, "Color," you can set various objects to overprint using the Attributes panel. However, most composite printers (like laser printers and inkjets) don't support overprinting. Fortunately, you can simulate overprinting on these output devices by turning on the Simulate Overprint check box. Because this can change color definitions (spot colors get converted to process, for example), you *don't* want to turn this on for anything other than proofing your files on composite printers.

Ink Manager   The Ink Manager manages how colors trap with each other and how spot colors interact (for instance, you can use the Ink Manager to alias one spot color to another). We cover the Ink Manager in Chapter 10, "Color."

Graphics

The options in the Graphics pane control the way that InDesign prints the fonts and graphics in your publication (see Figure 11-6).

Send Data   The Send Data pop-up menu affects what InDesign does with bitmaps in TIFF, JPEG, and other explicitly bitmapped file formats. It has no effect on images inside imported EPS or PDF graphics.

Do you want to print that 30-megabyte color scan every time you proof a document on your laser printer? Probably not. The Send Data pop-up menu gives you four options to control what InDesign does with images when you print: All, Optimized Subsampling, Proxy, and None, each of which is described below.

All. Use this option when you want InDesign to send all of the image data from the image file to the printer. We recommend that you always use this option when printing the final copies of your pages.

Optimized Subsampling. This option tells InDesign to only send as much information from the image as is necessary to produce the best quality on the given output device using the current settings. It reduces the amount of data that has to be passed over the network and imaged by the printer. It can speed up printing immensely.

How InDesign pares down the data depends on whether the image is color/grayscale or black and white.

▸   **Color/Grayscale images.** As we mentioned in Chapter 7, "Importing and Exporting," there's no reason for the resolution

FIGURE 11-6
The Graphics Panel
of the Print Dialog Box

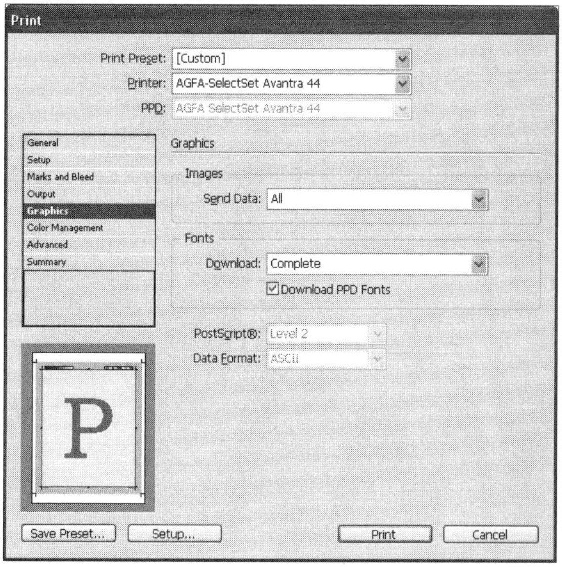

of grayscale and color images (in pixels per inch) to exceed two times the halftone screen frequency (in lines per inch). When you choose Optimized Subsampling from the Send Data pop-up menu, InDesign reduces the resolution of grayscale and color images to match the halftone screen frequency you've selected (in the Output pane of the Print dialog box). If you've set up a 75-line screen (for instance), InDesign won't send more than 150 dots per inch of image resolution. Note that InDesign does not change the resolution of the images in your publication—it just reduces the amount of data that's sent to the printer.

▶ **Black-and-white (bi-level) images.** When you're printing bi-level, black-and-white images, and have selected Optimized Subsampling from the Send Data pop-up menu, InDesign matches the images it sends to the resolution of the output device. So if you've got a 600-pixels-per-inch black-and-white TIFF, and you're printing on a 300-dpi laser printer, InDesign reduces the resolution of the image to 300 pixels per inch before sending it to the printer. For those who really want to know, InDesign gets the printer's resolution from the DefaultResolution keyword in the PPD.

The real value of the Optimized setting lies in printing laser proof copies of jobs that are destined for high-resolution (hence high halftone screen frequency) output. If you're producing a document that will be printed with a 133-lpi screen, for instance, you may be working with images that have resolutions of 250 or even 300 ppi. But for proofing on a 600-dpi laser printer (which has a 85-lpi default screen frequency), you only need 106 dpi—maximum. By subsampling to this lower resolution, InDesign is sending *less than one fifth* of the information over the wire. Obviously, this can save you a lot of time. With high-resolution line art, InDesign might send only a sixteenth of the data.

Printing an image using the Optimized Subsampling option produces a more detailed printed image than using the Low Resolution option, but doesn't take as long to print or transmit as would the full-resolution version of the image.

While Optimized Subsampling might sound like the universal cure for perfect (speedy, high quality) printing, it isn't. Subsampling, by its nature, blurs and distorts images, especially in areas of high contrast. Therefore, we think you should use this option for proof printing, but not for printing the final copies of your pages.

Proxy. Choose Proxy from the Send Data pop-up menu to have InDesign send only the low-resolution preview images it displays on your screen to the printer. Again, this is an option to use when you're printing proof copies of your pages, not for final output.

None. When you choose this option, InDesign prints all of the imported graphics in your publication as boxes with Xs through them. As you'd expect, this makes it print faster. Proof printing is great when you're copy-editing the text of a publication—why wait for the graphics to print?

Note that you can speed things up a bit, without completely eliminating the graphics, by using the Proxy or Optimized Subsampling option on the Send Data pop-up menu. Also, note that you can turn off the printing of a particular type of imported graphic using the Omit EPS/PDF/Bitmap Images options in the Advanced pane of the Print dialog box.

Font Downloading

One of the best ways to speed up InDesign's printing is to manage downloaded fonts sensibly. You can save many hours over the course of a day, week, month, or year by downloading fonts to your printer in advance, and by understanding the way that InDesign handles font downloading.

The basic concept is pretty simple: Fonts can be either "resident" (which means that they're stored in your printer's memory or on a hard drive attached to the printer) or "downloadable" (which means they're stored somewhere on your system or network).

When you print, InDesign checks the printer PPD to see if the fonts are available on the selected printer. If the font is available, InDesign sends a reference to the font, but does not send the font itself, which means that the text will be printed in the font available on the printer.

What happens when a font is not available in the printer's memory or on its hard drive? That depends on the option you've selected in the Fonts section of the Graphics pane of the Print dialog box.

When you choose the None option, you're directing InDesign to refrain from including any fonts in the PostScript it's sending to the printer (or to disk). If text in your publication has been formatted using fonts that are not resident on the printer, that text will be printed using the printer's default font (usually Courier).

When you choose the Complete option, InDesign checks the state of the Download PPD Fonts option. If this option is on, InDesign sends all of the fonts used in the publication to the printer's memory. If the option is turned off, InDesign downloads all of the fonts used in the publication that are not listed in the PPD (PPDs contain lists of fonts available on a given make and model printer, plus any you've added by editing the PPD). InDesign downloads the fonts once for each page that's printed. As you'd expect, this increases the amount of time it takes to send the job to your printer.

To decrease the amount of your printer's memory that's taken up by downloaded fonts, or to decrease the amount of time it takes InDesign to send the fonts to your printer, choose the Subset option. When you do this, InDesign sends only those characters required to print the publication. This can speed up printing tremendously.

At the same time, subsetting fonts can cause problems with some printers. If you find that you are losing characters, that the wrong characters print, or that your printer generates a PostScript error when you're trying to print using the Subset option, use one of the other options. If you're printing a file to disk as PostScript for delivery to a service bureau or to create a PDF using Acrobat Distiller, do not use the Subset option.

Postscript Level   Adobe would love it if everyone had PostScript 3 or PDF print engine devices. Not only would they make money from licensing fees, but their software could also take advantage of all the cool features in PostScript 3 RIPs. However, currently many people only have PostScript Level 2 devices. (Please don't ask us why "PostScript 3" omits the "Level" moniker. We can only assume that Adobe's marketing strategists have their reasons.) In most cases, InDesign reads the PostScript version from the PPD, so you don't have to think about this. However, if you're making a device-independent PostScript file you will need to choose Level 2 or Level 3. (Here Adobe *does* use "Level.")

Data Format The Data Format feature controls how bitmapped images (like TIFF and JPEG) are sent to the printer. While sending the information in ASCII format is more reliable over some older networks, binary is almost always fine and has the benefit of creating a much smaller PostScript file (the images are half the size of ASCII). We usually use binary unless we're sending files to an output provider that we know requires ASCII.

Color Management

The features in the Color Management pane of the Print dialog box are complex enough that we need to cover them in a separate section. We discuss color management, including all these Print dialog box settings, in Chapter 10, "Color."

Advanced

We're not sure what makes this pane more "advanced" than the others, but it's where you specify how InDesign should print to non-PostScript printers, images in an OPI workflow, and objects that have transparency settings (see Figure 11-7).

Print as Bitmap If (and only if) you're printing to a non-PostScript/PDF device, your pages need to be rasterized (converted to a bitmap). You can control who does the conversion: If you turn on Print as Bitmap, InDesign rasterizes at a particular image resolution that you specify. If you turn it off, InDesign writes vectors to disk and lets the operating system do the conversion. In general, it works pretty well either way.

OPI Image Replacement When you're printing through an OPI server, you can direct the server to replace the low-resolution images you've used to lay out your document with the high-resolution images you've stored on the server. To do this, turn off the OPI Image Replacement option and turn on the appropriate Omit for OPI check boxes. This omits

FIGURE 11-7
The Advanced Panel
of the Print Dialog Box

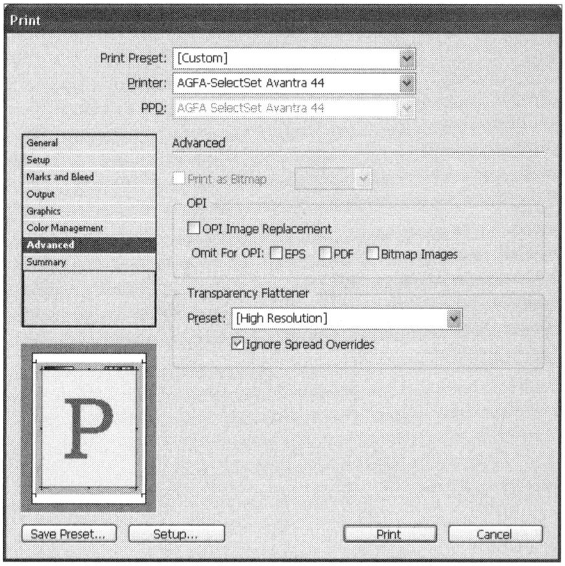

the images from the PostScript output, leaving only the OPI link information in their place.

Note that you can specify which types of images you want to replace with OPI comments: EPS, PDF, or Bitmap Images. When you turn on the EPS option, you're telling InDesign not to print any EPS graphics in the file, but if PDF and Bitmap Images are still turned off then the program will include that image data at print time.

When you turn on OPI Image Replacement, InDesign acts as an OPI server at print time, replacing the low-resolution OPI proxy images with the high-resolution versions. InDesign needs access to the server or drive containing the files for this to work. To retain OPI image links to images stored inside imported EPS graphics, make sure that you turn on the Read Embedded OPI Image Links option in the EPS Import Options dialog box.

Transparency Flattener

We hate to give you the runaround, but if you're reading this hoping to learn all about how the flattener works, you're out of luck. We cover all the issues regarding printing transparency later in this chapter. We will say, however, that you can use the Transparency Flattener section of the Advanced pane of the Print dialog box to choose a default Flattener setting for your print job, and to tell InDesign whether to ignore any Flattener settings you've applied to particular spreads in your document with the Pages panel.

Use Medium Resolution when printing proofs and High Resolution when printing final artwork. But "Medium" and "High" can mean different things depending on the Flattener settings, so you still need to go read that other section. Sorry.

Summary

The last pane of the Print dialog box, Summary, simply lists all the various settings in all the panes in one long text list. It's darn silly (not to mention difficult and time-consuming) to read through this unformatted list of settings on screen. Fortunately, you can click the Save Summary button to save this list to disk as a text file.

Print Presets

We don't know about you, but we find we print a typical InDesign publication (at least) three different ways. We print a proof copy on our laser printer, a color proof on a color printer, and then we print our final copies on an platesetter. In the first two instances, we print composites; when we print to an imagesetter, we may print color separations. You might think that for each type of printing we have to claw our way through the settings in the Print dialog box. Instead, we save our Print dialog box settings in a *print preset*—which means that switching from proof to final printing is as easy as selecting the appropriate print preset.

Print presets are like paragraph styles—they're bundles of attributes that can be applied in a single action. Almost all of the attributes in the Print dialog box and in the printer driver dialog boxes are included in a print preset.

Creating a Print Preset

It's easy to create a print preset; set up the Print dialog box with the options the way you want them, click the Save Preset button at the bottom of the dialog box, and then give the preset a name. You can then go ahead and print, or just cancel out of the Print dialog box (if you just wanted to set up the preset without printing).

InDesign also has a second method for making print presets, though we find it slightly more cumbersome.

1. Choose Define from the Print Presets submenu of the File menu. InDesign displays the Define Print Presets dialog box (see Figure 11-8).

2. Click the New button. InDesign displays the New Print Preset dialog box, which is nearly identical to the Print dialog box.

FIGURE 11-8
Creating a Print Preset

Choose Define from the Print Presets submenu of the File menu. InDesign displays the Print Presets dialog box.

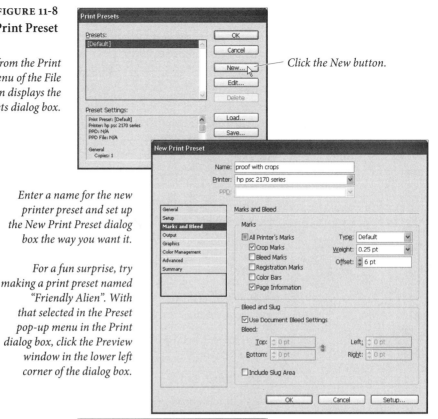

Click the New button.

Enter a name for the new printer preset and set up the New Print Preset dialog box the way you want it.

For a fun surprise, try making a print preset named "Friendly Alien". With that selected in the Preset pop-up menu in the Print dialog box, click the Preview window in the lower left corner of the dialog box.

InDesign adds the new print preset to the list of available presets.

To print using the printer preset, choose the preset name from the Print Presets submenu of the File menu (hold down Shift if you want to print without displaying the Print dialog box).

3. Enter a name for the print preset in the Name field, then set up the dialog box with the settings you want, and click the OK button. InDesign returns you to the Print Presets dialog box and adds the new print preset to the list of available presets.

To print using the settings in a print preset, you can choose the preset from the Print preset pop-up menu in the Print dialog box. Or, even easier, select the print preset name from the Print presets submenu of the File menu. InDesign displays the Print dialog box. Click the Print button (or the Save button, if you're printing to disk), and InDesign prints the specified pages.

To print without displaying the Print dialog box, hold down Shift as you choose the print preset name from the Print Presets submenu of the File menu.

Managing Print Presets

You can use the Print Presets dialog box to add presets, delete presets, rename presets, edit presets, or import or export print presets.

▶ To create a new print preset that is based on an existing preset, open the Print Presets dialog box, select a print preset, and then click the New button. Enter a name for your new print preset, then modify the settings in the panels of the Print dialog box. Note that this does not link the two presets—changes made to the "parent" print preset will not affect any presets you've based on it.

▶ To delete a print preset, select the preset name and click the Delete button.

▶ To export a print preset (or presets), select one or more presets and click the Save button. Specify a file name and location for the print presets document and click the OK button.

▶ To import a print preset or set of presets, open the Print Presets dialog box and click the Load button. Locate and select a print presets document (or an InDesign publication containing print presets), then click the OK button. If the print presets you're importing already exist in the publication, InDesign will create copies of the presets (InDesign will append a number—usually "1"—to the duplicate print presets).

▶ To edit a print preset, select the preset name in the Print Presets dialog box, then click the Edit button. InDesign displays the Print dialog box. Make the changes and click the OK button to save the edited preset.

Custom Printer Marks

If there's one thing we've learned about our fellow desktop publishers over the years, it's that you're picky about printer's marks. You want to control the offset of the crop marks and bleed marks from the edge of the page. You want to use star targets instead of, or in addition to, the standard registration marks. You want the color bars to print at the top, the bottom, the left, or the right of the page.

There is utterly no way for a page layout program to provide for all of your individual preferences—what's right for one person is not just wrong, but is probably offensive to another.

InDesign, in recognition of this fact, provides a (very obscure) way for you to define your own marks with printer's marks definition (also known as PMD or .mrk) files. They're text files that can be edited with any text editor (the free TextWrangler on the Mac OS or Notepad in Windows work quite well). Once you've saved a PMD file to a specific folder on your system, a new entry will appear in the Type pop-up menu in the Marks and Bleed panel of the Print dialog box. Choose the option, and InDesign will print using the marks defined in the file.

Instead of boring most of you with arcane code here, we've made this section, including example code, available as a PDF file for you to download here: *www.indesignsecrets.com/downloads/mrk.pdf*

Printing Booklets

As we mentioned earlier, there's an important difference between reader spreads and printer spreads. In reader spreads, page 2 and 3 appear opposite each other, as left and right facing pages. But if you want to print, fold up, trim, and bind a book or magazine, you need to print it using printer spreads. If you have an 8-page booklet, you need to print page 1 and 8 next to each other (the front and back cover), then page 2 and 7, then 3 and 6, and so on. The process of creating printer spreads is called *imposition*, and there are expensive, dedicated applications (such as Kodak PREPS, Farrukh Systems Imposition Publisher, and Impostrip from Ultimate) that can impose 8 or 12 or 32 document pages onto an enormous plate.

There are also a number of mid-range solutions—typically Acrobat plug-ins such as Quite Imposing (www.quite.com)—that can impose any PDF.

But what if you just want to print up a little booklet from inside InDesign? The answer is the Print Booklet feature, found at the bottom of the File menu. Print Booklet is perfect for pretty much any small publication you would print on a desktop printer—such as a saddle-stapled office telephone directory. Here's how to manage the Print Booklet dialog box (see Figure 11-9):

FIGURE 11-9
Print Booklet

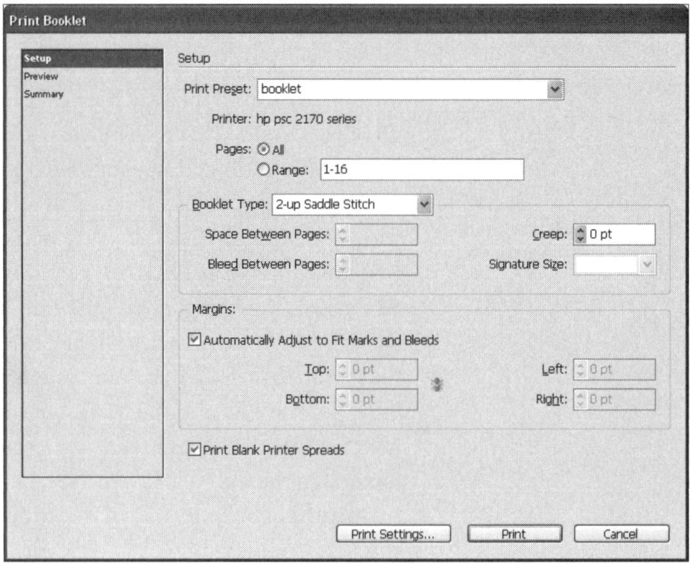

1. If you have already created a Print Preset for your output device, you can choose it from the pop-up menu at the top of the dialog box. Alternately, click the Print Settings button at the bottom of the dialog box to view the Print dialog box, pick a printer, and choose from all the features we've been talking about.

2. Choose a page range to print. For example, typing 1,6-11,18 will print pages 1, 6 through eleven, and 18.

3. Pick an arrangement from the Booklet Type pop-up menu:

   ▸ **Saddle Stitch.** In a saddle-stitched imposition, you end up folding all the sheets in half and stapling them in the middle (see Figure 11-10). InDesign can do 2-up saddle stitching, so you'd get two document pages printed on each side of the sheet of paper. In most cases, this is what you'll likely use.

   ▸ **Perfect Bound.** In a perfect bound imposition, you build signatures, then bind those signatures together (typically by gluing them inside spine a cover). InDesign only creates 2-up sheets (two pages on each side of the sheet). You need to specify how large each signature should be in the Signature Size pop-up menu.

   ▸ **Consecutive.** The Consecutive booklet type is for documents such as tri-fold brochures where you want the first three pages of your document to be on one side of a sheet, and the fourth through sixth pages to be on the opposite side. While

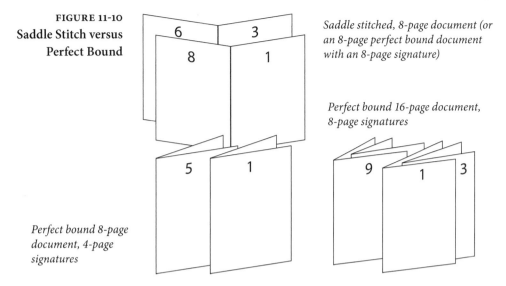

FIGURE 11-10
Saddle Stitch versus Perfect Bound

Saddle stitched, 8-page document (or an 8-page perfect bound document with an 8-page signature)

Perfect bound 16-page document, 8-page signatures

Perfect bound 8-page document, 4-page signatures

we can see the appeal of building your document this way, there are two problems. First, the third panel of a trifold typically has to be slightly narrower than the first two, or else it won't fold properly. The amazing PageControl plug-in from DTPtools lets you create different-sized pages in your InDesign document, but we're not sure how much to trust Print Booklet with these files.

4. Enter values, if necessary, for Creep, Space Between Pages, and Bleed Between Pages.

   ▸ **Creep.** Sheets of paper have thickness, so when you stack a bunch of them and fold them together, the sheets on the inside get pushed out a little. To accommodate for that, you can increase the Creep value, which pushes pages incrementally closer to the binding as they approach the middle of the booklet. The value you enter in the Creep field defines the full adjustment of pages at the middle of the booklet. The actual value you should use for Creep depends entirely on the thickness of the paper. If you have fewer than 6 or 8 sheets of paper, you probably don't even need to worry about it. And, yes, Nirvana fans, you can enter a negative creep value.

   ▸ **Space Between Pages/Bleed Between Pages.** If you know exactly how far apart you want two pages on your spreads to sit from each other, you can enter that in the Space Between Pages value (but only for perfect binding). And if you have increased the amount of Space Between Pages, you can also increase the Bleed Between Pages value (up to one half the amount of Space Between Pages)—this lets some of page 2 bleed into the blank space to the left of page 3, for example. In general, we feel that if you need these kinds of features, then you're likely outgrowing the usefulness of Print Booklet and should probably look around for a more robust imposition solution.

5. In most cases, you can leave the Automatically Adjust to Fit Marks and Bleeds checkbox turned on, letting InDesign figure out where to put your page marks.

6. Finally, click on the Preview pane to see how the final imposition will look (see Figure 11-11). Most importantly, check the Messages and Warning sections to see if InDesign had to add blank pages or if it expects any other problems printing. For example, if your document has only 6 pages, InDesign will have to add two blank pages in order to fill out two 2-up sheets (eight pages). Notice that you can scroll through the imposed document to see each spread.

    If InDesign tells you that the imposed page won't fit on your current page size, you can click Print Settings, change the page size in the Print dialog box, and click OK. This returns you to the Preview pane, where you can see the effects of your change.

7. When you're convinced that it will output correctly, click Print.

FIGURE 11-11
Print Booklet

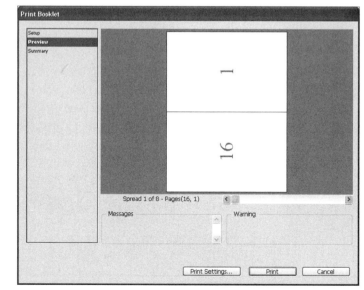

Note that Print Booklet does not let you create a new imposed InDesign document; it only prints the imposed pages and doesn't change your current document at all. If you find you need to impose your document yourself in order to send to someone else to print, you can always "print" using Print Booklet to a PDF file. However, you shouldn't send an imposed document to a printer unless they specifically ask you to—they should have software to do it better (especially for their press) than you do.

Here's another reason you may have to print the booklet to a PDF: If you don't have a duplex printer (one that can print on both sides of a sheet of paper). Instead, print the imposed file to a PDF file and open it in Acrobat. When you print from Acrobat you can choose to print just the odd pages. Then flip the printed pages over, put them back into the paper tray, and print all the even pages backward (with the Reverse checkbox turned on in Acrobat's Print dialog box).

Booklets of Books   Unfortunately, there is no way to use Print Booklet with a book. If you need to impose a book, it's better export the book as a PDF and then use a third-party Acrobat plug-in to do the imposition.

Separations Preview

If there's one feature we've longed for since desktop publishing programs gained the ability to print color separations (yes, Junior, there was a time when they didn't), it's a separations preview—a way that we could look at the individual separations of a document *before* committing them to expensive imagesetter film or printing plates.

We've tried all sorts of workarounds—rasterizing files in Photoshop and then splitting channels; printing separations to disk and then converting the PostScript to PDF using Acrobat Distiller...you name it, we've probably tried it in our quest to see what our separations would look like without having to print them.

That's all over now, thanks to InDesign's Separations Preview panel. With this modern marvel, you can see what your separations will look like without even having to leave InDesign.

To view your pages as separations, display the Separations panel (choose Separations from the Output submenu of the Window menu, or press Shift-F6). Choose Separations from the View menu in the Separations panel. Click the column to the left of the Ink names to turn the display of that ink off or on (see Figure 11-12). You can also use keyboard shortcuts, as shown in Table 11-3.

FIGURE 11-12
Separations Preview

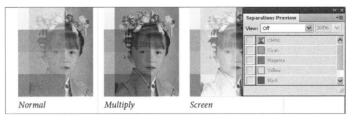

Separations preview off.

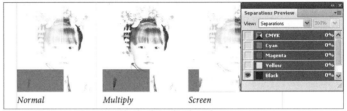

Separations preview on, Black plate displayed.

TABLE 11-3
Keyboard Shortcuts for Separations Preview

To Display:	Press:
First spot plate	Command-Shift-Option-5/Ctrl-Alt-Shift-5
Second spot plate	Command-Shift-Option-6/Ctrl-Alt-Shift-6
Third spot plate	Command-Shift-Option-7/Ctrl-Alt-Shift-7
Fourth spot plate	Command-Shift-Option-8/Ctrl-Alt-Shift-8
Fifth spot plate	Command-Shift-Option-9/Ctrl-Alt-Shift-9
All plates	Command-Shift-Option-` (accent grave) /Ctrl-Alt-Shift-` (accent grave)
Black plate	Command-Shift-Option-4/Ctrl-Alt-Shift-4
Cyan plate	Command-Shift-Option-1/Ctrl-Alt-Shift-1
Magenta plate	Command-Shift-Option-2/Ctrl-Alt-Shift-2
Yellow plate	Command-Shift-Option-3/Ctrl-Alt-Shift-3

FIGURE 11-13
Ink Limit

Choose Ink Limit…

…and enter a percentage in the associated field (the percentage should match the maximum ink coverage for the type of press and paper you're printing on).

InDesign highlights the areas in which the ink concentration is greater than the percentage you've entered (shown as black here, as we don't have color to work with).

All other objects are rendered using gray values corresponding to the intensity of ink coverage in the area.

FIGURE 11-14
Previewing
Overprinting

You can use the Separations Preview panel to view overprinting before you print.

Stroke greatly enlarged for illustrative purposes!

You can choose to display the separations in the ink color, or you can view the separations in black—to do the latter, choose Show Single Plates in Black from the Separations panel menu.

As you move the cursor over objects on the page, the Separations Preview panel displays the inks percentages used in the objects beneath the cursor.

The Separations Preview panel can also help you watch the ink densities of objects on your pages. Choose Ink Limit from the View pop-up menu in the Separations Preview panel, then enter an ink coverage percentage in the associated field. When the ink coverage in an area exceeds the percentage you entered, InDesign highlights the area in red (see Figure 11-13).

One really cool thing about the Separations Preview is that you can see the effect of overprinting, as shown in Figure 11-14. This feature alone is worth a great deal, as you can use it to preview simple text trapping and special overprinting effects without having to print the document.

Printing Transparency

Two of the most important figures in the desktop publishing revolution—Tim Gill (founder of Quark, Inc.) and John Warnock (co-founder of Adobe, Inc.)—each had a blind spot that led to a tragedy of unparalleled proportions. Well, maybe not quite that strong (they both retired quite happily in recent years). But the blind spots did have interesting results that caused their companies—and their customers—difficulties.

Tim Gill didn't believe that HTML or PDF was worth paying much attention to, and Quark suffered by being late to supporting the Web and the PDF standard. John Warnock didn't believe transparency was important in the print industry and so it took PostScript 20 years to support it. Today, everyone knows that vector transparency is important to designers, but because PostScript couldn't print it, programs couldn't support it.

But wait, you say, some programs have had transparency features for many years! Photoshop supported transparency because it only had to worry about pixels, not vector artwork. The transparency features of every other program (including Illustrator, FreeHand, and so on) worked by faking the effects at print time, "flattening" the transparent objects into a form that PostScript could handle.

In recent years, transparency has finally made its way into PostScript 3 by way of the PDF 1.4 specification. RIPs that support transparency in PDF (such as those based on the Adobe PDF Print Engine) can print transparency. For older equipment, however, InDesign users will still have to flatten files that include drop shadows, feathering, or any other cool transparency effects.

The Flattener Adobe's technology for turning transparent objects into a form suitable for older RIPs is called "the flattener." The flattener works by breaking up transparent objects into smaller non-transparent objects. It uses three basic methods to do this.

▸ **Divide and conquer.** If you have a 50-percent transparent magenta square partially over a cyan square, the flattener splits this into three objects: where the two squares overlap, it creates a rectangle made of cyan and magenta; where they didn't overlap, it makes two L-shaped objects, one cyan, the other magenta.

▸ **Clip it up.** Let's say you have a 20-percent transparent picture partially overlapping that cyan square (or vice versa, a partially transparent cyan square overlapping a picture). The flattener splits the picture into two (or more) pieces by drawing invisible frames (clipping paths) and putting pieces of the picture into them. The part of the picture that is inside the square gets cyan added to it to finish the effect.

▸ **Rasterize.** When all else fails, and InDesign realizes that it'll take too long to use the previous two methods (too long to flatten means the file will probably also take way too long to print), it punts and just turns the whole thing into a bitmapped picture (converting vectors into bitmaps is called rasterizing).

Again, all of this is done behind the scenes and only at print time (or when you export the file as an EPS or an Acrobat 4 PDF file, both of which also use the flattener). In most cases, you'd never know that InDesign was doing any of this if we hadn't told you, because the results are extremely clean. In some cases, primarily when InDesign ends up rasterizing part of your page, you may find the results only fine, okay, or (rarely) unacceptable.

Transparency Tricks

Transparency is all about accepting compromise, and if you can't deal with compromise then you might consider avoiding transparency altogether. The first compromise is time versus quality: the better the quality, the more time your files will take to print (or export). The next compromise is that if you want to play with transparency (or your clients want to, and you've agreed to print their documents), you need to pay attention to how your document is created and be prepared to proof the final results carefully.

Here are a few things you should pay attention to when messing with transparency:

▶ Transparency comes in all sorts of forms. If you use the Drop Shadow or any other feature in the Effects panel, you're introducing transparency. So does importing a native Photoshop, Illustrator, or PDF document that includes any transparent object. If the page icon in the Pages panel has a checkerboard icon under it, you can bet that the flattener will kick in.

▶ If you can avoid placing text or other vector objects (especially small text) behind a transparent object, you probably should. For example, a black drop shadow falling on top of black text looks the same whether the text is over or under the shadow, so you should definitely put the text on a layer higher than the shadow. But if your design depends on the text being beneath a transparency effect, then by all means go for it—and be prepared to proof it and make sure it prints correctly.

▶ If you're going to use transparent objects in Illustrator (including transparent brushes, most filters, drop shadows, and so on), make sure you're using version 9.02 or later (you should probably just use version 10 or later). Also, we suggest saving files in the native .ai format, the Acrobat 5 PDF format, or an .eps format compatible with Illustrator 9 or 10 (not earlier versions). This way InDesign handles flattening at print time instead of you worrying about Illustrator getting it right.

- ▶ If you're importing Illustrator documents that include images and use transparency effects, it's probably a good idea to embed the images in the Illustrator file itself rather than relying on linking to the file on disk.

- ▶ Set the Transparency Blend Space (in the Edit menu) to CMYK rather than RGB, and—if you've turned on color management— use Convert to Profile (Preserve Numbers) to convert the document working space to your final output space.

- ▶ Spot colors offer a number of opportunities for problems, especially the flattener converting spot colors to process colors (or worse, converting part of an object to process color and leaving the rest of the object a spot color). This typically happens when you use fancy transparency modes (such as Color, Saturation, Difference, and so on) or when you have spot color gradients involved with transparency.

- ▶ The flattener must work with high-resolution images on disk, which means that an OPI workflow—which relies on importing low-resolution images that get swapped out with high-resolution later—is out. (Of course, if you have OPI images that are not involved with transparency then you can still use them.) DCS files *do* work with transparency flattening. Adobe's documentation used to say that EPS duotones are also a no-no, but we haven't run into any problems with them.

- ▶ It's better not to mix overprint settings (such as Overprint Stroke or Overprint Fill) with transparency. If you're using transparency anyway, consider using the Multiply blend mode rather than turning on Overprint Fill.

- ▶ Most PostScript RIPs can handle the flattener tricks just fine, but we have encountered some RIPs that cause problems. For example, because older Scitex (now part of Creo) RIPs rely on separating continuous tone imagery from line work (vector) images, you can get some very bad results, especially where text interacts with transparent objects. Creo says they're working on a fix for this, but be extra careful when perusing your output if you (or your output provider) are using this sort of RIP.

- ▶ In fact, it would behoove you to always look over your final output carefully. Look for spot colors that were converted to process, overprinting instructions that were ignored, vector objects that were rasterized in unpleasant ways, unintentionally rasterized type, and text or strokes that became heavier.

Flattener Presets

As we said earlier, flattening is a matter of compromise. Fortunately, you have a say in the matter, by selecting among various flattener presets. A flattener preset essentially asks: how hard should InDesign try before giving up and rasterizing the artwork?

InDesign ships with three predefined flattener presets: Low Resolution, Medium Resolution, and High Resolution. You can mentally replace the word "resolution" with "quality." You should typically use Low or Medium when printing to a desktop laser printer and High when printing to an imagesetter or platesetter (see "Applying Flattener Presets," later in this chapter).

FIGURE 11-15
Creating a Flattener Preset

Select Transparency Flattener Presets from the Edit menu.

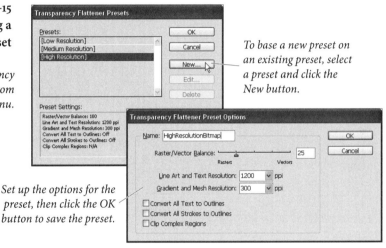

To base a new preset on an existing preset, select a preset and click the New button.

Set up the options for the preset, then click the OK button to save the preset.

Occasionally we find a need to create our own flattener preset. If you're doing a lot of proofs on a black-and-white desktop laser printer, you could probably get away with making a "Very Low" preset, which may print faster than Low Resolution with "good enough" quality. Or, if you're getting unacceptably slow printing, printing errors, or poor quality on an imagesetter with the High Resolution preset, you might want to create a custom preset that works better for you.

To make a custom flattener preset, select Transparency Flattener Presets from the Edit menu (see Figure 11-15). While you cannot edit the default presets, you can base a new one on a default preset by selecting the preset, then clicking the New button, which opens the Transparency Flattener Preset Options dialog box. Beyond the name of the preset (enter whatever you want), there are six controls here.

Raster/Vector Balance. The Raster/Vector Balance slider is a graphic representation of the quality/speed compromise. Push the slider all the way to the left and InDesign rasterizes everything on the page (we can't think of any good reason to do this). Push the slider all the way to the right and InDesign tries its best to maintain every vector in the document, even if that means taking a long time to flatten and a long time to print. As left-leaning as we tend to be, we always prefer pushing this to the far right when printing on imagesetters. However, on a complex page, this creates so many clipping paths that your file might not print at all. In that case, you'd need to take it down a notch.

Line Art and Text Resolution. When InDesign ends up rasterizing a vector object, it looks to the Line Art and Text Resolution setting in order to find the appropriate resolution. The Low Resolution flattener preset uses a flattener resolution of 288 ppi (pixels per inch), which will look very slightly jagged on a desktop laser printer. The High Resolution flattener preset uses 1200 ppi. If you were printing on newsprint, you could easily get away with creating a flattener preset that used 800 ppi. If you're printing on glossy stock for a coffee table book, you could probably raise this to 1600 ppi.

The flattener resolution also acts as an "upper boundary" when imported bitmapped images are involved with transparency. For example, let's say you import a 300 ppi image, put transparent text over it, and then print using the Low Resolution flattener preset. InDesign resamples the image down to 288 ppi. However, if you use the High Resolution flattener preset, InDesign will not upsample the image to 1200 (that would be crazy).

Gradient and Mesh Resolution. Sometimes objects get rasterized no matter what happens—for instance, soft drop shadows or feather effects. This setting determines the appropriate resolution for these sorts of raster effects. The Gradient and Mesh Resolution setting in the Low Resolution flattener preset defaults to 144 ppi, even though you typically don't need more than 100 ppi on any desktop printer. You generally don't need more than 200 ppi for high-resolution output. (After all, you need resolution to capture detail in an image, and these "images" have no detail).

InDesign may upsample images if they're involved with transparent areas of the page and they're lower resolution than the Gradient and Mesh Resolution setting. For example, if you import a 72 ppi image (like a JPEG saved from a Web site) and change its transparency setting, the flattener upsamples the image to the gradient resolution. Unfortunately, if you import a 200 ppi TIFF image (which is very reasonable for most printed artwork today), set its transparency, and print it using the High Resolution flattener preset, InDesign also upsamples it to 300 ppi—causing slower printing and possibly image degradation. (InDesign uses "nearest neighbor" interpolation, which results in pretty clunky images.)

Convert All Text to Outlines. When text gets involved with transparency (either it is transparent or something transparent is on top of it), the type almost always gets turned into paths that act as clipping paths. This slows down printing a bit, and sometimes that text appears heavier than the equivalent characters that aren't converted to outlines, especially on lower-resolution printers. If, for example, you had an image that was partially transparent on top of half a column of text, the text under the image might appear like it was very slightly more bold than the rest of the text. One answer would be to create a flattener preset in which the Convert All Text to Outlines option was turned on and apply that to this particular spread (we discuss applying flattener presets below). This way, all the text on that spread gets converted to outlines. The page prints even slower, but is more consistent. This is rarely a problem when imagesetting or platesetting, however, so we usually just ignore this feature.

Convert All Strokes to Outlines. The problem with type "heavying up" is also an issue around thin lines. The flattener converts lines involved with transparency effects into very thin boxes. These lines may appear thicker than other lines of the same stroke weight. Turning this feature on ensures that InDesign will convert all of the lines in the document, making them more visually equal. Again, this is rarely an issue on high-resolution printers.

Clip Complex Regions. When InDesign does resort to rasterizing vectors, it usually does so in rectangular areas, called "atomic regions" (sort of like the smallest regions the flattener deals with). The problem with this lies along the line between a rasterized area and an area drawn with vectors—in many cases, the step from raster to vector is visually obvious (sometimes called "stitching"), which sort of ruins the whole point. When you turn on the Clip Complex Regions check box, however, InDesign works extra hard to make the transitions between raster and vector occur only along the edges of objects. The result is a better-looking page that is more complex and prints more slowly (or not at all).

Applying Flattener Presets

After reading all of this, don't you wish you had an Adobe PDF Print Engine-enabled device that could print transparency effects without flattening? Until you have one, however, you'd better know about how to apply these flattener presets.

You can set the flattener preset to either the whole document (the "default preset") or specific page spreads (a "local preset"). To apply a default preset at print time, choose it from the Transparency Flattener Preset pop-up menu in the Advanced pane of the Print dialog box. You can also set the default preset in the Advanced panes of the Export as PDF and Export as EPS dialog boxes, as well as the Export as SVG dialog box (if you click More Options).

To apply a local flattener preset, select one or more page spreads in the Pages panel and select from among the choices in the Spread Flattening menu in the Pages panel menu: Default, None (Ignore Transparency), or Custom. If you choose None, InDesign prints this spread without any transparency effects. You might use this as a troubleshooting technique if your page isn't printing properly.

If, at print time, you want to override any and all flattener presets applied to the document with the default preset, you can turn on the Ignore Spread Overrides check box in the Print dialog box.

Flattener Preview   It's driving you crazy. The Pages panel is displaying the icon that means there's transparency on a page, but you can't figure out which object is transparent. This sort of thing often happens when you're working on a file created by someone else. Wouldn't it be great if you could see the transparent areas at a glance?

You've set up your flattener to encourage rasterization, but you want to be certain that text near transparent areas is not rasterized. Is there some way to see which areas will be rasterized?

The Flattener Preview panel is the answer to both questions. To display the Flattener Preview panel, choose Flattener from the Output submenu of the Window menu. Note that this panel has been misnamed; it's really more of a "flattener alert" than a preview. That is, it's not technically showing you what something will look like after it is flattened; it's just pointing out what will be flattened.

To use it, first choose from the Highlight pop-up menu to highlight the type of transparency you're looking for (see Figure 11-16). In the first example we described, you'd choose Transparent Objects; in the second, you'd probably want to choose All Rasterized Regions. The other options on the menu give you more specific control over the type of transparency you want to highlight.

You can have InDesign refresh the transparency highlight for you by turning on the Auto Refresh Highlight option, or turn it off to speed up your screen display and click the Refresh button as needed.

The Flattener Preview panel gives you a way to "audition" flattener presets, which can help you decide which preset will work best. Choose a preset from the Presets pop-up menu, and InDesign

FIGURE 11-16
Flattener Preview

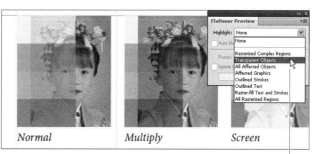

*Choose a flattener preview from
the Highlight pop-up menu.*

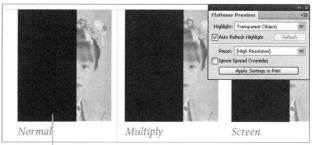

*InDesign highlights transparent areas on
the page in red (shown here in dark gray).*

*In this example, we've applied a
drop shadow to the text.*

*Choosing All Rasterized Regions
shows that the drop shadow will
be rasterized (according to the
currently selected flattener preset).*

*When we switch flattener
presets to a preset that encourages
rasterization, InDesign highlights
the rasterized text.*

highlights the appropriate areas based on the new preset (if you've turned off the Auto Refresh Highlight option, you'll have to click the Refresh button to see the effect). Turn on the Ignore Spread Overrides option to use the preset you've selected, rather than using the flattener applied to the spread, if necessary.

Once the preview looks good to you, you can apply the flattener preset to your print settings by clicking the Apply Settings to Print button (you'll see this change reflected in the Advanced panel of the Print dialog box).

Preparing an InDesign File for Imagesetting

We've listened long and carefully to the grievances of imagesetting service bureau customers and operators. We've heard about how this designer is suing that service bureau for messing up a job, and we've heard imagesetter operators talking about how stupid their clients are and how they have to make changes to the files of most of the jobs that come in. We've listened long enough, and we have only one thing to say: Cut it out! All of you!

There's no reason that this relationship has to be an adversarial one. We don't mean to sound harsh. We just think that we can all cooperate, to everyone's benefit.

Designers: You have to learn the technical chops if you want to play. That's just the way it is. The challenges are no greater than those you mastered when you learned how to use a waxer, an X-Acto knife, or a copy camera. (Or whatever it is designers learn nowadays.)

Your responsibility to your imagesetting service bureau is to set your file up so that it has a reasonable chance of printing and to communicate to your service bureau exactly how it is you want your publication printed.

Service bureau folks, you've got to spell out the limits of your responsibility. If you don't think you should be fixing people's files, don't do it. If you do think it's your responsibility, tell your customer up front you'll fix the files, and tell them what you'll charge for your time. And if you get customers who know what they're doing, give them a discount. This will encourage everyone else.

Okay, back to the book.

Sending Your File
You have three basic choices in transporting your document to an output provider: sending the file itself, sending a PDF, or sending a PostScript file. While our preference is to send a PDF file, many service providers want the InDesign file itself.

When we send an InDesign file off to be printed on someone else's system, we don't know whether their fonts are different, whether they'll forget to set up registration marks, and so on. If you send them a PDF (and you know what you're doing), you can be reasonably sure that the file will print correctly. The only things that can go wrong are related to film handling and processing—the wrong film's used, the film's scratched, or the film's been processed incorrectly.

However, no matter what you're going to send to your output provider, you have to be dead certain you've thought of everything before it goes, because it's difficult to change things after that. For instance, you need to make sure that any linked graphics in the publication are up to date.

Make certain that the Print dialog box is set up correctly: What screening are you using? Is tiling turned off? Do you need separations or composite color? What inks to print? Do you want spot colors or process colors? Your output provider should be able to help you with these decisions.

If you're sending a PDF for printing, *don't* create the PDF by printing PostScript to disk and then running that file through Acrobat Distiller. This is a recipe for disaster, and asking for it is a clue that your service provider doesn't know what they're doing. Instead, simply export PDF from within InDesign.

There is one file format that you should *never* provide to a service provider for printing, and that's INX. We've heard of cases where the service provider does not have the latest version of InDesign and asks for an INX file—don't do it. While INX provides "backward compatibility," it doesn't guarantee a perfect translation from one version of InDesign to another. If nothing else, it's almost certain that text composition will change when you open an INX file in a previous version of InDesign. If your service provider makes such a request, it's time to start looking for a new service provider.

Preflight and Package

Are all systems "go"? Do you know the number of kilometers, meters, and centimeters it'll take to get your publication safely in orbit around Mars? Or is it miles, feet, and inches?

Preflight   To make sure that your publication is really ready for "prime time," you use the Preflight panel (see Figure 11-17). To display the Preflight panel, double-click the Preflight icon at the bottom of the InDesign window (or choose Preflight from the Output submenu of the Windows menu, or press Command-Option-Shift-F/Ctrl-Alt-Shift-F).

You can work with Preflight "live" (always on), or turn it on only when you need to check your document. Having Preflight turned on can slow InDesign performance in some cases; experiment to see if it's a problem on your system.

When you turn preflight on, InDesign examines the publication for missing fonts, lost image links, and other conditions that might cause you problems and/or embarrassment when you print your document. When InDesign finds a problem, the indicator in

FIGURE 11-17
Preflight Panel

Choose Preflight Panel from the Preflight pop-up menu. Use the Preflight Document option turn the Preflight feature on or off.

If preflight is on, you can double-click the Preflight icon to display the panel.

Choose the preflight profile you want to use.

The Preflight panel gives you a quick look at the status of the preflight check. If anything is amiss (according to the current prflight profile), you'll see it reported here.

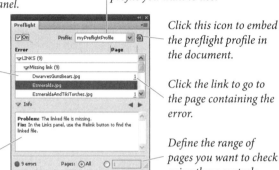

Click this icon to embed the preflight profile in the document.

Click the link to go to the page containing the error.

When you select an item in the Error list, the Info area shows more detail about the error.

Define the range of pages you want to check using these controls.

the Preflight icon turns red; if everything is okay, the indicator is green. To get more information on a specific problem, display the Preflight panel.

There's more to Preflight than just the default settings—Preflight can check for a large number of conditions in your document. The default "Basic" preflight profile covers only the most obvious of errors (missing/incomplete fonts, missing links, and overset text); it's up to you to define preflight profiles that match your documents and your workflow.

A key point here is that the preflight warnings do not, by themselves, mean that something is wrong with your document. Even the warnings produced by the Basic profile are not necessarily bad. It all depends on your workflow and printing process. For example, the Basic profile will always flag images that use the RGB color space. It might be that RGB images are fine in your workflow—it's up to you to decide whether to ignore the error message or not. In similar fashion, you might want to set up custom profiles that alert you to benign, but possibly unexpected, conditions in your documents.

Defining preflight profiles. To define a preflight profile, follow these steps (see Figure 11-18).

1. Display the Preflight panel.

2. Choose Define Profiles from the Preflight Panel menu. InDesign displays the Preflight Profiles dialog box.

3. Click the New Preflight Profile button ("+").

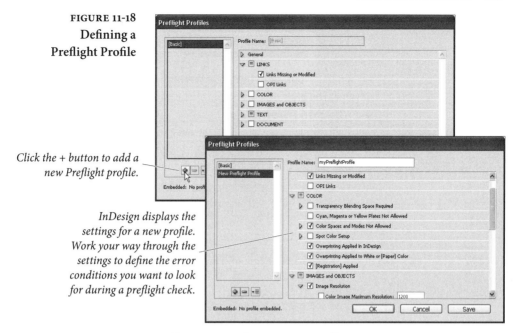

*Click the + button to add a
new Preflight profile.*

*InDesign displays the
settings for a new profile.
Work your way through the
settings to define the error
conditions you want to look
for during a preflight check.*

4. Enter a name for your new profile.

5. Work your way through the different areas of the dialog box, turning preflight checks on and off as necessary.

6. When the preflight profile includes all of the checks you want it to, click the OK button to save the profile.

To use the profile, select the profile name from the Profile pop-up menu in the Preflight panel. To edit the profile, return to the Preflight Profiles dialog box, select the profile name in the list of profiles. The Preflight panel will fill in with the conditions you've defined for the profile.

Performing a preflight check. Once you've selected a preflight profile, all you need to do is turn it on. To do this, display the Preflight panel (choose Preflight Panel from the Preflight pop-up menu), then turn on the On option. You can control the range of pages checked using the options at the bottom of the Preflight panel.

As InDesign checks your document against the preflight conditions defined in the profile, any errors found will appear in the Preflight panel. Links in the Preflight panel will take you to each error.

Embedding preflight profiles. You can embed a preflight profile in a document, which means that the document can travel to other systems and still be checked for the conditions you defined in the profile.

To embed a profile, select the profile from the Profile pop-up menu in the Preflight panel, then click the Embed Profile button.

Saving Preflight Reports. To save a preflight report (the list of errors shown in the Error section of the Preflight panel) as a text file or PDF, choose Save Report from the Preflight panel menu. InDesign displays a standard file dialog. Enter a file name and folder for the file, then choose the format you want to use to save the report from the Save As Type pop-up menu. Click the OK button to save the report.

Setting Preflight Options. The Preflight Options dialog box (choose Preflight Options from the Preflight panel menu) gives you a way to define various settings for the way that InDesign interprets and uses preflight profiles (see Figure 11-19).

Settings in this dialog box are pretty much self-explanatory: choose whether you want to use a profile as a default, whether you want the profile to check master pages and page items on the pasteboard, and so on. If you ever work with files created by others, we think you should keep the Use Embedded Profile option turned on. Without it, you might not notice the profile someone else has set up, and end up "correcting" mistakes that aren't mistakes at all.

Package   You can assemble all of the files needed to print the publication using the Package plug-in (this is similar to QuarkXPress' "Collect for Output" feature, or PageMaker's "Save For Service Provider" plug-in). InDesign also creates a report containing detailed information about your document, including fonts and pictures you used. Then all you have to do is get the folder to your output provider.

To "package" a publication, follow these steps (see Figure 11-20).

1. Choose Package from the File menu (or press Command-Option-Shift-P/Ctrl-Alt-Shift-P). InDesign displays the Printing Instructions dialog box.

2. Enter contact information in the Printing Instructions dialog box—this information will appear in the final text report that InDesign adds to the package you're creating.

3. Click the Continue button. InDesign displays the Create Package Folder dialog box. Set the options you want and enter a name for the folder that will contain the packaged publication.

   When you turn on the Copy Fonts or Copy Linked Graphics option, InDesign copies the files to the folder you specify. The Update Graphic Links in Package option tells InDesign to set

FIGURE 11-19
**Preflight Options
Dialog Box**

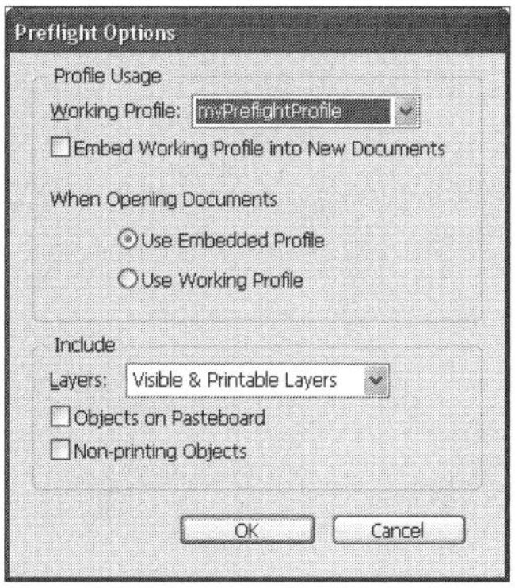

the links for non-embedded images to the images in the pack-aged folder (rather than leaving them linked to the original files). It's pretty rare that you'd want to turn this off. When you turn on the Use Document Hyphenation Exceptions Only option, InDesign flags this document so that it won't reflow when some-one else opens or edits it on a machine that may have different dictionaries and hyphenation settings. We generally turn this on when sending the file to an output provider.

4. Click the Package button. InDesign creates the folder and copies the publication and the files you specified into it. If the Copy Fonts option was turned on, InDesign also alerts you that copy-ing fonts may be a violation of your rights. Adobe fonts can be copied to send to an output provider, but some font vendors don't allow this (though we've never heard of anyone being taken to court for this).

When you send this folder full of files to your printer or ser-vice bureau, make sure you remind them that there is a file called Instructions.txt in there that they should read.

Finally, if you're working on really large files with hundreds of megabytes of images, you need to be careful with the Package feature so that you don't run out of hard disk space.

**Document
Installed Fonts**

The Package command can generate a Document Fonts folder when you want to move your document to another computer. Fonts in the Document Fonts folder are temporarily installed when the docu-ment is opened, and uninstalled when the document is closed. Fonts installed by one document are not available to other documents. Document installed fonts are listed in a submenu of the Font menu.

You don't need to use the Package command to generate the Doc-ument Fonts folder. You can create a Document Fonts folder that's in the same location as an InDesign document, and add fonts to it.

FIGURE 11-20
Packaging a Publication for Remote Printing

When you choose Package from the File menu (or click the Package button in the Preflight dialog box), InDesign displays the Printing Instructions dialog box.

After you click the Continue button, InDesign displays the Package Publication dialog box.

Enter a name and location for the package (the publication file and any other files you choose to copy).

Enter your contact information and any notes you want to include in the fields; these instructions will be saved as a text file.

Choose the files you want to copy to the package folder.

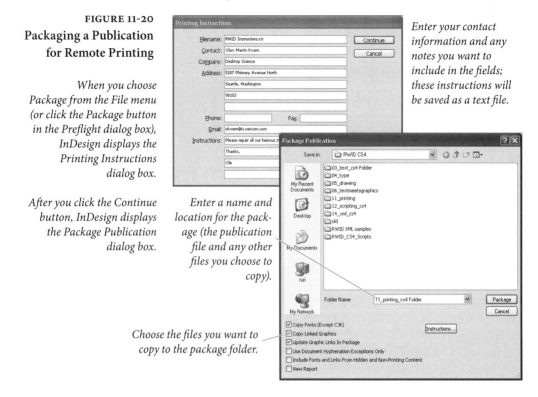

Some fonts can't be installed temporarily as document fonts, including some Type 1 fonts, Mac Postscript fonts, and dfont packages or some older TrueType fonts with Mac-specific encodings.

InDesign looks first in the Document Fonts folder, then in InDesign's Fonts folder, then in the Adobe Application Support Fonts folder, then in the user fonts folder (on a Mac), then in the general Library folder (on a Mac), then finally, in the operating system fonts folder. If there are duplicate fonts and something doesn't look right, open the Find Fonts dialog box, select the font, and then choose Reveal in Finder/Explorer to view the file location.

All the News That Prints to Fit

Printing is all about thinking ahead. When you create a new publication, you really should be thinking "How the heck are we going to print this thing?" By the end of the production process, you'll be tired, cranky, and less able to deal with any problems that come up— so make your decisions about paper size, color selection, and graphic file types as early as you can.

Scripting

12

Most of the time, we tell a program (an application, a plug-in, or our system software) what to do by manipulating the program's user interface—we click, drag, and type. Scripting is a way of telling a program to perform the same tasks and accomplish the same things. The difference is that, with scripting, we don't have to click the buttons, type the characters, or choose the menu items. The script does it for you. Scripting is what computing is supposed to be *about*: having your computer take over boring, repetitive tasks so that you can spend more time playing *World of Warcraft*. Er, we mean, concentrating on your creative work.

Scripting also gives you the ability to add the features you need to InDesign *now*, rather than waiting for Adobe to give them to you. Even better than that, scripting gives you a way to customize InDesign to match your publications and habits to a degree that Adobe is *never* going to provide.

We're convinced that the reason many people have not taken up scripting is that they're scared. They think scripting is difficult, and is only for people with advanced computer science degrees. And they tell themselves that they're too "intuitive" and "artistic" to master the minimal analytical skills required to write a script.

Be Not Afraid

You do not need to know how to *write* scripts to be able to *run* scripts. This is a misunderstanding that prevents many people from even trying scripting, even though existing scripts might save them enormous amounts of time and trouble.

Even if you don't want to write scripts, or know anything about how they're written, you can use scripts. For that matter, chances are quite good that you know someone who *is* interested in writing scripts for you, and would be willing to do so for the occasional expression of admiration (or beer).

Installing Scripts

All you need to know is how to install scripts—and that's very simple: just put the script in the Scripts Panel folder in the Scripts folder inside your InDesign folder. When you do this, the script will appear in the Scripts panel in InDesign.

Here's a tip for finding the Scripts panel folder. Open the Scripts panel, select a folder such as User, and then choose Reveal in Finder or Reveal in Explorer. That's where you keep your scripts.

That's pretty simple, right? If not, we're not certain you should be using a computer at all (or driving a car, for that matter).

Running a Script

To run a script, double-click the script name in the Scripts panel. There are a few other options, as discussed in "Using the Scripts Panel and the Script Label Panel," later in this chapter. Many scripts will display a dialog box (or other user interface item).

Writing Scripts: How Hard Could It Be?

Next, we encourage everyone to consider learning to write scripts.

Ole says: "Look. I'm practically a high school dropout, and my background is in illustration, not computer science. I have never taken a single class on programming. As a rebellious teenager I did my best to ignore the sciences and to panic at the sight of even simple equations (in psychoanalytical terms this makes sense: my father was a high school algebra teacher).

"I got over it. These days, I write scripts. You can, too."

System Requirements

What do you need to write and run scripts for InDesign? The following things:

▶ The InDesign scripting documentation and sample scripts.

▶ A good understanding of the way InDesign works.

▶ The standard scripting system for your computer (if you plan to use the platform-specific scripting languages rather than JavaScript). You probably already have this.

▶ Confidence.

It also helps to have a repetitive task that you wish you would never have to do again. This is not required, but it helps.

JavaScript   InDesign supports an Adobe version of JavaScript called Extend-Script. ExtendScript complies with the ECMA JavaScript 1.5 standard, and adds a few features to make it more useful for scripting a desktop application (as opposed to a web browser).

InDesign JavaScripts are cross-platform—they run in both the Windows and Mac OS versions of InDesign. There are a few minor differences between platforms—but they're limited to the way that the scripts work with files and the operating system (as you'd expect).

If JavaScript is cross-platform, why does Adobe bother supporting the platform-specific languages? First, because scripters might prefer those languages. Adobe's goal should be to *increase* the number of languages that can be used, not to limit them. Next, because InDesign's JavaScript does not know how to communicate with other applications on your system (such as FileMaker or Access); the platform-specific languages do that very well.

Luckily, we can use both, and we can tie the platform-specific and platform-independent languages together with InDesign's "do script" method, which lets scripts run other scripts. A JavaScript, for example, can run an AppleScript, or a VBScript can run a JavaScript.

Note: Some InDesign JavaScripts have the file extension ".js", which is the standard extension for JScripts in Windows, they will not work if run from the operating system (at best, you'll get an error message). Instead, run these scripts using InDesign's Scripts panel. Try to get in the habit of using the ".jsx" extension, rather than ".js".

Mac OS   On the Mac OS, all you need is AppleScript. You almost certainly already have it installed, but in case you don't, it comes on the Mac installation CD. If you can't find your installation CD, you can download AppleScript directly from Apple (http://www.apple.com). What's the easiest way to tell if it's installed? Search for a file named "Script Editor" (this is the application you use to write and run AppleScripts). If you can't find it, you'll have to install it from the Mac OS X installation CD.

Alternative script editors are available—if you're planning to do serious AppleScript development, we strongly recommend Script Debugger, from Late Night Software (http://www.latenightsw.com). Script Debugger is an astonishingly good piece of software, well worth its purchase price. And no, we are not paid to say this.

InDesign can run uncompiled AppleScripts—script files saved as text. To use an uncompiled AppleScript, save the file with the file extension ".applescript" (or ".as") in the Scripts Panel folder inside the Scripts folder in your InDesign folder, and then run the script from the Scripts panel.

Windows   On the Windows side, you've got a number of options. There are (at least) three different scripting systems claiming to be the system standard: Visual Basic Script (VBScript), Visual Basic for Applications (VBA), and various forms of Visual Basic (VB)—including Visual Basic 6, Visual Basic .NET, and Visual Basic 5 Control Creation Edition (VB5 CCE). They're all from Microsoft, and they're all variants of the Basic programming language. Almost all of them work.

Our Recommendation: Use VBScript. To write a VBScript, all you need is a text editor. Notepad does the job quite handily. You don't need anything to run a VBScript—you can run them from Explorer or from InDesign's Scripts panel. If you run them from InDesign's Scripts panel, though, they'll run much faster.

Using VBScript makes distributing and deploying your scripts easier, too. Since they're just text, they're easy to post on web pages or send to other people.

The InDesign sample scripts are provided in VBScript, so you'll have a lot of code to work with that won't require much translation (as it would if you were to try to use them in VB.NET, for example).

Our Further Recommendation: Use VBA to develop VBScripts. Troubleshooting (debugging) VBScripts can be difficult. All you can do is run the script and then note any error messages that appear— and they're not particularly useful. What you need is a real programming environment, where you can step through the lines of your script one by one, as you can when you use Visual Basic.

Visual Basic for Applications, the version of Visual Basic that's built into most Microsoft Office applications, works quite well for developing VBScripts for InDesign. Chances are pretty good that you've already got an Office application.

VBA works very well for developing VBScripts for use in InDesign. You can write your VBScript in VBA, making certain that you don't use part of Visual Basic that does not exist in VBScript; debug the script, and then, when everything works the way you want it to, copy the contents of the subroutine to a text editor and save it as a VBScript (.vbs) file. We'll talk more about this later in the chapter.

Other Scripting Languages   We know of InDesign scripters who are using C#, C, C++, Perl, Python, JScript, OSA JavaScript, Delphi, and other languages to drive InDesign. If your favorite programming language can connect to the platform standard means of passing messages between applications (that's OSA/AppleEvents on the Mac OS and DDE/COM in Windows), it can probably communicate with InDesign.

We're not going to spend any time on those languages, however, because, frankly, we have more than enough to do explaining VBScript, AppleScript, and JavaScript. Forgive us.

Learning About InDesign Scripting

Once you've gathered and installed the software you need to start scripting, you need to learn about how InDesign implements scripting. You're in luck—you'll find the scripting documentation, sample scripts, on the InDesign scripting home page:

```
http://www.adobe.com/products/indesign/scripting/index.html
```

Once you're there, you'll need to click the Scripting Resources tab to display the scripting-specific goodies.

The *Adobe InDesign CS5 Scripting Tutorial* is a PDF that contains an introduction to scripting, and basic tutorials (including introductory scripts). The *Adobe InDesign CS5 Scripting Guide* comes in three flavors: AppleScript, JavaScript, and Visual Basic. Pick the one that matches the language you want to work with.

In addition, the InDesign scripting forum is at:

```
http://forums.adobe.com/community/indesign/indesign_scripting
```

The forum is a great source of scripting information—it's the center of the InDesign scripting community. The forum is the place to find example scripts (literally hundreds of them), ask questions, and generally hang out with other scripters. Do not be afraid to ask "newbie" questions—we've all been there!

Example Scripts   You'll find a number of sample scripts in the Scripts Panel folder inside the Scripts folder in your InDesign folder (you can also see them in the Scripts panel). Even if you don't intend to write scripts of your own, you might find something useful in the sample scripts. Note that the InDesign scripting home page mentioned above also contains a downloadable archive of these scripts.

▶ **AddGuides.** Draws guides around the currently selected object or objects. This script shows you how to get positioning information back from InDesign, and how to create ruler guides.

▶ **AddPoints.** Adds points to a path: each point is added at the midpoint of each line segment in a path. This script demonstrates simple Bezier math and path and point manipulations.

▶ **AdjustLayout.** Moves the page items of even/odd pages by specified distances. Use this script to move objects back into the correct position after adding pages or applying master pages.

▶ **AlignToPage.** How many times have you wanted to position an object in the center of the page? This script does that, and many other page alignments—including the ability to align the objects relative to the page margins.

▶ **AnimationEncyclopedia.** Creates a new document with a number of different buttons and animated objects. Use the Preview panel to see the animated objects in action.

▶ **BreakFrame.** Removes the selected text frame and its contents from the story. This feature has been frequently requested by PageMaker users. Doesn't really work when tables span multiple text frames.

▶ **CornerEffects.** Ever want to round one or two corners of a rectangle, while leaving the other corners square? If you have, then this script is for you. The script redraws the path and applies a corner effect to a pattern of corners you specify.

▶ **CreateCharacterStyle.** When you create a character style in InDesign by basing the style on the selected text, InDesign records only those attributes that differ from the default formatting of the surrounding text. While this is a powerful and flexible way of working with character styles, it's also different from the way that other applications (such as QuarkXPress and FrameMaker) work. In those applications, character styles apply every formatting attribute. The CreateCharacterStyle script creates a new character style based on the selected text and defines every formatting attribute.

▶ **CropMarks.** Draws crop and registration marks around the selected object or objects. Like AddGuides, this script shows how to create new objects around existing objects.

▶ **ExportAllStories.** Exports all of the stories in a document to a specified folder using the file format of your choice (RTF, tagged text, or text only). Shows how to traverse all stories in a document and how to export text.

▶ **FindChangeByList.** Runs a sequence of find/change operations on the selected text. The find/change parameters are stored in a tab-delimited text file (it should be in a folder named Find-ChangeSupport inside the same folder as the sample script). By default, these searches cover the standard stuff: changing double spaces to single spaces, changing double returns to single returns, changing double dashes to em dashes, and so on—but you can add your own favorite searches to the text file (including the ability to find/change formatting). You'll find instructions at the beginning of the script, and in the corresponding find/change file.

▶ **ImageCatalog.** Places all of the graphics in a folder in a grid in an InDesign document.

▶ **MakeGrid.** Splits the selected frame into a grid of frames. If the frame contains content, the script can duplicate the frame.

▶ **Neon.** Creates a simple "glow" effect by duplicating the selected path or paths. Each copy of the path is slightly smaller than the original, and slightly lighter. The final duplicate path is a white hairline. The resulting group of paths is something like an Illustrator blend.

▶ **PathEffects.** This script includes the ever-popular Illustrator, path effects "Bloat" and "Punk," as well as a few others. If you want to learn about scripting InDesign paths, path points, control handles, and Bezier math, this is a good place to start.

▶ **PlaceMultipagePDF.** InDesign can place all of the pages in a multi-page PDF, but it's a manual process—you have to click the place icon for each PDF page you want to place. This script places all of the pages of a PDF on sequential pages, placing one PDF page per page, adding pages to the document if necessary as it does so.

▶ **SelectObjects.** Selects all of the objects on a spread that belong to a specific object type (or set of types). This script is only slightly useful by itself, but it shows you how to traverse the objects on a spread to find objects based on their type or content. It's a great starting point for any graphic "search and replace" operation.

▶ **SortParagraphs.** Alphabetically sorts the paragraphs in the selection. Shows how to sort text using a simple "bubble sort" algorithm, and how to move text in an InDesign story.

▶ **SplitStory.** Converts each text frame in the selected story to an independent text frame (story), retaining the content in the frames. Doesn't really work when tables span multiple text frames.

▶ **TabUtilities.** This script automates two tasks: setting a right tab stop at the right margin of a paragraph, and setting a left tab at the current cursor position.

InDesign Scripting Philosophy

When you launch InDesign, you're probably aware that you're not really launching a single program—you probably know that you're starting a plug-in manager and several hundred plug-ins.

What you probably don't know is that each plug-in is responsible for its own scripting support, and that InDesign's scripting object model—the library of objects and the properties and methods of those objects that make scripting work—is created anew each time you change your plug-in configuration.

In other applications that support scripting, the developers try to determine what features users of their product might want to automate. They then provide scripting support for those features. The trouble with this approach, of course, is that they always miss something—and their users, in the field, are stymied. The users then complain, and are generally given the response, "Why would anyone want to do that?" (Translation: "We didn't think of that.")

InDesign scripting doesn't work that way. InDesign provides scripting access to everything (well, almost everything) you can do to the database that is an InDesign document.

Thinking About Scripting

Because scripting is a great tool for automating large, repetitive tasks, many of us think that that's *all* it's good for. But there's far more to scripting than that. Scripting is also good at little things—operations that might save you only a few seconds a day, but can make your work easier or more precise.

By "little things," we means scripts that save you only a few mouse clicks, drags, or key presses at a time. It's these tiny tasks, repeated dozens, hundreds, or even thousands of times day by day, that add up to fatigue, irritation, and repetitive motion injuries. When you take a common task that involves some number of actions and replace it with a simple double-click or keystroke (all it takes to run a script), you reduce the difficulty and complexity of your work.

Scripting, which many of us think of as being somehow *opposed* to the creative process, can be a powerful creative tool. We often imagine effects we'd like to use in a publication layout that would be difficult to accomplish by hand. When there's time, we turn to scripting for help. Frequently, in the course of working on a script, we'll find a variation on the effect that leads us in an entirely new creative direction. Scripting gives us time to experiment—and we think experimentation has a lot to do with creativity.

What we're getting at here is that scripting is what you make of it, and how you think about it. If you only think of scripting as something applicable to massive projects, you're missing out on many of the benefits—and most of the fun.

Using the Scripts Panel and the Script Label Panel

InDesign includes two scripting-related plug-ins: the Scripts panel and the Script Label panel. The Scripts panel gives you a way to run scripts without leaving InDesign, and significantly speeds script execution; the Script Label panel gives you a way to enter text into the Label property of a page item.

Scripts Panel   To display the Scripts panel, choose Scripts from the Utilities submenu of the Window menu (see Figure 12-1). The Scripts panel displays the scripts (and folders) stored inside the Scripts Panel folder inside the Scripts folder in your InDesign folder.

In general, we think it's better to store your scripts somewhere else, and place aliases (on the Mac OS) or shortcuts (in Windows) in this folder. Why? We've accidentally deleted all of our scripts by reinstalling InDesign more than once. It's painful.

To run a script, double-click the script in the Scripts panel. To edit a script, hold down Option/Alt and double-click the script. InDesign will open the script in your script editor (or in the ExtendScript Toolkit, for JavaScript files). To delete scripts from the Scripts panel, open the Scripts Panel folder inside the Scripts folder in your InDesign folder and move the scripts to another location (or delete them).

FIGURE 12-1
Scripts Panel

*To run a script,
double-click the
script name in the
Scripts panel.*

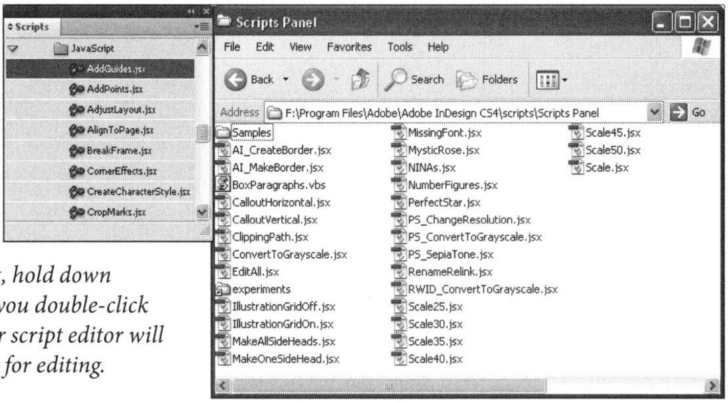

*To edit a script, hold down
Option/Alt as you double-click
the script. Your script editor will
open the script for editing.*

*"Install" scripts in the Scripts panel by adding them
to the Scripts Panel folder in the Scripts folder in your
InDesign application folder.*

To open the folder containing a script, hold down Command-Shift/Ctrl-Shift and double-click the script name in the Scripts panel. InDesign will open the folder containing the script in the Finder or Windows Explorer.

Adding Keyboard Shortcuts to Scripts. You can add keyboard shortcuts to scripts, just as you can to menu items. When you open the Edit Shortcuts dialog box, you'll find a list of installed scripts in the Scripts section. You assign a keyboard shortcut to a script in the same way that you assign any other keyboard shortcut.

There's a catch. The keyboard shortcut you apply is tied to a specific location in the list of scripts displayed in the Scripts section of the Edit Shortcuts dialog box. If you add or remove scripts, the shortcut could very well end up pointing to a different script.

Controlling Script Order. You can control the order in which scripts appear in the Scripts panel by entering numbers (from 00 to 99) followed by a close parenthesis character (")") before the first character of the file name. The Scripts panel hides the numbers, leaving only the name of the script visible. In any folder in the Scripts Panel folder, the file or folder with a name beginning with "00)" will appear first in the Scripts panel; the file beginning with "01)" will appear next.

Script Label Panel   To display the Script Label panel, choose Script Label from the Utilities submenu of the Window menu (see Figure 12-2). The Script Label panel has only one purpose—it gives you a way to enter text into the label of an object. Once you work with scripting for a bit, you'll realize how useful the label property of a page item is.

Choose Script Label from the Automation submenu of the Window menu to display the Script Label panel.

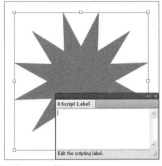

Select an object.

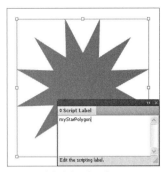

Enter a label for the object. Adding the label does not change the object in any visible way.

An object's label can store an apparently unlimited amount of text, so you could store quite complex scripts (which are just text, after all) inside an object. Or a label could contain an XML representation of the object, or any other type of text data you can think of.

A page item can have more than one label, thanks to the "insert label" method and the corresponding "extract label" method. If a single label on an object isn't enough for your needs, you can always add your own.

Getting Started

Work through the *Adobe InDesign CS5 Scripting Tutorial.* Don't type the scripts yourself—download the Zip archive from the scripting home page. Use your script editor to open the first script file—Hello-World—in the language or your choice. Try running it. Once you've gotten it working, you can move on to the more advanced scripts.

There are only three scripts in the tutorial. They're short, they show you how to create a new document, create a new text frame, add text to the text frame, and apply formatting to that text.

Once you're done with the tutorial, start thinking about the tasks in your work that you'd like to automate, and look through the example scripts for something related to the things you'd like to do.

At this point, you're ready to move on to the *Adobe InDesign CS5 Scripting Guide* for the scripting language of your choice. When you need to look something up, use the bookmarks in the PDF and/or Acrobat's search feature to find likely terms. Scripting terms tend to mirror the terms you see used in the user interface.

Again, use the scripts from the Zip archive (there are around 200 of them for each language). Don't try to copy/paste from the *Scripting Guide* PDF. Not only does copying/pasting from a PDF introduce extra characters and line breaks that can cause the script to fail, but most of the scripts shown in the *Scripting Guide* are not complete scripts—they're "snippets," intended to show only the feature or technique being discussed.

Where to Get the Scripts

You can download all of the scripts listed in this chapter from the web site David co-hosts. Don't type them yourself—most of the scripts shown here are not complete.

```
http://www.indesignsecrets.com/downloads/RWCS5scripts.zip
```

We're only able to show the JavaScript version of the scripts, but you can find AppleScript and VBScript versions online (see "Where to Get the Scripts," earlier in this chapter)

Overriding All Overrides

We admit that we feel a thrill of pride when we look at our neatly ordered lists of paragraph styles in the Paragraph Styles panel. We don't get out enough. But a "+" (plus sign, indicating a local formatting override) after a style name drives us crazy. What's that doing there? Evil, local formatting is interfering with our dream of formatting and organizational goodness!

It doesn't matter how the local formatting crept into the document (be it something in a Word file or an errant co-worker)—it's easy to get rid of, as long as you use the following script. It's very short, but it can save you hours of work.

Follow the steps shown earlier in this chapter for creating a JavaScript, then enter the following text or download the script (see "Where to Get the Scripts," earlier in this chapter).

To create the JavaScript, follow these steps.

1. Start the ExtendScript Toolkit and target InDesign. If InDesign is not already running, you'll be prompted to start it.

2. Enter the following text (note that it's *one line*).

   ```
   app.documents.item(0).stories.everyItem().clearOverrides();
   ```

3. Save the script as a plain text file with the file extension ".jsx" to the Scripts Panel folder inside the Scripts folder in your InDesign folder.

4. To test the script, double-click the script in the Scripts panel.

A Short, But Useful, Example

When you want to get an object or series of objects out of a frame you've pasted them into, you end up doing a lot of selecting, cutting, and pasting. A script that could remove all of the objects from a frame (while maintaining the positions they occupied in the frame) would save you time and trouble. Right? Let's go!

This script assumes you have an object selected, and that the object contains at least one other object. The script will not ungroup a group as it processes the objects.

Follow the same steps as above to create the script. Don't worry about the indents, JavaScript doesn't care about them—they're just here to make reading the script a little bit easier.

```
//CutContents.jsx
//An InDesign CS5 JavaScript
//Cuts the contents of the selected page items and places
//them in the proper page position and stacking order.
var myObjectList = new Array;
if(app.documents.length != 0){
  if(app.selection.length != 0){
    for(var myCounter = 0; myCounter < app.selection.length;
    myCounter ++){
      switch(app.selection[myCounter].constructor.name){
        case "Rectangle":
        case "Oval":
        case "Polygon":
        case "GraphicLine":
          //If the item is a page item, add the item to the list.
          if(app.selection[myCounter].pageItems.length != 0){
            myObjectList.push(app.selection[myCounter]);
          }
          break;
      }
    }
    //If there were qualifying items in the selection, pass them
    //on to the myCutContents routine for processing.
    if(myObjectList.length != 0){
      myCutContents(myObjectList);
    }
  }
}
function myCutContents(myObjectList){
  var myPageItem;
  var myGeometricBounds;
  for(var myCounter = 0; myCounter < myObjectList.length;
  myCounter ++){
    var myDone = false;
    myPageItem = myObjectList[myCounter];
    do{
      if((myPageItem.constructor.name != "Group")&&
      (myPageItem.pageItems.length != 0)){
        myPageItem = myPageItem.pageItems.item(0);
        app.select(myPageItem, SelectionOptions.replaceWith);
        app.cut();
        app.pasteInPlace();
        myPageItem = app.selection[0];
      }
```

```
      else{
        myDone = true;
      }
    } while(myDone == false);
  }
}
```

**Testing the
CutContents Script**

Now that you've saved the script, switch to InDesign. Select a path that contains one or more objects. Double-click the script name in the Scripts panel. InDesign will remove each nested object inside the frame and paste it into the same position as it occupied while inside the frame (see Figure 12-3).

**FIGURE 12-3
CutContents Script**

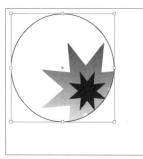

Once you've entered and saved a script, select an object you've pasted other objects into.

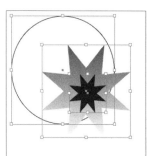

Run the script, and InDesign will "un-nest" the objects while retaining their original positions.

More Fun with Scripting

It's a shame that we're under so much pressure to reduce our page count, because there are a lot of other things we'd like to show you. Instead, we'll talk about a couple of creative things you can do with scripting, and show examples. You can find the script files online (see "Where to Get the Scripts," earlier in this chapter).

Drawing NINAs

Have you ever played with a Spirograph? Or been fascinated by one of the geometric patterns created by M. C. Escher? The authors admit a fondness (well, more like an obsession) for geometric art. While writing this book, we stumbled across a very interesting web site: http://www.washington.edu/bibsys/mattf/nina/. Matt Freedman, at the University of Washington, invented (or is it "discovered"?) a very nifty new algorithm for drawing shapes he's named NINAs (NINA being an acronym for "Nina Is Not An Acronym"). NINAs are fascinating shapes, and we had to see if we could write InDesign scripts that make use of the NINA algorithm (with Mr. Freedman's permission). Figure 12-4 shows some of the NINAs drawn by our script.

FIGURE 12-4
Various NINAs

Adding a User Interface InDesign scripts can create their own dialog boxes, and can populate those dialog boxes with static text labels, check box controls, pop-up menus, text entry fields, and a variety of number entry fields (measurement units, integers, percentages, and real numbers).

There's good news and bad news about InDesign script dialog boxes. The good news is that InDesign takes care of all spacing and sizing issues. The bad news? InDesign takes care of all spacing and sizing issues. This means that you don't have to worry about setting pixel coordinates for every control, but it also means that you have very little control over the appearance of your dialog boxes. At the same time, it's easy to create a dialog box (see Figure 12-5).

By adding a user interface to your script, you can make it much easier to use. This example dialog box was generated by InDesign—no DialogDirector, no AppleScript Studio, no Visual Basic form. How cool is that?

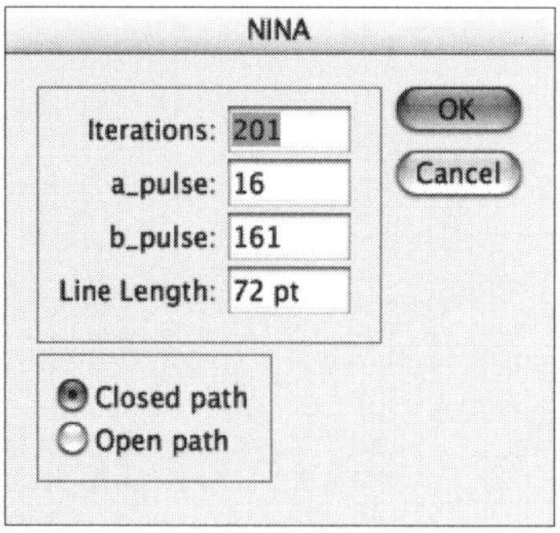

InDesign dialog boxes can include a range of controls not shown in this example, including pop-up menus, check boxes, and a variety of other number and text entry fields (only measurement edit box controls and integer edit box controls are shown here). As in all other InDesign numeric entry fields, you can do arithmetic and enter measurement overrides in these fields.

Mystic Rose

Another interesting geometric figure is the "Mystic Rose"—a polygon where every point connects to every other point. Ole thought it would be fun to have a script that would draw these, so he wrote one (see Figure 12-6). We've included this script with the other scripts in the Zip archive you can download from David's web site (see "Where to Get the Scripts in this Chapter," earlier in this chapter).

FIGURE 12-6
Mystic Rose

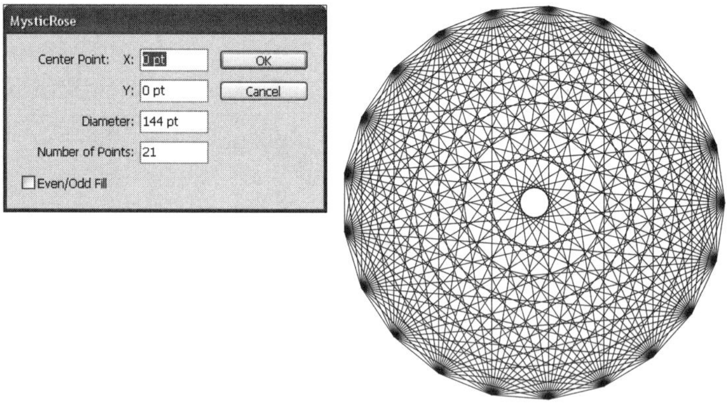

End Script

Scripting is all about *empowerment*. Don't just sit around telling yourself that the reason you're working late is that InDesign can't do something you'd like it to do. Sure, there are things in every program we'd like the manufacturer to fix, but, with InDesign's scripting features, we've finally got the tools we need to *fix them ourselves*.

By urging you to take up scripting, we're urging you to take control of InDesign, your publications, your work, and your life. We know you can do it!

Interactive Documents

13

A hundred years ago, when David was a young pup, he turned in a school essay he had typed using an amazing new device called a personal computer and printed on that technological marvel, the dot-matrix printer. His teacher was so impressed that she wrote her copious corrections on a separate page, so as not to spoil the appearance of David's "professionally published" work. Today, a school report printed on a color laser or inkjet printer is *de rigueur,* and teachers may question a student's work ethic if they don't have a corresponding Web site and public relations team.

Communication has come a long way, and while print is far from dead, you can bet that the future of publishing isn't solely a matter of throwing more ink at paper. Today's communicators have to be adept at creating both print and interactive documents—files that include buttons, sounds, animation, page transitions, and movies. Fortunately, InDesign offers a number of features for the "rich media" producer. Many of these tools don't produce any visible effect on your InDesign pages, but change the behavior of the PDF or Flash SWF files that you export.

Interactive Only
After Export

The key thing to understand about InDesign's interactive features is that they work only when you export the file to a format that can support them, such as PDF, SWF, FLA, or XHTML. And, different formats support different features.

Acrobat PDF. Interactive PDF files can include buttons, movies and sounds, hyperlinks, bookmarks, and page transitions. When you export an interactive document to PDF, select the Adobe PDF (Interactive) option, which uses the Acrobat 8/9 (PDF 1.7) version. If you select the Adobe PDF (Print) option, your document won't include any interactive elements.

Note that you should use Acrobat Reader or Acrobat Pro to view interactive PDF files—while other PDF readers (such as Preview in Mac OS X) can open them, most of the media features won't work.

We cover how to export PDF files in "Exporting interactive PDFs" later in this chapter.

XHTML and ePub. InDesign has very limited support for XHTML and ePub documents. However, hyperlinks that you create in InDesign are exported properly. We cover how to export XHTML and .epub documents from InDesign in Chapter 7, "Importing and Exporting."

SWF. InDesign can export one or more pages from your document directly to the SWF (Shockwave Flash) format. Exporting to SWF is great for interactive presentations and simple SWF files for the web, but if you need to create small web banners or more advanced SWF files, export using the FLA format. We'll discuss SWF export in more detail later in this chapter.

FLA. InDesign's SWF export is cool for simple projects, but limited. If you know ActionScript, or you're working with a Flash developer, you're going to want to export your InDesign document in the FLA format. (In InDesign CS4, the equivalent format was XFL.) FLA is a format that can be opened in Flash CS5 Professional. When you export to FLA, page transitions, buttons, and animation remain in effect. Hyperlinks are broken in FLA files. Movies and sound clips are also broken; only the posters are included. However, supported media files appear in a resources folder saved in the same location as the exported FLA file so that the Flash developer can reconnect the media.

Hyperlinks

What is an interactive page without links? Links help your readers explore your file, jumping between pages, to other documents, or even to Web sites. You can also add links to files that your readers can download, and you can add links for sending email.

A hyperlink is essentially a button—it's a "hot" area that performs some action when you click it. There are two big differences between a hyperlink and a button: First, you can apply a hyperlink directly to a range of text—though behind the scenes, InDesign is still more or less drawing a button around that text. Second, you can save a hyperlink destination and use it more than once.

To make a hyperlink, you'll need to open the Hyperlinks panel from the Interactive submenu under the Window menu. The Hyperlinks panel also includes the Cross-References panel; we discuss cross-references in Chapter 3, "Text."

Named versus Unnamed Hyperlinks

When you make a hyperlink, you need to decide whether it should be a hyperlink that can be used multiple times (which InDesign calls a "Shared Hyperlink Destination"), or a one-off link. Because these are similar in concept to named and unnamed color swatches, we tend to call these named and unnamed hyperlinks.

Named hyperlinks are actually easier to make, but they can slow you down if you're going to make dozens (or hundreds) of them, because each one you add takes a position on the Hyperlink panel's URL pop-up menu. Searching through 100 URLs is a hassle. Therefore, although we tend to eschew unnamed *color* swatches, we actually use unnamed hyperlinks most of the time.

On the other hand, if you are going to use a hyperlink several times in a document, it's great to make it named. That way, if you need to edit the link, you can change it once and it gets updated everywhere in the file.

Fast Hyperlinks

The fastest way to make a hyperlink is to select some text (with the Type tool) or a frame (with the Selection tool) and type a Web address into the URL field at the top of the Hyperlinks panel (see Figure 13-1). After you press Return/Enter, you'll see the link appear in the list in the middle of the Hyperlinks panel.

Unfortunately, this method has several significant drawbacks: First, this always creates a named hyperlink; there is no choice here. Second, InDesign usually places a big, ugly black rectangle around the text or object. Third, you can only make links to URLs (no page

FIGURE 13-1

New Named
Hyperlink

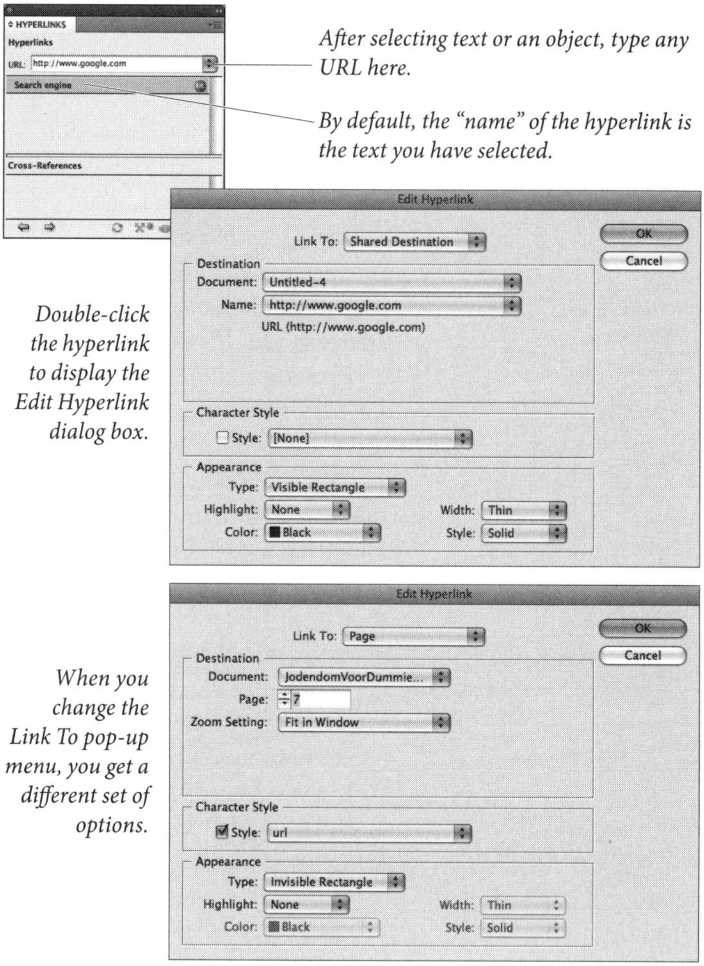

After selecting text or an object, type any URL here.

By default, the "name" of the hyperlink is the text you have selected.

Double-click the hyperlink to display the Edit Hyperlink dialog box.

When you change the Link To pop-up menu, you get a different set of options.

links, and other goodies we'll explain in a minute). Finally, if you selected a frame, the link appears in the panel as something generic, like "Hyperlink." If you selected some text, the text itself appears in the list, often causing confusion.

Converting URLs to Hyperlinks

You can search your document for URLs such as www.adobe.com, http://indesignsecrets.com, and president@whitehouse.gov, and convert them to hyperlinks. If you want to apply a character style to the hyperlinks, create a character style with the appropriate attributes, such as blue and underlined, before you do the conversion. For some reason, the InDesign team didn't add a New Character Style option to the pop-up menu in the dialog box.

Choose Hyperlinks & Cross-References from the Type menu, and then choose Convert URLs to Hyperlinks (see Figure 13-2). Select

FIGURE 13-2
Convert URLs

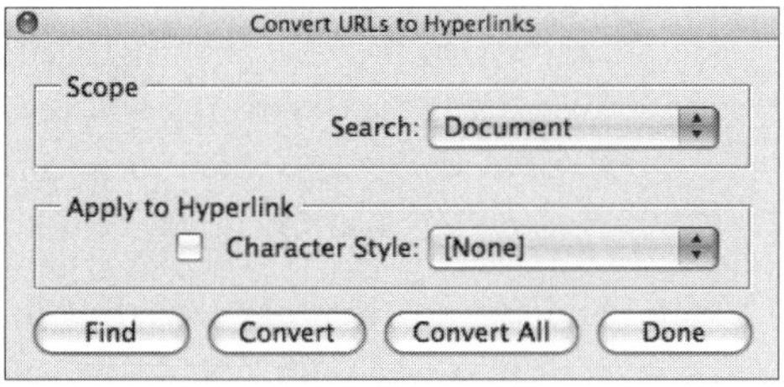

whether you want to convert the URLs in the document, story, or current selection. If you decide you want to convert URLs only in the selection, you can select text while the dialog box is still open.

Select a character style if you want visual indicators for the URL hyperlinks. Click Find to locate the first URL, and then click Convert or Convert All. These options are similar to the Change and Change All options in the Find/Change dialog box. InDesign creates named hyperlinks.

If you change your mind after the conversion, keep in mind that Undo undoes only one change, even if you choose Convert All. So press Ctrl/Command+Z for as many URLs as you converted.

Editing Hyperlinks

If you want to make a named hyperlink, using the URL field works fine. But immediately after making the link you should edit it. First, you can rename any link in the Hyperlinks panel by clicking on it and choosing Rename Hyperlink from the panel menu. If you do this a lot, make yourself a custom keyboard shortcut.

Then, double-click on the link in the Hyperlinks panel to open the Edit Hyperlink dialog box. You have several options.

Link To and Destination. You can tell InDesign what to link to by choosing one of the six options in the Link To pop-up menu. The first three let you make unnamed or named links; the last is for shared, named links. If you have already made a named link with the URL field, you can convert the link to a local link, but the original named link you made still remains in the URL list—we'll explain how to remove it later in the chapter.

▶ **URL.** To target a URL, choose URL from the Link To pop-up menu and type the address into the Destination URL field. A URL is typically a place on the Internet, like an HTTP or FTP site. Note, however, that Acrobat or Flash just passes this URL to the default Web browser to deal with.

(By the way, if you open a SWF with a hyperlink in it on your local hard drive, the Flash plug-in will likely throw up an alert saying that there's a potential security risk. However, you can avoid the alert by clicking Settings, then telling the Flash settings to always trust your local computer. If you place the SWF on the Web, you shouldn't see the alert.)

► **File.** If you want your hyperlink to open another PDF or file on your disk or on the server, you can choose File from the Link To pop-up menu. Unfortunately, Acrobat and Flash also hand these links to your Web browser to open, which is kind of crazy. If the browser knows what to do with it, it'll display it; if not, the file will likely be downloaded. To jump from one PDF to another, it's usually better to use a button, which we discuss in a later section.

► **Email.** If you want your link to send you an email, you could make a URL link that begins with *mailto://*, but it's easier to set the Link To pop-up menu to Email, then fill in the Address and Subject Line fields. When the viewer clicks on this kind of link, Acrobat launches your default Web browser and creates a new, addressed email message.

► **Page.** To link to another page within your document (but not to specific text or an object on the page), choose Page from the Link To pop-up menu. Enter the page number you want to link to in the Page field and which magnification you want to use to view that page from the Zoom Setting pop-up menu. Most of the zoom settings (such as Fit Width in Window) are pretty self-explanatory; the only two that we find confusing are Inherit Zoom and Fixed. Inherit Zoom leaves the viewer's magnification setting alone. Fixed is supposed to remember the zoom setting in InDesign when you created the hyperlink destination, but it only seems to produce the same effect as Inherit Zoom. The Zoom Settings are ignored in SWF files.

You can also choose a different file from the Document pop-up menu (if you have another InDesign document open). This sounds good, but it doesn't really work—you're asking Flash or Acrobat to open your other InDesign file, which it cannot do.

► **Text Anchor.** If there is some text you want to target, you should choose a Text Anchor from the Link To pop-up menu. We discuss how to make a text anchor later in this chapter.

► **Shared Destination.** If you want your hyperlink to point to a link you have already created as a named link, choose Shared Destination, then choose the link from the Name pop-up menu.

Character Style. If your hyperlink is on selected text, you can tell InDesign to apply a character style to it. For example, you might want to give the text a light blue underline to indicate to the reader that this is "clickable." Very helpful. What you can *not* do is make a character style that automatically applies a hyperlink. We hope to see that in a future version of InDesign.

Appearance. Remember that a hyperlink is technically a button in the PDF. The Appearance section lets you control how that object appears in the PDF file. If you want it to be invisible, set the Type pop-up menu to Invisible Rectangle. If you do this, you should be sure to apply some character style to the text; otherwise, the only way anyone will know that the link is there is that the cursor will change when it moves over it.

The other Appearance options are pretty dorky. Maybe someday InDesign will offer cooler hyperlink options, such as making the text highlight when you hover over it and then glow or burst into flame when you click it. Until then, only buttons provide interesting link effects (see "Buttons," later in this chapter).

By the way, if you import a Word document that has lots of words surrounded by rectangles, they're probably hyperlinks. You can make all those rectangles disappear quickly by selecting all the hyperlinks in the Hyperlinks panel (click on the first and then Shift-click on the last), choosing Hyperlink Options from the panel menu, and then changing the Type pop-up menu in the Appearance section from Visible Rectangle to Invisible Rectangle.

Making a New Unnamed Hyperlink

If you want to bypass making a named hyperlink entirely, select the text or frame and click the Create New Hyperlink button in the Hyperlinks panel (or choose New Hyperlink from the panel menu). This opens the New Hyperlink dialog box, which offers all the same features that we discussed in the last section.

Making a New Hyperlink Destination

InDesign also lets you make a named hyperlink without actually applying it to any text or objects. Of course, these links won't do anything, but it might be helpful if you have a list of known destinations you'll be targeting multiple times as you lay out your file. To do this, select New Hyperlink Destination from the Hyperlinks panel menu (see Figure 13-3). You can choose from among three types of hyperlink destinations: Page, Text Anchor, and URL.

▶ **Page.** After you choose Page from the Type pop-up menu, you can choose which page and zoom setting to use. Now give your

FIGURE 13-3
Creating a New
Hyperlink Destination

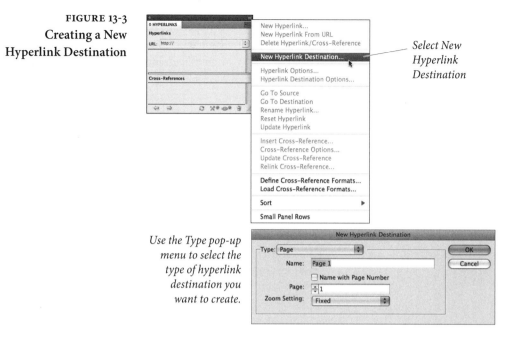

Use the Type pop-up menu to select the type of hyperlink destination you want to create.

Page hyperlink destination a name. Or, better yet, turn on the Name with Page Number check box, which names it automatically. This name is what you'll later use to apply this hyperlink destination to the text or object on your page.

▶ **URL.** The URL hyperlink destination lets you enter two values: The Web site or mailto address you want to target, and a name for this destination. Again, you'll be using this name later when you create the hyperlink.

▶ **Text Anchor.** The Text Anchor option lets you create an anchor to a specific piece of text in your document. Once you have created a text anchor, you can target it when making a hyperlink (which we talked about earlier). To do this, first place the cursor in the destination text (or select one or more characters of the text), or else this option will be grayed out. Then, in the New Hyperlink Destination dialog box, simply give the anchor a name. This is identical to how most HTML authoring programs create text anchors, too.

Editing Hyperlink Destinations Unfortunately, while the URL pop-up menu in the Hyperlnks panel gives you a list of all the named hyperlink destinations you've built in a document, it won't let you edit them or delete them. To do that, choose, Hyperlink Destination Options from the Hyperlinks panel menu—this displays the Hyperlink Destination Options dialog box.

From here, you can view and select the existing hyperlink destinations using the Destination pop-up menu. To edit a hyperlink destination, select it from the pop-up and click the Edit button. To delete a named hyperlink, select it and click the Delete button.

Hyperlinks from URLs in the Text

If you've already typed a URL in a text frame and now you want to make that URL a hyperlink, use the Text tool to select the URL and choose New Hyperlink from URL from the Hyperlinks panel menu. This is a two-for-one: InDesign first makes a URL destination (giving it the same name as the URL itself), and then applies that destination to the selected text or object, also using the URL as the hyperlink source name that appears in the panel. Cool, huh?

However, note that Acrobat 8 will now automatically create clickable links from anything that looks like a URL, so you may not need to convert these to InDesign hyperlinks yourself.

Deleting and Resetting Hyperlinks

We've already mentioned that you can delete a hyperlink destination, but what about the hyperlink on the page? If you delete the source itself (the text or object marked as a hyperlink), the hyperlink disappears. You can also select the hyperlink in the Hyperlinks panel and click the panel's Delete button. This leaves the text or page object alone, but it no longer has a hyperlink attached to it.

If you need to delete two or more hyperlinks, you can select discontiguous items by Command/Ctrl-clicking on them individually. Or—to select them all—select the first and then Shift-click on the last in the list. Then click Delete.

What if you applied a hyperlink to the wrong text or object? No problem—select the correct text or object, select the hyperlink name in the Hyperlinks panel, and then choose Reset Hyperlink from the Hyperlinks panel menu. The link is moved from the old source to the selected source.

Navigating Hyperlinks

Once you have a bunch of hyperlink sources in your document, you need some way to navigate through them. If you set the Appearance of the hyperlinks to Visible, you can view them by choosing Show Hyperlinks from the Extras submenu on the View menu.

If you can't find the source of a hyperlink, select the link in the Hyperlinks panel and click the Go to Source button (or choose Go to Source in the panel menu).

Alternatively, you can select a hyperlink name in the panel and click the Go to Destination button (or choose Go to Destination from the panel menu) to invoke the hyperlink itself. This means you can use hyperlinks to navigate around your document (or documents) even if you never plan on exporting the files as PDF or SWF at all!

Don't forget that you can put hyperlinks on a master page so that they'll show up on all the document pages based on that master.

Updating Hyperlinks   If you've used named hyperlink destinations from another document and those hyperlink destinations later change (perhaps a URL changes, for instance), then you'll need to update your hyperlink source. To do that, select the hyperlink source in the Hyperlinks panel and choose Update Hyperlink from the panel menu. If the other document isn't currently open, you'll need to hold down the Option/Alt key when choosing Update Hyperlink.

Exporting Hyperlinks   As we noted earlier, hyperlinks are only "live" in your exported PDF or SWF files (with the exception of the Go to Hyperlink Destination button in the Hyperlinks panel). However, your hyperlinks will only be included in the PDF or SWF if you turn on the Hyperlinks checkbox in the PDF Export or SWF Export dialog box.

Bookmarks

Any PDF file longer than a few pages should have bookmarks, which appear in the Bookmarks tab on the left side of the screen in Acrobat. Bookmarks make it easy for the viewer to find a particular section of the document. In InDesign, bookmarks appear in (surprise) the Bookmarks panel, shown in Figure 13-4 (choose Bookmarks from the Interactive submenu in the Window menu).

Whenever you build a table of contents in a document, you can automatically add those entries to the Bookmarks panel by turning on the Create PDF Bookmarks check box in the Table of Contents dialog box (see Chapter 8, "Long Documents"). You can also add a bookmark anywhere in your document by selecting an object or placing the text cursor in some text and then clicking the New Bookmark button in the Bookmarks panel. You can name the bookmark anything you want.

As with the hyperlinks in the Hyperlinks panel, you can use the bookmarks to navigate around your InDesign document, even without exporting as PDF. To jump to a bookmark, double-click the bookmark name in the Bookmarks panel.

As with hyperlinks, you can build bookmarks all day long, but they won't show up in your PDF files unless you turn on the Bookmarks checkbox in the Export PDF Options dialog box.

FIGURE 13-4
Bookmarks Panel

Believe it or not, these are actual bookmarks from one of David's other book projects!

What if you want bookmarks generated from a table of contents to appear in the Bookmarks panel, but you don't want the actual TOC? In InDesign CS3, you can simply place the table of contents on the pasteboard or on a hidden layer, and the bookmarks still show up in the PDF. That trick doesn't work in later versions. Instead, generate the TOC on the pasteboard, and make sure that an edge of the TOC text frame overlaps a page.

Sorting and Editing Bookmarks

You can move a bookmark by dragging it up or down in the list. Note that, as you drag, InDesign displays a black bar indicating where the bookmark will land when you let go of the mouse button. If you drag the bookmark on top of another bookmark, the bookmark becomes a sub-bookmark (or a second-level bookmark or a nested bookmark, or whatever). To "unnest" the bookmark, drag it out again.

If you add one or more custom bookmarks to a document and then update your table of contents, the custom bookmarks will appear at the bottom of the list again. Oops! One way to fix this is to select Sort Bookmarks from the panel menu—this sorts the list of bookmarks chronologically by page, and alphabetically for multiple bookmarks within each page.

To rename a bookmark, select it and move the cursor slightly, or wait for a second. InDesign should highlight the bookmark name so you can edit it. If that doesn't work, select it and choose Rename Bookmark from the panel menu.

Buttons

Buttons are only useful in interactive PDF or SWF files, but they can do all kinds of things—jump to another page, play a movie, sound or animation, or hide or show another button.

You can make any selected frame or line into a button (except for frames that contain movies or sounds)—just choose Convert to Button from the Interactive submenu, under the Object menu or in the Context menu. Or, click the Convert Object to a Button button in the Buttons panel (which you can find in the Interactive submenu, under the Window menu). You can also turn a button back into an object by selecting Convert from Button.

An object turned into a button acts like any other object—you can even print it. But the object comes to life when you turn on the Include All option in the Export to Interactive PDF dialog box or the Export SWF dialog box.

The Way of Buttons

It's important to remember that buttons are containers, like a special kind of frame. When you turn an object into a button, InDesign actually puts that object inside a button "frame." This means you can select that nested frame (with the Direct Selection tool or by clicking the Select Content button in the Control panel), move it around, delete it, replace it with something else, and so on.

Behavioral Modification

To make a button actually do something—react when the user clicks it—you have to change the button's behavior in the Buttons panel (see Figure 13-5).

1. Enter a descriptive name for the button (at the top of the Buttons panel).

2. Choose a trigger from the Event pop-up menu: On Release (that's when the user lets go of the mouse button), On Click (when the mouse button is down), On Roll Over (when the cursor is above the button), On Roll Off (when the cursor leaves the button), On Focus (when the button is selected—either by a click or by a press of the Tab key), or On Blur (when a click or press of the Tab key moves the focus to another field).

3. Select one of the actions you want to associate with the Event from the Actions pop-up menu.

   ▶ **Go To Destination.** If you used the Hyperlinks panel to make a text anchor in this or another document, use this action to jump to that point. If the document that contains the anchor isn't open, you can click Browse to select it.

   ▶ **Go To First/Last/Next/Previous Page.** Use any of these actions to jump to the first, last, next, or previous page. For example, you might assign these as navigation buttons, and put them on a master page of a document. Buttons work well on master pages because they appear on every document page tagged with that master.

FIGURE 13-5
Adding Behaviors
to a Button

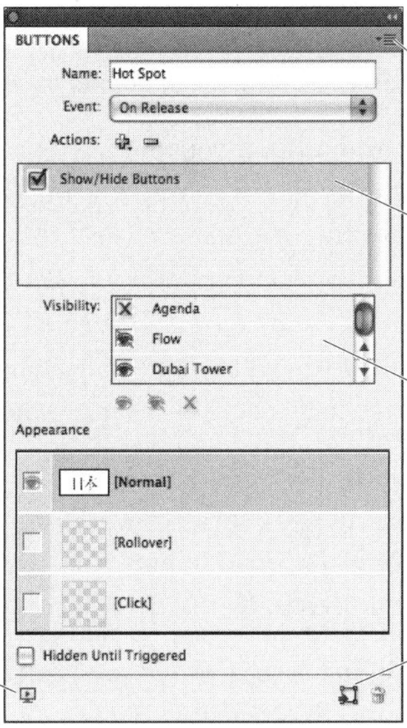

InDesign ships with a library full of sample buttons you can use: Choose Sample Buttons from the panel menu.

As you add Actions, InDesign adds them to the list.

Button behaviors can affect all other buttons in a document. In this example, other buttons are affected by clicking the button.

This button converts objects to buttons or vice versa

Preview button

► **Go To URL.** Like a URL hyperlink, the Go To URL action hands off the URL you specify to the default Web browser. This can be any URL, including http://, file://, or mailto:.

► **Show/Hide Buttons.** Buttons are a kind of "field" (in PDF parlance). While Acrobat has several different kinds of fields (such as text entry fields, check box fields, and so on), InDesign currently supports only button fields. Whenever you want objects to appear or disappear on your page, make them into buttons. Even if those buttons have no behavior of their own, they can still be controlled (made visible or hidden) using the Show/Hide Buttons action. When you select Show/Hide Buttons, the panel lists all the fields (buttons) in your document (not just the fields on the current page). You can click once in the box to the left of the field name to make the button visible (you'll see a little eyeball), or click again to make the button hidden (InDesign draws a red line through the eyeball). Click a third time to make it neutral (this action won't affect the button at all).

► **Sound.** After you import a sound file into your document, you can Play, Pause, Stop, or Resume it with this action. In exported SWF files, you can stop all sounds.

► **Video.** If you placed a movie file (see "Audio and Video," later), you can control it using the Video action. After selecting Video, select a movie, and then specify what you want to do to it: Play, Pause, Stop, Resume, or Play from Navigation Point. Use the Media panel to set navigation points.

▶ **Animation.** If you animated an object (see "Animation," later), you can control it using the Animation action. After selecting Animation, select the animation name, and then specify what you want it to do: Play, Stop, Pause, Resume, Reverse, and Stop All. Turn on the Reverse on Roll Off check box if you want, say, an animated object that flies onto the page to fly back off the page when you mouse off the button.

▶ **Go To Page.** Go To Page (which jumps directly the page number you specify), works only when exported in a SWF file. If you want to jump to a particular page in a PDF file, you need to use Go To Anchor.

▶ **Go To State.** If you created a multi-state object (see "Multi-State Objects," later), you can jump to a specific state. For example, use the Go To Previous State and Go To Next State actions in navigation buttons that let users click through images in a slide show.

▶ **Go to Previous View.** This action returns to the last page the viewer displayed. If you jump from page 5 to page 20, Go to Previous View would jump back to page 5.

▶ **Go to Next View.** This action only works if someone has already invoked a "Previous page" action; it's like the Forward feature in a Web browser.

▶ **Open File.** Use this action to open another file. You need to specify the file using an absolute file path; it's much simpler to click the Browse button to let InDesign figure out the path for you.

▶ **View Zoom.** A button can control the current view settings in Acrobat. After selecting the View Zoom behavior, choose from among the many options in the Zoom pop-up menu, including Zoom In, Zoom Out, Fit in Window, Rotate Clockwise, and Single Page.

After creating an action, you can select another Event/Action combination and add it to the button. This means one button click can do a bunch of things at once: go to another page, show a hidden object on that page, and immediately start playing a movie. To remove an action, select it and click the Delete Action button.

Tab Order   When you open a PDF in Acrobat and press the Tab key, the focus jumps to the first field on the page; press Tab again, and it skips to the next field. If the field is a button, you can press Return/Enter to "click" the button. But who specifies the order of the buttons? You do. As long as you have more than one button on a page, you can choose Set Tab Order from the Interactive submenu (under the Object menu). To reorder a field in the list, select it and click the Move Up or Move Down buttons—or better, just drag it into the correct position.

Rollovers and States   Multimedia designers love rollovers. A rollover is an image on an interactive page (like a PDF or a SWF) that changes in some way when the user moves the cursor over it. The rollover may appear to change color or shape; or maybe it lights up to indicate that it's a hotspot. When you move the cursor away, the image returns to its original form. InDesign supports both normal rollovers and two-state buttons (buttons that change when you click on them). It also lets you make "hot spot" rollovers—where you roll over or click a button and an image changes somewhere else on the page.

We use the term "image," but rollovers can involve text or lines as easily as images; it's up to you. However, if you are using images, you need to create the graphics for each state of the rollover: the original image on the page (the "off" state), and the image you see when the cursor is over the image (the "on" state).

Remember that buttons are just containers, typically with objects nested in them—a text frame, a graphic frame, a line, or even a group of objects. The Buttons panel gives you a way to change the content of a button container depending on two events: the user moving the cursor over the button or clicking on it.

It's easy to add and change states (see Figure 13-6):

1. Select the button and the Buttons panel. (You can open this panel if it's not visible by double-clicking the button).

2. To add a Rollover state, click the [Rollover] tile in the State Appearance section of the Buttons panel. If you want to add a state for when the mouse is clicked, click the [Click] tile. If you later decide you don't want a state, select it and click the Delete button at the bottom of the panel.

   If the thumbnails in the panel aren't big enough, make them larger by choosing Panel Options from the panel menu.

3. Click the state you want to alter, and then, on the document page, make a change to the content of the button. Let's say you have a button with a picture in it. You can click on the Rollover

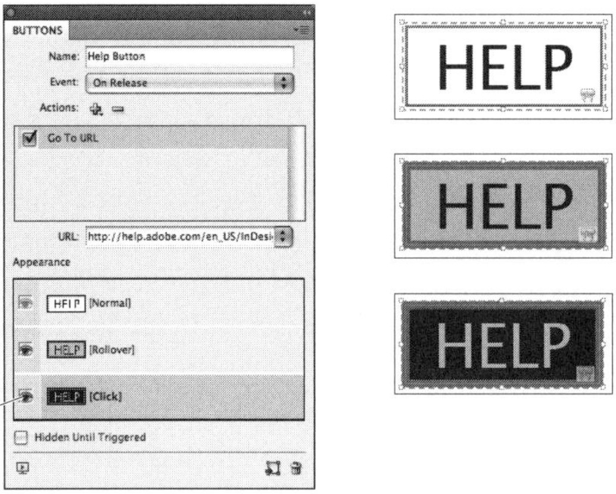

FIGURE 13-6
Button Rollovers

Create separate appearances in the exported file for when the mouse rolls over the button, and for when it clicks it.

Select the state, and then change the appearance of the button object.

Normal state

Rollover state

Click state

state, and replace the picture with a different one (just the way you normally would; with the File > Place command). Or, you could make the edge of the button turn red.

Each state actually contains a different object and the Buttons panel gives you a way to make each one visible—one at a time—almost like the Conditional Text panel. So you can add a drop shadow to the object inside the Rollover state and when you switch back to the Normal state, the drop shadow disappears.

4. Test the states using the Preview panel.

Hot Spots Making a rollover that affects objects elsewhere on the page involves creating a set of actions: Convert all of the relevant objects to buttons and then use the On Roll Over and On Roll Off events to make those objects Visible or Hidden at the appropriate time(s). You could, for example, have one button that, when rolled over, makes two other buttons visible.

Why have an invisible button? Don't think of buttons as just something you click; if you want a picture to appear when you click a button, you make two buttons: a visible one that you click and a hidden one that appears when you click the other button.

For example, let's say you want an image of a dog to appear when you mouse over a text button. For the dog image, you convert it to a button, and you select the Hidden Until Triggered check box in the Buttons panel, This hides the dog image in the SWF or PDF file until it's made visible. For the text button, you choose On Roll Over for Event and Show/Hide Buttons for Action, and set the dog image to become visible. To make the dog image disappear again, create an On Roll Off event that makes the dog image invisible when the mouse leaves the text button.

Tool Tips   What about creating a tooltip for a button in the PDF file? Choose PDF Options from the Buttons panel menu, and then type a description, such as "Turn to next page." Whatever you type in the Description field appears as a tooltip when you mouse over the button.

You can also use the PDF Options dialog box to determine whether the button is printed. For example, you may want a "Submit" button to appear on the screen but not print when the PDF is printed. Turn off the Button Is Printable option.

Multi-State Objects

The purpose of the Object States panel is to let you create little slide shows within an interactive document. Here's the way it works. You insert a bunch of images that act as slides in a slide deck. Then you arrange them on top of each other, select them, and use the Object States panel to convert them into a multi-state object, with each image becoming a state. Finally, you create navigation buttons for cycling through the images (see Figure 13-7).

There is no limit to the number of states that you can include in a multi-state object. Only one state is visible on the page at a time. For print and PDF output, only the active state appears in the final output. That means you can use multi-state objects as a way to create conditional images in your document. Just make sure you have the right state selected when you print or export.

To create a multi-state object, follow these steps:

1. Place or create the objects that will be part of the multi-state object. If you're creating a slide show, you probably want the image frames to be the same size. By the way, a state does not have to be a single item—it can be a collection of items, such as an image and its caption.

2. To stack the images, select them, and click Align Horizontal Centers and Align Vertical Centers in the Control panel.

3. With the images still selected, click the New button in the Object States panel. (To open the Object States panel, choose Object States from the Interactive submenu on the Window menu.)

A dashed frame appears around the multi-state object.

FIGURE 13-7
**Create a Multi-State
Slide Show**

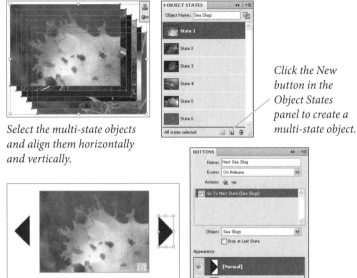

*Select the multi-state objects
and align them horizontally
and vertically.*

*Click the New
button in the
Object States
panel to create a
multi-state object.*

*Create navigation buttons that cycle
through the images (or states) in the
SWF file.*

4. Use the Buttons panel to create navigation buttons that trigger the Go To Next State and Go To Previous State actions when the mouse button is released.

5. Use the Preview panel to test the navigation buttons.

6. Export the document to SWF format. (Unfortunately, it doesn't work in PDF.)

Edit States   Editing a multi-state object is fairly intuitive. If you resize or rotate the selected multi-state object, all the states are transformed as well.

One tricky issue is figuring out the difference between adding a slide to a slideshow and adding an object to a state. For either task, select both the object and multi-state object. Click the Add Objects to Visible State button to add an object to the selected state. Click the New button to add a whole new state to the multi-state object.

To paste objects into an existing state, cut or copy one or more objects, select the multi-state object, click the state in the Object States panel, and choose Paste Into State from the panel menu.

To duplicate a state, select a state to base the new state on, and choose New State from the panel menu.

To convert a single state in a multi-state object back to a set of independent objects, select the state in the Object States panel and choose Release State To Object from the panel menu. To convert all states in the multi-state object to objects, choose Release All States To Objects.

To hide the multi-state object in the exported file until it's triggered by a button, choose Hide Until Triggered from the panel menu.

To reset all multi-state objects in the document to the first state, choose Reset All Multi-State Objects To First State from the panel menu. When you select a state, the object remains in that state, even if you close and reopen the document. This option is a quick way to reset all the multi-state objects.

Audio and Video

Sometimes movies and sounds in PDF and SWF files do a better job of explaining things than plain ol' quiet, static print. For instance, watching a movie about how to change the oil in your car might help more than trying to figure it out from ten pages of printed diagrams and explanations.

For movies, you should place FLV, F4V, SWF, or any video file with H.264 encoding, such as MP4. For sounds, place MP3 files. These formats take advantage of the rich media support offered in Acrobat 9 or later and Flash Player 10 or later.

But what about AVI, MOV, and MPEG videos and WAV, AIF, and AU sound files? They should play just fine in interactive PDF files, but they don't work in exported SWF files. Use the Adobe Media Encoder application to convert video file formats to FLV or F4V. Adobe Media Encoder doesn't convert audio files, but you can use a program like Apple iTunes to do that.

Importing Sounds and Movies

You import a sound or a movie file in the same way that you import text and graphics—use the Place feature or drag the file from a Finder/Explorer window (see Figure 13-8). To place the file on a page, click the place icon to create a frame that is the size of the original file. If you drag the place icon (to specify the size of the frame), then immediately choose Fit Frame to Content to scale the frame. Placed movies and sounds are automatically embedded.

By the way, when you import a sound or a movie, make sure you don't put any other text or graphics on top of it. Acrobat isn't smart enough to play rich media behind other objects (see "Movie Limitations," late in this chapter).

FIGURE 13-8
Placing a Movie

Choose Place from the File menu, select a movie file, and then click the Open button to import the movie.

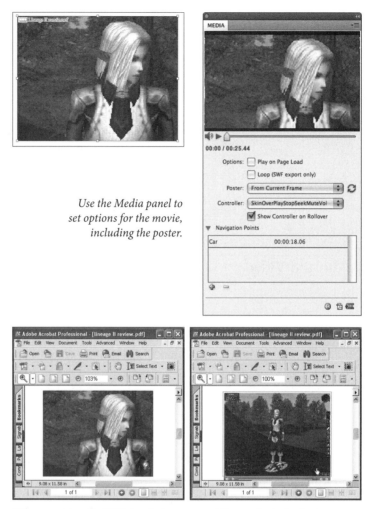

Use the Media panel to set options for the movie, including the poster.

When you view the PDF, Acrobat displays the poster...

...and the movie starts playing.

Linking to Web Videos

Instead of placing a movie, you can link to a movie on a Web site (via a URL). Linking to an online movie is useful if the movie will change after you export the PDF file, or if the movie is large and you don't want to transport it along with (or inside of) your PDF or SWF file.

Draw a rectangle of any size—you'll resize it later—and then select it and choose Video from URL from the Media panel menu. Specify the URL containing the a video file that Flash supports: FLV, F4V, or H.264-encoded MP4. You can use either the standard http:// URL or an rtmp:// URL, which is Adobe's proprietary protocol developed specifically for streaming video over the Web. Click OK. If the movie is valid, InDesign finds the movie on the Web and gets its dimensions (you need a live Internet connection for this to work, obviously).

After you click OK, use the Fitting features to make sure the frame is the same size as the movie. You can scale the movie, but don't try to clip or mask it. There doesn't appear to be any way to link to a streaming audio file; just video.

Movie Options   When you select a movie object, the Media panel displays options for that movie (see Figure 13-8). To open the Media panel, choose Interactive from the Window menu, and then choose Media.

> ► **Play on Page Load.** When you turn on this check box, the movie begins playing as soon as the page it's on is displayed.

> ► **Loop.** When you turn on this check box, the movie plays in a continuous loop in the SWF file.

> ► **Poster options.** A *poster* is a still image associated with a movie or sound—basically what you see on the InDesign page and in the PDF file (before you activate the movie). If you choose From Current Frame, InDesign grabs the first frame of the movie. If you don't want the first frame, drag the slider to "scrub" the movie until you see the frame you want to use. Then click the icon to the right of the Poster pop-up menu to use that frame as the poster. If you're creating a document that will be used for both print and onscreen web, then you should probably select Choose Image—this lets you pick a high-resolution image (like a PSD or a TIFF file) to stand in for the movie, both as a poster and when you print.
>
> You can use any size poster you want, but posters are always cropped to the size of the movie itself. It's best to make sure that the poster and the movie have the same dimensions.

> ► **Controller.** This option determines which controller buttons appear while the movie is playing. If the movie file is a Flash Video (FLV or F4V) file or an H.264-encoded file, you can choose from a number of controller skins that vary in style, but they all do essentially the same thing—let users play, pause, and stop the video and control volume. The controller is hidden. If you want the controller to appear when the user mouses over the movie, turn on Show Controller on Rollover.
>
> If you've placed an AVI, MPEG, or other legacy file, you can display a basic controller that appears in the PDF file. Note that SWF files you place may have their own controller skins applied.
>
> Use the Preview panel to see what the selected controller looks like.

▶ **Navigation Points.** Navigation points are useful if you want to play the movie from a different starting point. To create a navigation point, advance the video to a specific frame, and then click the plus sign icon. For example, in a training video, you could set navigation points at the beginning of each section. Create separate buttons that start the movie at each navigation point. (When you create a button that triggers a video action, select Play from Navigation Point, and then specify the point.)

▶ **PDF Options.** Choose PDF Options from the Media panel menu. The Description you type appears as a tool tip when you mouse over the movie in Acrobat (but only if the movie has a poster). If you want the movie to play in a floating window rather than on the page itself, turn on Floating Window, and specify the size and position of the window.

Sound Options   Use the Media panel to set sound options for the selected sound object, usually an MP3 file (see Figure 13-9).

▶ **Play on Page Load.** When you turn on this check box, Acrobat begins playing the sound as soon as the page it's on is displayed.

▶ **Stop on Page Turn.** Stop playing the sound when someone turns to a different page. This option isn't available if the audio file is a non-MP3 file.

▶ **Loop.** Play the sound file continuously. This option isn't available if the audio file is a non-MP3 file.

▶ **Poster.** You only need to give a sound a poster image when you want the viewer to be able to click on it to play the sound. If you

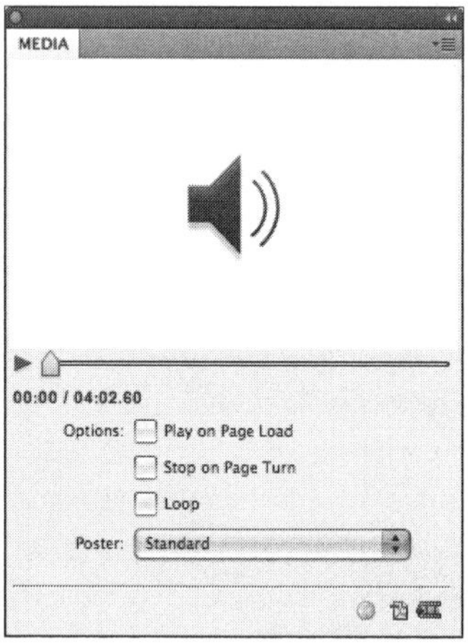

FIGURE 13-9
Sound Options in
Media Panel

have set up another button to play the sound, you can leave the Poster pop-up menu set to None. If you do want to use a poster image, choose Standard (which gives you a silly little speaker icon image) or Choose Image to select an image from a standard file dialog box.

To change the default Standard image, save an image in the JPEG format to a file named StandardSoundPoster.jpg, and put it inside the Images folder in the Presets folder inside your InDesign folder.

Media Limitations

Some aspects of exported movies and sounds are still a bit clunky. For example, there's usually a pause before and after a movie plays, making it hard to have seamless loops of movies. (A pain when you want to have a soundtrack looping in the background.)

Here are a few other limitations Acrobat and Flash Player have, and how they affect making interactive documents using InDesign:

▶ You can scale a movie on your page and it does appear scaled when you play it. However, you cannot crop a movie, even though you can crop the movie's poster image on your InDesign page—the movie will scale itself to fit inside the cropped area.

▶ Similarly, you can't clip movies into nonrectangular shapes. Acrobat and Flash Player can't deal with nonrectangular movies, so they'll appear as full-frame rectangles in the PDF or SWF file.

▶ As exciting as it might feel to rotate or shear movies and sounds, all that goes away in the final exported document. Oh well.

▶ You can use the Hyperlinks panel to apply a hyperlink to a movie or sound frame (or to a button), but, unfortunately, they're not active in the exported document.

▶ While it might appear that you can apply transparency effects to movies and buttons, these effects will not appear in the exported file. Drop shadows, however, work (because drop shadows are images behind the movie).

Animation

The Animation feature gives you the feeling that you can be a Flash developer without knowing a thing about scripting. In a matter of seconds, you can make an object appear to fly in from off the page, spin around, or fade into view.

Animation works only in an exported SWF file, not in a PDF file. But there's a workaround to animate a PDF, which we'll get to later.

Let's quickly define our terms. In InDesign, animation consists of the animated object and, in some cases, a motion path, which is the path along which the object travels (see Figure 13-10). The circle end of the motion path is where the animation begins; the arrow end is where the animation ends. Of course, some animations, such as Fade In and Shrink, don't move along a path.

Motion Presets   InDesign includes motion presets that make it easy to animate an object quickly. For example, you can draw a red ball, select it, and choose the Bounce and Smoosh motion preset in the Animation panel, and . . . that's all there is to it. When you export the document to SWF, turning to that page makes the red ball drop, appear to flatten out as it hits bottom, and rise.

Animation Panel   The Animation panel has plenty of options to sort through, but don't be intimidated. Most of the options are easy to figure out.

▶ **Preset.** Choose the motion preset you want to apply. You can then modify the settings, and you can use the Pen tool and Direct Selection tool to edit the motion path. If you want to reuse these settings, save the motion preset. You can use saved presets in other documents and even in Flash Pro.

▶ **Event(s).** Use the Event(s) option to determine what triggers the animation in the SWF file, such as clicking the animated object or mousing over it. You can trigger the animation using more than one event. In fact, be aware that turning on one event doesn't turn off another. For example, if you choose On Self Click (which starts the animation when you click the object), On Page Load remains selected.

If you choose On Roll Over, you can create a cool effect by selecting Reverse on Roll Off. In other words, if the animated object flies in from the left when the object is moused over, the object flies back where it came from when the mouse is moved off the object.

▶ **Speed.** Do you want the animation speed to be a steady rate? Choose None. Do you want it to start slowly and speed up? Choose Ease In. The object moves faster where points on the motion path are closer together.

FIGURE 13-10
Animated Objects

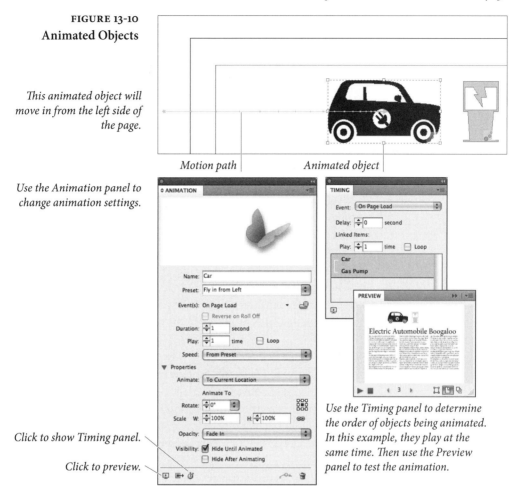

This animated object will move in from the left side of the page.

Motion path   Animated object

Use the Animation panel to change animation settings.

Click to show Timing panel.

Click to preview.

Use the Timing panel to determine the order of objects being animated. In this example, they play at the same time. Then use the Preview panel to test the animation.

► **Animate.** The Animate pop-up menu options help you print the animated object properly.

For example, suppose you want an object to fly in from off the page, but you want the object to appear on the page for printing. If you choose To Current Appearance from the Animate pop-up menu, the object's properties are used as the ending point of the animation. That way, the object appears on the page at the start, and can be printed. This option is especially useful in slide shows.

But what if you want to print an animated object that flies in from off the page and then blurs? If you choose To Current Appearance, the printed object is blurry. Instead, choose To Current Location from the Animate pop-up menu. This option uses the current object's properties (not blurry) as the starting point of the animation and the object's position as the ending point.

> ▶ **Opacity.** Choose None if you want the animated object to remain solid. Choose Fade In if you want the object to gradually become visible or Fade Out to gradually become invisible.

> ▶ Visibility Select Hide Until Animated or Hide After Animating to make an object invisible before or after playback.

Custom Animation

Create a custom animation by selecting an object and a path and clicking the Convert to Motion Path button in the Animation panel (see Figure 13-11). Then change the settings in the Animation panel. If you selected two closed paths, such as two rectangles, the path on top becomes the motion path. You can't convert more than two selected objects.

When you convert selected objects to a motion path, the path start moves to the center of the object. This means the path may flip to the opposite site of the object, depending on the path direction. If you don't like the direction, undo the animation and choose Reverse Path from the Paths submenu on the Object menu. Then try again.

Edit Motion Paths

Edit the motion path the same way you edit other paths. Use the Direct Selection tool to select the path and move points. Use the Pen tool to add and remove points.

The points on the path determine the speed of the object; the object moves faster where points are further apart. To slow down the object at a certain point of the path, add more points in that area.

Button Launch

Buttons and animation play nicely together. In the Buttons panel, you can create buttons that play, pause, stop, and reverse an animated object. See "Buttons" earlier in this chapter.

Complex Animation

What if you want to animate the same object multiple times? For example, let's say you want a headline to fly in from off the page, spin around, and fly off the other side of the page. Although you can apply only one animation to an object, you can copy and paste the object, and then use the Paste in Place command to make sure the object appears in the same place.

Think of it like a relay race. In this example, the first animated object uses the Fly in from Left preset with Hide After Animating selected. The next copied object uses the Rotate preset with both Hide Before Animating and Hide After Animating selected. The last copied object uses the Fly out Right preset with Hide Before Animating selected. It's a little clumsy, but there's always Flash Pro...

FIGURE 13-11
Draw a Motion Path

Draw a path using the Pen tool or Pencil tool, and insert the object that you want to move along the path...

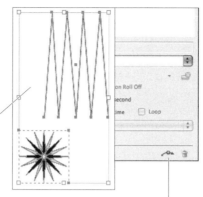

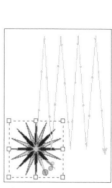

...Select the drawn path and object, and click the Convert to Motion Path button.

The motion path moves next to the newly animated object.

The Timing Panel

By default, animated objects play in the order in which they were added. Use the Timing panel to change the order, play animation effects at the same time, or delay animation (see Figure 13-12).

Turn to the spread containing multiple animated objects and display the Timing panel (choose Timing from the Interactive submenu on the Window menu).

The Timing panel shows the animations on the current spread based on page events. If you have one set of animations that occur when the page is turned to and another set of animations that occur when the page is clicked, you can change the timing of each event. To do this, choose Page Load or Page Click from the Event menu. Page Load and Page Click appear only if at least one item on the page uses that event.

Drag items up and down in the list to change their order. The items at the top of the list are animated first.

To play multiple animated objects at the same time, select the items in the list and click the Play Together button to link the items.

FIGURE 13-12
Timing Panel

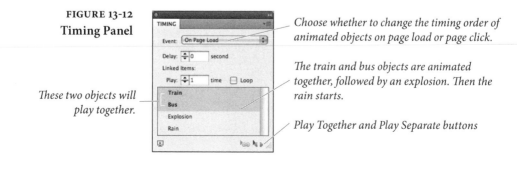

These two objects will play together.

Choose whether to change the timing order of animated objects on page load or page click.

The train and bus objects are animated together, followed by an explosion. Then the rain starts.

Play Together and Play Separate buttons

If you change your mind and decide you don't want one or more of the linked items to play together, select them and click the Play Separately button.

To play a group of items a specific number of times or to play them in a loop, select the items and then specify the number of times the animations play, or select Loop.

You can change which event triggers the animation either in the Timing panel or the Animation panel. In the Timing panel, select the item and choose Reassign To On Page Load or Reassign To On Page Click from the panel menu.

Animation in PDFs

Animated objects are not included when you export a document to interactive PDF. However, if you want your InDesign animation to appear in the exported PDF, there is a fairly simple workaround.

To get animation in a PDF file, you can select an animated object in InDesign, export the selection to SWF format, and then place the SWF file in the InDesign document. Depending on your circumstances, you may want to use different layers for the original animation and the placed SWF file, or you may want to move the original animation to the pasteboard. When you export to PDF, the SWF file can be played in the exported PDF.

Reuse Motion Presets

The motion presets you see in the Animation panel are the same ones that appear in Flash Professional CS5. In fact, when you create a custom motion preset in InDesign, you can save it as an XML file and import it into Flash Pro for use there, or you can send it to your InDesign pals.

To save an animation, select the animated object, and choose Save from the Animation panel menu. Type the name and click OK.

If you want to make the saved preset available on another computer, in Flash Pro, or to someone else, save the preset as an XML file. Choose Manage Presets from the Animation panel menu (see Figure 13-13). Select a preset and click Save As. Specify the name and location of the motion preset, and click Save. When you do this, the motion path is saved, along with the Duration, Speed, Scale, Rotate, and Opacity settings.

To import motion presets that have been exported from either InDesign or Flash Professional as XML files, click Load in the Manage Presets dialog box, and then double-click the XML file you want to import.

FIGURE 13-13
Manage Presets

Saved custom presets

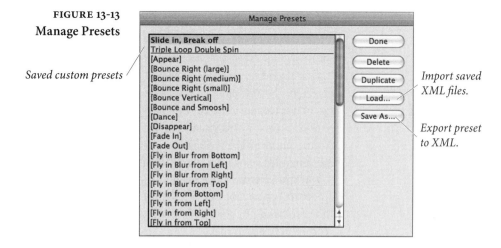

*Import saved
XML files.*

*Export preset
to XML.*

Page Transitions

Normally, if you switch from one page to another in your interactive document, the transition is (more or less) instantaneous—like flipping from one channel to the next. But you have the option to spice up your multi-page PDF and SWF files by adding more interesting transitions. You can find the Page Transitions panel in the Interactive submenu under the Window menu (see Figure 13-14).

The Page Transitions panel gives you two ways to choose a type of transition: You can pick from the Transition pop-up menu, or you can choose Choose from the panel menu. Both do the same thing, but the latter displays a dialog box that shows you all the transitions at the same time. In either case, you can get a preview of the transition by placing your cursor over the displayed graphic. The transition is applied to the current page.

FIGURE 13-14
Page Transitions panel

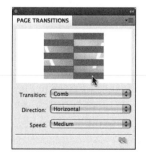

*Tired of transitions?
You can clear your
document of them by
choosing Clear All
from the panel menu.*

Most transitions also let you specify one or two parameters, such as which way a wipe wipes or how fast a dissolve dissolves. You can control those in the lower half of the panel.

If you want every page to have the same transition, you can turn on the Apply to All Spreads checkbox in the Page Transitions dialog box, or click Apply to All Spreads at the bottom of the panel. You can override those transitions later on a page-by-page basis.

You can use the Preview panel to test transitions (make sure in Document Mode, not Spread Mode).

You can also choose Page Transitions for all the spreads in the Export to Interactive PDF or Export SWF dialog box. The Export SWF also has an Interactive Page Curl option, which lets people drag a corner to turn the page.

To view transitions of an exported PDF in Acrobat, make sure that you're in Full Screen Mode. In the Export to Interactive PDF dialog box, you can select the Open in Full Screen Mode option. In Acrobat, choose Full Screen Mode from the View menu; press the Escape key to exit.

Previewing Interactive Documents

If you've worked with interactivity features in versions of InDesign before CS5, you'll be especially happy about the Preview panel. It means you don't have to export to PDF or SWF whenever you want to test your interactive objects. You can preview buttons, hyperlinks, media, page transitions, and animated objects from within InDesign (see Figure 13-15).

To display the Preview panel, choose Preview from the Interactive submenu on the Window menu. You can also click the Preview button in the lower left corner of the Animation, Timing, and Buttons panels.

In its default state, the Preview panel is too small. You'll want to drag it out to enlarge it. In the lower right corner of the panel, click a button to determine whether you're previewing the selection, spread, or document. If you're previewing the document, you can click the Go To Previous Page and Go To Next Page arrows at the bottom of the panel to move to different pages.

You can change the settings to determine what displays in the Preview panel. Choose Edit Preview Settings from the panel menu. The options are the same as those in the SWF Export dialog box.

You can also preview the document in your default web browser by choosing Test in Browser.

FIGURE 13-15
Preview Panel

Click an interactive object, such as this button, to make sure it works.

Click the Play button to start previewing.

Click this icon to preview the document instead of the selection or spread.

Presentation Mode

Presentation Mode is like Preview Mode on steroids. All the panels, menus, and toolbars are hidden. Only the content appears. Does it preview interactive objects? Unfortunately, no. As its name implies, it's especially useful for giving presentations. Presentation Mode can turn your document into a slide show—especially useful if you're using Adobe Connect (choose Share My Screen from the File menu),

Press Shift-W to turn Presentation Mode on and off (if there's a text cursor, pressing Shift-W just inserts a capital W). Or, choose Presentation Mode from the Screen Mode submenu on the View menu. Table 13-1 shows which shortcut keys work in Presentation Mode.

You can't edit the document in Presentation Mode. But with a dual screen monitor, you can have two windows open on the same document (choose New Window from the Arrange submenu on the Window menu), and put one of them into Presentation Mode.

TABLE 13-1
Presentation Mode
Shortcuts

To do this:	Press:
Turn on/off Presentation Mode	Shift+W
Go to next spread	Mouse click, Right arrow, or Page Down
Go to previous spread	Shift-click, Right-click, Left Arrow, or Page Up
Exit Presentation Mode	Esc
First/Last spread	Home/End
Black background	B
White background	W
Gray background	G

Interactive PDF Export

There are now separate commands for creating print PDF files and interactive PDF files. You export an interactive PDF by selecting Export from the File menu and choosing Adobe PDF (Interactive) from the Format or Save as Type pop-up menu. InDesign displays the Export to Interactive PDF dialog box (see Figure 13-16).

Embed Page Thumbnails. Create a thumbnail preview for each page being exported. Thumbnails are displayed in file dialog boxes and in Bridge. Turn off this option if you want a smaller file size.

Create Acrobat Layers. Save each InDesign layer as an Acrobat layer within the PDF. The layers are fully navigable, which lets Acrobat readers generate multiple versions of the file from a single PDF.

Create Tagged PDF. During export, InDesign can tag text elements based on a subset of the Acrobat tags that InDesign supports. This includes recognition of paragraphs, basic text formatting, lists, and tables. If you want more control over the tags, use the Tags panel to apply tags before you export. See "XML" in Chapter 7, "Importing and Exporting."

View and Layout. Determine the initial view settings and layout of the PDF when it's opened.

FIGURE 13-16
**Interactive PDF
Export Options**

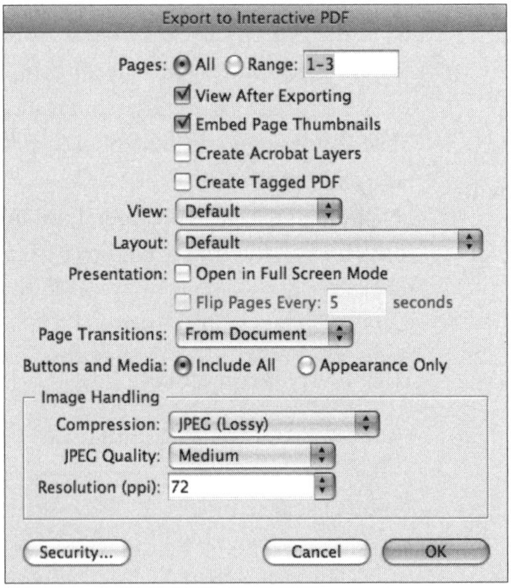

Open In Full Screen Mode. Display the PDF in Acrobat or Reader without menus or panels. To advance the pages automatically in a presentation, select Flip Pages Every and specify the number of seconds between page turns.

Page Transitions. If you used the Page Transitions panel to specify transitions, choose the From Document option to use those settings, or override them by selecting one page transition for all pages.

Buttons And Media. Select Include All to allow movies, sounds, and buttons to be interactive in the exported PDF. Select Appearance Only to include the normal state of buttons and the video posters without interactivity.

Compression, JPEG Quality, and Resolution. To keep file size down, images are compressed. You can control the trade-off between quality and file size in these three pop-up menus.

SWF Export

We've been babbling on for the past 20 pages about creating interactive SWF files; it's time we get down to actually making one. To export a document in the SWF format, choose Export from the File menu, and choose Flash Player (SWF) from the pop-up menu. After clicking Save, you'll see the Export SWF dialog box (see Figure 13-17).

Most of the features in this dialog box are self-explanatory: For example, you can choose a size (in pixels, or by a percentage of the current document size). Remember that one pixel equals one point. You can choose which pages to export, and if your document is set up for facing pages, you can choose whether or not to treat each spread as a single page.

We can never remember how to write the HTML for embedding a SWF file into a Web page. Fortunately, the Generate HTML checkbox does all that for us. And, if you turn that checkbox on, you can also turn on the View SWF after Exporting checkbox to open it (the HTML with the embedded SWF) in your default Web browser. There are several other features of this dialog box that require a tad more explanation.

Interactivity. Have you made buttons, hyperlinks, and page transitions in your document? If so, you need to turn on these checkboxes

FIGURE 13-17
SWF Export Options

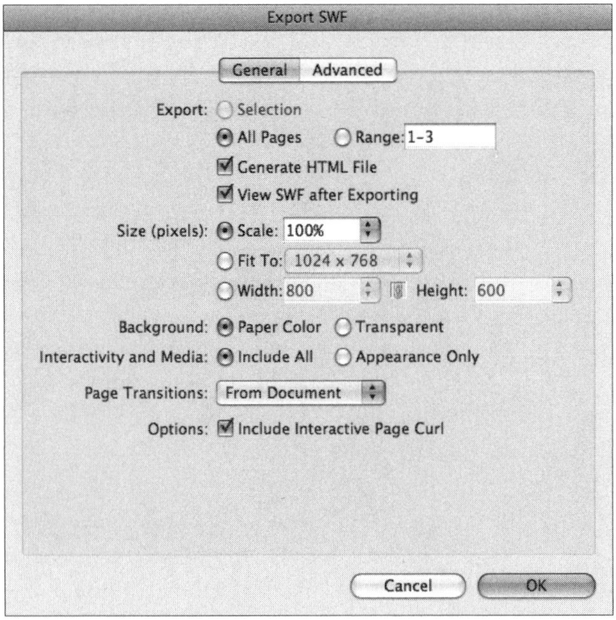

Note that when creating a document for SWF export (or for an interactive PDF), you get a better onscreen view of transparency and color effects if you first choose Document RGB from the Transparency Blend Space submenu, under the Edit menu.

to make them live in the SWF. If you turn on the fourth checkbox, Include Interactive Page Curl, people viewing your SWF will be able to "turn the page" by dragging a corner (as in a book).

Rasterize Pages (Advanced tab). You can turn all vector objects (including text) into a bitmap by turning on the Rasterize Pages checkbox. That removes interactive elements and tends to make a large SWF file. It's very rare you'd want to do this.

Flatten Transparency (Advanced tab). This option removes live transparency from the SWF and preserves the transparency appearance. But if you select this option, all interactivity is removed from the SWF file.

Text (Advanced tab). InDesign and Flash compose text differently, so if you choose Flash Classic Text in the Text pop-up menu, your text may appear different in the final SWF. Nevertheless, in most cases, this is the option you want, as it keeps file size down and makes the text visible to search engines. You can also choose to convert text to vector paths (outlines) or to bitmaps (pixels), which maintains the look and feel, but at significant cost.

Compression and Quality (Advanced tab). To keep file size down, bitmapped images are usually compressed using JPEG and complex vector curves are sometimes simplified in the SWF. You can control the quality of these algorithms in the final three pop-up menus.

FLA Export

As we said at the start of the chapter, if you really want cool SWF files, you're going to need Adobe Flash CS5 Professional. But you can still use your InDesign layouts—just export them to the Flash format, FLA (which was called XFL in CS4). When you do this, you'll see the Export Flash CS5 Professional (FLA) dialog box (see Figure 13-18).

Most of the features are the same as the options for creating SWF files. Flatten Transparency requires explanation, though. Flash does not share the same transparency engine with InDesign, so transparent objects may look very different after you open the FLA in Flash. If the look of the object is more important than your ability to animate it in Flash, you can turn on the Flatten Transparency checkbox.

Text conversion is similar to SWF export, but there is another option, Flash TLF Text, that maintains links between text frames. If this option is turned on, you can select Insert Dictionary Hyphenation Points to allow hyphenation.

Whoever edits the FLA file in Flash Pro will be happy that, unlike in CS4's XFL output, buttons, page transitions, hyperlinks, and animation transfer to Flash Pro. Only the appearance of movies and sounds are passed on in the FLA file, but the media files are packaged

FIGURE 13-18
FLA Export Options

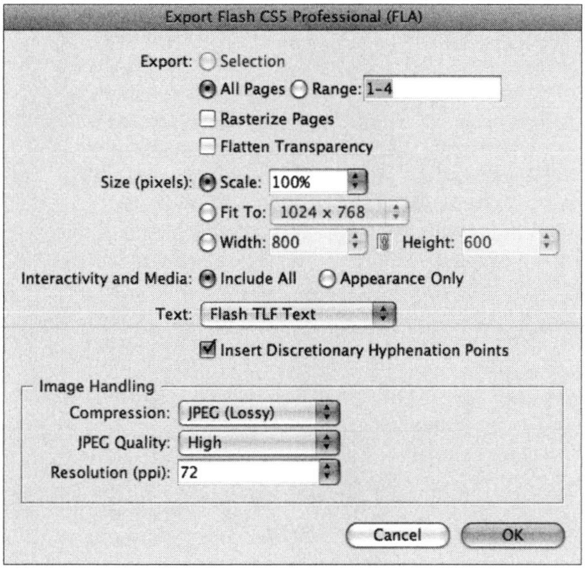

in a resource folder, making it easy for the Flash developer to hook them back up.

Web Publishing

Someday, possibly today, you're going to thank your lucky stars that InDesign can create rich media PDF and SWF files. Even if today most of us are still making money with print projects (or trying to, anyway), we still think that getting interactive files, complete with buttons and movies, is pretty dang cool.

INDEX

A

C

D

E

E

G

F

F

G

H

I

L

M

N

O

P

P

P

P

S

S

S

T

V